AP® U.S. HISTORY
PREMIUM PREP

2021 Edition

The Staff of The Princeton Review

PrincetonReview.com

Penguin
Random
House

The Princeton Review
110 East 42nd St, 7th Floor
New York, NY 10017
Email: editorialsupport@review.com

Terms of Service: The Princeton Review Online Companion Tools ("Student
Tools") for retail books are available for only the two most recent editions
of that book. Student Tools may be activated only once per eligible book
purchased for a total of 24 months of access. Activation of Student Tools
more than once per book is in direct violation of these Terms of Service
and may result in discontinuation of access to Student Tools Services.

ISBN: 978-0-525-56968-8
eBook ISBN: 978-0-525-57003-5
ISSN: 2691-1469

AP is a trademark registered and owned by the College Board, which is
not affiliated with, and does not endorse, this product.

The Princeton Review is not affiliated with Princeton University.

The material in this book is up-to-date at the time of publication. However,
changes may have been instituted by the testing body in the test after this
book was published.

If there are any important late-breaking developments, changes, or corrections to the materials in this book, we will post that information online in
the Student Tools. Register your book and check your Student Tools to see
if there are any updates posted there.

Editor: Orion McBean
Production Editors: Becky Radway and Emma Parker
Production Artist: Deborah Weber
Content Contributors: Jason Morgan and Christopher Stobart

Printed in the United States of America.

10 9 8 7 6 5 4 3 2 1

2021 Edition

Editorial

Rob Franek, Editor-in-Chief
David Soto, Director of Content Development
Stephen Koch, Student Survey Manager
Deborah Weber, Director of Production
Gabriel Berlin, Production Design Manager
Selena Coppock, Managing Editor
Aaron Riccio, Senior Editor
Meave Shelton, Senior Editor
Chris Chimera, Editor
Eleanor Green, Editor
Orion McBean, Editor
Patricia Murphy, Editorial Assistant

Penguin Random House Publishing Team

Tom Russell, VP, Publisher
Alison Stoltzfus, Publishing Director
Amanda Yee, Associate Managing Editor
Ellen Reed, Production Manager
Suzanne Lee, Designer

Acknowledgments

The Princeton Review would like to thank Jason Morgan and Christopher Stobart for their valuable contributions to the 2021 edition of this book.

As always, we are also very grateful to Deborah Weber, Becky Radway, and Emma Parker for their time and attention to each page.

Contents

Get More (Free) Content

at **PrincetonReview.com/prep**

As easy as **1 · 2 · 3**

1 Go to PrincetonReview.com/prep and enter the following ISBN for your book:

9780525569688

2 Answer a few simple questions to set up an exclusive Princeton Review account. *(If you already have one, you can just log in.)*

3 Enjoy access to your **FREE** content!

Once you've registered, you can...

- Get our take on any updates to the AP U.S. History Exam

- Access and print out Practice Tests 5 and 6 as well as the corresponding Answers and Explanations

- Get valuable advice about the college application process, including tips for writing a great essay and where to apply for financial aid

- If you're still choosing between colleges, use our searchable rankings of *The Best 386 Colleges* to find out more information about your dream school

- Access comprehensive study guides and a variety of printable resources, including bubble sheets for the practice tests in this book, and a handy list of key concepts, people, policies, and events

- Check to see if there have been any corrections or updates to this edition

Need to report a potential **content** issue?

Contact **EditorialSupport@review.com** and include:

- full title of the book
- ISBN
- page number

Need to report a **technical** issue?

Contact **TPRStudentTech@review.com** and provide:

- your full name
- email address used to register the book
- full book title and ISBN
- Operating system (Mac/PC) and browser (Firefox, Safari, etc.)

Look For These Icons Throughout The Book

 ONLINE ARTICLES

 ONLINE PRACTICE TESTS

 PROVEN TECHNIQUES

 APPLIED STRATEGIES

 TIME-SAVING TIP

 ASK YOURSELF

 OTHER REFERENCES

Part I
Using This Book to Improve Your AP Score

- Preview: Your Knowledge, Your Expectations
- Your Guide to Using This Book
- How to Begin

PREVIEW: YOUR KNOWLEDGE, YOUR EXPECTATIONS

Your route to a high score on the AP U.S. History Exam depends a lot on how you plan to use this book. To help you determine your approach, respond to the following questions.

1. Rate your level of confidence about your knowledge of the content tested by the AP U.S. History Exam:

    A. Very confident—I know it all
    B. I'm pretty confident, but there are topics for which I could use help
    C. Not confident—I need quite a bit of support
    D. I'm not sure

2. Circle your goal score for the AP U.S. History Exam:

    5   4   3   2   1   I'm not sure yet

3. What do you expect to learn from this book? Circle all that apply to you.

    A. A general overview of the test and what to expect
    B. Strategies for how to approach the test
    C. The content tested by this exam
    D. I'm not sure yet

YOUR GUIDE TO USING THIS BOOK

This book is organized to provide as much—or as little—support as you need, so you can use this book in whatever way will be most helpful to improving your score on the AP U.S. History Exam.

*   The remainder of **Part I** will provide guidance on how to use this book and help you determine your strengths and weaknesses.

*   **Part II** of this book contains Practice Test 1, and its answers and explanations. (Bubble sheets can be found in the very back of the book for easy tear-out.) We strongly recommend that you take this test before going any further, in order to realistically determine:
    o your starting point right now
    o which question types you're ready for and which you might need to practice
    o which content topics you are familiar with and which you should carefully review

Once you have nailed down your strengths and weaknesses with regard to this exam, you can focus your test preparation, build a study plan, and be efficient with your time.

Access your Student Tools for a free diagnostic answer key for Practice Test 1, which includes targeted study recommendations. See pages viii–ix for more information.

- **Part III** of this book will:
  - provide information about the structure, scoring, and content of the AP U.S. History Exam
  - help you to make a study plan
  - point you toward additional resources

- **Part IV** of this book will explore the following strategies:
  - attacking multiple-choice and short-answer questions
  - writing effective essays
  - managing your time to maximize the number of points available to you

- **Part V** of this book covers the content you need for the AP U.S. History Exam.

- **Part VI** of this book contains Practice Tests 2, 3, and 4, and their answers and explanations. (Bubble sheets can be found in the very back of the book for easy tear-out.) If you skipped Practice Test 1, we recommend that you take both Practice Tests 1 and 2 (with at least a day or two between them) so that you can compare your progress between the two before taking the other tests. Additionally, this will help to identify any external issues. If you answered a certain type of question wrong both times, you probably need to review it. If you answered it wrong only once, you may have run out of time or been distracted by something. In either case, comparing the two exams will allow you to focus on the factors that caused the discrepancy in scores and to be as prepared as possible on the day of the test.

You may choose to use some parts of this book over others, or you may work through the entire book. Your approach will depend on your needs and how much time you have. Let's now look at how to make this determination.

Don't Forget!
To take Practice Tests 5 and 6, be sure to register your book online following the instructions on pages viii–ix. You'll also gain access to a wealth of other helpful Student Tools, including study guides, printable bubble sheets, and the Chapter 15 Key Terms list.

HOW TO BEGIN

1. **Take a Test**

   Before you can decide how to use this book, you need to take a practice test. Doing so will give you insight into your strengths and weaknesses, and the test will also help you make an effective study plan. If you're feeling test-phobic, remind yourself that a practice test is a tool for diagnosing yourself—it's not how well you do that matters but how you use information gleaned from your performance to guide your preparation.

   So, before you read further, take Practice Test 1 starting on page 9 of this book. Be sure to do so in one sitting, following the instructions that appear before the test.

2. **Check Your Answers**

Using the answer key on page 36, count the number of multiple-choice questions you answered correctly and the number you missed. Don't worry about the explanations for now, and don't worry about why you missed questions. We'll get to that soon.

3. **Reflect on the Test**

After you take your first test, respond to the following questions:

- How much time did you spend on the multiple-choice questions?
- How much time did you spend on the short-answer questions?
- How much time did you spend on each essay?
- How many multiple-choice questions did you miss?
- Do you feel you had the knowledge to address the subject matter of the short-answer questions and essays?
- Do you feel you wrote well-organized, thoughtful essays?
- Circle the content areas that were most challenging for you, and draw a line through the ones in which you felt confident/did well.

Puritanism/Early Colonization
Colonial Era
English Oppression and the Revolutionary War
The U.S. Constitution and Early American Politics
The Louisiana Purchase and Westward Expansion
The War of 1812
Women's Rights and Suffrage Movement
Slavery and the Abolitionist Movement
Manifest Destiny
Civil War
Reconstruction
The Gilded Age (Reconstruction–1900)
The Industrial Revolution
World War I
Prohibition
The Great Depression and New Deal
World War II
The Cold War
McCarthyism
The Civil Rights Movement
Great Society
Vietnam War
The 1970s—Clash of Cultures and Political Scandals
The Reagan Revolution and the New Right
End of the Cold War
America's Rise as a Global Power and 21st Century Challenges

4. Read Part III of this Book, and Complete the Self-Evaluation

As discussed in "Your Guide to Using this Book," Part III will provide information on how the test is structured and scored. It will also set out areas of content that are tested.

As you read Part III, reevaluate your answers to the questions above. At the end of Part III, you will revisit and refine the questions you answered on page 4. You will then be able to make a study plan based on your needs and time available that will allow you to use this book most effectively.

5. Engage with Parts IV and V as Needed

Notice the word *engage*. You'll get more out of this book if you use it intentionally than if you read it passively, hoping for an improved score through osmosis.

Strategy chapters in Part IV will help you think about your approach to the question types on this exam. This part opens with a reminder to think about how you approach questions now and then closes with a reflection section asking you to think about how/whether you will change your approach in the future.

Content chapters in Part V are designed to provide a review of the content tested on the AP U.S. History Exam, including the level of detail you need to know and how the content is tested. You will have the opportunity to assess your mastery of the content of each chapter through test-appropriate questions and a reflection section.

6. Take Practice Tests 2 Through 6, and Assess Your Performance

Once you feel you have developed the strategies you need and gained the knowledge you lacked, you should take Practice Test 2, which starts on page 385 of this book. You should do so in one sitting, following the instructions at the beginning of the test.

When you finish, check your answers to the multiple-choice sections. See if a teacher will read your essays and provide feedback.

Once you have taken the test, reflect on what areas you still need to work on, and revisit the chapters in this book that address those deficiencies. Repeat this process with Practice Tests 3, 4, 5, and 6. Through this type of reflection and engagement, you will continue to improve.

7. Keep Working

As we'll discuss in Part III, there are other resources available to you, including a wealth of information on AP Students (apstudent. collegeboard.org/home). You can continue to explore areas that can stand improvement and engage in those areas right up to the day of the test.

Part II
Practice Test 1

- Practice Test 1
- Practice Test 1: Answers and Explanations

Practice Test 1

AP® United States History Exam

SECTION I, PART A: Multiple Choice

DO NOT OPEN THIS BOOKLET UNTIL YOU ARE TOLD TO DO SO.

At a Glance

Time
55 minutes
Number of Questions
55
Percent of Total Score
40%
Writing Instrument
Pencil required

Instructions

Section I, Part A of this exam contains 55 multiple-choice questions. Fill in only the ovals for numbers 1 through 55 on your answer sheet. Because this section offers only four answer options for each question, do not mark the (E) answer circle for any question.

Indicate all of your answers to the multiple-choice questions on the answer sheet. No credit will be given for anything written in this exam booklet, but you may use the booklet for notes or scratch work. After you have decided which of the suggested answers is best, completely fill in the corresponding oval on the answer sheet. Give only one answer to each question. If you change an answer, be sure that the previous mark is erased completely. Here is a sample question and answer.

Sample Question

The first president of the United States was
(A) Millard Fillmore
(B) George Washington
(C) Benjamin Franklin
(D) Andrew Jackson

Sample Answer

Ⓐ ● Ⓒ Ⓓ

Use your time effectively, working as rapidly as you can without losing accuracy. Do not spend too much time on any one question. Go on to other questions and come back to the ones you have not answered if you have time. It is not expected that everyone will know the answers to all of the multiple-choice questions.

Your total score on the multiple-choice section is based only on the number of questions answered correctly. Points are not deducted for incorrect answers or unanswered questions.

SECTION I, PART B: Short Answer

At a Glance

Time
40 minutes
Number of Questions
3
Percent of Total Score
20%
Writing Instrument
Pen with black or dark blue ink
Questions 1 and 2
Mandatory
Question 3 or 4
Choose one question

Instructions

For Section I, Part B of this exam, answer Question 1 and Question 2 and **either** Question 3 **or** Question 4. Write your responses in the Section I, Part B: Short-Answer Response booklet. You must write your response to each question on the lined page designated for that response. Each response is expected to fit within its designated page. Fill in the circle on the Section I, Part B: Short-Answer Response booklet indicating whether you answered Question 3 or Question 4. Failure to do so may delay your score.

GO ON TO THE NEXT PAGE.

UNITED STATES HISTORY
SECTION I, Part A
Time—55 minutes
55 Questions

Directions: Each of the questions or incomplete statements below is followed by four suggested answers or completions. Select the one that is best in each case and then blacken the corresponding space on the answer sheet.

Questions 1–4 refer to the excerpts below.

"Those whose condition is such that their function is the use of their bodies and nothing better can be expected of them, those, I say, are slaves of nature. It is better for them to be ruled thus."

Juan de Sepulveda, *Politics*, 1522

"When Latin American nations gained independence in the 19th century, those two strains converged, and merged with an older, more universalist, natural law tradition. The result was a distinctively Latin American form of rights discourse. Paolo Carozza traces the roots of that discourse to a distinctive application, and extension, of Thomistic moral philosophy to the injustices of Spanish conquests in the New World. The key figure in that development seems to have been Bartolomé de Las Casas, a 16th-century Spanish bishop who condemned slavery and championed the cause of Indians on the basis of a natural right to liberty grounded in their membership in a single common humanity. 'All the peoples of the world are humans,' Las Casas wrote, and 'all the races of humankind are one.' According to Brian Tierney, Las Casas and other Spanish Dominican philosophers laid the groundwork for a doctrine of natural rights that was independent of religious revelation 'by drawing on a juridical tradition that derived natural rights and natural law from human rationality and free will, and by appealing to Aristotelian philosophy.'"

Mary Ann Glendon, "The Forgotten Crucible: The Latin American Influence on the Universal Human Rights Idea," 2003

1. The above excerpts support which one of the following generalizations?

    (A) After European and Latin American populations interacted economically, most Europeans were more compassionate toward the interests of non-whites.

    (B) There was some degree of debate by Spanish explorers over how to treat natives in the New World.

    (C) The appeal to natural rights and natural law succeeded in abolishing slavery in the New World.

    (D) The European belief in white superiority was used to justify the doctrine of natural rights.

2. Which one of the following statements about the Spanish conquest of the Americas is most accurate?

    (A) African slavery was a direct result of Spanish settlements in Florida.

    (B) Early native civilizations in Mexico introduced Spanish explorers to cattle ranching and wheat cultivation.

    (C) Christopher Columbus was not the first European to have explored North America.

    (D) Because of racial prejudice, Spanish explorers shunned intermarriage with native people.

3. Which of the following presidents was most involved in Latin American politics in the 20th century?

    (A) James K. Polk
    (B) James Monroe
    (C) Theodore Roosevelt
    (D) Chester Arthur

4. Maize cultivation among the native peoples of Mexico is most analogous to which of the following?

    (A) Buffalo hunting among the Lakota Sioux
    (B) Wolf domestication by the Algonquians
    (C) Mixed agriculture among the Iroquois
    (D) Seal hunting among the Inuit

GO ON TO THE NEXT PAGE.

Questions 5–9 refer to the excerpt below.

"I observe the great and wonderful mistake, both our own and our fathers, as to the civil powers of this world, acting in spiritual matters. I have read…the last will and testament of the Lord Jesus over many times, and yet I cannot find by one tittle of that testament that if He had been pleased to have accepted of a temporal crown and government that ever He would have put forth the least finger of temporal or civil power in the matters of His spiritual affairs and Kingdom. Hence must it lamentably be against the testimony of Christ Jesus for the civil state to impose upon the souls of the people a religion, a worship, a ministry, oaths (in religious and civil affairs), tithes, times, days, marryings, and buryings in holy ground…."

Roger Williams, *The Hireling Ministry None of Christ's,* 1652

5. The Puritans believed that the freedom to practice religion should be extended to

   (A) Puritans only
   (B) all Protestants only
   (C) all Christians only
   (D) all Jews and Christians only

6. Consistent with the excerpt above, Roger Williams was banished from Massachusetts Bay in 1636 for advocating

   (A) the separation of church and state
   (B) women's suffrage
   (C) bigamy
   (D) the export of tobacco

7. The First Great Awakening can be seen as a direct response to which of the following?

   (A) Puritanism
   (B) The Enlightenment
   (C) Transcendentalism
   (D) Existentialism

8. Puritan emigration from England came to a near halt between the years 1649 and 1660 because, during that period,

   (A) most English Puritans were imprisoned for heresy
   (B) most Puritans converted to Catholicism
   (C) the New England settlement had become too overcrowded, and colonial legislatures strongly discouraged immigration
   (D) the Puritans controlled the English government

9. Which of the following documents encouraged church membership in the Massachusetts Bay Colony?

   (A) The Mayflower Compact
   (B) The Fundamental Orders
   (C) The Halfway Covenant
   (D) The Cambridge Agreement

GO ON TO THE NEXT PAGE.

Questions 10 and 11 refer to the excerpt below.

"Permit us, then, earnestly to recommend these articles to the immediate and dispassionate attention of the legislatures of the respective states. Let them be candidly reviewed under a sense of the difficulty of combining in one system the various sentiments and interests of a continent divided into so many sovereign and independent communities, under a conviction of the absolute necessity of uniting all our councils and all our strength, to maintain and defend our common liberties...."

Journals of the Continental Congress, 1777

10. A major weakness of the Articles of Confederation was that they

    (A) created a too-powerful chief executive
    (B) did not include a mechanism for their own amendment
    (C) made it too difficult for the government to raise money through taxes and duties
    (D) denied the federal government the power to mediate disputes between states

11. The most notable achievement of the United States under the Articles of Confederation was

    (A) the creation of a strong executive office to lead the national government
    (B) the empowerment of Congress to regulate commerce
    (C) the empowerment of Congress to collect taxes
    (D) the provision for land sales in the Northwest that would benefit the entire nation

Questions 12–14 refer to the excerpt below.

"Whereas it is expedient that new provisions and regulations should be established for improving the revenue of this kingdom, and for extending and securing the navigation and commerce between Great Britain and your Majesty's dominions in America, which, by the peace, have been so happily enlarged: and whereas it is just and necessary, that a revenue be raised, in your Majesty's said dominions in America, for defraying the expenses of defending, protecting, and securing the same; we, your Majesty's most dutiful and loyal subjects, the commons of Great Britain, in parliament assembled, being desirous to make some provision, in this present session of parliament, towards raising the said revenue in America, have resolved to give and grant unto your Majesty the several rates and duties herein after-mentioned...."

The Sugar Act of 1764

12. The Sugar Act of 1764 represented a major shift in British policy toward the colonies in that, for the first time, the British

    (A) attempted to control colonial exports
    (B) offered the colonists the opportunity to address Parliament with grievances
    (C) required the colonies to import English goods exclusively
    (D) levied taxes aimed at raising revenue rather than regulating trade

13. In harmony with the sentiments expressed in the excerpt, which of the following does NOT represent the views of Prime Minister Grenville after the French and Indian War?

    (A) He felt that the Crown needed to control trade and raise revenue.
    (B) He felt that the colonists should help pay the debt incurred by the war.
    (C) He felt that Parliament had the right to increase taxes on the colonies.
    (D) He wanted to reward the colonies through his extension of "salutary neglect."

14. The goals presented in the excerpt have the most in common with which of the following?

    (A) Antitrust reforms of the Progressive Era
    (B) Free trade policies of the 1970s
    (C) Increasing federal income tax rates after World War I
    (D) Decreasing federal income tax rates in the 1980s

GO ON TO THE NEXT PAGE.

Questions 15 and 16 refer to the excerpt below.

"Society in every state is a blessing, but government even in its best state is but a necessary evil; in its worst state an intolerable one; for when we suffer, or are exposed to the same miseries *by a government,* which we might expect in a country *without government,* our calamity is heightened by reflecting that we furnish the means by which we suffer. Government, like dress, is the badge of lost innocence; the palaces of kings are built on the ruins of the bowers of paradise. For were the impulses of conscience clear, uniform, and irresistibly obeyed, man would need no other lawgiver; but that not being the case, he finds it necessary to surrender up a part of his property to furnish means for the protection of the rest; and this he is induced to do by the same prudence which in every other case advises him out of two evils to choose the least. *Wherefore,* security being the true design and end of government, it unanswerably follows that whatever *form* thereof appears most likely to ensure it to us, with the least expense and greatest benefit, is preferable to all others."

Thomas Paine, *Common Sense,* 1776

15. Which of the following is most harmonious with the sentiment expressed in the excerpt?

(A) Government is unnecessary, since humanity is capable of guiding itself by personal conscience.
(B) A limited republican government is preferable to a monarchy.
(C) Government is a necessary check against the corrupting influence of society.
(D) Security is the only justification for government.

16. Which of the following "miseries" alluded to above were most condemned by Anti-Federalists of the post-Revolutionary era?

(A) Organized response to Bacon's Rebellion
(B) Federal response to Shays's Rebellion
(C) Federal response to the Whiskey Rebellion
(D) Federal response to Pontiac's Rebellion

GO ON TO THE NEXT PAGE.

Questions 17–22 refer to the excerpt below.

"The far-reaching, the boundless future will be the era of American greatness. In its magnificent domain of space and time, the nation of many nations is destined to manifest to mankind the excellence of divine principles; to establish on earth the noblest temple ever dedicated to the worship of the Most High—the Sacred and the True. Its floor shall be a hemisphere—its roof the firmament of the star-studded heavens, and its congregation a Union of many Republics, comprising hundreds of happy millions, calling, owning no man master, but governed by God's natural and moral law of equality, the law of brotherhood—of 'peace and good will amongst men.'"

John L. O'Sullivan, "The Great Nation of Futurity," 1839

17. Which of the following best states the principle described above?

    (A) Colonists were destined to leave the British Empire because of the distance between the New World and England.
    (B) Women are biologically predestined to lives of child rearing and domestic labor.
    (C) America's expansion to the West Coast was inevitable and divinely sanctioned.
    (D) The abolition of slavery in the United States was certain to come about because slavery was immoral.

18. Between 1820 and 1854, the greatest number of immigrants to the United States came from

    (A) France
    (B) Russia
    (C) England
    (D) Ireland

19. Which of the following best describes the effect of the American rail system in the 19th century?

    (A) Government subsidy of the railroads enabled markets to expand and production to become more efficient.
    (B) The entire national system was planned before the first railway was constructed.
    (C) The development of the rails had little effect on the development of American industry.
    (D) A more highly developed rail system gave the Confederacy a decided advantage in the Civil War.

20. Which of the following changes in westward migration is most likely to have occurred in the 1840s?

    (A) The number of pioneers headed for the Oregon territory decreased while the number headed for California greatly increased.
    (B) The first great wave of migration ended, and the number of migrants remained extremely low until after the Civil War.
    (C) For the first time, pioneers began to settle areas west of the Mississippi River.
    (D) Large numbers of free blacks, unwelcome in the East, began to resettle in the West.

21. By what means did the United States take possession of the Oregon Territory?

    (A) The United States was granted the territory in a postwar treaty with France.
    (B) The United States bought it from the Native Americans who lived there.
    (C) U.S. settlers were the first to arrive in the region; they claimed it for their country.
    (D) Great Britain ceded it to the United States as part of a negotiated treaty.

22. Which of the following presidents is most closely associated with the concept of Manifest Destiny?

    (A) James K. Polk
    (B) Andrew Johnson
    (C) Woodrow Wilson
    (D) Ronald Reagan

GO ON TO THE NEXT PAGE.

Questions 23–27 refer to the excerpt below.

"In one view the slaveholders have a decided advantage over all opposition. It is well to notice this advantage—the advantage of complete organization. They are organized; and yet were not at the pains of creating their organizations. The State governments, where the system of slavery exists, are complete slavery organizations. The church organizations in those States are equally at the service of slavery; while the Federal Government, with its army and navy, from the chief magistracy in Washington, to the Supreme Court, and thence to the chief marshalship at New York, is pledged to support, defend, and propagate the crying curse of human bondage. The pen, the purse, and the sword, are united against the simple truth, preached by humble men in obscure places."

Frederick Douglass, "The Dred Scott Decision," 1857

23. In his opinion on the case *Dred Scott v. Sandford,* Chief Justice Roger Taney upheld the sentiment above by stating that

  (A) "separate but equal" facilities for people of different races was constitutional
  (B) corporations were entitled to the same protections guaranteed to individuals under the Fourteenth Amendment
  (C) school prayer violated the principle of "separation of church and state"
  (D) Congress had no right to regulate slavery in United States territories

24. In what way did the actions of Abraham Lincoln in 1860 contradict Douglass's sentiments in the excerpt above?

  (A) Lincoln promoted the freedom of settlers within territories to determine the slave status of their new state.
  (B) Lincoln passed the Homestead Act to give free land to all western settlers.
  (C) Lincoln favored the exclusion of slavery from any of the new territories.
  (D) Lincoln enacted the policy of giving newly freed slaves "forty acres and a mule."

25. The excerpt from Frederick Douglass is most clearly an example of which of the following developments in the mid-19th century?

  (A) The gradual replacement of indentured servants with African slaves
  (B) The preservation of African culture through cultural adaptation
  (C) Southern influence upon the federal government to defend the institution of slavery
  (D) The success of abolitionists to sway majority public opinion

26. Which of the following groups would be most likely to support the perspective of Frederick Douglass?

  (A) Southern Democrats in the 1880s
  (B) Western ranchers in the 1850s
  (C) Southern farmers in the 1830s
  (D) Northern Republicans in the 1860s

27. Frederick Douglass was most influenced by which of the following social movements?

  (A) First Great Awakening
  (B) Second Great Awakening
  (C) Manifest Destiny
  (D) Popular Sovereignty

GO ON TO THE NEXT PAGE.

Questions 28–32 refer to the excerpt below.

"We have witnessed for more than a quarter of a century the struggles of the two great political parties for power and plunder, while grievous wrongs have been inflicted upon the suffering people. We charge that the controlling influences dominating both these parties have permitted the existing dreadful conditions to develop without serious effort to prevent or restrain them. Neither do they now promise us any substantial reform. They have agreed together to ignore, in the coming campaign, every issue but one. They propose to drown the outcries of a plundered people with the uproar of a sham battle over the tariff, so that capitalists, corporations, national banks, rings, trusts, watered stock, the demonetization of silver and the oppressions of the usurers may all be lost sight of. They propose to sacrifice our homes, lives, and children on the altar of mammon; to destroy the multitude in order to secure corruption funds from the millionaires.

"Assembled on the anniversary of the birthday of the nation, and filled with the spirit of the grand general and chief who established our independence, we seek to restore the government of the Republic to the hands of 'the plain people,' with which class it originated. We assert our purposes to be identical with the purposes of the National Constitution; to form a more perfect union and establish justice, insure domestic tranquillity, provide for the common defence, promote the general welfare, and secure the blessings of liberty for ourselves and our posterity."

Populist Party Platform, 1892

28. The sentiments expressed in the excerpt above about political parties are most similar to those expressed by

   (A) George McGovern, Democratic Party, 1972
   (B) Theodore Roosevelt, Progressive Party, 1912
   (C) Andrew Jackson, Democratic Party, 1829
   (D) H. Ross Perot, Reform Party, 1996

29. The "free silver" campaign of 1896 received its greatest popular support from

   (A) New England businessmen, who were discriminated against under the existing banking system
   (B) Southern women, who incorporated it into a larger campaign for economic equality
   (C) bankers, who had run out of paper currency to invest
   (D) farmers, who hoped that a more generous money supply would ease their debt burdens

30. Which one of the following political movements most closely shared many of the goals outlined by the Populist Party?

   (A) Progressivism of the early 1900s
   (B) Neoconservatism of the 1980s
   (C) Federalism of the late 1700s
   (D) Jacksonian Democracy of the early 1800s

31. Which of the following is LEAST associated with the Populist movement?

   (A) Support of labor unions
   (B) Secret ballot elections
   (C) Free coinage of silver
   (D) Deregulation of railroads and utilities

32. Which of the following was most directly a cause of the success of the Populist party?

   (A) Western farmers and ranchers favored conservation and organized to promote the National Parks system.
   (B) The growth of corporate power and banking interests inspired rural activists to lobby for political reform.
   (C) Western farmers resisted the mechanization of agriculture and resented government interference in rural affairs.
   (D) After the Civil War, westward migration slowed, causing a long-term recession in many Western territories.

GO ON TO THE NEXT PAGE.

Questions 33 and 34 refer to the excerpt below.

"With 78 percent of the Union electorate casting ballots, Lincoln was reelected in an Electoral College landslide, 212 to McClellan's 21. The 55% popular vote for the president was the third largest in the nineteenth century, surpassed only by Jackson's first victory in 1828 and Grant's reelection in 1872. McClellan won only New Jersey, Delaware, and Kentucky. Republicans drew support from native-born farmers, skilled and professional workers, those of New England descent, younger voters, and military personnel. Democrats were strongest in the cities and among Irish- and German-Americans (the most populous immigrant groups). It has been estimated that Lincoln received 78% of the vote of Union soldiers and sailors. The figure was not necessary for his reelection, but was perhaps the margin of victory in a few close states and, more importantly, of great symbolic value. Republicans also gained seats in Congress to retain unassailable control, 149 to 42 in the House and 42 to 10 in the Senate; took back several state legislatures; and lost only the governorship of New Jersey (McClellan's home state)."

"1864: Lincoln v. McClellan," Harpweek.com

33. Which of the following conclusions is best supported by the excerpt above?

(A) Lincoln received more votes in the heavily populated states of the North, while McClellan won more sparsely populated states.

(B) Lincoln won the Election of 1864 because of Union successes during the Civil War.

(C) The Emancipation Proclamation mobilized black voters in the South to vote for Lincoln in the Election of 1864.

(D) Republicans managed to gain control of Congress through the efforts of Lincoln to campaign on their behalf.

34. Which of the following provides the best explanation for why Radical Republicans opposed Lincoln in 1861?

(A) Lincoln's decision to issue the Emancipation Proclamation was done without congressional oversight.

(B) The Radical Republicans wanted immediate emancipation of slaves, but Lincoln refused to cooperate.

(C) Lincoln's Ten Percent Plan provided no assurance of black suffrage.

(D) Lincoln's appointment of Andrew Johnson as vice president clashed with the Reconstruction goals of the Senate.

GO ON TO THE NEXT PAGE.

Questions 35–39 refer to the excerpt below.

"The conscience of the people, in a time of grave national problems, has called into being a new party, born of the nation's sense of justice. We of the Progressive party here dedicate ourselves to the fulfillment of the duty laid upon us by our fathers to maintain the government of the people, by the people and for the people whose foundations they laid. We hold with Thomas Jefferson and Abraham Lincoln that the people are the masters of their Constitution, to fulfill its purposes and to safeguard it from those who, by perversion of its intent, would convert it into an instrument of injustice. In accordance with the needs of each generation the people must use their sovereign powers to establish and maintain equal opportunity and industrial justice, to secure which this Government was founded and without which no republic can endure.

"This country belongs to the people who inhabit it. Its resources, its business, its institutions and its laws should be utilized, maintained or altered in whatever manner will best promote the general interest. It is time to set the public welfare in the first place."

Progressive Party Platform, 1912

35. Of the following policies, which was NOT a main objective of American Progressives?

   (A) Passage of the Pure Food and Water Act
   (B) Creation of national forests and protected wildlife reserves
   (C) Initiation of antitrust lawsuits against various corporate monopolies
   (D) Intervention in the affairs of Central American governments

36. "Muckraking" author Jacob A. Riis's *How the Other Half Lives* best exemplifies which of the following quotes from the excerpt above?

   (A) "the duty laid upon us by our fathers"
   (B) "masters of their Constitution"
   (C) "an instrument of injustice"
   (D) "without which no republic can endure"

37. Which of the following regulatory laws was passed as a result of Upton Sinclair's *The Jungle*?

   (A) The Clayton Antitrust act
   (B) The Hepburn Act
   (C) The Sherman Antitrust Act
   (D) The Pure Food and Drug Act

38. In harmony with the sentiments of the excerpt above, which of the following best characterizes the "Square Deal" of Theodore Roosevelt?

   (A) Conservation, trust-busting, consumer protection
   (B) Protective tariffs, centralized banking, conservation
   (C) Equal opportunity, women's suffrage, laissez-faire economics
   (D) Laissez-faire economics, support of labor unions, conservation

39. Would the Underwood-Simmons Tariff of 1913 be generally endorsed by Progressives of that era?

   (A) Yes, because they were largely supporters of Teddy Roosevelt's "Square Deal"
   (B) Yes, because most Democrats advocated lower duties
   (C) No, because they were largely supporters of Teddy Roosevelt's "New Nationalism"
   (D) No, because they were largely opponents of Woodrow Wilson

GO ON TO THE NEXT PAGE.

Questions 40–44 refer to the cartoon below.

Strike-Breaking

40. The 1933 political cartoon shown above makes the point that

   (A) infighting within and among unions prevented their rise to economic power

   (B) government inspectors turned their backs to illegal repression of labor unions

   (C) attacks on unions were so well concealed that the government did not know where to begin its investigations

   (D) from their beginnings, labor unions were controlled by organized crime

41. Which of the following acts was the most beneficial to the labor movement?

   (A) The Clayton Antitrust Act, which legalized strikes and picketing

   (B) The Sherman Antitrust Act, which prevented corporations from monopolizing markets

   (C) The Elkins Act, which provided greater regulation of railroads

   (D) The Hepburn Act, which regulated public modes of transportation

42. Which of the following best accounts for the successes of labor unions?

   (A) Throughout the early 1900s, Congress promoted the interests of labor unions over captains of industry.

   (B) Immigrants helped to promote a more diverse workforce less reliant on child labor.

   (C) Sharecroppers in the South largely voted for Democrats who championed labor causes.

   (D) Locally and nationally, organizations such as the American Federation of Labor negotiated directly with corporations to effect change in the workplace.

GO ON TO THE NEXT PAGE.

43. Which of the following best describes the conflict between management and labor illustrated in the cartoon?

(A) Tradition vs. innovation
(B) Native-born vs. immigrant
(C) Christian vs. atheist
(D) Urban vs. rural

44. How was the Red Scare in post–World War I America connected to organized labor movements?

(A) Unrestricted immigration after World War I flooded the job markets with low-wage workers, leading to resentment by union members and accusations of communist sympathies.
(B) California migrant workers were largely Italian immigrants, many of whom had anarchist leanings.
(C) Labor unions were largely thought to be controlled by liberals with Marxist sympathies.
(D) Senator Joseph McCarthy, a Wisconsin Republican, was hostile to both Communism and labor unions, fueling suspicion among American Conservatives.

GO ON TO THE NEXT PAGE.

Questions 45–48 refer to the excerpt below.

"We conclude that, in the field of public education, the doctrine of 'separate but equal' has no place. Separate educational facilities are inherently unequal. Therefore, we hold that the plaintiffs and others similarly situated for whom the actions have been brought are, by reason of the segregation complained of, deprived of the equal protection of the laws guaranteed by the Fourteenth Amendment."

Brown v. Board of Education, 1954

45. In which decision did the Supreme Court validate the practice of "separate but equal" facilities for blacks and whites?

(A) *Marbury v. Madison*
(B) *Bradwell v. Illinois*
(C) *Plessy v. Ferguson*
(D) *Holden v. Hardy*

46. Which of the following best represents an effect of the legal decision described above?

(A) Continuing white resistance slowed efforts at desegregation, sparking a series of social conflicts throughout the South.
(B) The Supreme Court decision *Brown v. Board of Education* led to increased enrollment in colleges and universities.
(C) During the 1960s, increasing numbers of high-school graduates rejected the notion that a college education was desirable.
(D) In the 20th century, jobs in advanced technical and medical industries generally require postgraduate degrees.

47. All of the following are social movements inspired by the Civil Rights movement EXCEPT

(A) women's rights
(B) gay and lesbian rights
(C) states' rights
(D) Native American rights

48. Desegregation of schools was, in part, a response to un-fulfilled promises from which of the following initiatives?

(A) The Great Society
(B) The Square Deal
(C) The New Deal
(D) Reconstruction

GO ON TO THE NEXT PAGE.

Questions 49 and 50 refer to the excerpt below.

"If you analyze it I believe the very heart and soul of conservatism is libertarianism. I think conservatism is really a misnomer just as liberalism is a misnomer for the liberals—if we were back in the days of the Revolution, so-called conservatives today would be the Liberals and the liberals would be the Tories. The basis of conservatism is a desire for less government interference or less centralized authority or more individual freedom and this is a pretty general description also of what libertarianism is. Now, I can't say that I will agree with all the things that the present group who call themselves Libertarians in the sense of a party say, because I think that like in any political movement there are shades, and there are libertarians who are almost over at the point of wanting no government at all or anarchy. I believe there are legitimate government functions. There is a legitimate need in an orderly society for some government to maintain freedom or we will have tyranny by individuals. The strongest man on the block will run the neighborhood. We have government to ensure that we don't each one of us have to carry a club to defend ourselves. But again, I stand on my statement that I think that libertarianism and conservatism are traveling the same path."

Ronald Reagan, Interview published in *Reason* magazine, 1975

49. All of the following are factors that contributed to the prominence of conservatism in the late 1970s and 1980s EXCEPT

(A) the success of the Libertarian party in national elections

(B) the growth of religious fundamentalism

(C) perceived economic and foreign policy failures under President Carter

(D) social changes following the Civil Rights movement and Vietnam War

50. Which of the following groups would be most opposed to the sentiments expressed in the excerpt above?

(A) Neoconservatives

(B) Reagan Democrats

(C) Progressive Liberals

(D) Populists

GO ON TO THE NEXT PAGE.

Questions 51–55 refer to the excerpt below.

"The challenge of the next half century is whether we have the wisdom to use wealth to enrich and elevate our national life, and to advance the quality of our American civilization…. The Great Society rests on abundance and liberty for all. It demands an end to poverty and racial injustice, to which we are totally committed in our time. But that is just the beginning. The Great Society is a place where every child can find knowledge to enrich his mind and to enlarge his talents. It is a place where leisure is a welcome chance to build and reflect, not a feared cause of boredom and restlessness. It is a place where the city of man serves not only the needs of the body and the demands of commerce but the desire for beauty and the hunger for community. It is a place where man can renew contact with nature. It is a place which honors creation for its own sake and for what it adds to the understanding of the race. It is a place where men are more concerned with the quality of their goals than the quantity of their goods. But most of all, the Great Society is not a safe harbor, a resting place, a final objective, a finished work. It is a challenge constantly renewed, beckoning us toward a destiny where the meaning of our lives matches the marvelous products of our labor."

Lyndon Johnson, Remarks at the University of Michigan, Ann Arbor, 1964

51. Which of the following programs is most related to Johnson's claim that the Great Society is "a place where man can renew contact with nature"?

(A) Urban Mass Transportation Act
(B) Endangered Species Preservation Act
(C) Public Broadcasting Act
(D) Higher Education Act

52. All of the following were part of Johnson's Great Society program EXCEPT

(A) the Civil Rights Act of 1964
(B) Medicare and Medicaid
(C) the establishment of the Department of Housing and Urban Development
(D) the balanced budget mandate

53. Along with his goals of establishing a Great Society, Johnson was also engaged in which of the following initiatives?

(A) Undermining Communism in Cuba with the Bay of Pigs Invasion
(B) Undermining Communism in Vietnam after the Tet Offensive
(C) Undermining Communism in Turkey and Greece using economic aid
(D) Undermining Communism in the Eastern Block by demanding a removal of the Berlin Wall

54. Johnson's Great Society most represented an extension of which of the following initiatives?

(A) The New Deal
(B) The Square Deal
(C) The Truman Doctrine
(D) The Monroe Doctrine

55. Which one of the following was an unintended consequence of the liberal successes of the 1960s?

(A) Liberal Democrats abandoned antiwar protests in a show of support for President Johnson.
(B) Conservative Republicans mobilized to defend traditional mores and curb government authority.
(C) Economic recession catalyzed by increased government spending causing "stagflation."
(D) A majority of Northern black voters abandoned the Democrat party, siding with Republicans.

GO ON TO THE NEXT PAGE.

UNITED STATES HISTORY
SECTION I, Part B
Time—40 minutes

Directions: Answer Question 1 **and** Question 2. Answer **either** Question 3 **or** Question 4.

Write your responses in the Section I, Part B: Short-Answer Response booklet. You must write your response to each question on the lined page designated for that response. Each response is expected to fit within the space provided.

In your responses, be sure to address all parts of the questions you answer. Use complete sentences; an outline or bulleted list alone is not acceptable. You may plan your answers in this exam booklet, but no credit will be given for notes written in this booklet.

Question 1 is based on the excerpts below.

"Constitutionalism is descriptive of a complicated concept, deeply imbedded in historical experience, which subjects the officials who exercise governmental powers to the limitations of a higher law. Constitutionalism proclaims the desirability of the rule of law as opposed to rule by the arbitrary judgment or mere fiat of public officials…. Throughout the literature dealing with modern public law and the foundations of statecraft the central element of the concept of constitutionalism is that in political society government officials are not free to do anything they please in any manner they choose; they are bound to observe both the limitations on power and the procedures which are set out in the supreme, constitutional law of the community. It may therefore be said that the touchstone of constitutionalism is the concept of limited government under a higher law."

Philip P. Wiener, Ed., *Dictionary of the History of Ideas: Studies of Selected Pivotal Ideas*, 1973

"I do not say that democracy has been more pernicious on the whole, and in the long run, than monarchy or aristocracy. Democracy has never been and never can be so durable as aristocracy or monarchy; but while it lasts, it is more bloody than either…. Remember, democracy never lasts long. It soon wastes, exhausts, and murders itself. There never was a democracy yet that did not commit suicide. It is in vain to say that democracy is less vain, less proud, less selfish, less ambitious, or less avaricious than aristocracy or monarchy. It is not true, in fact, and nowhere appears in history. Those passions are the same in all men, under all forms of simple government, and when unchecked, produce the same effects of fraud, violence, and cruelty. When clear prospects are opened before vanity, pride, avarice, or ambition, for their easy gratification, it is hard for the most considerate philosophers and the most conscientious moralists to resist the temptation. Individuals have conquered themselves. Nations and large bodies of men, never."

John Adams, letter to John Taylor, 1814

1. Using the excerpts above, answer parts (a), (b), and (c).

    a) Briefly explain the point of view made by Passage 1.
    b) Briefly explain the point of view made by Passage 2.
    c) Provide ONE piece of evidence about New England government before 1800, and explain how it either supports the interpretation in the first passage OR refutes the interpretation in the second passage.

GO ON TO THE NEXT PAGE.

Question 2 is based on the following image.

2. Use the image above and your knowledge of history to answer parts (a), (b), and (c).

   a) Explain the point of view in the image regarding ONE of the following:
      • Commerce
      • American Indians
      • European exploration

   b) Explain how ONE element of the image expresses the point of view you identified in part (a).

   c) Explain how a SECOND element of the image expresses the point of view you identified in part (a).

Question 3 or 4

Directions: Answer **either** Question 3 **or** Question 4.

3.   Answer parts (a), (b), and (c).

   a)   Briefly explain ONE example of how freedom of religion brought about new ideas in politics and society at any time prior to 1800.

   b)   Briefly explain a SECOND example of how freedom of religion brought about new ideas in politics and society in the same period.

   c)   Briefly explain ONE example of how religious people or groups resisted new ideas in politics and society in the same period.

4.   United States historians have debated the role of collective security in determining U.S. foreign policy in the late 20th century. Using your knowledge of United States history, answer parts (a), (b), and (c).

   a)   Briefly explain the basic principles of collective security.

   b)   Choose ONE of the organizations listed below and explain to what extent membership in this organization was a continuation or departure from U.S. foreign policy earlier in the century. Provide at least ONE piece of evidence to support your explanation.
   - The UN
   - NATO
   - SEATO

   c)   Briefly explain why ONE of the other options is not as persuasive as the one you chose.

END OF SECTION I

AP® United States History Exam

SECTION II: Free Response

DO NOT OPEN THIS BOOKLET UNTIL YOU ARE TOLD TO DO SO.

Instructions

The questions for Section II are printed in the orange Questions and Documents booklet. You may use that booklet to organize your answers and for scratch work, but you must write your answers in this Section II: Free Response booklet. No credit will be given for any work written in the Questions and Documents booklet.

The proctor will announce the beginning and end of the reading period. You are advised to spend the 15-minute period reading the question and planning your answer to Question 1, the document-based question. If you have time, you may also read Questions 2, 3, and 4. Do not begin writing in this booklet until the proctor tells you to do so.

Section II of this exam requires answers in essay form. Write clearly and legibly. Circle the number of the question you are answering at the top of each page in this booklet. Begin each answer on a new page. Do not skip lines. Cross out any errors you make; crossed-out work will not be scored.

Manage your time carefully. The proctor will announce the suggested time for each part, but you may proceed freely from one part to the next. Go on to Question 2, 3, or 4 if you finish Question 1 early. You may review your responses if you finish before the end of the exam is announced.

After the exam, you must apply the label that corresponds to the long-essay question you answered—Question 2, 3, or 4. For example, if you answered Question 2, apply the label ②. Failure to do so may delay your score.

At a Glance

Total Time
1 hour, 40 minutes
Number of Questions
2
Percent of Total Score
40%
Writing Instrument
Pen with black or dark blue ink

Question 1 (DBQ): Mandatory

Suggested Reading and Writing Time
60 minutes
Reading Period
15 minutes. Use this time to read Question 1 and plan your answer. You may begin writing your response before the reading period is over.
Suggested Writing Time
45 minutes
Percent of Total Score
25%

Question 2, 3, or 4: Choose One Question

Answer Question 2, Question 3, or Question 4
Suggested Writing Time
40 minutes
Percent of Total Score
15%

GO ON TO THE NEXT PAGE.

UNITED STATES HISTORY
SECTION II
Total Time—1 hour, 40 minutes

Question 1 (Document-Based Question)
Suggested reading and writing time: 1 hour

It is suggested that you spend 15 minutes reading the documents and 45 minutes writing your response.

Note: You may begin writing your response before the reading period is over.

Directions: Question 1 is based on the accompanying documents. The documents have been edited for the purpose of this exercise.

In your response, you should do the following.

- Respond to the prompt with a historically defensible thesis or claim that establishes a line of reasoning.
- Describe a broader historical context relevant to the prompt.
- Support an argument in response to the prompt using at least six documents.
- Use at least one additional piece of specific historical evidence (beyond that found in the documents) relevant to an argument about the prompt.
- For at least three documents, explain how or why the document's point of view, purpose, historical situation, and/or audience is relevant to an argument.
- Use evidence to corroborate, qualify, or modify an argument that addresses the prompt.

GO ON TO THE NEXT PAGE.

1. When World War I broke out, the United States declared its policy of neutrality. To what extent did the United States follow a policy of neutrality between 1914 and 1917?

Document 1

Source: President Woodrow Wilson, message to Congress (August 19, 1914)

The effect of the war upon the United States will depend upon what American citizens say and do. Every man who really loves America will act and speak in the true spirit of neutrality, which is the spirit of impartiality and fairness and friendliness to all concerned.

The people of the United States are drawn from many nations, and chiefly from the nations now at war. It is natural and inevitable that there should be the utmost variety of sympathy and desire among them with regard to the issues and circumstances of the conflict.

Such divisions amongst us would be fatal to our peace of mind and might seriously stand in the way of the proper performance of our duty as the one great nation at peace, the one people holding itself ready to play a part of impartial mediation and speak the counsels of peace and accommodation, not as a partisan, but as a friend.

Document 2

Source: Hugo Munsterberg, Harvard University professor, letter to Woodrow Wilson (November 19, 1914)

Dear Mr. President:

[I] ask your permission to enter into some detail with regard to the neutrality question. But let me assure you beforehand that I interpret your inquiry as referring exclusively to the views which are expressed to me by American citizens who sympathize with the German cause or who are disturbed by the vehement hostility to Germany on the part of the American press. My remarks refer in no way to the views of official Germany....

First, all cables sent by and received by wire pass uncensored, while all wireless news is censored. This reacts against Germany, because England sends all her news by cable, whereas Germany alone uses the wireless....

Second, the policy of the administration with regard to the holding up, detaining and searching of Germans and Austrians from neutral and American vessels is a reversal of the American policy established in 1812. It has excited no end of bitterness.

Third, the United States permitted the violation by England of the Hague Convention and international law in connection with conditional and unconditional contraband.... [O]n former occasions the United States has taken a spirited stand against one-sided interpretations of international agreements. The United States, moreover, [previously] insisted that conditional contraband can be sent in neutral or in American [ships] even to belligerent nations, provided it was not consigned to the government, the military or naval authorities.... By permitting this new interpretation the United States practically supports the starving out policy of the Allies [and seriously handicapping] Germany and Austria in their fight for existence....

Many of the complaints refer more to the unfriendly spirit than to the actual violation of the law. Here above all belongs the unlimited sale of ammunition to the belligerents....

GO ON TO THE NEXT PAGE.

Document 3

Source: Robert Lansing, *War Memoirs* (1935)

The author was acting secretary of state during the period described below.

The British authorities…proceeded with their policy [of blockading American ships headed for mainland Europe] regardless of protests and complaints. Neutral ships were intercepted and, without being boarded or examined at sea, sent to a British port, where their cargoes were examined after delays, which not infrequently lasted for weeks. Even a vessel which was finally permitted to proceed on her voyage was often detained so long a time that the profits to the owners or charterers were eaten up by the additional expenses of lying in port and by the loss of the use of the vessels during the period of detention.

Document 4

Source: Secretary of State William Jennings Bryan, letter to the Chairman of the Senate Committee on Foreign Relations (January 20, 1915)

Dear Mr. Stone:

I have received your letter…referring to frequent complaints or charges made…that this Government has shown partiality to Great Britain, France, and Russia against Germany and Austria during the present war…. I will take them up…

(1) Freedom of communication by submarine cables versus censored communication by wireless.

The reason that wireless messages and cable messages require different treatment by a neutral government is as follows: Communications by wireless can not be interrupted by a belligerent. With a submarine cable it is otherwise. The possibility of cutting the cable exists…. Since a cable is subject to hostile attack, the responsibility falls upon the belligerent and not upon the neutral to prevent cable communication.

A more important reason, however, at least from the point of view of a neutral government is that messages sent out from a wireless station in neutral territory may be received by belligerent warships on the high seas. If these messages…direct the movements of warships…the neutral territory becomes a base of naval operations, to permit which would be essentially unneutral.

(4) Submission without protest to British violations of the rules regarding absolute and conditional contraband as laid down in the Hague conventions, the Declaration of London, and international law.

There is no Hague convention which deals with absolute or conditional contraband, and, as the Declaration of London is not in force, the rules of international law only apply. As to the articles to be regarded as contraband, there is no general agreement between nations….

The United States has made earnest representations to Great Britain in regard to the seizure and detention by the British authorities of all American ships…. It will be recalled, however, that American courts have established various rules bearing on these matters.

(9) The United States has not interfered with the sale to Great Britain and her allies of arms, ammunition, horses, uniforms, and other munitions of war, although such sales prolong the conflict.

There is no power in the Executive to prevent the sale of ammunition to the belligerents.

The duty of a neutral to restrict trade in munitions of war has never been imposed by international law….

(20) General unfriendly attitude of Government toward Germany and Austria. If any American citizens, partisans of Germany and Austria-Hungary, feel that this administration is acting in a way injurious to the cause of those countries, this feeling results from the fact that on the high seas the German and Austro-Hungarian naval power is thus far inferior to the British. It is the business of a belligerent operating on the high seas, not the duty of a neutral, to prevent contraband from reaching an enemy….

I am [etc.]

W.J. Bryan

GO ON TO THE NEXT PAGE.

Document 5

Source: *New York Times*, notice (May 1, 1915)

NOTICE!

TRAVELLERS intending to embark on the Atlantic voyage are reminded that a state of war exists between Germany and her allies; that the zone of her waters includes the waters adjacent to the British Isles; that, in accordance with formal notice given by the Imperial German Government, vessels flying the flag of Great Britain, or of any of her allies, are liable to destruction in those waters and that travellers sailing in the war zone on ships of Great Britain or her allies do so at their own risk.

IMPERIAL GERMAN EMBASSY

Document 6

Source: Report from the American Customs Inspector in New York (1915)

Q: Did the *Lusitania* have on board on said trip 5400 cases of ammunition? If so, to whom were they consigned?

A: The *Lusitania* had on board, on said trip, 5468 cases of ammunition. The Remington Arms-Union Metallic Cartridge Co. shipped 4200 cases of metallic cartridges, consigned to the Remington Arms Co., London, of which the ultimate consignee was the British Government. G. W. Sheldon & Co. shipped three lots of fuses of 6 cases each, and 1250 cases of shrapnel, consigned to the Deputy Director of Ammunition Stores, Woolwich, England.

GO ON TO THE NEXT PAGE.

Document 7

Source: Woodrow Wilson, speech to Congress (March 24, 1916)

…I have deemed it my duty, therefore, to say to the Imperial German Government, that if it is still its purpose to prosecute relentless and indiscriminate warfare against vessels of commerce by the use of submarines, notwithstanding the now demonstrated impossibility of conducting that warfare in accordance with what the Government of the United States must consider the sacred and indisputable rules of international law and the universally recognized dictates of humanity, the Government of the United States is at last forced to the conclusion that there is but one course it can pursue; and that unless the Imperial German Government should now immediately declare and effect an abandonment of its present methods of warfare against passenger and freight carrying vessels, this Government can have no choice but to sever diplomatic relations with the Government of the German Empire altogether.

This decision I have arrived at with the keenest regret; the possibility of the action contemplated I am sure all thoughtful Americans will look forward to with unaffected reluctance. But we cannot forget that we are in some sort and by the force of circumstances the responsible spokesmen of the rights of humanity, and that we cannot remain silent while those rights seem in process of being swept utterly away in the maelstrom of this terrible war. We owe it to a due regard to our own rights as a nation, to our sense of duty as a representative of the rights of neutrals the world over, and to a just conception of the rights of mankind to take this stand now with the utmost solemnity and firmness….

END OF DOCUMENTS FOR QUESTION 1

GO ON TO THE NEXT PAGE.

Question 2, 3, or 4 (Long Essay)

Suggested writing time: 40 minutes

Directions: Answer Question 2 **or** Question 3 **or** Question 4.

In your response, you should do the following:

- Respond to the prompt with a historically defensible thesis or claim that establishes a line of reasoning.
- Describe a broader historical context relevant to the prompt.
- Support an argument in response to the prompt using specific and relevant examples of evidence.
- Use historical reasoning (e.g., comparison, causation, continuity or change over time) to frame or structure an argument that addresses the prompt.
- Use evidence to corroborate, qualify, or modify an argument that addresses the prompt.

2. To what extent did the American Revolution represent change and/or continuity over time in relation to how colonists reacted to the British imperial authority?

3. Evaluate the extent to which the assassination of James Garfield marked a turning point in the Gilded Age.

   In the development of your argument, explain what changed and what stayed the same from the period immediately before James Garfield's assassination (1870s) to the period immediately after his assassination (1880s).

4. To what extent did the social and political actions of Americans during the 1960s represent change and/or continuity over time?

WHEN YOU FINISH WRITING, CHECK YOUR WORK ON SECTION II IF TIME PERMITS.

STOP

END OF EXAM

Practice Test 1:
Answers and
Explanations

PRACTICE TEST 1 ANSWER KEY

Section I, Part A: Multiple-Choice Questions

1. B	20. A	39. B
2. C	21. D	40. B
3. C	22. A	41. A
4. C	23. D	42. D
5. A	24. C	43. A
6. A	25. C	44. C
7. B	26. D	45. C
8. D	27. B	46. A
9. C	28. D	47. C
10. C	29. D	48. D
11. D	30. A	49. A
12. D	31. D	50. C
13. D	32. B	51. B
14. C	33. A	52. D
15. B	34. B	53. B
16. C	35. D	54. A
17. C	36. C	55. B
18. D	37. D	
19. A	38. A	

Once you have checked your answers, remember to return to page 4 and respond to the Reflect questions.

Access your Student Tools for a free diagnostic answer key for Practice Test 1, which includes targeted study recommendations.

SECTION I, PART A: MULTIPLE-CHOICE QUESTIONS

Questions 1–4

Early interactions among native peoples and Europeans challenged the worldviews of each group. European overseas expansion and sustained contacts with native peoples shaped European views of social, political, and economic relationships among and between white and non-white peoples. With little experience dealing with people who were different from themselves, Spanish and Portuguese explorers poorly understood the native peoples they encountered in the Americas, leading to debates over how natives should be treated and how "civilized" these groups were compared to European standards. Many Europeans developed a belief in white superiority to justify their subjugation of Africans and American Indians, while others took a more humanitarian approach.

1. **B** The two quotations represent two vastly different views of non-white natives. The quote by Juan de Sepulveda rules out (A). Neither quote mentions the abolition of slavery, so rule out (C), and the concept of natural rights would tend to discourage white supremacy, so rule out (D).

2. **C** Although many people assume Columbus to be the first European to explore North America, Scandinavians had previously explored areas in the northern part of this continent. The Spanish were not directly responsible for slavery, so rule out (A). Early Mexicans did not raise cattle or wheat, so rule out (B). And the Spanish did, in fact, intermarry extensively with native peoples throughout Mexico and South America, so rule out (D).

3. **C** Theodore Roosevelt was most known for key foreign policy strategies in Latin America, particularly the Spanish-American War. Choice (A), Polk, was more concerned with domestic expansion. Choice (B), James Monroe, originator of the Monroe Doctrine, may have inspired Roosevelt, but Monroe was not involved in Latin American affairs during his presidency from 1817 to 1825. Chester Arthur is irrelevant to this question, so rule out (D). (Additionally, if you know that all choices but (C) are 19th-century presidents, "20th century" is a giveaway.)

4. **C** The spread of maize cultivation from present-day Mexico northward into the American Southwest and beyond supported economic development in these areas and allowed tribes to remain in fixed communities. This is most similar to the fixed agricultural and fishing communities of the Iroquois. Buffalo and seal hunting would require some degree of migration, so rule out (A) and (D), while (B), wolf domestication, would not provide a steady supply of food.

Questions 5–9

The Puritans came to the New World to escape religious and political persecution in England. In their communities, freedom of worship was solely a Puritan right. Non-Puritans were limited politically as well: only property-owning male Puritans were allowed to vote in the colonial assemblies (which, oddly, were quite democratic, within the extremely limited parameters of their membership). Those who questioned the church too aggressively—as did Roger Williams and Anne Hutchinson—were banished from the community. Williams went on to found the colony of Rhode Island, which for decades was the only place in New England where religious liberty was granted.

5. **A** Believing that theirs was the one true church, the Puritans saw no contradiction in denying others the same rights they had sought in England.

6.   **A**   Williams was quite a radical thinker for his time and place. After accepting a position as teacher in the Salem Bay settlement, Williams both taught and published a number of controversial principles. He believed, for example, that the king of England had no power to give away land that clearly belonged to the Native Americans. He also felt that the state was an imperfect vehicle for the imposition of God's will on Earth, so he advocated religious tolerance and the separation of church and state. Such ideas were pure anathema to the Puritans, who had settled Massachusetts Bay to establish precisely the type of state that Williams preached against. Neither easygoing nor good sports, the Puritans eventually banished Williams. Williams moved to what is now Rhode Island, received a charter, and founded a new colony. Rhode Island's charter allowed for the free exercise of religion; it did not require voters in its legislature to be church members.

7.   **B**   The term "First Great Awakening" refers to a period of resurgence of religious fundamentalism that took place between the 1730s and the 1760s. Its most prominent spokesmen were Congregationalist preacher Jonathan Edwards and Methodist preacher George Whitefield. From 1739 until his death in 1770, Whitefield toured the colonies preaching what has since come to be known as "revivalism." The period was marked by the creation of a number of evangelical churches, emphasis on the emotional power of religion, and briefly, a return of the persecution of witches. Whitefield was a native of England, where the Enlightenment was in full swing; its effects were also beginning to be felt in the colonies. The Enlightenment was a natural outgrowth of the Renaissance, during which Europe rediscovered the great works of the ancient world and began to assimilate some of its ideals. While European thinkers of the time did not turn their backs on religion, they also entertained ideas about the value of empirical thought and scientific inquiry that were not entirely consonant with contemporary religious beliefs. Further, they began to view humanity as a more important— and God as a less important—force in shaping human history. The First Great Awakening is usually characterized as a response to the threats posed by the intellectual trends of the Enlightenment.

8.   **D**   The period between 1649 and 1660 is often referred to as the "Interregnum," Latin for "between kings," because during that brief period England had no king. Rather, it was governed as a republican Commonwealth, with its leader, Oliver Cromwell, named "lord protector." The English Civil Wars, between 1642 and 1648, are often called the Puritan Revolution because they pitted the Puritans against the Crown. Royalists fought for the divine right of the king to rule and the maintenance of the Church of England (which later became known as the Episcopal Church in the United States) as the official church of state. The Puritans fought for a republican Commonwealth and a greater level of state tolerance for freedom of religion. The Puritans won and, for a little over a decade, ruled England. The death of Cromwell (1658) robbed the Puritans of their best-known and most respected leader, and by 1660 the Stuarts were restored to the throne. During the Interregnum, Puritans had little motive to move to the New World. Everything they wanted—freedom to practice their religion, representation in the government—was available to them in England. With the restoration of the Stuarts, many Puritans sought the opportunities and freedoms of the New World, bringing with them the republican ideals of the revolution.

9. **C** The Halfway Covenant extended the privilege of baptism to all children of baptized people, not just those who had the personal experience of conversion. The Covenant was an attempt to bring more people into the church and do away with some of the distinctions between the "elect" and all others.

Questions 10–11

During the fight for liberation against the English monarchy, the colonists were leery of establishing a too-powerful national government. They erred too much on the side of caution, however; by severely limiting the government's ability to levy taxes and duties, the framers of the Articles essentially hobbled the fledgling government. The Articles also curtailed the government's ability to regulate international trade, enforce treaties, and perform other tasks necessary to international relations. Havoc ensued. The British refused to abandon military posts in the states, and the government was powerless to expel them. Furthermore, the British, French, and Spanish began to restrict U.S. trade with their colonies. That, coupled with the government's reluctance and inability to tax its citizens, nearly destroyed the country's economy.

10. **C** Choice (A) is incorrect because the Articles did not create an executive, just a unicameral legislature. Choice (B) is incorrect because the Articles could be amended, but only by unanimous approval of the states. Choice (D) is incorrect; the Articles gave the government the power to mediate such disputes, on appeal raised by the states.

11. **D** The land sales in the Northwest were structured so that they would benefit the entire nation and gave newly created states equal status with the older states. None of the other choices were actually accomplished under the Articles of Confederation, which did not provide for a strong central government.

Questions 12–14

Throughout the colonial period, the English subscribed to the economic theory of mercantilism, which held, among other things, that a nation's wealth rested on colonial holdings, a favorable balance of trade, and a large store of precious metals. Mercantilists held that governments must regulate trade through taxes so as to preserve their self-interest. Accordingly, English taxes and levies on the colonists (prior to the Sugar Act) were proposed and accepted as acts of mercantilist protectionism. The Sugar Act was something different.

12. **D** England accrued a large war debt during the French and Indian War. Since, it was argued, the war was fought to protect the colonists, the colonists should share in its expense. Revenues from the Sugar Act were earmarked toward repaying that debt. The colonists saw things differently, however. Many argued that Englishmen could not be taxed without their consent, and since the colonists had no representatives in Parliament, they simply could not be taxed. The Sugar Act is often regarded as a major catalyst in the chain of events that led to the Revolutionary War.

13. **D** British treatment of the colonies during the period preceding the French and Indian War (also called the Seven Years' War) is often described as "salutary neglect" (or "benign neglect"). Although England regulated trade and government in its colonies, it interfered in colonial affairs as little as possible. Grenville's policies put an end to salutary neglect, rather than extending it.

14. **C** Since the Sugar Act was designed to raise funds necessary to pay off war debts, increased taxes following World War I would be most similar to this.

Questions 15–16

Before the Revolution, the rebels needed a masterpiece of propaganda that would rally colonists to their cause. They got it in *Common Sense*, a pamphlet published in January of 1776 by an English printer named Thomas Paine. Paine not only advocated colonial independence but also argued for the merits of republicanism over monarchy.

15. **B** Since Paine describes government as a "*necessary* evil," (A) is too extreme. Choice (C) is wrong because Paine states that society is a "blessing." The word "only" makes (D) too extreme.

16. **C** The key to this question is its reference to the Anti-Federalists. The Anti-Federalists were suspicious of centralized government power and were leery of Washington's military response to the Whiskey Rebellion in 1794. The response to Shays's Rebellion was weak; it would not have posed a perceived threat, so eliminate (B). Choice (A), Bacon's Rebellion, and (D), Pontiac's Rebellion, occurred prior to the Revolution, so these answers can be ruled out immediately.

Questions 17–22

The idea of Manifest Destiny was originally advanced by a newspaper editor in the 1840s, and it quickly became a part of the public's—and government's—vocabulary. Part and parcel with the doctrine of Manifest Destiny was the notion that Europeans, especially English-speaking Europeans, were culturally and morally superior to those whom they supplanted, and so they were entitled to the land even if others were already living on it. Manifest Destiny was later invoked as a justification for the Spanish-American War.

17. **C** O'Sullivan makes reference to God and the tone of the passage is clear and confident, so (C) is the best choice. No mention is made of distances, so rule out (A). Neither women nor slaves are mentioned, so rule out (B) and (D), respectively.

18. **D** Overpopulation and poor harvests in Ireland fueled a steady stream of immigration to the United States. Between the years 1820 and 1854, the Irish made up the single largest immigrant group for all but two of the years. The peak immigration period was between 1847 and 1854, when the potato famine struck Ireland; during those years, well over one million Irish left for America. In 1854, German immigrants began to outnumber the Irish, although Irish immigration remained at such a level that, by 1900, there were more Irish in the United States than in Ireland.

19. **A** During the century, the federal government gave over 180 million acres to railroad companies; state and local governments gave away another 50 million. For the federal government, the goal was the completion of a national rail system in order to promote trade. Local governments often wanted the railroad to come to a specific town because a rail station was a great boon to growth.

The incorrect answers are all entirely false. The nation's railroads grew haphazardly, and frequently different lines could not be joined because the tracks were of different gauges, so rule out (B). The transcontinental railroad was the single greatest factor in the growth of the American steel industry, so rule out (C). The North had a much more sophisticated rail system than the South, which gave the Union a great advantage in the Civil War, so rule out (D).

20. **A** In January 1848, a carpenter discovered gold at Sutter's Mill, California. Word spread quickly, and soon the Gold Rush was on. Western migrants continued to travel west on the Oregon Trail until they reached Fort Hall (in modern Idaho), but then they turned south on the California Trail and headed for where the gold was supposed to be. Most wound up disappointed, as only a very few found much gold. In seven years, California's population grew from 15,000 to 300,000. One observer noted that, by 1849, the western section of the Oregon Trail (which led into the Oregon Territory) "bore no evidence of having been much traveled."

21. **D** The United States almost fought a war over the Oregon Territory, which consisted of present-day Oregon, Washington, and parts of Montana and Idaho. Originally, American expansionists and settlers demanded all the territory up to the 54°40′ boundary, and they were willing to fight the British (who held it as part of their Canadian territories) to get it. Contemporaneous conflicts near Mexico caused President Polk to reconsider war with Great Britain; he feared that two wars would spread forces dangerously thin, as well as damage his popularity with voters. Therefore, Polk decided to negotiate a settlement with the British—the United States accepted a boundary at the 49th parallel—and directed his military activities southward. The United States subsequently entered a war with Mexico, which netted them much of the territory that makes up the Southwestern states.

22. **A** James K. Polk is known as the "Manifest Destiny" president; it was during his term that the country extended so many of its borders.

Questions 23–27

In the 1840s, Frederick Douglass began publishing his influential newspaper *The North Star*. Douglass, an escaped slave, gained fame as a gifted writer and eloquent advocate of freedom and equality.

23. **D** Dred Scott was a slave whose owner had traveled with him into the free state of Illinois and also into the Wisconsin Territory, where slavery was prohibited. Scott declared himself a free man, and a series of court cases ruled variously for and against his claim. The case finally reached the Supreme Court in 1857. Taney's ruling was remarkable in that it far exceeded the scope of the case. Taney could simply have ruled on the merits of the case; instead, he decided to establish a wide-ranging precedent. Slaves, he said, were property, and as such could be transported anywhere. Because slaves were not citizens, Taney further reasoned, they could not sue in federal court (thereby eliminating the possibility of the court reviewing any such cases in the future). Taney topped off his decision by stating that Congress could neither prevent settlers from transporting their slaves to western territories nor could it legislate slavery in those areas, thus nullifying the Missouri Compromise and rendering the concept of popular sovereignty unconstitutional. Taney's decision is infamous for its lack of compassion for Scott and slaves, and it is significant in that it hastened the inevitable Civil War. Choice (A) describes *Plessy v. Ferguson,* (B) describes many Supreme Court cases of the 1890s, and (C) describes *Engle v. Vitale.* You should know the *Plessy* and Dred Scott decisions, but not *Engle,* by name.

24. **C**   In the excerpt, Douglass asserts that slaveholders have an advantage because they control all aspects of government. He states that "the Federal Government…is pledged to support, defend, and propagate the crying curse of human bondage." This may have been true in 1857, but Lincoln turned the tables in 1860 by running on a Free-Soil platform, thus opposing the institution of slavery. He did not promote popular sovereignty, so rule out (A). The Homestead Act is irrelevant to this question, so rule out (B). The slaves were not freed in 1860, so rule out (D).

25. **C**   Many white Americans in the South asserted their regional identity through pride in the institution of slavery, insisting that the federal government should defend that institution. Indentured servants had long been replaced by slaves before 1857, so rule out (A). Douglass does not appear to be "adapting," so rule out (B). And, although Douglass was an abolitionist, he has not apparently swayed the opinion of Southerners, according to his own words, so rule out (D).

26. **D**   Northern Republicans were most prone to abolitionist sentiments in 1857. Southerners in general were more likely to defend or tolerate slavery, so rule out (A) and (C). Western ranchers, (B), were not known for having strong abolitionist views, although many were no doubt sympathetic to Douglass. Choice (D) is a better answer.

27. **B**   In the Northeast, the Second Great Awakening gave birth to numerous societies dedicated to the task of saving humanity from its own worst impulses. Much of the language of reform had a religious tone. For example, drinking and poverty were considered social evils. The religious and moral fervor that accompanied the Second Great Awakening also persuaded more and more Northerners that slavery was a great evil.

Questions 28–32

The Populists fought for the rights of the farmers and supported the free coinage of silver instead of the traditional reliance on the gold standard (which was seen as favoring bankers and lenders). Their leader, William Jennings Bryan, gave his most memorable speech in which he stated that the poor were being "crucified on a Cross of Gold." The Populists also believed in government ownership of railroads and utilities and opposed the tariff policies of William McKinley.

28. **D**   The excerpt specifically decries the "two great political parties" and asserts that "grievous wrongs have been inflicted upon the suffering people." This is most similar to the third-party presidential candidate H. Ross Perot, who ran for office twice in the 1990s, lambasting both Democrats and Republicans in his bid for independent-minded voters. Choices (A), George McGovern, and (C), Andrew Jackson, were not critics of political parties per se. Theodore Roosevelt is a close choice, since Progressives did adopt some Populist ideals, but he was not as much of an outlier as Perot. Choice (D) is the best choice.

29. **D**   The "free silver" campaign aimed to increase the money supply through the free coinage of silver. It was the great cause of the Populist party, which argued that the existing monetary practices favored the wealthy and elite, particularly in the Northeast. Free coinage of silver, the party argued,

would cause inflation but would also put more money in circulation, making it easier for farmers to pay off their debts. Furthermore, Populists felt that a larger money supply was appropriate to the United States' tremendous growth rate at that time. The policy was naturally quite popular with farmers, but not with bankers, who would have had their loans repaid with devalued currency. Free silver was a central issue in the 1896 election, during which the Populists and the Democratic Party joined forces.

30.   **A**   Progressives adopted some Populist causes, such as better conditions for working people and government regulation of certain industries, so (A) is the best choice. Although some Populists had conservative leanings, neoconservatism is a very different ideology, so rule out (B). Jackson was not reform-minded in the same way Populists were, so rule out (D).

31.   **D**   Western Populists resented the control that the railroads exerted over transportation of goods across the country and wished to see railroads more tightly controlled by the federal government. All other answers represent Populist causes.

32.   **B**   The Populists generally resented big business and banking interests and saw their power as working contrary to the interests of farmers, ranchers, and working people in general. Most Populists lived in rural areas, although later Populists championed the causes of urban factory workers. Conservation was not a prominent concern for Populists, so rule out (A). Western farmers did not resent government interference; in fact, they often welcomed it, so rule out (C). Westward migration did not slow after the Civil War; it increased, so rule out (D).

Questions 33–34

Abraham Lincoln ran as the Republican nominee against Democratic candidate George B. McClellan, who ran as the "peace candidate" without personally believing in his party's platform. Lincoln was re-elected president. Electoral College votes were counted from 25 states. Since the election of 1860, the Electoral College had expanded with the admission of Kansas, West Virginia, and Nevada as free-soil states. As the American Civil War was still raging, no electoral votes were counted from any of the eleven Southern states. Lincoln won by more than 400,000 popular votes on the strength of the soldier vote and military successes such as the Battle of Atlanta.

33.   **A**   This question is all about Process of Elimination (POE). There is no mention of black voters, so rule out (C). Choice (D) is tempting, but we don't know for sure if Lincoln was campaigning for any other Republicans. Choice (B) is likewise unsupported. Choice (A) must be true because Lincoln won so many Electoral College votes. New Jersey and Delaware are relatively small states, while Kentucky was rural in 1864.

34.   **B**   When the Union dissolved and the South left Congress, Lincoln was faced with a legislature much more progressive in its thoughts on slavery than he was. The Radical Republican wing of Congress wanted immediate emancipation. Choices (A), (C), and (D) are all post-1861.

Questions 35–39

Progressives were primarily concerned with domestic reform; their agenda was the greater empowerment of labor, women, and the poor. The successes of the Progressive Era include those mentioned in the answer choices, the beginning of direct elections for the U.S. Senate, and the establishment of three popular political tools: the ballot initiative, the referendum, and the recall.

35. **D** The Progressives pursued no coherent foreign policy per se. Although Theodore Roosevelt was interested in Central American affairs, he was not representing primarily Progressive ideals with this initiative.

36. **C** Photojournalist Jacob Riis exposed the misery of tenement life in his book *How the Other Half Lives*, published in 1890. Muckrakers in general were concerned with "injustice," so the answer is (C).

37. **D** The Pure Food and Drug Act was passed after Sinclair wrote *The Jungle*, which exposed the filth and disease that was rampant throughout the slaughterhouses of Chicago.

38. **A** Theodore Roosevelt's "Square Deal" program was designed to conserve the earth's resources, control corporations through government regulation, and protect the consumer.

39. **B** The Underwood-Simmons Tariff was passed under Woodrow Wilson. (Hint: "Under," then "w" for Wilson.) Although Wilson was one of the three Progressive presidents (Roosevelt and Taft being the other two), he was the only Democrat. The Republican Party has supported big business since the end of the 19th century, and therefore, high protective tariffs are usually enacted when Republicans are in office. The Underwood-Simmons Tariff, however, actually *lowered* duties on imported goods; thus the answer is (B).

Questions 40–44

Labor unions have had a very rough go of it for many decades. At first, government policy and law were directed only at the protection of corporations and their property. Eventually, legislature passed bills protecting the rights of workers to organize and to bargain collectively. Enforcement of those protections, however, was lax to nonexistent; as a result, many union workers were subject to all sorts of harassment. The use of scabs and strike-breaking thugs was common; workers who dared to organize could lose their jobs and even their lives.

40. **B** The cartoon depicts the government conducting a misdirected fact-finding mission at a time when abuses against labor unions were obvious. The attack is not "well-concealed," so rule out (C).

41. **A** Samuel Gompers once referred to the Clayton Antitrust Act as "The Magna Carta of Labor," because in addition to strengthening the Sherman Antitrust Act, it also exempted labor unions from antitrust prosecution and legalized strikes and picketing.

42. **D** Congress did not consistently promote the interests of labor unions, so rule out (A); Republicans, in particular, tended to try to curb the power of labor. Immigrants were not a large part of labor union membership, nor did they displace child workers (laws banning child labor accomplished this), so rule out (B). Black sharecroppers may have voted for Democrats, but they did not have a direct influence, so rule out (C). Thus, the success of labor unions was largely due to their own efforts.

43. **A** Labor unions met with resistance, in part, because they were new to America, a change from the traditional relationship between employer and employee. Many conservatives did not trust this new attempt to organize the workforce. Both union organizers and employers tended to be largely native-born, so (B) does not represent a contrast. Religion is not a factor here, so rule out (C). And most union AND employers were urban, so (D) does not represent a contrast.

44. **C** Although it was by no means universal, many early 20th-century union leaders were, in fact, Communists, or sympathetic to socialist ideologies. (This tendency reversed after World War II.) Choice (A) may have some kernel of truth, but is not the primary cause of the antilabor sentiment. Choice (D) is incorrect because McCarthy was most vocal in the 1950s.

Questions 45–48

In 1954, the Supreme Court ruled invalid the "separate but equal" standard approved by the court in *Plessy v. Ferguson* (1896). In a 9 to 0 decision, the court ruled that "separate educational facilities are inherently unequal." The suit was brought on behalf of Linda Brown, a black school-age child, by the NAACP. Then-future Supreme Court Justice Thurgood Marshall argued the case.

45. **C** About the other cases mentioned here: (A), *Marbury v. Madison*, is the case that established the principle of judicial review. Choice (B), *Bradwell v. Illinois*, is an 1873 decision in which the court upheld the right of the state of Illinois to deny a female attorney the right to practice law simply on the basis of gender. That case represented a setback for both women's rights and the Fourteenth Amendment. In (D), *Holden v. Hardy*, the Court ruled that states could pass laws regulating safety conditions in privately owned workplaces.

46. **A** Liberalism, based on a firm belief in the efficacy of governmental and especially federal power to achieve social goals at home, reached its apex in the mid-1960s and generated a variety of political and cultural responses. Southern Conservatives did not accept the goals of Civil Rights liberals without a struggle. Riots and protests erupted throughout the South, while Little Rock, Arkansas, refused to integrate its high school for some time. Choices (B) and (C) are unsupportable, while (D) cannot be directly attributed to *Brown*.

47. **C** Many formerly oppressed groups were inspired to take action after the successes of the Civil Rights movement. States' rights, however, was never a social movement in the same manner as the others.

48. **D** Reconstruction had originally intended to integrate freed slaves into Southern white society, but it largely failed to do so. Civil Rights leaders picked up the banner and sought to get the equal rights they had legally earned after the Civil War.

Questions 49–50

In the 1980s, a new conservatism grew to prominence in U.S. culture and politics, defending traditional social values and rejecting liberal views about the role of government. Reduced public faith in the government's ability to solve social and economic problems, the growth of religious fundamentalism, and the dissemination of neo-conservative thought all combined to invigorate conservatism.

49.   **A**   Public confidence and trust in government declined in the 1970s in the wake of economic infla-tion, political scandals, and foreign policy crises, such as the Iranian hostage crisis, so rule out (C). The rapid and substantial growth of evangelical and fundamentalist Christian churches and organizations, as well as increased political participation by some of those groups, encouraged sig-nificant opposition to liberal social and political trends—rule out (B) and (D). Libertarians never had much success in national elections, so (A) is the exception.

50.   **C**   Progressive Liberals would have been most opposed to Reagan's conservative principles. Choice (B), Reagan Democrats, were more moderate in their views, while (D), Populists, were not entirely liberal in their views.

Questions 51–55

The legislation passed during 1965 and 1966 represented the most sweeping change to U.S. government since the New Deal. Johnson's social agenda was termed the "Great Society."

51.   **B**   The mention of renewing "contact with nature" should call to mind wildlife and the preservation of natural habitats. Choice (B) is the only answer that connects to these ideas. An act related to mass transportation would not likely renew contact with nature. Eliminate (A). The Public Broad-casting Act and Higher Education Acts also have aims that are not directly related to nature, so (C) and (D) are incorrect.

52.   **D**   All choices, except (D), were indeed part of the Great Society program. Rather than balancing the budget, the Great Society reforms meant a significant increase in federal spending, which grew faster than government revenues through taxes.

53.   **B**   Under the Lyndon B. Johnson Administration, U.S. involvement in Vietnam accelerated. Choice (A) is associated with Kennedy. Choice (C) is associated with Truman and Eisenhower. Choice (D) occurred in the late 1980s and early 1990s under Reagan and George H. W. Bush.

54.   **A**   Today's social welfare system stems from the New Deal; those who feel that the current American system has failed can point to Roosevelt as the man who started it all.

55.   **B**   Liberal ideals were realized in Supreme Court decisions that expanded democracy and individual freedoms, Great Society social programs and policies, and the power of the federal government, yet these unintentionally helped energize a new conservative movement that mobilized to defend traditional visions of morality and the proper role of state authority.

SECTION I, PART B: SHORT-ANSWER QUESTIONS

Question 1

a) American constitutionalism is a group of ideas elaborating upon the principle that the authority of government derives from the people, and it is limited by a body of fundamental law. Constitutionalism is a bulwark against monarchy, totalitarianism, or pure democracy. In the first excerpt, Philip Wiener mentions such key ideas as the "rule of law," "officials are not free to do anything they please," "limitations on power," and "limited government."

b) Democracy is a form of government in which all eligible citizens participate equally—either directly or indirectly through elected representatives—in the proposal, development, and creation of laws. In his letter, John Adams seems to presuppose the drawbacks of pure democracy. He likens it to monarchy, though acknowledging that it is more short-lived. Democracy, "when unchecked, produces the same effects of fraud, violence, and cruelty…it is hard for the most considerate philosophers and the most conscientious moralists to resist the temptation" to descend into tyranny.

c) In your response to this question, you could have mentioned any one of the following:

Constitutionalism

- The Mayflower Compact—This document is not a constitution in the strictest sense because it does not provide for an actual government. Still, it was an important forerunner to constitutional government in the New World. Those who signed it agreed to self-government and to abide by the laws they passed.
- The Fundamental Orders of Connecticut—the formal constitution written by Connecticut settlers and enacted in 1639. (If you knew its name and date, give yourself bonus points.) You do have to know that this document was the first formal constitution in the New World and that it stated that the power of government rests in the consent of those being governed. In this assertion, the Connecticut settlers distinguished themselves from the royalists, who often argued that the king, and therefore the government, ruled by Divine Right (that is, that the king's power came from God, who chose the king).

Give yourself extra credit for mentioning the following:

- The Massachusetts Bay Charter—Acting as a constitution of sorts, it provided the mechanism for self-government. As mentioned above, Massachusetts Bay was technically ruled by the king, but actually, it was governed by the company's general court, established in the company charter. All property holders—thus, nearly all the white males in the settlement—voted for deputies (representatives) to the general court. The charter also required the company's proprietors to seek the advice and consent of all freemen before making laws.
- English traditions—(1) The Magna Carta (1215) established a few fundamental, inalienable rights for property holders. (2) The concept of limited government—the idea that the king ruled by the people's consent, and not by Divine Right—was gaining wider acceptance in England at the time. (3) The existence of a bicameral legislature—the House of Lords and the House of Commons— gave the colonists a tradition in both representative government and constitutional government.
- The English Civil War—In the early 17th century, Parliament, backed by reform forces that included the Puritans, began to demand changes to make government more responsive to and

representative of the people. King Charles responded by dissolving Parliament in 1629. When he finally recalled Parliament in 1640 (because his government was failing), Puritans demanded major constitutional reforms. Charles refused and a long, bloody war followed. When Puritan forces won in 1649, Charles lost his head and England, briefly, had a constitution. The whole episode demonstrates that the Puritans were strongly committed to constitutionalism.

- The New England Confederation—Founded in 1643, the confederation of New England colonies was mostly powerless because it had no executive power. However, it did settle some border disputes, and it represented the people's willingness to create governmental agencies and to (sort of) abide by their decisions.

Democracy

- All the New England colonies had elected legislatures by 1650.
- Most had bicameral legislatures, with a lower house elected by all freemen and an upper house usually made up of appointees. Freemen also usually elected the governor.
- New England had a tradition of town meetings at which many of the decisions concerning local government were made.
- Women, indentured servants, and slaves could not vote.
- Except in Rhode Island, only Puritans had the right to vote.
- Otherwise, voting rights were extended to all property holders. Because most settlers were enticed to the New World by the prospect of owning land and because in the early years land was plentiful, nearly all the white male colonists could vote.

Give yourself extra credit for mentioning the following:

- The Massachusetts Bay Company, while technically controlled by the king, had little contact with England. It was empowered to make almost all important decisions. It set an early precedent for self-government in the New World.
- Although initially governed by the owners of the company, Massachusetts Bay's governors soon extended democratic rights to all Puritan property-owning settlers. The colony was ruled by a general court to which all towns were allowed to elect delegates.
- The Plymouth settlement formed a legislature as soon as the settlement expanded beyond a couple of towns.
- The Puritans valued the ideal of the covenant. They believed they had a covenant with God, and they used the covenant as a model for their secular behavior. Accordingly, the Puritans expected everyone to work for the communal good and that everyone would have a voice in how the community was run.
- When settlers moved into the Connecticut Valley, they had their first run-in with Native Americans. The settlers essentially tried to bully the natives out of their land. In the resulting Pequot War, settlers torched villages and killed women and children. You might mention this as evidence of the settlers' rather limited sense of fair play and justice, which are usually considered democratic ideals.

About the Structure of Your Essay

For part (c), you want a short statement that allows you to discuss both of the basic characteristics of early American democracy. One way to achieve this is to discuss these developments in the context of their contribution to later developments in American self-governance. For example, you might phrase your statement in the following manner: "Because of their distance from England, the English colonists in New England were in a situation that largely allowed them to govern themselves. Other factors—English traditions, Puritan beliefs, the wide availability of land—helped create the communities that in many ways laid the foundation for American government. However, these communities also differed in significant ways from what we usually identify as the "American ideal." Then follow it up with ONE pertinent fact with regard to your chosen themes (supporting the first excerpt or refuting the second excerpt). A one-sentence conclusion, perhaps mentioning the similarities and differences between Puritan society and the more pluralistic democratic societies that followed it, would also be helpful.

Question 2

The name of this work is "English Trade with Indians" by Theodor de Bry, painted in 1634. (Notice that the College Board does not tell you this; they want to see if you can interpret the drawing on your own.)

This picture shows you one interpretation of a trading session between the English and Native Americans. Theodor de Bry was one of the first to create such drawings of the New World. Are there any European biases about Native Americans in this drawing? That might make good fodder for your essay.

a) For this question, you may have mentioned some of the following:

Commerce

* Make a nod to the Columbian Exchange, a series of interactions and adaptations among societies across the Atlantic.
* The Spanish introduced new crops and livestock to natives.

American Indians

* Iroquois and Algonquian Indians were not nomadic. They had permanent villages built around agriculture and fishing. This enabled them to engage in serious commerce with the English.
* Many Europeans had deeply ingrained beliefs about racial superiority.
* The English eventually established American colonies based on agriculture; large numbers of settlers came, often having relatively hostile relationships with American Indians.
* Early conflicts: The Beaver Wars, the Chickasaw Wars, King Philip's War.

European Exploration

* Spanish and Portuguese exploration and conquest of the Americas led to widespread deadly epidemics.
* New sources of mineral wealth facilitated the European shift from feudalism to capitalism.
* New sailing technology: the sextant.

b) and c) For these questions, describe the contrasts in how each group is portrayed, Indian and English traders. Explain the significance of any objects depicted. The traders seem to be interacting in a positive way, but we know that relationships between the English and native peoples were not always easy. What might have happened after the exchange depicted?

Question 3

a) and b) For these questions, you may have discussed some of the following:

- Spain was particularly successful in converting much of Meso-America to Catholicism through the Spanish mission system, thus introducing the idea that Natives could be Europeanized through religion. Christians in the Northeast tried this tactic and largely failed.
- The Puritans sought a new life and religious freedom in Massachusetts, thus setting the stage for the eventual republic.
- The Pilgrims created the Mayflower Compact, which is important not only because it created a legal authority and an assembly, but also because it asserted that the government's power derives from the consent of the governed.
- John Winthrop delivered a now-famous sermon, "A Model of Christian Charity," urging the colonists to be a "city upon a hill"—a model for others to look up to. All Puritans believed they had a covenant with God. Government was to be a covenant among the people.
- The First Great Awakening: Congregationalist minister Jonathan Edwards and Methodist preacher George Whitefield came to exemplify the period. Edwards preached the severe doctrines of Calvinism and became famous for his graphic depictions of Hell; his most famous speech was "Sinners in the Hands of an Angry God." Whitefield preached a Christianity based on emotionalism and spirituality, which today is most clearly manifested in Southern evangelism. The First Great Awakening is often described as the response of devout people to the Enlightenment.

c) For this question, you may have mentioned some of the following:

- Explorers, such as Juan de Oñate, swept through the American Southwest, determined to create Christian converts by any means necessary—including violence. Oñate was resisted by the natives.
- The Salem Witch Trials are often thought to be a product of the Puritan resistance to changes in their power within Massachusetts and declining support for Puritanism within the younger generation.
- Even though the Puritans had fled England because of religious persecution, they did not allow freedom of religion in their colonies.
- Roger Williams—Williams came to the New World to teach in the Salem Bay settlement (part of the Massachusetts Bay Colony). His writings and teachings advocated separation of church and state and the free practice of all religions in the New World. He also had some other radical ideas, such as suggesting that the English had no right to take land away from Native American tribes. The Puritans banished Williams from the colony in 1636. He moved to modern-day Providence and received a charter for the colony of Rhode Island in 1642. The charter specified that Rhode Island would protect the freedom of religion. By 1650, Rhode Island was still the only New England colony that allowed individuals to follow their religious faiths in freedom.
- Anne Hutchinson—Hutchinson fell from favor with the Puritans because of her ideas. She believed in the power of grace and also that God spoke directly to certain, chosen people. Those people, she argued, did not need Puritan ministers or the Church because God assured those He spoke to that they would be saved. Her position was known as "antinomianism." Hutchinson's message appealed to many Puritans because of its assurances of salvation. She was considered dangerous, doubly so because she was becoming a powerful woman in a society in which women were definitely second-class citizens. The General Court of Massachusetts brought her up on charges of defaming the ministry, found her guilty, and banished her. She started a settlement in Portsmouth, Rhode Island.
- There was no separation of church and state, as evidenced by the charges against Anne Hutchinson.

Question 4

This essay requires you to demonstrate an understanding of the concept of collective security and then provide historical examples that illustrate the role of collective security in the formation of U.S. foreign policy in the postwar period. That's the easy part, however. Remember that if you're aiming to get a 4 or 5 on this exam, you need to write analytical, not merely descriptive, essays. The College Board often utilizes this continuation/departure format in a social or foreign policy question, asking you to determine if the U.S. government is doing the same thing it always has or if this is a new policy. A really strong essay will not only answer the last part of this question but also discuss why the United States chose to alter its course at this time in history.

a) For this part, you merely have to describe what is meant by *collective security*. In simple terms, it is the cooperation of multiple nation-states for mutually beneficial security. To move your score higher, give an example or two on how this has been used by the United States. You may touch on the alliance systems from the two world wars, for instance.

b) For this question, you may have mentioned some of the following:

- In his Farewell Address, George Washington had urged the new nation to avoid permanent entangling alliances. Subsequent administrations followed Washington's advice throughout the entire 19th and early 20th centuries. We did not enter a major military alliance until World War I, and even then, we attempted to retreat to our traditional policy of isolationism when the war was over.
- How about the Senate's defeat of the Treaty of Versailles and the failure of the United States to join the League of Nations? This will enable you to argue that U.S. foreign policy following World War II was a *departure* from previous policy.
- If you choose the UN as one of the two alliances about which to write in your essay, you should mention the wartime conferences that established the UN at the conclusion of World War II.
- If you plan to write about NATO, then you should mention the uneasy alliance between the Soviet Union and the United States during World War II. You should also discuss the decisions reached at Yalta and the subsequent Soviet takeover of Eastern Europe. Be careful not to go into too much detail here. This is only a short essay! But this information answers the "Why at this time?" question and will strengthen your essay.
- It is not necessary to provide the historical background to SEATO. A brief discussion of NATO, however, might provide the rationale as to why the United States formed SEATO in 1954.
- Be sure to include a definition of collective security somewhere in your essay. It is usually a good idea to define the terms you will use in whatever essay you are writing. For example, it never hurts to define terms such as *democracy, nationalism,* and *imperialism.*
- A strong essay should answer a why question; so in this case, you should not only state that these international alliances were a clear departure from previous U.S. foreign policy, but you might also blame them on Stalin, for example. Don't be afraid to say something slightly unusual, as long as you have historical evidence to support what you are writing. Don't just say "We created the UN because we didn't join the League of Nations after World War I." This is a weak and boring statement.

Here is some in-depth info on each organization:

The UN

Many historians believe that the Treaty of Versailles was one of the major causes of World War II. Others see the failure of collective security to prevent another world war and blame the impotence of the League of Nations for its failure to stop German, Italian, and Japanese aggression throughout the 1930s. Some critics argue the

League would have been stronger had the United States been a member. You should remember that the League of Nations was proposed by Woodrow Wilson in his Fourteen Points as a means of maintaining world peace. The United Nations was formed after World War II in part to replace the League of Nations and in response to the horrors committed during World War II.

The most obvious choice here is the Korean War. You should begin this paragraph with a brief discussion of the Truman Doctrine and the articulation of the policy of containment by George Kennan. The Korean conflict is often considered the first test case of containment. Mao's forces won a victory in China in 1949, and when Soviet-supported North Korean troops invaded South Korea the following year, the UN Security Council declared North Korea an aggressor and voted to send in troops. Although the United States provided the majority of manpower, we went into Korea in 1950 under the protective umbrella of the United Nations. The Soviets had successfully tested an atomic bomb in 1949. Given the threat of atomic warfare, the United States felt more secure as part of an international peacekeeping organization.

NATO

In 1949, the United States, Canada, Great Britain, France, Italy, Belgium, the Netherlands, Luxembourg, Portugal, Denmark, Norway, and Iceland signed the North Atlantic Treaty. Each nation agreed that it would view an attack on any one nation as an attack on them all. Greece and Turkey were admitted to the Organization three years later. Unlike the UN, which is an international peacekeeping organization, NATO is an international, defensive military alliance. The United States' entrance into NATO was a significant departure from traditional U.S. foreign policy and marked the first peacetime military alliance in U.S. history. If the Truman Doctrine was an ideological response to the establishment of Soviet satellites following World War II, and the Marshall Plan "put our money where our mouth is," then NATO may be seen as the military component of this equation. You might mention either the war in Bosnia or the Persian Gulf War to illustrate NATO in action.

SEATO

In 1954, eight nations—including the United States and its major western allies, Great Britain and France—signed a collective defense treaty with the Philippines, Thailand, and Pakistan to form what became known as the Southeast Asia Treaty Organization. In essence, it was basically a Southeast Asian version of NATO. Each member nation pledged to come to the defense of another member nation in the event it was attacked. However, unlike NATO, an attack on one nation would not necessarily be viewed as an attack on them all. The United States agreed to the provisions of the treaty on the condition that the aggressor be a member of the communist bloc. Although the organization was intended to provide an "anticommunist shield" to the nations of Southeast Asia, SEATO was not invoked to protect Cambodia, Laos, or Vietnam during the Vietnam War, as one would have suspected. In fact, the Geneva Accords specifically precluded South Vietnam, Cambodia, and Laos from joining the organization. France lost interest almost immediately and did not feel bound to the other member nations after Vietnam gained its independence following the French defeat in the battle of Dien Bien Phu. The United States tried to make the situation in Vietnam a collective security issue, as evidenced by the rhetoric of the domino theory, but was unsuccessful. In effect, SEATO never had the teeth or muscle that NATO had, and it was dissolved in 1977.

c) This question can be answered by using any of the facts cited for part (a), while demonstrating that the organization was NOT a strong continuation or departure from prior U.S. foreign policy OR by simply explaining why it is LESS of a continuation or departure from the choice you made in part (a).

SECTION II, QUESTION 1: DOCUMENT-BASED QUESTION

The document-based question begins with a mandatory 15-minute reading period. During these 15 minutes, you should (1) come up with some information not included in the given documents (your outside knowledge) to include in your essay, (2) get an overview of what each document means, (3) decide what opinion you are going to argue, and (4) write an outline of your essay.

This DBQ concerns U.S. neutrality prior to World War I. You will have to explore to what extent the United States followed a policy of neutrality between 1914 and 1917. On the following pages, we will talk about how you might successfully explore this topic.

The first thing you want to do, BEFORE YOU LOOK AT THE DOCUMENTS, is brainstorm for a minute or two. Try to list everything you remember about the period leading up to the United States' entry into World War I. This list will serve as your reference to the outside information you must provide in order to earn a top grade.

Next, read over the documents. As you read them, take notes in the margins and underline those passages that you are certain you are going to use in your essay. If a document helps you remember a piece of outside information, add that information to your brainstorming list. If you cannot make sense of a document or it argues strongly against your position, relax! You may omit mention of <u>one</u> of the documents and still score well on the DBQ.

You need to look for the following in each document to get the most out of it:

- the author
- the date
- the audience (for whom was the document intended?)
- the significance

Remember: while readers are looking for as much in-depth document analysis as possible, it does help to bring in some outside information. They will not be able to give you a high score unless you have both! What readers really don't like is a laundry list of documents: that is, a paper in which the student merely goes through the documents, explaining each one. Those students are often the ones who forget to bring in outside information, because they are so focused on going through the documents.

Here is what you might see in the time you have to look over the documents.

The Documents

Document 1 is an excerpt from Wilson's declaration of neutrality. It makes several important points you can use.

Neutrality is defined as "impartiality and fairness and friendliness to all concerned." This standard will enable you to argue that the United States was, or was not, neutral.

The American people come from the different nations at war. The political implication is that even if the U.S. government wanted to enter World War I, the varied national backgrounds of the electorate would make it difficult to rally the nation to one side or the other. Even before Vietnam, American politicians knew the risks of entering an unpopular war.

Wilson envisions a prominent role for the United States resulting from neutrality. He sees the United States as "the one people holding itself ready to play a part of impartial mediation and speak the counsels of peace and accommodation, not as a partisan, but as a friend." This point argues that the United States entered the war as a neutral force, or, at the very least, intended to.

Document 2 is an excerpt from a letter a respected German-American intellectual wrote to Wilson early in the war. It describes German-American perceptions of U.S. favoritism toward the Allies.

This document persuasively argues that U.S. policies at the time favored the Allies. The details are important, but they are less important than the overall point; the document illustrates that an intelligent critique of U.S. policy, held up to its own definition of neutrality, is possible. In fact, when Wilson received this letter, he sent it to his secretary of state with a note essentially saying, "This letter makes a pretty strong case."

Munsterberg's second point, regarding the detention and searching of Germans and Austrians, is not often mentioned in discussions of the events leading up to World War I, and you are not expected to have heard of this policy. However, it does provide ammunition for those arguing that the United States was never neutral; searching civilians is, at the very least, an act of aggressive mistrust. If Allied travelers were not being treated the same way—and the letter implies they were not—then it indicates favoritism.

The issue of contraband could lead you to discuss the British blockade. (Document 3 provides more evidence of the effect of the British blockade.) Contraband is illegal merchandise. During war, contraband always includes weapons and other supplies necessary to the successful execution of war. The notion that contraband is illegal does not preclude the United States from selling arms to Europe; this same document demonstrates that the United States did just that. It does mean, however, that a country executing a successful blockade has the right to confiscate contraband. Munsterberg is saying that England defined contraband very broadly, including on its list of contraband items supplies that the German civilian population needed to survive. He complains that the United States was not aggressive enough in protesting this practice.

The last paragraph talks about the U.S. sale of arms to belligerents. This information can be interpreted in many ways. You could argue that to sell arms is essentially non-neutral, even if you sell to both sides. To make this argument, you would have to equate neutrality with pacifism (something Wilson does in Document 1) and then assert that arms sales prolong the war, and so they are counterproductive to the goals of neutrality. On the other hand, you could argue that because of the successful British blockade, arms sales were predominantly to the Allies; arms shipments to Germany never made it through the blockade. Again, Document 3 will help bolster this position.

Document 3, an often-quoted passage, comes from the memoirs of Robert Lansing, acting secretary of state and, later, secretary of state under Wilson.

Lansing describes the effects of the British blockade. Note that merchants are losing profits, and Americans are being terribly inconvenienced.

You might use this to argue favoritism toward the British. Since the British were interfering with U.S. trade, why didn't we go to war against them? To the contrary, you could point out that as it became clear that U.S. commercial interests were at stake, U.S. involvement in the war became more likely. In other words, the United States started out neutral, but the British blockade and German submarine warfare slowly forced America into the war. (See Documents 5, 6, 7, and 8.) You can also use this document to further discuss the effects of the British blockade on (1) the Allies and (2) the Central Powers. As you do, ask yourself whether the United States' response to the blockade was consistent with its policy of neutrality.

Document 4, a report from then-Secretary of State William Jennings Bryan (he would soon resign in protest) to the Senate. It is still early in the war.

Do not be intimidated by the length of this passage! The main point is simple. The government felt that its actions were neutral. This letter can be seen as a response to the complaints voiced in Munsterberg's letter.

Bryan discusses communication, the blockade, arms sales, and perceived hostility toward the governments of the Central Powers. In almost every case, he argues that England's advantages in geographic location and naval power are causing America's perceived breaches of neutrality.

If you are arguing that the United States was neutral, you might mention (if you remember) that Bryan, a pacifist, was committed to neutrality. His feeling that U.S. actions were neutral could be presented as strong evidence for your case.

If you are arguing that the United States was not neutral, you might contend that because Bryan is reporting to the Senate, he paints the rosiest picture he can. You might also mention (if you remember) that Bryan resigned not long after because of his disagreements with U.S. policy.

Document 5 is an advertisement that ran in fifty American newspapers just before the *Lusitania* sailed.

This document gives you the opportunity to discuss German submarine warfare. The British blockade was too effective for the Germans to fight it conventionally. The Germans therefore turned to the U-boat, or submarine. Submarines gave the Germans the advantage of surprise, as the British had no means of detecting them. You could argue that because submarine attacks resulted in the deaths of U.S. citizens, the use of submarines constituted a hostile act that ultimately forced the neutral United States into war. You might mention that Wilson regarded submarines as a violation of international law (see Chapter 11) and, as such, repeatedly asked the Germans to curtail their usage.

On the contrary, you might claim that the British blockade forced Germany to use submarines, and that by not opposing the blockade more aggressively, the United States was essentially siding with the Allies.

This document, along with Document 6, also gives you the opportunity to discuss the sinking of the *Lusitania* and its effects, both on U.S. policy and on anti-German sentiments in the general population. The shift in American public opinion away from neutrality is a factor you might mention in your discussion of U.S. entry into the war.

Document 6 is a customs report that provides evidence that the *Lusitania* carried weapons.

This document can be paired with Munsterberg's complaint about arms sales (Document 2) to support the argument that the United States was not neutral. Note that the shipment is headed for England. Your outside knowledge that the sinking of the *Lusitania* led to William Jennings Bryan's resignation as secretary of state would also be helpful here. Remember, the United States protested the sinking vigorously and demanded reparations. Bryan pointed out that the ship carried arms and quietly assured the Germans that the United States understood why the ship was sunk. In short, Bryan was at odds with official government policy, and he resigned when he realized that his advice to the president was going unheeded. His replacement, Robert Lansing, more active in defending American interests than Bryan, was willing to trade a reduction in American commerce for peace.

If you are arguing for neutrality, it is best to mention this document only in passing. Note that in Document 4, Bryan explains how the United States reconciles arms sales and neutrality. His justification, in short, is that international law does not outlaw such sales.

Document 7: Wilson gave this speech after the Germans sank the *Sussex*, an unarmed French channel steamer. The document is from 1916, almost a year after the sinking of the *Lusitania*.

Wilson threatens to break off diplomatic relations with Germany—a first step toward war.

Wilson invokes international law. Because Wilson interpreted international law as severely restricting submarine warfare, submarine attacks by Germany particularly angered him. Wilson considered himself and the United States the defenders of international law.

Wilson continues to declare America's international role as a mediator and peacemaker, as he did in his neutrality speech (Document 1). This insistence indicates that Wilson still considers the United States a neutral force.

You might point out that a year after the sinking of the *Lusitania* and that of several other ships, the United States is still not at war. This fact strongly argues for neutrality through early 1916.

Outside Information

We have already discussed much more than you could possibly include in a 45-minute essay. Do not worry. You will not be expected to mention everything or even most of what we have covered in the section above. You will, however, be expected to include some outside information—that is, information not mentioned directly in the documents.

Here is some outside information you might have used in your essay. The information is divided into two groups: general concepts and specific events.

General Concepts

- Even before the war, the United States relied more on trade with the British than with Germany. After the war began, this dependence became even heavier as the British blockade decreased American trade with Germany. The war effort also resulted in an increase in British orders for American goods. This increase occurred because the war had decreased British productivity. The British had taken men out of factories and put them in the army, and they also had converted some commercial manufacturing to munitions manufacturing.

- When the war started, official U.S. policy stated that American banks should not lend money to any nation at war. However, bankers pressured the administration to change this policy because Europe did not have the money to pay for the American goods it was ordering. Also, the loans were profitable, and American banks feared losing a lucrative opportunity to banks in other neutral nations. The majority of these loans went to the Allies.

- Wilson hoped the war would end in a draw. He thought a victorious Germany "would change the course of our civilization and make the United States a military nation." He also felt that an Allied victory would shift the balance of power too favorably toward England and France. Many of Wilson's advisors, however, were both pro-British and anti-German.

- "Wilsonianism," Wilson's idealized vision of the future, included universal, nonexploitative, free market capitalism; universal political constitutionalism, which would lead to the disappearance of empires; and universal cooperation and peace through the offices of the League of Nations. Wilson was also anxious to create a world leadership role for the United States. Many of his actions can be explained as the pursuit of these goals.

- Wilson held very strong views concerning international law, and those views favored the British. According to international law, an attacker had to warn a passenger or merchant ship before attacking. Submarines did not do this, for the obvious reason that it would cancel the greatest advantage submarines had—the element of surprise. Germany argued that submarines provided their only means of breaking British control of shipping channels, but this assertion did not persuade Wilson.

Specific Events

- The British blockade—From the beginning of the war, the British used their advantage at sea. They blocked shipping channels and confiscated any contraband headed for a Central Power country. Furthermore, England defined contraband very broadly, including some food and commercial products on its contraband list. The United States lodged numerous complaints against the practice, but the British government always paid for what it confiscated. The payment satisfied merchants and took enough pressure off Washington that the U.S. government never forced the issue.

- The sinking of the *Lusitania*, May 7, 1915—You will lose big points if you say that this event caused the United States to enter the war; the United States waited another two years before it started to fight. The *Lusitania* was a luxury liner that sailed from New York to England. When it sank, it took with it 1,198 passengers, among them 128 Americans. As

Document 6 illustrates, the *Lusitania* was carrying a considerable amount of contraband, including over 4 million rounds of rifle ammunition. Still, Wilson and most of his advisors considered Germany's attack on the ship barbaric. As a result of the attack, anti-German sentiments among voters grew stronger and more widespread.

- William Jennings Bryan's resignation—Bryan resigned in the aftermath of the *Lusitania* incident. An ardent pacifist, Bryan wanted the United States to respond to the incident with a strongly worded letter of protest to both the English and the Germans. Bryan also suggested that the United States ban American passengers from any ship flying the flag of a belligerent country. Wilson rejected both recommendations. He sent a letter of protest only to the Germans, and he refused to restrict American travel abroad. Bryan resigned in protest. In response to Wilson's letter, the Germans temporarily halted U-boat attacks on passenger ships.

- The sinking of the *Arabic*—In mid-August 1915, the Germans sank another passenger liner. This time only two Americans died, but the government was furious about the breach of etiquette. The Germans pledged again never to attack a passenger liner without advance warning, a promise they did not keep.

- Gore-McLemore resolution—After the sinking of the *Arabic*, Congress began to seriously consider a resolution prohibiting Americans from traveling on armed merchant ships or on ships carting contraband. Wilson fought this Gore-McLemore resolution. Wilson remained adamant that neutral nations should have free access to international waters. The resolution was defeated.

- The sinking of the *Sussex* and the Sussex Agreement—In February 1917, the Germans sank a French channel steamer called the *Sussex*. No Americans died, although four were injured. However, the incident had a big impact because the *Sussex* was neither armed nor was it carrying contraband. In short, its sinking convinced many people that either (1) German submarines could not tell what they were shooting at, or (2) the Germans did not care that they were killing civilians. Either way, it supported the widespread sentiment that submarine warfare was barbaric. Germany again agreed not to attack passenger ships without warning. Wilson was still resolutely determined to stay out of the war, so he accepted the agreement.

- The presidential election of 1916—Despite the many quarrels with England and Germany, most Americans still wanted no part of the European hostilities. All the major candidates campaigned against entry into the war. The Republican, Hughes, courted German-American votes and depicted Wilson as partial to the Allies. Wilson campaigned on the slogan "He kept us out of war." As the campaign wore on, however, he also began to stress "preparedness" for the possibility of war. Wilson won by a narrow margin.

- Details about the Zimmermann note—By the time this telegram was leaked to the press, Germany had already warned the United States of its plans to resume unrestricted submarine warfare. The reason for the shift in policy is that the Germans realized that without the submarines they would soon lose the war. The resumption of submarine warfare greatly angered Wilson. When the British intercepted the telegram, Wilson had already severed diplomatic ties with Germany and was considering his future options. Wilson received the telegram on February 24, 1917, and the newspapers received it four days later.

The telegram represents a last-ditch effort on Germany's part to keep the United States out of the war. Germany knew that its resumption of submarine warfare would draw the United States into the war. Planning to distract the United States with a border skirmish, Germany hoped to buy enough time to win the war in Europe before U.S. reinforcements could arrive. Because the Mexican Revolution had just replaced a government friendly to the United States with one much more hostile, the U.S. government took the threat of a German-backed Mexican attack in the Southwest very seriously.

It particularly galled the United States that Zimmermann sent the telegram through U.S. State Department channels. The United States had opened those channels to him in hopes of bringing the Germans back to the negotiating table. When he used those same channels to plot war against the United States, it was regarded as an act of extreme hostility and bad manners.

The United States did not immediately declare war. In the weeks that followed, Wilson asked Congress for a policy of "armed neutrality," which would allow American merchant ships to mount offensive weapons. Debate was fierce, showing how strong antiwar sentiment was even at the time. The United States did not officially declare war until the following month, on April 2, 1917.

- The Nye Commission investigations of 1933—The Nye Commission, investigating American business practices in the years leading up to World War I, revealed that American arms merchants had lobbied intensely for entry into the war. The commission also discovered that these merchants had reaped enormous profit from arms sales, first from whomever they could get them to in Europe and then from the U.S. government.

Choosing a Side

We have just covered an intimidating amount of material. Do not worry; your essay has to cover only some of the points mentioned above. This review mentions nearly everything you might include in a successful essay, not everything that must be in a successful essay.

Your next task is to choose a position to argue and then construct a strong justification from your notes on the documents and outside information. Document-based questions are written so that there is no one right answer, and there are many different defensible positions to this question. There are also many different ways to argue the same point; that is, there is no one right way to write an essay for any given argument.

Here are some positions you might argue:

- The United States was neutral at the beginning of the war, but a combination of factors—such as economic interests, German transgressions of international law, and America's predisposition toward England—ultimately drew America into the war.

- The United States was neutral at the beginning of the war but was provoked to fight by German aggression.

- The United States claimed neutrality, and maybe its leaders even convinced themselves that their actions were neutral, but in reality, U.S. actions helped the Allies. Consequently, the United States was never really neutral.

- The United States was correct in claiming neutrality because its policies adhered to its standards of neutrality. However, the Central Powers legitimately accused the United States of acting in a way that assisted the Allies and so were justified in regarding the United States as non-neutral. The question is semantic; whether the United States was neutral depends on how you define neutrality.

The only position you should certainly avoid is the claim that the United States had always sided fully with the Allies and lied about neutrality in order to help them. There is simply too much evidence of Wilson's commitment to neutrality to support that argument.

Planning Your Essay

Unless you read extremely quickly, you probably will not have time to write a detailed outline for your essay during the 15-minute reading period. However, it is worth taking several minutes to jot down a loose structure of your essay; it will actually save you time when you write. First, decide on your thesis and write it down in the test booklet. (There is usually some blank space below the documents.) Then, take a minute or two to brainstorm all the points you might put in your essay. Choose the strongest points and number them in the order you plan to present them. Lastly, note which documents and outside information you plan to use in conjunction with each point. If you organize your essay before you write, the actual writing process will go much more smoothly. More importantly, you will not write yourself into a corner and suddenly find yourself making a point you cannot support or heading toward a weak conclusion (or worse still, no conclusion at all).

For example, if you are going to argue that the United States was neutral at the start of the war, but a combination of factors eventually forced America's entry, you might write down an abbreviated version of that thesis, such as the following:

Started neutral, forced into war

Then you would brainstorm a list of ideas and events you wanted to mention in your essay, such as these.

Started neutral
British blockade
Business losing money from blockade
Wilson didn't want Germany to win war
U-boats violate international law
U-boats kill U.S. civilians
Zimmermann telegram
Lusitania
Sussex
American people were against war
Americans a little more favorable to war by 1917

Next, you would want to figure out which of your brainstorm ideas could be the main idea of a paragraph, which could be used as evidence to support a point, and which should be eliminated. You would probably want to begin your first paragraph by stating your thesis and then discussing how the United States was neutral at the start of the war. Your first point, "Started neutral," could be the main idea of that paragraph. That the "American people were against the war" would help explain why the United States was neutral, so you could use that as evidence. At this point, your list might look like this.

Started neutral	1
British blockade	
Business losing money from blockade	
Wilson didn't want Germany to win war	
U-boats violate international law	
U-boats kill U.S. civilians	
Zimmermann telegram	
Lusitania	
Sussex	
American people were against war	evidence for point 1
Americans a little more favorable to war by 1917	

What else would you want to mention in this paragraph? Certainly refer to Document 1, Wilson's statement of American neutrality and his definition of neutrality. Use that definition to explain how each of America's ensuing actions was either neutral or favorable to the Allies. You might also mention Wilson's desire to turn the United States into a world power and how he viewed neutrality as a means toward that end. Mentioning this point helps you fulfill the requirement to include outside information.

Next you might want to discuss the British blockade and America's response to it. That would make "British blockade" the subject of paragraph 2; "business losing money from blockade" is something you might want to mention in this paragraph. Now your list might look like this:

Started neutral	1
British blockade	2
Business losing money from blockade	evidence for point 2
Wilson didn't want Germany to win war	
U-boats violate international law	
U-boats kill U.S. civilians	
Zimmermann telegram	
Lusitania	
Sussex	
American people were against war	evidence for point 1
Americans a little more favorable to war by 1917	

In this paragraph, you probably also want to mention Documents 2, 3, and 4. Document 4, Bryan's letter to the Senate, gives the strongest evidence of U.S. neutrality. You might want to use Documents 2 and 3 (Munsterberg's complaint to Wilson and Lansing's description of the effects of the blockade) to explain how the United States found itself more involved in Europe's war than it perhaps had expected to be.

Proceed in this way until you have finished planning your strategy. Try to fit as many of the documents into your argument as you can, but do not stretch too far to fit one in. An obvious, desperate stretch will only hurt your grade.

As you write, remember that you do not have to fall entirely on one side or another of this issue. History is complex, and simple explanations are rarely accurate ones. If your essay argues that the United States intended to remain neutral and then discusses the events referred to by the documents in the context of neutrality, you will get a 9 on your DBQ essay, even if it does not characterize each U.S. action as neutral or non-neutral.

Arguing Against Neutrality

If you choose to argue that the United States was not neutral, you should concentrate on Documents 1, 2, and 3. Use Document 1, Wilson's congressional address, for the definition of neutrality, and then use the other documents and outside knowledge to argue that the United States did not meet its own definition. Document 2, Munsterberg's letter, really helps your position as it points out how U.S. actions appeared non-neutral at the time these events were taking place. Use Document 3, Lansing's criticism of the British blockade, to argue that the United States put up with abuses from the British at the same time they were denouncing Germany for similar abuses. Focus also on Document 6, which describes the substantial arms shipment aboard the *Lusitania*. You might then incorporate the other documents by claiming that Germany responded reasonably to its situation and that the United States, as a neutral nation, should have understood its actions. That position, by the way, is how William Jennings Bryan felt; if you knew that and included it in your essay, you would have gotten major bonus points for outside knowledge.

What You Should Have Discussed

Regardless of what side of the issue you argued, your essay should have discussed all of the following:

- Wilson's declaration of neutrality and his definition of neutrality
- Munsterberg's letter
- Bryan's response to Munsterberg
- the British blockade
- German submarine warfare
- the sinking of the *Lusitania*
- Zimmermann telegram

Give yourself very high marks for outside knowledge if you mentioned any three of the following:

- Wilsonianism
- U.S. balance of trade with the Allies and the Central Powers
- U.S. loans to England and France
- Wilson's cabinet and its predisposition toward England
- Wilson's interpretation of international law regarding submarine warfare
- Bryan's resignation
- the sinking of the *Sussex*
- the Gore-McLemore resolution
- the sinking of the *Arabic*
- "armed neutrality"
- the Nye Commission

SECTION II: THE LONG ESSAY QUESTION

Question 2

If you choose this question, keep in mind the three major theories concerning the issue. One holds that the Revolution was truly radical in its ideological quest for liberty and in the social and economic changes it brought about. A second theory holds that, on the contrary, simple economic and material interests, led by the colonists' desire to control their own economy, propelled the Revolution. A third holds that both ideology and material interests inspired our Revolution and that only by understanding the relationship between the two can we fully comprehend it.

If you decide to write about how the American Revolution was a radical break with the past, your essay pretty much has to mention the following:

- the establishment of representative government in the new United States and the expansion of voting rights
- the political changes that resulted from our new republican form of government, including the concept of Federalism, a written constitution, and the delicate balance between the rights of the state and those of the individual
- the notion that the colonists were spurred to revolution by their study of the ideas of the Enlightenment and their dislike of British rule

Give yourself extra points for mentioning any of the following:

- Thomas Paine's *Common Sense* and how it swayed public opinion in favor of independence by stating that it was against common sense for people to pledge loyalty to a corrupt and distant king whose laws were unreasonable
- the social changes brought about by the Revolution, such as the abolition of aristocratic titles and the separation of church and state

- the economic opportunities that resulted from our no longer being a British colony and the rise our independence gave to free enterprise and capitalism
- any of the relevant Revolutionary theorists or historians, such as Bailyn, Beard, Nash, or Boorstin

If you decide to write about how the American Revolution was a conservative attempt to maintain the status quo, then your essay pretty much has to mention the following:

- that some of the colonists' most important motives for seeking independence were based on economic self-interest, such as their desire to escape British taxes and British control of trade
- that the colonists sought to maintain the same social structure that existed under British rule, which included patronage and a devotion to patriarchal authority
- that the status of women and blacks remained pretty much unchanged after the Revolution

Give yourself bonus points for mentioning any of the following:

- the class aspect of the Revolution, including the idea that the Revolution wasn't only about "home rule" but about "who should rule at home" (in other words, the Revolutionaries thought that American aristocrats should rule instead of British aristocrats)
- the issue of slavery and how this war "for freedom" did nothing to abolish it, and, in fact, gave rise to a nation that enshrined slavery in its Constitution, with the notorious "Three-Fifths Clause" in Article I
- that the Revolution did not make great strides in the status of women. Extra bonus points for including Abigail Adams's letter to her husband, John, in which she writes, "Remember the ladies, and be more generous and favorable to them than your ancestors."
- that American distribution of wealth was not radically changed by the Revolution, which meant that those at the top of the social ladder were able to hold on to what they had

About the Structure of Your Essay

Remember that the best essays make the reader aware that you know both sides of the argument, even though you support one side more than the other. Try to take one side, and support it with as many details as you can (names, dates, documents, publications). Before your conclusion, you should include a paragraph in which you explain why the other side is wrong. For instance, if you were to write a glowing essay about how revolutionary the American Revolution was, one of your paragraphs should include the fact that, yes, certain lives, like those of women and blacks, were not radically altered by the Revolution, but that nonetheless this doesn't undermine the Revolution's many other radical achievements, because…. You are showing here that you understand the question well enough to have taken either side, but have chosen one over the other because you are an AP student who has learned to think for yourself! Don't forget to end with a strong conclusion that reinforces your original thesis.

Question 3

James Garfield's violent death no doubt placed a spotlight on corruption in both federal and local governments. Your job in this essay is to both enumerate the ways and analyze why this event was a catalyst for change. Your essay should describe the corruption caused by the spoils system. While the president's assassination was the act of a lone (perhaps crazed) gunman, it is a symptom of the frustration felt by many toward an unfair system. You will also discuss how reforms were necessary after the event: it was the newly appointed president, Chester A. Arthur, who was tasked with starting to clean up the mess.

Begin the essay with a brief discussion of the Gilded Age—both the wealth and the corruption. Then, lead your introduction to a claim that establishes how much the system changed following the 1881 assassination. Your body paragraphs should elaborate on the American system both before and after James Garfield's presidency.

What you may want to write about the Gilded Age before Garfield's assassination:

Rutherford B. Hayes

- Tammany Hall was the center of New York's Democratic political machine. Tammany Hall provided resources to local residents, particularly immigrants, in exchange for electoral loyalty.
- Graft, or using a political office for personal gain, was rampant in 19th-century politics.
- Boss Tweed was the most notorious of political bosses. As head of Tammany Hall, Tweed engaged in fraud and even received kickbacks from large government projects, such as the Erie Railroad. Tweed was arrested in 1871 for profiting from city contracts.
- In the spoils system, each new president would be tasked with filling hundreds of jobs. These appointments were not required to be based on merit, and were often a result of political loyalty.
- Those with opinions on the spoils system could be categorized into one of two groups: Stalwarts, who supported the system of appointing political supporters to government jobs, and Half-Breeds, who advocated civil service reform toward a merit-based system.

Give yourself bonus points for mentioning any of the following:

- George Washington Plunkitt was another boss of Tammany Hall. He distinguished between dishonest graft (motivated by selfish aims) and honest graft (for the good of the community).
- The New York Custom House, where federal duties on imports were collected, was an important symbol in the spoils system debate. The Custom House was employed entirely by political appointees.
- Roscoe Conkling, a New York senator, resigned from the body after feuding with James Garfield over New York Custom House patronage.

Things to mention about the Gilded Age following the assassination:

- President Garfield, shortly after handing out political appointments to his supporters, was killed by a supporter who was denied a job that he desired. The murder led to widespread calls for civil service reform.

- Chester A. Arthur, a longtime beneficiary of the spoils system was in the awkward position of rising to the presidency when Americans wanted nothing more from the government than to end the spoils system. Arthur ultimately signed the Pendleton Act, which was intended to do just that.
- The weak presidency that continued in the years immediately following the Pendleton Act shows us the little power the office held in the Gilded Age when the spoils system was eliminated.
- The corporate control of Congress throughout the Gilded Age, as evidenced by a toothless Sherman Antitrust Act, shows us that perhaps little had changed following the assassination.

Give yourself extra points for mentioning the following:

- Perhaps you want to make it clear that Muckrakers fixed the corrupt system, not the Pendleton Act. Lincoln Steffens's *Shame of the Cities* makes it clear that local corruption was alive and well into the early 20th century.
- Thomas Nast, the cartoonist, took great pride in exposing corruption. His cartoons of Boss Tweed were heavily influential to later satirists.

About the Structure of Your Essay

This topic can be tricky because, while some things did change following Garfield's assassination, much stayed the same. Don't worry—that can actually be your claim. If you feel that the Pendleton Act is not enough change to argue a clear difference before and after the assassination, then claim that little changed in terms of government corruption. On the other hand, the severity of misdeeds from political bosses such as Plunkett and Tweed were not as blatant following civil service reform. If you choose to say that little changed, be sure to mention what did, in fact, change the deep corruption of the Gilded Age. Perhaps you want to chalk it up to the Progressives and Muckrakers, after all.

Keep your facts plentiful, but relevant. Let your analysis do the hard work, though. Convince your reader of the power (or ineffectiveness) of the events surrounding James Garfield's assassination.

Question 4

This essay asks you to discuss that amazing decade, the 1960s. In it, you should describe the politics and social fabric of the country, giving specific examples, and then choose which two or three issues had the most impact on this decade. The 1960s are often described as a "turbulent" decade, and the reasons for that turbulence are where you want to begin. The social upheaval that was brought about by domestic and international issues, combined with the "generation gap" that defined the era, needs to be discussed. Although both the civil rights movement and the war in Vietnam began in the 1950s, the 1960s were defined by a rising tide of change and resistance to what had been readily accepted during the decades before. In contrast to the 1950s, known for its conformity and cold war jitters, the decade that followed, ushered in by the youngest president, John F. Kennedy, was one of the most mercurial in U.S. history.

You would have to begin with a solid description of the "stormy" sixties, with specific examples of the social changes that came about, and then move on to an in-depth analysis of two or three major issues. You would also be wise to mention the assassinations of John F. Kennedy, Robert F. Kennedy, and Martin Luther King, Jr., and the difficult presidency of Lyndon B. Johnson.

NOTE: It is much easier to build a case that the 1960s *did* represent a time of great change. In order to support the opposite position, you would need to find examples of turbulent events that began before the 1960s, a MUCH more difficult task. Go with the task that you can more easily defend!

The Civil Rights Movement

- Martin Luther King Jr. and his "I Have a Dream" speech
- Malcolm X and the Black Muslims
- the Southern Christian Leadership Conference, CORE, the Student Nonviolent Coordinating Committee, the NAACP, and the Black Panthers
- the voter registration drives, the "sit-ins" in the South, and the Freedom Riders
- Johnson's War on Poverty and Great Society programs
- the desegregation attempts made by Kennedy and Johnson, as compared with those made by Eisenhower and previous leaders
- the segregationist politicians and law "enforcers" in the South
- the Civil Rights Act of 1964
- the Voting Rights Act of 1965
- urban violence, "race riots"
- the shift to a more militant movement after the death of King

Give yourself extra points for mentioning the following:

- King's "Letter from a Birmingham Jail"
- the march from Selma to Montgomery, Alabama
- "Freedom Summer" in Mississippi
- the Greensboro, North Carolina, sit-ins at Woolworths
- the assassinations of Medgar Evers, Emmett Till, the three civil rights workers in Mississippi (Schwerner, Chaney, and Goodman), and the four little girls at the 16th St. Baptist Church in Birmingham
- the integration of "Ole Miss" by James Meredith, and Mississippi Governor Ross Barnett, who tried to stop him
- Governor George Wallace (and his candidacy for president in 1968), police chief Eugene "Bull" Connor, and the use of police dogs and fire hoses in Alabama
- the Mississippi Freedom Democratic Party (MFDP) at the Democratic Convention of 1964
- Stokely Carmichael, H. Rap Brown, Huey Newton, Bobby Seale, Eldridge Cleaver, and the Black Power movement
- Robert Weaver, who became the first black cabinet member (secretary of housing and urban development)
- the 1967 Kerner Commission, which concluded that black riots were a result of poverty and lack of job opportunities

The Vietnam War

- "Hawks" vs. "Doves"
- John F. Kennedy, Lyndon Johnson, Richard Nixon, Eugene McCarthy, Robert Kennedy
- Vietminh, Ho Chi Minh, South Vietnam, and Diem

- the Tet Offensive
- the war being broadcast on television to a national audience
- the Pentagon Papers
- Johnson's decision not to seek reelection
- the moratoriums and other demonstrations against the war
- the student antiwar movement

Give yourself extra points for mentioning the following:

- the Berkeley Student Movement, "hippies"
- the Students for a Democratic Society (SDS)
- "The Weathermen" (and you can add two points if you mentioned the fact that they got their name from a line in a Dylan song: "You don't need a weatherman to know which way the wind blows.")
- Hubert Humphrey
- the Democratic National Convention, Mayor Daley, the Chicago Seven
- Laos, Cambodia
- "Vietnamization"
- the burning of draft cards and the draft resistance movement
- antiwar music and Woodstock

The Women's Movement

- "Feminism" and the "Women's Liberation Movement"
- the Equal Rights Amendment and the Equal Pay Act
- National Organization for Women (NOW)
- abortion rights controversy (though *Roe v. Wade* wasn't until 1973)
- "Sexual Revolution," the birth control pill, "free love"

Give yourself extra points for mentioning the following:

- Betty Friedan's *The Feminine Mystique*
- the "glass ceiling"
- "Sexual Politics" (and the book by Kate Millett that gave it its name)
- the Kinsey Report
- Gloria Steinem, Bella Abzug, Shirley Chisholm (Chisholm could be mentioned under civil rights also)
- Woodstock and the "Counterculture"

About the Structure of Your Essay

You would need to describe the times by delving into the issues that caused the changes. But don't forget: the essays that look "easy" are often the most difficult. Don't forget to include *lots of facts* (don't let them go "blowin' in the wind...") that focus on how society and politics changed so dramatically in the 1960s.

Part III
About the AP U.S. History Exam

- The Structure of the AP U.S. History Exam
- How the AP U.S. History Exam Is Scored
- Overview of Content Topics
- Understanding Content with Thematic Learning Objectives
- How AP Exams Are Used
- Other Resources
- Designing Your Study Plan

THE STRUCTURE OF THE AP U.S. HISTORY EXAM

The AP U.S. History Exam consists of two main sections: a multiple-choice and short-answer section and an essay questions section.

The multiple-choice and short-answer section comprises 55 multiple-choice questions covering the breadth of U.S. history, and three short-answer questions. Students are provided with a total time of 95 minutes to complete this section. The multiple-choice questions are arranged in sets of two to five questions, which are tied to a primary- or secondary-source material. Students are allowed to spend 55 minutes completing the multiple-choice questions. The short-answer questions will explore one or more of the course thematic learning objectives. Students are expected to write a short response to three of four questions centered on a provided primary source, secondary source, or a prompt with no stimulus provided. Students are allowed to spend 40 minutes completing the short-answer questions.

The Latest on the AP U.S. History Course and Exam

The revised AP U.S. History test was scheduled to debut in May 2020, but because of the COVID-19 outbreak, the testing format was changed. The first administration of the new test is now planned for May 2021, so please refer to your free online student tools to see if there have been any breaking updates regarding the wording of questions or the representation of each content area within the test.

The essay questions section of the exam consists of two essays to be completed in a total of 100 minutes. After a 15-minute reading period, students may divide up the remaining time as desired, spending more or less time on each essay. AP recommends 45 minutes for the document-based question (DBQ) and 40 minutes for the long essay. The document-based question is an essay for which students will have to answer a question based on seven primary source documents provided. For the long essay, students will be asked to select an essay prompt from three different options. Unlike the DBQ, there will be no outside sources provided. This question requires the development of a thesis and/or historical argument supported by student-provided evidence.

Structure of the AP United States History Exam				
Section	Description	Number of Questions	Time Allotted	Percentage of Total Exam Score
Section I	Part A: Multiple-choice	55	55 min	40%
	Part B: Short-answer	3	40 min	20%
Reading Period			15 min	
Section II	Part A: DBQ	1	45 min	25%
	Part B: Long essay	1	40 min	15%

HOW THE AP U.S. HISTORY EXAM IS SCORED

AP U.S. History Exam scoring is based on the performance of the student on each of the four exam parts. The raw scores from each section will be weighted and summed to generate an overall AP grade of 1–5. Scoring of the multiple-choice section is based solely on the raw score of the number of correct answers. There is no penalty for guessing. The multiple-choice question section constitutes 40 percent of the total exam score. The short-answer questions will be evaluated for accuracy and useful application of historical thinking skills to address each question. The short-answer questions represent 20 percent of the total exam score.

The essay questions are graded against very clear rubrics outlined by the College Board, which we'll show you in Chapter 3. Both essays will be evaluated for development of a central thesis, contextualization, evidence, and analysis. The document-based question is scored with a maximum score of 7 possible points allocated across the following areas: thesis (1 point), contextualization (1 point), historical evidence (3 points), and analysis (2 points). The DBQ score represents 25 percent of the total exam score. The long essay is scored with a maximum score of 6 points allocated across the following areas: thesis (1 point), use of evidence in support of argument (2 points), contextualization (1 point), and analysis (2 points). The long essay constitutes 15 percent of the total exam score.

Incorporating the depth and content necessary to get high scores on the AP Exam requires practice and good time management. We will discuss approaches to maximize your score in Chapter 4.

For your reference, here is the College Board's score distribution data from the 2019 AP U.S. History Exam administration.

Score	Percentage
5	12.1%
4	18.7%
3	23.5%
2	22.0%
1	23.7%
Total	100%

OVERVIEW OF CONTENT TOPICS

The College Board provides a breakdown of assessment weighting of material for the exam by historical periods. These periods and their relative weights are shown below. It is important to remember that many events in history span multiple periods and are connected by overarching themes. You will notice that in the table below, several of the periods recognized by the College Board overlap. As you begin to evaluate the material, strive to make adequate connections between the periods rather than treating them as separate isolated entities. We will begin to look at how the College Board views connections in the next section about thematic learning objectives.

Historical Periods Covered on the AP U.S. History Exam			
Historical Period	Date Range	Suggested Instructional Time	Approximate Percentage of Questions on the AP Exam
1	1491–1607	6%	4–6%
2	1607–1754	10%	6–8%
3	1754–1800	12%	10–17%
4	1800–1848	12%	10–17%
5	1844–1877	12%	10–17%
6	1865–1898	13%	10–17%
7	1890–1945	15%	10–17%
8	1945–1980	14%	10–17%
9	1980–Present	6%	4–6%

Excelling on the AP U.S. History Exam requires a thorough knowledge of the events of American history and their significance. We have provided a review of this material in Part V of this text. Listed below is an overview of the specific topics that will be covered on the AP U.S. History Exam and should be reviewed in a course.

1. Pre-Columbian Societies
2. Transatlantic Encounters and Colonial Beginnings, 1492–1690
3. Colonial North America, 1690–1754
4. The American Revolutionary Era, 1754–1789
5. The Early Republic, 1789–1815
6. Transformation of the Economy and Society in Antebellum America
7. The Transformation of Politics in Antebellum America
8. Religion, Reform, and Renaissance in Antebellum America
9. Territorial Expansion and Manifest Destiny
10. The Crisis of the Union
11. Civil War
12. Reconstruction

content

13. The Origins of the New South
14. Development of the West in the Late 19th Century
15. Industrial America in the Late 19th Century
16. Urban Society in the Late 19th Century
17. Populism and Progressivism
18. The Emergence of America as a World Power
19. The New Era: 1920s
20. The Great Depression and the New Deal
21. The Second World War
22. The Home Front During the War
23. The United States and the Early Cold War
24. The 1950s
25. The Turbulent Sixties
26. Politics and Economics at the End of the 20th Century
27. Society and Culture at the End of the 20th Century
28. The United States in the Post–Cold War World

UNDERSTANDING CONTENT WITH THEMATIC LEARNING OBJECTIVES

The College Board has focused the breadth of historical developments and events covered in the AP U.S. History course and exam into eight key themes. All questions on the AP U.S. History Exam will evaluate student understanding of one or more of these learning objectives. As you begin to review the content covered in Part V, pay particular attention to these themes. The following are the thematic learning objectives:

1. **American and National Identity.** This theme explores how the American identity has formed and been transformed by the development of group identities throughout U.S. history. Particular emphasis is placed on understanding developments in gender, racial, class, and ethnic identities and how different groups have interacted with each other to form the modern American identity.

2. **Work, Exchange, and Technology.** This theme evaluates the development of American economies based on advances and developments in the fields of agriculture, commerce, and manufacturing. The exam will evaluate your understanding of how different economic and labor platforms and technological developments have revolutionized and shaped American society.

3. **Geography and the Environment: Physical and Human.** This theme explores how the environment, weather, and geography have transformed decisions that have shaped the country.

4. **Migration and Settlement.** This theme targets the movement and transformation of peoples over time. Particular emphasis is placed on understanding the motivating factors for migration and the impact of movement on American society today.

5. **Politics and Power.** This theme explores the relationship between political views and processes and society. You should have a firm understanding of the powers of different levels of government and how those powers are important in providing rights and freedoms to the American public.

6. **America and the World.** This theme investigates the influence of other cultures on American development, society, and culture and, alternatively, the impact of America on the rest of the world.

7. **American Regional Culture.** This theme explores how various regions of the United States have developed their own distinct identities and cultures and how those differences have impacted American history.

8. **Social Structures.** This theme focuses on how and why systems of social organization develop and change as well as the impact that these systems have on the broader society.

HOW AP EXAMS ARE USED

Different colleges use AP exams in different ways, so it is important that you go to a particular college's website to determine how it uses AP exams. The three items below represent the main ways in which AP exam scores can be used:

- **College Credit.** Some colleges will give you college credit if you score well on an AP Exam. These credits count toward your graduation requirements, meaning that you can take fewer courses while in college. Given the cost of college, this could be quite a benefit, indeed.

- **Satisfy Requirements.** Some colleges will allow you to "place out" of certain requirements if you do well on an AP Exam, even if they do not give you actual college credits. For example, you might not need to take an introductory-level course, or perhaps you might not need to take a class in a certain discipline at all.

- **Admissions Plus**. Even if your AP Exam will not result in college credit or even allow you to place out of certain courses, most colleges will respect your decision to push yourself by taking an AP Course or even an AP Exam outside of a course. A high score on an AP Exam shows mastery of content more difficult than that taught in many high-school courses, and colleges may take that into account during the admissions process.

OTHER RESOURCES

There are many resources available to help you improve your score on the AP U.S. History Exam, not the least of which are your teachers. If you are taking an AP class, you may be able to get extra attention from your teacher, such as obtaining feedback on your practice essays. If you are not in an AP course, reach out to a teacher who teaches U.S. History (or another AP history teacher) and ask if the teacher will review your essays or otherwise help you with content.

Another wonderful resource is **AP Students**, the official student site of the AP Exams. The scope of the information at this site is quite broad and includes the following materials:

- The updated course and exam description, which includes details on what content is covered and sample exam questions
- The latest AP U.S. History Free-Response and Scoring Guidelines
- Reading and Writing Study Skills to help you with the DBQ and free-response section of the test
- Updates on future changes to the AP U.S. History Exam and access to AP Classroom if you are enrolled in a course (teacher assistance required).

The AP Students home page address is apstudent.collegeboard.org/home

The AP U.S. History Exam Course home page address is apstudent.collegeboard.org/apcourse/ap-united-states-history

Finally, **The Princeton Review** offers tutoring and small group instruction for the AP U.S. History Exam. Our expert instructors can help you refine your strategic approach and add to your content knowledge. For more information, call 1-800-2REVIEW.

Check out The Princeton Review's college guidebooks, including *The Best 386 Colleges, The Complete Book of Colleges, Paying for College,* and many more!

Break up your review into manageable portions. Download our helpful study guide for this book, once you register online (see pages viii–ix for details).

DESIGNING YOUR STUDY PLAN

In Part I, you identified some areas of potential improvement. Let's now delve further into your performance on Practice Test 1, with the goal of developing a study plan appropriate to your needs and time commitment.

Read the answers and explanations associated with the multiple-choice questions (starting on page 35). After you have done so, respond to the following questions:

- Review the content topics on pages 72–73 and, next to each one, indicate your rank of the topic as follows: "1" means "I need a lot of work on this," "2" means "I need to beef up my knowledge," and "3" means "I know this topic well."

- How many days/weeks/months away is your AP U.S. History Exam?

  20 days

- What time of day is your best, most focused study time?

  eh anytime

- How much time per day/week/month will you devote to preparing for your AP U.S. History Exam?

  1 – 1.5 hr

- When will you do this preparation? (Be as specific as possible: Mondays and Wednesdays from 3:00 to 4:00 P.M., for example.)

  M – Sun   8 – 9:30

- Based on the answers above, will you focus on strategy (Part IV) or content (Part V) or both?

- What are your overall goals in using this book?

  pass

Part IV
Test-Taking
Strategies
for the AP U.S.
History Exam

PREVIEW

Understanding your current testing approach is an integral part of finding ways to maximize your efficiency and improve your studying effectiveness. Review your responses to the questions on page 4 of Part I and then respond to the following questions:

- How many multiple-choice questions did you miss even though you knew the answer?

- On how many multiple-choice questions did you guess blindly?

- How many multiple-choice questions did you miss after eliminating some answers and guessing based on the remaining answers?

- For how many of the short-answer questions did you have no clue where to start?

- Did you plan out your essay prompts before writing them? Did you create an outline for either of them?

- How did you approach the long essay question?

- Did you find any of the essay prompts easier or harder than the others—and, if so, why?

HOW TO USE THE CHAPTERS IN THIS PART

Before you read the following Strategy chapters, think about what you are doing now. As you read and engage in the directed practice, be sure to appreciate the ways you can change your approach. At the end of Part IV, you will have the opportunity to reflect on how you will change your approach.

Chapter 1
How to Approach
Multiple-Choice
Questions

THE BASICS

The multiple-choice part of the test will consist of sets of two to five questions, which are tied to primary sources, secondary sources, or historical issues. The directions will be pretty simple. They will read something similar to the following:

> **Directions:** Each of the questions or incomplete statements below is followed by four suggested answers or completions. Select the one that is best in each case and then fill in the corresponding space on the answer sheet.

In short, you are being asked to evaluate a provided document or source and answer a series of questions. Once you select an answer, you will fill in the appropriate bubble on a separate answer sheet. You will *not* be given credit for answers you record in your test booklet (e.g., by circling them) but not on your answer sheet. Part A of Section I consists of 55 questions, which are expected to take you approximately 55 minutes to complete. Time management will be a key part of this section, as you are also expected to complete three of four short-answer questions (in Part B) in the 105 minutes allotted for the entire section.

TYPES OF SOURCES

Unlike several of the other AP Exams, the multiple-choice questions on this test appear in sets associated with a primary source, secondary source, or historical issue. Primary sources are original materials, which provide a firsthand account or perspective. Many of the primary sources that you are likely to see on the exam will include direct excerpts from famous works, legislation, or speeches. Secondary sources are pieces of information, which relate to or are discussed in reference to information presented elsewhere (not firsthand information). Examples of secondary sources include historical perspectives on events, historical criticisms, artworks or cartoons, books or perspectives on historical events, or retrospective analyses. Additional sources used on the exam may include charts or graphs, which depict key historical relationships.

Here is an example of a primary source as it may appear on the AP Exam.

Questions 9–11 refer to the excerpt below.

"Can we forge against these enemies a grand and global alliance, North and South, East and West, that can assure a more fruitful life for all mankind? Will you join in that historic effort?

In the long history of the world, only a few generations have been granted the role of defending freedom in its hour of maximum danger. I do not shrink from this responsibility—I welcome it. I do not believe that any of us would exchange places with any other people or any other generation. The energy, the faith, the devotion which we bring to this endeavor will light our country and all who serve it—and the glow from that fire can truly light the world.

And so, my fellow Americans: ask not what your country can do for you—ask what you can do for your country.

John F. Kennedy, Inaugural Address, 1961

The speech by President Kennedy, excerpted on the previous page, outlines the American dream and the American vision. On the exam, you will be given primary sources that address key events or issues in U.S. history and be given questions that will evaluate these sources from the perspective of the thematic learning objectives described in Part III of this book. Throughout this section, we have provided additional examples, which represent the diversity of different sources you may see on the exam. We will now discuss how to tackle the questions stemming from these sources.

TYPES OF QUESTIONS

The questions in the multiple-choice section will center on one or more key themes addressed by the source document provided for each set of questions. The majority of the questions will be pretty straightforward once the context of the source is understood. For instance, an example question stemming from the Kennedy excerpt may appear as follows:

10. The excerpt provided discusses global turbulence and the desire for freedom of mankind in reference to which of the following events?

   (A) Civil Rights Movement
   (B) Women's Suffrage Movement
   (C) The Cold War
   (D) The Great Depression

However, the College Board often makes the questions a little trickier. One way it does this is by phrasing a question so that three answers are correct and one is incorrect. We call these questions "NOT/EXCEPT" questions because they usually contain one of those words (in capital letters, so they're harder to miss). A simple way to handle these types of problems is by treating them as "true" or "false." The answer choice that is false is correct. Here is an example of another primary source and an EXCEPT-type question:

Questions 6–10 refer to the excerpt below.

"Two months ago we were facing serious problems. The country was dying by inches. It was dying because trade and commerce had declined to dangerously low levels; prices for basic commodities were such as to destroy the value of the assets of national institutions such as banks, savings banks, insurance companies, and others. These institutions, because of their great needs, were foreclosing mortgages, calling loans, refusing credit. Thus there was actually in process of destruction the property of millions of people who had borrowed money on that property in terms of dollars which had had an entirely different value from the level of March, 1933. That situation in that crisis did not call for any complicated consideration of economic panaceas or fancy plans. We were faced by a condition and not a theory...."

Franklin Delano Roosevelt, Fireside Chat, 1933

6. The New Deal included programs for achieving all of the following goals EXCEPT

(A) developing an interstate highway system
(B) stabilizing agricultural prices
(C) insuring bank deposits
(D) providing employment for the unemployed

A few times during the multiple-choice section, you will be asked to interpret an illustration source, often a map or a political cartoon. These are usually pretty easy. The key is not to try to read too much between the lines. To save time, read the question first, and then go to the illustration, map, or political cartoon. This way you know what you are looking for!

Here is an example of a political cartoon source and associated question.

Questions 29–30 refer to the illustration below.

Hanna to McKinley: That Man Clay was an Ass.
It's Better to be President than to be Right!

29. The political cartoon above implies that

(A) McKinley was the first president to favor big business interests openly
(B) by the 1890s, Henry Clay's political approach had lost favor with the electorate
(C) McKinley's presidential campaign was masterminded by Marcus Hanna
(D) Marcus Hanna single-handedly controlled all three branches of the federal government

Finally, there will be a few questions on your test asking you to interpret a graph or chart source. Again, these are usually very straightforward, unless they are "EXCEPT" or "NOT" questions. Those tend to be time-consuming, and even strong students should probably do those at the end, if time permits. When you answer one of these chart or graph questions, realize that more than one answer might be valid, but only one will be supported by the information in the chart or graph.

An example of a chart source and question is shown below.

Questions 41–45 refer to the table below.

Average, Highest, and Lowest Approval Ratings, by Percentage of All Eligible Voters, for American Presidents, 1953 to 1974			
	Average	High	Low
Eisenhower	65	79	48
Kennedy	70	83	56
Johnson	55	79	35
Nixon	49	67	24

Source: Gallup Polls

43. Which of the following conclusions can be drawn from the information presented in the chart above?

   (A) Eisenhower was the most consistently popular president in the nation's history.
   (B) Kennedy received greater congressional support for his program than did any other president during the period in question.
   (C) Nixon's approval rating was the result of the Watergate scandal.
   (D) The difference between Johnson's highest and lowest approval ratings was the greatest for any president during the period in question.

Answers to these and other sample questions appear at the end of this chapter.

No Military History and No Trivial Pursuit

Here's some good news: the AP U.S. History Exam doesn't ask about the details of military history, such as the military strategy or exact death toll of a specific battle. You will never see a question on the AP Exam like the one below:

14. Union general Ulysses S. Grant was intent on capturing Vicksburg, Mississippi, because

   (A) Vicksburg was the munitions capital of the Confederacy
   (B) whoever controlled the city could control transportation along the Mississippi River
   (C) Grant hoped to use the city as a supply depot for Union troops stationed throughout the South
   (D) the city was poorly defended, and the Union desperately needed a victory for morale purposes

Although Grant's siege of Vicksburg in 1863 marked an important moment in the Civil War, you won't be asked about it on the test. The AP U.S. History Exam does not ask about important battles, military strategy, or advances in weapons technology. When it asks about war, the questions concern the political, diplomatic, or social implications of a war or battle, rather than the details of warfare. For example, you might have a question about the significance of the Battle of

Saratoga in the Revolutionary War. (It helped lead to the French providing direct aid to the colonists.) The correct answer to the question above, by the way, is (B).

Also, AP U.S. History questions never test rote memorization *only*. While you have to know your facts to do well on this test, the questions always ask for information in the context of larger historical trends. Therefore, you will never see a question like this one:

15. The treaty that ended the War of 1812 was called the

   (A) Treaty of Versailles
   (B) War of 1812 Treaty
   (C) Jay Treaty
   (D) Treaty of Ghent

The Big Picture

One of the most important characteristics of the AP U.S. History multiple-choice section is that the questions and answers are designed to illustrate **basic principles** of American history. These principles are evaluated through the seven thematic learning objectives described in Part III. Multiple-choice questions will NOT ask about exceptions to historical trends; the test ignores these because the test writers are trying to find out whether you have mastered the important generalizations that can be drawn from history. They do not want to know whether you have memorized your textbook (they already know that you haven't). Talk of historical exceptions is welcome in the essay section, though. Students who discuss exceptions in their essays often impress the readers. More on that later.

Overall, you should always keep the **big picture** in mind as you take this exam. As you approach questions, use the sources provided to help you focus on the key points or themes that are being questioned. Even if you cannot remember the specific event or concept being tested, you should be able to answer the question by remembering the general social and political trends of the era and using the information that may be ascertained from the source.

Let's look at a couple of illustrative examples.

Always keep the big picture in mind.

Questions 52–54 refer to the excerpt below.

"Whenever the [Federal Trade] Commission shall have reason to believe that any such person, partnership, or corporation has been or is using any unfair method of competition or unfair or deceptive act or practice in or affecting commerce, and if it shall appear to the Commission that a proceeding by it in respect thereof would be to the interest of the public, it shall issue and serve upon such person, partnership, or corporation a complaint stating its charges in that respect and containing a notice of a hearing upon a day and at a place therein fixed at least thirty days after the service of said complaint."

Excerpted from 15 U.S. Code § 45—*Unfair methods of competition unlawful; prevention by Commission*

53. During the Harding and Coolidge administrations, the Federal Trade Commission

   (A) greatly increased the number of court cases it brought against unethical business

   (B) controlled the rationing of food, rubber, and gasoline

   (C) generally worked to assist businesses, rather than regulate them

   (D) saw its regulatory powers expanded

Harding and coolidge were pro-business

Here's How to Crack It

At first glance, this question appears to require you to remember the history of the Federal Trade Commission. It's not that tricky, though. To answer this question correctly, you really need only to remember the big picture. What was the attitude of the Harding and Coolidge administrations toward business? Harding and Coolidge were presidents after both the Progressive Era and World War I ended; the country grew more conservative during their administrations, and both pursued policies favorable to business. Because pro-business governments weaken regulations, you should have been able to eliminate (A) and (D). Now let's look at the remaining answer choices. Was there rationing during the 1920s? No, rationing occurred during World War II, in the early 1940s. Eliminate (B). The correct answer is (C), which illustrates a "big picture" principle; the 1920s were a pro-business era.

Apply the Strategy
Use the big picture to help you find the correct answer!

Questions 17–18 refer to the excerpt below.

"[This legislative body declares] that it views the power of the Federal Government as resulting from the compact to which states are parties, as limited by plain sense and intention of the instrument constituting the compact…and that, in case of a deliberate, palpable, and dangerous exercise of other powers, not granted by the said compact, the states…have the right, and are duty bound, to interpose, for arresting the progress of the evil, and for maintaining…the authorities, rights, and liberties, pertaining to them."

17.   The quotation above appears in which of the following?

   (A)   The Wealth of Nations
   (B)   *Common Sense*
   (C)   Virginia Resolutions of 1798
   (D)   *The Liberator*

wrong

Here's How to Crack It

The first thing you may notice is that this question is pretty difficult; the quotation is one long sentence filled with archaic language and syntax. However, if you key in on the big picture, this question isn't all that hard, provided you've prepared for the exam. The central concept of the quotation is that the states have the right to try to stop the federal government when it tries to exercise too much power (particularly when it exceeds the constitutional limitations on it). Sound familiar? It's the doctrine of *nullification*. If you remembered that the source of the doctrine of nullification was the Virginia and Kentucky Resolutions, you would already be on your way to the next question. If not, look at the other answer choices. *The Wealth of Nations* is a treatise on capitalism; *Common Sense* was written before there even were states, let alone state assemblies; and *The Liberator* was an abolitionist newspaper. Looking at the big picture, you should realize that only the Virginia Resolutions and *The Liberator* could conceivably be right. If you don't know, guess. A fifty-fifty shot is pretty good on question 17. (Only about 30 percent of students taking the test will get this question right.)

Proven Technique
Use POE to boost
your score!

PROCESS OF ELIMINATION (POE)

If it seems that we are focusing more on eliminating incorrect answers than on finding the correct answers, it is because that is the most efficient way to take a multiple-choice exam. Use **Process of Elimination (POE)** to whittle down the answer choices to one on all but the easiest questions (on easy questions, the correct answer will be obvious), because incorrect answers are much easier to identify than correct ones. When you look for the correct answer among the answer choices, you have a tendency to try to justify how each answer *might* be correct. You'll adopt a forgiving attitude in a situation in which tough assertiveness is rewarded. Eliminate incorrect answers. Terminate them with extreme prejudice. Remember that half wrong is all wrong, and mark up the test as you do this. You are probably used to teachers telling you not to write on the test. This test, however, is yours to mark up, and that will make it easier for you to decide what to guess. If you have done your job well, only the correct answer will be left standing at the end.

Common Sense Can Help

Sometimes an answer on the multiple-choice section contradicts common sense. Eliminate those answers. Common sense works on the AP U.S. History Exam. Evaluate the question below, which stems from a source on early farming. Which of the answer choices to the question below don't make common sense?

19. Which of the following best explains the most important effect tobacco cultivation had on the development of the Chesapeake Bay settlements during the 17th century?

(A) Because tobacco cultivation requires large tracts of fertile land, it led to the rapid expansion of settled areas in the region.

correct

(B) The immediate commercial success of tobacco forced the settlers to defend against attacks by Spanish and French settlers, who wanted to take control of the tobacco trade.

(C) Tobacco provided the settlers a lucrative crop to trade with nearby Native American tribes.

(D) British customs houses established in the region to regulate tobacco trade led to widespread resentment of the British by the colonists.

Here's How to Crack It

Common sense should allow you to eliminate (C) immediately. Nearby Native American tribes lived on farmland similar to that held by the Chesapeake Bay settlers; why would they trade for something they could have easily grown themselves? Now let's consider the other answer choices. Did the Spanish or the French attack the Maryland/Virginia region during the 17th century? It would have been a pretty big deal if they had, right? You would remember if there had been a war for the control of Virginia in the 1600s, wouldn't you? You don't remember it because it didn't happen; eliminate (B). Choice (D) is anachronistic. The period of colonial resentment toward England was still 100 years away during the 17th century. The correct answer is (A).

Context Clues

Some questions contain context clues or vocabulary words that will either lead you to the correct answer or at least help you eliminate an incorrect answer. Look at the passage and question below.

Questions 36–39 refer to the excerpt below.

"It has been enacted by the Senate and House of Representatives of the United States of America in Congress assembled, That if, during the present or any future insurrection against the Government of the United States, after the President of the United States shall have declared, by proclamation, that the laws of the United States are opposed, and the execution thereof obstructed,...any person or persons, his, her, or their agent, attorney, or employee, shall purchase or acquire, sell or give, any property of whatsoever kind or description, with intent to use or employ the same, or suffer the same to be used or employed, in aiding, abetting, or promoting such insurrection or resistance to the laws, or any person or persons engaged therein;...all such property is hereby declared to be lawful subject of prize and capture wherever found; and it shall be the duty of the President of the United States to cause the same to be seized, confiscated, and condemned."

Section 1, The Confiscation Act of 1861

37. The Confiscation Act of 1861 authorized the Union to

(A) divert commercial production in the North toward the war effort

(B) negotiate a settlement to the Civil War with ambassadors from the Confederacy

(C) liberate those slaves used by the Confederacy "for insurrectionary purposes"

(D) stop merchant ships headed for Europe and seize their cargo

Here's How to Crack It

If you don't remember the exact purpose of the Confiscation Act of 1861, the word *confiscation* might give you enough of a context clue to answer this question correctly anyway. Which answer choices have nothing to do with confiscation? Clearly, (B). The dictionary definition of confiscation is "the seizure of private property." Choice (A) seems pretty unlikely too. It indicates that the government used industry for the war effort, not that it confiscated the factories. Choice (D) looks good, except when you ask "For what purpose would the Union be stopping ships headed away from the Confederacy?" This answer would much more likely be correct if it discussed the confiscation of property headed for the Confederacy. The correct answer, (C), is a little tricky because we don't normally think of human beings as private property. Slaves, however, were exactly that: the private property of slave holders. In order to liberate them, the Union had to "confiscate" them.

―――――――――――――○―――――――――――――

Finally, here are the answers to the questions that appear in this chapter.
10: (C); 6: (A); 29: (C); 43: (D); 53: (C); 17: (C); 19: (A); 37: (C).

Summary

o The multiple-choice section consists of sets of two to five questions, which are tied to primary sources, secondary sources, or historical issues.

o Familiarize yourself with the different types of questions that will appear on the multiple-choice section. Be aware that you will see many questions about political and social history, some questions about international relations, and relatively few about economic and cultural trends. Tailor your studies accordingly.

o Look for "big picture" answers. Correct answers on the multiple-choice section confirm important trends in American history. This section will not ask you about weird exceptions that contradict those trends. It also will not ask you about military history featured on the History Channel. You will not be required to perform miraculous feats of memorization; however, you must be thoroughly familiar with all the basics of American history. (And there are a lot of them! See our content review later in the book.)

o Use Process of Elimination (POE) on all but the easiest questions. Once you have worked on a question, eliminated some answers (by scratching them out in your packet of questions), and convinced yourself that you cannot eliminate any other incorrect answers, you should guess and move on to the next question.

o Use common sense. Look for context clues.

Chapter 2
How to Approach Short-Answer Questions

OVERVIEW

The short-answer part of Section I involves answering three of four short-answer questions. Two of the four provided questions will involve an element of choice, which will allow you to pick the topic or theme you feel most confident writing about. All of the questions will be tied to a primary source, historical argument, data or maps, or general propositions of U.S. history. Since these are short-answer prompts, you are not required to develop and support a thesis statement.

TIME CRUNCH

Probably the biggest challenge you have in answering the short-answer essays is the time allotment. You have a total of 40 minutes to answer three short-essay prompts, which means you have about 3 minutes to brainstorm ideas and about 10 minutes in which to write each one. You'll be given up to a page to write on. It is not necessary to fill all the allotted space. Quality matters more than quantity, though a longer essay will look more impressive to the reader. So there is no time to dawdle on the short essays. You must keep brainstorming to a minimum, and keep your pencil moving!

Here are the steps you should follow for each short-answer essay:

Choose, think, write: your short-answer strategy!

1. **Choose.** For one of the four essays you can choose a topic that best fits your knowledge base. Chances are, one of the choices will resonate more with your level of expertise. You can also decide in what *order* you wish to write the essays.

2. **Think**. Write down all the facts and details that you know about the topic. Try to rank them according to their importance in history and their relevance to the prompt question.

3. **Write.** Steps 1 and 2 should not take much more than 2 minutes. Writing is where you will spend the bulk of your time. Each of your essays should be two to three paragraphs, though the paragraphs need not be long. You have about 10 minutes of writing time, so don't feel the need to get too bogged down in minutiae.

STRATEGY FOR THE SHORT-ANSWER QUESTIONS

The short-answer questions will consist of multiple parts, which center on a key learning objective. You are required to answer questions 1 and 2 and are allowed to *choose* between questions 3 and 4.

The scoring guide determined by the College Board for each short-answer question is 0–3 points:

- 3 points: Response accomplishes all three tasks set by the question.
- 2 points: Response accomplishes two of the tasks set by the question.
- 1 point: Response accomplishes one of the tasks set by the question.
- 0 points: Response accomplishes none of the tasks set by the question.

Many of these questions will resemble the example shown below.

> "Convinced that the Revolution was the work of a full few miscreants who had rallied an armed rabble to their cause, they expected that the revolutionaries would be intimidated.... Then the vast majority of Americans, who were loyal but cowed by the terroristic tactics...would rise up, kick out the rebels, and restore loyal government in each colony."
>
> Jeremy Black, *Crisis of Empire: Britain and America in the Eighteenth Century* (2008)

Answer parts (a), (b), and (c).

a) Briefly explain ONE example of rebellion during the time period described in Black's quote.
b) Briefly explain ONE cause of the rebellion you chose.
c) Briefly explain ONE effect of the rebellion you chose.

Here's How to Crack It

1. **Choose.** If you remember all those Revolutionary War notes from the beginning of the year, then this one should be a slam dunk. There were many events during the period of 1754–1775 that prompted anti-British sentiment and ultimately led to the push for independence including the Stamp Act (1765), the Townshend Revenue Act (1767), the Sugar Act (1764), and the Tea Act of 1773. Let's say you don't remember what the Townshend Revenue Act was (two tax laws imposed on imports of common products into the colonies), but you remember the Stamp Act and the Tea Act. Which one provoked a strong response from the colonists and an even stronger counter-response from the British? I'll have my tea with lemon and sugar, please!

2. **Think.**
   - East India Tea Company
   - Boston Tea Party
   - Sons of Liberty
   - Intolerable Acts
   - Closing of Boston Harbor

Apply the three-step strategy to answer this question

3. **Write.** Here is a sample essay using some of the ideas outlined above:

> Under the principle of mercantilism, Britain frequently put the interests of its corporations ahead of the interests of American colonists. The Tea Act of 1773 was an attempt to force colonists to purchase tea from the East India Company rather than from cheaper sources. This hurt many colonial merchants, so the Sons of Liberty, dressed as Indians, initiated the Boston Tea Party; the protesters boarded Company ships and dumped many pounds of tea into Boston Harbor, thus sending a message to the King that his economic tactics were not welcome.
>
> The King did not ignore the Boston Tea Party. Governor George Grenville implemented the Intolerable Acts, which were designed to punish Massachusetts for its willful spirit and included such harsh measures as closing the port of Boston and required the quartering of soldiers in private homes. Little did Grenville realize that the people of Massachusetts would soon become instrumental in the defeat of British rule in North America.

Freedom of Choice

One beneficial aspect of the short-answer section in Part I is that you are allowed to choose between Questions 3 and 4. This allows you to play up your strengths, while avoiding topics that are less familiar. Questions 3 and 4 will always draw from different time periods (Question 3 always from an earlier time period than Question 4) and subjects, so you can choose the time period or subject that you know the most about.

Consider the following two prompts. Which one would be most suitable for you based upon your own knowledge?

Directions: Answer **either** Question 3 **or** Question 4.

3. Answer (a), (b), and (c). Confine your response to the period from 1600 to 1800.

   a) Briefly describe ONE specific historical difference between the types of people who settled and colonized New England and those who settled the South.

   b) Briefly describe ONE specific historical similarity between the types of people who settled and colonized New England and those who settled the South.

   c) Briefly describe ONE specific historical effect of the differences between the types of people who settled and colonized New England and those who settled the South.

4. Answer (a), (b), and (c).

    a) Briefly describe ONE specific historical difference between the immigration policies of the United States in the period 1920–1965 and the immigration policies in the period 1965 to the present.

    b) Briefly describe ONE specific historical similarity between the immigration policies of the United States in the period 1920–1965 and the immigration policies in the period 1965 to the present.

    c) Briefly explain ONE specific historical impact of the immigration policies in either time period.

Here's How to Crack It

1. **Choose.** Perhaps you're a little foggy about immigration policies throughout the 20th century. Sure, they changed, but how is 1965 significant? If you have no idea, then Question 3 is safer. The differences between the New England colonies and the Southern colonies were fairly well-defined, and the "South" could even include the Chesapeake region, if you so choose. And there had to be similarities, too. The most obvious one might be that most colonists in both the North and South were from the British Isles. One important thing to note is that this prompt limits you to the years 1600 to 1800. So, the "historical effect" you choose for part (c) should be relevant to this time period.

2. **Think.**

Similarity: mostly Protestant, with the exception of Maryland. Difference: Puritans in New England

New England: religious freedom; South: cash crops, leading to widespread use of indentured servants and slaves

Both North and South maintained cultural separation from Indians. New England had more early conflicts with and made more of an attempt to convert Indians to Christianity.

Focus on town-meeting-style democracy in New England

Mercantilism

Joint-stock companies in the South

Similarity: strong British identity

Effects: more New England independence from the crown, fewer economic strings; dependence on slavery in the South; differences in views on French and Indian War and Northwest Ordinance

3. **Write.** Here is a sample essay using some of the ideas outlined above:

The English started to emigrate to the New World in the early 1600s. The first successful colony was Jamestown, Virginia, settled in 1607 by a joint-stock company. Not too long after, the Pilgrims and Puritans settled The Massachusetts Bay area in order to seek religious freedom. From then on, the New England colonies and the colonies from the Chesapeake south were characterized by cultural and economic differences. While New Englanders were largely subsistence farmers and merchants who had left England to seek religious and political freedom, the colonists in southern areas were either wealthy farmers, agricultural investors, or, at the bottom of society, indentured servants and slaves. Though most of the colonists in the North and South were Protestant Christians, the Pilgrims and Puritans were more devout, perhaps even radical, in their vision of a perfect Christian society. John Winthrop's admonition to Puritan society to establish themselves as a "city upon a hill" would not have been delivered by a tobacco farmer whose goals were more mercenary. Despite religious differences, though, almost all colonists in the North and South had a strong sense of themselves as English citizens. Loyalty to the crown persisted in both regions. These loyalties were tested later, though, when the differences between New England and the remaining colonies became more apparent: talk of Revolution began in independent Massachusetts, while many Loyalists in the South were uncomfortable with the notion of risking trading partnerships with England.

Summary

- Spend a few minutes reading the questions carefully, and choose a historical event, perspective, or view that addresses the questions completely and for which you have a thorough understanding.

- When you have an option, think carefully about which would be easiest to write about in reference to all parts of the question.

- Make sure your responses are clear, succinct, and fully address all parts of the questions.

- Be mindful of your time. The first section of the test is shared with the multiple-choice questions. Consider doing the short-answer questions first before attempting the multiple-choice questions.

Chapter 3
How to Approach the Document-Based and Long Essay Questions

OVERVIEW

There are two types of essay questions on the AP U.S. History Exam. The first is the document-based question (DBQ), which requires you to answer a question based on six or seven primary source documents and your knowledge of the subject and time period. The second is the long essay question, which is more like typical essay questions on any other history exam. The era addressed in the long essay question shifts depending on what era the DBQ covers. Hence, if the DBQ concerns progressivism, then the long essay prompt might concern the road to the Civil War and elections in the mid-20th century. You are provided a total of 100 minutes to read the documents for the DBQ question, choose your long essay prompt from three available options, and write both essays. We will discuss each of these question types in greater detail in this chapter. First, let's talk about the basics of writing a successful AP essay.

What Are the AP Essay Graders Looking For?

Here is what one AP grader said:

> "My most basic advice to students taking the AP U.S. History Exam would be the same advice I give to college students facing an essay exam: ANSWER THE QUESTION, begin with a thesis, and follow a reasonable outline. Questions usually suggest a basic thesis statement and a logical outline, so look for them and follow them. The less a writer confuses his or her reader, the better."
>
> Pamela Riney-Kehrberg, Illinois State University

In other words, be straightforward. Do not try to fudge your way through the essay; the graders are all experts in history, and you will not be able to fool them into thinking you know more than you actually do.

It is also very important to focus on the phrasing of the question. Some students are so anxious to get going that they start writing as soon as they know the general subject of the question, and many of these students lose points because their essays do not answer the question being asked. Take, for example, an essay question that asks you to discuss the effects of the Great Depression on working-class citizens. The overanxious test-taker might start rattling off everything he or she knows about the Depression: its causes, its effect on the presidential election of 1932, the New Deal programs that helped alleviate its effects, and so on. No matter how well this essay is written, points are going to be lost for one simple reason—the writer did not answer the question!

Second, a good essay does more than rattle off facts. It reveals an understanding of the general principles or the "big picture" of American history. Professor Keith Edgerton at Montana State University in Billings grades AP essays, and here's what he says:

"The best essays that I encountered were the ones that wove an understanding of content with some critical analysis. I am impressed with some originality of thought too; so few students possess it these days. Students should be willing to take something of a chance with the essays and not simply provide recitation of the few 'facts' that they have memorized. Longer essays, though not necessarily better, are usually more thorough in their coverage rather than the quick, I-need-to-get-this-done-because-I'm-tired-and-sick-of-this-test essays. It is a cliché, to be sure, but there still is no substitute for hard work. It can be painful and awfully grinding sometimes to learn history well, and it seems that there are not many students who want to devote much time to it. It does not provide instant gratification and cannot be mastered quickly, and it certainly does not happen in 23 minutes with appropriate commercial interruption. Students should read everything they can get their hands on and turn off the television. That is the best advice I can give."

If all this sounds intimidating, read on! There are a few simple things you can do to improve your grade on your AP essays.

Reasons to Be Cheerful

AP graders know that you are given only 100 minutes to plan and write two separate essays. They also know that is not enough time to cover the subject matter tested by the question. The fact is, many very long books have been written about any subject that you might be asked about on the DBQ and the long essay questions. That is why the College Board includes this statement:

"As with the long essay, responses to the document-based question will be judged on students' ability to formulate a thesis and support it with relevant evidence."

In other words, expressing good ideas and presenting valid evidence in support of those ideas are important. Making sure you mention every single relevant piece of historical information is not so important, or even possible.

Remember that the graders are not given a lot of time to read your essays. One of them explains the grading experience this way:

"There were about 545 graders drawn from colleges, universities, high schools, and prep schools. We had about 70 tables of readers. A table leader presides over each group. A typical schedule looks like this: 8:30 A.M. to 10:00 reading; 10:00 to 10:20 break; 10:20 to 12:00 reading; 12:00 to 1:00 lunch; 1:00 to 3:00 reading; 3:00 to 3:20 break; 3:20 to 5:00 reading. We read for six and a half days. Before grading the essays, we read sample packets selected by the table leaders, who arrive a few days before the rest of us.

With the sample packets we try to establish standards using a 0 to 9 scale. When the table leader believes we all have 'locked into' the standards, we commence reading. The table leader occasionally samples our finished product in order to ensure accuracy. Also, a computer correlates the essay scores with the grade received on the multiple-choice section. The AP authorities emphasize accuracy rather than speed. In the six and a half days, I read 995 essays. I do not know how this rate relates to other readers…. We look for responsiveness to the question. For the DBQ, we seek a clear thesis statement and supporting evidence."

Charles Quirk, University of Northern Iowa

Think about it. Professor Quirk averaged almost 150 essays a day—a little more than two minutes per essay. True, they are not writing comments, but at any rate, readers cannot look for anything profound or subtle. What they can do is look for evidence that you have something reasonably intelligent to say and that you know how to say it. Furthermore, the graders read many awful essays. (Not everyone, remember, is preparing for this test as well as you are.)

It is true that you can get the best possible score only if you have mastered the material. However, regardless of how well-prepared you are, you can improve your score if you follow the guidelines on the following pages. They will tell you how to avoid the mistakes all graders hate and how to use writing and organizational techniques they love.

Before we get to those guidelines, a final word from Darril Wilburn, a high-school history teacher in Bardstown, New York. We think it is inspirational:

"On essay questions I stress two things: using detail and staying positive. You must be able to substantiate your ideas and thoughts with detail (factual, of course). This will go very far in impressing the reader that you do indeed know what you are talking about….On staying positive, I ask the students not to think of the essay questions (or any part of the exam for that matter) as something you lose points on. Think of each question and each bit of detail and each morsel of fact as an addition to your score; do not think of everything you leave out as being a subtraction from your score. This helps you stay focused and keeps stress levels lower (unless, of course, you do not know anything; then you deserve to be nervous). You can also play a mind game with yourself: 'How many points can I gather on this question?' This also keeps stress low."

Focus on what you know, rather than on what you do not know. Turn the test into a game.

Things That Make Any Essay Better

There are two essential components to writing a successful timed essay. First, plan what you are going to write before you start writing! Second, use a number of tried-and-true writing techniques that will make your essay appear better organized, better thought-out, and better written. This section is about those techniques. Remember: an essay that is better written and better organized usually earns a higher score than an essay that rambles but is packed with facts.

Choose, think, outline, write: your essay strategy!

1. Choose

Read the question carefully. For the DBQ, read each of the documents. You will be required to write one DBQ and one long essay. While there is no choice regarding the DBQ, you will be asked to select one question from a pair of long essay questions. The DBQ requires you to interpret a variety of documents and integrate your interpretation of these documents with your knowledge of the topic or time period. Being familiar with these instructions is useful in preparing for the exam, but you should reread all of the instructions very carefully on the actual day you take the exam to ensure that you are doing what is required of you.

2. Think

Brainstorm for one or two minutes. In your test booklet, write down everything that comes to mind about the subject. (There is room in the margins and at the top and bottom of the pages.) Look at your notes, and consider the results of your brainstorming session as you decide what point you will argue in your essay; that argument is going to be your thesis. Remember: your thesis must respond to the question. Utilize your notes to prove your thesis, but do not choose an argument that you know is wrong or with which you disagree. Finally, sort the results of your brainstorm. Some of what you wrote down will be "big picture" conclusions, some will be historical facts that can be used as evidence to support your conclusions, and some will be garbage.

3. Outline

Try to have at least three body paragraphs. You should go into special detail in each of the paragraphs on the DBQ. (Remember: you will have the documents and your outside knowledge to discuss on the DBQ.) Your first paragraph should contain your thesis statement as the last sentence. Your second, third, and fourth paragraphs (if there are three topics in the prompt) should contain three arguments that support that statement, along with historical evidence to back those arguments. The fifth paragraph should contain your conclusion, and you must specifically answer the question here if you have not already done so. Before you start to write your outline, you will have to decide what type of argument you are going to make. The following is a list of some classic arguments:

- **Three Good Points**

  This is the simplest strategy. Look at the results of your brainstorming session, and pick the three best points supporting your position. Make each of these points the subject of one paragraph, respectively. Make the weakest of the three points the subject of the second paragraph, and save the strongest point for the fourth paragraph. If your three points are interrelated and there is a natural sequence to arguing them, then by all means use that sequence, but otherwise, try to save your strongest point for last. Begin each paragraph with a topic sentence that tells the reader which topic you are going to address in that paragraph. Then spend the rest of the paragraph supporting it. Use specific historical examples whenever possible. Your first paragraph should state what you intend to argue; your final paragraph should explain why you have proven what you set out to prove. Don't forget to use transitions to make your examples and argument more cohesive and stronger.

- **The Chronological Argument**

   Many questions lend themselves to a chronological treatment. Questions about the development of a political, social, or economic trend can hardly be answered any other way. When you make a chronological argument, look for important transitions and use them to start new paragraphs. A five-paragraph essay about the events leading up to the Civil War, for example, might start with an introductory discussion of slavery and regional differences in the early 19th century. This is also where you should state your thesis. The second paragraph might then discuss the Missouri Compromise and other efforts to avoid the war. The third paragraph might mention the expansionism of the Polk era and how it forced the slavery issue, and the fourth paragraph might cover the collapse of the Missouri Compromise and how the events that followed—the Compromise of 1850, the Kansas-Nebraska Act, and the Dred Scott case—led the country into war. Your conclusion in this type of essay should restate the essay question and answer it. For example, if the question asks whether the war was inevitable, you should answer "yes" or "no" in this paragraph. However, remember that simply writing "The Civil War was inevitable" is not a thesis.

- **Comparison**

   Some questions, particularly on the free-response section, ask you to compare events, issues, and/or policies. Very often, the way the question is phrased will suggest the best organization for your essay. Take, for example, a question asking you to compare the impact of three events and issues on the United States' decision to enter World War II. This question pretty much requires you to start by setting the historical scene prior to the three events/issues you are about to discuss. Continue by devoting one paragraph to each of the three, and conclude by comparing and contrasting the relative importance of each.

   Other questions will provide options. If you are asked to compare the political philosophies of two presidents, you might use each paragraph to compare and contrast both presidents' views on a single subject. For example, you might compare the two presidents' philosophies regarding the interpretation of the Constitution (loose or strict) in one paragraph, their differing approaches to foreign policy in one paragraph, and their ideas about the American economy in another paragraph. In the final paragraph, you can draw your conclusion (e.g., "their similarities were more significant than their differences," or vice versa), but be certain you state your argument in your thesis at the beginning of the essay.

- **The "Straw Man" Argument**
  In this essay-writing technique, choose a couple of arguments that someone taking the position opposite yours would take. State their arguments, and then tear them down. Remember that proving that your opposition is wrong does not mean that you have proved you are correct; that is why you should choose only a few opposing arguments to refute. Summarize your opponent's arguments in paragraph two, dismiss them in paragraph three, and use paragraph four to make the argument for your side. Or, use one paragraph to summarize and dismiss each of your opponent's arguments, and then make the case for your side in your concluding paragraph. Acknowledging both sides of an argument, even when you choose one over the other, is a good indicator that you understand that historical issues are complex and can be interpreted in more than one way—which teachers and readers like to see.

No matter which format you choose, remember to organize your essay so that the first paragraph addresses the question and states how you are going to answer it. (That is your thesis.) The second, third, and fourth paragraphs should each be organized around a single argument that supports your thesis, and each of these arguments must be supported by historical evidence. Your final paragraph then ties the essay up into a nice, neat package. Your concluding paragraph should also answer the question.

4. Write

- **Keep sentences as simple as possible.** Long sentences get convoluted very quickly and will give your graders a headache, putting them in a bad mood. Do not antagonize your reader! Remember that good writing does not have to be complicated; some great ideas can be stated simply. NEVER use a word if you are unsure of its definition or proper usage. A malapropism might give your graders a good laugh, but it will not earn you any points, and it will probably cost you.

- **Write clearly and neatly.** As long as we are discussing your graders' moods, here is an easy way to put them in good ones. Graders look at a lot of chicken scratch; it strains their eyes and makes them grumpy. Neatly written essays make them happy. When you cross out, do it neatly. If you are making any major edits—if you want to insert a paragraph in the middle of your essay, for example—make sure you indicate these changes clearly.

- **Define your terms.** Most questions require you to use terms that mean different things to different people. One person's "conservative" is another person's "liberal" and yet another person's "radical." What one person considers "expansionism," another might call "colonialism" or "imperialism." The folks who grade the test want to know what you think these terms mean. When you use them, define them. Take particular care to define any such terms that appear in the question. The introductory paragraph is a good place to include any definitions. Almost all official College Board materials stress this point, so do not forget it. Be sure to define any term that you suspect can be interpreted in more than one way.

- **Use transition words between paragraphs and within paragraphs to show where you are going.** When continuing an idea, use words such as *furthermore, also,* and *in addition.* When changing the flow of thought, use words such as *however* and *yet.* Transition words make your essay easier to understand by clarifying your intentions. Better yet, they indicate to the graders that you know how to make a coherent, persuasive argument.

- **Use structural indicators to organize your paragraphs.** Another way to clarify your intentions is to organize your essay around structural indicators. For example, if you are making a number of related points, number them ("First… Second… And last…"). If you are writing a compare/contrast essay, use the indicators "on the one hand" and "on the other hand."

- **Stick to your outline.** Unless you get an absolutely brilliant idea while you are writing, do not deviate from your outline. If you do, you will risk winding up with an incoherent essay.

- **Try to prove one "big picture" idea per paragraph.** Keep it simple. Each paragraph should make one point and then substantiate that point with historical evidence.

- **Back up your ideas with examples.** Yes, we have said this already, but it bears repeating. Do not just throw ideas out there and hope that you are right (unless you are absolutely desperate). You will score big points if you substantiate your claims with specific, historical examples.

- **Try to fill the essay form.** An overly short essay will hurt you more than one that is overly long. Try to write five solid paragraphs.

- **Make sure your first and last paragraphs directly address the question.** Nothing will cost you points faster than if the graders decide you did not answer the question. It is always a safe move to start your final paragraph by answering the question. If you have written a good essay, that answer will serve as a legitimate conclusion.

CRACKING THE DOCUMENT-BASED QUESTION

The DBQ is an essay question that requires you to interpret a mix of textual and visual *primary source* documents. (There are six or seven documents in a DBQ.) These documents will include many, if not all, of the following: newspaper articles and editorials, letters, diaries, speeches, excerpts from legislation, political cartoons, charts, and graphs. The documents will *not* include excerpts from current textbooks. Occasionally, one or two of the documents will be taken from something "classic" that you may have previously seen, but generally the documents will be new to you. However, they will discuss events and ideas with which you should be familiar. All the documents will pertain to a single subject. The documents are usually between a quarter and a half page long, although occasionally you will see something longer.

The DBQ, which is approximately 60 minutes long, is part of the second section of the test. At the beginning of the DBQ, you will be handed a green booklet, in which the essay question and documents are printed, as well as a separate form on which to write your essay. You are advised to spend the first 15 minutes of the section reading the documents and planning your essay.

To give you an idea of what you can expect on your DBQ, let's look at what appeared on a recent test. The question asked students to decide whether liberal opponents, conservative opponents, or President Woodrow Wilson bore the responsibility for the Senate's defeat of the Treaty of Versailles. The seven documents included excerpts from the following:

- A speech by a conservative senator, denouncing the League of Nations

- A letter from Herbert Hoover to Wilson, urging him to compromise with the Senate

- An editorial cartoon from a newspaper, opposing the League of Nations

- An article by economist John Maynard Keynes, discussing the European victors' opposition to Wilson's Fourteen Points

- A 1920 speech by Wilson, asking voters to support the League of Nations

- A 1921 article by W. E. B. Du Bois, criticizing Wilson for his handling of the treaty negotiations with the Senate

- A 1922 article by Jane Addams, discussing the necessity of the League of Nations

As you can see, a typical DBQ may contain documents you might have seen prior to the exam. However, the DBQ also includes documents you certainly have not seen before. Each of the documents, though, represents a political position you have studied. Many are written by famous people about whom you should know quite a bit (Keynes, Addams, Du Bois, Hoover), even if you do not know precisely how they felt about the Treaty of Versailles before reading the documents. In other words, you will not be starting from square one, even when the documents are new to you. Each document should trigger a memory of some historical figure, event, or trend in U.S. history.

Is There a "Right" Answer to Each DBQ?

No. DBQs are worded in such a way that you can argue any number of positions, and often the question is a historiographical one that historians have been debating for years. In the example on the previous page, the documents provide evidence for those who would blame the failure of the Treaty of Versailles on Wilson, liberals, conservatives, or some combination of the three. So long as you support your argument with evidence, you can argue whatever thesis you want. Often, however, the documents will "drive" a particular thesis, and it becomes more difficult to try to argue the other side.

Similarly, there is no "checklist" of facts and ideas against which DBQs are graded. Here's an excerpt from the College Board's official material:

> "The document-based question will typically require students to relate the documents to a historical period or theme and, thus, to focus on major periods and issues."

Readers are supposed to take into account the strength of your argument and the evidence you offer in support of it. In other words, if you forget to mention a good, illustrative historical event but manage to back up your point in some other way, you will not be penalized.

However, in order to earn the most credit for your essay, you must include *outside information*. You will notice that your DBQ contains the following instruction:

> Use at least one additional piece of specific historical evidence
> (beyond that found in the documents) relevant to an argument about the prompt.

Use the Documents AND Your Knowledge of the Subject

The outside information includes historical facts and ideas that are relevant to the question but not mentioned in the DBQ documents. For example, in the Treaty of Versailles DBQ described on the previous page, any information offered about the writers' backgrounds would count as outside information, as would information about the war itself. Of course, to receive credit, that information would have to help explain who was responsible for the failure of the Treaty of Versailles in the United States. Some students make the mistake of throwing everything they know about a subject into their essays, whether or not it pertains to the question. That type of information receives partial credit, at best.

GETTING STARTED ON THE DBQ: THE QUESTION

Start by reading the question. This direction may seem obvious, but it obviously is not, given the number of students who write essays on subjects that are only marginally related to the question being asked. Students miss the question because they become anxious during the exam. They panic. They think they are going too slowly. In an effort to speed up, they read half the question, say to themselves, "A-ha! I know what they're going to ask!" and stop reading. Do NOT make this mistake! The question is probably the shortest thing you have to read on the DBQ. Take your time; savor it. Explore its nuances. Essays that address the question fully earn huge bonuses; essays that ignore parts of the question are doomed to much lower scores.

Here's a sample question:

1. To what extent did the constituencies and agenda of the Progressive movement of the early 1900s represent continuity and/or change in relation to both the reform movements of the 1830s and 1840s and the Populist movement of the 1890s?

The first question you should ask yourself is this: do I have an opinion about this subject? The second question is this: what must I discuss in order to write a successful essay?

Of the two questions, the second is much more important. You can construct a position later, after you have gathered the information you want to include in your essay. First, you need to figure out what issues you must address and what data you will use in your discussion.

To begin with, you should notice that the question asks you to compare three movements—the Progressives, the Populists, and the reformers of the 1830s and 1840s. Your essay will obviously have to mention all three groups. Equally important, the question asks you to consider the constituencies and the agendas of these three groups in drawing your comparisons. Also, you must decide whether the Progressives were more similar to the Populists or to the reformers. Finally, you must include a discussion of the given documents and your outside knowledge in your essay.

Some people find it helpful to circle and underline key elements of an essay question. If you did that, your question probably looked something like this:

1. To what extent did the constituencies and agenda of the Progressive movement of the early 1900s represent continuity and/or change in relation to both the reform movements of the 1830s and 1840s and the Populist movement of the 1890s?

However you decide to approach the question, it is essential that you do not rush. Read carefully to make sure that you understand what issues must be addressed in your essay. Then determine how to organize the information you are going to collect from the documents and from memory for inclusion in the essay.

Drawing a grid can help you to quickly organize your ideas.

Organizing Your Essay: Grids and Columns

Many DBQs ask you to draw comparisons. For those questions, you can always organize your thoughts in a grid. Drawing a grid helps in seeing all sides of an argument, which is important because DBQ graders will reward you for acknowledging arguments other than your own. Consider the question from earlier; here is how you could grid this question:

	Constituency	Agenda
Antebellum Reformers		
Populists		
Progressives		

As you remember appropriate outside information and as you read the documents, take notes in the appropriate boxes. When it comes time to write your essay, you will find it easier to compare and contrast the three movements because your information will already be organized in a way that makes similarities and differences more obvious.

If you cannot draw a grid for a question, you can instead set up column headings. Because every DBQ can be argued from at least two different positions, you can always set up two (or more) columns, designating one for each position. Consider the DBQ about the Treaty of Versailles, which we discussed earlier in the chapter. You could create one column entitled "It was Wilson's fault," one entitled "It was liberals' fault," a third entitled "It was conservatives' fault," and even a fourth for information that you know belongs in your essay but that you cannot yet classify (give that the title "To be classified").

Good essays do not just flow out of your pen by accident. They happen when you know what you are going to say *before you start writing*. Although, given the time constraints, it is difficult (if not impossible) to prepare your entire DBQ essay before you begin writing, pre-organization and a good outline will get you much closer to that goal.

A Sample Question

Let's take a look at another question. Circle and/or underline the key elements of the question; then create a grid (or columns) in which to organize your information.

1. From the end of World War II through the Eisenhower administration, many Americans feared that communism threatened the existence of the United States. Using BOTH the documents AND your knowledge of the 1940s and 1950s, assess the reasons for and the validity of those fears.

Your question should look something like this:

1. From the end of World War II through the Eisenhower administration, many Americans feared that communism threatened the existence of the United States. Using BOTH the documents AND your knowledge of the 1940s and 1950s, assess the reasons for and the validity of those fears.

Your thesis must address the reasons for and validity of the Cold War fears, and your essay will have to address the Red Scare, the widespread fear of a communist takeover that Americans experienced during the early Cold War. (Remember that the second Red Scare in the age of McCarthyism during the 1950s followed the first Red Scare in the 1920s.) You will, of course, have to include analysis of both the documents and outside information, and your essay should cover the years between the end of the war and the end of the Eisenhower administration. Last (and what most students miss), you must answer two questions: Why did Americans fear a communist takeover? And, how valid were their fears?

Because the question does not ask you to draw any comparisons, you might want to organize your information in columns titled "Valid reason," "Not a valid reason," and "Maybe valid/maybe not." However, the question naturally lends itself to comparisons among the various perceived and real threats to the United States, which means that you could use a grid instead. Americans feared communist attacks both from communist nations and from subversives in the government. You could, therefore, draw a grid, giving your rows the headings "Threats from other countries" (e.g., the USSR and China), and "Threats from within the United States" (e.g., the Communist Party of the United States of America). This analysis would leave you with a grid that looks like the following:

	Valid	Not valid	Maybe valid/ maybe not
Threats from other countries			
Threats from within the United States			

Once you have created your grid, begin collecting information for your essay. At this point, you are probably eager to start reading the documents. Resist the temptation. You have one more important job to do before you start reading.

Gather Outside Information

Most students read the DBQ documents first and then try to think of outside information to supplement their essays. This is a mistake. The reason? *The power of suggestion*. Once you have read the documents—a chore that can take six to eight minutes—those documents will be on your mind. If you wait until after you have read them to think of outside information, you will not be able to get the documents out of your head. Invariably, you will think of things you have already read about, rather than things you *have not* read about, which is precisely what outside information means.

Plus, reading and processing the documents is a big task. Once you have accomplished that, you will want to get started right away on organizing and writing your essay while the documents are fresh in your mind. You *do not* want to stop to think of outside information to include in your essay. And you certainly do not want to be trying to come up with outside information *while* you are writing your essay. So do it *before* you read the documents. The only exception to this strategy is the unlikely event that you are totally unfamiliar with a topic. In that case, the documents might jog your memory.

Look at your grid or columns and brainstorm. In a separate blank space in your green booklet (*not* in your grid/columns), write down everything you can think of that relates to the question. Spend two or three minutes on this task, then look at what you have written, cross out what you know you cannot use, and enter the rest into your grid/columns in the appropriate spaces.

Chances are that some of the outside information you think of will be mentioned in the documents, which means that it will not be outside information anymore.

That is no big deal. In fact, you should think of it as something good. If some of what you remembered shows up in the documents, that means you are on the right track toward answering the question!

This is what a brainstorming grid for the communism question might look like:

	Valid	Not valid	Maybe valid/ maybe not
Threats from other countries	–Soviets develop H-bomb –U.S.-Soviet confrontations: containment, Greece, Marshall Plan, Truman Doctrine –Korean War heightens tensions –fall of Cuba		–Chinese revolution –fall of Hungary: Soviet aggression, or Soviets protecting border? –U.S. involvement in Vietnam –Guatemala's ties to USSR
Threats from within the United States	–there was an American Communist party –though small, party was influential in powerful labor unions –some evidence of espionage: the Rosenbergs	–Rosenbergs' punishment too great for crime, shows U.S. paranoia –Loyalty Review Board; McCarthy's list of State Dept. subversives; blacklisting; bomb shelters –postwar affluence made Americans more conservative	–Alger Hiss case

1. Choose

After you have gathered outside information to include in your essay, you are ready to read the documents. As you read, keep the following things in mind:

- **The order in which documents appear is almost always helpful.**
  Very often, the documents in the DBQ appear in chronological order. When they do, it often indicates that the College Board wants you to trace the historical development of the DBQ subject. On such questions, you do not have to write an essay that adheres strictly to chronological order, but chronology should play an important part in the development of your thesis. When the documents appear in an order other than chronological, they are usually organized so that you can easily compare and contrast different viewpoints on a particular event or issue. On these questions, one of your main goals should be to draw those comparisons.

- **Watch for inconsistencies within and among the documents.** The documents will not necessarily agree with one another. In fact, they are almost certain to present different viewpoints on issues and almost as certain to present conflicting accounts of a historical event. Some documents might even contradict themselves! This is intentional. The AP is testing your ability to recognize these contradictions. You are expected to resolve these conflicts in your essay. To do so, you will have to identify the sources of the documents. (See below.)

- **Identify the sources of the documents.** Why do two accounts of the same event contradict each other? Why do two economists, looking at the same data, come up with dissimilar interpretations? It is because the people giving these accounts—the sources of the documents—have different perspectives. Identify the sources and explain why their opinions differ. As you explain these differences, look for the following differences between sources:

    o political ideology
    o class
    o race
    o religion
    o gender

Consider the question of whether communism posed a serious threat to the United States in the 1940s and 1950s. An urban Northeastern intellectual, a wealthy Midwestern industrialist, and a Chinese immigrant on the West Coast would offer very different answers to that question. The graders will be looking specifically to see if you have tried to explain those differences.

To make sure you're giving an in-depth document analysis (and the best way to get full credit!) use HIPA.

H – historical context
I – intended audience
P – purpose
A – author or artist's point of view

- **Look for evidence that could refute your argument.** Once you have decided what your thesis will be, you will be looking through the documents for evidence to support your argument. Not all the documents will necessarily back you up. Some may appear to contradict your argument. Do not simply ignore those documents! As you read them, try to figure out how you might incorporate them into your argument. Again, let's consider the communism DBQ. Suppose you argue that Americans overreacted to the communist threat. Now suppose that one of the documents presents evidence of subversive communist activity in the United States. You might be tempted to pretend that the document does not exist. However, you will be better off if you incorporate the document into your essay. For example, acknowledge that America was not immune to communist subversion but that the threat was nowhere near as great as most anticommunists claimed. By doing this, you will be acknowledging that this historical issue, like all historical issues, is complex and multifaceted. This acknowledgment is good. AP readers are instructed to look for evidence that you understand that history has no simple answers and to reward you for it.

As you read the documents, be aware that each one holds a few morsels of information for your essay. Do not fixate on any one document, as you can't afford to waste the time. Try to use all, or all but one, of the documents. Don't panic if you are initially confused by a document. Remember: the AP puts each document in the DBQ to serve one or two purposes, rather than five. Think about it and try to figure out why they've included this document, and you'll have a pretty good idea of why it's in the DBQ and how to fit it into your essay. Unless you are clueless (which is unlikely), you will be able to find a way to include each document in your essay, which is better than leaving it out entirely. However, it is better to leave a document out than to misinterpret it. And be confident. If you're in an AP History course, you're smart enough to figure out why the document has been included in the DBQ. Often, the documents "speak" to one another. You, the historian, should enter that dialogue.

Also, as you read the documents, take note of any outside information that the document reminds you of, scribble it into the margins around the document, and enter it into your grid/columns. Again, don't panic if, after you read the question, you can't think of any outside information. Stay calm; you will remember more after looking at the documents. Even though brainstorming first is best, if you freeze, you should go to the documents, and let the documents get you going on the outside info.

2. Think

As you finish reading the documents and prepare to formulate your thesis, remember that while you do not have to answer this question by falling squarely on one side or the other of the issue, it's best to lean one way, with a nod to the other side. A safe, effective route to take on your DBQ essay is to indicate that there is evidence to support both sides of the argument. A good lawyer acknowledges there is other evidence, but he or she is confident that there is stronger evidence to support his or her side of the case. Try to develop a case as you write your essay, using the documents and outside knowledge as mounting evidence. "To what extent" questions should prompt you to determine if something is more this way than that way. Most questions can be rephrased as "to what extent" questions and doing so is often a useful strategy in developing a thesis.

Before you decide on your thesis, GO BACK AND READ THE QUESTION ONE MORE TIME! Make sure that your thesis addresses all the pertinent aspects of the question.

3. Outline

Having a distinct outline for your essay will better ensure that all of the material flows properly and that you address all of the parts of the essay questions. Create an outline with one Roman numeral for each paragraph. Decide on the subject of each paragraph and on what information you will include in each paragraph. Do not rely on your grid/columns if you do not have to. The grid/columns are good for organizing your information but are less efficient for structuring an essay.

4. Write

Go back and reread the section in this chapter titled "Things That Make Any Essay Better" to review good essay-writing techniques. Follow this advice: don't write flowery introductions or conclusions—just say what you are going to say. The readers want to get right to the point and see how much you know. Remember to back up your thesis statement with lots of facts, even if you are stretching it, because the graders want to hear solid evidence and not a lot of fluff. Also, make sure to remember what is being asked in the question, and refer to the question several times during the essay writing, as it is easy to wander away from your main point.

Stay confident. Everyone else taking the test, all across the country, is at least as nervous about it as you are.

GRADING OF YOUR DBQ ESSAY

The document-based question (DBQ) is scored with a maximum score of 7 possible points allocated across the following areas: thesis/claim (1 point), contextualization (1 point), evidence (3 points), and analysis and reasoning (2 points). The DBQ score represents 25 percent of the total exam score. Your essay is being graded with a rubric similar to the one shown below. Remember that the graders are looking quickly for the elements of the essay, which address the core themes in this rubric.

The general grading approach is described in Part III of this book. We have included the rubric here to assist you in optimizing your writing approach.

DBQ Scoring Rubric		
Task	**Points Possible**	**Description**
A: Thesis/Claim	1	Respond to the prompt by creating a logically and historically defensible claim. (**1 point**)
B: Contextualization	1	Offer a larger historical context that is rooted in the prompt. (**1 point**)
C: Evidence	3	1. Connecting at least three documents to the **topic** will yield 1 point, whereas… 2. Developing an **argument** with at least six documents will yield **2 points**. Incorporating at least one relevant piece of evidence outside those offered in the documents will earn **the third point**.
D: Analysis and Reasoning	2	1. Explain the relevance of at least three of the documents in terms of the thesis. (**1 point**). 2. Show a complex understanding of the issue (comparison, causation, and continuity and change over time) with the use of relevant evidence. (**1 point**).

CRACKING THE LONG ESSAY QUESTION

The other essay question in Section II of the test is a long essay question. You will be asked to choose one of three different essay prompts. The options for the essay prompts fall under three time periods: option one is 1491–1800, option two is 1800–1898, and option three is 1890–present. These questions will usually take the form of a historical statement or stance. You must support, modify, or refute its interpretation in a written essay. Similar to the DBQ, you are expected to develop and defend a relevant thesis. Many of the design and outlining approaches for the DBQ described earlier in this chapter are applicable for this essay. However, unlike the DBQ, you are provided no documents. In other words, all information you use will be that which you come up with. You are expected to take approximately 40 minutes to write your essay, and the long essay question will constitute 15 percent of your total AP Exam score.

A simple, defendable thesis, accompanied by an organized essay filled with strong analysis of the given subject, should result in a high score. Do not write an essay that is simply descriptive, in which you regurgitate everything you know about the essay prompt. Purely descriptive essays rarely get scored well as they fail to analyze, assess, and evaluate the given subject.

Here is an example of a long essay question:

1. Compare and contrast the impact of religion on the American colonies during the First Great Awakening and in the Second Great Awakening (1800–1860).

   In the development of your argument, explain the reasons for the similarities and differences.

As you can see, long essay questions are designed to prompt analysis and evaluation of subject matter that you have learned in class. The subjects should be familiar; the questions are straightforward. The long essay is scored with a maximum score of 6 points allocated across the following areas: thesis (1 point), use of evidence in support of argument (2 points), contextualization (1 point), and analysis (2 points). Similar to the DBQ, a grading rubric is available and will be similar to the one shown on the following page.

Long Essay Scoring Rubric		
Task	**Points Possible**	**Description**
A: Thesis/Claim	1	Respond to the prompt by creating a logically and historically defensible claim. **(1 point)**
B: Contextualization	1	Offer a larger historical context that is rooted in the prompt. **(1 point)**
C: Evidence	2	1. Offering evidence related to the **topic** will yield 1 point, whereas… 2. Developing an **argument** with specific, relevant pieces of evidence will yield **2 points**.
D: Analysis and Reasoning	2	1. Structuring the argument around historical reasoning will yield 1 point, whereas… 2. Showing a complex understanding (comparison, causation, and continuity and change over time) of the issue that is backed up with relevant evidence will yield **2 points**.

Choose

Choose the question about which you know the most, NOT the one that looks easiest at first glance. The more you know about the subject, the better your final grade will be.

Think, Outline, Write

Because we have already covered this information, here are brief directions to structure your essay. First, read the question and analyze it. Second, create a grid or columns and take notes. Third, assess your information and devise a thesis. Fourth, write a quick outline. Lastly, write your essay. If any of these instructions are unclear, reread the previous parts of this chapter.

A Final Note

This section is short because we have already discussed what you need to know to write successful AP essays, not because the long essay questions are unimportant. The long essay question is worth 15 percent of your total test score and is very important. Many students are tempted to ease up or invest all of their time in the DBQ, because it is so challenging. Do not make this mistake. Reach down for the last bit of energy and finish strong.

Summary

Overview

o Read the questions carefully. You must answer the specific question asked in order to receive full credit.

o Do not start writing until you have brainstormed, developed a thesis, and written an outline.

o Follow your outline. Stick to one important idea per paragraph (say, comparisons only or social issues only). Support your ideas with historical evidence.

o Write clearly and neatly. Do not write in long, overly complex sentences. When in doubt, stick to simple syntax and vocabulary.

o Use transition words to indicate continuity of thought and changes in the direction of your argument.

o Proofread your essay to make sure you have answered the question and to catch any errors or omissions. Watch out for any careless errors in names or years. Did you write Theodore Roosevelt when you meant to write Franklin Roosevelt? Did you say that the Declaration of Independence was written in 1876 when you meant to write 1776?

The Document-Based Question

o The DBQ consists of an essay question and 6 or 7 historical documents. Most likely, you will not have seen most of the documents before, but they will all relate to major historical events and ideas and will remind you of what you have learned about this topic. The DBQ is expected to take you 1 hour (including the time of planning and reading the documents).

o There is no single "correct" answer to the DBQ. DBQs are framed so that they can be successfully argued from many different viewpoints.

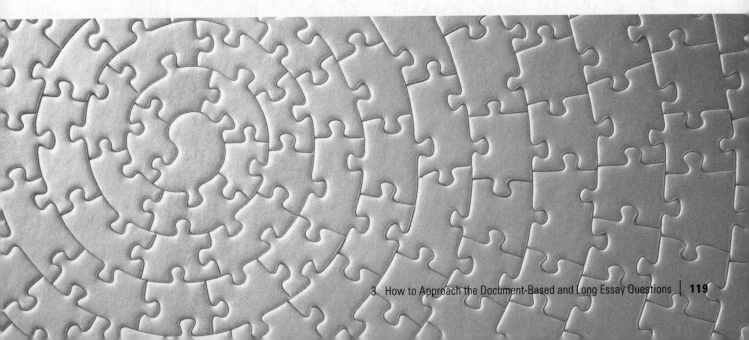

o   Read the essay question carefully. Circle and/or underline important words and phrases. Once you understand the question, create a grid or columns in which to organize your notes on the essay.

o   Before you start reading the documents, brainstorm about the question. This way you will gather the all-important outside information before you submerge yourself in the documents.

o   Read the documents. Read them in order, as there is usually a logic to the order in which they are presented. Pay attention to contradictions within and among the documents and to who is speaking and what sociopolitical tradition he or she represents. If you have already decided on a thesis, keep an eye out for information that might refute your thesis, and be prepared to address it in your essay.

o   Decide on a thesis; then write an outline for your essay.

o   Try to summarize key points from as many of the documents as you can in your essay. Weave in as much outside information as you can.

The Long Essay Question

o   The long essay section consists of three questions. You must answer one question from the three. The eras covered in this section will depend upon what eras were covered on your DBQ.

o   Choose the questions about which you know the most, not the ones that look easiest.

o   Analyze each question you choose. Circle and/or underline important words and phrases. Once you understand the question, create a grid or columns in which to organize your notes on the essay.

o   Decide on a thesis; then write an outline for your essay.

o   Follow your outline. Stick to one important idea per paragraph. Support your ideas with historical evidence.

o   Write clearly and neatly. Do not write in overly complex sentences. Toss in a couple of "big" words that you know you will not misuse. When in doubt, stick to simple syntax and vocabulary.

o   Use transition words to indicate continuity of thought and changes in the direction of your argument.

Chapter 4
Using Time Effectively to Maximize Points

Very few students stop to think about how to improve their test-taking skills. Most assume that if they study hard, they will test well, and if they do not study, they will do poorly. Most students continue to believe this even after experience teaches them otherwise. Have you ever studied really hard for an exam and then blown it on test day? Have you ever aced an exam for which you thought you weren't well prepared? Most students have had one, if not both, of these experiences. The lesson should be clear. Factors other than your level of preparation influence your final test score. This chapter will provide you with some insights that will help you perform better on the AP U.S. History Exam and on other exams as well.

PACING AND TIMING

A big part of scoring well on an exam is working at a consistent pace. The worst mistake made by inexperienced or unsavvy test-takers is that they come to a question that stumps them, and rather than just skip it, they panic and stall. Time stands still when you're working on a question you cannot answer, and it is not unusual for students to waste five minutes on a single question (especially a question involving a graph or the word EXCEPT) because they are too stubborn to cut their losses. It is important to be aware of how much time you have spent on a given question and on the section you are working. There are several ways to improving your pacing and timing for the test:

- **Know your average pace.** While you prepare for your test, try to gauge how long you take on 5, 10, or 20 multiple-choice questions. Knowing how long you spend on average per question will help you identify the number of questions you can answer effectively and how best to pace yourself for the test.

- **Have a watch or clock nearby.** You are permitted to have a watch or clock nearby to help you keep track of time. It is important to remember, however, that constantly checking the clock is in itself a waste of time and can be distracting. Devise a plan. Try checking the clock after every 15 or 30 questions to see if you are keeping the correct pace or whether you need to speed up; this will ensure that you're cognizant of the time but will not permit you to fall into the trap of dwelling on it.

- **Know when to move on.** Since all multiple-choice questions are scored equally, investing appreciable amounts of time on a single question is inefficient and can potentially deprive you of the chance to answer easier questions later on. If you are able to eliminate answer choices, do so, but don't worry about picking a random answer and moving on if you cannot find the correct answer. Tests are like marathons; you do best when you work through them at a steady pace. You can always come back to a question you don't know. When you do, very often you will find that your previous mental block is gone, and you will wonder why the question perplexed you the first time around (as you gleefully move on to the next question). Even if you still don't know the answer, you will not have wasted valuable time you could have spent on easier questions.

- **Be selective.** You don't have to do any of the questions in a given section in order. If you are stumped by an essay or multiple-choice question, skip it or choose a different one. In the section below, you will see that you may not have to answer every question correctly to achieve your desired score. Select the questions or essays that you can answer, and work on them first. This will make you more efficient and give you the greatest chance of getting the most questions correct.

- **Use Process of Elimination on multiple-choice questions.** Many times, one or more answer choices can be eliminated. Every answer choice that can be eliminated increases the odds that you will answer the question correctly. The section on multiple-choice questions (Chapter 1) presented strategies to find these incorrect answer choices and increase your odds of getting the question correct.

Remember: when all the questions on a test are of equal value, no one question is that important; your overall goal for pacing is to get the most questions correct. Finally, you should set a realistic goal for your final score. In the next section, we will break down how to achieve your desired score and ways of pacing yourself to do so.

GETTING THE SCORE YOU WANT

Depending on the score you need, it may be in your best interest *not* to try to work through every question. Check with the schools to which you are applying. Do you need a 3 to earn credit for the test? With the recently updated formatting of the test, it remains unclear how the College Board will calculate score distributions. However, you will likely be able to skip one or two of the sets of questions in the multiple-choice section completely and still be able to attain a 3. The key to scoring what you need is knowing approximately how many questions you, on average, get correct out of the number of questions attempted. For instance, do you normally get 75 percent of the multiple-choice questions correct? If so, then you would need to attempt far fewer questions than someone who averages only 50 percent correct. The only way to know for sure is practice. Remember, however, that you are not penalized for guessing, so you should never leave a question blank. If, for example, you do not attempt 12 questions but rather guess at random, you would expect to get an additional 3 questions correct based on random chance.

You have nothing to lose by guessing.

Of course, obtaining a 5 is not impossible, but it will require good performance on all sections of the test. As described in Part III, there are a lot of different ways to score points. The test evaluates your understanding of AP U.S. History from multiple perspectives. Scoring a 5 requires a thorough understanding of the material (which we will address in the next part of this text) and the ability to utilize provided sources and historical perspectives to synthesize a thesis around a central question or argument.

More Great Books
Check out The Princeton Review's test prep titles for ACT and SAT: *Princeton Review ACT Premium Prep, Princeton Review SAT Premium Prep, ACT Elite, SAT Elite,* and many more!

TEST ANXIETY

Everybody experiences anxiety before and during an exam. To a certain extent, test anxiety *can* be helpful. Some people find that they perform more quickly and efficiently under stress. If you have ever pulled an all-nighter to write a paper and ended up doing good work, you know the feeling.

However, *too much* stress is definitely a bad thing. Hyperventilating during the test, for example, almost always leads to a lower score. If you find that you stress out during exams, here are a few preemptive actions you can take.

- **Take a reality check.** Evaluate your situation before the test begins. If you have studied hard, remind yourself that you are well prepared. Remember that many others taking the test are not as well prepared, and (in your classes, at least) you are being graded against them, so you have an advantage. If you didn't study, accept the fact that you will probably not ace the test. Make sure you get to every question you know something about. Don't stress out or fixate on how much you don't know. Your job is to score as high as you can by maximizing the benefits of what you do know. In either scenario, it is best to think of a test as if it were a game. How can you get the most points in the time allotted to you? Always answer questions you can answer easily and quickly before you answer those that will take more time.

- **Try to relax.** Slow, deep breathing works for almost everyone. Close your eyes, take a few, slow, deep breaths, and concentrate on nothing but your inhalation and exhalation for a few seconds. This is a basic form of meditation, and it should help you to clear your mind of stress and, as a result, concentrate better on the test. If you have ever taken yoga classes, you probably know some other good relaxation techniques. Use them when you can (obviously, anything that requires leaving your seat and, say, assuming a handstand position won't be allowed by any but the most free-spirited proctors).

- **Eliminate as many surprises as you can.** Make sure you know where the test will be given, when it starts, what type of questions are going to be asked, and how long the test will take. You don't want to be worrying about any of these things on test day or, even worse, after the test has already begun.

The best way to avoid stress is to study both the test material and the test itself. Congratulations! By buying or reading this book, you are taking a major step toward a stress-free AP U.S. History Exam.

Chapter 5
Pacing Drills

In this chapter, you'll have the opportunity to put to use the strategies you've learned. Let's get cracking!

Multiple-Choice Drill

As you work through the following questions, try to apply everything you learned in Chapter 1. Make sure to keep the big picture in mind as you consider the answer choices. Use POE. If you can get rid of one or more answer choices and can go no further, guess and move on. Use common sense and context clues. Answers and explanations for these questions follow the drills in this chapter.

Questions 1–3 refer to the excerpt below.

"As for the lawfulness of keeping slaves, I have no doubt, since I hear of some that were bought with Abraham's money, and some that were born in his house.—And I cannot help thinking, that some of those servants mentioned by the Apostles in their epistles, were or had been slaves. It is plain, that the Gibeonites were doomed to perpetual slavery, and though liberty is a sweet thing to such as are born free, yet to those who never knew the sweets of it, slavery perhaps may not be so irksome."

George Whitefield, 1751

1. Whitefield's statements suggest that many colonists' opinions on slavery in the 1700s were most directly shaped by
   (A) Christian biblical interpretations
   (B) commerce and business interests
   (C) trade with the Gibeonites
   (D) agricultural interests

2. Whitefield's revival meetings contributed most directly to which of the following trends?
   (A) Republican Motherhood
   (B) Political and religious independence
   (C) Back-to-the-land migration
   (D) Progressive social reforms

3. The speaker above would be most associated with which of the following social or political movements?
   (A) Republicanism
   (B) Abolitionism
   (C) The Age of Reason
   (D) The First Great Awakening

Questions 4–6 refer to the excerpt below.

"Neither here, nor in any other part of the world, is the right of suffrage allowed to extend beyond one of the sexes. This universal exclusion of woman…argues, conclusively, that, not as yet, is there one nation so far emerged from barbarism, and so far practically Christian, as to permit woman to rise up to the one level of the human family."

U.S. Representative Gerrit Smith, 1848

4. The ideas expressed in the excerpt most directly challenged the prevailing ideal in the 19th century that

   (A) women should enjoy full and equal rights with men

   (B) women's political interests were sufficiently represented by their husbands and fathers

   (C) the presence of women in industry and agriculture was a positive step toward independence

   (D) women were responsible for the education of their children

5. According to the sentiments expressed, which of the following trends in the late 19th century would Gerrit most support?

   (A) Women's suffrage

   (B) The Gospel of Wealth

   (C) Prohibition

   (D) The Second Great Awakening

6. Many supporters of the sentiments expressed above would also ally themselves with which of the following ideologies?

   (A) Social Darwinism

   (B) States' rights

   (C) Abolitionism

   (D) Isolationism

Questions 7–9 refer to the excerpt below.

"The battle, sir, is not to the strong alone; it is to the vigilant, the active, the brave. Besides, sir, we have no election. If we were base enough to desire it, it is now too late to retire from the contest. There is no retreat but in submission and slavery! Our chains are forged! Their clanking may be heard on the plains of Boston! The war is inevitable—and let it come! I repeat it, sir, let it come!

"It is in vain, sir, to extenuate the matter. Gentlemen may cry, 'Peace! Peace!'—but there is no peace. The war is actually begun! The next gale that sweeps from the north will bring to our ears the clash of resounding arms! Our brethren are already in the field! Why stand we here idle? What is it that gentlemen wish? What would they have? Is life so dear, or peace so sweet, as to be purchased at the price of chains and slavery? Forbid it, Almighty God! I know not what course others may take; but as for me, give me liberty, or give me death!"

7. The excerpt above was from a speech by which of the following?

    (A) Dred Scott
    (B) John Brown
    (C) Patrick Henry
    (D) Samuel Adams

8. The excerpt is most clearly an example of advocating for which of the following?

    (A) Abolition of slavery
    (B) Equal civil rights for African Americans
    (C) Freedom from Great Britain
    (D) Joining the war effort during World War II

9. Which of the following groups would be most likely to support the perspective presented in the excerpt?

    (A) Northern abolitionists
    (B) Southern plantation owners
    (C) Loyalists
    (D) Patriots

Short-Answer Drill

Question 1 is based on the following image.

XVth Amendment—"Shoo, fly, don't bother me!"

1. Use the image above to answer parts (a), (b), and (c).

   a) Briefly explain the point of view expressed through the image about ONE of the following:
      - Voting Rights
      - Emancipation
      - The Constitutional Amendment process

   b) Briefly explain ONE outcome of the Civil War that led to the historical change depicted in the image.

   c) Briefly explain ONE way in which the historical change you explained in part (b) was challenged in the period between 1866 and 1896.

"It is a solemn sight to see so many Christians lying in their blood, some here, and some there, like a company of sheep torn by wolves, all of them stripped naked by a company of hell-hounds, roaring, singing, ranting, and insulting, as if they would have torn our very hearts out; yet the Lord by His almighty power preserved a number of us from death, for there were twenty-four of us taken alive and carried captive."

Mary Rowlandson, taken captive during King Philip's War, 1675

"How different would be the sensation of a philosophic mind to reflect that instead of exterminating a part of the human race by our modes of population that we had persevered through all difficulties and at last had imparted our Knowledge of cultivating and the arts, to the Aboriginals of the Country by which the source of future life and happiness had been preserved and extended."

Henry Knox to George Washington, 1790s

2. Using the excerpts above, answer parts (a), (b), and (c).

a) Briefly explain ONE major difference between Rowlandson's and Knox's interpretations.

b) Briefly explain how someone supporting Rowlandson's interpretation could use ONE piece of evidence from the period between 1600 and 1800 not directly mentioned in the excerpt.

c) Briefly explain how someone supporting Knox's interpretation could use ONE piece of evidence from the period between 1600 and 1800 not directly mentioned in the excerpt.

DBQ Drill

1. From the end of World War II through the Eisenhower administration, many Americans feared that communism threatened the existence of the United States. Using BOTH the documents AND your knowledge of the 1940s and 1950s, assess the reasons for and the validity of those fears.

Document 1

Source: Decoded telegram from a KGB agent, New York to Moscow. Intercepted by U.S. intelligence.

November 14, 1944

To VIKTOR,

LIBERAL has safely carried through the contracting of Kh' YuS. Kh' YuS is a good pal of METR's. We propose to pair them off and get them to photograph their own materials having given them a camera for this purpose… LIBERAL will receive the film from METR for passing on….

OSA has agreed to cooperate with us in drawing in ShMEL'…with a view to ENORMOUS. On summons from KALIER she is leaving on 22 November for the Camp 2 area….

_____

Notes:

VIKTOR = Lt. Gen. P. M. FITIN [KGB Moscow]

LIBERAL = Julius ROSENBERG

Kh' YuS = probably Joel BARR or Alfred SARANT

OSA = Ruth GREENGLASS

ShMEL'/KALIER = David GREENGLASS

ENORMOUS = Atomic Energy Project

Document 2

Source: Representative John F. Kennedy, speech to Congress, January 1949.

Mr. Speaker, over this weekend we have learned the extent of the disaster that has befallen China and the United States. The responsibility for the failure of our foreign policy in the Far East rests squarely with the White House and the State Department.

The continued insistence that aid would not be forthcoming unless a coalition government with the Communists was formed, was a crippling blow to the National Government.

So concerned were our diplomats and their advisers…with the imperfection of the democratic system in China…and the tales of corruption in high places that they lost sight of our tremendous stake in a non-Communist China….

This House must now assume the responsibility of preventing the onrushing tide of communism from engulfing all of Asia.

Document 3

Source: President Harry Truman, speech, July 29, 1951.

This malicious propaganda has gone so far that on the Fourth of July…people were afraid to say they believed in the Declaration of Independence. A hundred and twelve people were asked to sign a petition that contained nothing except quotations from the Declaration of Independence and the Bill of Rights. One hundred and eleven of these people refused to sign that paper—many of them because they were afraid that it was some kind of subversive document and that they would lose their jobs or be called Communists.

Document 4

Source: Advertisement, *Civil Defender* magazine, 1955.

TO: CIVIL DEFENSE AUTHORITIES, EDUCATORS, AND PARENT-TEACHER ASSOCIATIONS

STUDENT IDENTIFICATION DURING AN "ATOMIC" ALERT

NEED: Is Civil Defense needed? If the answer to this question is yes, then we must entertain the thought of evacuation. Since the advent of the Hydrogen Bomb, the only safety lies in not being "there."

EVACUATION: Should it be necessary to evacuate the children during school hours, it is also necessary to identify them. Many educators feel that this identification is more necessary for the grades from sixth down through kindergarten.

IDENTIFICATION: Identification must be positive, practical, and nontransferable. Identification must be kept in the school, to be used only during the time of the actual alert or drill. Identification must be inexpensive, since neither the schools nor the Civil Defense people have a lot of money to spend.

How do we of NATIONAL SCHOOL STUDIOS fit into this picture?

We offer the solution to the Identification problem...

We will furnish the Identification Card, chain, and pin (pictured in this ad) for the small sum of sixty cents per student.... We will furnish the Identification Card...free of charge if we are permitted to submit our envelopes of pictures to the parents for possible purchase of these envelopes by the parents. Incidentally, this entails absolutely NO OBLIGATION on the part of the parent to purchase the envelope of pictures. We submit the envelope of pictures 100% on speculation....

Document 5

"COME UNTO ME, YE OPPREST!"

Document 6

Source: Senator Joseph McCarthy, Lincoln Day speech to the Republican Women's Club of Wheeling, West Virginia, 1950.

The State Department is infested with communists. I have here in my hand a list of 205—a list of names that were made known to the Secretary of State as being members of the Communist Party and who nevertheless are still working and shaping policy in the State Department.

Document 7

Source: Edward R. Murrow, broadcast journalist, 1954.

No one familiar with the history of this country can deny that congressional committees are useful. It is necessary to investigate before legislating, but the line between investigating and persecuting is a very fine one, and the junior Senator from Wisconsin has stepped over it repeatedly. His primary achievement has been in confusing the public mind, as between the internal and the external threats of Communism. We must not confuse dissent with disloyalty. We must remember always that accusation is not proof and that conviction depends upon evidence and due process of law. We will not walk in fear, one of another. We will not be driven by fear into an age of unreason, if we dig deep in our history and our doctrine, and remember that we are not descended from fearful men—not from men who feared to write, to speak, to associate and to defend causes that were, for the moment, unpopular.

Long Essay Drill

Below is a drill based upon a long essay question. During the actual exam, you will have the option to choose between one of three different questions. Since the long essay questions provide no outside information, you will have to provide all of the relevant outside information you can come up with. Develop an outline and an approach to how you would write an essay based on the following prompt:

1. Assess the causes and consequences of the abolition movement of the 1840s and 50s.

EXPLANATIONS FOR THE MULTIPLE-CHOICE DRILL

1. **A** Along with Jonathan Edwards, George Whitefield was a leading Methodist preacher and star of the First Great Awakening, a religious movement that gained in popularity in the mid-18th century. He was known for leading revival tent meetings. He was known mostly for his evangelism, but as you can see from this quote, he was also tolerant of slavery. Notice that Whitefield makes frequent references to the Bible ("Abraham," "apostles," "Gibeonites") and claims that slavery is not so "irksome" to those who have been born into it.

2. **B** This one is pure Process of Elimination (POE). Choices (A) and (C) are unrelated to both the First Great Awakening and the issue of slavery. Choice (D), progressive social reforms, don't come until many years later. Choice (B) is the best answer because the First Great Awakening did encourage a more personal experience of religious faith. Preachers tended to be charismatic individuals rather than formally educated drones.

3. **D** If you recognized Whitefield's name, then this one is a slam dunk. Otherwise, use POE. Choice (B) is the opposite of what we're looking for. Choices (A) and (C) are unrelated to the topic.

4. **B** Gerrit Smith was a fiery Free-Soil member of Congress who was active in both the abolition and temperance movements of the mid-19th century. In the quote, he is advocating for women's suffrage (his cousin was Elizabeth Cady Stanton). Those who opposed women's suffrage at this time justified their opinions by asserting that women need not vote since their husbands and other male relatives would make sure their interests were represented politically.

5. **A** Choice (A) is closest to the sentiment expressed in the quote. Although Smith was in favor of Prohibition, as in (C), this is not mentioned in the quote. Choice (D) may be true, but, again, it is not directly supported by the quote.

6. **C** Many supporters of women's suffrage were also abolitionists. In fact, Gerrit Smith was a big defender of John Brown.

7. **C** This question asks you to identify the source of the excerpt provided. Any time a question asks for a source, the excerpt is likely from a famous quote or speech. Upon reading the excerpt, there are several key clues provided. First, the provider alludes to the clanking of chains in Boston. Slavery and abolition had already occurred in Boston by the time of Dred Scott and John Brown, making (A) and (B) incorrect. Therefore, the excerpt must have come from a colonist. At the end of the excerpt, we see the famous line: "give me liberty, or give me death." This is an excerpt from Patrick Henry's passionate liberty speech, making (C) the correct answer.

8. **C** This question asks for the nature of the speech. Freedom and liberty in Boston were passionate cries for freedom and independence from British rule, making (C) correct. Although it is very tricky to fall into the trap of associating his pleas for freedom from chains with African American freedom, it is important to evaluate all of the answer choices.

9. **D** This question asks you to identify the group most likely to sympathize with the speech in the excerpt. The speech calls for Boston to stand up and fight for freedom and liberty. These are not (B), passionate cries of a Southerner, nor are they (C), the words of a loyalist to the British crown. Since the speech describes having "no election" and the clanking of chains in Boston, the nature of the speech is more revolutionary than of abolitionist nature, making (D) the better answer.

EXPLANATION FOR THE SHORT-ANSWER DRILL

1. The cartoon shows a black man poised to cast his ballot as flies hover around harassing him. He tells the flies to "Shoo!" with a smile on his face. The name of the cartoon is "XVth Amendment." Here are some facts relevant to this cartoon:

    -   The Fifteenth Amendment guaranteed universal suffrage to blacks after the Civil War. Keep in mind, though, that some Freedmen in some states had voting rights even before the Civil War.

    -   All amendments to the Constitution must be ratified by the states. Not all states ratified the Fifteenth Amendment immediately. In fact, the flies in this cartoon are labeled with the abbreviations of the Northern states that delayed ratification.

    -   New York had the most restrictive laws against black suffrage. (This is why the biggest fly is labeled "NY," perhaps represented by Democrat governor John Hoffman.)

    -   In some Southern states after the Civil War, black voters temporarily outnumbered disenfranchised Confederates.

    -   The voter in this cartoon appears to be casting his ballot in public into a clear glass bowl, perhaps representing the lack of privacy afforded to voters at that time. Yet, he has a smile on his face, so he will not be dissuaded by either the "flies" or the public nature of his act.

2. Mary Rowlandson was a colonial woman who was captured and held hostage by Wampanoag Indians during the series of raids known as King Philip's War. After her ransom, she wrote a detailed narrative of her experiences, which became one of the most read books of the late 17th century. Her account is filled with atrocities committed by her captors and no doubt fueled suspicions in the colonists about the trustworthiness of local tribes. As you can see from this quote, she shared a view of Indians that many people had at the time: Indians were lawless savages, and God was on the side of the Protestant settlers. There are numerous examples of Indian aggression throughout the 17th and 18th centuries that could support this view.

    Henry Knox took the more modernist view that Indians could be "tamed" and taught to assimilate into American society and that warfare was not the answer. No doubt Knox's views were popular among some throughout the 19th century, eventually leading to the reservation system and the Dawes Act. Since we are sticking to events prior to 1800, it would be useful to discuss Indian cooperation with Europeans throughout the Seven Years' War.

EXPLANATION FOR THE DBQ DRILL

Document 1 is a good example of a document that starts out confusing but ends up being pretty straightforward. At first glance, this document makes very little sense; it is just a jumble of words and names. Do not panic; look for familiar elements. First, look at the source information. It is a telegram from a KGB agent. Therefore, it must have something to do with Soviet espionage. Now, look at the notes, and notice that they mention Julius Rosenberg and the Atomic Energy Project. Those references are probably all you need to know to understand why this document is included in the DBQ. It presents evidence that the Soviets were spying on the United States while it was developing the atomic bomb.

When you write your essay, do not fall into the trap of explaining every detail of this telegram. Your job is to analyze the importance of the document, not to describe exactly what it contains. This is true of every document in a DBQ, but it is particularly tempting here. You will be so proud that you have figured out what this document is all about that you might be tempted to spend a paragraph describing your achievement. Forget it. You have bigger fish to fry.

You probably asked yourself why this DBQ starts with a document from 1944, given that the question is about the period from 1945 through 1960. The document is here to demonstrate that there was some foundation for America's anticommunist fears after World War II. You can use this document as a springboard to discuss other reasons for that fear, such as the relative popularity of the American Communist Party (CPUSA) in the 1930s and the party's disproportionate representation in some labor unions. Mentioning unions then allows you to discuss labor problems in the postwar era. (Labor held more than 5,000 strikes in 1946 and 1947, which spurred the antiunion Taft-Hartley Act.)

This document can also be incorporated easily into an "America was too paranoid" essay because it raises the issue of the Rosenberg trial and the controversy over their sentence. Many people believe their execution resulted from anticommunist paranoia, not from reasoned consideration of their alleged crimes. (Albert Einstein testified that the Rosenbergs gave the Soviets nothing that they wouldn't have figured out on their own.) Of course, the Rosenberg trial generated a national debate, which illustrates the nation's preoccupation with communism during this period.

You may have thought of other issues that this document raises. That is good, and it highlights an important point: most DBQ documents will be adaptable to a discussion of many different events and ideas. Consequently, you have a lot of leeway in your essay. (Remember that there is no single correct answer to the DBQ.) It also means you cannot possibly discuss every event that relates to this question. There is simply too much to discuss. Believe it or not, that is good too. DBQ topics are so large that no one *expects* you to write the definitive essay on the subject. Hence, you will not be penalized for forgetting one or another event that illustrates your point as long as you back your points with other evidence.

Document 2 is taken from a speech in Congress by John F. Kennedy, and it raises several important issues. Primarily, it brings up the Chinese Revolution, which gives you an opportunity to discuss the expansion of communist power in other parts of the world. Using Document 2 as a starting point, you could discuss the Korean War, the crises in Eastern Europe in the 1950s (e.g., Hungary), and the fall of Cuba and other Latin American nations to communist insurgents. All of these events support the position that America's fear of communism was valid, especially if you choose to attribute these events to communist expansionism.

On the other hand, you might argue that this speech shows Kennedy demonstrating the same Cold War paranoia that later inspired the Bay of Pigs fiasco. You might attribute this speech to his political skills and argue that Kennedy is exploiting a sensitive issue for his own political gain. (Remember, many early "Cold Warriors" gained political support by accusing the government of "giving away" China to the Communists.) Interestingly, Kennedy felt it so important to keep China from communist control that he was willing to overlook the flagrant corruption of Chiang Kai-shek's government. If you think he was right, this document justifies American fears; if you argue that he was wrong, you can use it to illustrate how anticommunism distorted America's judgment.

Document 3 clearly supports the argument that Americans were paranoid about communism and that this paranoia was the result of propaganda. President Truman's reference to people "losing their jobs" opens the door for you to talk about blacklisting during the 1950s and, by extension, McCarthyism and other excesses of this anticommunist era. His description of those citizens who thought that the Declaration of Independence was a "subversive document" illustrates the conservatism of the era. However, Document 3 also gives you a chance to discuss Truman's anticommunism. Remember, he established loyalty boards with tremendous power to fire government employees merely on the suspicion of communist tendencies. Plus, his foreign policy initiatives, from containment to the Marshall Plan and the Truman Doctrine, might all be considered the ideas of an overzealous anticommunist. You certainly could argue that those policies antagonized communist countries and therefore exacerbated tensions. You could even say that the growing American-communist tension *resulted* from Truman's policies. As usual, nothing is cut-and-dried in the DBQ, which means that you have many options available to you.

Document 4 addresses two important issues, the hydrogen bomb and its chilling effect on America. The document is an advertisement that very clearly tries to exploit parents' fears as a means of selling them pictures of their children. While it is exploitative, it also indicates just how far fear of the H-bomb had infiltrated the American psyche. You can use this document as a starting point to discuss air-raid shelters, atomic bomb drills in school, the "Duck and Cover" propaganda campaign, and civil defense organizations. All of these events stem from American fear of the Communists. Most Americans were afraid of the USSR primarily because the USSR had the H-bomb. For many Americans, it was conceivable and even likely that the Soviets would use that bomb against the United States.

Document 5 is a cartoon depicting a European immigrant anarchist arriving in New York, poised to stab and bomb the Statue of Liberty. The cartoon satirizes the American pledge to welcome immigrants, some of whom are either a threat to American politics or perceived to be so by the public. The immigrant is sneaking up behind the Statue, so she is unaware of the threat. Most likely this cartoon was published in the early 1920s, when Italian anarchists were suspect, but the First Red Scare certainly influenced the sentiments of the Second Red Scare.

Document 6 is a quote from Senator Joseph McCarthy who claimed to have information regarding Communists who had infiltrated powerful positions in the military and government bureaucracies. McCarthy staged hearings to try to ferret out the Communists, but he was gradually discredited when proof of Communists could not be produced

Document 7 is an excerpt from a live broadcast by Edward R. Murrow. Murrow was a highly respected journalist with Democrat leanings who was at times vocal about his criticisms of society and the government. In this quote, he points out that McCarthy had gone too far in his accusations of Communist sympathizers, engaging in a witch hunt.

That's it for the documents. Now formulate a thesis. There are any number of positions you can argue on our sample question. The best route, as we just said, would be to attribute America's fear of the Communists to a combination of justifiable and exaggerated reasons. Furthermore, there are a number of ways you can choose to construct an essay that demonstrates this thesis. You might want to argue chronologically, indicating which events caused justifiable alarm and which were blown out of proportion by anticommunist propagandists. You might wish to divide the body of your essay into two large paragraphs, one dealing with the communist threat posed from abroad and the other dealing with the threat posed by American Communists.

Once you've figured out how and where to fit all your information into your argument, create an outline, and write your essay.

EXPLANATION FOR THE LONG ESSAY DRILL

As you begin to think about this prompt, you realize that the theme and therefore thesis of the essay should focus on the connection between slavery and the start of the war. You should begin by making notes or a set of columns of events related to slavery that occurred specifically during this period preceding the Civil War and how they may have contributed to the war. For instance, you could include some of the following key events in your essay:

- Compromise of 1850 (admission of California as a free state; popular sovereignty in territories; banning of slave trade in Washington, D.C.; Fugitive Slave Law)

- *Uncle Tom's Cabin* by Harriet Beecher Stowe, 1852 (antislavery novel, fostered abolitionist sentiment)

- Election of 1852 (slavery was a key issue and caused intra- and interparty conflict)

- Kansas-Nebraska Act, 1854 (popular sovereignty in Kansas/Nebraska territories, negated the Missouri Compromise)

- Bleeding Kansas, 1855 (war between pro- and antislavery factions; Pottawatomie Creek Massacre)

- Election of 1856 (party lines are drawn on views of slavery)

- *Dred Scott v. Sanford*, 1857 (made the Missouri compromise unconstitutional)

- Lincoln-Douglas Debates, 1858 (Lincoln's house divided speech, open discussion on slavery in territories)

- Harper's Ferry Raid, 1859 (attempt to start an armed slave revolt)

- Election of 1860 (split of democratic party over views on slavery, election of pro-abolitionist Lincoln)

After you have assembled your list of events, you will need to evaluate which events share a common theme and can be written together to form paragraphs and the start of an outline. For the example above, you may have noticed that several of the events involve issues related to the stance of political parties. This could become the focus of one of your paragraphs. Two possible additional themes include pre-Civil War armed confrontations (such as Bleeding Kansas and the Harper's Ferry Raid) and the role of Popular Sovereignty in new states and territories. Remember that, as you write essays, you must structure your outline and arguments to a central theme, in this case, the connection between slavery and the start of the Civil War. Since you have only approximately 40 minutes to structure and write the long essay question, your sentences should be succinct, and your essay should have a clear thesis supported by your outside information. Be confident, pace yourself, and most importantly, stay on target.

REFLECT

Think about what you've learned in Part IV, and respond to the following questions:

- How long will you spend on multiple-choice questions?

- How will you change your approach to multiple-choice questions?

- What is your multiple-choice guessing strategy?

- How will you change your approach to the short-answer questions?

- How will you manage your time on the short-answer questions?

- How much time will you spend on the DBQ? The long essay question?

- Will you spend 15 minutes reading and planning? Or will you jump right into writing your essay?

- How will you change your approach to the essays?

- Will you seek further help, outside of this book (such as a teacher, tutor, or AP Students) on how to approach multiple-choice questions, the essays, or a pacing strategy?

Part V
Content Review for the AP U.S. History Exam

HOW TO USE THE CHAPTERS IN THIS PART

The history review is meant to serve as a supplement to the textbook you use in class. It is not a substitute for your textbook. However, it does cover all major subjects and terms that are likely to appear on the AP U.S. History Exam. If you are familiar with everything in this review, you should do very well on the AP Exam.

In the following content review chapters, you will find a summary of those events and actions that the writers of the AP Exam consider important. Because historical events often exemplify economic, social, and political trends, and because that's what makes those events important to historians (and to test writers), this review focuses on those connections. We have tried to make this section as interesting and as brief as possible while remaining thorough.

You may need to come back to these chapters more than once. Your goal is to obtain mastery of the content you are missing, and a single read of a chapter may not be sufficient. At the end of each chapter, you will have an opportunity to reflect on whether you truly have mastered the content of that chapter.

Additionally, we've provided review questions at the end of each chapter to quiz your retention of what you've read. Please note that these multiple-choice questions differ from the ones you'll see on the AP U.S. History Exam in that they refer to the content covered in the chapter and NOT to a specific source document. For source-based multiple-choice questions, see our Practice Tests as well as the drills in Chapter 5.

Chapter 6
Unit 1: Early Contact with the New World (1491–1607)

Unit 2: Colonization of North America (1607–1754)

NATIVE AMERICANS IN PRE-COLUMBIAN NORTH AMERICA

Historians refer to the period before **Christopher Columbus's** arrival in the "New World" as the **pre-Columbian** era. During this period, North America was populated by **Native Americans**—not to be confused with native-born Americans, a group that includes anyone born in the United States. Five percent of multiple-choice questions test you on this era, so it is important to understand the clash of cultures that occurred between the European settlers and the Native Americans, as well as their subsequent conflicts throughout American history.

Most historians believe that Native Americans are the descendants of migrants who traveled from Asia to North America. The migration likely occurred in multiple waves, from as early as 40,000 years ago to as recently as 15,000 years ago. During this period, the planet was significantly colder, and much of the world's water was locked up in vast polar ice sheets, causing sea levels to drop. The ancestors of the Native Americans could therefore simply walk across a **land bridge** from Siberia (in modern Russia) to Alaska. As the planet warmed, sea levels rose and this bridge was submerged, forming the **Bering Strait.** These people and their descendants eventually migrated south, either by boat along the Pacific coast or possibly along an ice-free corridor east of the Rocky Mountains, and went on to populate both North and South America.

At the time of Columbus's arrival, between 1 million and 5 million Native Americans lived in modern Canada and the United States; another 20 million populated Mexico. Native American societies in North America ran the gamut from small groups of nomadic hunter-gatherers to highly organized urban empires. In the year 1500, the Aztec capital of Tenochtitlan was more populous than any city in Europe, and both the Aztecs and the Maya are noted for their advances in astronomy, architecture, and art. While these civilizations were located in Mesoamerica, the territory that would become the United States was home to urban cultures as well, such as the **Pueblo people** of the desert southwest with their multistory stone houses consisting of hundreds of rooms and the **Chinook people** of the Pacific Northwest who subsisted on hunting and foraging or the nomadic **Plains Indians.** The first Native Americans to encounter Europeans were smaller tribes, such as the Iroquois and Algonquian, who had permanent agriculture and lived along the Atlantic Ocean; Columbus, mistakenly believing he had reached the East Indies, dubbed them "Indians," and the name stuck for centuries.

True or False?

Q: Native American cultures tended to have limited or minimal impact on the environment.

Maize

The domestication and cultivation of maize, or corn, began thousands of years ago in Mexico. The indigenous people of the region depended on this staple crop for much of their livelihood and the reliance on maize soon spread to much of North America. The transition from hunting and gathering to maize production enabled stable economies and organized societies to prosper throughout Mesoamerica and the Southwest region of the modern-day United States. Maize production also encouraged advancements in irrigation and other advanced agricultural practices.

EARLY COLONIALIZATION OF THE NEW WORLD (1491–1607)

The Early Colonial Era: Spain Colonizes the New World

Christopher Columbus arrived in the New World in 1492. He was not the first European to reach North America—the Norse had arrived in modern Canada around 1000—but his arrival marked the beginning of the Contact Period, during which Europe sustained contact with the Americas and introduced a widespread exchange of plants, animals, foods, communicable diseases, and ideas in the **Columbian Exchange**. Columbus arrived at a time when Europe had the resources and technology to establish **colonies** far from home. (A *colony* is a territory settled and controlled by a foreign power.) When Columbus returned to Spain and reported the existence of a rich new world with easy-to-subjugate natives, he opened the door to a long period of European expansion and colonialism.

During the next century, Spain was *the* colonial power in the Americas. The Spanish founded a number of coastal towns in Central and South America and in the West Indies, where the **conquistadors** collected and exported as much of the area's wealth as they could. Under Spain's **encomienda** system, the crown granted colonists authority over a specified number of natives; the colonist was obliged to protect those natives and convert them to Catholicism, and in exchange, the colonist was entitled to those natives' labor for such enterprises as sugar harvesting and silver mining. If this sounds like a form of slavery, that's because it was.

Spanish and Portuguese colonization of North America was also marked by liberal mixing of cultures, leading to a racial caste system, with Europeans at the top of the hierarchy, followed by **Mestizos** (those of mixed European and Native blood), **Zambos** (those of mixed African and Native American heritage), and full-blooded Africans at the bottom of the ladder. Meanwhile, the strength of Spain's navy, the **Spanish Armada**, kept other European powers from establishing much of a foothold in the New World. In 1588, the English navy defeated the Armada, and consequently, French and English colonization of North America became much easier.

> Much of early American history revolves around the conflict between Native Americans and European settlers. Europeans were generally victorious. Why? One seemingly obvious answer is that the Europeans had more advanced technology, but this wasn't actually a major factor. In fact, in many ways, the Native Americans' technology was superior: their canoes were far better at navigating North American rivers than any European ship, and their moccasins offered better footing than clumsy European boots. The most important factor, by a wide margin, was disease. Native Americans had never been exposed to European microbes and had never developed immunities to them. Epidemics, such as **smallpox**, devastated Native American settlements, sometimes killing 95% of the population.

True or False?
A: False! Even Native American societies that hadn't developed much in the way of agriculture often transformed the landscape through the strategic use of fire, which encouraged the growth of useful plants and attracted game animals. Many early European immigrants to North America remarked that the areas they were settling resembled parkland; this wasn't the natural condition of these regions, but it reflected the cultivation of the local environment by the Native Americans who had preceded them.

True or False?
Q: Pre-Columbian societies used horses and cows for transportation and agriculture.

Competition for Global Dominance

Once Spain had colonized much of modern-day South America and the southern tier of North America, other European nations were inspired to try their hands at New World exploration. They were motivated by a variety of factors: the desire for wealth and resources, clerical fervor to make new Christian converts, and the race to play a dominant role in geopolitics. The vast expanses of largely undeveloped North America and the fertile soils in many regions of this new land, opened up virtually endless potential for agricultural profits and mineral extraction. Concurrently, improvements in navigation, such as the invention of the **sextant** in the early 1700s, made sailing across the Atlantic Ocean safer and more efficient.

Intercontinental trade became more organized with the creation of **joint-stock companies**, corporate businesses with shareholders whose mission was to settle and develop lands in North America. The most famous ones were the British East India Company, the Dutch East India Company, and later, the **Virginia Company,** which settled **Jamestown.**

Increased trade and development in the New World also led to increased conflict and prejudice. Europeans now debated how Native Americans should be treated. Spanish and Portuguese thinkers, such as **Juan de Sepúlveda** and **Bartolomé de Las Casas,** proposed wildly different approaches to the treatment of Native populations, ranging from peace and tolerance to dominance and enslavement. The belief in European superiority was nearly universal.

Some American Indians resisted European influence, while others accepted it. Intermarriage was common between Spanish and French settlers and the natives in their colonized territories (though rare among English and Dutch settlers). Many Indians converted to Christianity. Spain was particularly successful in converting much of Mesoamerica to Catholicism through the **Spanish mission system**. Explorers, such as **Juan de Oñate,** swept through the American Southwest, determined to create Christian converts by any means necessary—including violence.

As colonization spread, the use of African slaves purchased from African traders from their home continent became more common. Much of the Caribbean and Brazil became permanent settlements for plantations and their slaves. Africans adapted to their new environment by blending the language and religion of their masters with the preserved traditions of their ancestors. Religions such as **voodoo** are a blend of Christianity and tribal animism. Slaves sang African songs in the fields as they worked and created art reminiscent of their homeland. Some, such as the **Maroon** people, even managed to escape slavery and form cultural enclaves. Slave uprisings were not uncommon, most notably the Haitian Revolution.

The English Arrive

Unlike other European colonizers, the English sent large numbers of men and women to the agriculturally fertile areas of the East. Despite our vision of the perfect Thanksgiving table, relationships with local Indians were strained, at best. English intermarriage with Indians and Africans was rare, so no new ethnic groups emerged, and social classes remained rigid and hierarchical.

England's first attempt to settle North America came a year prior to its victory over Spain, in 1587, when **Sir Walter Raleigh** sponsored a settlement on Roanoke Island (now part of North Carolina). By 1590, the colony had disappeared, which is why it came to be known as the **Lost Colony**. The English did not try again until 1607, when they settled **Jamestown**. Jamestown was funded by a **joint-stock company**, a group of investors who bought the right to establish New World plantations from the king. (How the monarchy came to sell the rights to land that it clearly did not own is just the kind of interesting question that this review will not be covering. Sorry, but it is not on the AP Exam!) The company was called the **Virginia Company**—named for Elizabeth I, known as the Virgin Queen— from which the area around Jamestown took its name. The settlers, many of them English gentlemen, were ill-suited to the many adjustments life in the New World required of them, and they were much more interested in searching for gold than in planting crops. (The only "gold" to be found in Virginia was iron pyrite, aka "fool's gold," which the ignorant aristocrats blithely gathered up.) Within three months, more than half the original settlers were dead of starvation or disease, and Jamestown survived only because ships kept arriving from England with new colonists. **Captain John Smith** decreed that "he who will not work shall not eat," and things improved for a time, but after Smith was injured in a gunpowder explosion and sailed back to England, the Indians of the **Powhatan Confederacy** stopped supplying Jamestown with food. Things got so bad during the winter of 1609–1610 that it became known as "the **starving time**": nearly 90 percent of Jamestown's 500 residents perished, with some resorting to cannibalism. The survivors actually abandoned the colony, but before they could get more than a few miles downriver, they ran into an English ship containing supplies and new settlers.

One of the survivors, **John Rolfe,** was notable in two ways. First, he married Powhatan's daughter **Pocahontas**, briefly easing the tension between the natives and the English settlers. Second, he pioneered the practice of growing **tobacco**, which had long been cultivated by Native Americans, as a cash crop to be exported back to England. The English public was soon hooked, so to speak, and the success of tobacco considerably brightened the prospects for English settlement in Virginia.

Because the crop requires vast acreage and depletes the soil (and so requires farmers to constantly seek new fields), the prominent role of tobacco in Virginia's economy resulted in rapid expansion. The introduction of tobacco would also lead to the development of plantation slavery. As new settlements sprang up around Jamestown, the entire area came to be known as the **Chesapeake** (named after the bay). That area today comprises Virginia and Maryland.

Many who migrated to the Chesapeake did so for financial reasons. Overpopulation in England had led to widespread famine, disease, and poverty. Chances for improving one's lot during these years were minimal. Thus, many were attracted to the New World by the opportunity provided by **indentured servitude**. In return for free passage, indentured servants typically promised seven years' labor, after which they would receive their freedom. Throughout much of the 17th century, indentured servants also received a small piece of property with their freedom, thus enabling them (1) to survive and (2) to vote. As in Europe, the right to vote was tied to the ownership of property, and indentured servitude in America opened a path to land ownership that was not available to most working class men

[handwritten margin note: Original colonist escaped poverty and Ramine]

[handwritten note, left margin: most colonists were indentured servants]

[handwritten note, left margin: colonists encouraged by land ♢ $$$]

[handwritten note, left margin: First government]

in populous Europe. However, indenture was extremely difficult, and nearly half of all indentured servants—most of whom were young, reasonably healthy men—did not survive their term of service. Still, indenture was common. More than 75 percent of the 130,000 Englishmen who migrated to the Chesapeake during the 17th century were indentured servants.

In 1618, the Virginia Company introduced the **headright system** as a means of attracting new settlers to the region and to address the labor shortage created by the emergence of tobacco farming, which required a large number of workers. A "headright" was a tract of land, usually about 50 acres, that was granted to colonists and potential settlers.

In 1619, Virginia established the **House of Burgesses**, in which any property-holding, white male could vote. All decisions made by the House of Burgesses, however, had to be approved by the Virginia Company. That year also marks the introduction of **slavery** to the English colonies. (See the section later in this chapter, "Slavery in the Early Colonies.")

French Colonization of North America

At first glance, the French colonization of North America appears to have much in common with Spanish and English colonization. While the English had founded a permanent settlement at Jamestown in 1607, the French colonized what is today Quebec City in 1608. Like the Spanish missionaries, the French Jesuit priests were trying to convert native peoples to Roman Catholicism, but they were much more likely to spread diseases, such as smallpox, than to convert large numbers to Christianity. Like colonists from other European countries, the French were exploring as much land as they could, hoping to find natural resources, such as gold, as well as a shortcut to Asia.

Unlike the Spanish and English, however, the French colonists had a much lighter impact on the native peoples. Few French settlers came to North America, and those who did tended to be single men, some of whom intermarried with women native to the area. They also tended to stay on the move, especially if they were *coureurs du bois* ("runners in the woods") who helped trade for the furs that became the rage in Europe. True, the French ultimately did play a significant role in the French and Indian War (surprise!) from 1754–1763; however, their chances of shaping the region soon known as British North America were slim from the outset and faded dramatically with the **Edict of Nantes** in 1598.

[handwritten note: upheld protestant freedom]

The four main colonizing powers in North America interacted with the native inhabitants very differently:

- **Spain** tended to conquer and enslave the native inhabitants of the regions it colonized. The Spanish also made great efforts to convert Native Americans to Catholicism. Spanish colonists were overwhelmingly male, and many had children with native women, leading to settlements populated largely by mestizos, people of mixed Spanish and Native American ancestry.

- **France** had significantly friendlier relations with indigenous tribes, tending to ally with them and adopt native practices. The French had little choice in this: French settlements were so sparsely populated that taking on the natives head-on would have been very risky.

- **The Netherlands** attempted to build a great trading empire, and while it achieved great success elsewhere in the world, its settlements on the North American continent, which were essentially glorified trading posts, soon fell to the English. This doesn't mean they were unimportant. One of the Dutch settlements was New Amsterdam, later renamed New York City.

- **England** differed significantly from the three other powers in that the other three all depended on Native Americans in different ways: as slave labor, as allies, or as trading partners. English colonies, by contrast, attempted to exclude Native Americans as much as possible. The English flooded to the New World in great numbers, with entire families arriving in many of the colonies rather than just young men, and intermixing between settlers and natives was rare. Instead, when English colonies grew to the point that conflict with nearby tribes became inevitable, the English launched **wars of extermination**. For instance, the Powhatan Confederacy was destroyed by English "Indian fighters" in the 1640s.

The Métis

Métis (pronounced may-tee) is a term to describe people of Canada and parts of the northern United States who are of mixed Native American and European (usually French) descent.

The Métis are originally descended from 17th-century French trappers and traders who married Native, usually Algonquian, women. The Métis are a legally recognized indigenous people in modern-day Canada.

The Pilgrims and the Massachusetts Bay Company

During the 16th century, English Calvinists led a Protestant movement called **Puritanism** in England. Its name was derived from its adherents' desire to purify the Anglican church of Roman Catholic practices. English monarchs of the early 17th century persecuted the Puritans, and so the Puritans began to look for a new place to practice their faith.

One Puritan group, called **Separatists**—because they thought the Church of England was so incapable of being reformed that they had to abandon it—left England around this time. First, they went to the Netherlands but ultimately decided to start fresh in the New World. In 1620, they set sail for Virginia, but their ship, the *Mayflower*, went off course and they landed in modern-day Massachusetts. Because winter was approaching, they decided to settle where they had landed. This settlement was called **Plymouth**.

While on board, the travelers—called **Pilgrims** and led by William Bradford—signed an agreement establishing a "body politic" and a basic legal system for the colony. That agreement, **the Mayflower Compact**, is important not only because it created a legal authority and an assembly, but also because it asserted that the government's power derives from the consent of the governed and not from God, as some **monarchists** known as **Absolutists** believed.

Like the earlier settlers in Jamestown, the Pilgrims received life-saving assistance from local Native Americans. To the Pilgrims' great fortune, they had happened to land at the site of a Patuxet village that had been wiped out by disease; one inhabitant of that village, a man named Tisquantum, better known as **Squanto**, had been spared this fate because he had been captured years before and brought to Europe as a slave. He wound up in London, where he learned English and then returned to his homeland only to find it depopulated. Shortly thereafter, the Pilgrims arrived, and Squanto became their interpreter and taught them how best to plant in their new home.

In 1629, a larger and more powerful colony called **Massachusetts Bay** was established by Congregationalists (**Puritans** who wanted to reform the Anglican church from within). This began what is known as The Great Puritan Migration, which lasted from 1629 to 1642. Led by Governor **John Winthrop**, Massachusetts Bay developed along Puritan ideals. While onboard the ship *Arabella*, Winthrop delivered a now-famous sermon, "A Model of Christian Charity," urging the colonists to be a **city upon a hill**—a model for others to look up to. All Puritans believed they had a **covenant** with God, and the concept of covenants was central to their entire philosophy, in both political and religious terms. Government was to be a covenant among the people; work was to serve a communal ideal, and, of course, the Puritan church was always to be served. This is why both the Separatists and the Congregationalists did not tolerate religious freedom in their colonies, even though both had experienced and fled religious persecution.

The settlers of the Massachusetts Bay Colony were strict **Calvinists**, and Calvinist principles dictated their daily lives. For example, much has been written about the "Protestant work ethic" and its relationship to the eventual development of a market economy. In fact, some historians believe the roots of the Civil War can be traced back to the founding of the Chesapeake region and New England, as a plantation economy dependent on slave labor developed in the Chesapeake and subsequent southern colonies, while New England became the commercial center.

Two major incidents during the first half of the 17th century demonstrated Puritan religious intolerance. **Roger Williams**, a minister in the Salem Bay settlement, taught a number of controversial principles, among them that church and state should be separate. The Puritans banished Williams, who subsequently moved to modern-day Rhode Island and founded a new colony. Rhode Island's charter allowed for the free exercise of religion, and it did not require voters to be church members. **Anne Hutchinson** was a prominent proponent of *antinomianism*, the belief that faith and God's grace—as opposed to the observance of moral law and performance of good deeds—suffice to earn one a place among the "elect." Her teachings challenged Puritan beliefs and the authority of the Puritan clergy. The fact that she was an intelligent, well-educated, and powerful woman in a resolutely patriarchal society turned many against her. She was tried for heresy, convicted, and banished.

Puritan immigration to New England came to a near halt between 1649 and 1660, the years during which **Oliver Cromwell** ruled as Lord Protector of England. Cromwell's reign represented the culmination of the **English Civil Wars**, which the Puritans won. During the **Interregnum** (literally "between kings"), Puritans had little motive to move to the New World. Everything they wanted—freedom to practice their religion, as well as representation in the government—was available to them in England. With the restoration of the Stuarts, many English Puritans again immigrated to the New World. Not coincidentally, these immigrants brought with them some of the republican ideals of the revolution.

The lives of English settlers in New England and the Chesapeake differed considerably. Entire families tended to immigrate to New England; in the Chesapeake, immigrants were often single males. The climate in New England was more hospitable, and so New Englanders tended to live longer and have larger families than Chesapeake residents. A stronger sense of community, and the absence of tobacco as a cash crop, led New Englanders to settle in larger towns that were closer to one another; those in the Chesapeake lived in smaller, more spread-out farming communities. While both groups were religious, the New Englanders were definitely *more* religious, settling near meetinghouses. Another important difference between New England and the Chesapeake was in the use of slavery. New England farms were small and required less labor. Slavery was rare. Farms in middle and southern colonies were much larger, requiring large numbers of African slaves. In fact, at one time, South Carolina had a larger proportion of African slaves than European settlers.

Other Early Colonies

Several colonies were proprietorships; that is, they were owned by one person, who usually received the land as a gift from the king. **Connecticut** was one such colony, receiving its charter in 1635 and producing the **Fundamental Orders**, usually considered the first written constitution in British North America. **Maryland** was another, granted to Cecilius Calvert, Lord Baltimore. Calvert hoped to create a haven colony for Catholics, who faced religious persecution in Protestant England, but he also hoped to make a profit growing tobacco. In order to populate the colony's land more quickly, Calvert offered religious tolerance for all Christians, and Protestants soon outnumbered Catholics, recreating England's old tension between the faiths. After a Protestant uprising in England against a Catholic-sympathizing king, Maryland's government passed the **Act of Toleration** in 1649 to protect the religious freedom of most Christians, but the law was not enough to keep the situation in Maryland from devolving into bloody religious civil war for much of the rest of the century.

New York was also a royal gift, this time to James, the king's brother. The Dutch Republic was the largest commercial power during the 17th century and, as such, was an economic rival of the British. The Dutch had established an initial settlement in 1614 near present-day Albany, which they called New Netherland, and a fort at the mouth of the Hudson River in 1626. This fort would become New Amsterdam and is today New York City. In 1664, Charles II of England waged a war against the Dutch Republic and sent a naval force to capture New Netherland. Already weakened by previous clashes with local Native Americans, the Dutch governor, Peter Stuyvesant, along with 400 civilians, surrendered peacefully. Charles II's brother, James, became the Duke of York, and when James became king in 1685, he proclaimed New York a royal colony. The Dutch were allowed to remain in the colony on generous terms, and they made up a large segment of New York's population for many years. Charles II also gave **New Jersey** to a couple of friends, who in turn sold it off to investors, many of whom were Quakers.

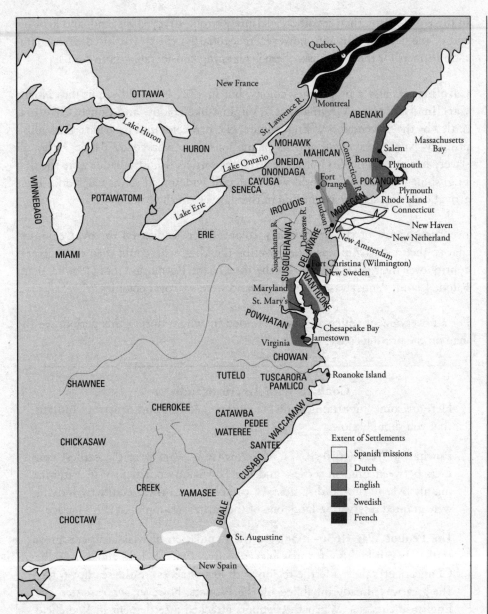

European Settlements in North America, 1650

Ultimately, the Quakers received their own colony. William Penn, a Quaker, was a close friend of King Charles II, and Charles granted Penn what became **Pennsylvania**. Charles, like most Anglicans, perceived the egalitarian Quakers as dangerous radicals, but the two men's friendship (and Charles's desire to export the Quakers to someplace far from England) prevailed. Penn established liberal policies toward religious freedom and civil liberties in his colony. That, the area's natural bounty, and Penn's recruitment of settlers through advertising, made Pennsylvania one of the fastest growing of the early colonies. He also attempted to treat Native Americans more fairly than did other colonies and had mixed results. His attitude attracted many tribes to the area but also attracted many European settlers who bullied tribes off of their land. An illustrative story: Penn made a treaty with the Delawares to take only as much land as could be walked by a man

Geography = Destiny?
Here's a good general guide for remembering which colonies were established for what reasons: the northern colonies were mostly established for religious reasons, the southern for commercial gain.

in three days. Penn then set off on a leisurely stroll, surveyed his land, and kept his end of the bargain. His son, however, renegotiating the treaty, hired three marathon runners for the same task, thereby claiming considerably more land.

Carolina was also a proprietary colony, but in 1729 it officially split into **North Carolina**, settled by Virginians as a Virginia-like colony, and **South Carolina**, settled by the descendants of Englishmen who had colonized Barbados. Barbados's primary export was sugar, and its plantations were worked by slaves. Although slavery had existed in Virginia since 1619, the settlers from Barbados were the first Englishmen in the New World who had seen widespread slavery at work. Their arrival truly marked the beginning of the slave era in the colonies.

Eventually, most of the **proprietary** colonies were converted to **royal** colonies; that is, their ownership was taken over by the king, who could then exert greater control over their governments. By the time of the Revolution, only Connecticut, Rhode Island, Pennsylvania, and Maryland were *not* royal colonies.

For an overview of which areas were settled by whom during this period, see the map on the previous page.

Conflicts with American Indians

Here are some important conflicts between colonists and American Indians that you should know:

Powhatan Wars (1610–1677). The Powhatan Wars were the earliest conflicts between English settlers and the Powhatan confederacy in Virginia, mainly over territorial disputes. As a resolution to these conflicts, Indians were granted reservation land, one of the earliest examples of this practice.

The Pequot War (1636–1638). As the population of Massachusetts grew, settlers began looking for new places to live. One obvious choice was the Connecticut Valley, a fertile region with lots of access to the sea (for trade). The area was already inhabited by the Pequots, however, who resisted the English incursions. When the Pequots attacked a settlement in Wakefield and killed nine colonists, members of the Massachusetts Bay Colony retaliated by burning the main Pequot village, killing 400, many of them women and children. The result was the near-destruction of the Pequots in what came to be known as the Pequot War.

The Beaver Wars (1628–1701). The Iroquois Confederacy, spurred on by English allies, fought frequently with the French-backed Algonquian tribes of the Great Lakes region over fur and fishing rights. These conflicts were called the "Beaver" Wars because the beaver was an important fur animal hunted by Indians and European settlers throughout the region. When beaver numbers declined because of over-harvesting, territorial conflicts between trappers intensified. Though largely forgotten in popular history, the Beaver Wars were considered the bloodiest in North American history. (Hmm, where else did the French, English, and Indians fight over fur and fishing rights? Oh yeah, the Seven Years' War!)

Decline of the Huron Confederacy (1634–1649). At one time the Hurons numbered up to 40,000, living primarily near Lake Ontario and in parts of Quebec, with some groups as far south as West Virginia. During the 1630s, though, smallpox ravaged the tribes, and their numbers declined to around 12,000. Added to their woes were constant conflicts with other tribes for fur rights. The Huron were allies with the French and fought alongside them in the Seven Years' War.

King Philip's War (1675–1678). Metacomet, the leader of the Wampanoag tribe living near Narragansett Bay in Rhode Island, was neither a King nor named "Philip." The Wampanoags were surrounded by white settlements, and colonists were attempting to convert the Indians to English culture and religion. "Praying towns" were villages set up for the sole purpose of making converts to Christianity. Indians were also encouraged to give up their tribal clothing. Metacomet led attacks on several settlements in retaliation for this intrusion on Wampanoag territory. Soon after, he formed an alliance with two other local tribes. The alliance destroyed a number of English settlements but eventually ran out of food and ammunition. When Metacomet died, the alliance fell apart and the colonists devastated the tribes, selling many into slavery in the West Indies. King Philip's War marks the end of a formidable Native American presence among the New England colonists.

The Pueblo Revolt (1680). While the French and British played their political and economic chess games with Indian tribes in the East, the Spanish sought to maintain control of the Southwest. After years of domination by the fearsome Juan de Oñate, the Pueblo people of New Mexico led a successful revolt against the Spanish, killing hundreds and driving the remaining settlers out of the region. The Spanish returned in 1692, and though they regained control of the territory, they were more accommodating to the Pueblo, the fear of continued conflicts driving the need for compromise.

The Chickasaw Wars (1721–1763). The Chickasaw tribe (allied with the British) fought the Choctaw (allied with the French) for control of the land around the Mississippi River. The Chickasaw Wars were deadlier and more devastating than previous conflicts, since the Indians were supplied with guns from the Europeans. These prolonged wars halted only when the Treaty of Paris was signed at the end of the Seven Years' War.

Decline of the Catawba Nation (1700s). The Catawbas were at one time the most powerful and numerous tribe in the Carolina Piedmont. The Catawbas were allied with colonists and even fought alongside the Patriots during the Revolutionary War, but were engaged in constant warfare with other tribes, such as the Iroquois, the Algonquian, and the Cherokee. Catawba numbers were also weakened by smallpox epidemics. Eventually the Catawba were so decimated by war and disease that they temporarily ceded land and tribal status. Today, there are a few thousand Catawba still living in North Carolina.

Slavery in the Early Colonies

As mentioned above, the extensive use of African slaves in the American colonies began when colonists from the Caribbean settled the Carolinas. Until then, indentured servants and, in some situations, enslaved Native Americans had mostly satisfied labor requirements in the colonies. As tobacco-growing and, in South Carolina, rice-growing operations expanded, more laborers were needed than indenture could provide. Events such as Bacon's Rebellion (see Major Events of the Period for more on this) had also shown landowners that it was not in their best interest to have an abundance of landless, young, white males in their colonies either.

Enslaving Native Americans was difficult; they knew the land, so they could easily escape and subsequently were difficult to find. In some Native American tribes, cultivation was considered women's work, so gender was another obstacle to enslaving the natives. And as noted, Europeans brought diseases that often decimated the Native Americans, wiping out 85 to 95 percent of the native population. Southern landowners turned increasingly to African slaves for labor. Unlike Native Americans, African slaves did not know the land, so they were less likely to escape. Removed from their homelands and communities, and often unable to communicate with one another because they were from different regions of Africa, black slaves initially proved easier to control than Native Americans. The dark skin of the West Africans who made up the bulk of the enslaved population made it easier to identify slaves on sight, and the English colonists came to associate dark skin with inferiority, rationalizing Africans' enslavement.

The majority of the slave trade, right up to the Revolution, was directed toward the Caribbean and South America. Still, during that period more than 500,000 slaves were brought to the English colonies (of the over 10 million brought to the New World). By 1790, nearly 750,000 blacks were enslaved in England's North American colonies.

The shipping route that brought the slaves to the Americas was called the **Middle Passage** because it was the middle leg of the **triangular trade route** among the colonies, Europe, and Africa. Conditions for the Africans aboard were brutally inhumane, so intolerable that some committed suicide by throwing themselves overboard. Many died of sickness, and others died during insurrections. It was not unusual for one-fifth of the Africans to die on board. Most, however, reached the New World, where conditions were only slightly better. Mounting criticism (primarily in the North) of the horrors of the Middle Passage led Congress to end American participation in the Atlantic slave trade on January 1, 1808. Slavery itself would not end in the United States until 1865.

Slavery flourished in the South. Because of the nature of the land and the short growing season, the Chesapeake and the Carolinas farmed labor-intensive crops such as **tobacco**, **rice**, and **indigo**, and plantation owners there bought slaves for this arduous work. Slaves' treatment at the hands of their owners was often vicious and at times sadistic. While slavery never really took hold in the North the same way it did in the South, slaves were used on farms in New York, New Jersey, and Pennsylvania, in shipping operations in Massachusetts and Rhode Island, and as domestic servants in urban households, particularly in New York City. Although northern states would take steps to phase out slavery following the Revolution, there were still slaves in New Jersey at the outbreak of the Civil War. In both regions, only the very wealthy owned slaves. The vast majority of people remained at a subsistence level.

THE AGE OF SALUTARY NEGLECT (1650–1750)

British treatment of the colonies during the period preceding the **French and Indian War** (also called **the Seven Years' War**) is often described as **salutary neglect** or **benign neglect.** Although England regulated trade and government in its colonies, it interfered in colonial affairs as little as possible. Because of the distance, England set up absentee customs officials and the colonies were left to self-govern, for the most part. England occasionally turned its back to the colonies' violations of trade restrictions. Thus, the colonies developed a large degree of autonomy, which helped fuel revolutionary sentiments when the monarchy later attempted to gain greater control of the New World.

During this century, the colonies "grew up," developing fledgling economies. The beginnings of an American culture—as opposed to a transplanted English culture—took root.

English Regulation of Colonial Trade

Throughout the colonial period, most Europeans who thought about economics at all subscribed to a theory called **mercantilism**. Mercantilists believed that economic power was rooted in a favorable balance of trade (that is, exporting more than you import) and the control of **specie** (hard currency, such as gold coins). Colonies, they felt, were important mostly for economic reasons, which explains why the British considered their colonies in the West Indies that produced sugar and other valuable commodities to be more important than their colonies on the North American continent. The colonies on the North American continent were seen primarily as markets for British and West Indian goods, although they also were valued as sources of raw materials that would otherwise have to be bought from a foreign country.

In order to guarantee a favorable balance of trade, the British government encouraged manufacturing in England and placed **protective tariffs** on imports that might compete with English goods. A number of such tariffs, included in the **Navigation Acts**, were passed between 1651 and 1673. The Navigation Acts required the colonists to buy goods only from England, to sell certain of their products only to England, and to import any non-English goods via English ports and pay a duty on those imports. The Navigation Acts also prohibited the colonies from manufacturing a number of goods that England already produced. In short, the Navigation Acts sought to establish wide-ranging English control over colonial commerce. Also of note was the **Wool Act** of 1699, which forbade both the export of wool from the American colonies and the importation of wool from other British colonies. Some colonists protested this law by dealing only in flax and hemp. Likewise, the **Molasses Act** of 1733 imposed an exorbitant tax upon the importation of sugar from the French West Indies (thus protecting British merchants). New Englanders frequently refused to pay the tax, an early example of rebellion against the Crown.

The Navigation Acts were only somewhat successful in achieving their goal, as it was easy to smuggle goods into and out of the colonies. The colonists also did not protest aggressively against the Navigation Acts at the time, because they were entirely dependent on England for trade and for military protection.

Colonial Governments

Despite trade regulations, the colonists maintained a large degree of autonomy. Every colony had a **governor** who was appointed by either the king or the proprietor. Although the governor had powers similar to the king's in England, he was also dependent on colonial **legislatures** for money. Also, the governor, whatever his official powers, was essentially stranded in the New World. His power relied on the cooperation of the colonists, and most governors ruled accordingly, only infrequently overruling the legislatures.

Except for Pennsylvania (which had a unicameral legislature with just one house), all the colonies had **bicameral** legislatures modeled after the British Parliament. The lower house functioned in much the same way as does today's House of Representatives; its members were directly elected (by white, male property holders), and its powers included the "power of the purse" (control over government salaries and tax legislation). The upper house was made up of appointees, who served as advisors to the governor and had some legislative and judicial powers. Most of these men were chosen from the local population. Most were concerned primarily with protecting the interests of colonial landowners.

The British never tried to establish a powerful central government in the colonies. The autonomy that England allowed the colonies helped ease their transition to independence in the following century.

The colonists did make some small efforts toward centralized government. **The New England Confederation** was the most prominent of these attempts. Although it had no real power, it did offer advice to the northeastern colonies when disputes arose among them. It also provided colonists from different settlements the opportunity to meet and to discuss their mutual problems.

Major Events of the Period

Bacon's Rebellion took place on Virginia's western frontier in 1676. With virtually all coastal land having been claimed, newcomers who sought to start their own farms in the region were forced west into the back country. Encroaching on land inhabited by Native Americans made frontier farmers subject to raids. In response, the western settlers sought to band together and drive the native tribes out of the region. In this effort, they were stymied by the government in Jamestown, which did not want to risk a full-scale war. Class resentment grew as frontiersmen, many of whom had been indentured servants, began to suspect that eastern elites viewed them as expendable "human shields" serving as a buffer between them and the natives.

The farmers rallied behind **Nathaniel Bacon**, a recent immigrant who, despite his wealth, had arrived too late to settle on the coast. Bacon demanded that Governor **William Berkeley** grant him the authority to raise a militia and attack the nearby tribes. When Berkeley refused, Bacon and his men lashed out at the natives anyway, attacking not only the Susquehannock but also the Pamunkeys, who were actually allies of the English. The rebels then turned their attention to Jamestown, sacking and burning the city. The rebellion dissolved when Bacon suddenly died of dysentery, and the conflict between the colonists and Native Americans was averted with a new treaty, but Bacon's Rebellion is often cited as an early example of a populist uprising in America.

> Bacon's Rebellion is significant for other reasons not always discussed in most textbooks. Many disgruntled former indentured servants allied themselves with free blacks who were also disenfranchised—or unable to vote. This alliance along class lines, as opposed to racial lines, frightened many Southerners and led to the development of what would eventually become black codes following the Civil War. Bacon's Rebellion may also be seen as a precursor to the American Revolution. As colonists pushed westward, in search of land, but away from the commercial and political centers, they experienced a sense of alienation and desire for greater political autonomy. It is important to remember that Berkeley was the royal governor of Virginia, and the backcountry of Virginia was even farther from London.

Insurrections led by slaves did not begin until nearly 70 years later with the **Stono Uprising,** the first and one of the most successful slave rebellions. In September 1739, approximately 20 slaves met near the Stono River outside Charleston, South Carolina. They stole guns and ammunition, killed storekeepers and planters, and liberated a number of slaves. The rebels, now numbering about 100, fled to Florida, where they hoped the Spanish colonists would grant them their freedom. The colonial militia caught up with them and attacked, killing some and capturing most of the others. Those who were captured and returned were later executed. As a result of the Stono Uprising (sometimes called the **Cato Rebellion**), many colonies passed more restrictive laws to govern the behavior of slaves. Fear of slave rebellions increased, and New York experienced a "witch hunt" period, during which 31 blacks and 4 whites were executed for conspiracy to liberate slaves.

Speaking of witch hunts, the **Salem Witch Trials** took place in 1692. These were not the first witch trials in New England. During the first 70 years of English settlement in the region, 103 people (almost all women) had been tried on charges of witchcraft. Never before had so many been accused at once, however; during the summer of 1692, more than 130 "witches" were jailed or executed in Salem.

Historians have a number of explanations for why the mass hysteria started and ended so quickly. The region had recently endured the autocratic control of the **Dominion of New England**, an English government attempt to clamp down on illegal trade. In 1691, Massachusetts became a royal colony under the new monarchs, and suffrage was extended to all Protestants; previously only Puritans could vote, so this move weakened Puritan primacy. War against French and Native Americans on the Canadian border (called **King William's War** in the colonies and **the War of the League of Augsburg** in England) soon followed and further heightened regional anxieties.

To top it all off, the Puritans feared that their religion—which they fervently believed was the *only* true religion—was being undermined by the growing commercialism in cities like Boston. Many second- and third-generation Puritans lacked the fervor of the original Pilgrim and Congregationalist settlers, a situation that led to the **Halfway Covenant**, which changed the rules governing Puritan baptisms. (Prior to the passage of the Halfway Covenant in 1662, a Puritan had to experience the gift of God's grace in order for his or her children to be baptized by the church. With so many, particularly men, losing interest in the church, the Puritan clergy decided to baptize all children whose parents were baptized. However—here is the "halfway" part—those who had not experienced God's grace were not allowed to vote.) All of these factors—religious, economic, and gender—historians argue, combined to create **mass hysteria in Salem in 1692**. The hysteria ended when the accusers, most of them teenage girls, accused some of the colony's most prominent citizens of consorting with the Devil, thus turning town leaders against them. Some historians also feel that the hysteria had simply run its course.

As noted, the generations that followed the original settlers were generally less religious than those that preceded them. By 1700, women constituted the majority of active church members. However, between the 1730s and 1740s the colonies (and Europe) experienced a wave of religious revivalism known as the **First Great Awakening**. Two men, Congregationalist minister **Jonathan Edwards** and Methodist preacher **George Whitefield**, came to exemplify the period. Edwards preached the severe, predeterministic doctrines of Calvinism and became famous for his graphic depictions of Hell; you may have read his speech "Sinners in the Hands of an Angry God." Whitefield preached a Christianity based on emotionalism and spirituality, which today is most clearly manifested in Southern **evangelism**. The First Great Awakening is often described as the response of devout people to the **Enlightenment**, a European intellectual movement that borrowed heavily from ancient philosophy and emphasized rationalism over emotionalism or spirituality.

Whitefield was a native of England, where the Enlightenment was in full swing; its effects were also being felt in the colonies, especially in the cities. The colonist who came to typify Enlightenment ideals in America was the self-made and self-educated man, **Ben Franklin**. Franklin was a printer's apprentice who, through his own ingenuity and hard work, became a wealthy printer and a successful and respected intellectual. His ***Poor Richard's Almanack*** was extremely popular and remains influential to this day. (It is the source of such pithy aphorisms as "A stitch in time saves nine" and "A penny saved is a penny earned.") Franklin did pioneering work in the field of electricity. He invented bifocals, the lightning rod, and the Franklin stove, and he founded the colonies' first fire department, post office, and public library. Franklin espoused Enlightenment ideals about education, government, and religion and was, until Washington came along, the colonists' favorite son. Toward the end of his life, he served as an ambassador in Europe, where he negotiated a crucial alliance with the French and, later, the peace treaty that ended the Revolutionary War.

Franklin played a big social-poli pole.

Life in the Colonies

Perhaps the most important development in the colonies during this period was the rate of growth. The population in 1700 was 250,000; by 1750, that number was 1,250,000. Throughout these years, the colonies began to develop substantial non-English European populations. Scotch-Irish, Scots, and Germans all started arriving in large numbers during the 18th century. English settlers, of course, continued to come to the New World as well. The black population in 1750 was more than 200,000, and in a few colonies (South Carolina, for example) they would outnumber whites by the time of the Revolution.

The vast majority of colonists—over 90 percent—lived in **rural areas**. Life for whites in the countryside was rugged but tolerable. Labor was divided along gender lines, with men doing the outdoor work such as farming, and women doing the indoor work of housekeeping and childrearing. Opportunities for social interaction outside the family were limited to shopping days and rare special community events. Both children and women were completely subordinate to men, particularly to the head of the household, in this patriarchal society. Children's education was secondary to their work schedules. Women were not allowed to vote, draft a will, or testify in court.

Blacks, most of whom were slaves, lived predominantly in the countryside and in the South. Their lives varied from region to region, with conditions being most difficult in the South, where the labor was difficult and the climate less hospitable to hard work. Those slaves who worked on large plantations and developed specialized skills, such as carpentry or cooking, fared better than did field hands. In all cases, though, the condition of servitude was demeaning. Slaves often developed extended kinship ties and strong communal bonds to cope with the misery of servitude and the possibility that their nuclear families might be separated by sale. In the North, where black populations were relatively small, blacks often had trouble maintaining a sense of community and history.

Conditions in the **cities** were often much worse than those in the country. Because work could often be found there, most immigrants settled in the cities. The work they found generally paid too little, and poverty was widespread. Sanitary conditions were primitive, and epidemics such as smallpox were common. On the positive side, cities offered residents much wider contact with other people and with the outside world. Cities served as centers for progress and education.

Citizens with anything above a rudimentary level of education were rare, and nearly all **colleges** established during this period served primarily to train ministers.

Early colleges in the North include Harvard and Yale (established in 1636 and 1701, respectively). The College of William and Mary was chartered in the South in 1693.

The lives of colonists in the various regions differed considerably. **New England** society centered on trade. Boston was the colonies' major port city. The population farmed for subsistence, not for trade, and mostly subscribed to rigid Puritanism. The **middle colonies**—New York, Pennsylvania, New Jersey—had more fertile land and so focused primarily on farming (they were also known as the "bread colonies" because of their heavy exports of grain). Philadelphia and New York City, like Boston, were major trade centers. The population of the region was more heterogeneous than was that of New England. The **lower South** (the Carolinas) concentrated on cash crops, such as tobacco and rice. Slavery played a major role on plantations, although the majority of Southerners were subsistence farmers who had no slaves. Blacks constituted up to half the population of some Southern colonies. The colonies on the **Chesapeake** (Maryland and Virginia) combined features of the middle colonies and the lower South. Slavery and tobacco played a larger role in the Chesapeake than in the middle colonies, but like the middle colonies, the Chesapeake residents also farmed grain and thus diversified their economies. The development of major cities in the Chesapeake region also distinguished it from the lower South, which was almost entirely rural.

Thus, the colonies were hardly a unified whole as they approached the events that led them to rebel. How then did they join together and defeat the most powerful nation in the world? The answer to this and other exciting questions awaits you in the next chapter.

Reasons for the Founding of Selected Colonies

Virginia (1607): Economic gain
Plymouth (1620): Religious freedom (Separatist Pilgrims)
Massachusetts (1629): Religious freedom (Nonseparatist Puritans); later merged with Plymouth
Maryland (1633): Religious freedom (Catholics)
Connecticut (1636): Religious differences with Puritans in Massachusetts
Rhode Island (1636): Religious freedom from Puritans in Massachusetts
New York (1664): Seized from Dutch
New Jersey (1664): Seized from Dutch
Delaware (1664): Seized from Dutch, who took it from Swedes
Pennsylvania (1682): Religious freedom (Quakers)
Georgia (1732): Buffer colony and alternative to debtors' prison

Summary

Here are the most important concepts to remember from the Early Contact period.

o   Native populations in North America were not monolithic; they were diverse. Tribal groups varied widely in their economies, level of civilization, and interaction with each other and Europeans.

o   The Columbian exchange revolutionized both European and Native cultures by expanding trade and technology and creating a racially mixed New World, stratified by wealth and status.

o   African slavery started in this period, gradually replacing Native slavery and European indentured servitude.

o   The belief in European superiority was a key rationale for the colonization of North America.

Here are the most important concepts to remember from the Colonization period.

o   Europeans and Native Americans vied for control of land, fur, and fishing rights.

o   The Spanish, French, Dutch, and British had different styles of interacting with Native populations.

Chapter 6 Review Questions

See Chapter 14 for answers and explanations.

1. Which of the following statements about indentured servitude is true?

   (A) Indentured servitude was the means by which most Africans came to the New World.
   (B) Indentured servitude never attracted many people because its terms were too harsh.
   (C) Approximately half of all indentured servants died before earning their freedom.
   (D) Indenture was one of several systems used to distinguish house slaves from field slaves.

2. The Mayflower Compact foreshadows the U.S. Constitution in which of the following ways?

   (A) It posits the source of government power in the people rather than in God.
   (B) It ensures both the right to free speech and the separation of church and state.
   (C) It limits the term of office for all government officials.
   (D) It establishes three branches of government in order to create a system of checks and balances.

3. The first important cash crop in the American colonies was

   (A) cotton
   (B) corn
   (C) tea
   (D) tobacco

4. The philosophy of mercantilism holds that economic power resides primarily in

   (A) surplus manpower and control over raw materials
   (B) control of hard currency and a positive trade balance
   (C) the ability to extend and receive credit at favorable interest rates
   (D) domination of the slave trade and control of the shipping lanes

5. Colonial vice-admiralty courts were created to enforce

   (A) Puritan religious edicts
   (B) prohibitions on antimonarchist speech
   (C) import and export restrictions
   (D) travel bans imposed on Native Americans

6. All of the following are examples of conflicts between colonists and Native American tribes EXCEPT

   (A) Bacon's Rebellion
   (B) the Pequot War
   (C) the Stono Uprising
   (D) King Philip's War

7. Which of the following statements about cities during the colonial era is NOT true?

   (A) Poor sanitation left colonial cities vulnerable to epidemics.
   (B) Religious and ethnic diversity was greater in colonial cities than in the colonial countryside.
   (C) Most large colonial cities grew around a port.
   (D) The majority of colonists lived in urban areas.

8. Colleges and universities during the colonial period were dedicated primarily to the training of

   (A) medical doctors
   (B) scientists
   (C) political leaders
   (D) the clergy

9. Which of the following is the best explanation for why the British did not establish a powerful central government in the American colonies?

   (A) The British cared little how the colonists lived so long as the colonies remained a productive economic asset.
   (B) Britain feared that the colonists would rebel against any substantial government force that it established.
   (C) Few members of the British elite were willing to travel to the colonies, even for the opportunity to govern.
   (D) Britain gave the colonies a large measure of autonomy as a first step in transitioning the region to independence.

REFLECT

Respond to the following questions:

- For which content topics discussed in this chapter do you feel you have achieved sufficient mastery to answer multiple-choice questions correctly?

- For which content topics discussed in this chapter do you feel you have achieved sufficient mastery to discuss effectively in a short-answer question or an essay?

- On which content topics discussed in this chapter do you feel you need more work before you can answer multiple-choice questions correctly?

- On which content topics discussed in this chapter do you feel you need more work before you can discuss them effectively in a short-answer question or an essay?

- What parts of this chapter are you going to review again?

- Will you seek further help, outside of this book (such as a teacher, tutor, or AP Students), on any of the content in this chapter—and, if so, on what content?

Chapter 7
Unit 3: Conflict and American Independence (1754–1800)

Before 1754, most colonists still considered themselves English

In 1754, the colonists still considered themselves English subjects. Very few could have imagined circumstances under which they would leave the British Empire. The events that led from almost universal loyalty to rebellion are frequently tested on the AP U.S. History Exam. Here is what you need to know:

Albany Plan of Union

In 1754, representatives from seven colonies met in Albany, New York, to consider the **Albany Plan of Union**, developed by Benjamin Franklin. The plan provided for an intercolonial government and a system for collecting taxes for the colonies' defense. At that meeting, Franklin also tried to negotiate a treaty with the Iroquois. Franklin's efforts to unite the colonies failed to gain the approval of a single colonial legislature. The plan was rejected because the colonists did not want to relinquish control of their right to tax themselves, nor were they prepared to unite under a single colonial legislature. Franklin's frustration was well publicized in one of the first American political cartoons—his drawing of a snake broken into pieces, under which lie the words "Join or Die."

The Seven Years' War (1754–1763)

Yes, the Seven Years' War lasted for nine years. It is also called the **French and Indian War**, which is almost equally confusing because the French and Indians fought on the same side, not against each other. The Seven Years' War was the British name for the war. The colonists called it the "French and Indian War" because that's who they were fighting. It was actually one of several "wars for empire" fought between the British and the French, and the Americans got stuck in the middle. This was arguably the first world war.

The war was the inevitable result of colonial expansion. (It was also caused by a number of inter-European power struggles, which is how Spain, Austria, Sweden, Prussia, and others got involved, but that is on the European history test, so you can worry about it some other time.) As English settlers moved into the Ohio Valley, the French tried to stop them by building fortified outposts at strategic entry spots. The French were trying to protect their profitable fur trade and their control of the region. A colonial contingent led by **George Washington** attacked a French outpost and lost badly. Washington surrendered and was allowed to return to Virginia, where he was welcomed as a hero. Other skirmishes and battles ensued, and in 1756, England officially declared war on France. Most Native Americans in the region, choosing the lesser of two evils, allied themselves with the French who had traditionally had the best relations with Native Americans of any of the European powers and whom, based on Washington's performance, they expected to win the war. The war dragged on for years before the English finally gained the upper hand. When the war was over, England was the undisputed colonial power of the continent. The treaty gave England control of Canada and almost everything east of the Mississippi Valley. The French kept only two sugar islands, underscoring the impact of mercantilism since the French prioritized two small but highly profitable islands over the large landmass of Canada.

William Pitt, the English Prime Minister during the war, was supportive of the colonists and encouraged them to join the war effort, promising them pay and some autonomy (this helped to create one of the first real senses of intercolonial unity). When the leadership in Britain changed after the war, that led to resentment by the colonists against the British rule.

The English victory spelled trouble for Native Americans, who had previously been able to use French and English disputes to their own advantage. They negotiated their allegiances in return for land, goods, and the right to be left alone. The Native Americans particularly disliked the English, however, because English expansionism was more disruptive to their way of life. The French had sent few colonists, and many of those colonists were fur trappers who did not settle anywhere permanently. In the aftermath of the war, the English raised the price of goods sold to the Native Americans (they now had a monopoly, after all) and ceased paying rent on their western forts. In response, Ottawa war chief **Pontiac** rallied a group of tribes in the Ohio Valley and attacked colonial outposts. The attacks and resultant wars are known as **Pontiac's Rebellion** (or **Pontiac's Uprising**). In response to Pontiac's Rebellion, the **Paxton Boys**, a group of Scots-Irish frontiersmen in Pennsylvania murdered several in the Susquehanook tribe.

In response to the initial attacks, the British government issued the **Proclamation of 1763**, forbidding settlement west of the rivers running through the Appalachians. The proclamation came too late. Settlers had already moved west of the line. The proclamation did have one effect, however. It agitated colonial settlers, who regarded it as unwarranted British interference in colonial affairs.

Pontiac's Rebellion was, in part, a response to the colonists expanding into the Ohio River Valley and encroaching on the Native Americans' lands. (Recall similar events such as the Pequot War and Bacon's Rebellion.) The British were forced to quell this rebellion at great cost in addition to the costs of fighting the French. They used germ warfare, in the form of smallpox-infected blankets, to help defeat the Ottawa. The resulting Proclamation of 1763 is significant for a number of reasons. The year 1763 is often viewed as a turning point in British-colonial relations in that it marks the end of salutary neglect. The Proclamation of 1763 may be viewed as the first in a new series of restrictions imposed on the colonists by the British Parliament, and in that way, it marks the first step on the "road to revolution." Furthermore, it established a pattern of demarcating "Indian Territory," a pattern that would be adopted and pursued by the United States government long after the colonists gained their independence. (See for example the **Indian Removal Act,** 1830.)

The Scots-Irish were a group of Protestant colonial settlers who emigrated from Ireland but were ethnically Scottish. They settled mainly in the Appalachians, from Pennsylvania to Georgia. As in the case of the Paxton Boys, the Scots-Irish were known for early conflicts with local Indian tribes. Their culture and folkways remain an integral part of modern Appalachian life.

1763 - end of salutary neglect

Sugar act

The Sugar Act, the Currency Act, and the Stamp Act

One result of the Seven Years' War was that in financing the war the British government had run up a huge debt. The new king, **George III**, and his prime minister, **George Grenville**, felt that the colonists should help pay that debt. After all, they reasoned, the colonies had been beneficiaries of the war; furthermore, their tax burden was relatively light compared to that of taxpayers in England, even on the same goods. Meanwhile, the colonists felt that they had provided so many soldiers that they had fulfilled their obligation.

Accordingly, Parliament imposed new regulations and taxes on the colonists. The first was the **Sugar Act** of 1764, which established a number of new duties and which also contained provisions aimed at deterring molasses smugglers. Although Parliament had previously passed other acts aimed at controlling colonial trade and manufacturing, there was little colonial resistance prior to the decade leading up to the Revolutionary War. There were benefits to being part of the vast British Empire and most Americans accepted regulations of trade such as the **Navigation Acts** as part of **mercantilism**. Furthermore, although laws such as the Molasses Act of 1733 were on the books, smuggling was common practice and little revenue from taxes was actually collected. Some historians have gone so far as to suggest that Parliament never intended the Molasses Act to raise revenue but merely to function as a protective tariff aimed against French imports. Parliament was quite shrewd in passing the Sugar Act of 1764 in that this new act actually *lowered* the duty on molasses coming into the colonies from the West Indies. What angered the colonists the most was that this new regulation was to be more strictly enforced: duties were to be collected. It became more difficult for colonial shippers to avoid committing even minor violations of the Sugar Act. Furthermore, violators were to be arrested and tried in vice-admiralty courts, courts in which a single judge issued a verdict without the deliberation of a jury. It was this last provision of the Sugar Act that suggested to some colonists that Parliament was overstepping its authority and violating their rights as Englishmen.

Another Parliamentary act, the **Currency Act**, forbade the colonies to issue paper money. Collectively, the Sugar Act, Currency Act, and Proclamation of 1763 caused a great deal of discontent in the colonies, whose residents bristled at what they correctly viewed as British attempts to exert greater control. These acts signaled a clear end to Britain's long-standing policy of salutary neglect. That these acts came during a postwar economic depression further aggravated the situation. Colonial protest to these acts, however, was uncoordinated and ineffective.

That all changed when Parliament passed the **Stamp Act** the following year, 1765. The Stamp Act included a number of provocative elements. First, it was a tax specifically aimed at raising revenue, thus awakening the colonists to the likelihood that even more taxes could follow. The Stamp Act demonstrated that the colonies' tradition of self-taxation was surely being unjustly taken by Parliament, much to the dismay of many colonists. Second, it was a broad-based tax, covering all legal documents and licenses. Not only did it affect almost everyone, but it particularly affected a group that was literate, persuasive, and argumentative—namely, lawyers. Third, it was a tax on goods produced within the colonies.

Reaction to the Stamp Act built on previous grievances and, consequently, was more forceful than any protest preceding it. A pamphlet by James Otis, called *The Rights of the British Colonies Asserted and Proved*, laid out the colonists' argument against the taxes and became a bestseller of its day. Otis put forward the "No taxation without representation" argument that later became a rallying cry of the Revolution. Because the colonists did not elect members to Parliament, he argued, they were not obliged to pay taxes (following the accepted precept that no Englishman could be compelled to pay taxes without his consent). Otis did *not* advocate secession; rather, he argued for either representation in Parliament or a greater degree of self-government for the colonies. Neither the British nor the colonists had much interest in creating a colonial delegation to Parliament. The British scoffed at the notion, arguing that the colonists were already represented in Parliament. Their argument was rooted in the theory of **virtual representation**, which stated that members of Parliament represented all British subjects regardless of who elected them. The colonists, for their part, knew that their representation would be too small to protect their interests and so never pushed the issue. What they wanted, and what the British were refusing to give them, was the right to determine their own taxes.

Opponents of the Stamp Act united in the various colonies. In Virginia, Patrick Henry drafted the Virginia Stamp Act Resolves, protesting the tax and asserting the colonists' right to a large measure of self-government. (The Virginia legislature removed Henry's most radical propositions before passing the resolves.) In Boston, mobs burned the customs officers in effigy, tore down a customs house, and nearly destroyed the governor's mansion. Protest groups formed throughout the colonies, calling themselves **Sons of Liberty.** The opposition was so effective that, by the time the law was supposed to take effect, not one of the Crown's appointed duty collectors was willing to perform his job. In 1766, Parliament repealed the Stamp Act. Just as important, George III replaced Prime Minister Grenville, whom the colonists now loathed, with Lord Rockingham, who had opposed the Stamp Act. Rockingham oversaw the repeal but also linked it to the passage of the **Declaratory Act**, which asserted the British government's right to tax and legislate in all cases anywhere in the colonies. Thus, although the colonists had won the battle over the stamp tax, they had not yet gained any ground in the war of principles over Parliament's powers in the colonies.

The Townshend Acts

Rockingham remained prime minister for only two years. His replacement was William Pitt. Pitt, however, was ill, and the dominant figure in colonial affairs came to be the minister of the exchequer, Charles Townshend. Townshend drafted the eponymous **Townshend Acts**. The Townshend Acts, like the Stamp Act, contained several antagonistic measures. First, they taxed goods imported directly from Britain—the first such tax in the colonies. Mercantilism approved of duties on imports from other European nations but not on British imports. Second, some of the tax collected was set aside for the payment of tax collectors, meaning that colonial assemblies could no longer withhold government officials' wages in order to get their way. Third, the Townshend Acts created even more vice-admiralty courts and several new government offices to enforce the Crown's will in the colonies. Fourth, they suspended the New York legislature because it had refused to comply with a law requiring the colonists to supply British troops. Last, these acts instituted *writs of assistance*, licenses that gave the British the power to search any place they suspected of hiding smuggled goods.

The colonists got better at protesting with each new tax, and their reaction to the Townshend Acts was their strongest yet. The Massachusetts Assembly sent a letter (called the **Massachusetts Circular Letter**, written by Samuel Adams in 1768) to all other assemblies asking that they protest the new measures in unison. The British fanned the flames of protest by ordering the assemblies *not* to discuss the Massachusetts letter, virtually guaranteeing it to be all anyone *would* talk about. Governors of colonies where legislatures discussed the letter dissolved those legislatures, which, of course, further infuriated colonists. The colonists held numerous rallies and organized boycotts, and for the first time they sought the support of "commoners" (previously such protests were confined largely to the aristocratic classes), making their rallies larger and much more intimidating. The boycotts were most successful because they affected British merchants, who then joined the protest. Colonial women were essential in the effort to replace British imports with "American" (New England) products. After two years, Parliament repealed the Townshend duties, although not the other statutes of the Townshend Acts, and not the duty on tea.

Nonconsumption and Nonimportation

There were no police departments in colonial America. Communities were self-policing. If a man was beating his wife, groups of neighbors would gather and threaten him with dire consequences if he didn't stop. Patriot leaders leveraged this practice in organizing resistance to the Townshend and other duties. The colonists' only recourses were **nonconsumption** and **nonimportation**—in other words, to boycott British goods—but such a policy could be effective only if everyone participated. So it was that New England newspapers printed pleas to women in particular, who generally managed the family budget, not to buy British linen and tea, and exposed importers, such as one William Jackson who ran a shop called the Brazen Head. If these methods proved ineffective, then, yes, Patriot leaders would deploy thugs to get the point across. A few painful and humiliating tar-and-featherings went a long way, and imports from Britain dropped 40 percent by 1770.

The Quartering Act of 1765 stationed large numbers of troops in America and made the colonists responsible for the cost of feeding and housing them. Even after the Townshend duties were repealed, the soldiers remained—particularly in Boston. Officially sent to keep the peace, these soldiers in fact heightened tensions. For one thing, the detachment was huge—4,000 men in a city of only 16,000. To make matters worse, the soldiers sought off-hour employment and so competed with colonists for jobs. Numerous confrontations resulted, with the most famous on March 5, 1770, when a mob pelted a group of soldiers with rock-filled snowballs. The soldiers fired on the crowd, killing five—hence, the **Boston Massacre**. The propaganda campaign that followed suggested that the soldiers had shot into a crowd of innocent bystanders. Interestingly, John Adams defended the soldiers in court, helping to establish a tradition of giving a fair trial to all who are accused.

The Calm, and Then the Storm

Oddly enough, for the next two years, nothing major happened. The Boston Massacre shocked both sides into de-escalating their rhetoric, and an uneasy status quo fell into place during this period. Colonial newspapers discussed ways in which the relationship between the mother country and the colonies might be altered to satisfy both sides, but still, nobody except a very few radicals suggested independence.

Things picked up in 1772 when the British implemented the part of the Townshend Acts that provided for colonial administrators to be paid from customs revenues (and not by the colonial legislatures). The colonists responded cautiously, setting up groups called **Committees of Correspondence** throughout the colonies to trade ideas and inform one another of the political mood. The committees also worked to convince more citizens to take an active interest in the conflict. Writers such as **Mercy Otis Warren**, a friend of Abigail Adams and Martha Washington, published pamphlets calling for Revolution. *Letters From a Farmer in Pennsylvania* were a series of essays written by John Dickinson, uniting the colonists against the Townshend Acts.

Not long after, the British granted the foundering East India Tea Company a monopoly on the tea trade in the colonies as well as a portion of new duties to be collected on tea sales. The result was cheaper tea for the colonists, but the colonists saw a more important issue: Parliament was once again imposing new taxes on them. In Boston, the colonists refused to allow the ships to unload their cargo, and the governor refused to allow them to leave the harbor. On December 16, 1773, a group of Sons of Liberty, poorly disguised as Mohawks, boarded a ship and dumped its cargo into Boston Harbor. It took them three hours to jettison the approximately £10,000 worth of tea. The incident is known as the **Boston Tea Party.**

The English responded with a number of punitive measures, known collectively as the **Coercive Acts** (also called the **Intolerable Acts**). One measure closed Boston Harbor to all but essential trade (food and firewood) and declared that it would remain closed until the tea was paid for. Several measures tightened English control over the Massachusetts government and its courts, and a new, stricter Quartering Act put British soldiers in civilian homes. The Coercive Acts convinced many colonists that their days of semi-autonomy were over and that the future held even further encroachments on their liberties by the Crown. To make matters worse, at the same time Parliament passed the Coercive Acts, it also passed the **Quebec Act**, which, to the colonists' chagrin, (1) granted greater liberties to Catholics, whom the Protestant colonial majority distrusted, and (2) extended the boundaries of the Quebec Territory, thus further impeding westward expansion.

The colonists met to discuss their grievances. All colonies except Georgia sent delegates to the **First Continental Congress,** which convened in late 1774. All perspectives were represented—Pennsylvania's delegation included conservatives such as Joseph Galloway, while Virginia sent two radicals, Richard Henry Lee and **Patrick Henry.** The goals of the meeting were to enumerate American grievances, to develop a strategy for addressing those grievances, and to formulate a colonial position on the proper relationship between the royal government and the colonial governments.

The Congress came up with a list of those laws the colonists wanted repealed and agreed to impose a boycott on British goods until their grievances were redressed. The delegates also agreed to form a **Continental Association**, with towns setting up committees of observation to enforce the boycott; in time, these committees became their towns' de facto governments. Perhaps most important, the Congress formulated a limited set of parameters within which it considered Parliamentary interference in colonial affairs justified; all other spheres, the delegates agreed, should be left to the colonists themselves. This position represented a major break with British tradition and, accordingly, a major step toward independence.

Throughout the winter of 1774 and the spring of 1775, the committees of observation expanded their powers. In many colonies, they supplanted the British-sanctioned assemblies. They led acts of insubordination by collecting taxes, disrupting court sessions, and, most ominously, organizing militias and stockpiling weapons. As John Adams would later comment about the period, "The Revolution was effected before the war commenced. The Revolution was in the minds and hearts of the people.... This radical change in the principles, opinions, sentiments, and affections of the people was the real American Revolution."

The Shot Heard 'Round the World

The British underestimated the strength of the growing pro-revolutionary movement. Government officials mistakenly believed that if they arrested the ringleaders and confiscated their arsenals, violence could be averted. To that end, the English dispatched troops to confiscate weapons in Concord, Massachusetts, in April 1775. The troops had to first pass through Lexington, where they confronted a small colonial militia, called **minutemen** because they reputedly could be ready to fight on a minute's notice. Someone, probably one of the minutemen, fired a shot, which drew British return fire. When the **Battle of Lexington** was over, the minutemen had suffered 18 casualties, including 8 dead. The British proceeded to **Concord**, where a much larger contingent of minutemen awaited them. The Massachusetts militia inflicted numerous casualties on the British **redcoats** and forced them to retreat. That a contingent of colonial farmers could repel the army of the world's largest empire was monumental, which is why the **Battle of Concord** is sometimes referred to as "the shot heard 'round the world." The two opponents dug in around Boston, but during the next year only one major battle was fought. The two sides regrouped and planned their next moves.

For the colonists, the period provided time to rally citizens to the cause of independence. Not all were convinced. Among those remaining loyal to the Crown—such people were called **Loyalists**—were government officials, devout Anglicans (members of the Church of England), merchants dependent on trade with England, and many religious and ethnic minorities who feared persecution at the hands of the rebels. Many slaves believed their chances for liberty were better with the British than with the colonists, a belief strengthened when the royal governor of Virginia offered to free those slaves who escaped and joined the British army. The pre-Revolutionary War era saw an increase in the number of slave insurrections, dampening some Southerners' enthusiasm for revolution. The **patriots** were mostly white Protestant property holders and gentry, as well as urban artisans, especially

Big Man on Campus
Washington's future vice president, John Adams, once griped that "Washington was always selected by deliberative bodies to lead, whatever the cause, because he was always the tallest man in the room."

in New England, where Puritans had long shown antagonism toward Anglicans. Much of the rest of the population just hoped the whole thing would blow over. The Quakers of Pennsylvania, for example, were pacifists and so wanted to avoid war.

The **Second Continental Congress** convened during this period, just weeks after the battles of Lexington and Concord. Throughout the summer, the Congress prepared for war by establishing a **Continental Army**, printing money, and creating government offices to supervise policy. The Congress chose **George Washington** to lead the army because he was both well-liked and a Southerner (thus bolstering support in an area with many loyalists). There is a lot of interesting military history about Washington's command, but because the AP Exam ignores military history, so too does this review.

Not all delegates thought that war was inevitable, and many followed John Dickinson, who was pushing for reconciliation with Britain using the **Olive Branch Petition**. Adopted by the Continental Congress on July 5, 1775, following the skirmish at Breed's Hill, often known as Bunker Hill, the Olive Branch petition was a last-ditch attempt to avoid armed conflict. King George III, however, was hardly interested in the proposal since he considered the colonists to be in open rebellion given their boycotts, attacks on royal officials, and resistance at Lexington and Concord. Still, it is worth noting that just one year before the adoption of the Declaration of Independence, the colonial leaders were trying to reconcile with the mother country.

The Declaration of Independence

The rebels were still looking for the masterpiece of propaganda that would rally colonists to their cause. They got it in *Common Sense*, a pamphlet published in January of 1776 by an English printer named **Thomas Paine**. Paine not only advocated colonial independence, he also argued for the merits of republicanism over monarchy. The pamphlet was an even bigger success than James Otis's *The Rights of the British Colonies Asserted and Proved*. Though literacy rates in New England were somewhat higher, thanks to the Puritan legacy of teaching children to read the Bible, most of the nation's two million inhabitants could not read. Nevertheless, Paine's pamphlet sold more than 100,000 copies in its first three months alone, the proportional equivalent of selling 13 million downloads today. The secret to Paine's success was that *Common Sense* stated the argument for independence in plainspoken language accessible to colonists who couldn't always keep up with the lofty Enlightenment-speak of the Founding Fathers. It helped swing considerable support to the patriot cause among people who had worried about the wisdom of attacking the powerful mother country.

The preamble of the Declaration of Independence begins with "We hold these truths to be self-evident, that all men are created equal, that they are endowed by their Creator with certain unalienable Rights, that among these are Life, Liberty and the pursuit of Happiness." This opening statement reflects the Enlightenment ideals that Thomas Jefferson strongly believed in, and outlines the philosophy of government that the American colonies believe in. The bulk of the Declaration is a list of grievances about George III and the British government, including taxation without representation, dissolving local representative government, keeping standing armies in the colonies during peacetime, cutting off trade with the rest of the world, and depriving American colonists of the right to trial by jury.

In June, the Congress was looking for a rousing statement of its ideals, and it commissioned **Thomas Jefferson** to write the **Declaration of Independence.** He did not let them down. The Declaration not only enumerated the colonies' grievances against the Crown, but it also articulated the principle of individual liberty and the government's fundamental responsibility to serve the people. Despite its obvious flaws—most especially that it pertained only to white, propertied men—it remains a work of enormous power. With the document's signing on July 4, 1776, the Revolutionary War became a war for independence.

Chronology of Events Leading to Revolutionary War	
1763	–French and Indian War ends –Pontiac's Rebellion –Proclamation of 1763
1764	–Sugar Act –Currency Act
1765	–Stamp Act –Stamp Act crisis –Sons of Liberty formed
1766	–Grenville replaced by Rockingham as prime minister –Stamp Act repealed –Declaratory Act
1767	–Townshend Acts
1770	–Townshend duties repealed (except tea tax) –Boston Massacre
1772	–parts of Townshend Acts implemented –Committees of Correspondence formed
1773	–British give the Dutch East India Tea Company monopoly on tea in colonies –Boston Tea Party
1774	–Coercive (Intolerable) Acts –Quebec Act –First Continental Congress meets –Continental Association forms
1775	–Battles of Lexington and Concord –Second Continental Congress meets
1776	–Declaration of Independence

The Battle of Saratoga (October 17, 1777) in upstate New York was a turning point in the American Revolution, as it was a decisive victory of American troops against British troops, ending the British prominence in upstate New York and serving as a recruitment tool for the Americans. With this victory, the French government agreed to a formal alliance with the Continental Congress, and began sending military advisers, weapons, and financial assistance.

The Battle of Yorktown (October 1781) was the symbolic end to the American Revolution, even though the British remained in New York City until 1783 and other British troops remained active in the South until 1782. The major British general, Cornwallis, was surrounded by the French navy on the York River and George Washington's troops via land, and surrendered after a lengthy siege. Cornwallis's surrender began a long period of negotiations between the American colonies and Great Britain, which would finally end the war in October of 1783.

After several years of fighting, the British surrendered at Yorktown in October of 1781. You should remember a few other facts about the war. The Continental Army (as opposed to local militias) had trouble recruiting good soldiers. Eventually, the Congress recruited blacks, and up to 5,000 fought on the side of the rebels (in return, most of those who had been slaves were granted their freedom). The **Franco-American Alliance**, negotiated by **Ben Franklin** in 1778, brought the French into the war on the side of the colonists, after the battle of Saratoga. This was hardly surprising given the lingering resentment of the French toward the English after the French and Indian War. It would be three years before French troops landed in America, but the alliance buoyed American morale, and with the help of militia units, especially in the South, the colonists kept up a war of attrition until support could arrive from France. By then, much like the United States in Vietnam almost two centuries later, the British found themselves outlasted and forced to abandon an unpopular war on foreign soil. The **Treaty of Paris**, signed at the end of 1783, granted the United States independence and generous territorial rights. (This Treaty of Paris is not to be confused with the Treaty of Paris that ended the French and Indian War or the Treaty of Paris that ended the Spanish-American War in 1898. Paris was all the rage as a treaty name, apparently.)

Neither the Declaration of Independence, with its bold statement that "all men are created equal," nor the revolution with its republican ideology, abolished slavery. These events also did not bring about a more egalitarian society. Like blacks, many women played a significant role in the Revolutionary War, either as "camp followers" or by maintaining households and businesses while the men were off fighting the Revolution. Many women also served as spies, while the British offered their slaves freedom if they fought for them. It would take another war to end slavery (the Civil War) and centuries of hard work toward progress to help bring about greater political and economic equality for women.

George Washington Versus Volunteer Militias

George Washington was one of the wealthiest men in America, and to a great extent his involvement with the independence movement grew out of his dissatisfaction with the mercantile system, which he felt was keeping him from expanding his fortune as much as he might have liked. The tobacco he sent to Britain never fetched the price he wanted, and the goods he received in return were too expensive and of shoddy quality. He wanted relief from British taxes and the freedom to sell to and buy from whomever he liked. The American Revolution was fueled in large part by libertarian sentiments such as these.

But after becoming commander of the Continental Army, Washington found that libertarian ideals sound terrific when you're a rich planter trying to fill your coffers, but don't work so well when you're trying to build a country or win a war. Washington pressed for a professional standing army, and demanded that the states raise money to pay the troops, but the libertarian-dominated Continental Congress replied that those ideas were precisely what they were fighting against and that Washington would have to make do with volunteers who paid their own way.

The Articles of Confederation

The colonies did not wait to win their independence from England before setting up their own governments. As soon as the Declaration of Independence was signed, states began writing their own constitutions. In 1777, the Continental Congress sent the **Articles of Confederation**, the first national constitution, to the colonies for ratification. The colonists intentionally created little to no central government since they were afraid of ridding themselves of Britain's imperial rule only to create their own tyrannical government. The articles contained several major limitations, as the country would soon learn. For one, the Articles gave the federal government no power to raise an army (which hurt the colonies during Shays's Rebellion). Some of the Articles' other major limitations on the federal government included the following:

- It could not enforce state or individual taxation, or a military draft.
- It could not regulate trade among the states or international trade.
- It had no executive or judicial branch.
- The legislative branch gave each state one vote, regardless of the state's population.
- In order to pass a law, 9 of the 13 of the states had to agree.
- In order to amend or change the Articles, unanimous approval was needed.

After the Revolution, many new state constitutions made voting privileges, and even citizenship, contingent upon property ownership. This would not change entirely until the Andrew Jackson administration.

With the end of the war, the colonies had other issues to confront as well. The decrease in England's power in the region opened a new era of relations with Native Americans. This new era was even more contentious than the previous one because a number of tribes had allied themselves with the Crown. Second-class citizens and noncitizens—namely, women and blacks—had made sacrifices in the fight for liberation, and some expected at least a degree of compensation. **Abigail Adams** wrote a famous letter to her husband pleading the case for women's rights in the new government; she reminded John to "remember the ladies and be more generous and favorable to them than your ancestors." The number of free blacks in the colonies grew during and after the war, but their increased presence among free whites was also accompanied by a growth of racist publications and legislation. Such conditions led to the early "ghettoization" of blacks and, for similar reasons, other minorities.

The problems with the Articles of Confederation became apparent early on. The wartime government, unable to levy taxes, tried to finance the war by printing more money, which led, naturally, to wild inflation. After the war, the British pursued punitive trade policies against the colonies, denying them access to West Indian markets and dumping goods on American markets. The government, unable to impose tariffs, was helpless. A protective tariff would impose duties on imported goods; the additional cost would be added to the selling price, thereby raising the cost of foreign products. By making domestic products cheaper than imports, most tariffs protected American manufacturers. Having just fought a war in part caused by taxes imposed by a central authority, the newly independent Americans were reluctant to give this power to their new federal government. In fact, the first protective tariff in United States history wasn't passed until 1816. The issue of the tariff exposed another source of tension within the new country— economic sectionalism—a major conflict that eventually led the new nation to civil war and continues to play a role in partisan politics to this very day.

Translate the Answer Choice

(D) imposed high duties on foreign goods

Translation: *made it more expensive to buy stuff from other countries*

Furthermore, when state governments dragged their heels in compensating loyalists for lost property, the British refused to abandon military posts in the States, claiming that they were remaining to protect the loyalists' rights. The government, again, was powerless to expel them. Perhaps the rudest awakening came in the form of **Shays's Rebellion**. Daniel Shays was a Revolutionary War veteran who was not receiving his pay from the war. As the Massachusetts government was enforcing the ability of banks to repossess farms and foreclose on homes of people who could not pay, Shays was facing foreclosure. His plan was to take over the courthouses that were making these rulings. He and his men seized a weapons armory in Springfield and used those weapons to attack courthouses. The Massachusetts government couldn't mobilize any forces to stop Shays and his men, so private citizens organized to put the rebellion down. This was one of the leading reasons for the Constitutional Convention. As with the earlier **Bacon's Rebellion** and later **Whiskey Rebellion**, this rebellion revealed lingering resentment on the part of the backcountry farmers toward the coastal elite. One thing that especially worried the wealthy, though, was that the Articles of Confederation had created a national government that was essentially powerless to stop such rebellions.

The government under the Articles was not totally without its successes, though. Its greatest achievements were the adoption of ordinances governing the sale of government land to settlers. Best known is the **Northwest Ordinance of 1787**, which also contained a bill of rights guaranteeing trial by jury, freedom of religion, and freedom from excessive punishment. It abolished slavery in the Northwest territories (northwest of the Ohio River and east of the Mississippi River, up to the Canadian border), and it also set specific regulations concerning the conditions under which territories could apply for statehood. Thus, the ordinance is seen as a forerunner to the Bill of Rights and other progressive government policies. It was not so enlightened about Native Americans, however; in fact, it essentially claimed their land without their consent. War ensued, and peace did not come until 1795 when the United States gained a military advantage over the Miami Confederacy, its chief Native-American opponent in the area. The Northwest Ordinance remained important long after the Northwest territories were settled because of its pertinence to the statehood process and to the issue of slavery.

A New Constitution

By 1787, it was clear that the federal government lacked sufficient authority under the Articles of Confederation. **Alexander Hamilton** was especially concerned that there was no uniform commercial policy and feared for the survival of the new republic. Hamilton convened what came to be known as the **Annapolis Convention**, but only five delegates showed up! Subsequently, Congress consented to a "meeting in Philadelphia" the following May for the sole purpose of "revising the Articles of Confederation." This meeting would eventually become the now-famous Constitutional Convention, comprising delegates from all states except Rhode Island, which met throughout the long, hot summer of 1787.

Much has been written about the framers of the Constitution. There were 55 delegates: all men, all white, many of whom were wealthy lawyers or landowners, many of whom owned slaves. They came from many different ideological

A Controversial Interpretation

An Economic Interpretation of the Constitution of the United States by Charles Beard argues that the Constitution was written primarily to cater to the financial interests of the Founding Fathers. Beard's thesis has been important to constitutional scholars ever since its publication in 1913.

backgrounds, from those who felt the Articles needed only slight adjustments to those who wanted to tear them down and start from scratch. **The New Jersey Plan** called for modifications, and it also called for equal representation from each state. **The Virginia Plan**, largely the brainchild of James Madison, called for an entirely new government based on the principle of **checks and balances** and for the number of representatives for each state to be based upon the population of the state, giving some states an advantage.

The Virginia Plan called to create a three-tiered federal government with an executive branch led by a president, a legislative branch composed of a bicameral (two house) Congress, and a judicial branch composed of a Supreme Court. The legislature received the most attention from Madison. The new legislature would have expanded powers to enforce federal taxation, to regulate trade between the states, to regulate international trade, to coin and borrow money, to create a postal service, to authorize a military draft, and to declare war.

The president would be indirectly chosen by the Electoral College, a body of prominent political leaders that represented the popular vote of each state. In order to win a state's electoral votes, a presidential candidate must win a majority of the popular vote within that state. Each state's electoral count is the sum of their senators (two) and their representatives (determined by state population). The Electoral College gave states with larger populations more power in presidential elections.

The convention lasted for four months, over the course of which the delegates hammered out a bundle of compromises, including the **Great Compromise** (also known as the **Connecticut Compromise**), which blended the Virginia Plan and the New Jersey plan to have a bicameral legislature, and the **Constitution**. This bicameral legislature included a lower house (the House of Representatives) elected by the people and the upper house (the Senate) elected by the state legislatures. (Direct election of senators, believe it or not, is a 20th-century innovation.) The president and vice president were to be elected by the Electoral College, not the citizens themselves.

The delegates at the Constitutional Convention agreed that the international slave trade could not be ended until at least 1808. There was a debate about allowing Congress to place tariffs on exported goods, but the Southern states opposed this because they depended so much on foreign trade. A tax on imports was allowed to be passed (and will later cause much controversy in the argument over states' rights).

The Constitution also laid out a method for counting slaves among the populations of Southern states for "proportional" representation in Congress, even though those slaves would not be citizens. This became known as the **Three-Fifths Compromise**, because each slave counted as three-fifths of a person. It also established three branches of government—the **executive**, **legislative**, and **judicial**—with the power of checks and balances on each other. Only three of the 42 delegates who remained in Philadelphia to the end refused to sign the finished document (two because it did not include a bill of rights).

Ratification of the Constitution was by no means guaranteed. Opposition forces portrayed the federal government under the Constitution as an all-powerful beast. These opponents, known as **Anti-Federalists**, tended to come from the backcountry and were particularly appalled by the absence of a bill of rights. Their position rang true in many of the state legislatures where the Constitution's fate lay, and some held out for the promise of the immediate addition of the **Bill of Rights** upon ratification. The **Federalist** position was forcefully and persuasively argued in the **Federalist Papers**, anonymously authored by **James Madison**, **Alexander Hamilton**, and **John Jay**. The Federalist Papers were published in a New York newspaper and were later widely circulated. They were critical in swaying opinion in New York, a large and therefore politically important state. (Virginia, Pennsylvania, and Massachusetts were the other powerhouses of the era.) The **Constitution** went into effect in 1789; the **Bill of Rights** was added in 1791.

The Washington Presidency

The Electoral College unanimously chose **George Washington** to be the first president. Washington had not sought the presidency, but as the most popular figure in the colonies, he was the clear choice, and he accepted the role out of a sense of obligation.

Knowing that his actions would set precedents for those who followed him in office, Washington exercised his authority with care and restraint. He determined early on to use his veto only if he was convinced that a bill was unconstitutional. He was comfortable delegating responsibility and so created a government made up of the best minds of his time. Although the Constitution does not specifically grant the president the duty or even the power to create a cabinet, every president since George Washington has had one. The cabinet is made up of the heads of the various executive departments, which have grown in number over the years, and it functions as the president's chief group of advisors.

Prominent among his cabinet selections were **Thomas Jefferson** as secretary of state and **Alexander Hamilton** as secretary of the treasury. These two men strongly disagreed about the proper relationship between the federal government and state governments. Hamilton favored a strong central government and weaker state governments. Jefferson, fearing the country would backslide into monarchy, or tyranny, favored a weaker federal government empowered mainly to defend the country and regulate international commerce. All other powers, he thought, should be reserved to the states.

Their argument was not a mere intellectual exercise. The new government was still defining itself, and each man had a vision of what this nation was to become. The

The Bill of Rights in a Nutshell

1. Freedom of religion, speech, press, assembly, and petition

2. Right to bear arms in order to maintain a well-regulated militia

3. No quartering of soldiers in private homes

4. Freedom from unreasonable search and seizure

5. Right to due process of law, freedom from self-incrimination, double jeopardy (being tried twice for the same crime)

6. Rights of accused persons; for example, the right to a speedy and public trial

7. Right of trial by jury in civil cases

8. Freedom from excessive bail and from cruel and unusual punishment

9. Rights not listed are kept by the people

10. Powers not listed are kept by the states or the people

Jefferson:
Federalist

Hamilton:
Anti-Fed

debate came to the forefront when Hamilton proposed a **National Bank** to help regulate and strengthen the economy. Both houses of Congress approved Hamilton's plan, but Washington, uncertain of the bank's constitutionality, considered a veto. In the debate that followed, the two main schools of thought on constitutional law were established. On one side were the **strict constructionists**, led by Jefferson and **James Madison**. They argued that the Constitution allowed Congress only those powers specifically granted to it or those "necessary and proper" to the execution of its **enumerated powers**. While a bank might be "desirable" and perhaps beneficial, they argued, it was not "necessary," and thus its creation was beyond the powers of the national government. Hamilton took the opposing viewpoint, framing the **broad (loose) constructionist** position. He argued that the creation of a bank was an **implied power** of the government because the government already had explicit power to coin money, borrow money, and collect taxes. Hamilton put forward that the government could do anything in the execution of those enumerated powers—including create a bank—that was not explicitly forbidden it by the Constitution. Washington agreed with Hamilton and signed the bill.

Hamilton's tenure at treasury was a busy and successful one. Among his achievements was his successful handling of the **national debt** accrued during the war. Hamilton's financial plan called for the federal government to assume the states' debts (further increasing the federal government's power over them) and to repay those debts by giving the debt holders land on the western frontier. The plan clearly favored Northern banks, many of which had bought up debt certificates at a small portion of their worth. Northern states also had more remaining debt than Southern states, another reason why the plan drew accusations that Hamilton was helping the monied elite at the expense of the working classes. (Some issues are perennials of American politics; this is one of them. Opposition to tax increases is another.) Hamilton was able to strike a political deal to get most of his plan implemented. His concession was a Southern location for the nation's capital. In 1800, the capital was moved to **Washington, D.C.,** a city created to become the seat of government.

The **French Revolution** took place during the Washington administration, and it too caused considerable debate. Jefferson wanted to support the revolution and its republican ideals. Hamilton had aristocratic leanings and so disliked the revolutionaries, who had overthrown the French aristocracy. The issue came to the forefront when France and England resumed hostilities. The British continued to be America's primary trading partner after the war, a situation that nudged the United States toward neutrality in the French-English conflict. Even Jefferson agreed that neutrality was the correct course to follow. When French government representative **Citizen Edmond Genêt** visited America to seek its assistance, Washington declared the U.S. intention to remain "friendly and impartial toward belligerent powers." This was called the **Neutrality Proclamation**. Genêt's visit sparked large, enthusiastic rallies held by American supporters of the revolution.

Historians cite the differences between Hamilton and Jefferson as the origins of our two-party system. Those favoring a strong federal government came to be known as **Federalists** (not to be confused with the Federalists who supported ratification of the Constitution, even though they were often the same people),

The Global Struggle for Independence

Historians often consider the American Revolution a primary inspiration for the French Revolution of the late 18th century. Likewise, the Haitian slave revolt and various uprisings in Latin America can be traced to the philosophies espoused by the early Patriots and Founding Fathers.

while the followers of Jefferson called themselves the Republicans, later known as **Democratic-Republicans** to avoid confusion with members of the Republican Party created in the 1850s, a very different group which still survives today. The development of political parties troubled the framers of the Constitution, most of whom regarded parties as factions and dangerous to the survival of the Republic.

Our First Party System		
	Federalists	**Democratic-Republicans**
Leaders	Hamilton, Washington, Adams, Jay, Marshall	Jefferson, Madison
Vision	Economy based on commerce	Economy based on agriculture
Governmental Power	Strong federal government	Stronger state governments
Supporters	Wealthy, Northeast	Yeoman farmers, Southerners
Constitution	Loose construction	Strict construction
National Bank	Believed it was "necessary"	Believed it was merely "desirable"
Foreign Affairs	More sympathetic toward Great Britain	More sympathetic toward France

Note: The Federalist Party would die out after the **Hartford Convention**, following the War of 1812. Hamilton's vision and programs would be carried out by the nationalist program and **Henry Clay's American System** during the **Era of Good Feelings**. The **Second Party System** would emerge during the presidency of **Andrew Jackson** and would consist of the **Whigs**, who embraced many Federalist principles and policies, and the **Jacksonian Democrats**, who saw themselves as the heirs of the Jeffersonian Republicans.

Hamilton's financial program not only stirred controversy in Congress and helped to create our two-party system but also instigated the **Whiskey Rebellion** in 1791, which began in western Pennsylvania when farmers resisted an excise tax on whiskey. As part of his financial program, Hamilton imposed the tax in an attempt to raise revenue to defray the debt incurred by the Revolution. Washington, determined not to let his new government tolerate armed disobedience, dispatched the militia to disperse the rebels. After the opposition was dispelled, the rebels went home, and although there were some arrests and two convictions, Washington eventually pardoned both men. The Whiskey Rebellion is significant because, like Bacon's Rebellion and Shays's Rebellion before it, the uprising demonstrated the lasting class tensions between inland farmers and the coastal elites who ran the new government. But while Shays's Rebellion demonstrated that the national government of the time had lacked the power to respond, Americans noted that the new government had power it wasn't afraid to use. Some saw fairness in Washington's actions; others saw the makings of tyranny. James Madison, among others, would retreat from his support of the Federalists to back Jefferson's camp of Democratic-Republicans.

After the **Battle of Fallen Timbers** in 1794, Washington sent John Jay to England to negotiate a treaty concerning the evacuation of the British from the Northwest Territory, as stipulated in the Treaty of Paris that concluded the Revolutionary War, as well as to discuss British violations of free trade. Although **Jay's Treaty** prevented war with Great Britain, opponents of the treaty believed Jay made too many concessions toward the British, who in essence were not respecting our rights as a sovereign nation (the treaty also involved paying some war debts). In 1796, Congress attempted to withhold funding to enforce the treaty. The House of Representatives asked Washington to submit all documents pertinent to the treaty for consideration. Washington refused, establishing the precedent of **executive privilege**, which is the right of the president to withhold information when doing so would protect national security (e.g., in the case of diplomatic files and military secrets). Jay's Treaty is often considered to be the low point of Washington's administration, and Jay himself was burned in effigy in the streets of New York.

At the same time, Washington sent Thomas Pinckney to Spain to negotiate use of the Mississippi River, duty-free access to world markets, and the removal of any remaining Spanish forts on American soil. During this mission, Pinckney was able to extract a promise from Spain to try to prevent attacks on Western settlers from Native Americans. The **Treaty of San Lorenzo**, also known as **Pinckney's Treaty**, was ratified by the U.S. Senate in 1796 and is often considered to be the high point of Washington's administration.

The end of Washington's presidency was as monumental as its beginning. Wishing to set a final precedent, Washington declined to run for a third term. In his famous **farewell address**, composed in part by Alexander Hamilton, he warned future presidents to "steer clear of permanent alliances with any portion of the foreign world." Washington's Farewell Address was published in newspapers around the United States in the fall of 1796. It warned Americans against sectional divisions, as well as political party conflict. The most prominent portion of the address focuses on international relations, or "foreign entanglements." Washington promoted the notion of having friendly relationships with all nations, but to avoid any permanent alliances. This warning remained a prominent part of American foreign policy through the mid-20th century, when the United States joined the North Atlantic Treaty Organization in 1949.

Republican Motherhood

During the 1790s, women's roles in courtship, marriage, and motherhood were all reevaluated in light of the new republic and its ideals. Although women were largely excluded from political activity, they had an important civil role and responsibility. They were to be the teachers and producers of virtuous male citizens.

While public virtue had been a strictly masculine quality in the past, *private* virtue emerged as a very important quality for women, who were given the task of inspiring and teaching men to be good citizens through romance and motherhood. The idea here is that a woman should entertain only suitors with good morals, providing more incentive for men to be more ethical. Women also held a tremendous influence on their sons, leading advocates for female education to speak out, arguing that educated women would be better mothers, who would produce better citizens. Even though the obligations of women had grown to include this new political meaning, traditional gender roles were largely unchanged as the education of women was meant only in service to husbands and family.

The idea of **Republican Motherhood** emerged in the early 1800s, as the importance of education emerged in American society. The role of the mother became more prominent in child-rearing, as mothers were now expected to raise educated children who would contribute positively to the United States.

The Adams Presidency

The Electoral College selected **John Adams**, a Federalist, as Washington's successor. Under the then-current rules, the second-place candidate became vice president, and so Adams's vice president was the Democratic-Republican Thomas Jefferson.

Following the Washington era, Adams's presidency was bound to be an anti-climax. Adams, argumentative and elitist, was a difficult man to like. He was also a hands-off administrator, often allowing Jefferson's political rival **Alexander Hamilton** to take charge. The animosity between Jefferson and Hamilton and the growing belligerence between the Federalists and Democratic-Republicans set the ugly, divisive tone for Adams's term.

Perhaps Adams's greatest achievement was avoiding all-out war with France. After the United States signed the Jay Treaty with Britain, France began seizing American ships on the open seas. Adams sent three diplomats to Paris, where French officials demanded a huge bribe before they would allow negotiations even to begin. The diplomats returned home, and Adams published their written report in the newspapers. Because he deleted the French officials' names and replaced them with the letters X, Y, and Z, the incident became known as the **XYZ Affair**. As a result, popular sentiment did a complete turnaround; formerly pro-French, the public became vehemently anti-French to the point that a declaration of war seemed possible. Aware of how small the American military was, Adams avoided the war (a war Hamilton wanted) and negotiated a settlement with a contrite France although he was not able to avoid the Naval skirmishes called the Quasi-War.

The Alien Act wanted to lengthen the amount of time it took for immigrants to become citizens (and thus eligible to vote) from 5 to 15 years. It also allowed the president to deport any "dangerous aliens."

The low point of Adams's tenure was the passage and enforcement of the **Alien and Sedition Acts**, which allowed the government to forcibly expel foreigners and to jail newspaper editors for "scandalous and malicious writing." The acts were purely political, aimed at destroying new immigrants'—especially French immigrants'—support for the Democratic-Republicans. Worst of all, the Sedition Act, which strictly regulated antigovernment speech, was a clear violation of the First Amendment. In a scenario almost unimaginable today, Vice President Jefferson led the opposition to the Alien and Sedition Acts. Together with Madison, he drafted the **Virginia and Kentucky Resolutions** (which were technically anonymous), which argued that the states had the right to judge the constitutionality of federal laws. The resolutions went on to exercise this authority they claimed, later referred to as **nullification**, by declaring the Alien and Sedition Acts void. Virginia and Kentucky, however, never prevented enforcement of the laws. Rather, Jefferson used the laws and the resolutions as key issues in his 1800 campaign for the presidency. Even today, states often pass resolutions similar to these to express their displeasure with the federal government.

Summary

Here are the most important concepts to remember from the American Independence period.

- Britain's increased attempts to control the colonies and impose burdensome taxation led to the colonists' desire for revolution.

- France, Britain, Spain, and the new United States vied for control of land; the borders of the new United States were constantly expanding.

- The common people had changed their view of government. The belief in egalitarianism and democracy replaced trust in monarchy and aristocracy.

Chapter 7 Review Questions

See Chapter 14 for answers and explanations.

1. The Albany Plan of Union failed because

   (A) the plan required the Northeastern colonies to contribute a disproportionate share of the necessary troops and money

   (B) no political leader with national stature was willing to support the plan

   (C) there was no legitimate executive power to enforce it

   (D) none of the colonies was willing to share tax-collecting powers with a national entity

2. The American colonists objected to the policies imposed by Parliament after the French and Indian War for all of the following reasons EXCEPT

   (A) the new restrictions would hinder New England trade

   (B) their rights as Englishmen were being violated

   (C) they resented quartering British troops now that the French threat was removed

   (D) they believed they should be represented in Parliament if they were subjected to mercantilist restrictions

3. According to the theory of virtual representation,

   (A) colonists were represented in Parliament by virtue of their British citizenship

   (B) slaves were represented in Congress by virtue of the fact that their owners were voters

   (C) paper money has value by virtue of the fact that it is backed by the full faith and credit of the government

   (D) the best interests of criminal defendants are represented by their attorneys

4. The Stamp Act Congress of 1765 was historically significant in that it

   (A) represented a first step in colonial unity against Britain

   (B) demonstrated Parliament's determination to tax its American colonies

   (C) represented New England's determination to go to war against England

   (D) demonstrated the colonists' political and philosophical disagreement among themselves

5. Thomas Jefferson relied on the ideas of John Locke in writing the American Declaration of Independence in all of the following ways EXCEPT Locke's belief that

   (A) man is born free and equal

   (B) man must submit to the General Will to protect his natural rights

   (C) governments get their authority from the people, not God

   (D) the purpose of government is to protect man's natural rights

6. Historians often cite Shays's Rebellion (1786–1787) as a significant event in U.S. history because it

   (A) demonstrated the strength, yet fairness, of the newly created federal government

   (B) made many Americans realize that slavery could not last

   (C) made Americans realize that excessive taxation often leads to violence

   (D) demonstrated the weakness of the federal government under the Articles of Confederation

7. Under the Articles of Confederation, the national government had which of the following powers?

    I. The power to collect taxes
    II. The power to negotiate treaties
    III. The power to supercede state law

    (A) I only
    (B) II only
    (C) I and III only
    (D) I, II, and III

8. George Washington established the principle of executive privilege in a dispute with Congress over the

    (A) Alien and Sedition Acts
    (B) legality of political parties
    (C) Jay Treaty
    (D) Whiskey Rebellion

9. The Age of Salutary Neglect drew to a close with

    (A) the Boston Tea Party
    (B) the formation of the Republic of Texas
    (C) the Salem Witch Trials
    (D) the end of the French and Indian War

10. Which of the following best summarizes the strict constructionist position on the establishment of the National Bank?

    (A) All matters not clearly reconciled by the Constitution, such as the establishment of a national bank, must be arbitrated by the federal judiciary.
    (B) The establishment of the National Bank is necessary to strengthen the United States economy and therefore must be allowed even if it is technically unconstitutional.
    (C) The decision on whether to establish a National Bank, like all important governmental decisions, should be left in the hands of a powerful executive branch.
    (D) The Constitution forbids the establishment of the bank because creating a bank is not among Congress's enumerated powers.

11. All of the following were immediate social or economic consequences of the American Revolution EXCEPT

    (A) increased opportunities for land settlement in the West
    (B) reform of primogeniture inheritance laws
    (C) expanded rights for women to hold property
    (D) the opening of many areas of trade and manufacture

REFLECT

Respond to the following questions:

- For which content topics discussed in this chapter do you feel you have achieved sufficient mastery to answer multiple-choice questions correctly?

- For which content topics discussed in this chapter do you feel you have achieved sufficient mastery to discuss effectively in a short-answer question or an essay?

- On which content topics discussed in this chapter do you feel you need more work before you can answer multiple-choice questions correctly?

- On which content topics discussed in this chapter do you feel you need more work before you can discuss them effectively in a short-answer question or an essay?

- What parts of this chapter are you going to review again?

- Will you seek further help, outside of this book (such as a teacher, tutor, or AP Students), on any of the content in this chapter—and, if so, on what content?

Chapter 8
Unit 4: Beginnings of Modern American Democracy (1800–1848)

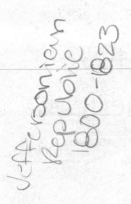

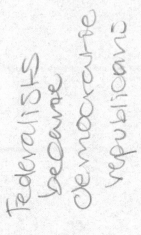

The "Revolution of 1800"

By 1800, the Federalist Party was split, clearing the way to the presidency for the Democratic-Republicans. Two men ran for the party nomination: **Thomas Jefferson** and **Aaron Burr**. Each received an equal number of votes in the Electoral College, which meant that the Federalist-dominated House of Representatives was required to choose a president from between the two. It took 35 ballots, but Jefferson finally won. Alexander Hamilton swallowed hard and campaigned for Jefferson, with whom he disagreed on most issues and whom he personally disliked, because he believed Burr to be "a most unfit and dangerous man." Burr later proved Hamilton right by killing him.

The election was noteworthy for two reasons. For the second time in as many elections, a president was saddled with a vice president he did not want. That problem was remedied in 1804 with the **Twelfth Amendment** to the Constitution, which allowed electors to vote for a **party ticket**. The other, more important reason the election was significant is that in America's first transfer of power—from the Federalists to the Democratic-Republicans—no violence occurred, a feat practically unprecedented for the time. Jefferson referred to his victory and the subsequent change-over as "the bloodless revolution."

THE JEFFERSONIAN REPUBLIC (1800–1823)

Note: The next two sections primarily review political history. They are followed by a review of social and economic history between 1800 and 1860 because many of the important socioeconomic trends of the era developed over the course of several decades. The economic and social conditions of this period also played a major role in bringing about the Civil War, and the AP Exam often tests them in this context. That's why we'll review them as we get closer, chronologically, to the Civil War.

Jefferson's First Term

The transition of power from the Federalists to the Democratic-Republicans may have been a bloodless one, but it was not a friendly one. Adams was so upset about the election that he left the capital before Jefferson took office in order to avoid attending the inauguration ceremony. Before he left town, however, he made a number of **midnight appointments,** filling as many government positions with Federalists as he could. Jefferson's response was to refuse to recognize those appointments. He then set about replacing as many Federalist appointees as he could. He dismissed some, pressured others to retire, and waited out the rest. By his second term, the majority of public appointees were Democratic-Republicans.

Jefferson's refusal to accept Adams's midnight appointments resulted in a number of lawsuits against the government. One, the case of *Marbury v. Madison* reached the Supreme Court in 1803. William Marbury, one of Adams's last-minute appointees, had sued Secretary of State James Madison for refusing to certify his appointment to the federal bench. Chief Justice **John Marshall** was a Federalist, and his sympathies were with Marbury, but Marshall was not certain that the court could force Jefferson to accept Marbury's appointment. Marshall's decision in the case established one of the most important principles of the Supreme Court: **judicial review**. The court ruled that Marbury did indeed have a right to his judgeship but that the court could not enforce his right. Why? The Judiciary Act of 1789 gave the Supreme Court the authority to order federal appointees (such as Madison) to deliver appointments such as William Marbury's. Marshall believed that this act gave too much power to the Judicial Branch at the expense of Congress and the Presidency, and thus it was unconstitutional. In one fell swoop, Marshall had handed Jefferson the victory he wanted while simultaneously claiming a major role for the Supreme Court: the responsibility for reviewing the constitutionality of Congressional acts. Throughout the rest of his tenure, Marshall worked to strengthen that doctrine and, thus, the court.

The major accomplishment of Jefferson's first term was the **Louisiana Purchase**. When Spain gave New Orleans to the French in 1802, the government realized that a potentially troublesome situation was developing. The French, they knew, were more likely to take advantage of New Orleans' strategic location at the mouth of the Mississippi, almost certainly meaning that American trade along the river would be restricted. In hopes of averting that situation, Jefferson sent James Monroe to France. Monroe's mandate was to buy New Orleans for $2 million. Monroe arrived at just the right time. Napoleon was gearing up for war in Europe, and a violent slave revolt in Haiti against the French further convinced him to abandon French interests in the New World. The French offered to sell Monroe the whole Louisiana territory for $15 million.

Spain gave the United States the right to trade in New Orleans in the 1794 Pinckney Treaty. In exchange, the United States agreed to acknowledge the border between Georgia and Spanish Florida.

Thomas Jefferson was now faced with a dilemma. As secretary of state under Washington, he had argued for a strict interpretation of the Constitution, thus limiting the power of the federal government to those powers specifically stated in the Constitution. Nowhere did the Constitution authorize the president to purchase land, yet clearly Jefferson could not pass up this opportunity to double the size of the United States. Jefferson thought about trying to get a constitutional amendment added allowing him to buy land from other countries. Ultimately, Jefferson resolved the issue by claiming his presidential power to negotiate treaties with foreign nations. His decision to purchase Louisiana without Congressional approval was not unanimously applauded: New England Federalists opposed the Louisiana Purchase because they feared (correctly) that more Western states would be more Democratic states, and that they would lose political power. They formed a group called the **Essex Junto,** planning to secede from the United States (and asked Aaron Burr to be their leader), but the plan never fully materialized. Some Republicans, led by John Randolph of Virginia, criticized Jefferson for violating Republican principles. This group became known as the Quids.

Jefferson sent explorers, among them **Lewis and Clark**, to investigate the western territories, including much of what was included in the Louisiana territory. This trip included Sacajawea as the Shoshoni guide who helped Lewis and Clark negotiate with other Native American tribes on the way up the Missouri River. All returned with favorable reports, causing many pioneers to turn their attentions westward in search of land, riches, and economic opportunities. Those early explorers also reported back to Jefferson on the presence of British and French forts that still dotted the territory, garrisoned with foreign troops that had been (deliberately?) slow to withdraw after the regime changes of the previous half-century.

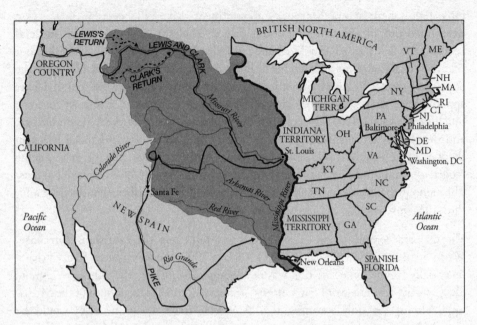

The Louisiana Purchase and the Lewis and Clark Expedition

In 1804, Jefferson won reelection in a landslide victory. During the 1804 elections, Aaron Burr ran for governor of New York. Again, Alexander Hamilton campaigned against Burr. When Burr lost, he accused Hamilton of sabotaging his political career and challenged him to a **duel** in which he killed Hamilton. Afterward, Burr fled to the Southwest, where he plotted to start his own nation in parts of the Louisiana Territory. He was later captured and tried for treason but was acquitted due to lack of evidence.

Jefferson's Second Term

Jefferson's second term did not go nearly as smoothly as his first. During these years, the United States got caught in the middle of yet another French-English dispute. The situation eventually led to the **War of 1812**.

In 1805, the British and French were at war and at a stalemate. In an effort to gain an advantage, each side began blockading the other's trade routes. The United States, dependent on both as trade partners, suffered greatly from the blockades. To add insult to injury, the British began stopping American ships and **impressing** sailors: that is, they declared, often with little or no proof, that those sailors had deserted from the British navy, and they forced them back into it. Unfortunately, the English were not as particular about whom they "reenlisted" as the Americans would have liked them to be. Tensions mounted and then boiled over when a British frigate attacked an American ship in American waters. Jefferson was at a loss. He couldn't go to war against the British because the U.S. Navy was no match for England's forces. So Jefferson responded with a boycott, biding his time while increasing military and naval appropriations.

Because both the British and the French continued to harass American ships, Jefferson lobbied for and won passage of the **Embargo Act of 1807**. The law

basically shut down America's import and export business, with disastrous economic results. New England's economy collapsed, and smuggling became widespread. The New England states strongly opposed the Embargo Act, as they were the ones most impacted by an end of international trade. Many continued to trade with British Canada regardless. The Embargo Act also led to the Democratic Republicans losing many Congressional seats in the 1808 elections. The **Non-Intercourse Act of 1809** reopened trade with most nations, but it still officially banned trade with the two most significant trade partners, Britain and France. In the end, Jefferson decided, as had Washington before him, that two terms as president were enough. He endorsed his secretary of state, **James Madison**, who handily defeated the ever-weakening Federalists.

Madison's Presidency and the War of 1812

Madison sought a solution to America's trade problems, and Congress responded with **Macon's Bill No. 2**, a bill that reopened trade with both France and England. However, Madison promised that if either country renounced its interference with American trade, he would cut off trade with the other one. Napoleon made that promise, forcing the United States to cut off trade with England, but France then continued to harass American ships.

The British, angry at the new embargo, stepped up their attacks on American ships, making a bad situation even worse. These developments helped build pro-war sentiments in the United States. Particularly anxious for a confrontation with the British were the Southern and Western **War Hawks**, who saw war as an opportunity to grab new territories to the west and southwest. There was also a strong desire among Western War Hawks to gain Canada from the British. Their leaders were **Henry Clay** and **John C. Calhoun**. Madison held out as long as he could but finally relented and asked Congress to declare war in 1812.

You should know several important points about the **War of 1812**. Once again, Native Americans aligned themselves with the British. The great chief **Tecumseh** unified area tribes in an effort to stop American expansion into Indiana and Illinois, both before and during the war. The British had been arming Native Americans in these Western territories against new American settlers. In an earlier battle against Tecumseh (the Battle of Tippecanoe), Gen. William Henry Harrison defeated Tecumseh's coalition of different tribes, and saw that they had British weapons. Meanwhile, his brother Tenskwatawa, also known as **the Prophet,** led an extensive revival of traditional Native American culture and religion. Tecumseh's coalition fell apart after he was killed in battle.

American forces were ill-prepared for the war, and much of the fighting went badly. The British captured Washington, D.C. in 1814 and set the White House on fire.

> **Effects of the War of 1812**
> - First and foremost, it represented the end of Native Americans' ability to stop American expansion.
> - The American economy, by necessity, became less reliant on trade with Britain.
> - It made Andrew Jackson into a celebrity and paved the way to his presidency.
> - The victory in New Orleans led to national euphoria.
> - The popularity of the war destroyed the Federalists, who had opposed it, and taught American politicians that objecting to going to war could be hazardous to their careers.

However, in most battles, America was able to fight to a stalemate. When English-French hostilities ended (with Napoleon's defeat), many of the issues that had caused the war evaporated, and the British soon negotiated peace. Unaware that the Treaty of Ghent had been signed in Belgium on December 24, 1814, and the war was over, General Andrew Jackson fought and won the Battle of New Orleans from January 8 until January 18, 1815, the only clear-cut U.S. victory of the war. The Federalists, opposed to the war because it disrupted trade and unaware that its end was coming, met in Hartford, Connecticut, to consider a massive overhaul of the Constitution or, failing that, secession. When the war ended soon after, most people considered the Federalists to be traitors, and their national party dissolved soon after the Hartford Convention (although the party continued to exert influence in some states through the next decade). The **Hartford Convention** itself brought many grievances, including the notion that two-thirds majority of Congress should be required to pass any laws dealing with trade, that a two-thirds majority be required to admit new states, and that no president can serve more than one four-year term and that two presidents in a row cannot come from the same state (all measures to retain some power for the Federalists).

The war had one clear positive result: it spurred **American manufacturing**. Cut off from trade with Europe, the states became more self-sufficient by necessity. New England became America's manufacturing center during the war, and after the war, the United States was less dependent on imports than it had been previously. (For more information on economic developments of the period, see pages 207–213.)

Throughout the rest of his tenure, Madison worked to promote national growth. At the same time, he remained true to his Democratic-Republican principles and so extended federal power only cautiously. Madison championed a combination of programs that included protective tariffs on imports, improvements to interstate roads (including expansion of the **National Road** from Maryland to Ohio), and the rechartering of the National Bank after the first National Bank's charter had expired. The National Bank was rechartered in 1816 and a new protective tariff was passed to protect the growing American industry. The programs were known collectively as the **American System**, sometimes referred to as the Nationalist Program. Speaker of the House **Henry Clay** lobbied for them so aggressively that many history books refer to "Henry Clay's American System."

Monroe's Presidency

The demise of the Federalists briefly left the United States with only one political party. This period of unity is referred to as the **Era of Good Feelings,** although the term belies the growing tension created by economic development and increased sectionalism. During this period, Chief Justice John Marshall's rulings continued to strengthen the federal government and its primacy. For example, *McCulloch v. Maryland* ruled that the states could not tax the National Bank, thus establishing the precedence of national law over state law. This case also reaffirmed the supremacy clause as the opposition was trying to challenge the constitutionality of the Bank of the United States.

The good feelings nearly came to an abrupt end in 1819 when a financial scare called the **Panic of 1819** threw the American economy into turmoil. The panic followed a period of economic growth, inflation, and land speculation, all of which had destabilized the economy. When the National Bank called in its loans, many borrowers couldn't repay them. The consequences included numerous mortgage foreclosures and business failures. Many people were thrown into poverty. Nonetheless, no nationally organized political opposition resulted from the panic, and Monroe easily won reelection in 1820.

The postwar period had also ushered in a new wave of westward expansion. As secretary of state under Monroe, **John Quincy Adams**, son of former president John Adams, deftly negotiated a number of treaties that fixed U.S. borders and opened new territories. The United States acquired Florida from the Spanish by the Adams-Onis Treaty in 1819. Adams also had to handle international tensions caused by a series of revolutions in Central America and South America, as the inhabitants of those regions won their independence from Spain. The U.S. was beginning to recognize the new South American nations largely to gain access to trade. Ultimately, events compelled Monroe and Adams to recognize the new nations. At the same time, they decided that America should assert its authority over the Western Hemisphere. The result was the **Monroe Doctrine**, a policy of mutual noninterference. You stay out of the Americas, Monroe told Europe, and we'll stay out of your squabbles. The Monroe Doctrine also claimed America's right to intervene anywhere in its own hemisphere, if it felt its security was threatened. No European country tried to intercede in the Americas following Monroe's declaration, and so the Monroe Doctrine *appeared* to work. Following the Napoleonic Wars, most European nations (particularly Spain) didn't have the military power to challenge the Monroe Doctrine or take back their colonies. No one, however, was afraid of the American military; Spain, France, and others stayed out of the Western Hemisphere because the powerful British navy made sure they did.

The **Adams-Onis Treaty** promised that in exchange for Florida, the United States would never try to take actions to gain Spanish-held Mexico. This was later nullified when Mexico gained independence from Spain in the 1820s.

The Monroe Doctrine is the first of several "doctrines" you should know for the AP Exam. In general, these doctrines were presidential statements that became foreign policy. For example, in 1823, President Monroe warned European nations that the Western Hemisphere was closed to future colonization. This policy, together with the advice given in Washington's Farewell Address, secured American neutrality all the way until World War I. (The **Truman Doctrine**, issued at the end of World War II, is especially important, but you should also familiarize yourself with the Eisenhower Doctrine, the Nixon Doctrine, and most recently, the Bush Doctrine.)

The new period of expansion resulted in a national debate over slavery, as would every period of expansion to follow until the Civil War resolved the slavery question. In 1820, the Union consisted of 22 states. Eleven allowed slavery; 11 prohibited it. Missouri was the first state to be carved out of the Louisiana Purchase, and its application for statehood threatened the balance, particularly in the U.S. Senate. Henry Clay brokered the **Missouri Compromise**, which (1) admitted Missouri as a slave state, (2) carved a piece out of Massachusetts—Maine—and admitted Maine as a free state, (3) drew a line along the 36°30′ parallel across the Louisiana Territory, and (4) established the southern border of Missouri as the northernmost point at which slavery would then be allowed in the western territories of the United

States, except of course for Missouri itself, which in a way violated the Missouri Compromise since it was north of the line. The compromise was the first in a series of measures forestalling the Civil War. It also split the powerful Democratic-Republican coalition, ending its 20-year control of national politics.

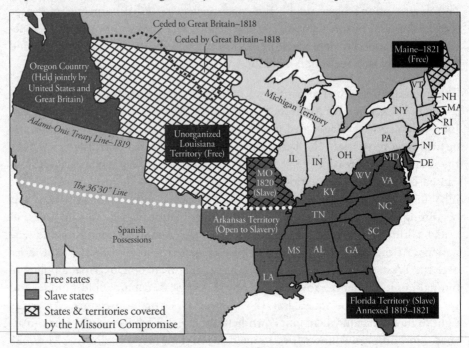

Missouri Compromise, 1820

POLITICAL EVENTS AND SOCIAL DEVELOPMENTS

The Election of 1824 and John Quincy Adams's Presidency

The **election of 1824** marked a major turning point in presidential elections. Prior to 1824, electors, who selected the president in the Electoral College, had been chosen by a variety of methods. State legislatures chose many electors, although with each election the number of states using this method decreased. By 1824, a majority of states allowed voters to choose their presidential electors directly. In earlier elections, **congressional caucuses**, or groups of U.S. Congressmen, had chosen their parties' nominees, and electors, often chosen by those same congressmen or by their friends, had not challenged the choices. With more people voting directly for presidential electors, however, there was less and less voter support for the candidates nominated by party leaders in this era before primaries and caucuses. When the Democratic-Republican caucus chose William H. Crawford in 1824, others—among them John Quincy Adams, Henry Clay, and Andrew Jackson—decided to challenge the nomination. Their opposition, along with their accusations that the party caucuses were undemocratic, brought about the **demise of the caucus system**. Of the four, Andrew Jackson received the greatest number of popular votes and electoral votes; however, as none of the four had won a majority, the election was decided in the House of Representatives. There, Speaker of the House Clay threw his support to Adams, thereby handing Adams the victory.

Adams subsequently named Clay secretary of state, a position whose previous holders included Adams, Monroe, and Jefferson and that was therefore considered the gateway to the presidency. Jackson and other opponents of Clay's appointment alleged that Adams and Clay had struck a **corrupt bargain** and immediately vowed to see both removed in the election of 1828. One other thing to note about the 1824 election is that the Constitution states that in cases where there is no majority winner in the Electoral College, the three top electoral winners go on to House election (Henry Clay came in fourth, and thus was out of the running). William Crawford suffered a stroke after the inital election, and was never a real contender for the House vote.

Adams's presidency was impeded by a contrary Congress. (Remember, more congressmen had initially supported Jackson than Adams.) He had also been a Federalist congressman and was the son of a Federalist president, and every effort he made to strengthen the central government was thus viewed with deep suspicion. Jackson's supporters strongly favored **states' rights** and thwarted all of Adams's efforts to initiate improvements through the federal government. His proposals to impose new protective tariffs, build interstate highways, and establish federal schools and research centers were all met with steep opposition, though he did go on to found a naval college and become an influential congressman.

John Quincy Adams and Postmillennialism

Postmillennialism was a belief, widespread among 19th-century Christians, that Jesus would return only after a thousand-year golden age brought about by humankind. It was therefore a major progressive force in America, with adherents such as John Quincy Adams. Here is our sixth president calling for the United States to adopt the metric system—in the 1820s!

"But if man upon earth be an improvable being; if that universal peace, which was the object of a Saviour's mission, which is the desire of the philosopher, the longing of the philanthropist, the trembling hope of the Christian, is a blessing to which the futurity of mortal man has a claim of more than mortal promise; if the Spirit of Evil is, before the final consummation of things, to be cast down from his dominion over men, and bound in the chains of a thousand years, the foretaste here of man's eternal felicity, then this system of common instruments to accomplish all the changes of social and friendly commerce, will furnish the links of sympathy between the inhabitants of the most distant regions; the metre will surround the globe in use, as well as in multiplied extension; and one language of weights and measures will be spoken from the equator to the poles."

The Jackson Presidency and Jacksonian Democracy

Despite the political incorrectness of his policies by today's standards and reevaluation of Andrew Jackson by modern-day historians, the era of Jackson as president is an important period in American history. There are always more than a few multiple-choice questions on this material, and one of the essay questions often pertains to Jackson's administration or the concept of Jacksonian democracy.

Furious that he had been denied the presidency in 1824 despite winning a plurality of the vote (more votes than any other candidate, but short of a majority), Jackson put together a support network to assure wide popular support. A coalition of state political organizations, newspaper publishers, and other community leaders rallied around the campaign. That group became the present-day **Democratic** Party. The campaign was vicious. While the candidates themselves stayed out of the fray—no presidential candidate would campaign on his own behalf until Stephen Douglas in

1860—their surrogates showed no restraint in slinging mud. Jackson's men accused Adams of being a corrupt career politician, while Adams's men accused Jackson of being a stupid and violent drunkard. Jackson was particularly infuriated by accusations that his wife was a bigamist—which was technically true, as she had married Jackson before her divorce was final. The **Coffin Handbill** accused Jackson of murdering his enlisted men during the Indian Wars. Those who consider today's smear campaigns unprecedented haven't studied much American history.

In 1828, Jackson won the election by a large margin; in so doing, he became the first president who wasn't either born in Virginia or named Adams. He was considered to have the interests of the West in mind, and he was seen as the epitome of a self-made man. Among his first acts, he dismissed numerous government officials and replaced them with political supporters. While almost every one of his predecessors had done exactly the same thing, because Jackson was the first true outsider-president, administration jobs that had previously circulated among a relatively insular circle of political supporters fell into new hands. Those who lost power criticized Jackson, but so too did the public, who noticed for the first time the cronyism already inherent in their government. Trading jobs for political favors came to be known as the **spoils system.** It was truly a case of "to the victor goes the spoils."

Jackson's popularity ushered in the age of **Jacksonian democracy**, which replaced Jeffersonian republicanism. Jefferson had conceived of a nation governed by middle- and upper-class educated property holders, in which the government would be only as large as necessary to provide an acceptable level of services. Jefferson also envisioned a nation of yeoman farmers—farmers who owned their land—whose liberty would be protected by limiting the power of the central government. Jacksonian democracy, on the other hand, benefited from **universal white manhood suffrage**, meaning the extension of voting rights to all white males, even those who did not own property. This, however, was the work of state legislatures; Jackson only benefited from it.

A strong presidency also characterized Jacksonian democracy. Jackson parlayed his wide popularity into a mandate to challenge both Congress and the Supreme Court in a way that none of his predecessors had. You should note that, unlike Jeffersonian republicanism, Jacksonian democracy is *not* a coherent vision of how a government should function. Jacksonian Democrats saw themselves as champions of liberty, but they did not always act as such. Jackson was not as great a thinker as Jefferson, the Enlightenment scholar.

No policy of Jackson's has received more criticism by modern scholars than Jackson's treatment of the Cherokees with the **Indian Removal Act,** passed by Congress in 1830. In some ways, this

When "the West" Wasn't That West

In colonial times, any settlement that wasn't located right on the Atlantic Ocean was said to be located in "the west." By the early 19th century, definitions had changed—but not to their modern meanings. "The Northwest" consisted of northern states west of the Appalachians, such as Ohio, Indiana, and Illinois, which are now considered "the Midwest." (This is why Northwestern University is located not in, say, Seattle, but in Chicago.) "The Southwest" consisted of southern states west of the Appalachians, such as Alabama and Mississippi, which are now considered "the Deep South." Henry Clay and Andrew Jackson were considered the foremost Westerners of the period, and they were respectively from Kentucky and Tennessee.

represented a natural continuation of policy toward American Indians. Originally, it had been the British who established the concept that Native Americans were "foreign nations," and as such, the government could go to war and make treaties with them. These treaties often established what the British termed "Indian territory," as was the case with the **Proclamation of 1763** issued at the close of the **French and Indian War**.

When the Americans gained their independence, the U.S. government continued the treatment of Native Americans that had been established by the British. Some Americans, however, among them Thomas Jefferson, suggested assimilation into American culture as a solution to the "Indian Problem." Jefferson and others believed that if the Native Americans gave up their "hunting and gathering" lifestyle and adopted American farming techniques and culture—in essence, "learned to live on less land"—then the Americans and Native Americans might coexist peacefully.

By the time of Jackson's presidency, there were "Five Civilized Tribes" living in the South in the area east of the Mississippi River, among those the Cherokee nation. The Cherokees had developed a written language, converted to Christianity, and embraced agriculture as a way of life. Some Cherokees even owned slaves. (How much more "civilized" could these Native Americans become?!) The Cherokees had developed their own government and deemed themselves to be an independent republic within the state of Georgia. The problem arose when gold was discovered on Cherokee land and the citizens of Georgia demanded that the Cherokees comply with the provisions of the Indian Removal Act, a policy suggested by Monroe but enacted during Jackson's tenure in office. This act demanded that the Native Americans resettle in Oklahoma, which had been deemed Indian territory. Jackson, for his part, argued that moving away from white society was the best way to protect themselves from white encroachment and maintain their traditional customs. The Cherokees refused and brought their case to the Supreme Court. Although John Marshall, Chief Justice at the time, sided with the Cherokees in two cases, *Cherokee Nation v. Georgia* (1831) and *Worcester v. Georgia* (1832), Andrew Jackson refused to comply with the Court's decision and is reputed to have sneered, "John Marshall has made his decision, now let him enforce it." Between 1835 and 1838, thousands of Cherokees walked to Oklahoma under the supervision of the U.S. Army in what has come to be known as the **Trail of Tears.** Thousands died of sickness and starvation along the way. The other side of that is related to the Seminole in Florida. Refusing to leave their land, they initiated the Seminole War which lasted until the late 1830s. It was incredibly expensive and eventually the U.S. government gave up, allowing the Seminole to stay on their land.

One of the major issues of Jackson's presidency focused on **nullification**. The doctrine of nullification, first expressed by Jefferson and Madison in the Virginia and Kentucky Resolutions, holds that the individual states have the right to disobey federal laws if they find them unconstitutional. John Marshall had established that only the Supreme Court had the power of **judicial review,** in the landmark decision of *Marbury v. Madison* (1803). The **Tariff of 1828**, also known as the **Tariff of Abominations**, was passed during the Adams administration, but it almost turned into a national crisis during Jackson's administration. In 1828,

The Bank of the United States

In the 19th century, paper money was issued not by the government but by private banks. If you went to a bank for a $100 loan, the bank would print some money for you. It didn't necessarily have to have $100 worth of gold in its vaults to do this. If it had $10,000 worth of gold in its vaults, a bank might issue $100,000 in paper money—and as long as no more than 10 percent of that money was cashed in at the same time, the bank would be fine.

What kept such a bank from printing up a million dollars, or a trillion? The main answer was that people could pay their taxes with paper money and that paper collected at the Bank of the United States. Fear that the Bank would attempt to cash in a huge amount of paper at once kept smaller banks from overusing the printing presses. Once Andrew Jackson killed the Bank of the United States, however, **wildcat banks** did indeed spring up and issue paper money with abandon. Add the fact that the government stopped accepting paper money in payment for land, and people realized that all their paper money was now nearly worthless—a recipe for a major depression.

With only gold and silver now considered to have value, the stage was set for the late 19th century, when arguments over these metals would dominate the debate over economic policy.

John C. Calhoun, a South Carolinian who was Jackson's vice president, anonymously published "The South Carolina Exposition and Protest," arguing that states who felt the 50 percent tariff was unfairly high could nullify the law. By 1830, southern states were openly discussing nullification, as such protectionist tariffs cut into the trade with Britain on which the South relied to sell its cotton and buy British wools and certain other raw materials in return. Jackson, though a strong supporter of states' rights, thought nullification endangered the Union and was thus too extreme. After the **Tariff of 1832** failed to lower rates to an acceptable level, South Carolina nullified the tariff. Jackson had Congress authorize a **Force Bill**, threatening to call in troops to enforce the tariff, but Calhoun and Henry Clay (remember the Missouri Compromise?) brokered a behind-the-scenes compromise, lowering the tariff and diffusing tensions. After the compromise tariff was approved and accepted by South Carolina, the legislature nullified the Force Bill, for no purpose except to support the doctrine of nullification.

Jackson's economic policies demonstrated his distrust of both big government and Northeastern power brokers. He spent much of his two terms "downsizing" the federal government and strengthening the office of the presidency through his extensive use of the presidential veto. He fought against the **reform** movements of the time that called for increased government activism against social and economic problems. He saw to it that the **Second Bank of the United States (BUS)** failed by vetoing Congress's attempt to recharter the bank and by withdrawing federal funds and depositing them in state "**pet**" **banks**. He felt that the BUS protected Northeastern interests at the expense of the West. Jackson argued that the bank was an unconstitutional monopoly, but the Supreme Court ruled against him using a loose interpretation of the commerce clause (*McCulloch v. Maryland*, **1819**). He was also suspicious of paper money, preferring "hard currency" such as gold or silver. His **Specie Circular**, which ended the policy of selling government land on credit (buyers now had to pay "hard cash"), caused a money shortage and a sharp decrease in the treasury, and it helped trigger the **Panic of 1837**. Congress overturned the circular in the last days of Jackson's final term.

Slavery grew to be an ever more controversial issue during the time of Jacksonian Democracy. As the Northern abolition movement grew stronger, the South experienced several slave revolts, which resulted in the use of more brutal disciplinary measures by slaveholders. The most famous of the insurrections was **Nat Turner's**

Rebellion. Turner, a well-read preacher, had a vision, and he took this vision as a sign from God that a black liberation movement would succeed. As a result, he rallied a gang that proceeded to kill and then mutilate the corpses of 60 whites. In retaliation, 200 slaves were executed, some with no connection at all to the rebellion. Fearful that other slaves would hear of and emulate Turner's exploits, Southern states passed a series of restrictive laws, known as **slave codes**, prohibiting blacks from congregating and learning to read. Other state laws even prevented whites from questioning the legitimacy of slavery. After Turner's Rebellion, Virginia's House of Burgesses debated ending bondage but did not pass a law.

The Election of 1836 and the Rise of the Whigs

Jackson's Democratic party could not represent the interests of all its constituencies (Northern abolitionists, Southern plantation owners, Western pioneers), and inevitably, an opposition party, the **Whigs**, was formed. By 1834, almost as many congressmen supported the Whig Party as the Democratic Party. The Whigs were a loose coalition that shared one thing in common: opposition to one or more of the Democrats' policies. For example, while the Democrats favored limited federal government, many Whigs believed in government **activism,** especially in the case of social issues. Many Whigs were also deeply religious and supported the temperance movement and enforcement of the Sabbath. Still, the defining characteristic of the Whigs was their opposition to the Democrats.

The Whigs had many of the same beliefs as the Federalists, especially support for manufacturing, opposition to new immigrants, and Westward Expansion.

In the election of 1836, Jackson supported his second vice president, Democrat **Martin Van Buren**. Van Buren had the misfortune to take over the presidency just as the country was entering a major economic crisis (the Panic of 1837). Van Buren made the situation worse by continuing Jackson's policy of favoring hard currency, thereby insuring that money would be hard to come by. The economic downturn lasted through Van Buren's term, practically guaranteeing that he would not be reelected.

In 1841, former military hero **William Henry Harrison** became the first Whig president. He died of pneumonia a month after taking office. His vice president, **John Tyler**, a former Democrat, assumed the presidency and began championing states' rights, much to his own party's chagrin. Tyler vetoed numerous Whig bills, which alienated Whig leadership; eventually his entire cabinet resigned in protest. Tyler is often referred to as the "president without a party," and his presidency lasted only one term.

ECONOMIC HISTORY (1800–1860)

This section discusses economic developments in the United States during the first part of the 19th century. These developments played an important role in the political events that led to the Civil War, and they helped to determine the different characteristics of the country's regions. Along with social developments (discussed in the next section), these economic factors laid the foundation for issues that would be important to American society for the following century (such as abolitionism, women's suffrage, and temperance).

Beginnings of a Market Economy

From the time they first arrived until the Revolutionary War era, most settlers in the United States raised crops for subsistence, rather than for sale at market. Most people made their own clothing and built their own furniture and homes, and they got by without many other conveniences. Cash transactions were relatively rare. Instead, people used ledgers to keep track of who owed what to whom and typically settled accounts when someone moved away or died.

Developments in manufacturing and transportation changed all that, however. By making it possible to mass produce goods and transport them across the country cheaply, a **market economy** began to develop. In a market economy, people trade their labor or goods for cash, which they then use to buy other people's labor or goods. Market economies favor those who specialize. For example, farmers who grow a single crop (monoculture) usually do better in a market economy than those who produce many different crops. One-crop farmers can offer buyers more of what they want. These farmers also do not have to look for different buyers for their many products. The trade-off, of course, is that these farmers are no longer self-sufficient. Instead, they become dependent on the market to provide some necessities. Furthermore, such farmers sometimes fall victim to overproduction, resulting in an unexpected, unwelcome drop in the price of their crop.

Market economies grow more quickly and provide more services than subsistence economies, and they also make people more interdependent. However, they are also much more prone to change. Any number of factors can halt a period of prosperity and throw the economy into a skid like the panics of 1819 and 1837. These changes are referred to as **boom-and-bust cycles.** During the first decades of the 19th century, the United States made a rapid transition from a subsistence economy to a market economy.

As stated earlier, the **War of 1812** and the events leading up to it forced the United States to become less dependent on imports and, consequently, to develop a stronger national economy. Two key advances, both developed by **Eli Whitney**, also played a major part in the process. The **cotton gin**, invented in 1793, revolutionized Southern agriculture by making it much easier to remove the seeds from cotton plants. (The machine was 5,000 percent more efficient than a human being.) The cotton gin made it easier and cheaper to use cotton for textiles, and as a result, the demand for cotton grew very rapidly into the early 1800s. As demand grew, so did cotton production in the South. Because cotton farming is labor intensive, the spread of cotton as the region's chief crop also intensified the South's dependence on slave labor. Other notable inventions that revolutionized agriculture include the steel plow and mechanical reaper.

Whitney's second innovation was the use of **interchangeable parts** in manufacturing. Whitney originally struck upon the idea while mass-producing rifles for the U.S. Army. Prior to Whitney's breakthrough, manufacturers had built weapons (and other machines) by hand, custom fitting parts so that each weapon was unique. The process was costly, time-consuming, and inconvenient, because replacing broken parts was extremely difficult. Whitney demonstrated the practicality of his invention to Thomas Jefferson and James Madison by disassembling a number of rifles, scrambling the parts, and then reassembling the rifles from whichever parts he picked out of the pile. Whitney's demonstration was a huge success, and soon his idea was being applied to all aspects of manufacturing.

Interchangeable parts gave birth to the **machine-tool industry**, which produced specialized machines for such growing industries as textiles and transportation. (Without interchangeable parts, such machines would have been impractical because they would have been too expensive to build and too difficult to fix.) Whitney's advances also helped promote the development of **assembly line production**. On an assembly line, products are constructed more efficiently by dividing the labor into a number of tasks and assigning each worker one task. Prior to assembly lines, each worker would create a product in its entirety. The result was a product that took longer to produce and was less uniform in quality.

The North and the Textile Industry

The above-mentioned developments first benefited the textile industry. Advances in machine technology, coupled with a U.S. embargo on British goods prior to and during the War of 1812—England was then America's chief source of textiles—spurred the development of textile mills in New England. During the first decade of the 19th century, mills produced thread and hired local women to weave the thread into cloth at home. The mills would then buy the finished cloth and sell it on the open market. The invention of the first **power loom**, in 1813, meant that textile manufacturers could produce both thread and finished fabric in their own factories quickly and efficiently. The resulting product was both of high quality and inexpensive—so much so that women who had previously woven their own fabrics at home started to buy cloth. **Samuel Slater**, the "Father of the American Industrial Revolution," designed the first American textile mills.

The rapid growth of the textile industry resulted in a shortage of labor in New England. Consequently, textile manufacturers had to "sweeten the pot" to entice laborers (almost all of whom were women from nearby farms) to their factories. The most famous worker-enticement program was called the **Lowell system** (or **Waltham system**), so named after the two Massachusetts towns in which many mills were located. The Lowell system guaranteed employees housing in respectable, chaperoned boardinghouses; cash wages; and participation in cultural and social events organized by the mill. The system, widely copied throughout New England, lasted until great waves of Irish immigration in the 1840s and 1850s made factory labor plentiful. Later, as working conditions started to deteriorate, workers began to organize **labor unions** to protect their interests. These early unions in the mid-1800s met with strong, frequently violent opposition from industry. Still, they ultimately succeeded. (We'll discuss labor unions in much more detail later, when we discuss the Gilded Age in the late 1800s and the Progressive era in the early 1900s.)

Other industries inevitably sprang up around the textile industry. **Clothing manufacturers**, also located primarily in the Northeast, transformed the textiles into finished products. **Retailers** sold the clothing and other manufactured products in their stores. **Brokers** acted as middlemen, buying and selling raw and finished products and trafficking them among manufacturers and retailers. **Commercial banks** lent money to everyone so that the wheels of commerce stayed well greased. Most significant, the **transportation industry** grew as a result of the need to ship these and other products across the country.

Transportation: Canals, Railroads, Highways, and Steamships

Prior to the 1820s, travel and shipping along east-west routes was difficult, and most trade centered on the north-south routes along the Ohio and Mississippi Rivers. The construction of the **National Road** from Maryland to West Virginia (and ultimately to central Ohio) made east-west travel easier, but the big change came with the completion of the **Erie Canal** in 1825. Funded entirely by the state of New York, the Erie Canal linked the Great Lakes region to New York and thus to European shipping routes. Suddenly, it became lucrative for a Midwestern merchant or farmer to sell his products to Eastern buyers, and as a result, the Northeast soon established itself as the United States' center of commerce. The Erie Canal was so successful that, by 1835, its width and depth had to be nearly doubled to handle the traffic. Other regions tried to duplicate the Erie Canal's success, and during the 1830s, thousands of miles of canals were constructed throughout the Northeast and Midwest. None performed as well as the Erie Canal, and a number of those canals failed. Meanwhile, the railroads developed into a convenient means of transporting goods; by 1850, the **canal era** had ended.

The end of this era, however, did not mark the end of shipping as an important industry. The invention of the steam engine allowed for **steamships**, which traveled faster than sailing vessels. Steamships became important freight carriers and replaced sailing ships for long sea voyages. By 1850, passengers could travel by steamship from New York to England in 10 days; by sail, the same trip had taken more than a month. Steamships were not without their problems though; exploding boilers, burning ships, and other disasters accompanied the technological advances.

Similarly, **railroads** redefined land travel. America's first railroads were built during the 1830s, the first typically connecting only two cities. As the nation's rail network grew, a major problem arose. Different railroad lines could not be connected to one another because the width, or **gauge**, of their tracks was different. As a result, rail development proceeded slowly. When different railways converted to compatible systems, the government often paid the bill even though the railroads were privately owned. This hastened progress, and by 1853, New York and Chicago were linked by rail, as were Pittsburgh and Philadelphia. (Southern rail development was much slower, and superior rails gave the North a huge advantage during the Civil War.) We'll discuss the railroads further in the post–Civil War period, during which railroad construction really "picked up steam."

Market Revolution (handwritten margin note)

The Market Revolution
The changes caused by the development of better transportation and manufacturing had permanent altering effects on American society. Increasing numbers of Americans no longer relied solely on agriculture for their livelihoods; instead, they supported themselves by working in factories. Coal mining, too, became an important industry during this era.

The Transportation Revolution
By 1855, the cost to send things across America had fallen to one-twentieth of what it had cost in 1825—and they arrived in one-fifth the time.

The increase in travel and shipping was helped considerably by the invention of the **telegraph**, which allowed immediate long-distance communication for the first time. The telegraph was like a primitive telephone, except that people communicated in **Morse code** rather than by speaking to one another. Americans quickly understood the benefits of telegraphic communications, and widespread use followed its invention almost immediately. Transatlantic telegraph cables, however, would not be successfully laid until 1866, after the Civil War.

Developments in transportation and communication during the first half of the 19th century revolutionized American commerce and culture but favored the Northeast and the West (today known as the Midwest). Products, people, and ideas traveled much faster in 1850 than they had in 1800.

Farming

Although American manufacturing grew at a rapid pace, agriculture remained by far the most common source of livelihood throughout the first half of the 19th century. Mechanization revolutionized farming during the period, as many machines came into common use during this time, including the mechanical plow, sower, reaper, thresher, baler, and cotton gin. The growth of the market economy also changed farming. In 1820, about one-third of all the food grown in the United States went to market. (The rest was kept for personal consumption.) By 1860, that fraction had doubled.

Farming continued in the Northeast, but not without difficulties. The region's rocky, hilly terrain was unsuitable to many of the machines that were making farming on the plains easier and cheaper. Furthermore, much of the farmland in the region had been over-farmed, and as a result, the quality of the soil had grown poor. Unable to compete with Midwestern grain farmers, some New England farmers quit cultivating grain and started raising livestock and growing fruits and vegetables. Others quit farming entirely and headed to the cities to take manufacturing jobs.

As mentioned above, the Midwest became America's chief source of grains, such as wheat and corn. Midwestern farms—much larger than New England farms—were also much more adaptable to the new technology that allowed farmers to nearly double production. Banks sprang up to lend farmers the capital necessary to buy modern equipment, and the trade routes created by rail and ship provided access to the markets these farmers needed to sell their crops in order to pay off their loans. The system worked well, except during the various financial crises of the first half of the century. The panics of 1819 and 1837 resulted in bank foreclosures on mortgages and other business loans, not just in the Midwest but all across the country. Not surprisingly, many people were thrown into poverty.

In the South, plantations focused primarily on cotton, especially in the Deep South; tobacco continued to be a major cash crop in the Upper South. The majority of Southerners owned small farms and did not own slaves. (In 1860, approximately one-quarter of white Southern families owned slaves.)

Westward Expansion

The Louisiana Purchase removed one major obstacle to U.S. western settlement, and the resolution of the War of 1812 removed another by depriving Native Americans of a powerful ally in Great Britain. By 1820, the United States had settled the region east of the Mississippi River and was quickly expanding west. Americans began to believe that they had a God-given right to the Western territories, an idea that came to be known as America's **Manifest Destiny**. Some took the idea of Manifest Destiny to its logical conclusion and argued that Canada, Mexico, and even all of the land in the Americas eventually would be annexed by the United States.

Western settlement was dangerous. The terrain and climate could be cold and unforgiving, and these settlers from the East were moving into areas that rightfully belonged to Native Americans and Mexicans, none of whom were about to cede their homes without a fight.

Texas presents a good case in point. When Mexico declared its independence from Spain in 1821, the new country included what is now Texas and much of the Southwest, including California. The Mexican government established liberal land policies to entice settlers, and tens of thousands of Americans (many of them cattle ranchers) flooded the region. In return for land, the settlers were supposed to become Mexican citizens, but they rarely did. Instead, they ignored Mexican law, including—and especially—the one prohibiting slavery. When Mexico attempted to regain control of the area, the settlers rebelled and declared independence from Mexico. It was during this period that the famous battle at the **Alamo** was fought (1836). For a while, Texas was an independent country, called the **Republic of Texas.** The existence of slavery in the area guaranteed a Congressional battle over statehood, and Texas was not admitted to the Union until 1845.

Farther west and north, settlers were also pouring into the **Oregon Territory**. During the early 1840s, thousands of settlers traveled to the Willamette Valley, braving a six-month journey on the Oregon Trail. Again, the Americans were not the first ones in; not only was there a large Native American population, but the British were also there, claiming the territory for Canada. The Russians also staked a claim, and both the British and the Americans saw them as a threat. The Polk administration eventually settled the territorial dispute by signing a treaty with England.

By the late 1840s, though, those heading along the Oregon Trail had a new destination—**California**. In 1848, the discovery of gold in the California mountains set off the **Gold Rush**, attracting more than 100,000 people to the Golden State in just two years. Most of these people did not strike it rich, but they settled the area after discovering that it was very hospitable to agriculture. Its access to the Pacific Ocean allowed major cities such as San Francisco to develop as important trade centers.

Economic Reasons for Regional Differences

Throughout the first half of the 19th century, three different sections of the country—North, South, and West, including what is today known as the Midwest—developed in very different directions. Accordingly, they did not see eye to eye on many issues; thus, historians often refer to **sectional strife** during this period.

The **North**, as mentioned earlier, was becoming industrialized. Technological advances in communications, transportation, industry, and banking were helping it become the nation's commercial center. Farming played less of a role in the Northeastern economy than it did elsewhere in the country, and legal slavery became increasingly uncommon in this region's states throughout the early 1800s.

The **South**, meanwhile, remained almost entirely agrarian. Its chief crops—tobacco and cotton—required vast acreage, and so Southerners were constantly looking west for more land. Anxious to protect slavery, which the large landholders depended on, Southerners also looked for new slave territories to include in the Union in order to strengthen their position in Congress and protect slavery from Northern legislators, who in ever-increasing numbers sought to make slavery illegal.

Western economic interests were varied but were largely rooted in commercial farming, fur trapping, and real-estate speculation. Westerners generally distrusted the North, which they regarded as the home of powerful banks that could take their land away. They had little more use for the South, whose rigidly hierarchical society was at odds with the egalitarianism of the West. Most Westerners wanted to avoid involvement in the slavery issue, which they regarded as irrelevant to their lives. Ironically, Western expansion was the core of the most important conflicts leading up to the Civil War.

Westward expansion leads to civil war

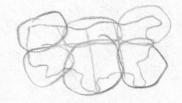

Know Your Regional Trends

Remember these regional generalizations; by using them (and some common sense), you can often answer specific AP questions. Take, for example, a question dealing with a specific tariff. Even if you do not remember the details of the tariff—and chances are you will not—you should remember that the North, as a commercial and manufacturing center, would probably support it because a tariff makes imports more expensive and therefore reduces competition with American goods. Southerners would probably oppose it because a tariff reduces competition and therefore raises prices. (Also, tariffs helped the North, and Southerners did not like the North.) Likewise, as the 19th century turned to the 20th, Republicans tended to support a high tariff and the Democrats a lower one, so pay attention to who's in office, i.e., McKinley, Teddy Roosevelt, or Wilson. Note: The AP Exam asks about events that illustrate important general trends in American history. If there was a 19th-century tariff that the South supported and the North opposed, the test would not ask about it!

SOCIAL HISTORY, 1800–1860

The growth of the American economy in the early 19th century brought about numerous social changes. The invention of the cotton gin, coupled with the advent of the Industrial Revolution in England, altered Southern agriculture, resulting in the region's increased reliance on slave labor. The development of commerce led to a larger middle class, especially in the North but also in Southern and Midwestern cities. Industrialization resulted in bigger cities with large (and often impoverished) migrant and immigrant neighborhoods. Westward migration created a new frontier culture as pioneers dealt with the uniqueness of the West's landscape and climate. Each of these sets of circumstances influenced people's attitudes and ambitions and set the scene for the social and political events of the era.

The North and American Cities

As we discussed previously, the North became the nation's industrial and commercial center during the first half of the 19th century. Accordingly, it became home to many of the nation's major cities. In their early years, American cities faced numerous problems, chiefly the lack of powerful urban governments to oversee their rapid expansion. Modern waste disposal, plumbing, sewers, and incineration were still a long way off, and as a result, cities could be extremely toxic environments. The proximity in which people lived and worked, coupled with sanitation problems, made epidemics not only likely but inevitable.

City life was not, however, without its benefits. First, cities meant jobs. Many Northern farmers, unable to compete with cheaper produce carted in from the West and South by steamship and rail, moved to cities to work in the new factories. Craftsmen, such as tailors, cobblers, and blacksmiths, also found it easier to make a living in cities. Second, cities offered more opportunities for social advancement. In the 1830s and 1840s, as municipal governments grew, cities began to provide important services, such as public schooling. Labor unions began to form; although it would be many decades until they would come close to matching the power of business management, these unions still fought to bring about improvements in the lives of working people, even though they had quite limited success. Middle- and upper-class Americans in cities formed clubs and associations through which they could exert more influence on government and in society. Finally, cities provided a wide variety of leisure-time options, such as theater and sports.

Still, as in the South, there was a great disparity in the **distribution of wealth** in Northern cities. An elite few controlled most of the personal wealth and led lives of power and comfort. Beneath them was the **middle class**, made up of tradesmen, brokers, and other professionals. They worked to reach the plateau at which the women in their families could devote themselves to homemaking instead of wage earning. (Many middle-class women in their teens and early twenties worked—as salesclerks, teachers, and such—before settling down to marriage.) As wage-earning labor was more often performed away from the home, in factories and offices, the notion developed that men should work while women kept house and raised children. That notion, known as the **cult of domesticity**, was supported by popular magazines and novels that glorified home life. The middle classes also

Lydia Maria Child (1802–1880) was an author dedicated to the cult of domesticity. Her most famous book, *The American Frugal Housewife,* championed the achievement of well-planned housekeeping for even her poorest readers. Child was also an outspoken abolitionist and promoter of women's rights.

constituted much of the market for luxury goods such as housewares and fine furniture. Members of the middle class often rose from the **working class**. In working-class families, men often worked in factories or at low-paying crafts; women often worked at home, taking in sewing. Others worked as domestic servants, and most worked throughout their lives. Such families lived just above the poverty level, and any calamity—loss of a job, injury, sickness, or a death in the family—could plunge them irretrievably into debt. Those in **poverty** were most often recent immigrants. Their numbers swelled in the 1840s and 1850s when the great **immigration waves** from **Ireland** (to the cities in the North) and then **Germany** (to the West) reached the United States. These immigration waves were met with hostility, especially from the working classes, who feared competition for low-paying jobs.

Occasionally tensions would boil over, and American cities were frequently the sites of riots. Particularly in the 1830s and 1840s, religious, ethnic, and/or class strife could escalate to violence and even result in fatalities. Such disturbances were largely responsible for the formation of municipal police departments, which replaced privately run security companies in enforcing the peace.

The South and Rural Life

There were few major urban centers in the South. The majority of Southerners lived instead in rural areas in near isolation. In 1860, the population density of Georgia was 18 people per square mile. Family, not surprisingly, played a dominant role in social life. After family came the church, and after the church, little else. There simply were not enough people around to support organized cultural and leisure events.

With almost no major cities, the South also had few centers of commerce, and while the North developed extensive networks of canals, railroads, and highways, the South's infrastructure remained fairly limited. The major city of the South, New Orleans, relied almost completely on waterways for its trade routes, and therefore grew much more slowly than did Northern cities such as New York and Boston. Consequently, the South did not develop a strong market economy, as did the North; many more Southerners made and grew most of their necessities for survival.

The wealthiest Southern citizens formed an aristocracy of plantation owners. As in the North, the wealthy made up a small minority, but in the South, this group dominated Southern society politically, socially, and economically. Less than one percent of the population owned more than 100 slaves. In fact, more than three-quarters of white Southerners owned no slaves. Of the rest, half owned five or fewer slaves. Only 10 percent of actual slaveholders—fewer than about 2 percent of the white population—held 20 or more slaves.

Plantation owners grew cotton throughout the Deep South and tobacco in the Middle Atlantic, alongside the crops they needed to support their families and slaves. Most convinced themselves that the slave system benefited all of its participants, *including* the slaves. This attitude, called **Southern paternalism**, relied on the perception of blacks as childlike and unable to take care of themselves. Many slaves discovered that life became easier for them when

Irish Immigration in the Early 19th century
In the early 19th century, Irish Catholic immigrants were primarily unskilled workers who settled in urban areas of the United States, getting jobs working on railroads and building canals. Many Irish also worked in the textile mills of the Northeast; some others worked as fishermen on the East Coast. The Know-Nothing party formed largely as a reaction to Catholic immigrants in the 1850s. Irish immigration continued to be prominent up until the turn of the century when numbers started to stabilize.

they reinforced such paternalistic instincts and adopted a submissive and grateful demeanor (which will be familiar to you if you've ever seen old Hollywood movies about this period). Slave owners almost always converted their slaves to Christianity, again convinced that they were serving the slaves' best interests. The slaves, in turn, adapted Christianity to their cultures and incorporated their own religions and traditions into their new faith.

Slaves lived in a state of subsistence poverty. They were usually housed in one-room cabins with their families and often with another family. Conditions were overcrowded and unsanitary. Although work conditions varied from region to region and farm to farm, most worked extremely long hours at difficult and tedious labor, and conditions tended to be worse in the Deep South. (Any concern that slaveholders had for their slaves' welfare could arguably be attributed to the fact that importing African slaves was banned in 1808, making it essential to keep one's slaves alive and reproducing. In addition, the purchase price of a slave remained fairly high or even increased.) Moreover, most slaves lived in fear that their families would be broken up by the sale of one or more of them, or they would be sold "down river." Many were subjected to the abuses of vicious overseers.

Most slaves survived the physical and psychological degradation of slavery by developing a unique culture that tended to blend aspects of their African roots with elements of Christianity. Likewise, although slave revolts were rarely successful, many slaves developed subtle methods of resistance that enabled them to maintain an aspect of their dignity. This might include violating a local slave code and sneaking out at night to meet a loved one or managing to learn to read and write despite codes forbidding them to do so.

The majority of Southerners farmed smaller tracts of land. Planters (those with 20 or more slaves) were in the minority—the remaining landholders were **yeomen**, who sometimes had a few slaves but often none at all, working their small tracts of land with their families. Most were of Scottish and Irish descent and farmed in the hills, which were unsuitable for plantation farming. They grew subsistence crops, raised livestock, and sometimes produced a few cash crops, though limited access to Northern markets hindered profit making. Less fortunate were **landless whites**, who either farmed as tenants or hired themselves out as manual laborers. Elevation from this social stratum to the level of yeoman proved very difficult.

The South was also home to more than 250,000 **free blacks**, the descendants of slaves freed by their owners or freed for having fought in the Revolutionary War. Slave codes prevented them from owning guns, drinking liquor, and assembling in groups of more than three (except in church). Prejudice was a constant fact of life. Some owned land or worked at a trade, but most worked as tenant farmers or day laborers. Some were "mulattoes" (biracial individuals), some of whom led lives of relative luxury and refinement in the Deep South, particularly in and around New Orleans.

The West and Frontier Living

During this period, the frontier's boundaries constantly changed. In 1800, the frontier lay east of the Mississippi River. By 1820, nearly all of this eastern territory had attained statehood, and the frontier region consisted of much of the Louisiana Purchase. Settlers also moved to Texas and then to a part of Mexico, in the late 1820s and 1830s. By the early 1840s, the frontier had expanded to include the Pacific Northwest. In 1849, the Gold Rush drew numerous settlers, **Forty-Niners**, to California.

The United States government actively encouraged settlers to move west. It gave away, or sold at reduced rates, large tracts of land to war veterans. The government also loaned money at reduced rates to civilians so that they too could move west. Some settlers, called **squatters**, ignored the requirement to buy land and simply moved onto and appropriated an unoccupied tract as their own.

Settlers in the Ohio Valley and points west soon found that the area was hospitable to grain production and dairy farming. As previously discussed, much of the area was flat and could easily be farmed by new farm implements such as mechanical plows and reapers. Transportation advances made shipping produce easier and more profitable, and soon the Midwest came to be known as "the nation's breadbasket."

Fur trading was another common commercial enterprise on the frontiers. Fur traders were also called "over-mountain men." They were often the first pioneers in a region, and they constantly moved west, one step ahead of farming families. When they reached Oregon, they ran out of places to go. Furthermore, they had hunted beaver to near extinction. A group of former trappers formed the first American government in the Oregon Territory and began lobbying for statehood. The western frontier was also home to **cattle ranchers** and **miners**.

Frontier life was rugged, to say the least. To survive, settlers constantly struggled against the climate, elements, and Native Americans who were not anxious for the whites to settle, having heard about their treatment of Eastern tribes. Still, the frontier offered pioneers opportunities for wealth, freedom, and social advancement—opportunities that were less common in the heavily populated, competitive East and the aristocratic South. Those women who could handle the difficulties of frontier life found their services in great demand, and many made a good living at domestic work and, later, running boardinghouses and hotels. Because of the possibilities for advancement and for "getting a new start in life," the West came to symbolize freedom and equality to many Americans.

Religious and Social Movements

The 19th century saw the beginnings of true social reform in the United States, and much of the impulse to improve the lives of others came from citizens' religious convictions. In fact, early social reform movements grew out of the **Second Great Awakening**, which, like the first, was a period of religious revival, mainly among Methodists, Presbyterians, and Baptists. In the early 1800s, the expansion of the Enlightenment in the United States encouraged more education, which led to more secularism and a decline in church attendance. Preachers like Charles Finney toured the rural regions of western New York and the rural South, spreading evangelical religious beliefs. The Second Great Awakening peaked in the 1820s and 1830s, as church membership soared in the Baptist, Methodist and Presbyterian churches. New religions like the Mormons and Shakers were inspired by the

The western and central regions of New York State were known as the **Burned-over District** for the spiritual fervor that figuratively set the area on fire.

Second Great Awakening, as were social reform movements like the temperance movement. Women were particularly inspired by the Second Great Awakening, and were encouraged to become active leaders in their new church communities.

Connections

The reform movements associated with The Second Great Awakening were a precursor to the later reform movements of the Progressive Era. Many of the issues debated in the early 19th century, such as women's suffrage and temperance, would not reach fruition until nearly one hundred years later.

Usually, the most active members of reform groups were women, particularly those of the middle and upper classes. **Temperance societies**, some of which tried to encourage people to sign the pledge not to drink and some of which sought outright prohibition of liquor, formed and remained powerful until the adoption of the Eighteenth Amendment in 1919 provided for nationwide prohibition. (Not coincidentally, prohibition finally succeeded at the same time it became evident to politicians that women would soon gain the right to vote.)

The temperance movement was largely promoted by Protestant churches and reformers, and tied to the rise in Irish and German immigrants who were mostly Catholic, representing the divide between the two branches of Christianity—this will later be expressed in the Nativist movement/Know-Nothing Party. These groups battled other vices as well, particularly **gambling**. By 1860, every state in the Union had outlawed **lotteries**, and many had prohibited other forms of gambling. Many Northern states also prohibited the manufacture or purchase of alcoholic beverages during this period. A group called "The Female Moral Reform Society" led the battle against **prostitution** in the cities, focusing not only on eliminating the profession but also on rehabilitating those women involved in it.

Reform societies also helped bring about **penitentiaries**, **asylums**, and **orphanages** by popularizing the notion that society is responsible for the welfare of its least fortunate. Asylums, orphanages, and houses of refuge for the poor were built to care for those who would previously have been imprisoned or run out of town. With leadership from Dorothea Dix, penitentiaries sought to rehabilitate criminals (rather than simply isolate them from society, as prisons do) by teaching them morality and a "work ethic."

Before we discuss the abolition movement, we need to mention a few other important movements of the period. **The Shakers**, a utopian group that splintered from the Quakers, believed that they and all other churches had grown too interested in this world and too neglectful of their afterlives. Shakers, followers of Mother Ann Lee, isolated themselves in communes where they shared work and its rewards; they also granted near-equal rights to women, even allowing them to attain priesthood. Believing the end of the world was at hand and that sex was an instrument of evil, the Shakers practiced celibacy; their numbers, not surprisingly, diminished. The Shaker revival ended during the 1840s and 1850s. Other Utopian groups included the Oneida community in New York and the New Harmony community in Indiana.

Perhaps the most well-known of these experimental communities was Brook Farm, established near Roxbury, Massachusetts, in 1841. Brook Farm was home to the Transcendentalists, a group of nonconformist Unitarian writers and philosophers who drew their inspiration from European romanticism. Transcendentalists believed that humans contained elements of the divine, and thus they had faith in man's, and ultimately society's, perfectibility. The most famous of these writers were Nathaniel Hawthorne, author of *The Scarlet Letter*; Ralph Waldo Emerson; and Henry David Thoreau. Thoreau is most noted for his publication of *Walden*, an account of the two years he spent living alone in a cabin on Walden Pond outside Concord, Massachusetts. Perhaps not as well-known, but equally significant, was Thoreau's demonstration of civil disobedience. Thoreau refused to pay taxes to a government that waged war against Mexico and subsequently enacted a Fugitive Slave Act as part of the **Compromise of 1850** (see the separate section on this in the next chapter).

Another important group involved in this American Renaissance was the **Hudson River School** painters, the first distinct school of American art. Their goal was to create a specific vision for American art, and they painted mostly landscapes that seemed to portray an awe for the wilderness and beauty of wild America. Like Thoreau and Emerson, the painters were influenced by European romanticism.

The **Mormons**, on the other hand, continue to thrive today. Joseph Smith formed the Church of Jesus Christ of Latter-Day Saints in 1830. Smith's preaching, particularly his acceptance of polygamy, drew strong opposition in the East and Midwest, culminating in his death by a mob while imprisoned in Illinois. The Mormons, realizing that they would never be allowed to practice their faith in the East, made the long, difficult trek to the Salt Lake Valley, led by Brigham Young. There, they settled and transformed the area from desert into farmland through extensive irrigation. The Mormons' success was largely attributable to the settlers' strong sense of community. Through their united efforts, they came to dominate the Utah territory.

The Second Great Awakening was only one source of the antebellum reform movements. By the 1820s and 1830s, most of the Founding Fathers were dead, but they left a legacy of freedom and equality, expressed in part in the Declaration of Independence as well as the Preamble to the Constitution. In the 1830s, "We, the People" still meant white males. Many women were active in the abolitionist movement, and it was their exclusion from participation at a worldwide antislavery convention held in London in 1840 that convinced women like Elizabeth Cady Stanton and Lucretia Mott to hold the first women's rights convention in 1848 in Seneca Falls in upstate New York (in the same Burned-over District from the Second Great Awakening). Stanton and Mott, along with other reformers, published the *Declaration of Rights and Sentiments of Women*, which they modeled after the American Declaration of Independence. The Declaration began, "We hold these truths to be self-evident, that all men *and women* are created equal...." Four years later, Stanton would team up with Susan B. Anthony, with whom she founded the **National Woman Suffrage Association** in 1869.

Finally, **Horace Mann** was instrumental in pushing for public education and education reform in general. He lengthened the school year, established the first "normal school" for teacher training, and used the first standardized books in education (*McGuffey's Reader* was used by 80 percent of public schools). Mann is noted for his belief that "Education is the great equalizer."

At about the same time that the members of the Hudson River School were busy capturing the transcendent elements of nature, **John James Audubon** was painting and cataloging birds for later publication in his seminal work on the subject, ***The Birds of America.*** Audubon discovered 25 new species of birds and was the inspiration for the Audubon Society, a nonprofit organization dedicated to the conservation of birds.

The Abolition Movement

Before the 1830s, few whites fought aggressively for the liberation of the slaves. The Quakers believed slavery to be morally wrong and argued for its end. Most other antislavery whites, though, sought gradual abolition, coupled with colonization, a movement to return blacks to Africa. For example, the **American Colonization Society**, established in 1816, sought to repatriate slaves to the newly formed country of Liberia in Africa. Many politicians supported the cause, including Henry Clay. The religious and moral fervor that accompanied the Second Great Awakening, however, persuaded more and more whites, particularly Northerners, that slavery was a great evil. As in other reform movements, women played a prominent role, such as the Grimke sisters from South Carolina, who were early abolitionists despite growing up in a slave-holding family.

White abolitionists divided into two groups. Moderates wanted emancipation to take place slowly and with the cooperation of slave owners. **Immediatists**, as their name implies, wanted emancipation at once. Most prominent among white immediatists was **William Lloyd Garrison,** who began publishing a popular abolitionist newspaper called the *Liberator* in 1831 and helped found the **American Antislavery Society** in 1833. His early subscribers were mostly free blacks, but as time passed, his paper caught on with white abolitionists as well.

Garrison fought against slavery and against moderates as well, decrying their plans for black resettlement in Africa as racist and immoral. Garrison's persistence and powerful writing style helped force the slavery issue to the forefront. His message, as you may imagine, did not go over well everywhere; some Southern states banned the newspaper, and others prohibited *anyone* from discussing emancipation. When congressional debate over slavery became too heated, Congress adopted a **gag rule** that automatically suppressed discussion of the issue. It also prevented Congress from enacting any new legislation pertaining to slavery. The rule, which lasted from 1836 to 1844, along with Southern restrictions on free speech, outraged many Northerners and convinced them to join the abolition movement.

The abolition movement existed prior to 1830, but it had been primarily supported by free blacks such as **David Walker**. A Bostonian, his Appeal to the Colored People of the World told all freed black people to work to end slavery. His work inspired William Lloyd Garrison. Abolition associations formed in every large black community to assist fugitive slaves and publicize the struggle against slavery; these groups met at a national convention every year after 1830 to coordinate strategies. In the 1840s, **Frederick Douglass** began publishing his influential newspaper *The North Star*. Douglass, an escaped slave, gained fame as a gifted writer and eloquent advocate of freedom and equality; his *Narrative of the Life of Frederick Douglass* is one of the great American autobiographies. Other prominent black abolitionists included **Harriet Tubman**, who escaped slavery and then returned south repeatedly to help more than 300 slaves escape via the **underground railroad** (a network of hiding places and "safe" trails); and **Sojourner Truth**, a charismatic speaker who campaigned for emancipation and women's rights.

Abolitionists' determination and the South's inflexibility pushed the issue of slavery into the political spotlight. Westward expansion, and the question of whether slavery would be allowed in the new territories, forced the issue further. Together, they set in motion the events that led up to the Civil War.

The AP and Retrospect

Abolitionism is an important topic on every AP U.S. History Exam. But it is worth noting that, right up to the Civil War, abolitionists were widely considered extremists. Far and away the leading reform movement of the time was the temperance movement. Nearly all abolitionists believed in temperance; few supporters of temperance were abolitionists. But as the abolition movement succeeded (slavery is now illegal), the success of the temperance movement was short-lived (Prohibition lasted only from 1920 to 1933), so you'll find a lot more questions about the former than about the latter.

Although slavery persisted in the United States, many European Enlightenment thinkers criticized slavery on human rights grounds. A member of the British Parliament, James Edward Oglethorpe, was among the first to argue against slavery. Granville Sharp, Hannah More, and William Wilberforce were also famous abolitionists.

Summary

Here are the most important concepts to remember from the American Democracy period.

o The new United States struggled to define its ideals as boundaries changed and regional opinions clashed.

o New developments in technology, agriculture, and commerce built wealth and infrastructure, transforming America from a wilderness to a developed society.

o Relationships with Britain and France were problematic, each country playing one off the other. After the War of 1812, relationships stabilized.

o Slavery became one of the most controversial issues in politics and the social sphere.

o Abolitionists, feminists, and temperance activists organized, published, and lectured to promote their ideas.

Chapter 8 Review Questions

See Chapter 14 for answers and explanations.

1. Although the Supreme Court was the weakest of the three branches of government in the early days of the new republic, John Marshall strengthened the Court by

    (A) establishing the principle of federalism, giving federal courts the power to declare laws unconstitutional
    (B) declaring the Virginia and Kentucky Resolutions, which asserted the right of states to nullify federal laws, unconstitutional
    (C) establishing the principle of judicial review in the case of *McCulloch v. Maryland*
    (D) establishing the principle of judicial review in the case of *Marbury v. Madison*

2. The Louisiana Purchase was an important factor in the development of U.S. trade because it

    (A) opened new markets among the western Indian nations
    (B) gave the country complete control of the Mississippi River
    (C) added numerous French factories in the Louisiana Territory to the U.S. economy
    (D) facilitated the immediate completion of the transcontinental railroad

3. As a result of the Hartford Convention following the War of 1812,

    (A) the Federalist Party lost credibility and eventually died out
    (B) the Constitution was amended to limit the president to two terms in office
    (C) the New England states threatened to secede
    (D) Congress passed the War Powers Act, limiting future presidents from gaining too much power during wartime, as Madison had

4. Andrew Jackson accused Henry Clay of using his influence to broker the "corrupt bargain" of 1824 (which cost Andrew Jackson the election) because Clay

    (A) was promised a cabinet position if John Quincy Adams was elected president
    (B) was promised the vice presidency if Jackson was defeated
    (C) knew Jackson did not support his "American System"
    (D) feared Jackson's pro-slavery stance on states' rights

5. The controversy over the tariff during the late 1820s and early 1830s demonstrated that

    (A) New Englanders were more radical than Southerners, as they had been since the days of the American Revolution
    (B) Andrew Jackson favored states' rights over federal supremacy
    (C) the system of checks and balances was flawed
    (D) economic sectionalism was a serious threat to national unity

6. Andrew Jackson's positions on the Second National Bank and the American System typified his

    (A) distrust of large national government programs
    (B) abhorrence of the spoils system
    (C) tendency to favor the interests of the Northeast
    (D) commitment to developing a national economy

7. The Cherokee of Georgia were forced off their land because

    (A) they refused to assimilate to the "American" way of life
    (B) gold was discovered in their territory and Georgians demanded that the Indian Removal Act be enforced
    (C) the Supreme Court refused to hear their cases
    (D) the Seminole tribe, their traditional enemy, conquered their territory

8. Brook Farm in Massachusetts, the Oneida Community in upstate New York, and New Harmony in Indiana were similar in that they

    (A) were religious communities inspired by the Second Great Awakening
    (B) demonstrated the attraction of communism to many Americans
    (C) failed because they practiced political and social equality within their own communities
    (D) were utopian communities designed to ameliorate the effects of a growing commercial society

REFLECT

Respond to the following questions:

- For which content topics discussed in this chapter do you feel you have achieved sufficient mastery to answer multiple-choice questions correctly?

- For which content topics discussed in this chapter do you feel you have achieved sufficient mastery to discuss effectively in a short-answer question or an essay?

- On which content topics discussed in this chapter do you feel you need more work before you can answer multiple-choice questions correctly?

- On which content topics discussed in this chapter do you feel you need more work before you can discuss them effectively in a short-answer question or an essay?

- What parts of this chapter are you going to review again?

- Will you seek further help, outside of this book (such as a teacher, tutor, or AP Students), on any of the content in this chapter—and, if so, on what content?

Chapter 9
Unit 5: Toward the Civil War and Reconstruction (1844–1877)

POLITICAL AND JUDICIAL ACTIVITY BEFORE THE WAR

The election of 1844 pitted **James Polk** against Whig leader Henry Clay. Though the differences between the Whig and Democratic platforms may seem hazy by modern standards, and there was more than a little overlap, in one respect the two parties were sharply opposed. Above all else, the Whigs stood for a policy of **internal improvements**: building bridges, dredging harbors, digging canals, and in short civilizing the lands the United States already possessed. Democrats tended to be expansionists, set on pushing the nation's borders ever outward. They also felt that it was not the government's place to do anything with newly added land, and it should instead be kept in private hands, even if that meant living in a country of meandering dirt roads instead of railways. Compare Whig-dominated New England, dotted with bustling towns and busy factories, to the heavily Democratic South with its isolated plantations, and you have a sense of the two parties' disparate visions for America. The election was close, but Polk won.

The Polk Presidency

Polk took office with four goals, and having pledged to serve only one term, had only four years in which to accomplish them. The first goal was to restore the practice of keeping government funds in the Treasury; Andrew Jackson had kept them in so-called **pet banks**, and the results had been disastrous. The second was to reduce tariffs. Both of these were accomplished by the end of 1846.

In the last days of his administration, President Tyler had proposed the annexation of Texas. Northern congressmen were alarmed: Texas was huge and lay entirely south of the Missouri Compromise line, raising the prospect that it might end up being divided into as many as five slave states. They demanded that Polk maintain the balance by annexing the entirety of the Oregon Country, which stretched from the Mexican territory of Alta California at 42° north up to the Russian territory of Alaska at 54°40′ north. "54°40′ or Fight," they demanded—yes, this was *not* Polk's slogan, but one directed *at* him—but Polk recognized that the United States could hardly afford to fight two territorial wars at the same time, particularly if one was against Great Britain, the other claimant to the Oregon Country. Consequently, he conceded on demands for expansion deep into Canada and set about instead to negotiate a more reasonable American-Canadian border. The **Oregon Treaty**, signed with Great Britain in 1846, allowed the United States to acquire peacefully what is now Oregon, Washington, and parts of Idaho, Wyoming, and Montana. It also established the current northern border of the region.

Reasonably certain that war in the Northwest could be avoided, Polk concentrated on efforts to claim the Southwest from Mexico. He tried to buy the territory, and when that failed, he challenged Mexican authorities on the border of Texas, provoking a Mexican attack on American troops. Mexico was already agitated over the annexation of Texas, which had gained its independence from Mexico in 1836 (remember the Alamo?). Polk then used the border attack to argue for a declaration of war. Congress granted the declaration, and in 1846 the **Mexican-American War** began. Whigs, such as first-term member of the House of Representatives Abraham Lincoln, questioned Polk's claim that the Mexicans had fired first, but Congress declared war anyway.

The Mexican-American War did not have universal support from the American public. Northerners feared that new states in the West would become slave states, thus tipping the balance in Congress in favor of proslavery forces. Opponents argued that Polk had provoked Mexico into war at the request of powerful slaveholders, and the idea that a few slave owners had control over the government became popular. Those rich Southerners who allegedly were "pulling the strings" were referred to as the **Slave Power** by suspicious Northerners. The **gag rule** in 1836 raised suspicions of a Slave Power and the defeat of the **Wilmot Proviso**, a congressional bill prohibiting the extension of slavery into any territory gained from Mexico, reinforced those suspicions. The main thing to remember about the Wilmot Proviso is the outcome of the vote:

> ### "Spot" Resolutions
> Whigs were almost universally opposed to the Mexican-American War, as were abolitionists and anti-imperialists. When the young Whig Abraham Lincoln was a Representative in the U.S. Congress, he proposed a series of "spot" resolutions, demanding that Democrat President Polk reveal the exact "spot" where American blood had been spilled by Mexican soldiers, Polk's main argument when asking for the War. Lincoln was later criticized by some for this persistent approach and was nicknamed "spotty Lincoln."

Wilmot Proviso House vote	Whigs	Democrats
Northern	all in favor	all but four in favor
Southern	all but two opposed	all opposed

As you can see, the vote fell along not *party* lines but *sectional* ones, an ominous sign. Over the course of the next decade, the Democrats would become even more Southern-dominated than before, while the Whigs would split between the anti-slavery, Northern "Conscience Whigs" and the pro-slavery, Southern "Cotton Whigs," and would thus follow the Federalists into extinction. New parties would rise to take its place, the first of which was the **Free-Soil Party**, a regional, single-issue party devoted to the goals of the Wilmot Proviso. It should be noted that the Free-Soil Party was largely opposed to the expansion of slavery not because they were abolitionists but because they didn't want white settlers to have to compete with slave labor in new territories.

While debate raged on, so too did the Mexican War, which went very well for American forces. The United States prevailed so easily in Texas that Polk not only ordered troops south to Mexico but also across the Southwest and into California, hoping to grab the entire region by war's end. When the United States successfully invaded Mexico City, the war was over. In the **Treaty of Guadalupe Hidalgo** (1848), Mexico handed over almost all of the modern Southwest: Arizona, New Mexico, California, Nevada, and Utah. This is known as the **Mexican Cession**. The United States, in return, paid $15 million for the land.

The addition of this new territory greatly increased the nation's potential wealth, especially when gold was found at Sutter's Mill during the year that the treaty was signed. However, it also posed major problems regarding the status of slavery. The chief problem was this. By an accident of geography, it just so happened that, east of the Mississippi, the territory of the United States was divided evenly between lands suited for plantation agriculture, where slavery flourished, and those that were not, and where slavery died out shortly after independence. Now the country extended all the way to the Pacific—but even south of the Missouri Compromise line, lands west of the Mississippi were not suitable for growing cotton, or tobacco, or any of the traditional plantation crops. Southerners saw a future in which slavery was confined, not to the *southern half* of the country, but to the *southeastern quarter* of it, and where they would therefore be greatly outvoted should free-soil advocates decide to ban slavery everywhere. Southerners therefore decided that the time had come to rip up the Missouri Compromise and attempt to open up more areas to slavery. Their first step was to introduce the concept of **popular sovereignty**. Popular sovereignty meant that the territories themselves would decide, by vote, whether to allow slavery within their borders.

The Compromise of 1850: Major Players

Henry Clay

- Whig Senator from Kentucky
- Drafted and formally proposed the Compromise of 1850
- Helped to clarify the final boundaries of Texas
- Originally proposed banning slavery in the entire Mexican Cession
- Wanted a stringent Fugitive Slave Act

John Calhoun

- Democrat Senator from South Carolina
- Defender of slavery
- Opposed the Compromise of 1850
- Advocate for states' rights and secession
- Spurred notion of popular sovereignty for Mexican Cession territories

Daniel Webster

- Whig Senator from Massachusetts
- Supported the Compromise in order to preserve the Union and avert Civil War
- In the Seventh of March speech, characterized himself "not as a Massachusetts man, nor as a Northern man, but as an American...."
- Risked offending his abolitionist voter base by accepting the Compromise

The Compromise of 1850

Sectional strife over the new territories started as the ink was drying on the Treaty of Guadalupe Hidalgo. During the Gold Rush, settlers had flooded into California, and the populous territory wanted statehood. Californians had already drawn up a state constitution. That constitution prohibited slavery, and so, of course, the South opposed California's bid for statehood. At the very least, pro-slavery forces argued, southern California should be forced to accept slavery, in accordance with the boundary drawn by the Missouri Compromise of 1820. The debate grew so hostile that Southern legislators began to discuss openly the possibility of secession.

Democrat **Stephen Douglas** (not to be confused with black abolitionist Frederick Douglass) and Whig Henry Clay hammered out what they thought to be a workable solution, known as the **Compromise of 1850**. When presented as a complete package, the compromise was defeated in Congress. Douglas, however, realized that different groups supported different parts of the compromise, and so he broke the package down into separate bills. He managed to organize majorities to support each of the component bills, and thus ushered the entire compromise through Congress. Together, the bills admitted California as a free state, at the price of the enactment of a stronger **fugitive slave law**. They also created the territories of Utah and New Mexico, but they left the status of slavery up to each territory to decide only when it came time for each to write its constitution, thus reinforcing the concept of **popular sovereignty**. The Compromise of 1850 abolished the slave *trade*, not slavery itself, in Washington, D.C. Proponents of this provision argued that it was immoral to "buy and sell human flesh in the shadow of the nation's capitol."

Instituting popular sovereignty and a new fugitive slave law posed serious problems. The definition of popular sovereignty was so vague that Northerners and Southerners could interpret the law entirely differently to suit their own positions.

The fugitive slave law, meanwhile, made it much easier to retrieve escaped slaves, but it required citizens of free states to cooperate in their retrieval. Abolitionists considered it coercive, immoral, and an affront to their liberty.

Antislavery sentiments in the North grew stronger in 1852 with the publication of **Uncle Tom's Cabin**, a sentimental novel written by Harriet Beecher Stowe, a then-obscure writer. Stowe, a Northerner, based her damning depictions of plantation life on information provided her by abolitionist friends. She wisely avoided political preaching, instead playing on people's sympathies. The book sold more than a million copies and was adapted into several popular plays that toured America and Europe. Like Thomas Paine's *Common Sense* during the Revolutionary War era, it was an extremely powerful piece of propaganda, awakening antislavery sentiment in millions who had never before given the issue much thought.

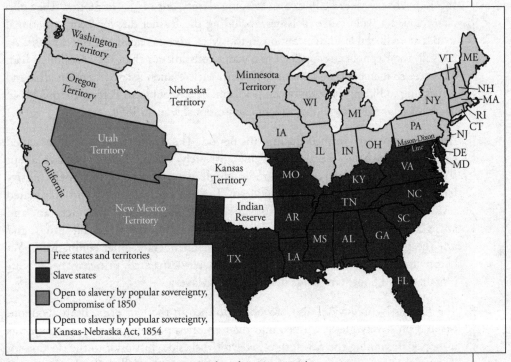

Kansas-Nebraska Act, 1854

The Kansas-Nebraska Act and "Bleeding Kansas"

After California, no new states would be admitted to the Union until 1858. However, the contentious status of the new territories proved increasingly problematic. Settlers entering the Kansas and Nebraska territories found no established civil authority. Congress also wanted to build railways through the territory, but they needed some form of government to impose order, secure land (a task that included driving out Native Americans), and supervise construction.

Illinois Senator Stephen Douglas promoted the Kansas-Nebraska Act because he wanted the transcontinental railroad to terminate in Illinois, which would bring money and jobs to his home state. Douglas worked to create a coalition of Southerners who would want to repeal the Missouri Compromise and Northerners who wanted the railroad to end in the Illinois region, getting the act passed through Congress over the strong objection of antislavery Whigs and antislavery Democrats. Northerners considered the new law a betrayal, regarding it as further evidence of the Slave Power's domination of government. In response, many Northern states passed laws weakening the fugitive slave act. These laws, called **personal liberty laws**, required a trial by jury for all alleged fugitives and guaranteed them the right to a lawyer. Southerners, who thought the fugitive slave law would be the final word on the issue, were furious.

The Kansas-Nebraska Act also drove the final stake into the heart of the Whig Party. Antislavery Whigs, growing more impassioned about the issue and more convinced that the national party would never take a strong stand, joined Northern Democrats and former Free-Soilers (whose single issue was effectively defeated by Kansas-Nebraska) to form a new party, the **Republicans**. Though not abolitionist, the Republicans were dedicated to keeping slavery out of the territories. They also championed a wide range of issues, including the further development of national roads, more liberal land distribution in the West, and increased protective tariffs. As a result, the Republicans appealed to a wider constituency than the Free-Soilers had. Midwestern merchants and farmers, Western settlers, and Eastern importers all found something to like in the Republican platform. The Republican Party grew quickly in the North, where it won a majority of congressional seats in 1854.

Another new party formed during this period. The **American** party, often called the **Know-Nothings** because they met privately and remained secretive about their political agenda, rallied around a single issue: hatred of foreigners (**nativism**), a perennial favorite in U.S. politics. The party grew quickly and dominated several state legislatures. It also spread some ugly anti-Irish, anti-German, and anti-Catholic propaganda. For a while it appeared that the Know-Nothings, and not the Republican Party, would become the Democrats' chief competition. Yet before it could reach that pinnacle, the party self-destructed, primarily because its Northern and Southern wings disagreed over slavery.

The Kansas-Nebraska Act also provoked violence in the territories. Both abolitionists and proslavery groups rushed into the territories, planning to form governments in hopes of winning the two future states for their side. Just prior to the election for Kansas's legislature, thousands of proslavery Missourians (called **Border Ruffians**) temporarily relocated in Kansas, resulting in rival constitutions being sent to Washington: an antislavery one from Topeka and a proslavery one from Lecompton. President Franklin Pierce, a "doughface" (as Northerners who supported pro-Southern policies were called), recognized the Lecompton Constitution and promptly declared Kansas a slave territory. Proslavery forces took Pierce's recognition as a license to expel the free-soilers, and they demolished the free-soil city of Lawrence. In retaliation, radical abolitionist **John Brown** led a raid on a proslavery camp, murdering five. After that, the gloves *really* came off, as gangs from both sides roamed the territory and attacked the opposition. More than 200 people died in the conflict, which is how Kansas came to be known as **Bleeding Kansas**, or **Bloody Kansas**, during this period.

The events in Kansas further polarized the nation. The passions raised were even reflected in Congress when Preston Brooks, nephew of proslavery Senator **Andrew Butler**, savagely beat abolitionist Senator Charles Sumner on the head with a cane for a speech in which Sumner attacked both the South and Butler, using lewd metaphors about slavery. The crisis destroyed Pierce's political career, and the Democrats chose **James Buchanan** as their 1856 candidate. Buchanan's greatest political asset was that he had been out of the country for the previous four years and so could avoid blame for the disastrous results of the Kansas-Nebraska Act. In a sectional vote, Buchanan won the election, carrying the South, while the North split between Buchanan and Republican John Frémont. The Know-Nothings ran Millard Fillmore, who won 20 percent of the vote. It was the Know-Nothings' last hurrah.

Buchanan, Dred Scott, and the Election of 1860

As president, **James Buchanan** tried to maintain the status quo. He worked to enforce the fugitive slave act and opposed abolitionist activism in the South and West. Like many of the nation's leaders at the time, he was at a loss when it came to a permanent solution to the question of slavery. He hoped merely to maintain the Union until a solution presented itself.

Two days after Buchanan took office, the crisis over slavery escalated when the Supreme Court ruled in *Dred Scott v. Sandford*. Scott, a former slave whose master had taken him to territories where slavery was illegal, declared himself a free man and sued for his freedom. Scott won the case but lost the appeal, and the case finally wound up in the Supreme Court where Scott lost. At a time when many wanted to ignore the big questions surrounding slavery, Chief Justice Roger Taney (who wrote the majority decision) chose to attack them head-on. Taney's one-sided, proslavery decision declared that slaves were property, not citizens, and further, that no black person could ever be a citizen of the United States. Because blacks were not citizens, Taney argued, they could not sue in federal courts, as Scott had done. Moreover, he ruled that Congress could not regulate slavery in the territories, as it had done in passing the Northwest Ordinance in 1787 under the Articles of Confederation government and again in 1820 with the Missouri Compromise. This part of the decision not only nullified the now obsolete Missouri Compromise but also the Kansas-Nebraska Act, and it ruled out any hope of reviving the Wilmot Proviso, which was still championed by many Northerners and abolitionists.

In exercising judicial review and declaring the Missouri Compromise unconstitutional, Taney and the Court were in essence saying that slavery could go anywhere; the Republicans' goal of preventing the spread of slavery into the new territories was destroyed by the Court's ruling. The *Dred Scott* decision was thus a major victory for Southerners and a turning point in the "decade of crisis."

In the North, the Supreme Court decision was viciously denounced. Even those who lacked strong abolitionist sentiments feared that the decision tilted the balance of power too far in the South's favor. Many, including the press, regarded the decision as further proof of a Slave Power that, if left unchecked, would soon dominate the entire country, perhaps even forcing slavery on those states that did not want it. Meanwhile, the Democratic Party was dividing along regional lines, raising the possibility that the Republicans might soon control the national government.

1858 was an off-year election, and it was in this politically charged atmosphere that the famous Lincoln-Douglas debates took place. Students often think the debates were for the presidential election, but they weren't. Douglas faced stiff competition for his Illinois Senate seat from **Abraham Lincoln**, a rising star in the newly formed Republican Party. The race for Illinois's Senate seat gained national attention in part because of the railroad and telegraph. Stephen Douglas was viewed as the leading Democrat in the United States Senate, while Lincoln had gained his reputation as a Whig opposed to the Mexican War and Kansas-Nebraska Act.

In many ways, the Lincoln-Douglas debates gave voice to the issues and concerns that divided a nation heading for civil war. It was in this campaign that Lincoln delivered his famous "House Divided" speech ("this government cannot endure, permanently, half slave and half free"), while Douglas destroyed his political career in his attempt to defend popular sovereignty in what became known as the **Freeport Doctrine**. Douglas tried to depict Lincoln as an abolitionist, but Lincoln skillfully backed Douglas into a corner when he pushed him to reconcile popular sovereignty with the *Dred Scott* decision. Douglas suggested that slavery could not exist where local laws did not protect it. In essence, he contended, voters and residents of a territory could exclude slavery simply by not protecting a man's "property." Douglas alienated both Northern and Southern voters by his ambiguous stance on popular sovereignty and effectively destroyed any chance he might have had for winning the presidency in 1860.

Adding fuel to the secessionist fire was **John Brown**'s raid on **Harper's Ferry** in 1859. Brown hoped to spark a slave revolt but failed. After his execution, news spread that Brown had received financial backing from Northern abolitionist organizations. Brown became a martyr for the cause, celebrated throughout the North.

When it came time for the Democrats to choose their 1860 presidential candidate, their convention split. Northern Democrats backed Douglas; Southerners backed John Breckinridge. The election showed that the nation itself was on the brink of fracture. In the North, the contest was between Douglas and Republican nominee Abraham Lincoln. In the South, Breckinridge faced off against Constitutional Union Party nominee John Bell; Lincoln didn't even appear on Southern ballots. But the North held the majority of the electoral votes, so when Lincoln achieved a clean sweep there, he won the election. The response in Southern legislatures was to propose bills of secession.

Immediately after the election, Southern leaders who wanted to maintain the Union tried to negotiate and came up with the Crittendon Compromise. All hope of resolution died, however, when Lincoln refused to soften the Republican demand that slavery not be extended to the territories. Lincoln probably had no other political option, as to do otherwise would have been to abandon the principles of those who had supported his election. Lincoln and other Northern leaders were banking on the hope that the South was bluffing and would not secede.

In December 1860, three months before Lincoln's inauguration, South Carolina seceded from the Union. Within months, six other states had joined South Carolina to form the **Confederate States of America**; the states chose **Jefferson Davis** to lead the Confederacy. Cautiously, Lincoln decided to maintain control of federal forts in the South while waiting for the Confederacy to make a move. On April 12, 1861, it did, attacking and capturing **Fort Sumter**. No one died in this first battle of America's bloodiest war, the **Civil War**.

Fire-Eaters

The Fire-Eaters were a group of radical pro-slavery Southerners who wanted secession and the creation of the Confederacy. The most prominent leader of this group was Robert Barnwell Rhett of South Carolina, but John C. Calhoun was its most famous member. The Fire-Eaters also sought to reinstate the international slave trade, thus expanding slavery and making it more profitable.

THE CIVIL WAR AND RECONSTRUCTION (1860–1877)

For many people of the era, the Civil War was not solely (or even explicitly) about slavery. It is worth noting that Missouri, Kentucky, Maryland, and Delaware, the **Border States**, were slave states that fought for the Union. Except for active abolitionists, most Northerners believed they were fighting to preserve the Union. Most Southerners described their cause as fighting for their **states' rights** to govern themselves. But slavery was the issue that had caused the argument over states' rights to escalate to war. Lincoln's views on slavery evolved throughout the 1850s and the Civil War, but as late as 1862, Lincoln stated, "If I could save the Union without freeing any slaves I would do it, and if I could save the union by freeing all the slaves I would do it.... What I do about slavery, and the colored race, I do because I believe it helps to save the Union."

The Civil War took place not only on the battlefields but also in political, economic, and social realms. Although you do not need to know the military details of any specific battles for the AP Exam, you should know the political or diplomatic consequences of battles like Gettysburg or Antietam, and you do need to know how political, social, and economic conditions influenced the outcome of the war.

The Civil War and the Confederacy

Ironically, as the Southern states fought to maintain the right to govern themselves locally, the Confederate government brought them under greater central control than they had ever experienced. Jefferson Davis understood the North's considerable advantages in population, transportation, and economics, and he knew that the weak, poorly organized state governments of the South could not mount an effective defense. Davis took control of the Southern economy, imposing taxes and using the revenues to spur industrial and urban growth; he took control of the railroads and commercial shipping; and he created a large government bureaucracy to oversee economic developments. Davis, in short, forced the South to compensate quickly for what it had lost when it cut itself off from Northern commerce. When Southerners opposed his moves, he declared martial law and suspended the writ of *habeas corpus*, a traditional protection against improper imprisonment, in order to maintain control. Lincoln was upsetting Northerners with some of the exact same steps, but the use of the presidential power chafed especially badly in the Confederacy, where many believed they had seceded precisely to avoid the federal government commanding too much power.

The Battle of Antietam, fought in September 1862, was the first battle fought in the East where the Union wasn't completely defeated. By forcing the Confederacy to retreat, the Union claimed the battle was a victory. This "victory" gave Lincoln the platform he needed to announce the Emancipation Proclamation. It was also important to show Britain and France that the Union wasn't a lost cause, and put off those countries possibly helping the Confederacy.

The Battle of Gettysburg was fought in southern Pennsylvania. It was the most northern point the Confederacy had reached at the time. Lee's troops suffered massive casualties and were forced to retreat. This served as a massive confidence boost for the Union.

Four months after the Battle of Gettysburg, President Lincoln delivered his most famous speech, the **Gettysburg Address**. In only two minutes, the Address helped to redefine the War as not only a struggle to preserve the Union, but also as a struggle for human equality.

Davis had some success in modernizing the Southern economy, but the Confederacy lagged too far behind in industrialization to catch up to the Union. Rapid economic growth, furthermore, brought with it rapid **inflation**. Prices rose so quickly that paychecks and payments for crops became worthless almost as soon as they were made, plunging many Southerners into poverty. In 1862, the Confederacy imposed **conscription** (a military draft), requiring many small farmers to serve in the Confederate Army. This act caused even greater poverty in the country, as many families could not adequately tend their farms without their men.

Confederate conscription also created class conflict. The government allowed the wealthy to hire surrogates to perform military service in their place and exempted anyone who owned more than 20 slaves from military service (on the grounds that the large plantations these men ran fed the Confederacy and its army). In effect, the wealthy did not have to serve, while the poor had no choice. As a result, **class tensions** increased, leading ultimately to widespread desertions from the Confederate Army. Toward the end of the war, it also led many Southerners in small towns to ignore the government and try to carry on as if there was no war. Many resisted when asked to feed, clothe, or house passing troops.

The Civil War and the Union

The Northern economy received a boost from the war as the demand for war-related goods, such as uniforms and weapons, spurred manufacturing. The loss of Southern markets harmed the economy at first, but soon the war economy brought about a boom period. A number of entrepreneurs became extremely wealthy; many succumbed to the temptations of greed, overcharging the government for services and products (**war profiteering**). Some sold the Union government worthless, shoddy food and clothing, while government bureaucrats looked the other way for the price of a bribe. Corruption was fairly widespread, eventually prompting a yearlong congressional investigation.

Like the South, the North experienced a period of accelerated inflation, although Northern inflation was nowhere as extreme as its Southern counterpart. (In the North, prices rose between 10 and 20 percent annually; in the South, the inflation rate was well over 300 percent.) Workers, worried about job security in the face of mechanization and the decreasing value of their wages, formed **unions**. Businesses, in return, blacklisted union members, forced new employees to sign contracts in which they promised not to join unions, and used violence to break strikes. The Republican Party, then (as now) believing that government should help businesses but regulate them as little as possible, supported business in its opposition to unions.

Lincoln, like Davis, oversaw a tremendous increase in the power of the central government during the war. He implemented economic development programs without waiting for congressional approval, championed numerous government loans and grants to businesses, and raised tariffs to protect Union trade. He also suspended the writ of *habeas corpus* in the border states, to make it easier to arrest secessionists, especially in Maryland. During the war, Lincoln initiated the printing of a **national currency**. Lincoln's able treasury secretary, Salmon P. Chase, issued **greenbacks**, government-issued paper money that was a precursor to modern currency.

Emancipation of the Slaves

As previously stated, neither the Union nor the Confederacy initially declared the Civil War to be a war about slavery. The Constitution protected slavery where it already existed, so many opponents (including Republicans) were opposed to the *extension* of slavery into the new territories. As a presidential candidate, Lincoln had argued for gradual emancipation, compensation to slaveholders for liberated slaves, and the colonization of freed slaves somewhere outside the United States, perhaps in Africa. When the Union dissolved and the South left Congress, Lincoln was faced with a legislature much more progressive in its thoughts on slavery than he was. The **Radical Republican** wing of Congress wanted immediate emancipation. To that end, the radicals introduced the **confiscation acts** in Congress. The first (1861) gave the government the right to seize any slaves used for "insurrectionary purposes." The second (1862) was much wider in scope, allowing the government to liberate any slave owned by someone who supported the rebellion, even if that support was limited to paying taxes to the Confederate government. The second confiscation act, in effect, gave the Union the right to liberate all slaves. This act had little effect, however, because Lincoln refused to enforce it.

Soon after, however, Lincoln took his first cautious steps toward emancipation. The primary reason was pretty simple: slaves indirectly supported the Southern war effort. They grew the crops and cooked the meals that kept the rebel troops fed. Therefore, any strategy the Union army adopted had to include capturing slaves as a key element. But what to do with them once they were captured? Lock them up somewhere and return them to their owners after the war? They had to be freed, or the government of the United States would become the world's biggest slaveholder. And there were other advantages of making the freedom of the slaves one of the side effects of Union victory. One was that it kept Britain and France out of the war. Jefferson Davis had hoped that these countries would support the Confederacy in order to keep receiving shipments of Southern cotton, but once Lincoln made it explicit that Union victory would mean freedom for the slaves, European governments dared not attempt to come to the aid of the rebels for fear of being quickly toppled by an outraged public. Another advantage was that emancipation would provide a new source of troops for the Union side: "The bare sight of 50 thousand armed and drilled black soldiers on the banks of the Mississippi would end the rebellion at once," Lincoln mused. But he dared not make this move until after a Northern victory, lest it appear like a desperate response to the defeats skilled Southern generals were inflicting upon the Union. The moment came in September 1862, with the Union victory at Antietam.

In the aftermath of the battle, Lincoln issued the **Emancipation Proclamation**. Note that the Emancipation Proclamation, for all intents and purposes, actually freed no slaves. Instead, it stated that on January 1, 1863, the government would liberate all slaves residing in those states still "in rebellion." Throughout the war, Lincoln refused to acknowledge secession and insisted on referring to the Confederate states as "those states in rebellion." The Proclamation did not liberate the slaves in the border states such as Maryland, nor did it liberate slaves in Southern counties already under the control of the Union Army. Again, legally, Lincoln had no power to abolish slavery in areas governed by the U.S. Constitution. Abolitionists complained that the Proclamation liberated slaves only where the Union had

Gradual Emancipation

Lincoln's notion of "gradual emancipation" was inspired by a law in Pennsylvania passed in 1780 which guaranteed that all children born in Pennsylvania were free persons regardless of the condition or race of their parents. This model of freeing slaves in the North was common before the Civil War settled the question of slavery nationwide.

no power to enforce emancipation and maintained slavery precisely where it could liberate the slaves. The Proclamation also allowed Southern states to rejoin the Union *without* giving up slavery. On the positive side, the Emancipation Proclamation finally declared that the Civil War was, for the Union, a war against slavery, and thus changed the purpose of the war, much as the Declaration of Independence had changed the purpose of the Revolutionary War.

Not until two years later, while campaigning for reelection, did Lincoln give his support to complete emancipation. Just before the Republican convention, Lincoln lobbied for a party platform that called for a constitutional amendment prohibiting slavery; the result was the **Thirteenth Amendment**. After his reelection, Lincoln considered allowing defeated Southern states to reenter the Union and to vote on the Thirteenth Amendment. He tried to negotiate a settlement with Southern leaders along those lines at the **Hampton Roads Conference**. Lincoln also offered a five-year delay on implementing the amendment if it passed, as well as $400 million in compensation to slave owners. Jefferson Davis's commitment to complete Southern independence scuttled any chance of compromise.

The Election of 1864 and the End of the Civil War

As the 1864 presidential election approached, popular opinion in both the North and South favored an end to the war. In fact, Lincoln's Democrat opponent, George McClellan, most likely lost his bid for the presidency by defying the will of the majority of Democrats who favored a cessation of hostilities and negotiation with the North.

It should be reemphasized that less than one percent of the Southern population owned more than 100 slaves, and as the war dragged on, many small, non-slaveholding farmers resented the Confederacy and the war, which they now believed was being waged merely to protect the planter aristocracy's lifestyle. In the North, some "War Democrats" conceded that the war was necessary to preserve the Union. Others, called the **Copperheads**, accused Lincoln of instigating a national social revolution and criticized his administration's policies as a thinly disguised attempt to destroy the South. Nowhere, however, was opposition to the war more violent than in New York City, where racial, ethnic, and class antagonisms exploded into draft riots in July of 1863. Irish immigrants, mostly the poor working class who were already victims of **nativism**, resented being drafted into a war being fought to end slavery. Many immigrants feared that once freed, former slaves would migrate into Northern cities and compete with them for low-paying labor jobs. And yet, both sides fought on.

Just when a stalemate might have forced an end to the war, things began improving for the North. Victories throughout the summer of 1864 played a large part in helping Lincoln gain reelection. By the early spring of 1865, a Union victory was virtually assured, and the government established the **Freedman's Bureau** to help newly liberated blacks establish a place in postwar society. The Bureau helped with immediate problems of survival (food, housing) and developed social institutions, such as schools. Some historians see the Freedman's Bureau as the first federal, social welfare program in U.S. history. In April 1865, the Confederate leaders surrendered. John Wilkes Booth assassinated Lincoln just five days later, with devastating consequences for the reunited nation.

The Civil War was fought at enormous cost. More than 3 million men fought in the war, and of them, more than 500,000 died. At least as many were seriously wounded. Both governments ran up huge debts during the war, and much of the South was ravaged by Union soldiers. During **Sherman's March** from Atlanta to the sea in the fall of 1864, the Union Army burned everything in its wake (to destroy Confederate morale and deplete the South's material resources), foreshadowing the wide-scale warfare of the 20th century. From a political perspective, the war permanently expanded the role of government. On both sides, government grew rapidly to manage the economy and the war.

Reconstruction and Johnson's Impeachment

At war's end, three major questions faced the reunited nation. First, under what conditions would the Southern states be readmitted to the Union? Second, what would be the status of blacks in the postwar nation? Black leaders hoped that their service in the military would earn blacks equal rights. The newly liberated slaves, called freedmen, were primarily interested in the chance to earn wages and own property. And third, what should be done with the rebels?

Reconstruction may be seen as both a time period and a process. As a time period, Reconstruction usually refers to the years between 1865 and 1877, that is, from the end of the Civil War until the end of military reconstruction when the Union army withdrew from the South. The *process* of reconstruction, however, was complicated and complex, and some argue it continues to this day. Reconstruction involved readmitting the Southern states that had seceded from the Union; physically reconstructing and rebuilding Southern towns, cities, and property that had been destroyed during the war; and finally, integrating newly freed blacks into American society. It is this last process that has proven to be most difficult.

The process of reconstruction had begun even before the Civil War ended, although not without controversy. As president of the United States and commander-in-chief of the armed forces, Lincoln had claimed that he had the authority to determine the conditions under which the Southern states might be readmitted to the Union. Lincoln had no intention of punishing the South and wanted to end the war and reunite the nation quickly and painlessly, as his immortal words from his second inaugural address indicate: "With malice toward none, with charity for all, with firmness in the right as God gives us to see the right, let us strive on to finish the work we are in, to bind up the nation's wounds, to care for him who shall have borne the battle and for his widow and his orphan, to do all which may achieve and cherish a just and lasting peace among ourselves and with all nations."

Lincoln's plan is usually referred to as the **Ten-Percent Plan** and simply required that 10 percent of those voters who had voted in the 1860 election swear an oath of allegiance to the Union and accept emancipation through the Thirteenth Amendment. These men would then reorganize their state government and reapply for admission into the Union. Congress had another vision, however. It viewed the Southern states as "conquered territory" and as such, **Radical Republicans** in Congress argued, were under the jurisdiction of Congress, not the President. Most Republicans agreed that Lincoln's plan was too lenient and enacted the

Wade-Davis Bill in July of 1864. This act provided that former Confederate states be ruled by a military governor and required 50 percent of the electorate to swear an oath of allegiance to the United States. A state convention would then be organized to repeal their ordinance of secession and abolish slavery within their state.

It should be noted that neither Lincoln's Ten-Percent Plan nor the Wade-Davis Bill made any provisions for black suffrage. Lincoln pocket-vetoed the Wade-Davis Bill, effectively destroying it. (A pocket veto can occur only at the end of a congressional session. If the president does not sign a bill within 10 days and Congress adjourns within those 10 days, the bill dies and must be reintroduced when Congress reconvenes. Unlike a regular veto, which requires the president to explain his objections to a bill and can subsequently be overridden, a pocket veto does not need to be explained nor is it subject to another congressional vote. It cannot be overridden.) Lincoln was assassinated the following year.

With Lincoln's assassination, Vice President **Andrew Johnson** assumed the presidency. Johnson, a Southern Democrat, had opposed secession and strongly supported Lincoln during his first term. In return, Lincoln rewarded Johnson with the vice presidency. When the war ended, Congress was in recess and would not reconvene for eight months. That left the early stages of Reconstruction entirely in Johnson's hands.

Johnson had lifted himself from poverty and held no great love for the South's elite planters, and at first he seemed intent on taking power away from the old aristocracy and giving it to the yeomen. **Johnson's Reconstruction Plan**, which was based on a plan approved by Lincoln, called for the creation of provisional military governments to run the states until they were readmitted to the Union. It also required all Southern citizens to swear a **loyalty oath** before receiving amnesty for the rebellion. However, it barred many of the former Southern elite (including plantation owners, Confederate officers, and government officials) from taking that vow, thus prohibiting their participation in the new governments. According to this plan, the provisional governments would hold state constitutional conventions, at which time the states would have to write new constitutions eliminating slavery and renouncing secession. Johnson did not require the states to enfranchise blacks by giving them the vote.

The plan did not work, mostly because Johnson **pardoned** many of the Southern elite who were supposed to have been excluded from the reunification process. After the states drafted new constitutions and elected new governments, former Confederate officials were again in positions of great power. Furthermore, many of their new constitutions were only slight revisions of previous constitutions. Southern legislators also passed new **black codes** limiting freedman's rights to assemble and travel, instituting curfews, and requiring blacks to carry special passes. Many of them required blacks in the South to sign lengthy labor contracts. In the most egregious instances, state legislatures simply took their old slave codes and replaced the word *slaves* with *freedmen*. When Congress reconvened in December 1865, the new Southern senators included the vice president of the Confederacy and other Confederate officials. Northern congressmen were not pleased. Invoking its constitutional right to examine the credentials of new members, Congress voted not to seat the new Southern delegations. Next, it set about examining Johnson's Reconstruction plan.

Congress was divided among conservative Republicans, who generally agreed with Johnson's plan; moderates, who were a large enough contingent to swing a vote in one or the other direction; and Radical Republicans. The Radical Republicans wanted to extend democracy in the South. Following the Civil War, most important political positions were held by appointees; very few officials were directly elected. (Of course, women could not vote and black men could vote only in a few northern states at this time.) The most radical among the Radical Republicans advocated a reconstruction program that punished the South for seceding. Historians of the time suggested that revenge was the real motivation behind the passage of the Thirteenth Amendment, although contemporary historians have dismissed this idea. Under General Sherman's **Special Field Order No. 15**, land seized from the Confederates was to be redistributed among the new freedmen, but President Andrew Johnson rescinded Sherman's order, and the idea of giving freedmen **40 acres and a mule** never regained much ground.

All Republicans agreed that Johnson's Reconstruction needed some modification, but Johnson refused to compromise. Instead, he declared Reconstruction over and done with, vetoing a compromise package that would have extended the life of the Freedman's Bureau and enforced a uniform civil rights code on the South. Congress overrode Johnson's vetoes, which only increased tension between the two branches of the federal government.

In response, the radicals drew up the plan that came to be known as **Congressional Reconstruction**. Its first component was the **Fourteenth Amendment** to the Constitution. The amendment (1) stated that if you are born in the United States, you are a citizen of the United States and you are a citizen of the state where you reside; (2) prohibited states from depriving any citizen of "life, liberty, or property without due process of law"; (3) prevented states from denying any citizen "equal protection of the law"; (4) gave states the choice either to give freedmen the right to vote or to stop counting them among their voting population for the purpose of congressional apportionment; (5) barred prominent Confederates from holding political office; and (6) excused the Confederacy's war debt.

The first three points remain the most significant, to this very day, and are the basis for most lawsuits involving discrimination and civil rights. In fact, through a series of cases over the years, most of the first 10 amendments have been extended to the states through the due process clause of the Fourteenth Amendment. It is helpful to remember that the Bill of Rights protects the individual from the federal government, while the Fourteenth Amendment protects you from the state government. The Fourteenth Amendment was intended to clarify the status of newly freed slaves, address the issue of citizenship raised by the *Dred Scott* decision, and limit the effects of the black codes. The radicals hoped to force states to either extend suffrage to black men or lose power in Congress. In the **Swing Around the Circle** public speaking tour, Johnson campaigned against the amendment and lost. In the congressional election of 1866, the North voted for a Congress more heavily weighted toward the radical end of the political spectrum.

The new Congress quickly passed the **Military Reconstruction Act of 1867**. It imposed martial law on the South; it also called for new state constitutional conventions and forced the states to allow blacks to vote for convention delegates. The act also required each state to ratify the Fourteenth Amendment and to send its new constitution to Congress for approval. Aware that Johnson would oppose the new Reconstruction, Congress then passed a number of laws designed to limit the president's power. As expected, Johnson did everything in his power to counteract the congressional plan. The conflict reached its climax when the House Judiciary Committee initiated **impeachment proceedings** against Johnson, ostensibly for violating the Tenure of Office Act (which stated that the president had to secure the consent of the Senate before removing his appointees once they'd been approved by that body; Johnson had fired Secretary of War Edwin Stanton, a Radical Republican) but really because he was getting in the way of Reconstruction. Johnson was acquitted by one vote in the Senate, but the trial rendered Johnson politically impotent, and he served the last few months of his presidency with no hope of re-election.

With a new president, **Ulysses S. Grant**, in office, Congress forged ahead in its efforts to remake the South. The **Fifteenth Amendment**, proposed in 1869, finally required states to enfranchise black men. (Women's suffrage would have to wait another half-century.) In fact, Grant's win was mainly due to black votes. One of the reasons the Republicans created the Fifteenth Amendment was the hope that their party would continue to flourish with the addition of new black voters. Ironically, the Fifteenth Amendment passed only because Southern states were required to ratify it as a condition of reentry into the Union; a number of Northern states opposed the amendment.

The Failure of Reconstruction

Reconstruction had its share of successes while the North occupied the South. New state constitutions officially allowed all Southern men to vote (previous constitutions had required voters to own property) and replaced many appointed government positions with elected positions. New Southern governments, directed mostly by transplanted Northern Republicans, blacks, and Southern moderates, created public schools and those social institutions such as orphanages popularized in the North during the reform movement of the 1830s. The new governments also stimulated industrial and rail development in the South through loans, grants, and tax exemptions. The fact that blacks were serving in Southern governments represented a huge step forward, given the seemingly insurmountable restrictions placed on blacks only a few years earlier, though it would prove to be only a temporary victory.

However, ultimately, Reconstruction failed. Although government industrialization plans helped rebuild the Southern economy, these plans also cost a lot of money. High tax rates turned public opinion, already antagonistic to Reconstruction, even more hostile. Opponents waged a propaganda war against Reconstruction, calling Southerners who cooperated **scalawags** and Northerners who ran the programs **carpetbaggers**. (The name came from the suitcases they carried, implying they had come to the South merely to stuff their bags with ill-gotten wealth.) Many who participated in Reconstruction were indeed corrupt, selling their votes for money and favors.

It should be noted that Northerners were just as guilty as Southerners of corruption. The period following the Civil War is also known as the **Gilded Age** to suggest the tarnish that lay beneath the layer of gold. This is the era of political machines and "bosses," which will be discussed in a later chapter. Political scandal was not new at the time, and in fact, Grant's administration was wracked with political scandals and intrigue; Grant himself was supposedly innocent and oblivious to the goings on in his administration. Grant had no political experience when he became president; in fact, he was elected because he was a popular war hero, not an experienced political leader. Like Jackson, Grant appointed his friends and supporters to governmental positions, not necessarily those men most qualified, let alone those with the most integrity.

Unfortunately, although Grant was honest, his friends were not. A series of scandals broke out in the early 1870s, and while you don't need to know the details to do well on the AP Exam, the sheer length of the list should get the idea across:

> **Black Friday, 1869**
> **Credit Mobilier scandal, 1872**
> **New York Custom House ring, 1872**
> **Star Route frauds, 1872–1876**
> **Sanborn incident, 1874**
> **Pratt & Boyd scandal, 1875**
> **Whiskey Ring, 1875**
> **Delano affair, 1875**
> **Trading post scandal, 1876**
> **Alexander Cattell & Co. scandal, 1876**
> **Safe burglary, 1876**

These scandals diverted the public's attention away from the postwar conditions in the South.

Though the Civil War was officially over, a war of intimidation began, spear-headed by insurgent groups ranging from secretive terrorist groups, such as the **Ku Klux Klan**, who focused on murdering freedmen, to openly operating paramilitary forces, such as the **White League**, who focused on murdering Republicans. "These combinations amount to war," declared attorney general Amos Akerman, who had been posted to the Carolinas to try to speed trials of Klansmen along—a problem because local judges tended to be Klansmen as well. In some towns, the entire adult male population was engaged in battle against Reconstruction. Southern officials explained their failure to do anything to protect blacks and Republicans by complaining that if they obeyed their orders to round up insurgents, there would be mass starvation because nobody would be left to work. Grant and the Republicans in Congress got the Enforcement Acts passed, which allowed Grant to send in federal troops to oppose the Klan, and were successful in limiting the Klan's violence.

Also, because Reconstruction did nothing to redistribute the South's wealth or guarantee that the freedmen would own property, it did very little to alter the basic power structure of the region. Southerners knew that when the Northerners left, as they inevitably would, things would return to a condition much closer to the way they were before Reconstruction. As early as 1869, the federal government began sending signals that it would soon ease up restrictions. President Grant

"A portion of our southern population hate the government of the United States, because they understand it emphatically to represent northern sentiment, and hate the negro because he has ceased to be a slave and has been promoted to be a citizen and a voter, and hate those of the southern whites who are looked upon as in political friendship with the north, with the United States Government and with the negro. These persons commit the violence that disturbs many parts of the south."
—Attorney General Amos Akerman

enforced the law loosely, hoping to lessen tensions and thereby hasten an amicable reunion. Worse, throughout the 1860s and 1870s, the Supreme Court consistently restricted the scope of the Fourteenth and Fifteenth Amendments. In the *Slaughter-House* cases, the court ruled that the Fourteenth Amendment applied only to the federal government, not to state governments, an opinion the court strengthened in *United States v. Cruikshank*. In *United States v. Reese*, the court cleared the way for "grandfather clauses," poll taxes, literary tests, property requirements, and other restrictions on voting privileges. Soon, nearly all Southern states had restrictive laws that effectively prevented blacks from voting. Finally, because Grant's administration was so thoroughly corrupt, it tainted everything with which it was associated, including Reconstruction.

During the 1872 election, moderates calling themselves Liberal Republicans abandoned the coalition that supported Reconstruction. Angered by widespread corruption, this group hoped to end federal control of the South. Although their candidate, Horace Greeley, did not defeat Grant, they made gains in congressional and state elections. As a result, Grant moved further away from the radical position and closer to conciliation. Several congressional acts, among them the Amnesty Act of 1872, pardoned many of the rebels, thus allowing them to reenter public life. Other crises, such as the financial Panic of 1873, drew the nation's attention away from Reconstruction. By 1876, Southern Democrats had regained control of most of the region's state legislatures. These Democrats called themselves **Redeemers,** and their use of the word redemption suggested they intended to reverse Republican reconstruction policies as they returned to power.

The election of 1876 was one of the more infamously contested elections in American history, with both political parties accusing the other of fraud. Samuel J. Tilden, then governor of New York and a political reformer who had gone after **"Boss" Tweed**, the most notorious among the political bosses of the time, won the popular vote by a small margin but needed to win the electoral vote to gain the presidency. (Remember that according to the Constitution, if no one candidate receives a majority of electoral votes, the election is thrown into the House of Representatives. You should remember, for example, that Andrew Jackson lost the presidency to John Quincy Adams through a "corrupt bargain" in 1824.) Republicans challenged the election returns that favored Tilden in South Carolina, Louisiana, and Florida. Congress eventually stepped in to resolve the disputed election and created a special bipartisan electoral commission consisting of senators, representatives, and Supreme Court justices. Through a series of informal negotiations, a deal was struck that has come to be known as the **Compromise of 1877**. It was agreed that if Rutherford B. Hayes won the presidential election, he would end military reconstruction and pull federal troops out of South Carolina and Louisiana, thereby enabling Democrats to regain control of those states. Military reconstruction was thus ended, and it was business as usual in the South. Many historians feel that the federal government dropped the ball in 1877, for in many ways, life for blacks became worse, and it would take almost another 100 years for the federal government to live up to the ideal expressed in the Declaration of Independence: "that all men are created equal."

After the Compromise of 1877, many Southern leaders sought to emulate the industrialization of the North, coining the term "New South." Despite these aspirations, though, sharecropping and tenant farming would continue to dominate the region for many years.

Southern Blacks During and After Reconstruction

At the end of the Civil War, the former slaves were thrust into an ambiguous state of freedom. Most reacted cautiously, remaining on plantations as sharecroppers where they had been relatively well treated but fleeing from those with cruel overseers. Many set out in search of family members from whom they had been separated. The Freedman's Bureau helped them find new jobs and housing, and provided money and food to those in need. The Freedman's Bureau also helped establish schools at all levels for blacks, among them Fisk University and Howard University. Unfortunately, the Freedman's Bureau was terribly underfunded and had little impact once military reconstruction came to an end.

When it became evident that the government would not redistribute land, blacks looked for other ways to work their own farms. The Freedman's Bureau attempted to establish a system in which blacks contracted their labor to whites, but the system failed. Instead, blacks preferred **sharecropping**, in which they traded a portion of their crop in return for the right to work someone else's land. The system worked at first, but unscrupulous landowners eventually used the system as a means of keeping poor farmers in a state of near slavery and debt. Abuses of the sharecropping system grew more widespread at the end of Reconstruction, at which point no court would fairly try the case of a sharecropper against a landowner. Sharecropping existed well into the middle of the 20th century and actually included more whites than blacks.

Not all blacks, however, suffered a dismal fate during Reconstruction. Mississippi, with its large black population, became the most progressive in its promotion of blacks to political office. **Hiram Revels** and **Blanche K. Bruce** of Mississippi became the first black senators in the U.S. Congress and were elected in 1870 and 1875, respectively, only a few short years after the end of the Civil War. **Robert Smalls** of South Carolina founded the Republican Party of that state and served in the U.S. House of Representatives in the 1880s.

Summary

Here are the most important concepts to remember from the Civil War/Reconstruction period.

o Regional tensions over slavery and states' rights led to the Civil War, an event that radically changed American society and the role of the federal government in state affairs.

o "Manifest Destiny" and a land acquisition from Mexico spurred America to fully settle the West.

o Northern European immigrants continued to enter the country, motivated by industrial and agricultural opportunity.

o It took many years for the South to fully recover from the economic and social upheaval of the Civil War.

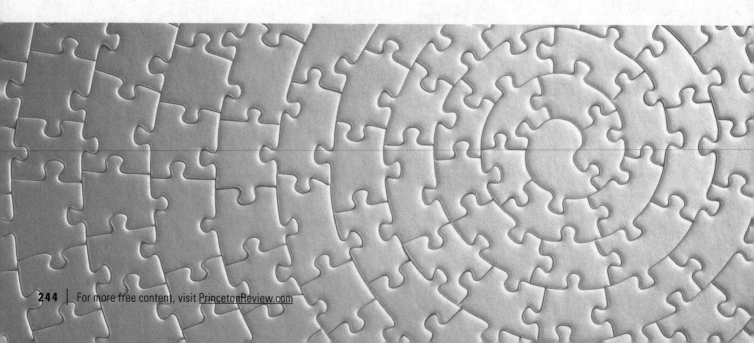

Chapter 9 Review Questions

See Chapter 14 for answers and explanations.

1. As a result of the Mexican-American War, all of the following became part of the United States EXCEPT

    (A) California
    (B) Nevada
    (C) New Mexico
    (D) Texas

2. "Bleeding Kansas" was a direct result of the doctrine of

    (A) judicial review
    (B) imperialism
    (C) containment
    (D) popular sovereignty

3. As a result of the Emancipation Proclamation,

    (A) all slaves in the Union and the Confederacy were declared free
    (B) nearly 200,000 free blacks and escaped slaves joined the Union Army
    (C) Maryland seceded from the Union
    (D) African Americans in the United States received the right to vote

4. Andrew Johnson was impeached because

    (A) he refused to carry out Lincoln's plan for reconstruction
    (B) he vetoed the Wade-Davis Bill
    (C) Congress was controlled by Republicans and he was a Democrat
    (D) he violated the Tenure of Office Act by firing Secretary of War Stanton

5. The dispute over electoral votes in the election of 1876

    (A) was similar to the election of 2000 in that the Supreme Court ultimately had to step in and decide the election
    (B) was resolved by a special bipartisan commission and resulted in the end of military reconstruction
    (C) led many members of Congress to push for a Constitutional amendment to abolish the Electoral College
    (D) was resolved when Samuel J. Tilden conceded the election to Rutherford B. Hayes

6. Following the Civil War, most freed slaves

    (A) stayed in the South and worked as sharecroppers
    (B) joined the pioneering movement as it headed West
    (C) moved to the North to work in factories
    (D) took work building the nation's growing railroad system

7. The Know-Nothing Party focused its efforts almost exclusively on the issue of

    (A) the right to bear arms
    (B) the prohibition of alcohol
    (C) women's rights
    (D) immigration

8. The Free-Soil party advocated which of the following?

   (A) The freedom of settlers within the territories to determine the slave status of their new state

   (B) Passage of the Homestead Act to give free land to all Western settlers

   (C) The exclusion of slavery from any of the new territories

   (D) The policy of giving newly freed slaves "40 acres and a mule" following the Civil War

9. The principle of popular sovereignty stated that

   (A) whenever a new area was settled, all United States citizens were required to vote on the slave status of that area

   (B) slavery would not be permitted in any area after 1848

   (C) the president, after meeting with public interest groups, was to decide on whether slaves would be allowed in a given territory

   (D) settlers in the Western territories, not Congress, would decide whether to allow slavery in their territories

10. Which of the following is NOT a requirement set by the Reconstruction Act of 1867 for Southern states' readmission to the Union?

   (A) Blacks had to be allowed to participate in state conventions and state elections.

   (B) The state had to ratify the Fourteenth Amendment to the Constitution.

   (C) The state had to pay reparations and provide land grants to all former slaves.

   (D) The state had to rewrite its constitution and ratify it.

REFLECT

Respond to the following questions:

- For which content topics discussed in this chapter do you feel you have achieved sufficient mastery to answer multiple-choice questions correctly?

- For which content topics discussed in this chapter do you feel you have achieved sufficient mastery to discuss effectively in a short-answer question or an essay?

- On which content topics discussed in this chapter do you feel you need more work before you can answer multiple-choice questions correctly?

- On which content topics discussed in this chapter do you feel you need more work before you can discuss them effectively in a short-answer question or an essay?

- What parts of this chapter are you going to review again?

- Will you seek further help, outside of this book (such as a teacher, tutor, or AP Students), on any of the content in this chapter—and, if so, on what content?

Chapter 10
Unit 6: The Industrial Revolution (1865–1898)

Technological advances increased economy

THE AGE OF INVENTION AND ECONOMIC GROWTH

In 1876, **Thomas A. Edison** built his workshop in Menlo Park, New Jersey, and proceeded to produce some of the most important inventions of the century. Edison's greatest invention was the **light bulb**. Edison's pioneering work in the development of **power plants** also proved immensely important. His advances allowed for the extension of the workday, which previously ended at sundown, and the wider availability of electricity. With that wider availability, Edison and other inventors began to create new uses for electricity, both for industry and the home. The last quarter of the 19th century is often called the **Age of Invention** because so many technological advances like Edison's were made. These advances, in turn, generated greater opportunities for **mass production**, which then caused the economy to grow at a tremendous rate. Not surprisingly, the people known as the "captains of industry" to their fans (and the "robber barons" to others), who owned and controlled the new manufacturing enterprises, became extremely rich and powerful during this period.

Industrialization, Corporate Consolidation, and the Gospel of Wealth

As more and faster machines became available to manufacturers, businessmen discovered that their cost per unit decreased as the number of units they produced increased. The more raw product they bought, the cheaper the suppliers' asking price. The closer to capacity they kept their new, faster machines running, the less the cost of labor and electricity per product. The lower their costs, the cheaper they could sell their products. The cheaper the product, the more they sold. That, simply put, is the concept of **economies of scale**.

The downside of this new business practice was that it required employees to work as efficiently, and repetitively, as machines. **Assembly line production** had begun to take hold when Eli Whitney developed interchangeable parts, but it reached a whole new level in Ford's plants in the early 20th century. This type of production required workers to perform a single task over and over, often (before labor reform) for 12 to 14 hours a day. Factories were dangerous; machine malfunctions and human error typically resulted in more than 500,000 injuries to workers per year.

The overriding concern for businessmen, however, was that profits continued to increase by huge margins. Although government made some efforts to regulate this rapid growth, these were tentative. Furthermore, the government remained uncertain as to how to enforce regulations, and widespread corruption existed among those bureaucrats charged with enforcing the regulations. Finally, the courts of the era (especially the Supreme Court) were extremely pro-business. With almost no restraint, businesses such as railroad companies followed the path that led to greater economies of scale, which meant larger and larger businesses. This was known as **corporate consolidation**.

One new form of business organization was called a **holding company**. A holding company owned enough stock in various companies to have a controlling interest in the production of raw material, the means of transporting that material to a factory, the factory itself, and the distribution network for selling the product. The logical conclusion is a **monopoly**, or complete control of an entire industry. One holding company, for example, gained control of 98 percent of the sugar refining plants in the United States. While the company did not control the entire sugar industry, it did control one very important aspect of it.

The most common forms of business consolidation at the end of the 19th century were **horizontal** and **vertical integration**. One is legal; one is not; both were practiced by "captains of industry" during the Gilded Age. For all intents and purposes, horizontal integration created monopolies within a particular industry, the best-known example being Standard Oil, created by John D. Rockefeller. In horizontal integration, several smaller companies within the same industry are combined to form one larger company, either by being bought out legally or by being destroyed through ruthless business practices such as cutthroat competition or pooling agreements. Many of these business practices are illegal today because of antitrust legislation passed at the turn of the 20th century. Vertical integration remains legal, however, provided the company does not become either a trust or a holding company, but rather allows other companies in the same industry to survive and compete in the marketplace. In vertical integration, one company buys out all the factors of production, from raw materials to finished product. For example, Swift Premium might control the stockyards, the slaughterhouse, and the processing and packaging plants but still compete with Oscar Mayer or Hebrew National.

Numerous problems arose because of this consolidation of power. First, rapid growth required lots of money. Businessmen borrowed huge sums, and when their businesses occasionally failed, bank failures could result. During the last quarter of the 19th century, the United States endured one major financial panic per decade. Although irresponsible investors caused the panics, the lower classes suffered the most, as jobs and money became scarce. Second, monopolies created a class of extremely powerful men whose interests clashed with those of the rest of society. As these businessmen grew more powerful, public resentment increased, and the government responded with laws to restrict monopolies (which the courts, in turn, weakened). The back-and-forth battle among the public, the government, and the courts is best exemplified by the **Sherman Antitrust Act of 1890**. Public pressure led to the passage of this law forbidding any "combination…or conspiracy in the restraint of trade."

Unfortunately, the wording of the Sherman Antitrust Act was ambiguous enough to allow the pro-business Supreme Court at the time to interpret the law as it saw fit. For example, in 1895, the Court ruled that E. C. Knight, the company that controlled 98 percent of the sugar refining plants in the United States, did not violate the Sherman Antitrust Act because local manufacturing was not subject to congressional regulation of interstate commerce. (*U.S. v. E. C. Knight Co.*, 1895.) On the other hand, labor unions were often found to be "in restraint of free trade" and declared illegal. This loophole was closed during Wilson's administration in 1914 with the passage of the Clayton Antitrust Act, which made allowances for collective bargaining.

Another "Gospel": The Social Gospel

Not to be confused with Carnegie's "Gospel of Wealth," the term "social gospel" was coined by Charles Oliver Brown in 1910. Some Protestants of the era articulated their social goals as the following:

"The great ends of the church are the proclamation of the gospel for the salvation of humankind; the shelter, nurture, and spiritual fellowship of the children of God; the maintenance of divine worship; the preservation of truth; the promotion of social righteousness; and the exhibition of the Kingdom of Heaven to the world."

Dismayed by poverty and urban slums, activists in the Social Gospel movement hoped that by promoting public health and education, the moral lives of the poor would begin to improve. Social Gospel activists also worked to abolish child labor and hoped to limit the number of hours employees could be required to work.

Another response to public pressure for reform came from industrialists themselves. Steel mogul **Andrew Carnegie** promoted a philosophy based on the work of Charles Darwin. Using Darwin's theory of evolution as an analogy, Carnegie argued that in business, as in nature, unrestricted competition allowed only the "fittest" to survive. This theory was called **Social Darwinism**. Aside from the fact that Carnegie's analogy to Darwin's theory was at best dubious, it also lacked consistency; while Carnegie argued against government regulation, he supported all types of government assistance to business (in the form of tax abatements, grants, tariffs, and so on). Carnegie further argued that the concentration of wealth among a few was the natural and most efficient result of capitalism. Carnegie also asserted that great wealth brought with it social responsibility. Dubbing his belief the **Gospel of Wealth**, he advocated philanthropy, as by building libraries and museums or funding medical research, but not charity. Some of his peers were as generous; others were not.

Factories and City Life

Manufacturers cut costs and maximized profits in every way they could imagine. They reduced labor costs by hiring **women** and **children**. In cities, where most factories were located, manufacturers hired the many newly arrived **immigrants** who were anxious for work. Because manufacturers paid as little as possible, the cities in which their employees lived suffered many of the problems associated with poverty, such as crime, disease, and the lack of livable housing for a rapidly expanding population. As mentioned before, factories were dangerous, and many families had at least one member who had been disabled at work. Insurance and workmen's compensation did not exist then, either.

The poverty level in cities also rose because those who could afford it moved away from the city center. As factories sprang up, cities became dirtier and generally less healthy environments. Advances in **mass transportation**, such as the expansion of railroad lines, streetcars, and the construction of subways, allowed the middle class to live in nicer neighborhoods, including bedroom communities in the suburbs, and commute to work. (The growing middle class was made up of managers, secretaries, bureaucrats, merchants, and the like.) As a result, immigrants and migrants made up the majority of city populations. Starting around 1880, the majority of immigrants arrived from Southern and Eastern Europe. (Prior to 1880, most immigrants to America came from northern and western Europe.) Prejudice against the new arrivals was widespread, and many immigrants settled in **ethnic neighborhoods** usually in **tenements**. Worse off still were **black** and **Latino** migrants. Many employers refused them any but the worst jobs.

Municipal governments of the era were not like those of today. In fact, such governments were practically nonexistent. Most Americans expected churches, private charities, and ethnic communities to provide services for the poor. However, many of those services were provided instead by a group of corrupt men called **political bosses**. Bosses helped the poor find homes and jobs; they also helped them apply for citizenship and voting rights. They built parks, funded auxiliary police and fire departments, and constructed roads and sewage lines. In return, they expected community members to vote as they were instructed. Occasionally, they also required "donations" to help fund community projects. Political bosses—whose organizations were called **political machines**—rendered services that communities would not otherwise have received. However, because the bosses resorted to criminal means to accomplish their goals, the cost of their services was high. The most notorious of these bosses was "Boss" Tweed of Tammany Hall in New York City.

William "Boss" Tweed became a New York City alderman in the 1850s. He expanded his influence by gaining a seat on New York's Board of Supervisors, which allowed him to embezzle millions of dollars through corruption in city construction projects. Tweed also became a prominent leader of Tammany Hall, the political machine of New York's Democratic Party. Tweed gave out jobs, homes, and protection to new immigrants in exchange for their votes in local elections. By the 1870s, Tweed's power became noticeable to leading journalists, including *The New York Times* and political cartoonist Thomas Nast. Nast drew images of Tweed's corrupt practices in *Harper's Weekly,* and *The New York Times* published ledgers proving that Tweed embezzled millions of dollars through extortion and fraudulent construction projects. One estimate claimed that Tweed charged the city of New York almost $180,000 ($2.5 million today) for 3 tables and 40 chairs, and that one worker earned over $130,000 ($1.8 million today) for two days' work. Tweed was eventually found guilty and died in prison in 1878, but not before escaping from prison and getting all the way to Spain, only to be recaptured because people recognized him from Nast's cartoons.

Widespread misery in cities led many to seek changes. Labor unions formed to try to counter the poor treatment of workers. Unions were considered radical organizations by many, and the government was wary of them; businesses and the courts were openly hostile to them. Hired goons and, in some cases, federal troops often broke strikes. Before the Civil War, the few unions that existed were small, regional, or local and represented workers within a specific craft or industry. One of the first national labor unions was the **Knights of Labor**, founded in 1869 by Uriah Stephens, a Philadelphia tailor.

The Knights organized skilled and unskilled workers from a variety of crafts into a single union. Their goals included (1) an eight-hour workday; (2) equal pay for equal work for men and women (this would not become a federal law until 1963); (3) child labor laws, including the prohibition of working under the age of 14; (4) safety and sanitary codes; (5) a federal income tax (not enacted until the ratification of the Sixteenth Amendment in 1913); and (6) government ownership of railroad and telegraph lines.

Identification

One important shift during the 19th century was that from vertical identification to horizontal identification. For example, in 1800, an apprentice shoemaker would likely think of himself as belonging to a class with journeyman shoemakers and master shoemakers. By 1850, he would be much more likely to think of himself as belonging to a class with apprentice tailors and apprentice blacksmiths.

Although the Knights advocated arbitration over strikes, they became increasingly violent in efforts to achieve their goals. By the 1880s, after a series of unsuccessful strikes under the leadership of **Terrence Powderly**, the popularity of the Knights began to decline. The American public began to associate unions with violence and political radicalism. Propagandists claimed that unions were subversive forces—a position reinforced in public opinion by the **Haymarket Square Riot**. During an 1886 labor demonstration in Chicago's Haymarket Square, a bomb went off, killing police. Many blamed the incident on the influence of radicals within the union movement, although no one knew who set off the bomb.

In 1892, workers at Carnegie's Homestead Steel factory went on strike, protesting a wage cut and the refusal of factory manager Henry Clay Frick to allow them to form a union. Frick locked out the workers when their contract expired, hired replacement workers, and then called in the Pinkerton Detective force to prevent the steel workers from protesting. The ensuing clash between the Pinkertons and the strikers led to several deaths and the retreat of the Pinkertons. Eventually, the Pennsylvania state militia ended the strike, and Frick hired new workers to replace the striking workers.

In 1894, workers at the Pullman Palace Car Factory faced a wage cut and an increase in the cost of their housing. They organized a strike, and the American Railway Union (ARU) joined their strike in May, leading to over 250,000 railway workers walking off the job, shutting down rail travel in 27 states. ARU president Eugene Debs refused to end the strike, even after President Cleveland ordered the Army to stop the strike and Debs was ordered to stop the strike because it was disrupting delivery of federal mail. Debs was convicted and jailed for refusing to follow a court order. While in jail, Debs is said to have read Karl Marx's *Communist Manifesto*. When released from jail, he became active in the socialist movement, and eventually became the leader of the American Socialist party.

Many early unions did indeed subscribe to utopian and/or socialist philosophies. Later on, the **American Federation of Labor**, led by **Samuel Gompers**, avoided those larger political questions, concentrating instead on such "bread and butter" issues as higher wages and shorter workdays, an approach that proved successful. Gompers also realized that his union could gain more power if it excluded unskilled workers; the AFL was formed as a confederation of **trade unions** (i.e., unions made up exclusively of workers within a single trade). The history of early unions is marred by the fact that most refused to accept immigrants, blacks, and women among their memberships.

Charitable middle-class organizations, usually run by women, also made efforts at urban reform. These groups lobbied local governments for building-safety codes, better sanitation, and public schools. Frustrated by government's slow pace, their members also founded and lived in **settlement houses** in poor neighborhoods. These houses became community centers, providing schooling, childcare, and cultural activities. In Chicago, for example, **Jane Addams** founded Hull House to provide such services as English lessons for immigrants, day care for children of working mothers, childcare classes for parents, and playgrounds for children. Addams also campaigned for increased government services in the slums. She was awarded the Nobel Peace Prize for her life's work in 1931.

While the poor suffered, life improved for both the wealthy and the middle class. Increased production and wealth meant greater access to luxuries and more leisure time. Sports, high theater, vaudeville (variety acts), and, later, movies became popular diversions. It was also during this period that large segments of the public began to read **popular novels** and **newspapers**. The growth of the newspaper industry was largely the responsibility of **Joseph Pulitzer** and **William Randolph Hearst**, both of whom understood the commercial value of bold, screaming headlines and lurid tales of scandal. This new style of sensational reporting became known as **yellow journalism**.

Jim Crow Laws and Other Developments in the South

Most of the advances made during the machine age affected primarily Northern cities. In the South, agriculture continued as the main form of labor. The industrialization programs of Reconstruction did produce some results, however. Textile mills sprang up around the South, reducing cotton farmers' reliance on the North. Tobacco processing plants also employed some workers. Still, the vast majority of Southerners remained farmers.

Postwar economics forced many farmers to sell their land, which wealthy landowners bought and consolidated into larger farms. Landless farmers, both black and white, were forced into **sharecropping**. The method by which they rented land was called the **crop lien system**; it was designed to keep the poor in constant debt. Because these farmers had no cash, they borrowed what they needed to buy seed and tools, promising a portion of their crop as collateral. Huge interest rates on their loans and unscrupulous landlords pretty much guaranteed that these farmers would never overcome their debt, forcing them to borrow further and promise their *next* crop as collateral. In this way, landlords kept the poor, both black and white, in a state of virtual slavery.

The advent of **Jim Crow laws** made matters worse for blacks. As the federal government exerted less influence over Southern states, towns and cities passed numerous discriminatory laws. The Supreme Court assisted the states by ruling that the Fourteenth Amendment did not protect blacks from discrimination by privately owned businesses and that blacks would have to seek equal protection from the states, not from the federal government. In 1883, the Court also reversed the Civil Rights Act of 1875 (which said that businesses and public facilities couldn't be segregated), thus opening the door to legal (*de jure*) segregation. In 1896, the Supreme

Excerpt from Booker T. Washington's Atlanta Compromise speech

"In conclusion, may I repeat that nothing in thirty years has given us more hope and encouragement, and drawn us so near to you of the white race, as this opportunity offered by the Exposition; and here bending, as it were, over the altar that represents the results of the struggles of your race and mine, both starting practically empty-handed three decades ago, I pledge that in your effort to work out the great and intricate problem which God has laid at the doors of the South, you shall have at all times the patient, sympathetic help of my race; only let this be constantly in mind, that, while from representations in these buildings of the product of field, of forest, of mine, of factory, letters, and art, much good will come, yet far above and beyond material benefits will be that higher good, that, let us pray God, will come, in a blotting out of sectional differences and racial animosities and suspicions, in a determination to administer absolute justice, in a willing obedience among all classes to the mandates of law. This, coupled with our material prosperity, will bring into our beloved South a new heaven and a new earth."

Court ruled in *Plessy v. Ferguson* that the role of the federal government was not to maintain social equality. It went on to establish that "separate but equal" facilities for the different races were legal. In so doing, the Court set back the civil rights gains made during Reconstruction.

In this atmosphere, integration and equal rights for blacks seemed to most a far-off dream. **Booker T. Washington** certainly felt that way. A Southern black born into slavery, Washington harbored no illusions that white society was ready to accept blacks as equals. Instead, he promoted economic independence as the means by which blacks could improve their lot. To pursue that goal, he founded the Tuskegee Institute, a vocational and industrial training school for blacks. Some accused Washington of being an **accommodationist** because he refused to press for immediate equal rights. Others believed that Washington simply accepted the reality of his time when he set his goals. In his Atlanta Exposition, a famous speech delivered in Atlanta, Georgia, in 1895, Washington outlined his view of race relations. Washington's more aggressive rival W. E. B. Du Bois (see Chapter 11) referred to the speech, which he deemed submissive, as "The Atlanta Compromise."

The Railroads and Developments in the West

On the western frontier, **ranching** and **mining** were growing industries. Ranchers drove their herds across the western plains and deserts, ignoring property rights and Native American prerogatives to the land. Individual miners lacked the resources to mine and cart big loads, so mostly they prospected; when they found a rich mine, they staked a claim and sold their rights to a mining company.

In the second year of the Civil War, Lincoln issued a challenge to America not unlike Kennedy's 1961 pledge to reach the Moon—that before the decade was out, America would have a Transcontinental Railroad connecting one side of the country to the other. From 1863 to 1869, former farmers, immigrants, freed slaves, and Civil War veterans worked to make Lincoln's vision a reality. The railroad's arrival changed the West in many ways. The railroads, although owned privately, were built largely at the public's expense, through direct funding and substantial grants of land to the railroads. Both federal and local governments were anxious for rails to be completed and so provided substantial assistance. Although the public had paid for the rail system, rail proprietors strenuously objected to any government control of their industry, and it took years for railroad rates to come under regulation. Until they were regulated, the railroads would typically overcharge wherever they owned a monopoly and undercharge in competitive and heavily trafficked markets. This practice was particularly harmful to farmers in remote areas.

As railroad construction crawled across the nation, rail companies organized massive hunts for buffalo (considered a nuisance). Railroad bounty hunters hunted the herds to near extinction, destroying a resource upon which local Native Americans had depended. Some tribes, such as the Sioux, fought back, giving the government an excuse to send troops into the region. While Native Americans won some battles (notably at **Little Big Horn**, where George Custer met his death), the federal army ultimately overpowered them.

The railroads brought other changes as well. Rails quickly transformed depot towns into vital cities by connecting them to civilization. Easier, faster travel meant more contact with ideas and technological advances from the East. Developments in railroad technology had applications in other industries and so accelerated the Industrial Revolution. In addition, "railroad time," by which rail schedules were determined, gave the nation its first standardized method of time telling with the adoption of time zones.

As the rails pushed the country westward, settlers started filling in the territory. By 1889, North Dakota, South Dakota, Washington, and Montana were populous enough to achieve statehood; Wyoming and Idaho followed in 1890. The result of the 1890 census prompted the Progressive historian Frederick Jackson Turner to declare that the American frontier was gone, and with it the first period of American history. Turner argued that the frontier was significant in (1) shaping the American character, (2) defining the American spirit, (3) fostering democracy, and (4) providing a safety valve for economic distress in urban, industrial centers by providing a place to which people could flee. Historians refer to these ideas collectively as the **Turner** or **Frontier Thesis**.

In the Great Plains, farming and ranching constituted the main forms of employment. New farm machinery and access to mail (and mail-order retail) made life on the plains easier, but it was still lonely and difficult. The government, realizing the potential of the region as the nation's chief agricultural center, passed two significant pieces of legislation in 1862—the **Homestead Act** and the **Morrill Land-Grant Act**. Anxious to attract settlers to develop the West, the federal government offered 160 acres of land to anyone who would "homestead" it (cultivate the land, build a home, and live there) for five years. It was quickly discovered that 160 acres wasn't enough to productively farm on some of the very dry land in the West or to compete with some of the large-scale commercial agricultural farms, so subsequent acts had to give out more land if farmers agreed to irrigate the land or plant trees on the land. Of course, the government was giving away land that belonged to Native Americans. Furthermore, private speculators and railroad companies often exploited the law for their own personal economic gain. The Morrill Land-Grant Act set aside land and provided money for agricultural colleges. Eventually, agricultural science became a huge industry in the United States.

The **Nez Perce** were an Indian tribe in northeast Oregon. As it did with many tribes, the U.S. government forced them to migrate to a small reservation in Idaho. **Chief Joseph** led his people in resistance to this removal, but eventually surrendered to federal power. Along with Sitting Bull, Chief Joseph became one of the most well-known Indians of his time.

With many families and corporations heading West, both government and conservation groups sought for added protection of natural resources. The **U.S. Fish Commission** was created in 1871 to study, monitor, and preserve wild fisheries. Today the Fish Commission is part of the U.S. Fish and Wildlife Service, a division of the Department of the Interior. In 1892, naturalist **John Muir** created the **Sierra Club**, one of the first large organizations devoted to conservation in the United States. Later, President Theodore Roosevelt would be known as a president who furthered environmental preservation of the West through the National Parks system.

In this expansionist era, those who lost out the most were, of course, the Native Americans. At first, pioneers approached the tribes as sovereign nations. They made treaties with them, which the settlers or their immediate successors broke. The result was warfare, leading the government to try another approach. The new tack was to force Native Americans onto reservations, which typically were made up of the least desirable land in a tribe's traditional home region. The reservation system failed for a number of reasons, including the inferiority of the land, the grouping of incompatible tribes on the same reservation, and the lack of autonomy granted the tribes in managing their own affairs. Moreover, some Westerners simply ignored the arrangement and poached on reservation lands. Helen Hunt Jackson's book *A Century of Dishonor* detailed the injustices of the reservation system and inspired reformers to push for change, which came in 1887 in the form of the **Dawes Severalty Act**.

The Dawes Severalty Act broke up the reservations and distributed some of the land to the head of each Native American family. Similar to the Homestead Act, the allotment was 160 acres of land. This time, however, it was required that the family live on the land for 25 years, after which time the land was legally theirs. And the grand prize was American citizenship! The Dawes Act was intended as a humanitarian solution to the "Indian problem"; its main goal was to accelerate the assimilation of Native Americans into Western society by integrating them more closely with whites. Native Americans, naturally, resisted. Furthermore, poverty drove many to sell their land to speculators, leaving them literally homeless.

Some displaced Indians turned to religion for comfort. The **Ghost Dance Movement** started in 1889, inspired by the visions of the prophet Wovoka. In his prophecies, Wovoka promised followers that, through proper ceremony and supernatural magic, federal expansion in the West would end and Indians would live peacefully on their native lands. Many Lakota Sioux were active in the Ghost Dance Movement and later met their bloody fate at the hands of federal agents during the **Wounded Knee Massacre**, a dispute started by cavalry troops intent on disarming the members of the Pine Ridge Reservation. Hundreds of Lakota were killed or injured and the site of the battlefield is now a National Historic Landmark.

National Politics

Mark Twain dubbed the era between Reconstruction and 1900 the **Gilded Age** of politics. Gilded metals have a shiny, gold-like surface, but beneath lies a cheap base. America looked to have entered a period of prosperity, with a handful of families having amassed unprecedented wealth, but the

Civil Service Reform

The "spoils system" pioneered by Andrew Jackson meant that every time a new president took office, thousands of government jobs opened up, and it was the president's responsibility to fill them. This is what the presidents of the mid-19th century did with their days. For instance, even as the Civil War raged, Abraham Lincoln spent morning, afternoon, and evening dealing with the job applicants who lined up outside his office, the line winding through the White House and out the door onto Pennsylvania Avenue.

Within the Republican Party, who dominated control of the White House following the Civil War, a split developed between **Stalwarts**, who believed that all government jobs should go to loyal Republicans, and **Half-Breeds**, who thought that qualified Democrats should be able to keep their jobs even after a Republican was elected. When a frustrated job-seeker assassinated President Garfield, it became clear that something had to be done about the way government employment was handled. His successor, Chester Arthur, had been a Stalwart, but he signed the **Pendleton Civil Service Reform Act** that began the dismantling of the old spoils system.

affluence of a few was built on the poverty of many. Similarly, American politics looked like a shining example of representative democracy, but just beneath the surface lay crass corruption and patronage. Political machines, not municipal governments, ran the cities. Big business bought votes in Congress and then turned around and fleeced consumers. Workers had little protection from the greed of their employers because the courts turned a deaf ear to worker complaints. In other words, Twain was right on the money.

The presidents of this era were generally not corrupt. They were, however, relatively weak. (The president is only as powerful as his support allows him to be; thus popular presidents, such as Andrew Jackson and Franklin Roosevelt, were able to accomplish so much.) Don't expect too many questions about the presidents of this period, but for the record, **Rutherford B. Hayes, James Garfield**, and **Chester A. Arthur** concerned themselves primarily with civil service reform (see the accompanying box on the previous page), while **Grover Cleveland** believed that government governed best which governed least. **Benjamin Harrison** took the opposite tack, and he and his allies in the Capitol passed everything from the nation's first meat inspection act to the banning of lotteries to the purchase of several battleships. Much of the legislation we have discussed, from the Sherman Antitrust Act to the second Morrill Land-Grant Colleges Act, was passed under Harrison's watch. But the public's discomfort with the activism of Harrison and the **Billion-Dollar Congress** of 1890 led to Grover Cleveland's return to the White House.

In response to the outcry over widespread corruption, the government made its first stabs at regulating itself and business. Many states imposed **railroad regulations** because railroads were engaging in price gouging. In 1877, the Supreme Court upheld an Illinois state law regulating railroads and grain elevators in the case of *Munn v. Illinois*. This was a surprising decision, given that railroads crossed state lines and only Congress can regulate interstate commerce. The Court argued that states had the power to regulate private industry that served the "public interest." Although the Supreme Court would reaffirm Congress's authority nine years later in the *Wabash* case, when it ruled that states could *not* establish rates involving interstate commerce, an important precedent for regulating business in the public's interest had been established.

In 1887, just one year after the *Wabash* decision, Congress passed the first federal regulatory law in U.S. history. The **Interstate Commerce Act** set up the Interstate Commerce Commission (ICC) to supervise railroad activities and regulate unfair and unethical practices. (The ICC wasn't disbanded until the 1980s under the Reagan administration, when, in attempts to save money, the federal government deregulated many forms of transportation.)

It was also during this period that **women's suffrage** became an important political issue. **Susan B. Anthony** led the fight, convincing Congress to introduce a suffrage amendment to the Constitution. The bill was introduced every year and rarely got out of committee, but the fight had begun in earnest. Meanwhile, organizations such as the **American Suffrage Association** fought for women's suffrage amendments to state constitutions. By 1890, they had achieved some partial successes, gaining the vote on school issues. (Women finally gained the right to vote with the ratification of the Nineteenth Amendment in 1920—fifty years after male suffrage became universal.)

The Silver Issue and the Populist Movement

In the period after the Civil War, production on all fronts—industrial and agricultural—increased. Greater supply accordingly led to a drop in prices. For many farmers, lower prices meant trouble, as they were locked into long-term debts with fixed payments. Looking for a solution to their problem, farmers came to support a more generous money supply. An increase in available money, they correctly figured, would make payments easier. It would also cause inflation, which would make the farmers' debts (held by Northern banks) worth less. Not surprisingly, the banks opposed the plan, preferring for the country to use only gold to back its money supply.

The farmers' plan called for the liberal use of silver coins, and because silver was mined in the West, this plan had the added support of Western miners along with that of Midwestern and Southern farmers. Thus, the issue had a regional component. Because it pitted poor farmers against wealthy bankers, it also had elements of class strife. Although a complicated matter, the money issue was potentially explosive.

Although the Grangers were the most influential group of united farmers, with chapters from New England to the West, there were other groups started by minority farmers that are less well known but which made an impact in their local regions. **Las Gorras Blancas** was founded in 1889 by New Mexican farmers whose land was being taken by Anglo-American settlers. Though their tactics were at times violent, several of their leaders ran for political positions under the banner of the Populist Party. In Texas, the **Colored Farmers' Alliance**, formed in 1886, invited black farmers to organize for their collective interests. Like Las Gorras Blancas, the Colored Farmers were largely Populists.

The "silver versus gold" debate provided an issue around which farmers could organize. They did just that. First came the **Grange Movement**, which, founded in 1867, boasted more than a million members by 1875. The Grangers started out as cooperatives, with the purpose of allowing farmers to buy machinery and sell crops as a group and, therefore, reap the benefits of economies of scale. Soon, the Grangers endorsed political candidates and lobbied for legislation. The Grangers ultimately died out because of a lack of money, but they were replaced by **Farmers' Alliances**. The Alliances allowed women to be politically active (Mary Elizabeth Lease was a huge organizer for them), and they had branches all around the nation. The Farmers' Alliances were even more successful than the Grange Movement, and they soon grew into a political party called the **People's Party**, the political arm of the **Populist** movement.

The Grangers were responsible for most of the laws regulating the railroads in the 1870s and 1880s. These are referred to as the Granger Laws.

The People's Party held a convention in 1892. (Their platform was called the Omaha Platform. It called for solidarity with industrial workers, opposition to immigration to help American workers, and trying to earn more support for Eastern laborers, among other things.) Aside from supporting the generous coinage of silver, the Populists called for government ownership of railroads and telegraphs, a graduated income tax, direct election of U.S. senators, and shorter workdays. Although their 1892 presidential candidate, James Weaver, came in third, he won more than 1 million votes, awakening Washington to the growing Populist movement.

As Cleveland took office in 1893, the country entered a four-year financial crisis. Hard economic times made Populist goals more popular, particularly the call for easy money. (Most people at the time, after all, had no money at all.) Times got so bad that even more progressive (some would say radical) movements gained popularity; in 1894, the **Socialists**, led by **Eugene V. Debs**, gained support. By 1896, the Populists were poised for power. They backed Democratic candidate **William Jennings Bryan** against Republican nominee **William McKinley**, and Bryan ran on a strictly Populist platform; he based his campaign on the call for **free silver**. He is probably best remembered for his "Cross of Gold" speech (a typical multiple-choice question). He argued that an easy money supply, though inflationary, would loosen the control that Northern banking interests held over the country. The Republicans, on the other hand, became solidly allied with big businesses, as McKinley received huge campaign contributions from large companies. Business leaders told their employees that they would lose their jobs if Bryan won the election. Bryan lost the campaign; this, coupled with an improved economy, ended the Populist movement.

Foreign Policy: The Tariff and Imperialism

Before the Civil War, most Americans earned their living by farming. By 1900, however, the United States had become the leading industrial power in the world. It is difficult for us to imagine the enormous controversy surrounding the issue of the tariff throughout U.S. history. Remember that there was no federal income tax until the Sixteenth Amendment was adopted in 1913. Clearly, the most infamous tariff was the **Tariff of Abominations** (1828). This ultimately triggered the nullification crisis during Jackson's first administration. Following the Civil War, the tariff came to dominate national politics, as industrialists competing in an international market demanded high tariffs to protect domestic industries. Farmers and laborers, on the other hand, were hurt by high tariffs. Generally, Democrats supported lower tariffs while Republicans advocated high, protective tariffs.

In 1890, Congress enacted the McKinley Tariff, which raised the level of duties on imported goods almost 50 percent. Certain products, however, such as unprocessed sugar, were put on a duty-free list. Then, in 1894, Congress passed the Wilson-Gorman Tariff, which essentially resembled the schedule established by the **McKinley Tariff**, despite heated debate between members of the House of Representatives and the Senate. The tariff issue not only dominated congressional debate, it also had a tremendous impact on foreign relations (see below). For example, the Wilson-Gorman Tariff is usually considered one of the causes of the **Spanish-American War**.

Throughout the machine age, American production capacity grew rapidly. As we have already discussed, not every American had enough money to buy the products he or she made at work. America began looking overseas to find **new markets**. Increased **nationalism** also led American business to look for new markets. America's centennial celebration in 1876 heightened national pride, as did awareness that the country was becoming a world economic power. As Americans became more certain that their way of life was best, they hoped to spread that around the globe. This philosophy led American influence to expand into a number of new arenas.

First, **William H. Seward**, secretary of state under Lincoln and Johnson, set the precedent for increased American participation in any and all doings in the Western Hemisphere. In particular, Seward engineered the purchase of Alaska and invoked the Monroe Doctrine to force France out of Mexico. In the following decade,

An easy way to remember the Populists is through the book *The Wizard of Oz* by L. Frank Baum. The novel is reportedly a political allegory, with Dorothy representing the common man, her silver shoes (the movie changed them into ruby slippers) representing the silver standard, the scarecrow representing the farmer, and the Tin Man representing the industrial worker. William Jennings Bryan was said to be the model for the Cowardly Lion.

Theodore Roosevelt was assistant secretary of the Navy in 1898 during the Spanish-American War, and he ordered the U.S. Pacific Fleet to the Philippines. He then resigned from the Navy and led a volunteer regiment of cavalry troops in Cuba.

American businesses began developing markets and production facilities in Latin America, and gradually they gained political power in the region.

As long as America moved into regions to do business, it was practicing **expansionism**, which most Americans supported. When the United States took control of another country, however, it was exercising **imperialism**, a more controversial practice. A book by naval Captain Alfred T. Mahan, called *The Influence of Sea Power Upon History* (1890), piqued the government's interest in imperialism. Mahan argued that successful foreign trade relied on access to foreign ports, which in turn required overseas colonies, and colonies in turn required a strong navy. The book popularized the idea of the **New Navy**, and after the United States invested in upgrading its ships, it turned its attention to foreign acquisitions.

The search for a port along the trade route to Asia attracted the United States to **Hawaii**. Foreign missionaries had arrived in Hawaii in the early 1800s, but significant U.S. involvement there began in the 1870s, when American sugar producers started trading with the Hawaiians. Due in large part to American interference, the Hawaiian economy collapsed in the 1890s. The United States had allowed Hawaii tariff-free access to American markets. Then, when Hawaii became dependent on trade with the United States, the government imposed high tariffs (the McKinley Tariff mentioned above), thereby greatly diminishing Hawaiian exports. The white minority overthrew the native government, and, eventually, the United States annexed Hawaii. Japan was outraged; more than 40 percent of Hawaii's residents were of Japanese descent. That anger would resurface during World War II.

Another opportunity for American expansion arose when Cuban natives revolted against Spanish control. The revolution in **Cuba**, like the Hawaiian revolution, was instigated by U.S. tampering with the Cuban economy (by imposing high import tariffs, as discussed above). A violent Cuban civil war followed, reported in all its gory detail in the sensational Hearst newspaper (see "yellow journalism," earlier in this chapter). When an American warship, the *Maine*, exploded in the Havana harbor under circumstances that remain a mystery, the drumbeats for war grew deafening. In the ensuing war, the United States not only drove Spain out of Cuba, but also sent a fleet to the Spanish-controlled **Philippines** and drove the Spanish out of there too. In the **Treaty of Paris**, Spain granted Cuba independence and ceded the Philippines, Puerto Rico, and Guam to the United States. Remember that Hawaii was annexed the same year but not because of the Spanish-American War. Also, note that this was the third Treaty of Paris that matters in U.S. history. The first ended the French and Indian War in 1763, while the second ended the Revolutionary War in 1783.

Despite the Teller Amendment, in which the United States claimed it would not annex Cuba after Spain's departure from the island in 1898, U.S. troops remained in Cuba for another few years. Then, in 1901, Cuba was compelled to include a series of provisions in its new constitution. The United States made it quite clear that its troops would not leave unless Cuba agreed to these provisions, collectively known as the **Platt Amendment**. The United States was basically given control over Cuba's foreign affairs. Under the guise of protecting Cuba's political and social stability and thus its independence, the following terms were established: (1) Cuba was not permitted to sign any foreign treaty without the consent of the United States, (2) the

United States could intervene in Cuban domestic and foreign affairs, and (3) the United States was granted land on which to build a naval base and coaling station. The Platt Amendment was ultimately repealed in 1934 during **FDR's** administration as part of his **Good Neighbor Policy**. The United States continues to operate a naval station at Guantanamo Bay, however. (Yes, *that* Guantanamo Bay.)

Control of the Philippines raised a tricky question: "Should the United States annex the Philippines, or should it grant the country the independence its people sought?" Proponents of annexing the Philippines argued that if the United States granted Filipinos their independence, the archipelago would simply be conquered by another European nation, with the only result being that the United States would lose a valuable possession. Perhaps most compelling, and certainly the best-known rationale for U.S. annexation of the Philippine Islands, was the belief that the United States had a moral obligation to "Christianize and civilize" the Filipinos, who were already overwhelmingly Christian—albeit Catholic, which didn't count for some Protestant imperialists—and preferred to achieve "civilization" in their own way. The notion that people not of European extraction were unfit to rule themselves came to be known as the "white man's burden," from the title of a poem written by Rudyard Kipling in response to the United States' annexation of the Philippines. Opponents felt that the United States should promote independence and democracy, both noble national traditions. To control the Philippines, they argued, would make the United States no better than the British tyrants they overthrew in the Revolutionary War. In the end, the Senate voted to annex the Philippines. It was a very close margin. The Senate needed 56 votes to get the two-thirds majority needed to ratify a treaty, and got 57, meaning that there were 27 senators who opposed the treaty. Filipino nationalists responded by waging a guerrilla war against the United States. In response, the United States used incredibly brutal tactics to subdue the Filipino revolt and inflict huge casualties on the civilian population. Although the United States eventually gained control of the country, the Philippines remained a source of controversy for decades. The United States granted the Philippines independence in 1946.

As the United States acquired an overseas empire, a fundamental question arose as to the legal status of the native population living in these territories: "Does the Constitution follow the flag?" In other words, were colonial subjects entitled to the same protections and privileges granted to U.S. citizens by the Constitution? The Supreme Court settled this issue by a series of rulings known collectively as the **Insular Cases** (1901–1903). The Court ruled that the Constitution did *not* follow the flag; Congress was free to administer each overseas possession as it chose, depending on the particular situation in any given foreign territory.

Finally, America hoped to gain entry into Asian markets. To that end, McKinley sought an **Open Door Policy** for all Western nations hoping to trade with Asia. The European nations that had colonized China were not so keen on the idea; to their way of thinking, they fought for those markets and planned to keep them. When Chinese nationalists (known as the **Boxers**) rose against European imperialism and besieged the Beijing legation quarter, the United States sent troops to help suppress the rebels. In return, Germany, France, and England grew more receptive to America's foreign policy objectives.

American imperialism would continue through Theodore Roosevelt's administration. We'll discuss that period in the next chapter.

Summary

Here are the most important concepts to remember from the Industrial Revolution period.

o   The Industrial Revolution changed not only industry, but also virtually every aspect of American daily life, ushering in urbanization and manufacturing, stimulating immigration and migration North.

o   Large businesses stimulated economic growth and largely thrived on little to no governmental regulation.

o   Work opportunities opened up for women and minorities—but also led to widespread child labor.

o   Corruption in government and corporate abuses of power led to social reformers calling for change.

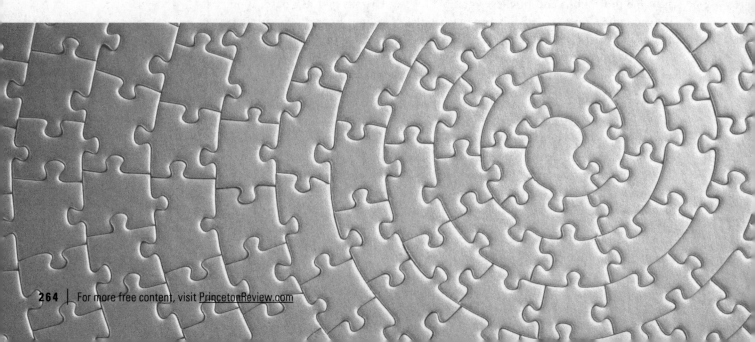

Chapter 10 Review Questions

See Chapter 14 for answers and explanations.

1. The scalawags were

    (A) another name for the Redeemers, who refused to accept the fact that the South had lost the Civil War

    (B) Northern politicians who traveled to the South after the Civil War to exploit the political and economic instability for their own personal gain

    (C) advocates of civil rights for the newly freed slaves

    (D) white Southerners who supported Republican policies during Reconstruction

2. Which of the following statements about Supreme Court decisions during the latter part of the 19th century is most accurate?

    (A) They reduced federal power over the states by narrowly defining the applicability of the Constitution to state law.

    (B) They cleared the way for the liberal reforms of the 20th century by broadly interpreting constitutional guarantees of individual rights.

    (C) They had little practical effect because the executive branch consistently refused to enforce the Court's rulings.

    (D) They used the Fourteenth Amendment to create numerous environmental regulations and human rights, stifling American business growth.

3. The term *vertical integration* refers to

    (A) Reconstruction-era efforts to assimilate newly freed slaves into all social strata of American society

    (B) an architectural movement that sought to blend urban skyscrapers with the natural landscape surrounding them

    (C) the industrial practice of assigning workers a single, repetitive task in order to maximize productivity

    (D) control of all aspects of an industry, from production of raw materials to delivery of finished goods

4. The passage of the Pendleton Act was a direct result of the

    (A) assassination of Abraham Lincoln

    (B) failure of Reconstruction

    (C) assassination of James A. Garfield

    (D) Supreme Court decision in *Plessy v. Ferguson*

5. The Haymarket Affair represented a major setback for the

    (A) women's suffrage movement

    (B) civil rights movement for African Americans

    (C) Knights of Labor

    (D) Temperance movement

6. Japan was outraged by the American annexation of Hawaii in 1898 primarily because

    (A) Japan depended heavily on trade with Hawaii to support its economy

    (B) the United States had signed a treaty with Japan granting Japan rights to Hawaii

    (C) the Japanese were committed to the principle of self-rule throughout the Pacific

    (D) nearly half of Hawaii's residents were of Japanese descent

7. The "new immigrants" who arrived in the United States after the Civil War were different from the "old immigrants" in that they

    (A) came mostly from Latin American countries

    (B) settled in rural areas in the Midwest where land was plentiful

    (C) were better prepared than previous immigrants had been to face the challenges of urban life

    (D) spoke different languages and had different customs than most Americans and thus were not easily assimilated

8. The "Ghost Dance" movement among Western Native Americans stressed all of the following EXCEPT

(A) the belief that the world would soon come to an end
(B) rejection of alcohol and other trappings of white society
(C) unity among Native Americans of different tribes
(D) nonviolence

9. In the late 19th century, political machines such as Tammany Hall were successful primarily because

(A) they operated primarily in rural areas, where the government could not monitor their activities
(B) they focused on accomplishing only a narrow set of human rights objectives
(C) they championed the suffragettes and received their support in return
(D) machine politicians provided needed jobs and services to naturalized citizens in return for their votes

10. Which of the following was the intended result of the Dawes Severalty Act of 1887?

(A) Railroad companies would be persuaded to stop unfair pricing through a number of government incentives.
(B) Recently arrived European immigrants would be enticed into settling in the less-populated West.
(C) Legislators would be less likely to accept bribes because of the severity of the penalty.
(D) Native Americans would be coaxed off reservations by land grants and would thus assimilate into Western culture.

REFLECT

Respond to the following questions:

- For which content topics discussed in this chapter do you feel you have achieved sufficient mastery to answer multiple-choice questions correctly?

- For which content topics discussed in this chapter do you feel you have achieved sufficient mastery to discuss effectively in a short-answer question or an essay?

- On which content topics discussed in this chapter do you feel you need more work before you can answer multiple-choice questions correctly?

- On which content topics discussed in this chapter do you feel you need more work before you can discuss them effectively in a short-answer question or an essay?

- What parts of this chapter are you going to review again?

- Will you seek further help, outside of this book (such as a teacher, tutor, or AP Students), on any of the content in this chapter—and, if so, on what content?

Chapter 11
Unit 7: The Early
20th Century
(1890–1945)

THE PROGRESSIVE ERA AND WORLD WAR I (1900–1920)

The Populist movement dissipated, but not before raising the possibility of reform through government. The Populists' successes in both local and national elections encouraged others to seek change through political action. Building on Populism's achievements and adopting some of its goals (e.g., direct election of senators, opposition to monopolies), the **Progressives** came to dominate the first two decades of 20th-century American politics. While the Populists were mainly aggrieved farmers who advocated radical reforms, the Progressives were urban, middle-class reformers who wanted to increase the role of government in reform while maintaining a capitalist economy.

The Progressive Movement

One of the reasons Populism failed is that its constituents were mostly poor farmers whose daily struggle to make a living made political activity difficult. The **Progressives** achieved greater success in part because theirs was an urban, middle-class movement. Its proponents started with more economic and political clout than the Populists. Furthermore, Progressives could devote more time to the causes they championed. Also, because many Progressives were Northern and middle class, the Progressive movement did not intensify regional and class differences, as the Populist movement had.

The roots of Progressivism lay in the growing number of associations and organizations at the turn of the century. The National Woman Suffrage Association, the American Bar Association, and the National Municipal League are some of the many groups that rallied citizens around a cause or profession. Most of these groups' members were educated and middle class; the blatant corruption they saw in business and politics offended their senses of decency, as did the terrible plight of the urban poor.

Progressivism got a further boost from a group of journalists who wrote exposés of corporate greed and misconduct. These writers, dubbed **muckrakers** by Theodore Roosevelt, revealed widespread corruption in urban management (**Lincoln Steffens**'s *The Shame of the Cities*), oil companies (**Ida Tarbell's** *History of Standard Oil*), and the meatpacking industry (**Upton Sinclair's** *The Jungle*). Their books and news articles raised the moral stakes for Progressives.

Over the course of two decades, Progressives achieved great successes on both the local and national levels. They campaigned to change public attitudes toward education and government regulation in much the same way reformers of the previous century had campaigned for public enlightenment on the plight of orphans, prostitutes, and the mentally infirm.

New groups arose to lead the fight against discrimination but met with mixed success. **W. E. B. Du Bois** headed the **National Association for the Advancement of Colored People** (**NAACP**) in the quest for racial justice, an uphill battle so strenuous that, after a lifelong struggle, Du Bois abandoned the United States and moved to Africa. Meanwhile, women's groups continued to campaign for suffrage. The adamant, conservative opposition they faced gave birth to the **feminist** movement. One early advocate, **Margaret Sanger**, faced wide opposition for promoting the use of contraceptives (illegal in most places). The movement's greatest success was in winning women the right to vote, granted by the **Nineteenth Amendment** in 1920.

Wisconsin governor **Robert La Follette** led the way for many Progressive state leaders. Under his leadership, Wisconsin implemented plans for direct primary elections, progressive taxation, and rail regulation. Many states extended greater power to voters by adopting the **ballot initiative**, through which the voters could propose new laws; the **referendum**, which allowed the public to vote on new laws; and the **recall election**, which gave voters the power to remove officials from office before their terms expired. Working-class Progressives also won a number of victories on the state level, including limitations on the length of the work day, minimum-wage requirements, child labor laws, and urban housing codes. Many states adopted progressive income taxes (taxes that charge higher percentages for people with higher incomes), which served partially to redistribute the nation's wealth.

The most prominent Progressive leader was President **Theodore Roosevelt**. In the 1900 election, Republican Party leaders chose Roosevelt to be McKinley's running mate because they feared McKinley might become too powerful. McKinley was a conservative president, and Roosevelt was expected to emulate his policies, though rumors had begun to circulate that Roosevelt harbored progressive sympathies. When McKinley was assassinated in 1901, Roosevelt succeeded him.

Roosevelt showed his more liberal tendencies early on. In 1902, he directed the Justice Department to investigate a major railroad company, and then broke it up following the Sherman Antitrust Act. That same year, he worked to negotiate a labor conflict between coal mine owners and coal workers, giving large concessions to the workers. After he convincingly won the 1904 election on the strength of his handling of Latin American affairs, Roosevelt began boldly enacting a progressive agenda. He was the first to successfully use the **Sherman Antitrust Act** against monopolies, and he did so repeatedly during his term, earning the nickname "the Trustbuster." As president, Roosevelt went beyond regulation corporations. Inspired by Upton Sinclair's groundbreaking book *The Jungle*, which described the dangerous conditions in America's meatpacking factories, Roosevelt encouraged Congress to pass the Meat Inspection Act, which created federal standards for meatpacking factories. Congress also passed the Pure Food and Drug Act, which required all processed food and drugs to include ingredient labels. Roosevelt's desire to conserve natural resources led him to preserve millions of acres of forested land and to encourage Congress to create the National Park Service and the National Forest Service. Presidents Taft and Wilson continued to promote Progressive ideals. **William Howard Taft**, who won the election of 1908, spearheaded the drive for two constitutional amendments, one that instituted a national income tax (the Sixteenth Amendment) and another that allowed for the direct election of senators (the Seventeenth Amendment). He pursued monopolies even more aggressively than Roosevelt. On the foreign policy front, Taft is best known for "**dollar diplomacy**," the attempt to secure favorable relationships with

Double Duty
William Howard Taft is the only former president to sit on the Supreme Court of the United States. He was the tenth Chief Justice, serving from 1921 to 1930.

Latin American and East Asian countries by providing monetary loans. Roosevelt wanted Taft to succeed him in the presidency, but when Taft took actions that Roosevelt opposed, Roosevelt challenged him for the 1912 Republican primary. Party bosses supported Taft's more conservative policies, leading Roosevelt to run for the presidency on the Progressive ticket. Roosevelt and Taft split the Republican vote.

The Progressive Era is a turning point in American history because it marks the ever-increasing involvement of the federal government in our daily lives. It's no coincidence that Prohibition took effect during this era. The third Progressive president was **Woodrow Wilson**, a Democrat who had to distinguish himself from Teddy Roosevelt, who ran for reelection (after Taft's one term) on the Bull Moose ticket in 1912. While Roosevelt's policies are often referred to as **New Nationalism**, Wilson referred to his ideas and policies as **New Freedom**. Thomas Jefferson had suggested limiting the power of the federal government in order to protect individual liberty, but Wilson now argued that the federal government had to assume greater control over business to protect man's freedom. For Roosevelt, there were "good trusts and bad trusts." For Wilson trusts were monopolies, which violated freedom for workers and consumers. Wilson was committed to restoring competition through greater government regulation of the economy and lowering the tariff.

Wilson created the **Federal Trade Commission**, lobbied for and enforced the **Clayton Antitrust Act of 1914**, and helped create the **Federal Reserve System**, which gave the government greater control over the nation's finances.

Progressivism lasted until the end of World War I, at which point the nation, weary from war and from the devastating **Spanish Flu** outbreak of 1918, stepped back from its moral crusade. The war had torn apart the Progressive coalition; pacifist Progressives opposed the war while others supported it. A **Red Scare**, heightened by the Russian Revolution, further split the Progressive coalition by dividing the leftists from the moderates. Moreover, the Progressive movement had achieved many of its goals, and as it did, it lost the support of those interest groups whose ends had been met. Some say that the Progressive movement was brought to an end, at least in part, by its own success.

Foreign Policy and U.S. Entry into World War I

Roosevelt differed from his predecessor on domestic policy, but he concurred with his foreign policy. Roosevelt was, if anything, an even more devout imperialist than McKinley had been. In 1903, the Roosevelt administration strong-armed Cuba into accepting the **Platt Amendment**, which essentially committed Cuba to American control. Under Platt's stipulations, Cuba could not make a treaty with another nation without U.S. approval, and the United States had the right to intervene in Cuba's affairs if domestic order dissolved. A number of invasions and occupations by the Marine Corps resulted. For 10 of the years between 1906 and 1922, the American military occupied Cuba, arousing anti-American sentiments on the island.

Roosevelt's actions were equally interventionist throughout Central America. During his administration, the country set its sights on building a canal through the Central American isthmus; a canal would greatly shorten the sea trip from the East Coast to California. Congress approved a plan for a canal through **Panama**, at the time a province of Colombia. Because Colombia asked for more than the government was willing to spend, the United States encouraged Panamanian rebels to revolt and then supported the revolution. Not surprisingly, the new Panamanian government gave the United States a *much* better deal. Because American commercial interests were so closely tied to the canal's successful operation, the United States military became a fixed presence throughout the region. During the next 20 years, troops intervened repeatedly, claiming that Latin American domestic instability constituted a threat to American security. This assertion came to be known as the **Roosevelt Corollary to the Monroe Doctrine** and is often referred to as the Big Stick Policy.

American foreign policy continued to adhere to the Monroe Doctrine, which asserted America's right to assume the role of an international police force and intervene anywhere in the Western Hemisphere where it felt its national security was at stake. It also stated that the United States wanted no part of Europe's internal disputes. American commitment to that aspect of the Monroe Doctrine would soon be tested, as Europe started down the path leading to **World War I**. Complicating matters was the fact that the United States and England were quickly forming a close alliance. To America's benefit, England had not opposed its many forays into Central American politics, although it could have. The British were not merely being friendly; they were trying to line up the United States as a potential ally in their ongoing rivalry with Germany, the other great European power of the era.

Fortunately, you do not need to know the tangled series of events that led Europe into war in 1914. You do, however, have to know about the United States' initial efforts to stay out of the war and the events that ultimately drew it into the conflict. Woodrow Wilson won the election of 1912, a three-way race in which the third-party candidate, Theodore Roosevelt, outpolled Taft, the Republican incumbent. Wilson entered office with less than a commanding mandate—only 40 percent of the electorate voted for him. However, with regard to the simmering European conflict, he and the electorate were of the same mind: the United States should stay out of it.

When war broke out in Europe in August 1914, Wilson immediately declared the U.S. policy of **neutrality**. Neutrality called for America to treat all the belligerents fairly and without favoritism. It was Wilson's hope that the United States would help settle the conflict and emerge as the world's arbiter. However, the neutrality policy posed several immediate problems, owing to America's close relationship with England and relatively distant relationship with Germany and Austria-Hungary. A number of Wilson's advisors openly favored the Allies (led by the British).

The situation quickly grew more complicated. England's strategic location and superior navy allowed it to impose an effective **blockade** on shipments headed for Germany, particularly those coming from the United States. Protests proved futile; the British government impounded and confiscated American ships. They then paid for the cargo, reducing the pressure that American merchants would otherwise have put on the U.S. government to take action against the blockade.

Germany attempted to counter the blockade with **submarines**, or **U-boats**. According to contemporaneous international law, an attacker had to warn civilian ships before attacking. Submarines could not do this because doing so would eliminate their main advantage. Furthermore, when the Germans attacked civilian ships, it was usually because those ships were carrying military supplies. The Germans announced that they would attack any such ship, but that did not satisfy Wilson, who believed that the Germans should adhere to the strict letter of international law. Thus, when the German submarines sank the passenger ship *Lusitania* in 1915 (killing 1,198 passengers, including 128 Americans), the action provoked the condemnation of both the government and much of the public. That the *Lusitania* was carrying tons of ammunition to the British was a fact that received much less public attention than did the loss of 1,198 innocent lives.

The sinking of the *Lusitania*, and the bad publicity it generated, led the Germans to cease submarine warfare for a while. Britain made steady gains, however, and as the U-boats were Germany's most effective weapon, the Germans resumed their use. In 1916, while Wilson was campaigning for reelection on the slogan "He kept us out of war," Germany sank another passenger liner, the *Arabic*. In response, Wilson, while still maintaining neutrality, asked Congress to put the military into a state of **preparedness** for war, just in case. While most Americans wanted to stay out of the war, popular support for entry was beginning to grow.

Then, in early 1917, the British intercepted a telegram from German Foreign Minister Zimmermann to the German ambassador to Mexico. The telegram, imaginatively called the **Zimmermann telegram**, outlined a German plan to keep the United States out of the European war. The telegram stated that *if* Mexico were to declare war on the United States, Germany would provide Mexico help in regaining the lands lost in the Mexican War. The telegram also suggested that Germany would help Japan if they, too, wanted to go to war against America. Published in newspapers around the country, the telegram convinced many Americans that Germany was trying to take over the world. Although the public was by no means universally behind the idea of war, the balance had shifted enough so that within a month, America would declare war on Germany.

World War I and Its Aftermath

As is often the case during wartime, the government's power expanded greatly during the three years America was involved in World War I. The government took control of the telephone, telegraph, and rail industries, and a massive bureaucracy arose to handle these new responsibilities. The **War Industry Board (WIB),** created to coordinate all facets of industrial and agricultural production, sought to guarantee that not only the United States but also the rest of the Allies would be well supplied. (European production had been drastically cut by the war.) The WIB had mixed success; like most large bureaucracies, it was slow and inefficient.

The government also curtailed individual civil liberties during the war. In response to the still-sizable opposition to U.S. involvement, Congress passed the **Espionage Act** in 1917 and the **Sedition Act** in 1918. The Espionage Act prohibited anyone from using the U.S. mail system to interfere with the war effort or with the draft that had been instituted under the **Selective Service Act of 1917** upon America's entry into the war. The Sedition Act made it illegal to try to prevent the sale of war bonds or to speak disparagingly of the government, the flag, the military, or the Constitution. Like the Alien and Sedition Acts in the late 1790s, both laws violated the spirit of the First Amendment but were worded vaguely, giving the courts great leeway in their interpretation.

In 1919, the Supreme Court upheld the Espionage Act in three separate cases, the most notable being *Schenck v. United States*. Schenck was a prominent socialist and ardent critic of American capitalism, who was arrested and convicted for violation of the Espionage Act when he printed and mailed leaflets urging men to resist the draft. Schenck argued that the draft was a blatant violation of the Thirteenth Amendment, whose ratification in 1865 had abolished slavery; the wording of the amendment, however, did not mention slavery but rather prohibited "involuntary servitude." Justice Oliver Wendell Holmes ruled that one's freedom of speech and other civil liberties were not absolute and could in fact be curtailed if one's actions posed a "clear and present danger" to others or the nation. In essence, you cannot yell "FIRE!" in a crowded theater if there is no fire.

These laws soon became useful tools for the suppression of anyone who voiced unpopular ideas. A mood of increased paranoia pervaded the era, heightened by the **Russian Revolution** in 1917, which placed Russia under Bolshevik control. Suddenly, Americans began to fear a communist takeover. Radical labor unions, such as the International Workers of the World, were branded enemies of the state, and their leaders were incarcerated. Eugene Debs, the Socialist leader, was also imprisoned for criticizing the war. A new government agency, the **Federal Bureau of Investigation**, was created to prevent radicals from taking over; **J. Edgar Hoover** headed the nascent agency (and continued to run it until the 1970s). Business assumed greater power, while unions lost power. Under the pretext of stamping out radicalism, businesses increased their use of strikebreakers and other forceful tactics against unions. In April of 1919, a series of bombs exploded in several American cities, one damaging the home of Attorney General A. Mitchell Palmer. Ongoing fears of radicalism and the spread of communism following the Russian Revolution encouraged Palmer to organize a series of raids on suspected radical groups around the country. In the **Palmer Raids** in early 1920, the government abandoned all pretext of respecting civil liberties as its agents raided union halls, pool halls, social clubs, and residences. Over 10,000 were arrested in over 30 cities, but very few weapons or bombs were found. About 500 immigrants were eventually deported at the conclusion of the Palmer Raids.

The government helped create this frenzied atmosphere through its wartime propaganda arm, the **Committee on Public Information** (**CPI**). As the war progressed, the CPI's messages grew more sensational. At lectures and movie theaters, in newspapers and magazines, the CPI created the image of the Germans as cold-blooded, baby-killing, power-hungry Huns. During this period, Americans rejected all things German; for example, they changed the name of sauerkraut to "liberty cabbage." More serious were the many acts of violence against German immigrants and Americans of German descent.

Wartime also presented new opportunities for women. Although the number of women in the workforce did not increase greatly during the war, their means of employment did change. Many women quit domestic work and started working in factories; at one point, 20 percent of factory-floor manufacturing jobs were held by women. (The symbol of Rosie the Riveter, however, belongs to World War II.) These workplace advances ended with the war, as veterans returned home and reclaimed their jobs.

Southern blacks, realizing that wartime manufacturing was creating jobs in the North, undertook a **Great Migration** to the big cities, like New York, Chicago, St. Louis, and Detroit. During the war, more than 500,000 blacks left the South in search of work. Many blacks joined the army; W. E. B. Du Bois encouraged blacks to enlist, hoping that military service would provide an inroad to social equality. Sadly, the army segregated blacks and assigned them mostly to menial labor. Fearful of the effects of integration, the army assigned black combat units to French command.

American participation in the war tipped the balance in the Allies' favor, and two years after America's entry, the Germans were ready to negotiate a peace treaty. Wilson wanted the war treaty to be guided by his **Fourteen Points**, his plan for world peace delivered to Congress in January of 1918, before the end of the war. The Fourteen Points called for free trade through lower tariffs and freedom of the seas; a reduction of arms supplies on all sides; and the promotion of self-determination, both in Europe and overseas—in other words, the end of colonialism. The plan also called for the creation of the League of Nations, a mechanism for international cooperation much like today's United Nations. Wilson's Fourteen Points served as a basis for initial negotiations, but the negotiations soon took a different direction.

The European Allies wanted a peace settlement that punished Germany, and ultimately they got it. Under the **Treaty of Versailles**, Germany was forced to cede German and colonial territories to the Allies, to disarm, to pay huge reparations, and to admit total fault for the war, despite other nations' roles in starting it. Most historians agree that by leaving Germany humiliated and in economic ruin, the Treaty of Versailles helped to set the stage for World War II. Although much of Wilson's plan was discarded, the Treaty of Versailles did create the League of Nations. Wilson hoped that the League would ultimately remedy the peace settlement's many flaws, but when he returned home, a rude surprise awaited him. According to the Constitution, the president has the power to negotiate treaties with foreign nations, but these treaties are subject to Senate ratification. This illustrates the principles of **separation of powers** and **checks and balances**.

At the center of the conflict was the debate over the League of Nations, particularly Article X of the League's covenant, which many people believed curtailed America's ability to act independently in foreign affairs, specifically Congress's power to declare war. The Senate split into three groups: Democrats, who sided with Wilson and were willing to accept America's entrance into the League of Nations; a group of Republicans who were totally opposed to the League and were known as the Irreconcilables; and the Reservationists, a group of Republicans led by **Henry Cabot Lodge**, Chairman of the Senate Foreign Relations Committee and Wilson's political nemesis and intellectual rival.

Much has been made of Wilson's stubbornness and inability to compromise, and in particular, his refusal to accept what were known as the Lodge Reservations.

Ultimately, the Democrats and Irreconcilables joined forces and defeated the treaty, which had been amended to include the changes suggested by Henry Cabot Lodge and the Reservationists. Thus, the United States was not a signatory of the Treaty of Versailles, nor did it ever join the League of Nations, an international organization envisioned by an American President to maintain world peace. Weary of war, America was receding into a period of isolationism. The public wanted less interaction with Europe, not more, as the League would have required. Wilson tried to muster popular support for the treaty. However, while campaigning, Wilson suffered a major stroke, thereby ending whatever chance the treaty may have had for ratification. Many people wonder whether the League of Nations would have been more successful in preventing World War II had the United States been a member.

THE JAZZ AGE AND THE GREAT DEPRESSION (1920–1933)

After World War I, the American economy went through a brief slump and then started to grow rapidly. By 1922, America was hitting new peaks of prosperity every day. The invention of a practical electric motor was largely responsible for the economic boom; like computers in the 1990s, electric motors became essential to work and home environments, driving industrial machines and household appliances. With the new prosperity, other industries arose to serve the growing middle class in its search for the trappings of affluence.

Pro-Business Republican Administrations

As the age of progressive reform ended, many Americans became more comfortable with the idea of large, successful businesses. Some of these businesses, such as department stores, offered both convenience and reasonable prices. Others, such as the automobile industry, offered products that made life more convenient and conferred status on their owners.

The government, which had worked closely with business leaders as part of the war effort, also grew to be more **pro-business** during the era. Government regulatory agencies (such as the Federal Trade Commission) more often assisted business than regulated it. Labor unions fell further out of public favor, particularly when they struck against industries necessary to keeping industrial America running smoothly. Unions striking for higher wages and safer work conditions in the steel, coal, and railroad industries were suppressed by federal troops. The Supreme Court overturned a minimum wage law for women and nullified child labor restrictions.

All three of the era's presidents—**Warren Harding**, **Calvin Coolidge**, and **Herbert Hoover**—pursued pro-business policies and surrounded themselves with like-minded advisors. Like Grant, Harding had the misfortune of surrounding himself with

Wilson and Race

For all his progressivism in other areas, Woodrow Wilson was an outspoken white supremacist. He issued executive orders to segregate the federal government, struck a clause on racial equality from the Covenant of the League of Nations, wrote admiringly of the Ku Klux Klan, and told racist jokes at Cabinet meetings.

corrupt advisors; several of his cabinet members wound up in prison. The most infamous incident of his administration was the **Teapot Dome Scandal**, in which oil companies bribed the secretary of the interior in order to drill on public lands. Conservative on economic issues, Harding proved more liberal than his predecessor Wilson on issues of civil liberty. He supported antilynching laws and tried to help farmers (who were benefiting less from the new economy than were middle-class city dwellers) by providing more money for farm loans. Harding died in office, and Coolidge, his vice president, assumed the presidency. When Coolidge ran for the presidency in 1924, he turned the election into a debate on the economy by running on the slogan "Coolidge prosperity." Coolidge won easily and, following his mandate, continued Harding's conservative economic policies. He also pushed for lower income-tax rates. We will discuss Hoover's presidency later, when we discuss the causes of the Great Depression.

The pro-business atmosphere of the era led to a temporary decline in the popularity of labor unions; membership levels dropped throughout the decade. Also contributing to this drop were the efforts of businesses to woo workers with pension plans, opportunities for profit sharing, and company parties and other events designed to foster a communal spirit at work. Businessmen hoped that, if they offered some such benefits, they could dissuade workers from organizing and demanding even more. Such practices were often referred to as **welfare capitalism**.

Modern Culture

No consumer product better typified the new spirit of the nation than the **automobile**. At first, automobiles were expensive conveniences, affordable only to the extremely wealthy; then, Henry Ford perfected the assembly line and mass production, which lowered the cost of automobiles. By the end of the decade, most middle-class families could afford a car. The automobile allowed those who worked in the cities to move farther away from city centers, thus giving birth to the **suburbs**, which, in turn, transformed the automobile from a convenience to a necessity. The impact of the automobile on the 1920s was tremendous, forcing areas to quickly develop roadways and the means of policing traffic. In 1929, with the population topping 100 million in the most recent census, more than 23 million automobiles were registered in the United States.

The **radio** followed automobiles in changing the nation's culture. Ten million families owned radios, and in cities it was not unusual for several families to gather at the home of a radio owner and settle in for the evening. As more houses gained access to electric power, household appliance sales boomed as well. The **advertising industry** grew up during the decade to hype all these new products. Although advertisements from that era look pretty goofy to us now, they were quite effective at convincing people to buy stuff they did not really need—not too different from today!

All this consumerism required money, and as single-earner households often couldn't afford to "keep up with the Joneses," more women entered the working world. While the vast majority of married women continued to stay at home, more than ever—about 15 percent—entered the work force. Women continued, as they had in the past, to work in predominantly female-dominated professions (often called "pink collar jobs"), such as school teaching or office-assistant work, and to earn much less than men.

Despite the persistence of traditional roles for women, a new image of American women emerged and became a symbol of the Roaring Twenties—the **flapper**. World War I, the allure of the "big city," the right to vote, and new attitudes brought about by the ideas of Sigmund Freud (whose ideas were just beginning to circulate in the United States during the 1920s) opened up a whole new world for this new generation of emancipated women. They discarded the corset, layers of petticoats and long, dark dresses worn by their Victorian grandmothers, in favor of waistless dresses worn above the knee (shocking!), flesh-colored silk stockings (brought back from Paris), cute little hats, strings of long beads, a wrist full of bracelets, and ruby-red lips. Many flappers risked ruining their reputation by smoking cigarettes; drinking in public (despite Prohibition); and dancing the tango, the lindy, and the shimmy.

The rapid modernization of American society was reflected in the way it entertained itself. **Movies** grew tremendously popular during the decade, reflecting back at the nation its idealized self-image; on movie screens, young, independent-minded, gorgeous heroes and heroines defied all odds to succeed in romance and—at the same time—strike it rich. Sports grew more popular as well, especially baseball, whose greatest player of the era, Babe Ruth, was idolized by millions. In literature, America gained international prominence through such world-class authors as **F. Scott Fitzgerald**, **Ernest Hemingway**, and playwright **Eugene O'Neill**. Ironically, many of these writers moved to Europe, where they chronicled their alienation from the modern era, which explains why they came to be known as the **lost generation**.

> F. Scott Fitzgerald's writings reflected disillusionment with the opulence and excess of the 1920s. *The Great Gatsby*, one of his most famous works, depicted an outsider's views of the lavish lifestyle of New York City's elite. Ernest Hemingway's experiences in World War I are reflected in many of his books, like *A Farewell to Arms* and *The Sun Also Rises*. Hemingway's realistic portrayal of war expressed his disillusionment with World War I, which is similar to many other Lost Generation writers.

In the largest black neighborhood of New York City, theaters, cultural clubs, and newspapers sprang up—a development called the **Harlem Renaissance**. W. E. B. Du Bois opened writers' centers, and his prominence helped draw attention to Harlem's cultural movement. Among the great figures of the Harlem Renaissance were the poets **Langston Hughes**, **Countee Cullen**, and **Zora Neale Hurston**. Another major black cultural development was the popularization of **jazz**. Because jazz featured improvisation and free-spiritedness, it came to be seen as emblematic of the era (which is how the decade came to be known as the **Jazz Age**). Probably the most popular and most gifted of the era's jazz musicians was trumpeter **Louis Armstrong**.

American Jewish culture also thrived in the early 20th century. There were a dozen Yiddish theaters in New York City alone, performing mostly satirical plays for Jewish audiences.

Backlash Against Modern Culture

Not all Americans were excited about the rapid transition into the modern age, and the 1920s were also a time of considerable reactionary backlash and renewed nativism. Most prominently, the **Ku Klux Klan** grew to more than 5 million members and widened its targets, attacking blacks, Jews, urbanites, and anyone whose behavior deviated from the Klan's narrowly defined code of acceptable Christian behavior. Anti-immigration groups grew in strength as well, targeting the growing number of southern and Eastern European immigrants. Accusations that America's newcomers were dangerous subversives intensified when two Italian immigrant anarchists, **Sacco and Vanzetti**, were arrested on charges of murder. (Their trial immediately became a cause célèbre for the political left, as the evidence against them was inconclusive. Nonetheless, they were convicted and executed.) At the start of the decade, the United States started setting limits and quotas to restrict immigration. The **Emergency Quota Act of 1924** set immigration quotas based on national origins and discriminated against the "new immigrants" who came from Southern and Eastern Europe. These limits were set to reduce "foreign influence" on the country.

Another famous trial also illustrated the societal tensions of the decade. In 1925, Tennessee passed a law forbidding teachers to teach the theory of evolution. **John Thomas Scopes** broke that law, and his trial (dubbed the **Scopes Monkey Trial**) drew national attention, due in part to the two prominent attorneys arguing the case—**Clarence Darrow** and **William Jennings Bryan**, who, you may recall, ran for president in 1896, 1900, and 1908. The case also captivated the nation because, for many, it encapsulated the debate over whether to stick with tradition or abandon it for progress's sake.

Nineteenth-century morals played a part in the institution of **Prohibition**, which banned the manufacture, sale, and transport of alcoholic beverages. The Prohibition movement had its roots in the reform campaigns of the 1830s and remained a mainstay of women's political agendas until, on the eve of women's enfranchisement (1917), the **Eighteenth Amendment** outlawed the American liquor industry. Many people soon came to resent the government's intrusion in what they considered a private matter. Prohibition was further weakened by the effectiveness of organized crime in producing and selling liquor, especially in the cities. Open warfare between competing gangs and between criminals and law enforcement earned this period the title of the **gangster era,** which inspired many movies and television series. Prohibition was repealed by the Twenty-first Amendment in 1933.

Herbert Hoover and the Beginning of the Great Depression

In 1928, the Republicans nominated **Herbert Hoover**. Like Coolidge, Hoover was able to parlay a strong economy into an easy victory. During his campaign, Hoover predicted that the day would soon come when no American would live in poverty. He turned out to be very wrong.

In October 1929, the bottom fell out of the stock market, and this was one of the reasons for the Great Depression, but not the main reason. Prices dropped, and no matter how far they dropped, nobody wanted to buy. Hoover and his advisers underestimated the damage that the stock market crash would eventually cause. Convinced that the economy was sound, Hoover reassured the public that only stock traders would be hurt because of their irresponsible speculation. (Traders had been allowed to buy on margin, which meant that they might have to put up only 10 or 20 percent of the cost of each stock, allowing them to borrow against future profits that might or might not materialize. Margin buying is a destabilizing practice that was made illegal soon after the crash.) Unfortunately, among those speculators were huge banks and corporations, which suddenly found themselves on the verge of bankruptcy and unable to pay employees or guarantee bank deposits.

Other factors contributed to plunging the nation into a deep depression. Immediately following World War I, the carnage of the conflict, along with Germany's disastrous attempts to satisfy its reparations obligations under the Treaty of Versailles, had put Europe's economy, and much of the rest of the world's, into a depression. Domestically, though, manufacturers and farmers had been overproducing for years, creating large inventories. This led factories to lay off workers and made the farmers' crops worth much less on the market. Furthermore, production of new consumer goods was outstripping the public's ability to buy them. Supply so exceeded demand for so many goods, that this might be the main underlying cause for the Great Depression, ultimately leading to deflation, unemployment, and business failures. Finally, government laxity in regulating large businesses had led to the concentration of wealth and power in the hands of a very few businessmen. When their businesses failed, many people were thrown out of work.

The Depression had a calamitous effect on tens of millions of Americans. People lost their jobs as their employers went bankrupt or, to avoid bankruptcy, laid off the majority of workers. People lost their life savings as thousands of banks failed, and many lost their homes when they could not keep up with mortgage payments. The homeless built shantytowns, sarcastically called **Hoovervilles.** In rural areas, farmers struggled to survive as produce prices dropped more than 50 percent. Furthermore, a prolonged drought afflicted the Great Plains area of the Midwest, turning the region into a giant **Dust Bowl**. The situation encouraged agrarian unrest; farmers fought evictions and foreclosures by attacking those who tried to enforce them. Farmers also conspired to keep prices at farm auctions low and then returned the auctioned property to its original owner. In addition, they formed the **Farmers' Holiday Association**, which organized demonstrations and threatened a nationwide walkout by farmers in order to raise prices.

At first, Hoover opposed any federal relief efforts because he believed they violated the American ideal of "rugged individualism," but as the Depression worsened, he initiated a few farm assistance programs and campaigned for federal works projects (such as the Hoover Dam and the Grand Coulee Dam) that would create jobs. He hoped that raising tariffs would help American business, but the **Hawley-Smoot Tariff** actually worsened the economy. The Hawley-Smoot Tariff was the highest protective tariff in U.S. history, and it was enacted during one of the worst economic depressions ever. After that, Hoover had Congress create the Federal Emergency Relief Administration. This provided government money to bail out large companies and banks, but only ones big enough to potentially pay the money back later on.

Hoover's most embarrassing moment came in 1932 when Congress considered early payment of benefits to World War I veterans. Tens of thousands of impoverished veterans and their families, calling themselves the **Bonus Expeditionary Force (BEF),** came to Washington to lobby for the bill. When the bill was narrowly defeated, many refused to leave. They squatted in empty government offices or built shanties and stayed through the summer. In July, Hoover ordered the Army to expel them, which Douglas MacArthur chose to do with excessive force. Employing the cavalry and attacking with tear gas, Army forces drove the veterans from D.C. and then burned their makeshift homes. Two people died during the attack, and thousands were injured.

News of the Army attack on the BEF killed any chance Hoover had for reelection, partly because he had taken the heat for MacArthur's actions. Nonetheless, by the summer of 1932, he had already secured the Republican nomination. He ran a campaign stressing his traditional conservative values. (His main concession was to accept the repeal of Prohibition; Hoover had opposed repeal during his first term.) His opponent, New York Governor **Franklin D. Roosevelt**, argued for a more interventionist government. Roosevelt also promised relief payments to the unemployed, which Hoover had opposed throughout his term. Roosevelt won the election easily.

THE NEW DEAL AND WORLD WAR II (1934–1945)

In his inaugural address, Roosevelt declared war on the Depression, and he asked the country to grant him the same broad powers that presidents exercise during wars against foreign nations. He also tried to rally the public's confidence. In the most famous line of the speech, Roosevelt declared, "The only thing we have to fear is fear itself—nameless, unreasoning, unjustified fear." Both a powerful presidency and the people's confidence in Roosevelt played a large part in the implementation of his sweeping reforms, called the **New Deal**.

The First New Deal

Early in 1933, Roosevelt summoned an emergency session of Congress to work out the details of his recovery plan. The period that followed is often called the **First Hundred Days** because (1) that's how long it lasted, and (2) it was during this time that the government implemented most of the major programs associated with the **First New Deal**. (The **Second New Deal** began two years later.)

Roosevelt first sought to reestablish America's confidence in its banking system. The **Emergency Banking Relief Bill** put poorly managed banks under the control of the Treasury Department and granted government licenses (which functioned as seals of approval) to those that were solvent. In the first of many **fireside chats** broadcast over the radio, Roosevelt reassured the public that the banks were once again secure. More than 60 million Americans listened, and they obviously took Roosevelt at his word. The following week, millions redeposited the savings they had withdrawn during the bank failures of the previous years. American banks, once on the verge of ruin, were again healthy and could begin to contribute to the economic recovery. Later during the first hundred days, the government passed the **Banking Act of 1933**, which created the **Federal Deposit Insurance Corporation (FDIC)** to guarantee bank deposits, which was a big deal since people used to lose all of the money in their accounts if a bank went bankrupt. Roosevelt also instituted a number of intentionally inflationary measures in order to artificially raise prices (to get more money flowing into the economy).

Roosevelt then set out to provide relief for the rural poor. At the time, farmers were overproducing. They hoped that by growing more they could make up for falling produce prices, but their efforts were futile; the more they produced, the further prices fell, just as they had in the 1800s during the time of the Populists. Roosevelt's solution was the **Agricultural Adjustment Act**, referred to as the **AAA**. (So many of Roosevelt's new agencies were referred to by their acronyms that the entire group became known as the **alphabet agencies**.) The AAA provided payments to farmers in return for their agreement to cut production by up to one-half; the money to cover this program came from increased taxes on meat packers, millers, and other food processors. A month later, Congress passed the **Farm Credit Act**, which provided loans to those farmers in danger of foreclosure.

Several other New Deal programs established government control over industry. The **National Industrial Recovery Act (NIRA)** consolidated businesses and coordinated their activities with the aim of eliminating overproduction and, by so doing, stabilizing prices. The NIRA also established the **Public Works Administration (PWA)**, which set aside $3 billion to create jobs building roads, sewers, public housing units, and other civic necessities. At the same time, the **Civilian Conservation Corps (CCC)** provided grants to the states to manage their own PWA-like projects. In one of the New Deal's most daring moves, the government took over the **Tennessee Valley Authority (TVA)**. Under government control the TVA (which provided energy to the Tennessee Valley region) expanded its operations greatly, which led to the economic recovery of the region.

In June 1933, Congress adjourned, ending the First Hundred Days. Most of the programs that made up the First New Deal were in place, although others, such as the creation of both the **National Labor Relations Board (NLRB)**—which mediated labor disputes—and the **Securities and Exchange Commission (SEC)**—which regulated the stock market—were not implemented until 1934. The First New Deal was an immediate success, both politically and economically; the

Keynesian Economics

Roosevelt's response to the Great Depression was guided by the work of the economist **John Maynard Keynes**. **Keynes** contended that depressions were the result of a vicious cycle in which people see that the economy is bad, so they fear that money will be hard to come by, so they don't spend the money they have, so businesses fail, so the economy worsens, so people fear that money will be hard to come by, and so on. The solution, Keynes argued, was for the government to step in and embark on a program of deliberate **deficit spending**, as the **multiplier effect** would ensure that every dollar spent would do several dollars' worth of good in reviving the economy. If the people who needed money the most received a little extra, they would spend it immediately on the things they needed; that money would go to businesses, who could afford to hire more people, who would start receiving paychecks and then spend that money, which would go to businesses, who could afford to hire more people, and so on. The success of Keynesian economics during the Roosevelt administration, especially as embodied in the United States' deficit spending during World War II, led to widespread acceptance of Keynes's theories, which resulted in nearly 30 years of economic expansion, from 1945 to 1973.

unemployment rate fell and wages rose. In the midterm elections of 1934, the Democrats increased their majorities in both houses.

The Second New Deal

Not everyone, however, was enamored of the New Deal. In fact, both ends of the political spectrum criticized Roosevelt. **Conservatives** opposed the higher tax rates that the New Deal brought; they also disliked the increase in government power over business, and they complained that relief programs removed the incentive for the poor to lift themselves out of poverty. Additionally, the government had to borrow to finance all of its programs, and its **deficit spending** was also anathema to conservatives. **Leftists,** such as Huey Long, complained that the AAA policy of paying farmers *not* to grow was immoral, given that many Americans were still too poor to feed themselves. They also felt that government policy toward businesses was too favorable; they wanted more punitive measures, as many on the left blamed corporate greed for the Depression. The despair caused by the Depression provided fodder for a more radical left, and the **Socialists** (and, to a lesser extent, the **Communist Party of America**) were gaining popularity by calling for the nationalization (that is, a takeover by the government) of businesses.

As a senator, and then governor, of Louisiana, Huey Long was a huge threat to FDR in 1934 and 1935 and strongly promoted a plan similar to Social Security, gaining him supporters around the country (and encouraging FDR to have Congress create the Social Security Act and increase income taxes). He was assassinated in the summer of 1935 by a man angry that Long had redistricted his father's judicial district.

Then, in 1935, the Supreme Court started to dismantle some of the programs of the First New Deal in a series of cases, one of which came to be known as the "sick chicken case." *Schechter Poultry Corp. v. United States* invalidated sections of the NIRA on the grounds that the codes created under this agency were unconstitutional. According to the Constitution, only Congress can make laws. However, the NIRA empowered an agency within the executive branch of government to set wage and price ceilings, maximum work hours, and regulations regarding labor unions. The court ruled that these codes were in effect "executive legislation" and beyond the limits of executive power.

Roosevelt had argued that like war, the Great Depression had created a national crisis that warranted the expansion of the executive branch of government. The following year, the Supreme Court struck down the AAA in *United States v. Butler*. In 1937, Roosevelt responded by attempting to "pack the court" with justices who supported his policies. The size of the Supreme Court had changed a few times since its creation, but Roosevelt's attempt to increase the size of the court from 9 justices to 15, giving him the power to pick justices whose views he liked, was too much for most Democrats, let alone Republicans. As a result, this **court-packing scheme** was rejected by Congress.

Roosevelt then continued with a package of legislation called the **Second New Deal**. First, he established the Emergency Relief Appropriation Act, which created the **Works Progress Administration** (**WPA**), whose name was later changed to the Works Project Administration. The WPA generated more than 8 million jobs, all paid for by the government. Along with public works projects, such as construction, the WPA also employed writers, photographers, and other artists to create travel guides and to record local and personal histories.

The summer of 1935 is often called Roosevelt's **Second Hundred Days** because the amount and importance of legislation passed then is comparable to that of the

First Hundred Days. During this period, Congress passed legislation that broadened the powers of the **NLRB**, democratized unions, and punished businesses with anti-union policies. During this time, Congress also created the **Social Security Administration** to provide retirement benefits for many workers, including the disabled and families whose main breadwinner had died. Furthermore, the government increased taxes on wealthy individuals and top-end business profits. The cumulative effect of these programs led to the creation of the **New Deal coalition**, made up of union members, urbanites, the underclass, and blacks (who had previously voted Republican, out of loyalty to the party of Lincoln). This new Democratic coalition swept Roosevelt back into office with a landslide victory in 1936 and held together until the election of Reagan in 1980.

Roosevelt's Troubled Second Term

Several problems marred Franklin Roosevelt's second term. The first major failure of his presidency came as the term began. Angry that the Supreme Court had overturned much of the First New Deal and worried that the same fate awaited the Second New Deal, Roosevelt drafted a **Judicial Reorganization** bill. The bill proposed that Roosevelt be allowed to name a new federal judge for every sitting judge who had reached the age of 70 and had not retired; if passed, it would have allowed Roosevelt to add six new Supreme Court justices and more than 40 other federal judges. A not-so-subtle effort at **packing the courts** with judges more sympathetic to Roosevelt's policies, the bill was soundly defeated in the Democratic Congress, and Roosevelt came under intense criticism for trying to seize too much power. Ultimately, the court situation worked itself out to Roosevelt's benefit. A number of justices retired not long after the incident, and Roosevelt was able to replace them with more liberal judges.

In 1937, the economy went into a **recession**, a period of continually decreasing output. The cause was twofold: Roosevelt, satisfied that the New Deal was doing its job, cut back government programs in an effort to balance the budget. At the same time, the Federal Reserve Board tightened the credit supply in an effort to slow inflation. Both actions took money out of circulation, resulting in a slower economy. The recession lasted for almost three years and caused a substantial increase in the unemployment rate.

To top off Roosevelt's second term, by 1938, it was becoming evident that Europe might soon be at war again. This situation forced Roosevelt to withdraw some money from New Deal programs in order to fund a military buildup. The administration succeeded in passing a second Agricultural Adjustment Act that met the standards set by the Supreme Court's rejection of the first AAA; it also secured the **Fair Labor Standards Act**, which set a minimum wage and established the 40-hour workweek for a number of professions. Not long after, however, the New Deal came to an end.

Did the New Deal work? Historians like to debate this question. Those who argue "yes" point to the many people who escaped life-threatening poverty because of government assistance, and especially to the immediate relief provided by the First New Deal. They also point to the many reforms of banking, finance, and management/union relations. In these areas, the New Deal remade America in ways that are still recognizable today. Finally, proponents of the New Deal argue that Roosevelt should be praised for taking bold chances in a conservative political climate; he risked new initiatives when it was clear that old solutions were failing.

On the other hand, those who assert that the New Deal failed can point to the unemployment rate, which remained in double digits throughout the New Deal. Conservative historians argue that the New Deal thus did not solve the unemployment problem. Some on the left agree, contending that the New Deal was too small and too short-lived—look at how unemployment began to spike in 1937 when Roosevelt took his foot off the gas—and that it wasn't until the truly massive deficit spending program put in place in response to World War II that the economy began to recover in earnest. Furthermore, today's social welfare system stems from the New Deal; those who feel that the current American system has failed can point to Roosevelt as the man who started it all. Lastly, the New Deal did not benefit all equally. Minorities, in particular, reaped fewer (and sometimes no) benefits. The AAA actually hurt blacks and tenant farmers by putting them out of work; some of the public works projects underhired blacks, and almost all were segregated.

Foreign Policy Leading up to World War II

In the decade that followed World War I, American foreign policy objectives were aimed primarily at promoting and maintaining peace and have been described as "independent internationalism" rather than "isolationism." The **Washington Conference** (1921–1922) gathered eight of the world's great powers; the resulting treaty set limits on stockpiling armaments and reaffirmed the Open Door Policy toward China. In 1928, a total of 62 nations signed the **Kellogg-Briand Pact**, which condemned war as a means of foreign policy. Although it contained no enforcement clauses, the Kellogg-Briand Pact was widely considered a good first step toward a postwar age.

In Latin America, the United States tried to back away from its previous interventionist policy and replace it with the **Good Neighbor Policy** in 1934. The name, however, is misleading; the United States continued to actively promote its interests in Latin America, often to the detriment of those who lived there. However, the Platt Amendment was repealed at this time. The United States achieved its foreign policy objectives mainly through economic coercion and support of pro-American leaders (some of whom were corrupt and brutal). The United States also figured out how to maintain a strong but less threatening military presence in the area, both by paying for the privilege of maintaining military bases in the countries and by arranging to train the nations' National Guard units.

In Asia, the United States had less influence. Consequently, when Japan invaded Manchuria in 1931 (and in so doing violated the Kellogg-Briand Pact, which Japan had signed), the League of Nations was powerless, and the American government could do little. When Japan went to war against China in 1937, the United States sold arms to the Chinese and called for an embargo on arms sales to Japan. However, fearful of provoking a war with Japan, the government did not order an embargo on commercial shipments to Japan from the United States.

Throughout the Republican administrations of the 1920s, the U.S. government kept tariffs high; this policy is called **protectionism**. Early in Franklin Roosevelt's presidency, the government devised a method of using economic leverage as a foreign policy tool. The **Reciprocal Trade Agreements Act** allowed the president to reduce tariffs if he felt doing so would achieve foreign policy goals. Countries granted **most favored nation (MFN) trade status** were eligible for the lowest tariff rate set by the United States, if they played their cards right. MFN trade status remains a foreign policy tool today.

Disenchantment with the results of World War I fed isolationist sentiment, a stance amplified by the findings of the **Nye Commission**. Led by Senator Gerald Nye, the commission's report in 1936 revealed unwholesome activities by American arms manufacturers; many had lobbied intensely for entry into World War I, others had bribed foreign officials, and still others were currently supplying fascist governments with weapons. Congress responded by passing a series of **neutrality acts**. The first neutrality act (1935) prohibited the sale of arms to either belligerent in a war. (Roosevelt sidestepped this act in the 1937 sale of arms to China by simply refusing to acknowledge that China and Japan were at war.) The second neutrality act banned loans to belligerents.

All the while, Roosevelt poured money into the military—just in case. As it became more apparent that Europe was headed for war, Roosevelt lobbied for a repeal of the arms embargo stated in the first neutrality act so that America could help arm the Allies (primarily England, France, and, later, the Soviet Union). When war broke out, Congress relented with a third neutrality act, which allowed arms sales and was termed "cash and carry." It required the Allies to (1) pay cash for their weapons, and (2) come to the United States to pick up their purchases and carry them away on their own ships. From the outset of the war until America's entry in 1941, Roosevelt angled the country toward participation, particularly when Poland fell to German troops and other countries followed in rapid succession. In 1940, Hitler invaded France, and a German takeover of both France and England appeared a real possibility. The chance that America might soon enter the war convinced Roosevelt to run for an unprecedented third term. Again, he won convincingly.

Within the limits allowed by the neutrality acts, Roosevelt worked to assist the Allies. He found creative ways to supply them with extra weapons and ships; he appointed pro-Ally Republicans to head the Department of War and the Navy; and he instituted the nation's first peacetime military draft. It becomes increasingly difficult to describe U.S. foreign policy as isolationist by the 1940s. In 1941, Roosevelt forced the **Lend-Lease Act** through Congress, which permitted the United States to "lend" armaments to England, which no longer had money to buy the tools of war. Roosevelt sent American ships into the war zone to protect Lend-Lease shipments, an act which could easily have provoked a German attack. Later in the year, Roosevelt and British Prime Minister Winston Churchill met at the **Atlantic Charter Conference**. The Atlantic Charter declared the Allies' war aims, which included disarmament, self-determination, freedom of the seas, and guarantees of each nation's security.

Given all this activity in the European theater, it seems odd that America's entry to the war came not in Europe but in Asia. Japan entered into an alliance (called the **Tripartite Pact**) with Italy and Germany in 1940. By 1941, France had fallen to Germany, and the British were too busy fighting Hitler to block Japanese expansion, which had continued south into French Indochina (modern-day Vietnam, Cambodia, and Laos). The United States responded to Japanese aggression by cutting off trade to Japan, which was dependent on foreign imports. The embargo included oil, which Japan needed to fuel its war machine. Despite peace talks in November of 1941 between the United States and Japan to avoid war, the United States had broken Japan's secret communication codes and knew that Japan was planning an attack but did not know the location. Secretary of War **Henry Stimson** encouraged Roosevelt to wait for the Japanese attack in order to guarantee popular support for the war at home. He did not have to wait long. The Japanese attacked **Pearl Harbor**, Hawaii, on December 7, and U.S. participation in the war began.

World War II

Complicated military strategy and the outcome of key battles played a big part in World War II. Fortunately, you do not have to know much about them for the AP Exam; nor do you need to know about the many truly unspeakable horrors the Nazis perpetrated on Europe's Jews, gypsies, homosexuals, and dissidents. You should know about the various wartime conferences, however, when the Allies met to discuss military strategy and the eventual postwar situation. It was no secret that the Grand Alliance between the Soviet Union and the West was tenuous at best, held together by the thread of a common enemy but threatened by Stalin's impatience at the Allies' delay in opening a "second front" while the Soviets bore the brunt of the Nazi onslaught.

> **Island-Hopping: Not Just a Vacation Strategy**
>
> "Island-hopping," also known as "leapfrogging," was a military strategy employed by the Allies in the Pacific War during World War II. Instead of attacking more obvious mainland targets first, this strategy sought to target Pacific islands that were not well defended but were later capable of providing access to the main islands of Japan. While General Douglas MacArthur took credit for inventing island-hopping, it was, in fact, a Naval innovation.

The first meeting of the "big three" (Roosevelt, Churchill, and Stalin) took place in the Iranian capital of Tehran in November of 1943. It was here that they planned the Normandy invasion, **D-Day**, and agreed to divide a defeated Germany into occupation zones after the war. Stalin also agreed to enter the war against Japan once Hitler had been defeated. The Allies fought the Germans primarily in the Soviet Union and in the Mediterranean until early 1944, when Allied forces invaded occupied France (on D-Day). The Soviet Union paid a huge price in human and material loss for this strategy and after the war sought to recoup its losses by occupying Eastern Europe. In the Pacific, both sides incurred huge numbers of casualties. The Allies eventually won a war of attrition against the Germans, and the Americans accelerated victory in the East by dropping two atomic bombs on Japan.

> **The Manhattan Project of 1942** was a concentrated research and development effort to develop the first atomic bombs. Based in Los Alamos, New Mexico, a team of more than 100,000 scientists and technicians created and tested nuclear bombs on the Pacific island of Bikini. Despite tight security measures, Soviet spies infiltrated the program, the most famous being **Ethel and Julius Rosenberg**.

> D-Day occurred on June 6, 1944, and was the largest amphibious landing of all time.

As it had during the Civil War, World War I, and the New Deal, the government acquired more power than it previously had. The War Production Board allowed the government to oversee the mobilization of industry toward the war effort; in return, businesses were guaranteed generous profits. **Rationing** of almost all consumer goods was imposed. The government sponsored scientific research directed at improving weaponry, developing **radar**, sonar, and the atomic bomb during this period. The government also exerted greater control over labor. The **Labor Disputes Act** of 1943 (passed in reaction to a disconcerting number of strikes in essential industries) allowed government takeover of businesses deemed necessary to national security, which gave the government authority to settle labor disputes. **Hollywood** was enlisted to create numerous propaganda films, both to encourage support on the home front and to boost morale of the troops overseas. Not surprisingly, the size of the government more than tripled during the war.

FDR signed the **Selective Training and Service Act of 1940**, which created the first peacetime draft in U.S. history and gave birth to the current incarnation of the Selective Service System, which ultimately provided about 10 million soldiers toward the war effort. (Although the draft was discontinued in 1973, after the United States' involvement in Vietnam, the Selective Service System remained in place and currently requires that all male citizens register for the draft within 30 days after turning 18.)

World War II affected almost every aspect of daily life at home and abroad. It created both new opportunities and new tensions within American society. More than a million African Americans served in the U.S. military during World War II, but they lived and worked in segregated units. The U.S. army was not desegregated until after the war, during the Truman administration in 1948. A popular image, familiar to most Americans, is that of Rosie the Riveter. Originally featured on a poster of the era, Rosie came to symbolize the millions of women who worked in war-related industrial jobs during World War II. Unfortunately for the cause of feminism, most women were expected to take off the coveralls and put the apron back on when the soldiers returned home.

Again, as during World War I, the government restricted civil liberties. Probably the most tragic instance was the **internment of Japanese Americans** from 1942 to the end of the war. Fearful that the Japanese might serve as enemy agents within U.S. borders, the government imprisoned more than 110,000 Asian Americans, over two-thirds of whom had been born in the United States and thus were U.S. citizens. Some were not even of Japanese descent. None of those interned was ever charged with a crime; imprisonment was based entirely on ethnic background. The government placed these Japanese Americans in desolate prison camps far from the West Coast, where they feared a Japanese invasion would take place. Most lost their homes and possessions as a result of the internment.

The Supreme Court upheld the constitutionality of both the evacuation and internment of Japanese Americans. As in the *Schenck* case of 1919, the Court ruled that a citizen's civil liberties can be curtailed and even violated in time of war. "Citizenship has its responsibilities as well as its privileges, and in time of war, the burden is always heavier. Compulsory exclusion of large groups of citizens from their homes, except under circumstances of direst emergency and peril, is inconsistent with our basic governmental institutions. But when under conditions of modern warfare our shores are threatened by hostile forces, the power to protect must be commensurate with the threatened danger," wrote Justice Hugo Black in *Korematsu v. United States* (1944). It wasn't until 1988 that a government apology was made and reparations of about $1.6 million were disbursed to surviving internees and their heirs.

The End of the War

As the war neared its end in Europe, the apparent victors—the Allies—met to discuss the fate of postwar Europe. In February of 1945, the Allied leaders met at **Yalta** and in effect redrew the world map. By this time the Soviet army occupied parts of Eastern Europe, a result of the campaign to drive the German army out of the USSR.

Stalin wanted to create a "buffer zone" between the Soviet Union and Western Europe; he wanted to surround himself with nations that were "friendly" toward the government in Moscow. Because of the presence of the Red Army, Stalin was given a free hand in Eastern Europe, a decision the other Allies would later regret, with the promise to hold "free and unfettered elections" after the war. Despite this promise, Soviet tanks rolled into Romania three weeks after Yalta, thus beginning the establishment of Soviet **satellites** and the descent of the **Iron Curtain**. (The Iron Curtain was a metaphor coined by Winston Churchill in 1946 to describe the symbolic division of Eastern and Western Europe, thus the origins of the Cold War following World War II.)

While at the Potsdam Conference, the Allies created the Potsdam Declaration, which established the terms for the surrender of Japan, which included the removal of the emperor from power. Many historians believe this term kept the Japanese from agreeing to surrender, which then provoked the dropping of the atomic bombs.

The Allies agreed on a number of issues concerning borders and postwar settlements. They also agreed that once the war in Europe ended, the USSR would declare war on Japan. Toward the end of the war, the Allies agreed to help create the **United Nations** to mediate future international disputes. The Allies met again at **Potsdam** to decide how to implement the agreements of Yalta. This time, **Harry S. Truman** represented the United States, as Roosevelt had died in April. Things did not go as well at Potsdam; with the war's end closer and the Nazis no longer a threat, the differences between the United States and the Soviet Union were growing more pronounced.

Some argue that American-Soviet animosity prompted Truman's decision to use the **atomic bomb** against the Japanese. (By this argument, America feared Soviet entry into the Asian war where the Soviets might then attempt to expand their influence, as they were doing in Eastern Europe. Along the same line of reasoning, one could assert that the United States wanted to put on a massive display of power to intimidate the Soviets.) However, the manner in which the war in the Pacific had been fought to that point also supported Truman's decision. The Japanese had fought tenaciously and remained powerful despite the long war; casualty estimates of an American invasion of Japan ran upward of 500,000. Some military leaders estimated that such an invasion would not subdue Japan for years. In August, the United States dropped two atomic bombs, first on **Hiroshima** and then three days later on **Nagasaki**. The Japanese surrendered soon after.

Summary

Here are the most important concepts to remember from the early-20th-century period.

- America transitioned from a largely rural and agricultural society to an urban industrialized society.

- Land in the West was largely settled and the boundaries of the Continental United States became fixed.

- America became embroiled in foreign conflicts.

- Isolationism and anti-immigrant sentiment collided with globalism and social reform.

- The Great Depression became the longest protracted economic challenge in American history.

- American Indians settled on reservations as sovereign nations under the oversight of the Bureau of Indian Affairs.

- Communications and transportation technologies revolutionized daily American life.

Chapter 11 Review Questions

See Chapter 14 for answers and explanations.

1. Muckrakers furthered the causes of the Progressive movement by

   (A) organizing grassroots campaigns for political reform at the state level
   (B) suing large companies and donating their court awards to Progressive campaigns
   (C) staging large, violent protests in support of Progressive goals
   (D) alerting the public to the social ills and corporate corruption targeted by Progressives

2. Prior to the administration of Theodore Roosevelt, the Sherman Antitrust Act had been used primarily to

   (A) dismantle corporate monopolies
   (B) suppress trade unions
   (C) impose import tariffs
   (D) enforce civil rights in the South

3. Following the Spanish-American War and the acquisition of territory overseas, in a series of cases known as the Insular Cases, the U.S. Supreme Court ruled that

   (A) natives living on American soil abroad were guaranteed the same rights and privileges as U.S. citizens living within the continental United States
   (B) colonial subjects within the American Empire were not entitled to the rights guaranteed by the U.S. Constitution
   (C) "the Constitution follows the flag"
   (D) Congress must relinquish control of these overseas possessions and honor their right of self-determination

4. Which of the following best summarizes the contents of the Zimmermann telegram, which was intercepted in 1917?

   (A) Germany offered Mexico a chance to regain the land it had lost in the Mexican Cession if Mexico attacked the United States and helped prevent the United States from assisting the Allies.
   (B) A British spy alerted the world to the existence of mass extermination camps in German-held territories.
   (C) The United States assured the British that it would join the war in Europe if the war were to continue for another year.
   (D) The owner of the Boston Red Sox revealed a plan to sell star player Babe Ruth to the New York Yankees for a large amount of cash.

5. Wilson's Fourteen Points plan for peace after World War I included all of the following EXCEPT

   (A) promotion of universal self-determination
   (B) lower tariffs to promote free trade
   (C) repayment of all Allied war expenses by Germany
   (D) across-the-board arms reductions

6. All of the following can be seen as clashes between traditional and modern culture during the post–World War I era EXCEPT

   (A) the rise of the Ku Klux Klan
   (B) the Teapot Dome Scandal
   (C) the Scopes Monkey Trial
   (D) the Emergency Quota Act of 1924

7. Buying "on margin" contributed to the stock market crash of 1929 because it

   (A) required investors to purchase only high-risk, volatile stocks
   (B) imposed high interest rates that discouraged trading
   (C) prevented traders from learning the true financial state of the companies in which they invested
   (D) allowed traders to pay for stock with projected future profits

8. Franklin Roosevelt invoked the Good Neighbor Policy in taking which of the following actions?

   (A) Providing England with munitions to defend itself against Germany
   (B) Creating the Tennessee Valley Authority to provide power in the poor rural South
   (C) Banning trade of war-related materials with Japan and freezing Japanese assets in the United States
   (D) Recalling U.S. troops from Nicaragua and Haiti

9. The Nye Commission report of 1936 reinforced American isolationism by

   (A) revealing unethical profiteering by American munitions companies during World War I
   (B) concluding that Germany had no interest in engaging the United States in war
   (C) listing the domestic programs that would have to be forfeited if the United States were to increase its overseas commitments
   (D) detailing deficiencies in all branches of the U.S. military

10. In its *Korematsu v. United States* decision, the Supreme Court ruled that

   (A) the wartime relocation of West Coast Japanese Americans was not unconstitutional
   (B) the Japanese government had no legitimate claim to reparations for the bombings of Hiroshima and Nagasaki
   (C) the U.S. government had violated the Constitution by entering the Korean War
   (D) immigration quotas based on race were unconstitutional

REFLECT

Respond to the following questions:

- For which content topics discussed in this chapter do you feel you have achieved sufficient mastery to answer multiple-choice questions correctly?

- For which content topics discussed in this chapter do you feel you have achieved sufficient mastery to discuss effectively in a short-answer question or an essay?

- On which content topics discussed in this chapter do you feel you need more work before you can answer multiple-choice questions correctly?

- On which content topics discussed in this chapter do you feel you need more work before you can discuss them effectively in a short-answer question or an essay?

- What parts of this chapter are you going to review again?

- Will you seek further help, outside of this book (such as a teacher, tutor, or AP Students), on any of the content in this chapter—and, if so, on what content?

Chapter 12
Unit 8: The Postwar Period and Cold War (1945–1980)

TRUMAN AND THE BEGINNING OF THE COLD WAR (1945–1953)

The end of World War II raised two major issues. The first concerned the survival of the combatants; with the exception of the United States, the nations involved in World War II had all seen fighting within their borders, and the destruction had been immense. The second issue involved the shape of the new world and what new political alliances would be formed. This question would become the major source of contention between the world's two leading political-economic systems, capitalism and communism.

The stakes in this power struggle, called the **Cold War** (because there was no actual combat as there is in a "hot war"), were high. Though the major powers (the United States and Soviet Union) didn't enter into combat in the Cold War, the United States did fight hot **proxy wars** in Korea and Vietnam during this time. The American economy was growing more dependent on exports; American industry also needed to import metals, a process requiring (1) open trade and (2) friendly relations with those nations that provided those metals. In addition, with many postwar economies in shambles, competition among the few reasonably healthy economies grew fiercer. Finally, those countries that were strongest before the war—Germany, Japan, and Great Britain—had either been defeated or seen their influence abroad greatly reduced. The United States and the Soviet Union emerged as the two new superpowers. Although they were allies during World War II, the war's end exposed the countries' many ideological differences, and they soon became enemies.

Truman and Foreign Policy

The differences between Soviet and American goals were apparent even before the war was over, but became even clearer when the Soviets refused to recognize Poland's conservative government-in-exile. (The Polish government had moved to England to escape the Nazis; this government was backed by the United States.) A communist government took over Poland. Within two years, pro-Soviet communist coups had also taken place in Hungary and Czechoslovakia. The propaganda in the United States and USSR during this period reached a fever pitch. In each country, the other was portrayed as trying to take over the world for its own sinister purposes.

Then, in 1947, communist insurgents threatened to take over both Greece and Turkey, but England could no longer prop up these nations. In a speech before Congress in which he asked for $400 million in aid to the two countries, Truman asserted, "I believe it must be the policy of the United States to support free peoples who are resisting attempted subjugation by armed minorities or outside pressures." This statement, called the **Truman Doctrine,** became the cornerstone of a larger policy, called **containment**, articulated by George Kennan. The idea of containment came from what is known as the **Long Telegram**, which Kennan sent to Washington from his duty station in Germany, in 1946. This policy said that the United States would not instigate a war with the Soviet Union, but it would come to the defense of countries in danger of Soviet takeover. The policy aimed to prevent the spread of communism and encourage the Soviets to abandon their aggressive strategies.

Meanwhile, the United States used a tried-and-true method to shore up its alliances—it gave away money. The **Marshall Plan**, named for Secretary of State

George Marshall, sent more than $12 billion to Europe to help rebuild its cities and economy. In return for that money, of course, countries were expected to become American allies. The countries were also required to work together to promote economic growth, and is the precursor to the European Union. Although the Marshall Plan was offered to Eastern Europe and the Soviet Union, no countries in the Soviet sphere participated in the program, as Stalin viewed the initiative as further evidence of U.S. imperialism. The United States also formed a mutual defense alliance with Canada and a number of countries in Western Europe called the **North Atlantic Treaty Organization** (**NATO**) in 1949. Truman did not have an easy time convincing Congress that NATO was necessary; remember, from the time of Washington's Farewell Address, American sentiment has strongly favored avoiding all foreign entanglements.

The crisis in **Berlin** the previous year, however, helped convince Congress to support NATO. The crisis represented a culmination of events after World War II. In 1945, Germany had been divided into four sectors, with England, France, the United States, and the USSR each controlling one. Berlin, though deep in Soviet territory, had been similarly divided. Upon learning that the three Western Allies planned to merge their sectors into one country and to bring that country into the Western economy, the Soviets responded by imposing a **blockade** on Berlin. Truman refused to surrender the city, however, and ordered airlifts to keep that portion under Western control supplied with food and fuel. The blockade continued for close to a year, by which point the blockade became such a political liability that the Soviets gave it up. Don't confuse the **Berlin Blockade** with the **Berlin Wall**. The Berlin Blockade occurred when the Soviets closed off access to the city during the Truman administration in 1948, while the Soviets erected the Berlin Wall in 1961 during the Kennedy administration to divide the city between the East and the West. Constructed of concrete and barbed wire, the wall separated the Soviet sector of Berlin from West Berlin and became a symbol of the Cold War. The wall was finally dismantled in 1989.

Not long after the United States joined NATO, the Soviets detonated their first atomic bomb. Fear of Soviet invasion or subterfuge also led to the creation of the **National Security Council** (a group of foreign affairs advisers who work for the president) and the **Central Intelligence Agency** (the United States' spy network).

National Security Council 68 was a document that said the United States should invest much more money into military spending because they couldn't trust other countries to help protect them against communism.

As if Truman didn't have enough headaches in Europe, he also had to deal with Asia. Two issues dominated U.S. policy in the region: the **reconstruction of Japan** and the **Chinese Revolution**. After the war, the United States occupied Japan, and its colonial possessions were divided up. The United States took control of the Pacific Islands and the southern half of Korea, while the USSR took control of the northern half of Korea. Under the command of General Douglas MacArthur, Japan wrote a democratic constitution, demilitarized, and started a remarkable economic revival. The United States was not as successful in China, where it chose to side with Chiang Kai-shek's Nationalist government against **Mao Zedong**'s Communist insurgents, during China's 20-year civil war (Mao having taken control of China in 1949). Despite massive American military aid, the Communists overthrew the Nationalists, whose government was exiled to Taiwan.

For decades, the United States refused to recognize the legitimacy of Mao's regime, creating another international "hot spot" for Americans. Truman also chose to aid the French during the Vietnamese war for independence in Indochina, although most Americans were not aware of this at the time.

McCarthyism

All this conflict with communists resurrected anticommunist paranoia at home, just as anticommunism had swept America during the Red Scare after World War I. In 1947, Truman ordered investigations of 3 million federal employees in a search for "security risks." Those found to have a potential Achilles' heel—either previous association with "known communists" or a "moral" weakness such as alcoholism or homosexuality (which, the government reasoned, made them easy targets for blackmail)—were dismissed without a hearing. In 1949, former State Department official **Alger Hiss** was found guilty of consorting with a communist spy (Richard Nixon was the congressman mostly responsible for Hiss's downfall). Americans began to passionately fear the "enemy within." Even the Screen Actors Guild, then headed by Ronald Reagan, attempted to discover and purge its own communists.

It was this atmosphere that allowed a demagogic senator named **Joseph McCarthy** to rise from near anonymity to national fame. In 1950, McCarthy claimed to have a list of more than 200 known communists working for the State Department. He subsequently changed that number several times, which should have clued people in to the fact that he was not entirely truthful. Unchallenged, McCarthy went on to lead a campaign of innuendo that ruined the lives of thousands of innocent people. Without ever uncovering a single communist, McCarthy held years of hearings with regard to subversion, not just in the government, but in education and the entertainment industry as well. Those subpoenaed were often forced to confess to previous associations with communists and name others with similar associations. Industries created lists of those tainted by these charges, called **blacklists**, which prevented the accused from working, just as blacklists had been used against union organizers at the turn of the last century. Eisenhower himself was worried about McCarthy and refused to speak against him, for fear that McCarthy would attack him. McCarthy's downfall came in 1954, during the Eisenhower administration, when he accused the Army of harboring communists. He had finally chosen too powerful a target. The Army fought back hard, and with help from **Edward R. Murrow**'s television show, in the **Army-McCarthy hearings**, McCarthy was made to look foolish. The public turned its back on him, and the era of **McCarthyism** ended, but public distrust and fear of communism remained.

"You've done enough. Have you no sense of decency, sir? At long last, have you left no sense of decency?"
—Army counsel Joseph Welch, speaking back to Joseph McCarthy at the hearings that would effectively end McCarthy's career.

Truman's Domestic Policy and the Election of 1948

The end of the war meant the end of wartime production. With fewer Jeeps, airplanes, guns, bombs, and uniforms to manufacture, American businesses started laying off employees. Returning war veterans further crowded the job market, and unemployment levels rose dramatically. At the same time, many people who had built up their savings during the war (since rationing had limited the availability of consumer goods) started to spend more liberally, causing prices to rise. In 1946, the inflation rate was nearly 20 percent. The poor and unemployed felt the effects the most. Truman offered some New Deal–style solutions to America's economic woes, but a new conservatism had taken over American politics. Most of his proposals were rejected, and the few that were implemented had little effect.

The new conservatism brought with it a new round of anti-unionism in the country. Americans were particularly upset when workers in essential industries went on strike, as when the coal miners' strike (by the **United Mine Workers**, or **UMW**) cut off the energy supply to other industries, shutting down steel foundries, auto plants, and more. Layoffs in the affected industries exacerbated tensions. Americans cared little that the miners were fighting for basic rights. Truman followed the national mood, ordering a government **seizure of the mines** when a settlement could not be reached. During a later railroad strike, Truman threatened to draft into the military those strikers who held out for more than he thought they deserved. Consequently, Truman alienated labor, one of the core constituencies of the new Democratic coalition. Labor and consumers, angry at skyrocketing prices, formed an alliance that helped the Republicans take control of the **Eightieth Congress** in the 1946 midterm elections.

Truman also alienated many voters (particularly in the South) by pursuing a civil rights agenda that, for its time, was progressive. He convened the **President's Committee on Civil Rights,** which in 1948 issued a report calling for an end to segregation and poll taxes, and for more aggressive enforcement of antilynching laws. Truman also issued an executive order forbidding racial discrimination in the hiring of federal employees and another executive order desegregating the Armed Forces. Blacks began to make other inroads. The NAACP won some initial, important lawsuits against segregated schools and buses; **Jackie Robinson** broke the color barrier in baseball; and black groups started to form coalitions with liberal white organizations, thereby gaining more political clout. These advances provoked an outbreak of flagrant racism in the South, and in 1948 segregationist Democrats, or **Dixiecrats,** abandoned the party to support Strom Thurmond for president.

With so many core Democratic constituencies—labor, consumers, Southerners— angry with the president, his defeat in 1948 seemed certain. Truman's popularity, however, received an unintentional boost from the Republican-dominated Congress. The staunchly conservative legislature passed several antilabor acts too strong even for Truman. The **Taft-Hartley Act**, passed over Truman's veto,

Let's Make A Deal

Both Theodore and Franklin Roosevelt, as well as FDR's successor Harry Truman, offered "deals" to the American public:

	President	What's the deal with this?
Square Deal	Theodore Roosevelt	Government promised to regulate business and restore competition
First New Deal	Franklin Roosevelt	Focused on immediate public relief and the recovery of banks
Second New Deal	Franklin Roosevelt	Addressed the shortcomings of the First New Deal and responded to a changing political climate
Fair Deal	Harry Truman	Extension of New Deal vision and provisions for reintegrating WWII veterans into society (e.g., the G.I. Bill)

prohibited "union only" work environments (called **closed shops**), restricted labor's right to strike, prohibited the use of union funds for political purposes, and gave the government broad power to intervene in strikes. The same Congress then rebuked Truman's efforts to pass health care reform; increase aid to schools, farmers, the elderly, and the disabled; and promote civil rights for blacks. The cumulative effect of all this acrimony made Truman look a lot better to those he had previously offended. Still, as election time neared, Truman trailed his chief opponent, Thomas Dewey. He then made one of the most brilliant political moves in American history. He recalled the Congress, whose majority members had just drafted an extremely conservative Republican platform at the party convention, and challenged them to enact that platform. Congress met for two weeks and did not pass one significant piece of legislation. Truman then went out on a grueling public appearance campaign, everywhere deriding the "do-nothing" Eightieth Congress. To almost everyone's surprise, Truman won re-election, and his coattails carried a Democratic majority into Congress.

The Korean War

The Korean War began in June of 1950, when communist North Korea invaded U.S.-backed South Korea. Believing the Soviet Union to have engineered the invasion, the United States took swift countermeasures. Originally intending only to repel the invasion, Truman decided to attempt a reunification of Korea after some early military successes. Under the umbrella of the United Nations, American troops attacked North Korea, provoking China, Korea's northern neighbor. (The Chinese were not too keen on the idea of hostile American troops on their border.) China ultimately entered the war, pushing American and South Korean troops back near the original border dividing North and South Korea. U.S. commander **Douglas MacArthur** recommended an all-out confrontation with China, with the objective of overthrowing the Communists and reinstating Chiang Kai-shek. Truman thought a war with the world's most populous country might be imprudent and so decided against MacArthur. When MacArthur started publicly criticizing the president, who was also the commander-in-chief, Truman fired him for insubordination. MacArthur was very popular at home, however, and firing him hurt Truman politically.

Although peace talks began soon after, the war dragged on another two years, into the Eisenhower administration. When the 1952 presidential election arrived, the Republicans took a page from the Whig playbook and chose **Dwight D. Eisenhower**, a war hero. By this point, the presidency had been held by the Democratic Party for 20 years. Truman was unpopular; his bluntness is now seen as a sign of his integrity, but during his terms, it offended a lot of potential constituents. In short, America was ready for a change. Eisenhower beat Democratic challenger **Adlai Stevenson** easily.

Democrats also wanted Eisenhower for their presidential candidate. He had been the President of Columbia University and the Supreme Commander of NATO before winning the presidency.

THE EISENHOWER YEARS (1953–1961)

The 1950s are often depicted as a time of **conformity**. Across much of America, a **consensus of values** reigned. Americans believed that their country was the best in the world, that communism was evil and had to be stopped, and that a decent job, a home in the suburbs, and access to all the modern conveniences (aka **consumerism**) did indeed constitute "the good life." Congress had enacted the Serviceman's Readjustment Act, commonly known as the **G.I. Bill of Rights**, in June of 1944. It provided an allowance for educational and living expenses for returning soldiers and veterans who wished to earn their high-school diploma or attend college. The G.I. Bill not only helped many Americans achieve the American dream but also helped stimulate postwar economic growth by providing low-cost loans to purchase homes or farms or to start small businesses. The 1950s also proved to be an era in which the civil rights movement built on the advances of the 1940s and met some violent resistance; an era plagued by frequent economic recessions; and an era of spiritual unrest that manifested itself in such emerging art forms as **Beat poetry and novels** ("Howl," *On the Road*), teen movies (*Blackboard Jungle, The Wild One, Rebel Without a Cause*), and **rock 'n' roll** (Elvis Presley, Little Richard, Jerry Lee Lewis, Chuck Berry).

The Kitchen Debate

Vice President Richard Nixon visited Moscow in 1959 for a cultural fair. While standing in a model American kitchen, Nixon ended up getting into an argument with Soviet leader Nikita Khrushchev that emblematized not only U.S.-Soviet relations but also common American attitudes toward gender in the 1950s. An excerpt:

Nixon: I want to show you this kitchen. It is like those of our houses in California.

Khrushchev: We have such things.

Nixon: This is our newest model. This is the kind which is built in thousands of units for direct installations in the houses. In America, we like to make life easier for women.

Khrushchev: Your capitalistic attitude toward women does not occur under communism.

Nixon: I think that this attitude toward women is universal.

Domestic Politics in the 1950s

Eisenhower arrived at the White House prepared to impose conservative values on the federal government, which had mushroomed in size under Roosevelt and Truman. He sought to balance the budget, cut federal spending, and ease government regulation of business. In these goals he was, at best, only partly successful. The military buildup required by the continuing Cold War prevented Eisenhower from making the cuts to the military budget that he would have liked. He reduced military spending by reducing troops and buying powerful weapons systems (thus shaping the **New Look Army**), but not enough to eliminate deficit spending. The popularity of remaining New Deal programs made it difficult to eliminate them; furthermore, circumstances required Eisenhower to increase the number of Social Security recipients and the size of their benefits. Under Eisenhower, the government also began developing the **Interstate Highway System**, partly to make it easier to move soldiers and nuclear missiles around the country. The new roads not only sped up travel, but they also promoted tourism and the development of the suburbs. The initial cost, however, was extremely high. As a result, Eisenhower managed to balance the federal budget only three times in eight years.

Some of the most important domestic issues during the Eisenhower years involved minorities. In 1953, Eisenhower sought to change federal policy toward Native Americans. His new policy, called **termination**, would liquidate reservations, end federal support to Native Americans, and subject them to state law. However, in devising this policy, Eisenhower did not take Native American priorities into account. He aimed simply to reduce federal responsibilities and bolster the power of the states. Native Americans protested, convinced that termination was simply a means of stealing what little land the tribes had left. The plan failed and was ultimately stopped in the 1960s but not before causing the depletion and impoverishment of a number of tribes.

The civil rights movement experienced a number of its landmark events during Eisenhower's two terms. In 1954, the Supreme Court heard the case of ***Brown v. Board of Education of Topeka***, a lawsuit brought on behalf of Linda Brown (a black school-age child) by the NAACP. Future Supreme Court Justice Thurgood Marshall argued the case for Brown. In its ruling, the Court overturned the "separate but equal" standard as it applied to education; "separate but equal" had been the law of the land since the Court had approved it in *Plessy v. Ferguson* (1896). In a 9 to 0 decision, the Court ruled that "separate educational facilities are inherently unequal" and that schools should desegregate with "all deliberate speed." Although a great victory for civil rights, *Brown v. Board of Education* did not immediately solve the school segregation problem. Some Southern states started to pay the tuition for white children to attend private schools in order to maintain segregation. Some states actually closed their public schools rather than integrate them. Although Eisenhower personally disapproved of segregation, he also opposed rapid change, and so did little. This inactivity encouraged further Southern resistance, and in 1957, the governor of Arkansas called in the state National Guard to prevent a group of black students, the **Little Rock Nine**, from enrolling in a Little Rock high school. Eisenhower did nothing until one month later, when the courts ordered him to enforce the law. Arkansas, in response, closed all public high schools in Little Rock for two years. Eisenhower supported the Civil Rights Acts of 1957 and 1960, which strengthened the voting rights protection of Southern blacks and the punishments for crimes against blacks, respectively.

Another key civil rights event, the **Montgomery bus boycott**, began in 1955 when **Rosa Parks** was arrested for refusing to give up her seat on a bus to a white man as was required by **Jim Crow** laws. Outrage over the arrest, coupled with long-term resentment over unfair treatment, spurred blacks to stay off Montgomery buses for more than a year. The boycott brought **Martin Luther King, Jr.** to national prominence. Barely 27 years old at the time, King was pastor at Rosa Parks's church. Although King was clearly groomed for greatness—his grandfather had led the protests resulting in the creation of Atlanta's first black high school, his father was a minister and community leader, and King had already amassed impressive academic credentials (Morehouse College, Crozer Theological Seminary, University of Pennsylvania, and finally a Ph.D. from Boston University)—the year-long bus boycott gave him his first national podium. In the end, a ruling by the Supreme Court resulted in the integration of city buses in Montgomery and elsewhere.

King encouraged others to organize peaceful protests, a plan inspired by his studies of Henry David Thoreau and Mohandas Gandhi. In 1960, black college students in **Greensboro**, **North Carolina**, tried just that approach, organizing a sit-in at a local Woolworth's lunch counter designated "whites only." News reports of the sit-in, and the resultant harassment the students endured, inspired a sit-in movement that spread across the nation to combat segregation.

America Versus the Communists

There are a number of terms associated with the Cold War policy of Eisenhower and Secretary of State **John Foster Dulles** that you need to know. The administration continued to follow the policy of containment but called it **liberation** to make it sound more intimidating. It carried the threat that the United States would eventually free Eastern Europe from Soviet control. Dulles coined the phrase **massive retaliation** to describe the nuclear attack that the United States would launch if the Soviets tried anything too daring. **Deterrence** described how Soviet fear of massive retaliation would prevent their challenging the United States and led to an arms race. Deterrence suggested that the mere knowledge of **mutually assured destruction (MAD)** prevented both nations from deploying nuclear weapons. Dulles allowed confrontations with the Soviet Union to escalate toward war, an approach called **brinksmanship**. Finally, the Eisenhower administration argued that the spread of communism had to be checked in Southeast Asia. If South Vietnam fell to communism, the nations surrounding it would fall quickly like dominoes—hence, the **domino theory**.

Cold War tensions remained high throughout the decade. Eisenhower had hoped that the death of **Joseph Stalin** in 1953 might improve American-Soviet relations. Initially, the new Soviet leader **Nikita Khrushchev** offered hope. Khrushchev denounced Stalin's totalitarianism and called for "peaceful coexistence" among nations with different economic philosophies. Some Soviet client states took Khrushchev's pronouncements as a sign of weakness; rebellions occurred in Poland and Hungary. When the Soviets crushed the uprisings, U.S.-Soviet relations returned to where they were during the Stalin era. Soviet advances in nuclear arms development (the USSR exploded its first hydrogen bomb a year after the United States blew up its first H-bomb) and space flight (the USSR launched the first satellite, *Sputnik*, into space, motivating the United States to quickly create and fund the **National Aeronautics and Space Administration**, or **NASA**) further heightened anxieties.

Meanwhile, the United States narrowly averted war with the other communists, the Chinese. American-allied Taiwan occupied two islands close to mainland China, **Quemoy** and **Matsu**. The Taiwanese used the islands as bases for commando raids on the communists, which eventually irritated the Chinese enough that they bombed the two islands. In a classic example of brinksmanship, Eisenhower declared that the United States would defend the islands and strongly hinted that he was considering a

The Arms Race

Size of bombs
- Atomic bomb dropped on Hiroshima, 1945: equal to 12,500 tons of TNT
- First hydrogen bomb test, 1952: equal to 10,400,000 tons of TNT
- Soviet Tsar Bomba test, 1961: equal to 57,000,000 tons of TNT

Number of warheads
- 1945: USA 6; USSR 0
- 1950: USA 369; USSR 5
- 1955: USA 3,057; USSR 200
- 1960: USA 20,434; USSR 1,605
- 1970: USA 26,119; USSR 11,643
- 1980: USA 23,764; USSR 30,062

nuclear attack on China. Tensions remained high for years, and Eisenhower's stance forced him to station American troops on the islands. During the 1960 presidential election, Kennedy used the incident as a campaign issue, arguing that the two small islands were not worth the cost of defending them.

Third World Politics

World War II resulted in the breakup of Europe's huge overseas empires. In the decades that followed the war's end, numerous countries in Africa, Asia, and South America broke free of European domination. These countries allied themselves with neither of the two major powers; for this reason they were deemed the **Third World**. Both America and the Soviets sought to bring Third World countries into their spheres of influence, as these nations represented potential markets as well as sources of raw materials. The two superpowers particularly prized strategically located Third World countries that were willing to host military bases.

Neither superpower, it turned out, was able to make major inroads in the Third World at first. **Nationalism** swept through most Third World nations, recently liberated from major world powers. Enjoying their newfound freedom, these countries were reluctant to foster a long-term alliance with a large, powerful nation. Furthermore, most Third World countries regarded both powers with suspicion. America's wealth fostered both distrust and resentment, prompting questions about U.S. motives. America's racist legacy also hurt it in the Third World, where most residents were nonwhite. Yet most Third World nations also saw how the Soviets dominated Eastern Europe and so had little interest in close relations with them. These new nations were not anxious to fall under the control of either superpower.

However, the United States tried to expand its influence in the Third World in other ways. For example, in 1956 in Egypt, the United States tried offering foreign aid, hoping to gain an ally by building the much-needed **Aswan Dam**. Egypt's nationalist leader Gamal Nasser suspected the Western powers of subterfuge; furthermore, he detested Israel, a Western ally. Eventually, he turned to the Soviet Union for that aid. Later that year, Israel invaded Egypt, followed by Britain and France, in an effort to gain control of the **Suez Canal**. President Eisenhower played the "good cop" and pressured Britain and France to withdraw. The American government also used **CIA covert operations** to provide a more forceful method of increasing its influence abroad. In various countries, the CIA coerced newspapers to report disinformation and slant the news in a way favorable to the United States, bribed local politicians, and tried by other means to influence local business and politics. The CIA even helped overthrow the governments of Iran and Guatemala in order to replace anti-American governments with pro-American governments. It also tried, unsuccessfully, to assassinate the communist leader of Cuba, **Fidel Castro**.

The 1960 Presidential Election

In 1960, Eisenhower's vice president, **Richard Nixon**, received the Republican nomination. The Democrats nominated Massachusetts senator **John F. Kennedy**. Similar in many ways, particularly in foreign policy, both candidates campaigned against the "communist menace" as well as against each other. Aided by his youthful good looks, Kennedy trounced an awkward Nixon in their first televised debate. Kennedy's choice of Texan **Lyndon Johnson** as a running mate helped shore up the Southern vote for the Northern candidate. Nixon, meanwhile, was hurt by his vice presidency, where he had often served the role of Eisenhower's "attack dog." The fact that Eisenhower did not wholeheartedly endorse Nixon also marred his campaign. Still, it turned out to be one of the closest elections in history, and some believe that voter fraud turned a few states Kennedy's way, without which Nixon would have won.

In his final days in office, Eisenhower warned the nation to beware of a new coalition that had grown up around the Cold War, which he called the military-industrial complex. The combination of military might and the highly profitable arms industries, he cautioned, created a powerful alliance whose interests did not correspond to those of the general public. In retrospect, many would later argue that in his final statement, Eisenhower had identified those who would later be responsible for the escalation of the **Vietnam War**.

THE TURBULENT SIXTIES

At the outset, the 1960s seemed the start of a new, hope-filled era. Many felt that Kennedy, his family, and his administration were ushering in an age of "Camelot" (the Broadway musical was very popular then). As Arthur had had his famous knights, Kennedy, too, surrounded himself with an entourage of young, ambitious intellectuals who served as his advisers. The press dubbed these men and one woman "the best and the brightest" America had to offer. Kennedy's youth, good looks, and wit earned him the adoration of millions. Even the name of his domestic program, the **New Frontier**, connoted hope. It promised that the fight to conquer poverty, racism, and other contemporary domestic woes would be as rewarding as the efforts of the pioneers who settled the West.

The decade did not end as it had begun. By 1969, America was bitterly divided. Many progressives regarded the government with suspicion and contempt, while many conservatives saw all dissidents as godless anarchists and subversives. Although other issues were important, much of the conflict centered on these two issues: the Vietnam War and blacks' struggle to gain civil rights. As you read through this summary of the decade, pay particular attention to the impact of both issues on domestic harmony.

Kennedy and Foreign Policy

Like Truman and Eisenhower, Kennedy perceived the Soviet Union and communism as the major threats to the security of the United States and its way of life. Every major foreign policy issue and event of his administration related primarily to these Cold War concerns.

Two major events during Kennedy's first year in office heightened American-

Soviet tensions. The first involved **Cuba**, where a U.S.-friendly dictatorship had been overthrown by communist insurgents led by **Fidel Castro**. When Castro took control of the country in 1959, American businesses owned more than 3 million acres of prime Cuban farmland and also controlled the country's electricity and telephone service. Because so many Cubans lived in poverty, Cuban resentment of American wealth was strong, so little popular resistance occurred when Castro seized and nationalized some American property. The United States, however, was not pleased. When Castro signed a trade treaty with the Soviet Union later that year, Eisenhower imposed a partial trade embargo on Cuba. In the final days of his presidency, Eisenhower broke diplomatic relations with Cuba, and Cuba turned to the Soviet Union for financial and military aid.

Taking office in 1961, President Kennedy inherited the Cuban issue. Looking to solve the dilemma, the CIA presented the ill-fated plan for the **Bay of Pigs invasion** to the new president. The plan involved sending Cuban exiles, whom the CIA had been training since Castro's takeover, to invade Cuba. According to the strategy, the army of exiles would win a few battles, and then the Cuban people would rise up in support, overthrow Castro, and replace his government with one more acceptable to the United States. Kennedy approved the plan but did not provide adequate American military support, and the United States launched the invasion in April 1961. The invasion failed, the Cuban people did not rise up in support, and within two days Kennedy had a full-fledged disaster on his hands. Not only had he failed to achieve his goal, but he had also antagonized the Soviets and their allies in the process. His failure also diminished America's stature with its allies.

Kennedy Wasn't a Donut

A popular urban legend holds that when President Kennedy went to the Berlin Wall in 1963 and declared, *"Ich bin ein Berliner,"* he made a grammatical error and inadvertently called himself a jelly donut. Sadly for high-school history teachers trying to get a laugh out of their classes, this isn't actually true. While the word *"ein"* is omitted when literally declaring one's residence, it is required for figurative statements such as Kennedy's. Kennedy made no error, and the donut legend didn't start circulating until a novelist joked about it 20 years later.

Later in the year, Kennedy dealt with a second foreign policy issue when the Soviets took aggressive anti-West action by erecting a wall to divide East and West Berlin. The **Berlin Wall**, built to prevent East Germans from leaving the country, had even greater symbolic significance to the democratic West. It came to represent the repressive nature of communism and was also a physical reminder of the impenetrable divide between the two sides of the Cold War.

In 1962, the United States and the Soviet Union came the closest they had yet to a military (and perhaps nuclear) confrontation. The focus of the conflict was once again Cuba. In October, American spy planes detected missile sites in Cuba. Kennedy immediately decided that those missiles had to be removed at any cost; he further decided on a policy of brinksmanship to confront the **Cuban missile crisis**. He imposed a naval quarantine on Cuba to prevent any further weapons shipments from reaching the island, and then went on national television and demanded that the Soviets withdraw their missiles.

By refusing to negotiate secretly, Kennedy backed the Soviets into a corner; if they removed the missiles, their international stature would be diminished, especially since the quarantine was effectively a blockade, which diplomats defined as an act of war on the part of the United States. Therefore, in return, the Soviets demanded that the United States promise never again to invade Cuba and that the United States remove its missiles from Turkey (which is as close to the USSR as Cuba is to the United States). When Kennedy rejected the second condition, he gambled that the Soviets would not attack in response. Fortunately, behind-the-scenes negotiations defused the crisis, and the Soviets agreed to accept America's promise not to invade Cuba as a pretext for withdrawing the missiles. In return, the United States secretly agreed to remove its missiles from Turkey a few months later, thus making it look like the United States had won. Recent scholarship suggests that it was the Soviet leader Khrushchev who prevented World War III and a nuclear holocaust.

The policy of containment even motivated such ostensibly philanthropic programs abroad as the **Peace Corps**. The Peace Corps' mission was to provide teachers and specialists in agriculture, health care, transportation, and communications to the Third World, in the hopes of starting these fledgling communities down the road to American-style progress. The government called this process **nation building**. The Peace Corps had many successes, although the conflict between its humanitarian goals and the government's foreign policy goals often brought about failures as well. Furthermore, many countries did not want American-style progress and resented having it forced upon them.

The greatest theater for American Cold War policy during this era, however, was **Vietnam**, which will be discussed in greater detail shortly.

Kennedy and Domestic Policy

Kennedy began his presidency with the promise that America was about to conquer a **New Frontier**. He pushed through legislation that increased unemployment benefits, expanded Social Security, bumped up the minimum wage, and aided distressed farmers, among other measures.

Kennedy's civil rights agenda produced varied results. Kennedy supported **women's rights**, establishing a presidential commission that in 1963 recommended removing all obstacles to women's participation in all facets of society. Congress enacted the **Equal Pay Act** in 1963, which required that men and women receive equal pay for equal work. Unfortunately, employers continue to get around this federal law by simply changing job titles. However, it was only late in his presidency that Kennedy openly embraced the black civil rights movement. After almost two years of near inaction, in September 1962, Kennedy enforced desegregation at the University of Alabama and the University of Mississippi, where James Meredith was the first integrated student. In the summer of 1963, he asked Congress for legislation that would outlaw segregation in all public facilities. After Kennedy's assassination in November, Lyndon Johnson was able to push that legislation—the **Civil Rights Act of 1964**—through Congress on the strength of the late president's popularity and his own skills as a legislator.

John F. Kennedy also ordered his Attorney General, Robert F. Kennedy, to have the Justice Department order the Interstate Commerce Commission to make all public transportation integrated in response to the Freedom Riders.

Still, Kennedy's presidency proved an active period for the civil rights movement as a number of nongovernmental organizations mobilized to build on the gains of the previous decade. Martin Luther King, Jr. led the **Southern Christian Leadership Conference (SCLC)**, which staged sit-ins, boycotts, and other peaceful demonstrations. The Congress of Racial Equality (CORE) organized the **Freedom Riders** movement; the Freedom Riders staged sit-ins on buses, sitting in sections prohibited to them by segregationist laws. They were initially an integrated group, as was the **Student Nonviolent Coordinating Committee (SNCC)**, which did grassroots work in the areas of voter registration and antisegregationist activism. Such groups met considerable resistance. In 1963, Mississippi's NAACP director, **Medgar**

Evers, was shot to death by an anti-integrationist. Not long after, demonstrators in Montgomery, Alabama, were assaulted by the police and fire department who used attack dogs and fire hoses against the crowd. News reports of both events horrified millions of Americans and thus helped bolster the movement. So, too, for reasons mentioned above, did Kennedy's assassination.

Lyndon Johnson's Social Agenda

Like Kennedy, Lyndon Johnson made an early commitment to the civil rights movement, but unlike Kennedy, Johnson took immediate action to demonstrate that commitment. From the time he took office, Johnson started to lobby hard for the **Civil Rights Act of 1964**, which outlawed discrimination based on a person's race, color, religion, or gender. If you can remember only one federal law in U.S. history, this is it! The Civil Rights Act of 1964 is the most comprehensive piece of civil rights legislation enacted in U.S. history and the basis of all discrimination suits to this day. The law prohibited discrimination in employment as well as in public facilities (thus increasing the scope of Kennedy's proposed civil rights act).

Not long after, Johnson oversaw the establishment of the **Equal Employment Opportunity Commission (EEOC)** to enforce the employment clause of the Civil Rights Act. Johnson signed the **Voting Rights Act of 1965** after he was elected in his own right in 1964. This law cracked down on those states that denied blacks the right to vote despite the Fifteenth Amendment. He also signed another civil rights act banning discrimination in housing, and yet another that extended voting rights to Native Americans living under tribal governments.

Johnson had grown up poor and believed that social injustice stemmed from social inequality, and therefore, he advocated civil rights in employment. Toward the same end, he lobbied for and won the **Economic Opportunity Act**, which appropriated nearly $1 billion for poverty relief. After his landslide victory in the 1964 presidential election, Johnson greatly expanded his antipoverty program. A number of programs combined to form Johnson's **War on Poverty. Project Head Start** prepared underprivileged children for early schooling; **Upward Bound** did the same for high-school students. **Job Corps** trained the unskilled so they could get better jobs, while **Volunteers in Service to America (VISTA)** acted as a domestic Peace Corps. In addition, **Legal Services for the Poor** guaranteed legal counsel to those who could not afford their own lawyers. To further assist the poor, Johnson founded the **Department of Housing and Urban Development (HUD)**, increased federal aid to low-income apartment renters, and built more federal housing projects, as well as establishing Medicare and Medicaid.

The legislation passed during 1965 and 1966 represented the most sweeping change to U.S. government since the New Deal. Johnson's social agenda was termed the **Great Society**. Best of all, taxpayers did not feel much pain. Increased tax revenues from a quickly expanding economy funded the whole package. Not everyone liked Johnson's agenda, however; many objected to any increase in government activity, and the extension of civil rights met with bigoted opposition, especially in the South. Thus, ironically, the huge coalition that had given Johnson his victory and his mandate for change started to fall apart because of his successes (and were hastened by a bitter national debate over American involvement in Vietnam).

The Civil Rights Movement

In the early 1960s, the civil rights movement made a number of substantial gains. Legislative successes such as those passed under Johnson's Great Society program provided government support. The movement also won a number of victories in the courts, particularly in the Supreme Court. Under Chief Justice **Earl Warren**, the Court, for a brief moment in history, was extremely liberal. The **Warren Court** worked to enforce voting rights for blacks and forced states to redraw congressional districts so that minorities would receive greater representation. The Warren Court expanded civil rights in other areas as well. Among its landmark rulings are those that prohibited school prayer and protected the right to privacy. The Warren Court also made several decisions concerning the rights of the accused. In *Gideon v. Wainwright*, the Court ruled that a defendant in a felony trial must be provided a lawyer for free if he or she cannot afford one. In ***Miranda v. Arizona***, the Court ruled that, upon arrest, a suspect must be advised of his or her right to remain silent and to consult with a lawyer.

On January 23, 1964, the Twenty-Fourth Amendment to the Constitution was ratified. This banned the use of the poll tax in all elections.

Civil rights victories did not come easily. Resistance to change was strong, as evidenced by the opposition of state governments, police, and white citizens. In Selma, police prevented blacks from registering to vote; in Birmingham, police and firemen attacked civil rights protesters. All over the South, the **Ku Klux Klan** and other racists bombed black churches and the homes of civil rights activists with seeming impunity. In Mississippi, three civil rights workers were murdered by a group that included members of the local police department.

With news reports of each event, outrage in the black community grew. Some activists abandoned Martin Luther King's strategy of nonviolent protest. Among the leaders who advocated a more aggressive approach was **Malcolm X**, a minister of the **Nation of Islam**. Malcolm X urged blacks to claim their rights "by any means necessary." (His autobiography is an essential document of the history of racism in America.) Later, two groups that previously had preached integration—the **SNCC** and **CORE**—expelled their white members and advocated the more separatist, radical program of **Black Power**, with the Black Panthers being at the forefront of this movement. By 1968, when King was assassinated, the civil rights movement had fragmented, with some continuing to advocate integration and peaceful change, while others argued for empowerment through self-imposed segregation and aggression.

The New Left, Feminism, and the Counterculture

Black Americans were not the only ones challenging the status quo in the 1960s. Young whites, particularly those in college, also rebelled. For these young adults, the struggle was one against the hypocrisy, complacency, and conformity of middle-class life.

In 1962, the **Students for a Democratic Society** (SDS) formed. Its leftist political agenda, laid out in a platform called the **Port Huron Statement**, set the tone for other progressive groups on college campuses; these groups collectively became known as the **New Left**. New Left ideals included the elimination of poverty and racism and an end to Cold War politics. One particularly active branch of the New

Beatniks

We usually associate cultural rebellion with the 1960s and early 1970s, but the **Beat Movement** got its start in the 1950s. Beat writers, such as Allen Ginsburg, William Burroughs, and Jack Kerouac, challenged the straight-laced conservatism of the Eisenhower era by publishing works championing bohemian lifestyles, drug use, and nontraditional styles of art. The Beatniks would later inspire the Hippies of the 1960s.

Left formed at the University of California at Berkeley. In 1964, students there protested when the university banned civil rights and antiwar demonstrations on campus. These protests grew into the **Free Speech movement**, which in turn fostered a number of leftist and radical political groups on the Berkeley campus.

Most New Left groups, however, were male-dominated and insensitive to the cause of women's rights. Women became frustrated with being treated as second-class citizens and started their own political groups. In 1963, Betty Friedan's book *The Feminine Mystique* openly challenged many people's assumptions about women's place in society. Friedan identified "the problem that has no name" and is credited with restarting the women's movement, a movement that had faded once women's suffrage was achieved with the Nineteenth Amendment in 1920. She was also one of the founders of **NOW**, the **National Organization for Women**, formed in 1966 to fight for legislative changes, including the ill-fated **Equal Rights Amendment** (ERA) to the Constitution. The modern movement for gay rights also began to solidify in the 1960s, with the first Gay Pride parades occurring on the anniversary of the **Stonewall riots,** an event at which gays fought back against the police in New York City.

Feminists fought against discrimination in hiring, pay, college admissions, and financial aid. They also fought for control of reproductive rights, a battle that reached the Supreme Court in the 1973 case *Roe v. Wade*, which enabled women to obtain abortions in all 50 states within the first trimester. Many states argued that they had an obligation to protect "life," as stipulated in the Fourteenth Amendment, and quickly passed state laws prohibiting a woman from having an abortion after the first three months of her pregnancy. Although there is no specific mention of a constitutional right to privacy, the Supreme Court had established this important precedent in 1965 in the case *Griswold v. Connecticut*. *Roe v. Wade* remains a controversial decision and continues to play a central role in American politics and society.

"There's a time when the operation of the machine becomes so odious, makes you so sick at heart, that you can't take part! You can't even passively take part! And you've got to put your bodies upon the gears and upon the wheels, upon the levers, upon all the apparatus, and you've got to make it stop! And you've got to indicate to the people who run it, to the people who own it, that unless you're free, the machine will be prevented from working at all!"

—Mario Savio, speaking from the steps of Sproul Hall at the University of California, Berkeley, on December 3, 1964

Rebellion against "the establishment" also took the form of nonconformity, a repudiation of the Eisenhower years. Hippies grew their hair long, wore tie-dyed shirts and ripped jeans, and advocated drug use, communal living, and "free love." Their way of life came to be known as the **counterculture** because of its unconventionality and its total contrast to the staid mainstream culture, which was typified by aging crooners and banal television variety shows. By the end of the 1960s, the counterculture became more widely accepted, and artists such as Andy Warhol, Bob Dylan, Jimi Hendrix, the Beatles, and the Rolling Stones were among the biggest moneymakers in the arts.

Concurrent with the rise in activism for civil rights and women's rights was the upsurge of interest in environmental issues. **Rachel Carson**, an American marine biologist wrote the seminal work of nonfiction, *Silent Spring*, a worldwide bestseller to this day. *Silent Spring* blew the whistle on the widespread use of the chemical pesticide DDT, leading to its eventual ban. Meanwhile, legislators responding to industrial pollution passed the **Clean Air Act** of 1955, the first law to control the use of airborne contaminants.

The New Left, feminists, the counterculture, and others in the growing left wing of American politics almost uniformly opposed American participation in the Vietnam War. These groups' vocal protests against the war and the fierce opposition they provoked from the government and pro-war Americans created a huge divide in American society by 1968. Before we discuss that fateful year, it is important to understand how and why America became involved in Vietnam.

American Involvement in Vietnam, World War II–1963

From the Truman administration until the fall of Soviet Communism in 1991, U.S. foreign policy leaders asserted an American right to intervene anywhere in the world to stop the spread of communism and to protect American interests. Nowhere did that policy fail more miserably than in Vietnam, where the United States maintained an economic and military presence for almost 25 years. The Vietnam War divided America as no war before had.

The origins of America's involvement in Vietnam stretch back to World War II. From the late 19th century until World War II, Vietnam was a French colony. France exported the country's resources—rice, rubber, and metals—for French consumption. This foreign exploitation of Vietnam helped foster a nationalist Vietnamese resistance called the **Vietminh**, led by **Ho Chi Minh**. Ho had been schooled in France and had joined the French Communist Party before returning home. In fact, Ho Chi Minh was in Paris during the Versailles Peace Conference in 1919 and approached Woodrow Wilson at the time. Ho asked Wilson to honor his commitment to the right of nations to **self-determination**, as expressed in Wilson's **Fourteen Points**, and to help the Vietnamese expel the French from their country. Wilson ignored Ho Chi Minh's appeal.

Japan invaded Vietnam during World War II and ended French control of the country. Faced with a common enemy, the Vietnamese helped the Allies defeat Japan and probably expected to be granted their independence at the conclusion of the war, as India was in 1947. Shortly after the Japanese surrender in 1945, Ho drafted the Vietnamese Declaration of Independence modeled on the United States Declaration of Independence and the French Declaration of Rights of Man and Citizens.

The United States did not recognize Vietnamese independence nor the legitimacy of Ho's government, in part because of America's alliance with France (which wanted its colony back), and in part because Ho was a communist. Instead, the United States recognized the government of Bao Dai, the Vietnamese emperor whom the French had installed in the South, which France still controlled. Subsequently, Vietnam fought a war for independence against the French from 1946 until 1954, when the French were defeated at the Battle of Dien Bien Phu. Although Ho appealed to President Truman for assistance on several occasions, Truman never responded. Ho hoped the United States would honor its commitment to the principle of self-determination and empathize with the Vietnamese rather than support the colonial power. Truman continued to aid the French. The United States financed more than 80 percent of France's war effort in Indochina, a fact few Americans knew then or know now.

In 1954, all of the involved parties met in Geneva, Switzerland, and drew up the **Geneva Accords**, which divided Vietnam at the 17th parallel, with Communist forces controlling North Vietnam and (so-called) democratic forces controlling the South. It was agreed that this division was to be temporary and that elections would be held in two years to reunite the country and determine who would rule a unified Vietnam. The elections never took place, however. The United States, certain that Ho Chi Minh would win an election, sabotaged the peace agreement. First, the United States made an alliance with another South Vietnamese leader named **Ngo Dinh Diem** and helped him oust Bao Dai (whom the United States felt was too weak to control the country). Then, the CIA organized commando raids across the border in North Vietnam to provoke a Communist response (which the South Vietnamese could then denounce). Diem pronounced South Vietnam an autonomous country and refused to participate in the agreed-upon national election. The United States rallied Britain, France, Thailand, Pakistan, the Philippines, New Zealand, and Australia to form the NATO-like **Southeast Asia Treaty Organization** (SEATO) to provide for South Vietnam's defense against Communist takeover.

Unfortunately, the situation continued its downward spiral. Diem, it turned out, was a vicious leader. He took despotic control of South Vietnam, imprisoning political enemies, persecuting Buddhist monks, and closing newspapers that criticized his government. As a result, many South Vietnamese citizens joined the North Vietnamese side. These communist South Vietnamese insurgents were called the **Vietcong**. Rather than cut its losses, the United States continued to support Diem and the South Vietnamese economically. Committed to the policy of containment and intent on nation building, President Kennedy increased America's involvement in Vietnam by sending in military advisors known as the Green Berets. Finally, in 1963, the CIA helped the South Vietnamese military stage a coup to overthrow Diem's government. During the coup, Diem and his brother were killed and Kennedy was appalled by the outcome. A few weeks later, Kennedy was assassinated, and Johnson took control of America's war efforts.

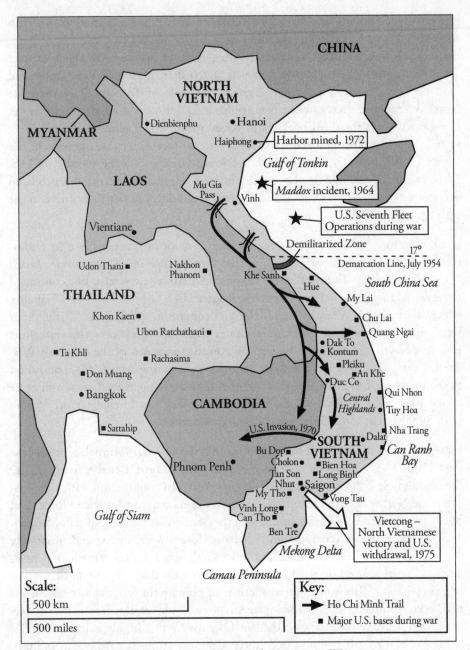

Southeast Asia During the Vietnam War

American Involvement in Vietnam, 1964–1968

Upon taking office, Johnson had the opportunity to withdraw American forces in a way that would not have embarrassed his administration. The United Nations, backed by France and the Vietcong, would have intervened and set up a coalition government to rule South Vietnam. Kennedy's advisers, however, convinced Johnson that U.S. forces could overwhelm any opposition in the region. He remained committed to using those forces to achieve "total victory."

In 1964, the United States supported a second coup in South Vietnam; apparently, the United States was not terribly selective as to who ran the country, so long as it was not the Communists. (The United States followed a similar pattern in Latin America.) The U.S. Army also started bombing the neighboring country of Laos, through which the North Vietnamese were shipping weapons to the Vietcong. Then, in August of the same year, reports stated that the North Vietnamese had fired on two American destroyer ships in the **Gulf of Tonkin**. (However, the North Vietnamese attack was never confirmed.) Johnson used the event to get Congress to pass the **Gulf of Tonkin Resolution**, which allowed the president to take any measures he deemed necessary to protect American interests in the region. The Tonkin Gulf resolution gave Johnson carte blanche to escalate U.S. participation in the war. It also is the closest Congress ever came to an official declaration of war in Vietnam. Thus, the first ground troops began to arrive in the early months of 1965.

Soon, Johnson had flooded the region with American troops. He also authorized massive Air Force bombing raids into North Vietnam. Those strikes, called "Operation Rolling Thunder," were supposed to last a few weeks, but continued for years. Many of them dropped chemical agents like Agent Orange and Napalm, which destroyed the Vietnamese jungles and contaminated the land. Throughout Johnson's administration, the United States essentially took over the war effort from the South Vietnamese—hence, the **Americanization** of the Vietnam War. As the war ground on and the draft claimed more young Americans, opposition to the war grew. Protest rallies grew larger and more frequent, and more and more young men either ignored their draft notices or fled to a foreign country (more than 30,000 went to Canada) to avoid military service.

Johnson's advisers continued to assure him that the war was "winnable" until January 1968, when the North Vietnamese launched the **Tet Offensive** (named after the Vietnamese holiday celebrating the New Year). In conjunction with the Vietcong, the North Vietnamese inflicted tremendous damage on American forces and nearly captured the American embassy in the South Vietnamese capital of Saigon. Though the North Vietnamese and Vietcong forces were, in the end, decisively driven back, the severity of the strikes was an ugly shock for the American people, who had been assured by the Johnson administration that the United States was winning the war. This would be a major turning point in the war, as most Americans had been confident their superior technology could easily defeat the underdeveloped Third World nation. The Tet Offensive was a highly calculated series of attacks carried out around the country, demonstrating that American military experts had vastly underestimated the sophistication of Vietnamese strategy. That the North Vietnamese and Vietcong could launch such a large-scale offensive and nearly succeed in taking the American embassy made the American public come to believe it was being lied to and that perhaps this war was not winnable.

The **My Lai Massacre** occurred the same year as the Tet Offensive. American soldiers were becoming more and more frustrated and began to act in unspeakable ways. The most publicized of these horrific events, although not an isolated occurrence, took place in a small village in South Vietnam, where U.S. soldiers abused, tortured, and murdered an estimated 347 to 504 innocent civilians, including women, children, and elderly Vietnamese too infirm to fight. When the story finally came to light in November 1969, the American public was outraged. Public opinion turned and protests against the war grew angrier and more frequent.

The Summer of 1968 and the 1968 Election

Johnson withdrew from the presidential race in large part because his association with the Vietnam War had turned many Americans against him, including many within his own party. Johnson's renomination would not have been easy; both **Eugene McCarthy** (no relation to Joseph McCarthy!) and **Robert Kennedy**, John F. Kennedy's brother and former attorney general, were poised to challenge him. Johnson's withdrawal opened the field to a third candidate, Vice President **Hubert Humphrey.**

Early in April 1968, a white assassin killed **Martin Luther King, Jr.** His murder ignited a massive wave of civil unrest, including arson and looting of largely white-owned businesses, in more than 150 towns and cities. In Chicago, where the Democratic convention would later be held, the mayor ordered the police to shoot arsonists on sight. To say that King's assassination heightened the already considerable tension surrounding race relations would be a huge understatement. During this time, the Kerner Commission report on race relations came out, stating that "our nation is moving toward two societies, one white and one black—separate and unequal."

Then, in June, frontrunner for the Democratic nomination **Robert Kennedy** was assassinated. Kennedy had come to represent the last bastion of hope for many Americans. Young, handsome, and vital (like his adored older brother), Kennedy was also an aggressive advocate for the poor and a harsh critic of the war in Vietnam. Together, the two assassinations convinced many that peaceful change from within the political system was impossible.

Many disenchanted young Americans came to Chicago in August to demonstrate at the Democratic Convention against government policy. The police were ordered to break up the crowds of protesters, which they did with tear gas, billy clubs, and rifles. Images of American policemen in gas masks clubbing American citizens reached millions of living rooms across the country through television and the newspapers, presenting a picture eerily reminiscent of the police states *against* which America supposedly fought. When the convention chose pro-war Vice President Humphrey over the antiwar McCarthy *and* refused to condemn the war effort, the Democrats alienated many of their core constituency on the left.

Meanwhile, the Republicans handed their nomination to former vice president **Richard Nixon** at a rather peaceful convention. Then, a third candidate entered the national election, Alabama governor **George Wallace**, who ran a segregationist third-party campaign, much like Strom Thurmond had done in 1948 against Harry Truman. Wallace was popular in the South, which had traditionally voted Democratic. Thus, Humphrey was twice cursed: he had alienated his progressive urban base in the North and Wallace was siphoning his potential support in the South. Humphrey denounced the Vietnam War late in the campaign, but it was too little, too late. In one of the closest elections in history, Richard Nixon was elected president.

The *Counter* Counterculture

It would be easy to stereotype the 1960s and 1970s as a rollicking party filled with free love, new social ideas, and worthy political causes for which young people could devote their time. Not everyone in America embraced the changes of the 1960s, though. Dismayed with what they perceived to be the excesses of the civil rights movement, the counterculture movement, and feminism, some Americans were eager to bring the country back to traditional values based on religious principles. Other Americans were alarmed by the rising cost of social welfare programs created by the New Deal and Johnson's Great Society. The conservative resurgence began in the 1970s at the grassroots level with a variety of groups that focused on single issues such as ending abortion, criticizing affirmative action, or emphasizing traditional gender roles and the nuclear family. Many older people were suspicious of the largely young contingent who had come to question the values of their parents and grandparents. Religious people distrusted the rejection of traditional morals and spiritual beliefs. Southern segregationists resisted the civil rights movement. And some Americans who did not have strong political leanings simply tired of marches and protests and wanted to return to a more peaceful way of life.

One notable leader in the Conservative reaction to the changes of the 1960s was **Phyllis Schlafly**. She is most well known for lobbying against the **Equal Rights Amendment** (ERA) to the Constitution. The ERA passed Congress, but was never fully ratified by the states, in part due to efforts to quell it by Schlafly and her supporters. Opponents to the ERA claimed that it could lead to the conscription of women into war (the Vietnam draft was already highly controversial), negatively affect women in divorce cases, and even allow men entry to women's-only colleges and clubs. Whatever the effects of the ERA would have been, these warnings influenced the opinions of many Americans and thus the ERA was never fully ratified.

When Richard Nixon ran for office, he sought to appeal to Americans who did not fully embrace the cultural and political changes of the 1960s and 1970. Conservatives voted for Nixon in large numbers, hoping that he would reverse the trend of encroaching federal power, as did some Southern Democrats who distrusted the newer liberal social policies of their party.

Nixon, "Vietnamization," and Détente

Nixon entered office promising to end American involvement in Vietnam by turning the war over to the South Vietnamese, a process he called "Vietnamization." He soon began withdrawing troops; however, he also increased the number and intensity of air strikes. Like his predecessors, Nixon was a veteran cold warrior who believed that the United States could, and must, win in Vietnam. He ordered bombing raids and ground troops into Cambodia, in hopes of rooting out Vietcong strongholds and weapons supplies. American involvement in Vietnam dragged on until 1973, when Secretary of State **Henry Kissinger** completed negotiations for a peace treaty with the North Vietnamese.

There are a couple of postscripts to the Vietnam story. First, the negotiated peace crumbled almost as soon as American troops started to vacate the country. In 1975, Saigon fell to the North Vietnamese Army, and Vietnam was united under communist rule. Second, Congress passed the **War Powers Resolution** in 1973 in order to prevent any future president from involving the military in another undeclared war. The War Powers Resolution requires the president to obtain congressional approval for any troop commitment lasting longer than 60 days.

Nixon did have success, however, in his other foreign policy initiatives, especially those concerning the world's two other superpowers, the USSR and China. During Nixon's first term, the United States increased trade with the Soviets, and the administration negotiated the first of a number of arms treaties between the two countries. Results were even more dramatic with China. After a series of secret negotiations, Nixon traveled to communist China, whose government the United States had previously refused to acknowledge. Nixon's trip eased tensions, partly because at the time of the trip, Americans trusted the anticommunist Nixon to improve relations with China, and his trip opened trade relations between the two countries. It also allowed Nixon to use his friendship with the Chinese as leverage against the USSR, and vice versa. (The Chinese and the Soviets, despite both being communist, hated each other.)

The Nixon years added two new terms to the vocabulary of foreign policy. Together, Nixon and Kissinger formulated an approach called **détente**, a policy of "openness" that called for countries to respect each other's differences and cooperate more closely. Détente ushered in a brief period of relaxed tensions between the two superpowers but ended when the Soviet Union invaded Afghanistan in 1979. The **Nixon Doctrine** announced that the United States would withdraw from many of its overseas troop commitments, relying instead on alliances with local governments to check the spread of communism.

Nixon's Domestic Policy

Nixon could not match his successes overseas at home. During Nixon's presidency, the economy worsened, going through a period of combined recession-inflation that economists called stagflation. Nixon attempted to combat the nation's economic woes with a number of interventionist measures, including a price-and-wage freeze and increased federal spending. None of his efforts produced their intended results.

Politically, American society remained divided among the haves and have-nots, the conservatives and the progressives. Much of the political rhetoric on both sides painted the opposition as enemies of the "American way." Several confrontations on college campuses heightened political tensions, most notably when national guardsmen shot and killed four protesters at **Kent State University** in Ohio who were protesting the United States' decision to invade Vietcong camps in neutral Cambodia. This incident became synonymous with the division between the youth and middle America. A similar incident occurred at the historically black Jackson State University in Mississippi, but the media failed to report the incident—further evidence of continued racial conflict in American society. Meanwhile, urban crime levels rose, causing many to flee to the relative tranquility of the suburbs.

Still, in 1972, Nixon won re-election in one of the greatest landslide victories in American political history, defeating liberal Senator George McGovern. Although Nixon won the election easily, both houses of Congress remained under Democratic control, an indication of the mixed feelings many Americans felt toward their political leaders.

Watergate and Nixon's Resignation

In the summer of 1971, two major newspapers published the **Pentagon Papers**, a top-secret government study of the history of U.S. involvement in Vietnam. The study covered the period from World War II to 1968, and it was not complimentary. It documented numerous military miscalculations and flat-out lies the government had told the public. Even though the documents contained nothing about the Nixon administration, Nixon fought aggressively to prevent their publication. The United States was involved in secret diplomatic negotiations with North Vietnam, the USSR, and China at the time, and both Nixon and Henry Kissinger (Nixon's Secretary of State) believed that the revelation of secret government dealings in the past might destroy their credibility in the present.

Nixon lost his fight to suppress the Pentagon Papers, a loss that increased Nixon's already considerable paranoia. In an effort to prevent any further leaks of classified documents, Nixon put together a team of investigators called the **plumbers.** The plumbers undertook such disgraceful projects as burglarizing a psychiatrist's office in order to gather incriminating information on Daniel Ellsberg, the government official who had turned the Pentagon Papers over to the press. During the 1972 elections, the plumbers sabotaged the campaigns of several Democratic hopefuls and then botched a burglary of Democratic headquarters in the **Watergate** Hotel.

When the plumbers were arrested at the Watergate Hotel, the White House began an all-out effort to cover up the scandal. A Senate hearing into the matter began in early 1973 and dragged on, keeping the story alive in the news for the next year and a half. Information was slowly revealed that incriminated the president's closest advisers. They would resign, and then most would be tried and convicted of felonies. (Perjury and destruction of evidence were two popular and successful charges against them.) At last, it was discovered that Nixon had secretly taped all conversations in the White House, including many concerning Watergate. For the next year, a legal battle over the tapes raged; the Senate demanded them, and Nixon refused to turn them over, claiming executive privilege. All the while, more damning evidence came to light—much of it in the pages of *The Washington Post,* courtesy of investigative journalists **Bob Woodward** and **Carl Bernstein**—and more former Nixon associates were jailed. When the president lost the battle over the tapes—the Supreme Court ordered Nixon to turn them over to the Senate—he knew his days were numbered, as the tapes revealed a number of unsavory aspects of Nixon's character. Rather than face impeachment proceedings, Nixon resigned in August 1974. His vice president, **Gerald Ford**, took office and almost immediately granted Nixon a presidential **pardon**, thereby preventing a trial.

Gerald Ford

Gerald Ford became president when Nixon resigned. Ford had replaced Nixon's first vice president, **Spiro Agnew**, who had resigned in the face of impending criminal charges (relating to corruption during his tenure as governor of Maryland). When Ford selected Nelson Rockefeller as his vice president, it was the first time that neither the president nor the vice president had been elected by the public.

Ford's controversial **pardon** of Nixon brought the Watergate era to a close, but it also cost Ford politically, as it raised suspicions that Nixon and Ford had struck a deal. Ford's political fortunes were further undermined by the weak economy. People were encouraged to wear "WIN" buttons: Whip Inflation Now. An oil embargo organized by Arab nations (under the leadership of **OPEC**) against the United States increased fuel prices, which in turn caused the price of almost everything else to rise. Inflation, coupled with an increasing unemployment rate, and the damage done to his credibility by the media, especially parodies by the actor Chevy Chase on *Saturday Night Live,* sealed Ford's fate. In 1976, he was defeated by Democrat **Jimmy Carter.**

Jimmy Carter

Carter inherited a weakening economy. During his presidency, inflation exceeded 10 percent, and interest rates on loans approached 20 percent. Slow economic growth was coupled with inflation to worsen the stagflation that began in Nixon's term. Carter tried to balance the federal budget but failed (as had every president since Eisenhower).

Many of the nation's economic problems resulted from the increased cost of OPEC petroleum. In response, President Carter increased funding for research into alternative sources of power. Carter created a new, cabinet-level government agency, the **Department of Energy,** to oversee these efforts. Many Americans saw nuclear power as a solution to the nation's energy woes. Opponents argued that nuclear power plant failures were potentially catastrophic; their fears were reinforced when a Pennsylvania plant at **Three Mile Island** failed, releasing radioactive materials into the atmosphere.

The high point of the Carter administration came when President Carter personally brokered a **peace agreement between Israel and Egypt**. Israeli-Egyptian conflict dated to the moment of Israel's founding in 1948, when Israel was besieged by hostile Arab neighbors. Tensions between Israel and Egypt were heightened by the 1967 **Six Day War**, during which Israel took control of the Sinai Peninsula, a desert region belonging to Egypt. In 1978, however, the leaders of the two countries agreed to meet with each other, in each other's countries. It was a major breakthrough in Israeli-Arab relations; most Arab nations refused even to acknowledge Israel's existence. President Carter hoped to capitalize on this breakthrough. He invited the two leaders to **Camp David** and personally brokered an agreement between the two nations. Ever since, the United States has actively participated in peace negotiations in the region.

Carter enjoyed some foreign policy successes. Along with negotiating the peace treaty between Israel and Egypt, he also concluded an arms agreement with the Soviets. However, Carter also suffered some major setbacks. When the USSR invaded Afghanistan, Carter's efforts proved powerless in forcing a withdrawal. Carter also flip-flopped in Nicaragua, where first he befriended the revolutionary **Sandinista** government and then turned against them as they allied themselves more closely with the USSR and Cuba. Carter's worst crisis involved Iran, when American hostages were taken in retaliation for America's decades-long support of the repressive, deposed Shah. Held for more than a year, the hostages were released only after Ronald Reagan took office.

Carter made the promotion of human rights one of the cornerstones of his foreign policy—he also negotiated a treaty between the United States and Panama that gave control of the canal zone back to Panama and got the Senate to ratify it. He spent his retirement working ceaselessly with organizations like Habitat for Humanity.

Summary

Here are the most important concepts to remember from the Postwar/Cold War period.

- After World War II, American life was economically prosperous—while fears of Communism dictated foreign policy.

- Left-wing liberalism promoted both a larger role for government in society and changing social norms.

- As industry and population grew, environmental concerns became more pressing.

Chapter 12 Review Questions

See Chapter 14 for answers and explanations.

1. All of the following threatened Harry Truman's chances for re-election in 1948 EXCEPT

   (A) Truman's positions on civil rights
   (B) rampant inflation
   (C) the Dixiecrat candidacy of Strom Thurmond
   (D) public dissatisfaction with the Korean War

2. Loyalty oaths, blacklists, and Alger Hiss are all associated with the

   (A) civil rights movement
   (B) New Deal
   (C) Red Scare
   (D) Great Society

3. John Foster Dulles, secretary of state under Eisenhower, intensified Cold War rhetoric with Washington's New Look defense program that emphasized

   (A) threatening Moscow with "massive retaliation"
   (B) containment
   (C) summit diplomacy
   (D) shuttle diplomacy

4. During the 1950s and early 1960s, the Warren Court was often criticized for

   (A) backing down from the Brown decision in its other civil rights rulings
   (B) exercising judicial restraint
   (C) protecting civil rights for African Americans while denying rights for political activists and communists
   (D) in effect, enacting "judicial legislation" through its rulings on individual rights

5. John F. Kennedy was unable to accomplish much of his stated civil rights agenda during his lifetime primarily because

   (A) the war in Vietnam demanded his full attention
   (B) African American leaders refused to work with him
   (C) his vice president, Lyndon Johnson, opposed any changes to civil rights law
   (D) Southern opposition to the civil rights movement made any association with it politically untenable

6. Which of the following does NOT accurately describe the presidential election of 1968?

   (A) The Democratic Party was fractured due to dissent over the Vietnam War.
   (B) A frontrunner for one of the major parties was assassinated during the primary season.
   (C) Both major-party candidates campaigned as Washington outsiders.
   (D) A third-party candidacy split the traditionally Democratic Southern vote.

7. Inflation throughout the 1970s was driven in large part by

   (A) the cost of funding the Vietnam War
   (B) rapidly increasing gasoline and oil prices
   (C) government investment in the space program
   (D) a dramatic reduction of income tax rates

8. The incident that began a chain of events that became one of the most infamous presidential scandals in American history and eventually led to the resignation of Richard Nixon was the

   (A) burglary of Daniel Ellsberg's psychiatrist's office
   (B) political sabotage of Nixon's opponent, George McGovern
   (C) illegal use of the CIA to hush up the FBI's investigation of the events surrounding the publication of the Pentagon Papers
   (D) break-in and attempted bugging of the Democratic Party's national headquarters

REFLECT

Respond to the following questions:

- For which content topics discussed in this chapter do you feel you have achieved sufficient mastery to answer multiple-choice questions correctly?

- For which content topics discussed in this chapter do you feel you have achieved sufficient mastery to discuss effectively in a short-answer question or an essay?

- On which content topics discussed in this chapter do you feel you need more work before you can answer multiple-choice questions correctly?

- On which content topics discussed in this chapter do you feel you need more work before you can discuss them effectively in a short-answer question or an essay?

- What parts of this chapter are you going to review again?

- Will you seek further help, outside of this book (such as a teacher, tutor, or AP Students), on any of the content in this chapter—and, if so, on what content?

Chapter 13
Unit 9: Entering into the 21st Century (1980–Present)

REAGAN, H. W., CLINTON, AND W. (1980–2001)

The Reagan Candidacy

By the late 1970s, many Americans had grown tired of the conflicts of the previous decade. Many were uncomfortable with the growing cynicism toward political leaders. Jimmy Carter hit a raw nerve—and disturbed many Americans—when he complained in a speech that the people were letting themselves be overtaken by a "crisis of confidence." This came to be known as "the malaise speech," though Carter never used the word "malaise" in it.

Ronald Reagan saw that the nation was ready for a major change. In the 1980 presidential campaign, Reagan, a former actor and governor of California, presented himself as Carter's opposite and a Washington "outsider," not tainted by events of the previous two decades, much as Carter had portrayed himself as an outsider in 1976. While Carter blamed American self-indulgence and consumerism for the country's problems, Reagan stressed the positive aspects of America. Furthermore, many Americans who disagreed with Reagan's conservative politics nonetheless voted for him because they liked him and his "can-do" attitude. Further damaging Carter's chances was the third-party candidacy of liberal Republican John Anderson, who attracted a sizable "protest vote" from those who might otherwise have supported Carter. In the end, Reagan won the 1980 election by a landslide.

Supply-Side Economics

Ronald Reagan tried to revive the economy by applying the theory of **supply-side economics**. Reagan believed that if corporate taxes were reduced, those corporations would earn greater profits. They would then use those profits, he believed, to buy new equipment and hire more employees. As a result, wealth would **trickle down** by creating more jobs and reinvigorating the economy. (George H. W. Bush would refer to this policy as "voodoo economics.") Reagan coupled this with large-scale deregulation, particularly in the areas of banking, industry, and the environment. He also successfully lobbied Congress for an across-the-board tax cut for all Americans. This policy increased his popularity with most Americans, although many complained that tax cuts hurt the poor, who pay little in income tax but depend on federal enfranchisement programs (such as welfare, food stamps, and Medicaid) to survive.

At first, Reagan's economic policies had little effect. The country continued in a recession for almost two years before the economy revived. Even then, results were mixed. Although inflation subsided, there was continued criticism that, under Reagan, the rich were getting richer while the poor were getting poorer. Rather than reinvesting in the economy, as supply-side economics suggested, the rich used the money saved on taxes to buy luxury items.

Military Spending and Budget Deficits

Ronald Reagan frequently claimed that he sought to decrease the size of the federal government. He called his plan the **New Federalism**, but it was quite the opposite of federalism—its goal was to shift power from the national government to the states. Reagan suggested that the states take complete responsibility for welfare, food stamps, and other social welfare programs currently funded at the national level; in return, the national government would assume the entire cost of Medicaid. Reagan's goal was never accomplished, however. The states feared that the shift would greatly increase the cost of state government, which would require unpopular tax increases at the state level.

At the same time, Reagan convinced Congress to greatly increase military spending. He funded research into a space-based missile shield system called the **Strategic Defense Initiative**, or **SDI** (the program was dubbed "**Star Wars**" by both supporters and detractors). Arguing that America needed to more quickly develop superior arms, Reagan also escalated the arms race with the USSR. Some historians have argued that the arms race bankrupted the Soviet Union and helped bring about an end to the Cold War, while others mainly credit Soviet leader Mikhail Gorbachev for the Cold War's end.

Tax cuts, increased military spending, and the failure of Reagan's New Federalism plan combined to escalate the **federal budget deficit**. Government spending increased while government revenues shrank, forcing the government to borrow money. Congress blamed the deficit on Reagan's tax cuts and called for a tax increase. Reagan, on the other hand, argued that the fault was with Congress, which refused to decrease funding for social welfare programs at the rate the president requested. Neither side budged, and as a result, the federal deficit reached record heights during the Reagan administration.

Foreign Policy Under Reagan

In foreign policy, Reagan sought to end the Cold War by winning it on every front he could in any way he could. He supported repressive regimes and right-wing insurgents in El Salvador, Panama, the Philippines, and Mozambique, all because they opposed communism. During the Reagan administration, the U.S. military led an international invasion of **Grenada** to topple a new Communist government there.

One of Reagan's top foreign policy priorities was support for a group of Nicaraguan insurgents called the **Contras**. Reports that the Contras were torturing and murdering civilians led Congress to cut off aid to the group, but the Reagan administration was so fully committed to them and opposed to the Sandinistas, who were communists, that it devised a plan to fund them through other channels. The government secretly sold weapons to Iran and then used the income to buy guns for the Contras. The entire process was eventually discovered; it came to be known as the **Iran-Contra affair**. Critics argued that Iran-Contra represented a constitutional crisis, pointing out that the plan had denied Congress the "power of the purse" central to the system of checks and balances. Supporters claimed that the president had broken no laws and that his goals were good ones. Reagan himself claimed that he had no knowledge of the plan; Oliver North, a member of the Security Council, took full credit.

Another foreign policy setback came when the Reagan administration sent marines to **Lebanon** as part of a United Nations peacekeeping force. A suicide bomb killed 240 servicemen and led to an eventual pullout of troops.

Reagan's greatest successes in foreign policy came in U.S.-Soviet relations. At first, Reagan's hard-line anticommunism led to deterioration in relations. The rhetorical war between the two enemies was fierce, Reagan calling the Soviet Union "the evil empire," and hitting an all-time low when he jokingly declared that he had outlawed the USSR, and added "we begin bombing in five minutes." Although not meant to be heard by the public, the joke was picked up by a microphone and later broadcast repeatedly. The escalated arms race further destabilized relations by constantly altering the military balance of power. Ultimately, however, the arms race helped bring the adversaries to the bargaining table, as neither side could afford the high cost.

American-Soviet relations were further helped when reformer **Mikhail Gorbachev** rose to power in the Soviet Union. Gorbachev is best known for his economic policy of *perestroika*, or restructuring, and his social reforms collectively referred to as *glasnost*, or openness. Gorbachev loosened Soviet control of Eastern Europe, increased personal liberties in the Soviet Union, and eventually allowed some forms of free-market commerce in the Communist country. Reagan and Gorbachev met frequently and ultimately negotiated a withdrawal of nuclear warheads from Europe.

George H. W. Bush

The election of 1988 convinced many Americans that progressive liberalism was finally destroyed, as George Bush easily defeated the Democratic candidate, Michael Dukakis, who was then governor of Massachusetts. In accepting his party's nomination, George Bush called for "a kinder, gentler nation," and he is most remembered for declaring, "Read my lips: No new taxes." "Liberalism" had become the "L word," and feminism had become the new "F word." The conventional wisdom held that Americans had settled back into traditional American lifestyles that celebrated values such as family and abstinence from sex and drugs (Nancy Reagan had urged kids your age to "Just say NO!"). It appeared as if the **moral majority** had spoken.

The most significant events of the Bush presidency were the ending of the Cold War (symbolized by the dismantling of the Berlin Wall and breakup of the Soviet Union) and the **Persian Gulf War**. If containment had been the guiding policy during the Cold War, but the Soviet Union no longer posed a threat to the world order, it would be left to George Bush to set the course for U.S. foreign policy into the 21st century. The test came in August 1990, when Saddam Hussein, the leader of Iraq, invaded Iraq's tiny but oil-rich neighbor Kuwait. When Saddam seized Kuwait's oil fields and threatened the world's access to Middle East oil, Washington reacted immediately. Having learned from Vietnam, Bush built a consensus in Congress and assembled an international coalition against Iraq in the UN.

Operation Desert Storm consisted mostly of massive air strikes against strategic Iraqi targets, and most Americans watched the war from the safety of their homes on television as if it were a video game. The war ended quickly with few American casualties. Although Iraq was required to submit to UN inspectors to insure that there were no **weapons of mass destruction** or chemical warfare production facilities, Saddam Hussein remained in power, a decision many foreign policy experts later came to criticize. It appeared that U.S. foreign policy in the post–Cold War era would focus on political stability in the Middle East and defending human rights.

War	Afghanistan	Iraq
Years	2001 to Present	2003 to 2011
Presidents	George W. Bush, Barack Obama, Donald Trump	George W. Bush, Barack Obama
Conflict	After the terrorist attacks of September 11, 2001, the Bush administration vowed to rout terrorist group Al-Qaida from its strongholds in Afghanistan while also curbing the power of the Taliban, a militant Islamic political organization. Osama bin Laden, the leader of Al-Qaida, was finally captured and killed, but the Taliban still holds influence in rural regions of Afghanistan.	Dubious allegations that Saddam Hussein had helped to orchestrate 9/11, as well as his ongoing human rights violations against his own people and rumors of weapons of mass destruction (which were later found to be false), led the Bush administration to invade Iraq in March of 2003. United States armed forces remained in Iraq until 2011. Both the war in Iraq and the war in Afghanistan fell under the United States' larger foreign policy known as the **War on Terror**.
Outcome	The Afghanistan War has not officially ended. U.S. troops are still stationed in the region. The Afghanistan War is now the longest one in U.S. history.	Although Iraq is no longer run by the Hussein family, it struggles to rebuild politically and economically. Without a strong-arm dictator, various factions vie for power. The Iraq War continues to be controversial in American politics.

Post-1980 Society

Though the 1980s were before you were born and may even seem like ancient history to you, historians assert that it can take as many as 50 years or more before enough time has elapsed for people to evaluate the past objectively. Keeping that in mind, let's take a look at some of the major trends and developments that historians have begun to identify in the past 20 or 30 years.

Changing Demographics

As was the case a century ago, when predominantly Eastern European immigrants arrived by the millions onto America's shores, immigration in recent decades has significantly affected the shape and tenor of American society. In 1890, 86 percent of immigrants to the United States were from Europe. From the 1970s through today, however, the fastest-growing ethnic minorities in the United States have been **Hispanics** and **Asians**, and according to the 2000 census, Hispanics now outnumber African Americans as the largest minority in the United States. Much of this growth among Asians and Hispanics has been fueled by immigration.

Who?	Hispanic	Asian
How many?	Population increased from 6 million in 1960 to 50 million today.	Population increased by 70% in the 1980s (about 3 million in the decade). Today, there are about 12.8 million Asian immigrants.
From where?	Mexico, Puerto Rico, Cuba, El Salvador, Guatemala, Honduras, and Nicaragua	Philippines, China, South Korea, India
To where?	California, Texas, Florida, Southwest	Largely settled in California

The **Immigration Act of 1965** contributed significantly to the increase in immigration by members of these population groups. This legislation phased out all national quotas by 1968 and set annual limits on immigration from the Western Hemisphere and the rest of the world, essentially relaxing restrictions on non-European immigration. It gave priority to reuniting families and to certain skilled workers (particularly scientists) and **political refugees**. Though the vast majority of immigrants who entered under this legislation did so in order to join family members, searching for employment and escaping from persecution still ranked high among the most common reasons people came to the United States. Several groups admitted under these regulations included Cuban and Southeast Asian refugees created by **Fidel Castro's** revolution and the Vietnam War, respectively.

At the end of the 20th century, from 1970 to 2000, the number of foreign-born people living in the United States went from 10 million to 31 million, or 11 percent of the total population. Fifty-one percent of those foreign-born were from Latin America, while 27 percent were from Asia, the second-largest group. Not since the turn of the 20th century has the United States experienced a comparable surge in immigration. In 1915, immigrants made up 15 percent of the total population, the largest percentage in our history so far.

What will all these changes mean for American society? The increasing racial and ethnic diversity of our population has sparked heated debate not only on immigration policy but also on issues such as bilingual education and affirmative action. Discussions of immigration policy have generally centered on illegal immigration, the role and impact that immigrants have on the economy, and the extent to which an influx of new cultures, attitudes, and ideas will reshape society. Tensions created by this new wave of immigration have resulted in various measures to curb **illegal immigration**, abolish bilingual education in some states, and allow both low-skilled and high-skilled workers into the United States on a temporary basis to provide needed labor and services. In 1986, for instance, Congress passed the **Simpson-Mazzoli Act**, which outlawed the deliberate employment of illegal immigrants and granted legal status to some illegal aliens who entered the United States before 1982. However, problems persist.

Guest worker programs were an attempt to curb illegal immigration by offering temporary employment to workers. Workers would then return to their home countries once the period of employment ended. The **Bracero** program was one such guest worker agreement between the United States and Mexico, in which the U.S. hosted migrant farm workers. The program lasted from 1942 until 1964, when pressure to end the program was put on the government by organized labor who were frustrated at the decrease in wages that the spike in agricultural employment brought with it.

Diversity, Asset, or Liability?

Whether you believe that immigrants place a burden on social services or support and enrich the development of our economy and society, it is clear that the United States is in the midst of major demographic changes that are visible today. With each new wave of immigration, ethnic enclaves sprout in big cities and neighborhoods, contributing to America's unique mixture of peoples. A century ago, there were communities such as Little Italy in New York City or Chinatown in San Francisco. Today, reflecting more recent population trends, there are places like Little Havana in Miami, Florida, and Little Saigon in Orange County, California. Americans have also seen an increase in multilingual services and the media catering to Hispanics and Asians, in particular. Even political parties openly attempt to attract Hispanics in recognition of their potential political influence. The impact of these changing demographics will be felt for generations to come.

Arguments for diversity as an asset	**Arguments for diversity as a liability**
• Immigrants enrich the development of the economy and society.	• Immigration places a burden on social services.
• American identity has always evolved with new waves of immigration. The U.S. economy and culture both benefit from increasing access to economic opportunities for previously excluded groups.	• There exists an American identity that is threatened by the presence of cultures that are not presumed to fit into that identity. This attitude can be observed in the frustration expressed by some groups over the increase in multilingual services and media outlets targeting Hispanics and Asians.

The Clinton Presidency (1993–2001)

William Jefferson Clinton was the first Democrat to be elected president since Jimmy Carter. After more than a decade of Republican control of the White House, Clinton and **Al Gore** took control in January 1993. Although it is doubtful that you would be required to write an essay that went through the 1990s, you could see a few multiple-choice questions about the major events that occurred during Clinton's two terms as president. The following is a brief review of those issues and events.

The close of the 20th century brought with it radical changes in the way Americans do business. The idea of a local economy could no longer be considered without considerations of how the larger global community affects it. Further, the economy was jump-started by a revolution in digital technology that brought about new business opportunities as well as fast-paced breakthroughs that quickly made relatively new technology obsolete.

One significant change from the 1990s was the acceleration of **globalism**. As opposed to nationalism, in which a nation's affairs are focused inward, globalism promotes an interconnectivity of nations by way of economic agreements (typically promoting free trade reducing tariffs), immigration, and military intervention.

The first significant event of the Clinton presidency was the establishment of the **North American Free Trade Agreement (NAFTA)**. Although the treaty had been negotiated by the previous Republican administration, Clinton signed it into law in 1993. In a way, it was similar to the global treaty from 1947, the **General Agreement on Tariffs and Trade (GATT)**, which sought to reduce trade barriers such as tariffs and preferential treatment. In the case of NAFTA, it did exactly what it sounds like it did—eliminated trade barriers among the United States, Mexico, and Canada. While the treaty was severely criticized by American labor unions, who feared American companies would move their factories elsewhere in order to reduce costs with lower wages and operation costs, corporate interests supported it enthusiastically. Despite often speaking favorably about the concept of free trade, and gradually reducing tariff barriers over time, the United States has historically interfered with trade, usually in the form of high, protective tariffs, when it was beneficial to certain political and economic groups, but always under the guise of protecting the "national interest."

Also notable during Clinton's presidency was the **1994 Congressional Election**. Speaker of the House **Newt Gingrich**'s Contract with America outlined a specific series of laws the Republican Party wished to pass, designed to reduce taxes, consolidate government programs, and reform welfare entitlement programs. The Republicans won back control of Congress, but their power was limited by Clinton's moderating Democrat executive power. Clinton cooperated with the Republicans in Congress on some matters, especially reforming welfare and giving the states more control over administering benefits. This led to his winning the 1996 presidential election over Bob Dole.

No doubt, the most infamous event of Clinton's presidency was the Clinton-Lewinsky scandal that led to Clinton's impeachment during his second term in office. Some Clinton supporters believe that special prosecutor Kenneth Starr had it in for the Clintons, beginning with his accusations of their dubious real-estate dealings in what came to be known as **Whitewater**. Regardless, the U.S. House of Representatives, which had a Republican majority at the time, impeached Clinton for perjury, obstruction of justice, and abuse of power. Remember that impeachment is the formal accusation of wrongdoing; it does not mean that the accused is thrown out of office. According to the Constitution, the House of Representatives has the "sole power of impeachment," and any federal official can be impeached for committing treason, bribery, or other "high crimes and misdemeanors." The United States Senate then has the "sole power to try all impeachments." Although Clinton was impeached, he was acquitted by the Senate and remained in office to finish his second term. Several federal judges have been impeached throughout American history, but Clinton was only the second president ever impeached. Lincoln's vice president, Andrew Johnson, was impeached, but he too was acquitted and was not thrown out of office. Students sometimes think that Nixon was impeached for his involvement in Watergate. Not quite. He resigned before the House of Representatives completed the process.

Clinton was really the first president to take office after the end of the Cold War, and he made it clear that one of his major foreign policy goals was the protection of human rights around the world, although some criticized his turning a blind eye to human rights violations in China, defending capitalism over democracy. In 1999, Clinton supported a bombing campaign in the former Yugoslavia under the auspices of NATO. Slobodan Milosevic, president of Serbia, was conducting a brutal policy of "ethnic cleansing" against Balkan Muslims. Milosevic was eventually tried and convicted for committing "crimes against humanity."

Other notable events that took place during the Clinton years include his "Don't ask, don't tell" policy pertaining to gays in the U.S. military and his appointments of Ruth Bader Ginsburg and Stephen Breyer to the Supreme Court. Two significant initiatives that failed were his proposal for a national health care program and campaign finance reform.

THE 2000 ELECTION

While it is incredibly unlikely that you will be asked to know anything specific about the George W. Bush administration, other than the obvious major events like 9/11 and the situation in Iraq (although certainly not in any detail), you may see a question about the 2000 election. According to the Constitution, a candidate must win a majority of electoral votes to win the presidential election. However, because of the "winner-take-all" system regarding the allotment of electoral votes in most states, it is possible for a candidate to win the majority of the popular vote nationwide but lose the presidency. Recall that this happened in 1824, when Jackson won a plurality of the popular vote, but John Quincy Adams became president, and again in 1876, when Samuel J. Tilden lost to Rutherford B. Hayes. On election night in November 2000, the major television networks erroneously reported that Al Gore had defeated George W. Bush. Through a convoluted series of mishaps with the voting procedure in Florida, Al Gore challenged the results of that election, but eventually the Supreme Court prevented a formal recount of the vote in Florida and George W. Bush, son of former president George H. W. Bush, was elected.

The George W. Bush presidency also marked the rise in **neoconservatism**, which literally means "new conservatism," a movement in sharp opposition to "paleoconservatism" or the conservatism of prior Republican administrations. Neoconservatives, such as Vice-President Dick Cheney, Secretary of State Donald Rumsfeld, and advisor Paul Wolfowitz, promoted the idea of spreading democracy worldwide and putting American corporate interests first through the use of military actions abroad. Global trade and open immigration is a net positive for America in neoconservative thought.

Some former Democrats latched onto neoconservatism, while both staunch liberals and paleo-conservatives criticized the Bush Administration. For liberals, the Bush policies were symptomatic of excessive corporate power and global imperialism, while traditional conservatives such as Patrick J. Buchanan lamented the cost of military adventures overseas, the loss of domestic jobs incurred by global free-trade agreements, and the ravages of unrestricted immigration. Americans on both sides of the aisle, it seemed, had lost faith in the ability of the federal government to solve social and economic problems.

AFRICAN AMERICANS IN POLITICS

The first African American governor was P.B.S. Pinchback, who served as governor of Louisiana for 15 days, from December 29, 1872, to January 13, 1873.

Following the accomplishments of Freedom Summer in 1964, the **Voting Rights Act of 1965**, and the **Twenty-fourth Amendment** to the Constitution, measures such as literacy tests and poll taxes that had been used by many Southern states to deny African Americans the right to vote were summarily banned. The results in the South were dramatic: in 1960, only 20 percent of eligible African Americans had been registered to vote, but by 1971, that number had jumped to 62 percent. Cities such as Los Angeles, Chicago, Washington, D.C., Atlanta, and New Orleans elected their first African American mayors in the 1980s. The nation's first African American governor in recent memory was elected in 1990 in Virginia.

In 1968, **Shirley Chisholm** was the first African American woman elected to Congress; in 1972, she also became the first African American to run for president. **Reverend Jesse Jackson** also ran for the Democratic presidential nomination in 1984 and 1988, winning many of the primary elections. According to the U.S. Census Bureau in 2000, there were 1,540 African American legislators, representing 10 percent of the total number of legislators nationwide. **Colin Powell** and **Condoleezza Rice**, both Secretaries of State under **President George W. Bush,** occupied the most powerful political office that African Americans had held since Thurgood Marshall was appointed to the Supreme Court by Lyndon Johnson in the 1960s. Of course, those records were surpassed with the historic 2008 election of Barack Obama as president of the United States.

Urban Problems

As in the past, people in the 1950s and 1960s flocked to the cities for employment and cheaper housing. African Americans continued to move to Northern and Western cities as they had done during World Wars I and II, while other minorities, including immigrants from Latin America, were drawn to cities for similar reasons. By the 1970s and 1980s, however, mounting urban problems—overcrowding, increasing unemployment and crime rates, and decaying and inadequate housing and commercial areas—initiated a trend of mostly white, middle-class Americans leaving the cities for the suburbs (a phenomenon nicknamed "white flight"); the open spaces, shopping malls, and better-funded schools of the suburbs also enticed people to move. When middle-class families moved to the suburbs, businesses and industries that once provided vital jobs and tax revenue for cities followed. The result was that poor people and racial minorities remained in cities where there were insufficient funds for housing, sanitation, infrastructure, and schools.

Meanwhile, televised **urban riots** in the 1960s, such as those in Los Angeles, Chicago, and New York after the assassination of Martin Luther King, Jr., only served to widen the gap between cities and suburbs and to heighten racial tensions. One of the worst urban riots occurred much later in 1992 in South Central Los Angeles, where many African Americans expressed outrage at the acquittal of four white police officers who were videotaped beating a black man, **Rodney King**.

Tensions between urban and suburban areas surfaced in ways that highlighted both racial and class animosity. During 1974–1975, the **forced busing** of students resulted in violence in South Boston when black students from a poorer section were bused into a predominantly white, working-class neighborhood school by court order. Buses were vandalized and attacked while riot police tried to quell the mob. White families moved from South Boston or sent their children to private schools, while even some black families opposed the forced busing, arguing instead that the schools in their black neighborhoods should receive better funding. Busing continued in many major cities through the late 1990s, and although many schools did achieve greater racial integration, the strategy was not without its critics. Indeed, the Supreme Court decision in **_Milliken v. Bradley_** (1974) held that an interdistrict remedy for unconstitutional segregation found in one district exceeded the scope of the violation.

But while the image of the scary inner city still has a hold on some imaginations, it is no longer supported by statistics. Both violent crime and property crime have plunged since the early 1990s, and crime in 2010 reached its lowest level in 40 years. In large urban areas, the drop in crime has been even more pronounced. Affluent young professionals have flocked back to city centers. There is an active debate over what has caused this encouraging trend—one theory credits falling levels of lead in the environment due to legislation in the early 1970s, as lead poisoning is linked to criminal activity. Whatever the reasons, the dramatic drop in crime has led to a revitalization of American cities over the course of the past 20 years.

AMERICA AND THE WAR ON TERROR

America entered a new phase of foreign policy when Osama bin Laden's Al Qaeda organization attacked the World Trade Center and the Pentagon on September 11, 2001. Two planes flew into the World Trade Center's Twin Towers, and one flew into the Pentagon. A fourth plane had allegedly planned to hit the White House, but passengers overcame the hijackers long enough to crash the plane into a field in Pennsylvania. In total, almost 3,000 civilians were killed on 9/11. The Bush Administration quickly got support from NATO (North Atlantic Treaty Organization) allies to launch an attack on the Taliban government in Afghanistan in October of 2001, where bin Laden and Al Qaeda were headquartered. The ensuing war led to the removal of the Taliban from power and a restoration of democracy in Afghanistan.

Allegations that Saddam Hussein helped to orchestrate 9/11, as well as his ongoing human rights violations against his own people and rumors of weapons of mass destruction, led the Bush administration to invade Iraq in March of 2003. American troops quickly seized Baghdad and Hussein went into hiding, leaving a power vacuum. American military leaders worked to establish a provisional government, but tensions between rival political and religious factions erupted, leading to a prolonged American occupation.

THE CONSERVATIVE RESURGENCE

Instrumental in energizing conservatives throughout the 1970s and 1980s were right-wing evangelical Christians, members of a branch of Protestantism that emphasized a "born-again" religious experience and adherence to strict standards of moral behavior taken from the Bible. **Evangelicalism**, particularly fundamentalist sects, became increasingly prominent in political life from the 1970s through the 1990s. Fundamentalists denounced the moral relativism of liberals and believed in a literal interpretation of the Bible. Evangelical groups also became increasingly political. Conservative evangelicals and fundamentalists such as **Billy Graham, Jerry Falwell,** and **Pat Robertson** helped to mobilize other like-minded citizens to support the Republican Party and bring together various conservative groups to form a movement known as the **New Right**. The growing strength of the New Right was evident in the key role it played in helping to elect **Ronald Reagan** in 1980, and in 1994 when the Republican Party under **Newt Gingrich** recaptured control of both houses of Congress under Democratic President **Bill Clinton**. Evangelical Christians continued to support Republicans with the election and re-election of George W. Bush.

DIGITAL REVOLUTION

Globalism's worldwide interconnectivity is both a cause and an effect of the **digital revolution**. As digital technology such as personal computers and cellular phones became easier to produce, they became cheaper to purchase. Americans turned to these new technologies for personal and business use as a result of the exponential increases in data storage offered by new devices. As you can probably guess, the 20 years between 1990 and 2010 saw significant changes in the ways Americans lived.

As access to the internet increased with the digital revolution, new business opportunities presented themselves. The "**dot-com bubble**" of the late 1990s involved widespread speculation on the value of internet-based companies before many of those sites were able to turn a profit. Predictably, the bubble burst by 2001, but not without creating its first wave of internet millionaires.

From 1990 until 2010, the number of manufacturing jobs in the United States decreased by a third. Around the turn of the century, these former manufacturing positions were replaced by retail jobs. However, the 2008–2009 recession reduced retail employment, and many Americans found new work in the booming healthcare industry.

DECLINE OF UNIONS

Throughout the second half of the 20th century, and in particular, its final three decades, union power and membership have declined. In addition to increased spending on the part of industry to advocate for anti-labor legislation, there are some other key factors at play.

The Taft Hartley Act of 1947—passed over Truman's veto—restricted the ability to strike as well as the preferential hiring of union members.

Union busting—President Reagan's 1981 mass firing of 3,000 striking air traffic controllers let industry know that union busting would not be tolerated.

The generational divide has no doubt also played a role in the decline of unions—younger generations have not experienced the struggles that unions encountered to secure workers' rights and often fail to see the benefits that older workers see.

Wage Stagnation

Economists have noted that one of the most prominent effects of a decline in union membership is the growth in income inequality starting in the latter part of the 20th century. The inability to collectively bargain on the scale that unions could from World War II through the 1970s has led to a stagnation in wages. As union membership decreased—from 34 percent in 1979 to 10 percent in 2010—there has been a notable consolidation of wealth in the upper echelon of American earners.

REPEAL OF GLASS-STEAGALL

In 1933, President Roosevelt signed the **Glass-Steagall Act** (also known as the **Banking Act of 1933**). The act stemmed from the volatility of American banks leading up to the Great Depression. Banks were able to use their commercial deposits (from individuals and businesses) to speculate in the investment market. Since the investment market was not always predictable, banks that used commercial deposits for this purpose were often unstable. The Glass-Steagall Act forced banks to avoid a conflict of interest by deciding whether they would be commercial banks or investment banks and prohibited them from participating in more than one of these operations.

The **Gramm-Leach-Bliley Act** of 1999 effectively did away with this provision. Many economists, such as Joseph Stiglitz, argue that it is no surprise that within a decade of the repeal of Glass-Steagall, the American economy was brought to its knees by a recession stemming from banks offering home loans based on speculation of the value of those homes.

GENDER ROLES

Women have taken on larger roles in professional settings in the 21st century. However, many claim the glass ceiling (unfulfilled promises of advancement) still remains. The fact that the average age for first marriage has increased points to the fact that women are prioritizing their careers before settling down to have families. Further, the 2008 recession affected jobs traditionally held by men more than it affected jobs traditionally held by women. Therefore, women were increasingly a family's primary breadwinner at the start of the second decade of the 2000s.

Along with changing gender roles, the United States has seen an increase in women elected to political office. Besides Hillary Clinton's presidential campaign in 2016, Geraldine Ferraro and Sarah Palin each were nominated as running mates in the presidential campaigns of 1984 and 2008, respectively. Further, the number of women elected to Congress has reached historic levels.

In addition to changing demographics, analysts have also noticed new patterns in family structures over the latter half of the 20th century. While 87% of children lived in a two-parent household in 1960, only 73% did in 2000, and 69% do today. Consistent with this is the rise in one-parent households: 9% of children lived in a one-parent household in 1960 compared with 26% today.

RECENT TRENDS

Another Course? Of Course!
If you can't get enough AP U.S. History and want to review this material with an expert, we also offer an online Cram Course that you can sign up for here: https://www.princetonreview.com/college/ap-test-prep?ceid=nav-1.

You are unlikely to see any questions on your test regarding the election of Barack Obama in 2008 or the election of President Donald Trump in 2016. In closing, however, it helps to know that the Bush and Obama administrations responded to the **financial crash of 2008** (exacerbated by the crisis in the mortgage industry) by providing financial assistance to major banks, popularly known as a "banker bailout." The most important piece of legislation passed under Obama's tenure was the **Affordable Care Act** or "Obamacare," a controversial set of laws that aimed to both regulate the medical industry and provide subsidies to uninsured Americans.

The **election of 2016** was a turbulent one, marked by ideological divisions within the Republican Party and a bitter rivalry between populist real-estate mogul Donald Trump and Democrat insider Hillary Clinton. Clinton won the national popular vote, while Trump won the Electoral College. While political analysts still struggle to understand the dynamics that propelled Trump to victory, the consensus may conclude that a **new populism** has emerged in the United States—one of skepticism for established institutions and optimism regarding political "outsiders." If the trend continues, no doubt many changes will come to both domestic and foreign policy.

Summary

Here are the most important concepts to remember from the pre-21st-century and early 21st-century period.

o   In response to a growing liberalization of government, Conservatives gained a new voice in public discourse.

o   After the collapse of the Soviet Union and the fall of the Berlin Wall, American fears shifted to the threat of Middle Eastern terrorism.

o   Immigration, both legal and illegal, grew exponentially, prompting internal debate.

o   The Internet revolution of the 1990s enhanced the economy and ushered in the Information Age, while domestic manufacturing jobs decreased. Many Americans were forced to seek alternative employment as large companies down-sized and outsourced jobs overseas.

o   The United States continued to pursue an interventionist foreign policy through the early 21st century.

o   Right-wing populism and left-wing socialism squared off before and during the Trump Administration.

Chapter 13 Review Questions

See Chapter 14 for answers and explanations.

1. The top goals of the Reagan presidency included

    (A) eliminating all social programs and balancing the federal budget
    (B) reducing the size of the federal government and increasing defense spending
    (C) using the federal government to enforce civil rights and reducing U.S. influence in Central America
    (D) increasing income tax rates and strengthening environmental regulations

2. Since the end of the Cold War, the continuing American impulse to intervene in the economic and political affairs of other nations around the world is motivated by all of the following EXCEPT

    (A) fears of renewed Soviet expansion
    (B) the protection of human rights
    (C) American economic interests
    (D) the desire to promote and develop democratic institutions in former communist and Third World nations

3. All of the following acts of President Ronald Reagan's administration are characterized as a return to conservative political values EXCEPT

    (A) cuts in the federal budget
    (B) the appointment of Sandra Day O'Connor to the Supreme Court
    (C) tax cuts for corporations
    (D) the loosening of government regulation

4. Which of the following did NOT contribute to the emergence of the New Right of the 1970s and 1980s?

    (A) The Moral Majority movement
    (B) The popularity of Ronald Reagan
    (C) The "stagflation" economic condition of the 1970s
    (D) A sudden drop in the stock market

5. In his 1985 State of the Union Address, Ronald Reagan articulated his foreign policy goals in what has come to be known as the Reagan Doctrine. Like Truman, Reagan pledged to

    (A) support anticommunist resistance movements, particularly in the Third World
    (B) sponsor covert military operations to overthrow communist regimes in Eastern Europe
    (C) ease tensions between the Soviet Union and the United States
    (D) broker a peace agreement between the Palestinians and the Israelis

6. During the 1990s, President George H. W. Bush

    (A) signed the welfare reform bill
    (B) persuaded Anwar Sadat and Menachem Begin to sign the Camp David Accords
    (C) sent troops to fight in the Persian Gulf War
    (D) cut taxes and social services

7. Which of the following actions by the Clinton administration was most harmonious with Liberal Democrat values?

    (A) Military peacekeeping interventions in the Balkans and Somalia
    (B) Welfare benefit reform to encourage young mothers to reenter the work force
    (C) Free trade agreements such as NAFTA and GATT
    (D) The effort to pass a universal health care legislation in the Congress

8. Which one of these presidents was best known for the campaign promise "Read my lips: No new taxes!"?

    (A) Jimmy Carter
    (B) Ronald Reagan
    (C) George H. W. Bush
    (D) Bill Clinton

REFLECT

Respond to the following questions:

- For which content topics discussed in this chapter do you feel you have achieved sufficient mastery to answer multiple-choice questions correctly?

- For which content topics discussed in this chapter do you feel you have achieved sufficient mastery to discuss effectively in a short-answer question or an essay?

- On which content topics discussed in this chapter do you feel you need more work before you can answer multiple-choice questions correctly?

- On which content topics discussed in this chapter do you feel you need more work before you can discuss them effectively in a short-answer question or an essay?

- What parts of this chapter are you going to review again?

- Will you seek further help, outside of this book (such as a teacher, tutor, or AP Students), on any of the content in this chapter—and, if so, on what content?

Chapter 14
Chapter Review
Questions:
Answers and
Explanations

CHAPTER 6 REVIEW QUESTIONS

1. **C** Indentured servitude promised freedom and a parcel of land to those who survived its seven-year term of service. Fewer than half did; most indentured servants worked in the fields performing grueling labor, and many died as a result. Indentured servitude was available only to the English, and nearly 100,000 took advantage of it.

2. **A** The Mayflower Compact states that government derives its power from the consent of the governed, not from divine mandate. This distinguishes government under the Mayflower Compact from the monarchial government the Pilgrims left behind in England.

3. **D** Virginia, one of the earliest colonies, developed around the tobacco trade; tobacco was the colonies' first important cash crop. Choice (A), cotton, did not become a major export until the early 19th century, when the invention of the cotton gin made large-scale cotton farming practical.

4. **B** During the colonial era, the British subscribed to the economic theory of mercantilism, which held that a favorable balance of trade and control of hard currency were the keys to economic power. Ultimately, the theory of capitalism, famously championed by Adam Smith, supplanted mercantilism as the predominant economic theory of the West.

5. **C** During the Age of Salutary Neglect, Britain regarded the colonies primarily as a market for exports and a resource of raw materials. England imposed numerous import and export restrictions on the colonies in an effort to maintain its monopoly on colonial markets. Naturally, the colonists tried to smuggle cheaper goods into the country and smuggled products out of the country in order to sell them. The British established their own military-style courts—called vice-admiralty courts—to enforce trade laws because they knew the colonists themselves would not.

6. **C** The Stono Uprising was an early slave rebellion (1739) in which African slaves rose against their oppressors. The Stono Uprising is sometimes referred to as the Cato Rebellion.

7. **D** The vast majority of colonists lived in rural areas. By 1750, roughly 5 percent of the colonial population resided in cities. Philadelphia, Boston, Williamsburg, Baltimore, and Boston were the most important cities of the era; all were built around ports.

8. **D** The purpose of America's first colleges was to train homegrown clergy so that the colonies would no longer have to import its clergy from England. The four oldest extant colonial universities—Harvard, William & Mary, Yale, and Princeton—were all originally affiliated with specific Protestant faiths.

9. **A** Provided the colonies continued to buy British goods and to supply the British with raw materials, England did not care how the colonies governed themselves. England did impose its will (through the vice-admiralty courts) when the colonies attempted to shirk their economic responsibilities but otherwise took a laissez-faire approach. As a result, the colonies developed a tradition of independence that contributed to their eventual rebellion against the Crown.

CHAPTER 7 REVIEW QUESTIONS

1. **D** Benjamin Franklin developed the Albany Plan, a first stab at a united colonial government empowered to collect taxes and raise a military. Although the delegations to Albany signed off on the plan, none of the colonial legislatures would have anything to do with it; they were uninterested in ceding any powers, even in the interest of strengthening the colonies as a whole. Franklin responded with his famous "Join or Die" cartoon, which showed the colonies as a snake cut into segments, each representing a colony.

2. **D** 1763, the year the Treaty of Paris ended the French and Indian War, is often considered to be a major turning point in British-colonial relations, as it marked the end of Britain's policy of salutary neglect. Beginning with the Proclamation of 1763, the colonists began to feel England tightening the screws. The passage of the Sugar and Stamp Acts set off a chain of new restrictions that set the colonists on the road to revolution. Although you no doubt know the phrase "No taxation without representation," the colonists did not actually want to send colonial representatives to sit in the British Parliament in London. Rather, as the resolutions of the Stamp Act Congress make clear, they believed that only their own colonial legislatures had the power to tax them. They initially understood that they were British subjects and that Parliament had the right to enact mercantilist restrictions to regulate trade. However, they soon voiced their concern that there was a significant difference between taxation and legislation.

3. **A** In the run-up to the Revolutionary War, colonists complained that Parliament had no business taxing them because the colonists lacked representation in the legislature. Their slogan, "No taxation without representation!" neatly summed up their argument (and it was catchy too!). The British responded with the theory of virtual representation, which stated that the colonists were represented in Parliament because members of Parliament represent all British citizens, not just the voters who elected them. Like most political debates, this one reeked of disingenuousness on both sides. The colonists knew that any delegation they sent to Parliament would be essentially powerless; what they really wanted was the right to set their own taxes, not to have them be set by a representative in the legislature. The British knew full well that their members of Parliament (MPs) did not give a tinker's damn about the colonists or their interests; what they wanted was for the colonists to shut up and pay their taxes.

4. **A** A recent DBQ on the AP Exam asked to what extent the colonists had developed a sense of unity by the eve of the Revolution. One could certainly argue that most colonists considered themselves to be loyal British subjects even after fighting had begun in Lexington and Concord in April 1775. Many historians view the Declaration of Independence, written in July 1776, as propaganda to convince those still loyal to England to fight for their independence. At the start of the French and Indian War, Benjamin Franklin had proposed the Albany Plan of Union, which was rejected by the colonists in favor of maintaining individual colonial sovereignty. The Stamp Act Congress of 1765 is historically significant because it marks the beginning of colonial unity and resistance against the British.

5. **B**   Much of the American Declaration of Independence is derived from the writings of John Locke, particularly his *Two Treatises of Government,* published in 1690, in which he challenged the theory of divine right of kings and put forth what is known as social contract theory. Both Locke and Rousseau believed that man was born free, but it was Rousseau who argued that "Man must be forced to be free" and submit to the "General Will."

6. **D**   The Articles of Confederation had intentionally created a weak central government, granting Congress few regulatory powers so as to avoid recreating an American Parliament. Shays's Rebellion threatened the survival of the newly established republic because the farmers in western Massachusetts were rebelling against their state government for the very same reason the colonists had rebelled against England—taxes. Under the Articles of Confederation, Congress could neither raise nor support a federal militia, so when Massachusetts requested federal assistance in squelching Daniel Shays and his farmer friends, no help was available. Had this question been about the Whiskey Rebellion during George Washington's administration, (A) would have been the correct answer. Choice (A) also demonstrates the difference between the limited power of the federal government under the Articles of Confederation and the stronger federal government established by the Constitution. Choice (C) is not correct, although excessive taxation was certainly one of the major causes of the American Revolution and subsequent rebellions. It is interesting to note that we did not have a federal income tax until the Sixteenth Amendment was ratified in the early 20th century.

7. **B**   The Articles of Confederation were established to provide a limited framework to organize the states under a single banner. However, they had very little power (purposefully) so that each state could decide its own legislation and government. States were expected to establish taxation, and Congress under the Articles of Confederation was not allowed to set up taxes (eliminating I). Furthermore, the whole purpose of the Articles of Confederation was to provide a legal document to enforce states' rights, not undermine them (eliminating III). The Articles of Confederation did, however, provide a framework for how the United States government would represent the states in foreign diplomatic matters such as treaties (making II correct).

8. **C**   Washington's presidency was all about establishing precedents. He was extremely conscious of this fact and proceeded cautiously throughout his two terms, aware that future presidents would follow his example. Thus, he rarely used his presidential veto, hoping to encourage future executives to accommodate the legislature on most matters. He didn't want the Congress to have complete control over the executive branch, though; he believed in the system of checks and balances. Thus, when the House of Representatives demanded all of Washington's papers regarding negotiations for the unpopular Jay Treaty, Washington refused. He reasoned that the papers were none of the House's business because only the Senate—with whom Washington did share the papers—is required to ratify treaties. His action established the precedent of executive privilege, a nebulous executive right to protect sensitive information and executive privacy. The right is occasionally invoked by the executive and almost as frequently challenged by the legislature, with the two typically working out a solution of compromise before the matter can reach the courts.

9. **D** The French and Indian War gave the British unchecked control over North America and a huge war debt. Searching for ways to repay the debt, the British sought greater contributions from, and subsequently greater control over, its American colonies. The Age of Salutary Neglect, an era during which the British basically allowed the colonies to govern themselves, was over.

10. **D** The strict constructionist interpretation of the Constitution is that Congress may use only those powers specifically enumerated in the Constitution. Other powers, regardless of how necessary they may be to national interests, are prohibited. The broad constructionist interpretation, in contrast, holds that Congress has numerous implied powers. For example, Congress has the power to print money, borrow money, and collect taxes; thus, the Constitution implies that Congress has the power to create a bank, the proper instrument for exercising these powers.

11. **C** First, cross out the "EXCEPT" and think "Yes" or "No" for each answer choice. The era is the American Revolution: think late 1700s, the colonies break from Great Britain, main disputes are taxing and trading laws, most people live on the Atlantic coast. Choices (A) and (D) are firmly within the era, and a "Yes" means to eliminate the choice. Maybe (B) leaves you a little clueless, but if you had to choose between (B) and (C), which one of these things is least like the others? Which answer choice stretches the era's boundaries? Obviously, (C) is the "No," the anti-era exception and the right answer. Women's rights did not become an issue until more than a century later, in the late 1800s, during the first women's movement.

CHAPTER 8 REVIEW QUESTIONS

1. **D** John Marshall was not the first Chief Justice of the Supreme Court, but he certainly was the man most responsible for giving the Court its teeth and much of the power it wields today. *Marbury v. Madison* was Marshall's first significant decision and established the principle of judicial review, which enables the Court to declare a federal or state law unconstitutional. Choice (C), *McCulloch v. Maryland,* was another landmark decision of the Marshall Court; this case dealt with the Second Bank of the United States and established the principle of federal supremacy. And it is important to note that while Marshall was an important Federalist, he did not establish the principle.

2. **B** The Louisiana Purchase grew out of the government's efforts to purchase New Orleans from the French; President Jefferson wanted control of the city because it sits at the mouth of the Mississippi River, an essential trade route. Jefferson sent James Monroe to France to negotiate the sale. The French, desperate for cash and nearly as desperate to divest themselves of New World holdings, offered to sell the entire massive Louisiana Territory, giving the United States control of both banks of the Mississippi River (as well as a tremendous amount of western land). As a result, American traders could travel the length of the river unimpeded, and trade subsequently boomed. Many of the incorrect answers to this question are anachronistic; the date of the purchase was too early for there to be "numerous French factories" in the territory, as in (C), or to allow for "the immediate completion of the transcontinental railroad," as in (D).

3. **A** The War of 1812 was very unpopular with New England Federalists who called the war "Mr. Madison's War." The economic policies of Jefferson and Madison disrupted trade, and as a result, were detrimental to New England merchants and shippers. Consequently, a group of New England Federalists met in Hartford, Connecticut, in 1814 to articulate a list of grievances against the Democratic-Republicans and their policies. While some men suggested secession, others suggested amending the Constitution to protect New England's commercial interests against what they perceived to be a dangerous, growing threat from the agrarian, Republican South. Because we "defeated" the British in what is often termed the Second War for Independence, the Federalists were seen as big babies and ultimately discredited. With the election of James Monroe in 1816, the United States had entered the Era of Good Feelings, a relatively brief period when there was only one political party—the Republicans. Although the War of 1812 damaged New England commerce initially, in the long run, the Embargo Act of 1807 and the War of 1812 forced Americans to be less dependent on British goods and indirectly stimulated the growth of industry in antebellum New England.

4. **A** The election of 1824 is one of the more infamous elections in American political history and exposes one of the unanticipated flaws in the Electoral College system. Because of the winner-take-all system of awarding electoral votes in most states, it is possible for a candidate to actually win the popular vote nationwide but lose the election. According to the Constitution, a candidate must win a majority, not a plurality, of electoral votes to win the presidential election. If no one candidate receives the requisite majority, the election is "thrown into the House," and the House of Representatives chooses the president from among the top three candidates. In the event this occurs, each state casts only one vote. Because there were five candidates running for president in 1824, it was almost impossible for anyone to receive a majority. Realizing that he did not have enough support to win the presidency, Henry Clay threw his support to John Quincy Adams in exchange for Adams's promise to make Clay his secretary of state. Jackson believed he lost the election because of this "corrupt bargain."

5. **D** The tariff in question here is the infamous Tariff of Abominations, so named by the Southern states that protested that this protective tariff benefited the New England manufacturers at the expense of cotton exporters in the South. The enactment of the Tariff of 1828 led to the nullification crisis a few years later when South Carolina declared the tariff null and void. (A similar situation had occurred in 1798 when Jefferson and Madison penned the Virginia and Kentucky resolutions in protest against the Alien and Sedition Acts.) In the case of *Marbury v. Madison*, Marshall had argued that only the Supreme Court, not individual states, could rule a law to be unconstitutional. Eventually, a compromise tariff was brokered, and the crisis was resolved. Nevertheless, the nullification crisis during Andrew Jackson's administration exposed the increasing tension of economic sectionalism that would propel the nation to civil war 30 years later.

6. **A** Andrew Jackson generally sided with the states on the issue of states' rights, preferring to limit the powers of the federal government to only those he perceived to be essential. He also favored his Western constituency to the power elite of the Northeast, whom he regarded with suspicion. Thus,

Jackson scuttled the Second National Bank, a large federal program championed by Northeastern bankers, and the American System, a large public works program.

7. **B**   The Cherokee were considered part of the "Five Civilized Tribes" living in the South, having established a republic in the state of Georgia. Unfortunately the discovery of gold within the Cherokee nation's borders was the catalyst for the tribe's forced relocation. Georgian citizens wanted to enforce the Indian Removal Act in order to have access to the territory. Although the Supreme Court ruled in favor of the Cherokees, President Andrew Jackson did not comply with the decision. States' rights were an important issue during Jackson's presidency, and he did not want to intervene on behalf of the Cherokee nation.

8. **D**   Brook Farm, the Oneida Community, and New Harmony were all utopian communities that arose during the antebellum period in response to what some people perceived to be the ill effects of a growing commercial society.

CHAPTER 9 REVIEW QUESTIONS

1. **D**   This is a trick question. Texas was annexed by the United States in 1845, prior to the start of the Mexican-American War. All the other territories mentioned in the answer choices came to the United States as a result of the Treaty of Guadalupe Hidalgo, which ended the war.

2. **D**   The term "Bleeding Kansas" refers to the battle in Kansas between pro-slavery and abolitionist forces. The doctrine of popular sovereignty had created the circumstances that led to the gruesome conflict; it left the slave status of each territory up to its residents, to be decided at the time when the territory was ready to write a constitution and apply for statehood. Both sides wanted Kansas badly, and both sent representatives into the territory to form governments. President Pierce recognized the pro-slavery government, but abolitionist forces cried "foul" and continued their fight to establish Kansas as a free state. More than 200 people died in the resulting skirmishes.

3. **B**   The Emancipation Proclamation did not free all the slaves. Instead, it freed only those slaves in rebel territories not controlled by the Union. In other words, it was completely unenforceable; it immediately took effect only in those places where Union forces had no power to act, but it ultimately had a significant impact as Union troops took over Confederate territory. The Emancipation Proclamation had a huge symbolic effect, though, as it clearly cast the Civil War as a war against slavery. Free blacks and escaped slaves rushed to join the cause; nearly 200,000 joined the Union army as a consequence of the Emancipation Proclamation.

4. **D**   Many historians argue that Andrew Johnson was neither the man nor the politician that Lincoln was. Johnson locked horns with the Radical Republicans in Congress over several issues pertaining to Reconstruction. Johnson had vetoed the Tenure of Office Act, which required a president to obtain Senate approval before firing an appointed official. The Senate argued that if it had the power to confirm nominations, it should also be allowed to have a say in the event a president

wanted to fire someone. Congress overrode Johnson's veto; Johnson fired his secretary of war, the Radical Republican Henry Stanton; and the House of Representatives impeached the President of the United States for the first time in American history. Johnson was acquitted, however, by one vote in the Senate and thus remained in office to finish his term.

5. **B** The election of 1876 is another one of the disputed elections in American political history. Although Samuel J. Tilden, then Governor of New York, won the popular vote nationwide, there were several states that contested the results of the election. Consequently, a special bipartisan commission was set up to determine the outcome of the election. In what became known as the "Compromise of 1877," Rutherford B. Hayes won the presidential election by a margin of one single electoral vote. Hayes had promised to remove federal troops still stationed in the South after the Civil War, thus ending military reconstruction.

6. **A** Remember that most slaves had no job skills and could neither read nor write. They had no money and nowhere to go when slavery was abolished. Some slaves took off in search of their scattered families, but most stayed exactly where they were and worked as tenant farmers or sharecroppers.

Under the new wage-labor system, plantations were subdivided into smaller farms of 30 to 50 acres, which were then leased to freedmen under a one-year contract. Tenants would work a piece of land and turn over 50 percent of their crops to the landlord. Often, other expenses, such as rent for a run-down shack or over-priced groceries, available only through the landowner, would be deducted from whatever was produced. One of the services initially provided by the Freedmen's Bureau was to help freed slaves who could neither read nor write understand the contracts they were about to sign. The system of sharecropping persisted well into the 20th century, keeping many blacks in positions of poverty and degradation.

Choice (C) is incorrect for reasons stated above. The Great Migration of Southern blacks into Northern cities did not take place until World War I, long after Reconstruction. Choice (D) is incorrect because Chinese immigrants were used to construct our nation's railroad system, much of which had been completed by the end of the Civil War.

7. **D** The Know-Nothings were a nativist group formed in response to the growing concentration of immigrants—particularly Italian and Irish Catholics—in Eastern cities. The party grew out of a number of secret societies whose members were instructed to tell outsiders nothing, hence the party's name. When asked anything about their groups, Know-Nothings would respond, "I know nothing." Their program included a 25-year residency requirement for citizenship; they also wanted to restrict all public offices to only those who were native-born Americans. By 1855, they had changed their name to the American Party, and in 1856, they fielded a presidential candidate (former president Millard Fillmore). Within a few years, the party had disbanded, destroyed by their disagreements over slavery. Most Northern Know-Nothings joined the Republican Party.

8. **C** The Free-Soil Party was created in the mid-1840s and was more like a faction or interest group than a political party. However, unlike a faction, it developed a political platform and nominated a candidate (Martin Van Buren) for the presidential election of 1844. The Free-Soil party attracted antislavery "Conscience" Whigs, former members of the Liberty party, and pro-Wilmot Proviso Democrats. The Wilmot Proviso was rejected by Congress but suggested that there be no slavery in

any territory acquired from Mexico. Free-Soilers were opposed to the extension of slavery into the new territories. Remember: The Constitution protected slavery where it already existed, but many people believed Congress could prevent the further spread of slavery as the United States acquired new land. Although the Free-Soil party did not exist for long, its major principles were adopted by the new Republican Party, which was formed in 1854 and was opposed to the extension of slavery into the new territories.

9. **D** In the election of 1848, the Democrats realized that their party was crumbling because its members could not agree on whether to allow slavery in the Western territories. They sought a policy to appease both abolitionists and slaveholders; the result of that search was the concept of popular sovereignty. By allowing the settlers to decide the slave status of an area, popular sovereignty took some pressure off Congress, which was growing increasingly divided over the issue. It also took pressure off the political parties, which were coming apart due to the irreconcilable regional differences of their members. Henry Clay invoked the notion of popular sovereignty in the Compromise of 1850, but the compromise contained a purposefully ambiguous interpretation of what popular sovereignty meant. While the ambiguous wording was necessary to make the Compromise of 1850 possible, it also made future disagreements over the issue inevitable.

10. **C** The Reconstruction Act of 1867, Congress's plan for the rehabilitation of the South, was much harsher than President Johnson's plan. Johnson, like Lincoln (who began planning the method for readmitting Southern states before his assassination), wanted a reconciliatory plan that punished only the most prominent leaders of the secession. Radical Republicans in Congress wanted something much tougher, and Johnson's plan was so lenient (in the first postwar Congress, Johnson's plan would have allowed the former president of the Confederacy to take a seat in the Senate) that it drove many moderates into the radicals' camp. The result was the Reconstruction Act, a punitive measure that imposed a number of strict requirements on Southern states as preconditions for their readmission to the Union. Choices (A), (B), and (D) list all of those preconditions; the fact that Congress did not impose any requirements such as the one described in (C) pretty much doomed postwar Southern blacks to poverty.

CHAPTER 10 REVIEW QUESTIONS

1. **D** The scalawags were white Southerners who supported Republican policies during Reconstruction. Carpetbaggers were Northerners who traveled south to exploit the turmoil following the Civil War for their own political gain. The Redeemers were white Democrats who were determined to get revenge on the Republicans for imposing their radical policies of Reconstruction on Southern states and thus hoped to "redeem" the South.

2. **A** If you remember that the Supreme Court of the late 19th century was extremely conservative and extremely pro-business—and you should remember that, because it's important—you should have been able to eliminate (B) and (D) immediately. If you remember the profound impact of such decisions as *Plessy v. Ferguson*—and you should also remember that—you could have eliminated (C).

3. **D** "Vertical integration" is another name for monopoly. Monopolies ran rampant in the late 1800s; the government did little to prevent them, and the courts actively encouraged them. Of the incorrect answers, (C) refers to assembly line production, and (A) and (B) are just made up.

4. **C** James A. Garfield's presidency is remembered for one thing: Garfield's assassination at the hands of a disgruntled office seeker. His assassin, Charles Guiteau, was actually a mentally disturbed individual who imagined himself an important player in Garfield's electoral success. Guiteau convinced himself that he deserved a big fat government job as a reward for his efforts, and when he received none he retaliated by shooting Garfield. Garfield's successor, Chester Arthur, signed the Pendleton Act, which replaced the spoils system Guiteau had hoped to exploit with a merit-based system for selecting civil servants.

5. **C** Although one might certainly make a valid claim that labor unions were necessary during the late 19th century when working conditions were dangerous, unsanitary, and exploitative, unions were very unpopular because they were associated with political radicalism and violence. The Haymarket Incident began as a mass meeting organized by anarchists, held in Haymarket Square in Chicago in 1886 in sympathy and protest of events related to striking workers at the McCormick Harvester Company plant nearby. When police tried to break up the meeting, someone threw a bomb into the crowd, leaving seven policemen dead and several wounded. This incident convinced the American public that unions were dangerous and ultimately led to the decline of the Knights of Labor.

6. **D** If you can't immediately identify the correct answer to this one, use common sense to eliminate incorrect answers. Japan is a huge nation relative to Hawaii; its economy couldn't realistically depend on trade with the island, so eliminate (A). Choice (B) contradicts one of the main themes of the period—the Age of Imperialism, when every Western power, including the United States, was gathering colonies in the East. Would the United States have ceded Hawaii to Japan during that period? Unlikely, and much less likely still that the AP Exam would ask about an anomalous agreement. Choice (C) suggests Japan was a bastion of democracy in the late 19th century; in fact, it was ruled by an emperor.

7. **D** Historians describe the immigrants who came to the United States before the Civil War as "old immigrants." These men and women came predominantly from countries in northwestern Europe. For the most part, they were Protestants and spoke English and easily became part of the melting pot we call America. Following the Civil War, however, the "new immigrants" came predominantly from nations in southeastern Europe, including Russians, Italians, and Poles. Many of these people were Catholics and Jews and were culturally very different from most Americans by that point. These new immigrants were not easily assimilated. They tended to settle among themselves

in ethnic neighborhoods in major cities like New York and Chicago where there was a demand for unskilled labor in the numerous factories of these big cities.

8.   **D**   The Ghost Dancers arose in the late 1800s when the sad fate awaiting the great Native American tribes of the era was becoming all too apparent. Wovoka, a Paiute Indian, started the Ghost Dance movement, which resembled a religious revival. It centered on a dance ritual that enabled participants to envision a brighter future, one in which whites no longer dominated North America. Wovoka preached unity among Native Americans and the rejection of white culture and its trappings, especially alcohol. He also preached the imminent end of the world, at which point the Indian dead would rise to reclaim the land that was rightfully theirs. Sioux Ghost Dancers believed in the power of "ghost shirts," garments blessed by medicine men that were capable of stopping bullets. This belief led to a rise in Sioux militancy and ultimately contributed to their massacre at Wounded Knee in 1890.

9.   **D**   Waves of European immigration throughout the 19th century swelled cities' populations. Governments of the time were nowhere near as activist as they are today, and only a very few provided even minimal services to immigrants as they accommodated themselves to their new homeland; ethnic communities and churches were expected to provide such services. A number of enterprising, unscrupulous men recognized in these immigrants the opportunity for great political power. Such men, known as political bosses, helped immigrants find homes and jobs and acquire citizenship and voting rights. In essence, these bosses created entire communities and then provided them with all sorts of services: food and loans for the poor, parks and protection for the community. In return, the communities were expected to provide loyal political support, which they did, originally out of loyalty, and later, as the machines became extremely powerful, out of both loyalty and fear. The bosses could then hand an election to a politician of their choice, in return for favors. Political machines filled a need, albeit in an expensive and unethical way. They fell from power when governments started to provide many of the services machines had provided.

10.   **D**   In the 1860s, the government initiated its reservation policy by which Native Americans were granted (usually less desirable) portions of the lands they inhabited. The policy failed on many fronts, and by the 1880s the government was searching for a different tack. Congress struck on the Dawes Severalty Act, which offered individual Native Americans 160-acre plots in return for leaving their reservations; through this program, Congress hoped to hasten the assimilation of Native Americans, whose cultures most congressmen held in contempt. The results were not good. Most American Indians preferred to remain among their tribes and did not accept the offer. Those who did accept usually ended up selling their land to whites, who often placed considerable pressure on them to do so.

CHAPTER 11 REVIEW QUESTIONS

1. **D** "Muckrakers" is a term Theodore Roosevelt coined to describe the investigative journalists of his day. They included Ida Tarbell, whose book on Standard Oil revealed corruption in the oil industry and big business in general; Upton Sinclair, whose stomach-turning account of the meatpacking industry drove public outcry for government regulation of food production (the Food and Drug Administration was created as a result of Sinclair's book *The Jungle*); and Lincoln Steffens, whose *The Shame of the Cities* exposed many Americans to the extent of urban poverty and corruption in urban government. Muckrakers helped fuel the public outcry for government reform, the main goal of the Progressive movement.

2. **B** Conservative courts and pro-business administrations allowed the Sherman Antitrust Act to be used to restrain labor but rarely to restrain business. Theodore Roosevelt changed all that. With public support Roosevelt transformed the Sherman Antitrust Act into a tool with which to break up monopolies. He focused his attention on corrupt monopolies whose activities countered the public interest, leaving alone trusts that operated more or less honestly. His approach garnered broad public acclaim, earning him the nickname "the Trustbuster."

3. **B** As a result of winning the Spanish-American War in 1898, the United States acquired Guam, Puerto Rico, the Philippines, and for all intents and purposes, Cuba. (Although we had claimed we had no interest in acquiring Cuba and could empathize with its colonial status, having once been a colony ourselves, the Platt Amendment rendered the island a virtual colony of the United States.) The situation in the Philippines created intense debate between business interests that saw the enormous economic benefits to acquiring "stepping stones" to profitable Chinese trade, and those Americans who believed having colonies contradicted our fundamental democratic principles. Once we acquired overseas possessions, a question arose as to the rights and privileges of the native peoples living within the American Empire. In a series of Supreme Court cases known as the Insular Cases, the Court ruled that the "Constitution did not follow the flag," and thus, colonial subjects were not entitled to the same rights as U.S. citizens living at home or abroad.

4. **A** This is a straight recall question. You either know what the Zimmermann telegram is or you don't. If you know it, you're going to get this question right. If you don't, use Process of Elimination to get rid of anachronistic answers, as in (B), or answers that seem un-AP-like because they don't reinforce important themes of U.S. history, as in (D). You should know, however, that the Zimmermann telegram was one of the reasons the United States entered World War I.

5. **C** In the aftermath of World War I, President Wilson favored a peace that would promote openness in international affairs, free trade, and diplomacy. He also sought universal arms reductions and a mechanism for enforcing world peace, which was to be achieved through the League of Nations. He did not seek a punitive treaty that forced Germany to pay heavy reparations; the European allies, however, insisted. Wilson was able to negotiate very little of his Fourteen Points plan, but he remained optimistic that the League of Nations would eventually broker a fairer postwar peace. Unfortunately, Wilson's hopes were never realized.

6. **B** The Ku Klux Klan evoked the execrable Southern traditions of racism and physical intimidation against the modern drive for expanded civil rights. The Scopes Monkey Trial pitted religion against the modern notion of evolution. The Emergency Quota Act of 1924 was passed to check immigration from non-western European countries; its champions felt the nation's western European traditions were threatened by immigrants from Southern Europe, Eastern Europe, South America, and Asia. Prohibition pitted religion against modern licentiousness. The Teapot Dome Scandal, on the other hand, was just an example of good old-fashioned political corruption.

7. **D** Buying "on margin" allowed investors to buy stock with only a small amount of cash; the rest was borrowed from stockbrokers and banks against the presumed profits from subsequent stock sales. The system worked only as long as stock prices kept rising; once they started to fall, all hell broke loose. In response to market weakness in the fall of 1929, investors who had long believed the market was overvalued started to sell off their stocks, causing prices to drop. Noting the market downturn, stockbrokers demanded that clients repay margin loans and, when their clients couldn't repay, dumped the stocks on the market in order to recoup some of their losses. The law of supply and demand sent stock prices spiraling uncontrollably downward. Over a period of two months, the market lost nearly half its value and many, many investors—including some of the nation's biggest banks—were ruined.

8. **D** Roosevelt coined the phrase "Good Neighbor Policy" to reflect a shift in American attitudes toward Latin America. In the past, American intervention in the region had incited great resentment of the United States. Roosevelt announced a new U.S. commitment to autonomy throughout the hemisphere and showed his intentions by withdrawing U.S. troops from Nicaragua and Haiti. He later resisted sending troops to Cuba to quell a revolution.

9. **A** Americans were already predisposed to isolationism by nature before they heard the results of the Nye Commission's investigations. They had been promised that World War I was "the war to end all wars." Less than 20 years later, Europe was apparently on the verge of another big confrontation. The sentiment in the United States was, "Let them sort this out themselves." Those feelings were strengthened when the Nye Commission revealed that many American munitions companies had violated an arms embargo in order to arm the nation's enemies. It further revealed that U.S. banks had lobbied for entry into the war in order to protect more than $2 billion in loans to Britain and its allies. The report left Americans more cynical about the motives of its leaders and less susceptible to calls for intervention overseas.

10. **A** Fred Korematsu was among the more than 110,000 Japanese Americans ordered to relocate from the West Coast to internment camps during World War II. Korematsu refused, was arrested, and took his case all the way to the Supreme Court. The Court ruled that the government had not exceeded its power, noting that extraordinary times sometimes call for extraordinary measures; three of the nine justices dissented. History has not judged Roosevelt's internment policy kindly. In 1998, Fred Korematsu was awarded the Presidential Medal of Honor.

CHAPTER 12 REVIEW QUESTIONS

1. **D** The Korean War didn't begin until 1950.

2. **C** Fear of communist infiltration and subversion reached hysterical proportions in the post–World War II era, making all sorts of excessive responses to the communist threat not only possible but likely. Loyalty oaths were instituted by private companies, state governments, and even the federal government, based on the apparent belief that communist spies are capable of espionage but not of lying under oath. Blacklists banned suspected subversives from work in many industries, destroying the lives of many innocent people. Alger Hiss was accused of passing government secrets to the Soviet Union. He professed his innocence to his dying day, although Soviet files released in the post-Soviet era suggest his guilt. The Hiss case was front-page news. Richard Nixon played a prominent role in Hiss's prosecution, thereby earning Nixon the national spotlight for the first time.

3. **A** The key to this question is the phrase "intensified Cold War rhetoric." Words like "massive retaliation" didn't exactly improve relations with the Soviet Union. While (B), containment, was the guiding principle of U.S. foreign policy throughout the Cold War, this question is asking something more specific. And although Dulles did forge many alliances with smaller nations (collective security), (A) is a better answer. Choice (C), summit diplomacy, was practiced by Reagan and Gorbachev, while the term "shuttle diplomacy," (D), was applied to Henry Kissinger under Nixon.

4. **D** You should be familiar with the important decisions of the Marshall Court (1801–1835) and the Warren Court (1953–1969). Marshall is remembered as a Federalist who strengthened the new federal government and encouraged economic development of the new nation. The Warren Court was an activist court, best remembered for increasing the rights of individuals, specifically the rights of the accused. (For example, the *Gideon* and *Miranda* cases were decided by the Warren Court.) According to the Constitution, only Congress can make laws, but in effect, many of the Warren decisions established social policy, which many conservative critics saw as "judicial legislation."

5. **D** Kennedy's victory in 1960 was by the tiniest of margins. He could not have won, or governed, without the support of Democrats in the South, many of whom opposed any federal strengthening of civil rights law. As a result, Kennedy had to tread carefully on the issue of African American civil rights, a cause he had supported forcefully during his campaign. He used the attorney general's office to bring suits to force desegregation of Southern universities and appointed African Americans to prominent positions in his administration but made no effort at civil rights legislation until his final year in office. After Kennedy's assassination, new President Lyndon Johnson invoked Kennedy's memory and commitment to civil rights to force the Civil Rights Act of 1964 through Congress.

6. **C**   The Republican candidate, Richard Nixon, was a former vice president. The Democratic candidate, Hubert Humphrey, was the current vice president and, before that, a longtime senator. Neither could have campaigned as a Washington outsider, and neither did. The Democrats were fractured over the war; the party was home to both aggressive cold warriors and the antiwar movement. Robert Kennedy was assassinated in June; many believe he would have won the nomination had he not been killed. George Wallace formed a third party and campaigned on states' rights and segregation, siphoning off key votes in the South, where the Democrats had traditionally done well. Nixon's only opposition in the Republican primaries came from Nelson D. Rockefeller, who campaigned halfheartedly, and Ronald Reagan, who, at the time, was seen as too extreme to ever win the presidency. Reagan never changed, but the country did.

7. **B**   Gasoline and oil prices shot through the roof in the 1970s, affecting a wide range of industries that relied on the fuels to run. The result was widespread inflation throughout the decade.

8. **D**   This is the event that started it all—the break-in to the Watergate complex in Washington, D.C., where the Democratic Party had its national headquarters. All of the other choices became part of the cover-up and are known collectively as "Watergate," which ultimately forced the resignation of Richard Nixon, the only president to resign in American history. Nixon resigned before he was impeached and was subsequently pardoned by Gerald Ford.

CHAPTER 13 REVIEW QUESTIONS

1. **B**   Reagan believed in limited federal government. Part of his goal in lowering tax rates was to reduce the federal budget (thus federal programs). But Reagan was also a stalwart cold warrior who believed that military strength was the best check against the Soviet Union and communism in general. He campaigned vigorously for new weapons systems, including the Strategic Defense Initiative, a space-based, antimissile system dubbed "Star Wars."

2. **A**   Though American relations with Russia remain uneasy, fears of Soviet expansion are a thing of the past; the Soviet Union ceased to exist in 1991, ending the Cold War.

3. **B**   In 1981, Ronald Reagan, in a move supported by various groups across the political spectrum, made Sandra Day O'Connor the first woman to serve on the Supreme Court. All the other choices represent typically conservative policy decisions by Reagan.

4. **D**   Although there was a brief drop in the stock market in 1987 (known as Black Friday), this was not a contributing factor to the emergence of the New Right. All of the other factors did lead to this renewal of conservatism.

5. **A** There are several presidential doctrines you should know for this exam—for example, the Monroe Doctrine and the Truman Doctrine. In most cases these "doctrines" were delivered as speeches to Congress but became statements of U.S. foreign policy. Alarmed by the establishment of Soviet satellites in Eastern Europe and the potential Soviet threat to Greece and Turkey following World War II, Truman pledged his support to prevent the spread of communism in Europe (although he did not use those exact words). As a cold warrior, Ronald Reagan was committed to providing covert and overt assistance to anticommunist resistance movements, particularly in nations like Afghanistan and Nicaragua.

6. **C** This is a factoid question. President George H. W. Bush led the brief Persian Gulf War in 1990. Choice (B) is Carter and (D) is Reagan. Choice (A) is President Clinton.

7. **D** Liberal Democrats would have mixed feelings about war and free trade, so rule out (A). Welfare benefit reform was in fact designed to get young mothers off welfare, so this was not necessarily a boon to the Democrats. The most ambitious effort by the Clinton administration was to pass a universal health care bill, but this ultimately did not pass Congress.

8. **C** This is another factoid question. This was President George H. W. Bush's campaign promise (though the promise was not kept).

Chapter 15
Key Terms and Concepts

A NOTE ON THE KEY TERMS

The list of key terms that follows provides a comprehensive review of U.S. history. We've separated the terms into categories: concepts, events, people, and policies (which includes major Supreme Court decisions and important federal legislation). Write a brief explanation or identification of each term in the space provided. Some students even find making flash cards helpful.

Keep the following suggestions in mind as you go through these terms. If it is a concept, do not simply write a definition; try to think of a historical example that illustrates the concept. For example, you might define *evangelicalism* and then cite the Great Awakening as an example. Be certain you can explain the causes and effects of each major event. This will help you with the essay questions for which you are required to showcase an analytical understanding of issues. The Supreme Court cases and major laws should be placed within their historical context. It is always useful to ask yourself the question, "Why at this time?" Again, you should not merely state what the Court decided or law required but also understand the case's or law's impact on American society at the time.

Most of these terms are printed in **bold**, *italic*, or ***bold italic*** type throughout the history review of the book (Chapters 6 through 13). If you cannot find a particular term in this book, use your textbook or the Internet.

Chapter 6: Early Contact with the New World and Colonization of North America

Concepts

Slave codes _____

City upon a hill _____

Encomiendas _____

Evangelicalism _____

Headright system _____

Indentured servitude _____

Joint-stock company _____

Mercantilism _____

Middle Passage _____

Praying towns _____

Proprietary colony _____

Puritanism _____

Royal colony _____

Salutary neglect _____

Slavery _____

Tariffs _____

Events

Bacon's Rebellion _____

Glorious Revolution in England _____

The Great Awakening _____

Huron Confederacy _____

King Philip's War _____

Pequot War _____

Pueblo Revolt _____

Salem witch trials _____

Spanish mission system _____

The "starving time" _____

Stono Uprising _____

People (Individuals and Groups)

Anne Hutchinson _____

Bartolomé de las Casas _____

Benjamin Franklin _____

Calvinists _____

Congregationalists _____

George Whitefield _____

Huguenots _____

John Rolfe _____

John Smith _____

Jonathan Edwards _____

Juan de Oñate _____

Maroons _____

Metacomet _____

Pilgrims _____

Pocahontas _____

Powhatan Confederacy _____

Puritans _____

Roger Williams _____

Separatists _____

Sir Walter Raleigh _____

Virginia Company _____

Wampanoags _____

Places

Cahokia _____

The Chesapeake _____

Jamestown _____

The Lower South _____

Massachusetts Bay Colony _____

Middle colonies _____

New England _____

Policies, Agreements, Court Rulings, Etc.

Act of Toleration _____

Dominion of New England _____

Fundamental Orders of Connecticut _____

Halfway Covenant _____

Maryland Toleration Act _____

Mayflower Compact _____

Navigation Acts _____

Chapter 7: Conflict and American Independence

Concepts

Checks and balances _____

Common Sense _____

Hamilton's Financial Plan _____

Kentucky and Virginia Resolutions _____

Loose constructionism _____

Mercantilism _____

Nullification _____

Republican Motherhood _____

Strict constructionism _____

Tariffs _____

Virtual representation _____

Washington's Farewell Address _____

Events

Battle of Concord _____

Battle of Fallen Timbers _____

Battle of Saratoga _____

Battle of Lexington _____

Boston Massacre _____

Boston Tea Party _____

French Revolution _____

Haitian Revolution _____

Pontiac's Rebellion _____

Seven Years' War (French and Indian War) _____

Shays's Rebellion _____

Whiskey Rebellion _____

XYZ Affair _____

People (Individuals and Groups)

Abigail Adams _____

Adam Smith_____

Alexander Hamilton_____

Anti-Federalists _____

Benjamin Franklin _____

Chief Little Turtle _____

Committees of Correspondence_____

Democratic-Republican Party _____

East India Tea Company _____

Federalists _____

George III _____

George Grenville _____

George Washington _____

Iroquois _____

James Madison_____

John Adams _____

John Jay _____

Loyalists_____

Mercy Otis Warren _____

Minutemen _____

Patrick Henry _____

Patriots_____

Paxton Boys _____

Redcoats _____

Sons of Liberty _____

Thomas Jefferson _____

Thomas Paine _____

Places

Concord and Lexington, Massachusetts _____

Washington, D.C. _____

Policies, Agreements, Court Rulings, Etc.

Three-Fifths Compromise _____

Albany Plan of Union _____

Alien and Sedition Acts _____

Annapolis Convention _____

Articles of Confederation _____

Bill of Rights _____

Constitution _____

Continental Army _____

Currency Act _____

Declaration of Independence _____

Declaratory Act _____

First Bank of the United States _____

First Continental Congress _____

Franco-American Alliance _____

Great Compromise (Connecticut Compromise) _____

Intolerable Acts _____

Jay's Treaty _____

National Bank _____

Navigation Acts _____

New Jersey Plan _____

Northwest Ordinance _____

Olive Branch Petition _____

Pinckney's Treaty _____

Proclamation of 1763 _____

Proclamation of Neutrality_____

Quebec Act _____

Second Continental Congress _____

Stamp Act _____

Sugar Act _____

Townshend Acts_____

Treaty of Paris _____

Virginia Plan _____

Chapter 8: Beginnings of Modern American Democracy

Concepts

"54°40' or Fight!"_____

American System _____

"Boom and bust"_____

Caucus system _____

"Corrupt bargain" _____

Cult of domesticity _____

Era of Good Feelings _____

Gag rule_____

Impressment _____

Jacksonian Democracy_____

Judicial review _____

Labor unions _____

Manifest Destiny _____

Monroe Doctrine_____

"Pet" banks _____

Revivalism _____

Second Great Awakening_____

Spoils system _____

States' rights_____

Temperance _____

Transcendentalism _____

Underground Railroad _____

Universal manhood suffrage _____

Utopian communities _____

Events

Battle of the Alamo _____

Election of 1824 _____

Lewis and Clark Expedition _____

Nat Turner's Rebellion _____

Nullification crisis _____

Panic of 1819 _____

Panic of 1837 _____

Seneca Falls Convention _____

Seminole Wars _____

Trail of Tears _____

War of 1812 _____

People (Individuals and Groups)

Aaron Burr _____

American Antislavery Society _____

American Colonization Society _____

Andrew Jackson _____

Charles G. Finney _____

David Walker _____

Democrat Party _____

Democratic-Republican Party _____

Dorothea Dix _____

Eli Whitney _____

Federalist Party _____

Frederick Douglass _____

Freedmen _____

Harriet Tubman _____

Henry Clay _____

Henry David Thoreau _____

Horace Mann _____

Hudson River School _____

James K. Polk _____

John C. Calhoun _____

John Marshall _____

John Quincy Adams _____

John Tyler _____

Lydia Maria Child _____

Martin Van Buren _____

Mormons _____

Mulattoes _____

Ralph Waldo Emerson _____

Samuel Slater _____

Shakers _____

Sojourner Truth _____

Tecumseh _____

War Hawks _____

Whig Party _____

William Henry Harrison _____

William Lloyd Garrison _____

Places

Brook Farm _____

Erie Canal _____

Lowell, Massachusetts _____

National Road _____

Oregon Territory _____

Republic of Texas _____

Policies, Agreements, Court Rulings, Etc.

Cherokee Nation v. Georgia _____

Embargo Act _____

Force Bill _____

Hartford Convention _____

Indian Removal Act _____

Louisiana Purchase _____

Marbury v. Madison _____

McCulloch v. Maryland _____

Missouri Compromise _____

Non-Intercourse Act _____

Oregon Treaty _____

Second Bank of the United States _____

Specie Circular _____

Tariff of 1828 (Tariff of Abominations) _____

Worcester v. Georgia _____

Chapter 9: Toward the Civil War and Reconstruction

Concepts

"40 acres and a mule" _____

Black codes _____

Conscription _____

Habeas corpus _____

Inflation _____

Loyalty oath _____

Nativism _____

Popular sovereignty _____

Segregation _____

Sharecropping _____

Uncle Tom's Cabin _____

Events

Battle of Fort Sumter _____

Battle of Gettysburg _____

Battle of Little Big Horn _____

Compromise of 1850 _____

Election of 1860 _____

Emancipation Proclamation _____

Bleeding Kansas _____

Gold Rush _____

Great Migration _____

Impeachment of Andrew Johnson _____

Mexican-American War _____

Minstrel shows _____

Sand Creek Massacre _____

Sherman's March to the Sea _____

People (Individuals and Groups)

Abraham Lincoln _____

Andrew Johnson _____

Carpetbaggers _____

Civil War _____

Copperheads _____

Dred Scott _____

Exodusters _____

Forty-Niners _____

Freedman's Bureau _____

Free-Soil Party _____

Harriet Beecher Stowe _____

Hiram Revels _____

James Buchanan _____

James K. Polk _____

Jefferson Davis _____

John Breckenridge _____

John Brown _____

John C. Calhoun _____

Know-Nothing Party _____

Ku Klux Klan _____

Matthew Perry _____

Millard Fillmore _____

Radical Republicans _____

Republican Party _____

Robert Smalls _____

Scalawags _____

Stephen Douglas _____

Ulysses S. Grant _____

Places

36°30' _____

54°40' _____

Confederate States _____

Fort Sumter _____

Harper's Ferry, West Virginia _____

Policies, Agreements, Court Rulings, Etc.

10% Plan _____

Thirteenth Amendment _____

Fourteenth Amendment _____

Fifteenth Amendment _____

Compromise of 1850 _____

Compromise of 1877 _____

Dred Scott v. Sandford _____

Hampton Roads Conference _____

Homestead Act _____

Fugitive Slave Act _____

Kansas-Nebraska Act _____

Personal liberty laws_____

Reconstruction Act _____

Treaty of Guadalupe Hidalgo_____

Wade-Davis Bill _____

Wilmot Proviso _____

Chapter 10: The Industrial Revolution

Concepts

Assembly line manufacturing_____

"Cross of Gold" speech _____

Economies of scale_____

Ghost Dance _____

The Gilded Age _____

The gold standard _____

Gospel of Wealth _____

Laissez-faire economics _____

Monopolies _____

The New South _____

Political bosses _____

Referendum _____

The silver standard_____

Social Darwinism_____

Social Gospel _____

Socialism _____

Temperance _____

Tenement housing _____

Trusts_____

Women's suffrage _____

Events

Haymarket Incident _____

Homestead Strike _____

Pullman Strike _____

Wounded Knee Massacre _____

People (Individuals and Groups)

American Federation of Labor (AFL) _____

American Socialist Party _____

American Suffrage Association _____

Andrew Carnegie _____

Benjamin Harrison _____

Booker T. Washington _____

"Boss" Tweed _____

Chester A. Arthur _____

Chief Joseph _____

Colored Farmers' Alliance _____

Cornelius Vanderbilt _____

Elizabeth Cady Stanton _____

Eugene V. Debs _____

Farmers' Alliances _____

Frederick Jackson Turner _____

The Grange _____

Grover Cleveland _____

Ida Wells-Barnett _____

James Garfield _____

John D. Rockefeller _____

John Muir _____

J.P. Morgan _____

Las Gorras Blancas _____

Mother Jones _____

Knights of Labor _____

Populist Party _____

Rutherford B. Hayes _____

Samuel Gompers _____

The Sierra Club _____

"Stalwarts and half-breeds" _____

Standard Oil _____

Susan B. Anthony _____

Tammany Hall_____

Thomas Edison _____

U.S. Steel_____

William H. Seward _____

William Jennings Bryan_____

William McKinley _____

Places

Alaska _____

Hawaii_____

Indian reservations_____

Land-grant colleges _____

Philippines_____

Settlement houses _____

Policies, Agreements, Court Rulings, Etc.

Civil Rights cases_____

Chinese Exclusion Act _____

Dawes Act _____

Interstate Commerce Act _____

Jim Crow laws _____

McKinley Tariff _____

Open Door Policy _____

Pendleton Civil Service Reform Act_____

*Plessy v. Ferguson*_____

Sherman Antitrust Act_____

Chapter 11: The Early 20th Century

Concepts

Christian Fundamentalism_____

Conservatism _____

Court-packing _____

Dollar Diplomacy _____

Fireside chats _____

Interventionism _____

Isolationism _____

Jazz _____

Labor strikes _____

Liberalism _____

New Deal _____

New Nationalism_____

Protectionism _____

Rationing_____

Roosevelt Corollary to the Monroe Doctrine_____

Sonar _____

Square Deal _____

Suburbs _____

Xenophobia _____

Yellow journalism _____

Events

Bombing of Hiroshima and Nagasaki _____

D-Day _____

Dust Bowl _____

First Red Scare_____

The Great Depression _____

Harlem Renaissance_____

Manhattan Project_____

Palmer Raids _____

Potsdam Conference _____

Russian Revolution _____

Sacco and Vanzetti Trial _____

Scopes "Monkey" Trial _____

Sinking of the *Lusitania* _____

Spanish-American War _____

Spanish Flu _____

Teapot Dome Scandal _____

World War I _____

Yalta Conference _____

Zimmermann telegram _____

People (Individuals and Groups)

Allied Powers _____

American Expeditionary Force _____

Axis Powers _____

Bonus Expeditionary Force _____

Calvin Coolidge _____

Communist Party of America _____

Countee Cullen _____

Ernest Hemingway _____

Eugene O'Neill _____

Flappers _____

Florence Kelley _____

Franklin D. Roosevelt _____

F. Scott Fitzgerald _____

Gangsters _____

Harry S. Truman _____

Henry Cabot Lodge _____

Herbert Hoover _____

Huey Long _____

Ida Tarbell _____

J. Edgar Hoover _____

Jane Addams _____

John Maynard Keynes _____

Joseph Pulitzer _____

Langston Hughes _____

Lost Generation _____

Louis Armstrong _____

Margaret Sanger _____

Muckrakers _____

National Association for the Advancement of Colored People (NAACP) _____

Progressive Party _____

Robert LaFollette _____

Theodore Roosevelt _____

Tripartite Pact _____

Upton Sinclair _____

Warren G Harding _____

W.E.B. Du Bois _____

William Howard Taft _____

William Randolph Hearst _____

Woodrow Wilson _____

Zora Neale Hurston _____

Places

"Hoovervilles" _____

Hull House _____

Japanese Internment Camps _____

Panama Canal _____

Pearl Harbor, Hawaii _____

Policies, Agreements, Court Rulings, Etc.

14 Points _____

Eighteenth Amendment (Prohibition) _____

Nineteenth Amendment _____

Agricultural Adjustment Act (AAA) _____

Atlantic Charter _____

Civilian Conservation Corps (CCC) _____

Clayton Antitrust Act _____

Emergency Banking Relief Bill _____

Emergency Quota Act _____

Fair Labor Standards Act _____

Federal Bureau of Investigation (FBI) _____

Federal Deposit Insurance Corporation (FDIC) _____

Federal Reserve Act _____

Federal Trade Commission (FTC) _____

Good Neighbor Policy _____

Hawley-Smoot Tariff _____

Immigration Act of 1924 _____

Labor Disputes Act _____

League of Nations _____

Lend-Lease Act _____

Most Favored Nation (MFN) trade status _____

National Industrial Recovery Act (NIRA) _____

Neutrality Acts _____

North Atlantic Treaty Organization (NATO) _____

Platt Amendment _____

Public Works Administration (PWA) _____

Schenck v. United States _____

Securities and Exchange Commission (SEC) _____

Selective Service Act _____

Sherman Antitrust Act _____

Social Security Act _____

Tennessee Valley Authority (TVA) _____

Treaty of Versailles _____

United Nations _____

Washington Naval Conference _____

Works Progress Administration (WPA) _____

Chapter 12: The Postwar Period and Cold War

Concepts

Baby boom _____

Blacklisting _____

Black Power _____

Cold War _____

Communism _____

Containment _____

Decolonization _____

Détente _____

Domino theory _____

Environmentalism _____

Fair Deal _____

Feminism _____

The Great Society _____

Hydrogen bomb _____

Military-industrial complex _____

Mutually assured destruction (MAD) _____

Nation-building _____

New Frontier _____

Proxy wars _____

Rock and roll _____

Sexual revolution _____

The Silent Majority _____

Space race _____

Truman Doctrine _____

Events

Bay of Pigs Invasion _____

Berlin Blockade/Airlift _____

Chinese Revolution _____

Civil Rights movement _____

Cuban Missile Crisis _____

Kent State Massacre _____

Korean War _____

Middle East oil crisis _____

Montgomery bus boycott _____

My Lai Massacre _____

Suez Crisis _____

Tet Offensive _____

Vietnam War _____

Watergate scandal _____

World War II _____

People (Individuals and Groups)

Adlai Stevenson _____

Alger Hiss _____

Beatniks _____

Black Panthers _____

Dixiecrats _____

Douglas MacArthur _____

Dwight D. Eisenhower _____

Earl Warren _____

Eugene McCarthy _____

Fannie Lou Hamer _____

Fidel Castro _____

Freedom Riders _____

George Wallace _____

Gerald Ford _____

Gloria Steinem _____

Henry Kissinger _____

Ho Chi Minh _____

Hubert Humphrey _____

Jackie Robinson _____

Jimmy Carter _____

John F. Kennedy _____

John Foster Dulles _____

John Lewis _____

Joseph McCarthy _____

Joseph Stalin _____

Lyndon Johnson _____

Malcolm X _____

Martin Luther King, Jr. _____

Mao Zedong _____

Medgar Evers _____

National Organization for Women (NOW) _____

Nikita Khrushchev _____

Phyllis Schlafly _____

Rachel Carson _____

Richard Nixon _____

Robert Kennedy _____

Rosa Parks _____

Southern Christian Leadership Conference (SCLC) _____

Students for a Democratic Society _____

Thurgood Marshall _____

Vietcong _____

Woodward and Bernstein _____

Places

Aswan Dam _____

Berlin Wall _____

Gulf of Tonkin _____

Suez Canal _____

Sun Belt _____

Policies, Agreements, Court Rulings, Etc.

Bakke v. University of California _____

Brown v. Board of Education _____

Camp David accords _____

Central Intelligence Agency (CIA) _____

Civil Rights Act _____

Clean Air Act _____

Department of Housing and Urban Development (HUD) _____

Equal Rights Amendment _____

Geneva Accords _____

Gideon v. Wainwright _____

Griswold v. Connecticut _____

Head Start _____

Interstate Highway Act _____

Marshall Plan _____

Miranda v. Arizona _____

National Aeronautics Space Administration (NASA) _____

National Security Council _____

Organization of the Petroleum Exporting Countries (OPEC) _____

Peace Corps _____

Roe v. Wade _____

Southeast Asia Treaty Organization (SEATO) _____

Taft-Hartley Act _____

Voting Rights Act _____

War Powers Resolution _____

Chapter 13: Entering into the 21st Century

Concepts

Amnesty (immigration) _____

Christian evangelical movement _____

Contract with America _____

"Don't Ask, Don't Tell" _____

Glasnost _____

Illegal immigration _____

Libertarianism _____

Militia movement _____

Moral majority _____

Neo-conservatism _____

Perestroika _____

"Read my lips: No new taxes!" _____

Stagflation _____

Star Wars missile defense system _____

Supply-side economics _____

Trickle-down economics _____

"War on Terror" _____

Events

9/11 _____

Afghanistan War _____

Bosnia conflict _____

Congressional Election of 1994 _____

Iraq War _____

Iran-Contra Affair _____

Iran Hostage Crisis _____

Los Angeles riots (Rodney King) _____

Monica Lewinsky scandal _____

Oklahoma City bombing _____

OPEC oil embargo _____

Persian Gulf War _____

Somalia conflict _____

Whitewater scandal _____

People (Individuals and Groups)

Al Gore _____

Bill Clinton _____

Colin Powell _____

Condoleezza Rice_____

Dick Cheney _____

Donald Rumsfeld_____

George H. W. Bush _____

George W. Bush_____

Janet Reno _____

Jesse Jackson _____

Mikhail Gorbachev _____

Newt Gingrich_____

Planned Parenthood_____

Ronald Reagan_____

Timothy McVeigh _____

Places

Grenada _____

Nicaragua_____

Policies, Agreements, Court Rulings, Etc.

Citizens United v. Federal Election Commission _____

General Agreement on Tariffs and Trade (GATT) _____

North American Free Trade Agreement (NAFTA)_____

Simpson-Mazzoli Act_____

Part VI
Additional
Practice Tests

Practice Test 2

AP® United States History Exam

SECTION I, PART A: Multiple Choice

DO NOT OPEN THIS BOOKLET UNTIL YOU ARE TOLD TO DO SO.

At a Glance

Time
55 minutes
Number of Questions
55
Percent of Total Score
40%
Writing Instrument
Pencil required

Instructions

Section I, Part A of this exam contains 55 multiple-choice questions. Fill in only the ovals for numbers 1 through 55 on your answer sheet. Because this section offers only four answer options for each question, do not mark the (E) answer circle for any question.

Indicate all of your answers to the multiple-choice questions on the answer sheet. No credit will be given for anything written in this exam booklet, but you may use the booklet for notes or scratch work. After you have decided which of the suggested answers is best, completely fill in the corresponding oval on the answer sheet. Give only one answer to each question. If you change an answer, be sure that the previous mark is erased completely. Here is a sample question and answer.

Sample Question   Sample Answer

The first president of the United States was   Ⓐ ● Ⓒ Ⓓ
(A) Millard Fillmore
(B) George Washington
(C) Benjamin Franklin
(D) Andrew Jackson

Use your time effectively, working as rapidly as you can without losing accuracy. Do not spend too much time on any one question. Go on to other questions and come back to the ones you have not answered if you have time. It is not expected that everyone will know the answers to all of the multiple-choice questions.

Your total score on the multiple-choice section is based only on the number of questions answered correctly. Points are not deducted for incorrect answers or unanswered questions.

SECTION I, PART B: Short Answer

At a Glance

Time
40 minutes
Number of Questions
3
Percent of Total Score
20%
Writing Instrument
Pen with black or dark blue ink
Questions 1 and 2
Mandatory
Question 3 or 4
Choose one question

Instructions

For Section I, Part B of this exam, answer Question 1 and Question 2 and **either** Question 3 **or** Question 4. Write your responses in the Section I, Part B: Short-Answer Response booklet. You must write your response to each question on the lined page designated for that response. Each response is expected to fit within its designated page. Fill in the circle on the Section I, Part B: Short-Answer Response booklet indicating whether you answered Question 3 or Question 4. Failure to do so may delay your score.

GO ON TO THE NEXT PAGE.

UNITED STATES HISTORY
SECTION I, Part A
Time—55 minutes
55 Questions

Directions: Each of the questions or incomplete statements below is followed by four suggested answers or completions. Select the one that is best in each case and then blacken the corresponding space on the answer sheet.

Questions 1–5 refer to the excerpt below.

"In the name of God, Amen. We, whose names are underwritten, the loyal subjects of our dread Sovereign Lord King James, by the Grace of God, of Great Britain, France, and Ireland King, Defender of the Faith, etc. Having undertaken for the Glory of God and advancement of the Christian Faith, and the Honor of our King and Country, a Voyage to plant the First Colony in the Northern Parts of Virginia, do by these presents, solemnly and mutually, in the presence of God and one another, covenant and combine ourselves together into a civil body politic, for our better ordering and preservation and furtherance of the ends aforesaid; and by virtue hereof do enact, constitute, and frame such just and equal Laws, Ordinances, Acts, Constitutions and Offices from time to time, as shall be thought most meet and convenient for the general good of the Colony, unto which we promise all due submission and obedience. In witness whereof we have hereunder subscribed our names at Cape Cod, the 11th of November, in the year of the reign of our Sovereign Lord King James, of England, France and Ireland the eighteenth, and of Scotland the fifty-fourth. Anno Domini 1620."

William Bradford, *Of Plymouth Plantation*, 1646

1. Consistent with the excerpt above, the pilgrims settling in Plymouth would NOT be expected to support which of the following views?

   (A) A strong desire to remove Catholic beliefs from the Anglican Church
   (B) A commitment to the Calvanist principles of daily life
   (C) A desire to establish a society of religious freedom
   (D) A belief that governance should be derived from the will of the governed

2. The teachings of which of the following early colonists would be most consistent with the 17th-century views of the Massachusetts Bay Colony?

   (A) Roger Williams
   (B) John Cotton
   (C) William Penn
   (D) Anne Hutchinson

3. The First Great Awakening was marked by a period of

   (A) political activism in the early colonies
   (B) philosophical enlightenment
   (C) religious fervor
   (D) increased commercialization

4. The English Civil Wars had which of the following direct impacts on Puritan New England?

   (A) "Heightened" religious hysteria resulting from a fear that increased urban commercialism would undermine their way of life
   (B) Increased taxation and economic turmoil to pay for costs associated with the English Civil Wars
   (C) Reduced access of trade between colonists and Native Americans
   (D) Reduced immigration due to increased religious tolerance and political representation in England

5. While Massachusetts Bay Colony was established by Protestants seeking religious freedom, which of the following colonies was established as a destination and haven for Catholics fleeing religious persecution?

   (A) Pennsylvania
   (B) Maryland
   (C) Virginia
   (D) New York

GO ON TO THE NEXT PAGE.

Questions 6–7 refer to the excerpt below.

"It is important for us, my brothers, that we exterminate from our lands this nation which seeks only to destroy us. You see as well as I that we can no longer supply our needs, as we have done from our brothers, the French…and when we wish to set out for our winter camp they do not want to give us any credit as our brothers the French do…. Therefore, my brothers, we must all swear their destruction and wait no longer. Nothing prevents us; they are few in numbers, and we can accomplish it."

Chief Pontiac of the Ottawa, speaking to a war council, 1763

6. In addition to the Ottawa, Pontiac's speech was delivered to several other tribes present at the war council meeting including which of the following?

   (A) Huron
   (B) Iroquois
   (C) Seminoles
   (D) Cherokee

7. Pontiac's rebellion led directly to

   (A) onset of the Seven Years' War
   (B) a proclamation forbidding settlement west of the Appalachian Mountains
   (C) the passage of the Intolerable Acts
   (D) the ending of the fur trade in North America

Questions 8–9 refer to the excerpt below.

"Whereas by an Act made in the last session of Parliament, several duties were granted, continued, and appropriated, towards defraying the expenses of defending, protecting, and securing, the British Colonies and Plantations in America: and whereas it is just and necessary, that Provision be made for raising a further revenue within your Majesty's Dominions in America, towards defraying the said expenses: We, your Majesty's most dutiful and loyal Subjects, the Commons of Great Britain in Parliament assembled, have therefore resolved to give and grant unto your Majesty the several rates and duties herein after mentioned."

Stamp Act, 1765

8. The justification to raise the Stamp Act "towards defraying the said expenses" is largely in response to

   (A) the high costs to produce and import paper into the British colonies
   (B) the high costs to support and maintain a standing army in the British colonies
   (C) the high costs of Indian removal and resettlement
   (D) the high costs of the French and Indian War

9. The revenue-generating measures imposed by the British in the mid-18th century were largely opposed by the colonists for all of the following reasons EXCEPT

   (A) a lack of representation in British Parliament
   (B) a perceived infringement upon the rights of the colonies to self-govern
   (C) a post-war economic depression was already limiting economic growth in the colonies
   (D) a desire to declare independence from Great Britain

GO ON TO THE NEXT PAGE.

Questions 10–13 refer to the image and excerpt below.

Join, or Die, Benjamin Franklin, 1754

"It is in vain, sir, to extenuate the matter. Gentlemen may cry, 'Peace, Peace,' but there is no peace. The war is actually begun! The next gale that sweeps from the north will bring to our ears the clash of resounding arms! Our brethren are already in the field! Why stand we here idle? What is it that gentlemen wish? What would they have? Is life so dear, or peace so sweet, as to be purchased at the price of chains and slavery? Forbid it, Almighty God! I know not what course others may take; but as for me, give me liberty or give me death."

Patrick Henry, speaking at the Second Virginia Convention, 1775

10. The political cartoon "Join, or Die" by Ben Franklin was designed to unite the colonies in response to

    (A) rising anti-British sentiment over taxation without representation in Parliament
    (B) conflicts over territorial rights with the French and Native Americans
    (C) increased conflict over religious differences between the colonies
    (D) an economic downturn resulting from the Seven Years' War

11. Consistent with his speech, Patrick Henry would have been identified at the time as a(n)

    (A) loyalist
    (B) conservative
    (C) radical
    (D) isolationist

12. Which of the following statements below most accurately reflects colonial attitudes regarding the declaration of independence from Great Britain?

    (A) Most colonists considered the war against Great Britain necessary and openly supported its efforts.
    (B) Most colonists viewed the declaration of independence with apprehension and were sympathetic to British interests in the colonies.
    (C) Most colonists were largely indifferent and wished for resolution of the rising hostilities as fast as possible.
    (D) Most colonists were slaves and resisted for calls of independence viewing the British as more likely to grant them liberty.

13. Which of the following Acts of Parliament was passed in direct response to the events of the Boston Tea Party?

    (A) Coercive Acts
    (B) Tea Act
    (C) Townshend Acts
    (D) Currency Act

GO ON TO THE NEXT PAGE.

Questions 14–16 refer to the image below.

Declaration of Independence, John Trumbull, 1818

14. Which of the following was NOT included in the Declaration of Independence?

    (A) The laws of governance to be used in the newly formed United States
    (B) Principles of individual liberties and rights of people
    (C) Grievances against the British crown
    (D) Justification for why the American colonies should independently self-govern

15. The preamble to the Declaration of Independence, which included the language "all men are created equal," was used as a partial justification by many Northerners to push for the adoption of the

    (A) 13th Amendment
    (B) 19th Amendment
    (C) Articles of Confederation
    (D) U.S. Constitution

16. Which of the following was seen as a major weakness of the Articles of Confederation?

    (A) It lacked laws to oversee any governance of the nation.
    (B) It limited the ability of the nation to levy taxes and tariffs.
    (C) It prevented the establishment of a legislative branch of government.
    (D) It was unable to form and adopt new laws and resolutions.

GO ON TO THE NEXT PAGE.

Questions 17–19 refer to the excerpt below.

"After an unequivocal experience of the inefficiency of the subsisting federal government, you are called upon to deliberate on a new Constitution for the United States of America. The subject speaks its own importance; comprehending in its consequences nothing less than the existing of the union, the safety and welfare of the parts of which it is composed, the fate of an empire in many respects the most interesting in the world. It has been frequently remarked that it seems to have been reserved to the people of this country, by their conduct and example, to decide the important question, whether societies of men are really capable or not of establishing good government from reflection and choice, or whether they are forever destined to depend for their political constitutions on accident and force. If there be any truth in the remark, the crisis at which we are arrived may with propriety be regarded as the era in which that decision is to be made; and a wrong election of the part we shall act may, in this view, deserve to be considered as the general misfortune of mankind."

The Federalist Papers, 1788

17. Regarding adoption and ratification of the U.S. Constitution, the writer of the excerpt above would be most likely to agree with which of the following statements?

 (A) A more established central government as proposed in the U.S. Constitution would lead to despotism and a possible return to monarchical rule.
 (B) Adoption and ratification of the proposed U.S. Constitution would result in the loss of states' rights to self-govern.
 (C) Failure to include adoption of a Bill of Rights along with the U.S. Constitution would result in loss of individual rights and threatened public liberties.
 (D) The U.S. Constitution should be ratified and does not need an additional Bill of Rights.

18. This excerpt was most likely written by

 (A) Alexander Hamilton
 (B) Patrick Henry
 (C) Thomas Jefferson
 (D) Samuel Adams

19. The Federalist Party of the early 1800s supported which of the following views?

 (A) A national bank was necessary to encourage foreign investment and maintain national economic security.
 (B) The provisions of the U.S. Constitution should be applied strictly as written.
 (C) The French Revolution would result in a more just form of government with more governance provided to the people.
 (D) Agriculture and farming are the backbone of the American economy.

GO ON TO THE NEXT PAGE.

Questions 20–21 refer to the excerpt below.

"The cession of Louisiana and the Floridas by Spain to France works most sorely on the U.S. On this subject the Secretary of State has written to you fully. Yet I cannot forbear recurring to it personally, so deep is the impression it makes in my mind. It completely reverses all the political relations of the U.S. and will form a new epoch in our political course. Of all nations of any consideration France is the one which hitherto has offered the fewest points on which we could have any conflict of right, and the most points of a communion of interests.... There is on the globe one single spot, the possessor of which is our natural and habitual enemy. It is New Orleans, through which the produce of three-eighths of our territory must pass to market, and from its fertility it will long yield more than half of our whole produce and contain more than half our inhabitants. France placing herself in that door assumes to us the attitude of defiance."

Thomas Jefferson, a letter written to U.S. Ambassador (to France) Robert Livingston, 1802

20. Consistent with the excerpt above, which of the following was NOT a reason that France ultimately agreed to sell their New World holdings in the Louisiana Purchase?

(A) The city and port of New Orleans were too costly to continue to protect and maintain.

(B) The French needed money to raise armies and prepare for war on the European continent.

(C) Failure to arrest a slave revolt led to fears among European powers of similar uprisings throughout the New World.

(D) American exploration and expansionism would apply increasing pressure on the French colony.

21. The decision of the United States to purchase the Louisiana Territory from France was not universally supported. Among those opposing this decision were the Quids who felt that

(A) Jefferson had paid far too much for the territory

(B) Jefferson lacked the authority as president under the U.S. Constitution to purchase the land from France

(C) Jefferson risked starting war with Spain over territorial rights

(D) Jefferson would use the territory to support the addition of new pro-Republican states limiting Federalist power

GO ON TO THE NEXT PAGE.

Questions 22–24 refer to the excerpt below.

"Sir, if you wish to avoid foreign commerce; give up all your prosperity. It is the thing protected, not the instrument of protection, that involves you in war. Commerce engenders collision, collision war, and war, the argument supposes, leads to despotism. Would the councils of that statesman be deemed who would recommend that the nation should be unarmed—that in the art of war, the material spirit, and martial exercises, should be prohibited...and that the great body of the people should be taught that the national happiness was to be found in perpetual peace alone? No, sir."

Henry Clay, a speech in the House of Representatives, 1812

22. This excerpt would be most likely supported by

   (A) The Federalists
   (B) The War Hawks
   (C) The British
   (D) The French

23. The War of 1812 directly led to which of the following?

   (A) The downfall of the Federalist Party
   (B) Greater dependence on trade with Great Britain and France
   (C) An increase in American territory
   (D) The Monroe Doctrine

24. Henry Clay would later broker the Missouri Compromise which stated that

   (A) all new U.S. states would vote on whether they would support slavery in their territory
   (B) states admitted in the North would enter as free states and those entering in the South would be slave states
   (C) slavery would be prohibited in all new states admitted to the Union
   (D) slave trade would be abolished in all new states, but slavery would be permitted

Questions 25–26 refer to the excerpt below.

"Mr. Adams is the Constitutional President and as such I would myself be the last man in the Commonwealth to oppose him upon any other ground than that of principle.... As to his character also, it is hardly necessary for me to observe, that I had esteemed him as a virtuous, able and honest man; and when rumor was stamping the sudden union of his and the friends of Mr. Clay with intrigue, barter and bargain I did not, nay, I could not believe that Mr. Adams participated in a management deserving such epithets.... But when these strange rumors became facts, when the predicted stipulation was promptly fulfilled, and Mr. Clay was Secretary of State, the inference was irresistible—I could not doubt the facts. It was well known that during the canvass Mr. Clay had denounced him as an apostate, as one of the most dangerous men in the union, and the last man in it that ought to be brought into the executive chair."

Andrew Jackson, in a letter to Henry Lee, 1825

25. John Quincy Adams became president of the United States because of

   (A) a win of the Electoral College
   (B) a win of the popular vote, but not the electoral college
   (C) a vote of the House of Representatives
   (D) the death of the existing president of the United States

26. The Election of 1824 saw nominees for president from which of the following political parties?

   I. The Federalists
   II. The Whigs
   III. Democratic-Republicans

   (A) II only
   (B) III only
   (C) I and III only
   (D) II and III only

GO ON TO THE NEXT PAGE.

Questions 27–30 refer to the image below.

King Andrew the First, Unknown Artist, c. 1833

27. This political cartoon of Andrew Jackson was least likely to have been sketched by a supporter of which of the following political parties?

(A) Whig
(B) National Republican
(C) Anti-Masonic
(D) Democratic

28. Which of the following famous court cases was used in defense of the constitutionality of the Second Bank of the United States?

(A) *Gibbons v. Ogden*
(B) *Marbury v. Madison*
(C) *McCulloch v. Maryland*
(D) *Chisholm v. Georgia*

29. The Nullification Crisis was triggered in response to

(A) paper money being prohibited for payment of debts or services
(B) Turner's Rebellion
(C) arguments over the constitutionality of Jackson's Indian Removal Act
(D) the passage of tariffs, which disproportionally affected Southern states

30. Which of the following was NOT a primary cause of the Panic of 1837?

(A) Andrew Jackson's policy of depositing federal funds in state "pet banks"
(B) Establishment of the Specie Circular for purchase of western lands
(C) Discovery of gold in western territories
(D) Overspeculation on the strength of commodities and investments

GO ON TO THE NEXT PAGE.

Questions 31–34 refer to the excerpts below.

"The whole continent of North America appears to be destined by Divine Providence to be peopled by one nation, speaking one language, professing one general system of religious and political principles, and accustomed to one general tenor of social usages and customs. For the common happiness of them all, for their peace and prosperity, I believe it is indispensable that they should be associated in one federal Union."

John Quincy Adams, letter to his father, 1811

"In assuming responsibilities so vast I fervently invoke the aid of that Almighty Ruler of the Universe in whose hands are the destinies of nations and of men to guard this Heaven-favored land against the mischiefs which without His guidance might arise from an unwise public policy. With a firm reliance upon the wisdom of Omnipotence to sustain and direct me in the path of duty which I am appointed to pursue, I stand in the presence of this assembled multitude of my countrymen to take upon myself the solemn obligation 'to the best of my ability to preserve, protect, and defend the Constitution of the United States'."

James Polk, Inauguration Speech, 1845

31. The nature of both Adams' and Polk's excerpts above best reflect which of the following common views of the 19th century?

  (A) Laissez-faire economics
  (B) Social Darwinism
  (C) Manifest Destiny
  (D) Nativism

32. The Polk presidency oversaw all of the following major events in U.S. history EXCEPT

  (A) the annexation of Texas into the United States
  (B) the addition of California and Oregon as new states
  (C) war with Mexico
  (D) the Compromise of 1850

33. The Wilmot Proviso was both a unique and significant bill brought during the presidency of Polk before Congress because it

  (A) addressed that status of slavery in new states and territories
  (B) represented the first proposal to use popular sovereignty to decide the status of slavery
  (C) was supported or rejected strictly on territorial lines rather than party lines
  (D) provided both legal protections and rights to slaves

34. Despite requests for admission as early as 1836, the annexation of Texas into the Union was delayed until 1845 mostly due to which of the following?

  I. Opposition to territorial growth and expansion into the West
  II. Concern over how to manage slavery in the territory
  III. Fear of war with Mexico

  (A) III only
  (B) I and III only
  (C) II and III only
  (D) I, II, and III

GO ON TO THE NEXT PAGE.

Questions 35–37 refer to the image below.

Density of Distribution of the Natives of Ireland: 1890, Government release of 11th Census Results, 1898

35. Consistent with the image above, Irish immigrants into the United States during the 19th century largely sought out settlement within

(A) industrialized towns and cities
(B) plantations and mostly agrarian society
(C) the American western frontier
(D) port cities

36. How did European immigrants of the early and mid-19th century largely differ from those of the late 19th century?

(A) Earlier immigrants were generally fleeing religious and social persecution, whereas later immigrants were typically seeking out improved opportunities for work.
(B) Earlier immigrants were mostly from Western Europe, whereas later immigrants included more from Southern and Eastern Europe.
(C) Earlier immigrants were mostly Catholics, whereas later immigrants generally were more often Protestants.
(D) Earlier immigrants were highly educated, whereas later immigrants were poorly educated.

37. Which of the following would have the greatest impact on curbing immigration into the United States?

(A) Passage of the 13th and 14th Amendments
(B) The Chinese Exclusion Act of 1882
(C) The Quota Act of 1924
(D) The Naturalization Act of 1870

GO ON TO THE NEXT PAGE.

Questions 38–41 refer to the excerpt below.

"Some man who seemed to be a stranger (a United States officer, I presume) made a little speech and then read a rather long paper—the Emancipation Proclamation, I think. After the reading we were told that we were all free, and could go when and where we pleased. My mother, who was standing by my side, leaned over and kissed her children, while tears of joy ran down her cheeks. She explained to us what it all meant, that this was the day for which she had been so long praying, but fearing that she would never live to see."

Booker T. Washington, *Up From Slavery: An Autobiography*, 1907

38. The Emancipation Proclamation had which of the following impacts?

    (A) It declared that all slaves in the United States were granted citizen rights.
    (B) It declared that all slaves in states in open rebellion were free.
    (C) It declared that slavery in Union-held territories was illegal.
    (D) It declared that slavery throughout the United States was illegal.

39. Copperheads viewed the Emancipation Proclamation as

    (A) a necessary step to end the Civil War
    (B) an egregious attempt by the president to push unneeded social revolution
    (C) a precursor to open rebellion by Southern states over the nature of slavery
    (D) an overly sympathetic gesture to the South

40. Which of the amendments to the U.S. Constitution provided direct Federal legitimacy and support to the Emancipation Proclamation?

    (A) The 13th Amendment
    (B) The 14th Amendment
    (C) The 15th Amendment
    (D) The 16th Amendment

41. Establishment of the Freedmen's Bureau provided all of the following EXCEPT

    (A) support for the establishment of schools and institutions of higher education for African Americans
    (B) public assistance to freed slaves to find jobs and housing
    (C) reallocation of land and property to freed slaves
    (D) aiding freed slaves with money and food for those in need

GO ON TO THE NEXT PAGE.

Questions 42–45 refer to the excerpt below.

"Every contract, combination in the form of trust or otherwise, or conspiracy, in restraint of trade or commerce among the several States, or with foreign nations, is declared to be illegal.... Every person who shall monopolize, or attempt to monopolize, or combine or conspire with any other person or persons, to monopolize any part of the trade or commerce among the several States, or with foreign nations, shall be deemed guilty of a felony."

Sherman Antitrust Act, 1890

42. Andrew Carnegie's opinion of the Sherman Antitrust Act would have been

   (A) favorable, because it sought to prevent the formation of highly influential monopolies and trusts
   (B) favorable, because it ensured that competition between companies would continue to allow for regulation of prices and political influence
   (C) unfavorable, because it restricted capitalism
   (D) unfavorable, because it concentrated the majority of wealth in the hands of a few

43. The Sherman Antitrust Act is most closely associated with the policies and actions of which U.S. president?

   (A) William McKinley
   (B) Benjamin Harrison
   (C) Theodore Roosevelt
   (D) Calvin Coolidge

44. Which of the following failed to strengthen the legality of the Sherman Antitrust Act?

   (A) Passage of the Clayton Antitrust Act
   (B) Passage of the Interstate Commerce Act
   (C) Formation of the Federal Trade Commission
   (D) Implementation of the McKinley Tariff

45. Which of the following business magnates is accurately paired with his theater of industry?

   (A) Cornelius Vanderbilt—Steel
   (B) J.P. Morgan—Oil
   (C) John D. Rockefeller—Railroads
   (D) John Jacob Aster—Furs

GO ON TO THE NEXT PAGE.

Questions 46–48 refer to the excerpt below.

"It is not enough to be well-meaning and kindly, but weak; neither is it enough to be strong, unless morality and decency go hand in hand with strength. We must possess the qualities which make us do our duty in our homes and among our neighbors, and in addition we must possess the qualities which are indispensable to the make-up of every great and masterful nation— the qualities of courage and hardihood, of individual initiative and yet of power to combine for a common end, and above all, the resolute determination to permit no man and no set of men to sunder us one from the other by lines of caste or creed or section. We must act upon the motto of all for each and each for all. There must be ever present in our minds the fundamental truth that in a republic such as ours the only safety is to stand neither for nor against any man because he is rich or because he is poor, because he is engaged in one occupation or another, because he works with his brains or because he works with his hands. We must treat each man on his worth and merits as a man. We must see that each is given a square deal, because he is entitled to no more and should receive no less."

Theodore Roosevelt, a speech to farmers in New York, 1903

46. The "square deal" referred to by Roosevelt in the excerpt above was a program of

   (A) reduced taxation on the lower class, enhanced protections for businesses, and isolationism on the global market
   (B) increased federal regulation of banking, tighter restrictions on trusts, and more support for domestic infrastructure
   (C) conservation of natural resources, control of corporations, and protection of consumers
   (D) radical social change, including enfranchisement of women and the prohibition of alcohol

47. Which of the following works had a critical role in shaping policy decisions within Roosevelt's Square Deal?

   (A) L. Frank Baum's *The Wizard of Oz*
   (B) Upton Sinclair's *The Jungle*
   (C) John Steinbeck's *The Grapes of Wrath*
   (D) William Faulkner's *As I Lay Dying*

48. In contrast to Roosevelt's Square Deal, FDR's First New Deal program aimed to

   (A) improve crumbling domestic infrastructure
   (B) provide work and stabilize the labor force
   (C) restore confidence in the economy and banking system
   (D) ensure financial support for retired and disabled workers

GO ON TO THE NEXT PAGE.

Questions 49–50 refer to the excerpt below.

"The Allied and Associated Governments affirm and Germany accepts the responsibility of Germany and her allies for causing all the loss and damage to which the Allied and Associated Governments and their nationals have been subjected as a consequence of the war imposed upon them by the aggression of Germany and her allies."

The Treaty of Versailles, Article 231, 1919

49. This excerpt from Article 231 of the Treaty of Versailles has been credited by some historians as contributing to the rise of Nazism and the later onset of World War II. All of the following have been provided as justifications of this view EXCEPT

(A) legally justifying the demand for war reparations, leading to rampant inflation in Germany

(B) establishing public indignation towards Allied governments for attributing full blame on Germany for World War I

(C) political instability with the abdication of the German monarchy

(D) formation of new formalized multinational alliances for protection and mutual interests

50. As a major part of the Treaty of Versailles, President Wilson sought to establish a League of Nations to

(A) assemble an international forum for settling disputes through diplomacy and arbitration rather than war

(B) provide a stabilizing multinational security force to protect and defend international law

(C) counter future German aggression in Europe and Africa

(D) establish a common currency and international regulatory body for trade and economic growth

GO ON TO THE NEXT PAGE.

Questions 51–53 refer to the excerpt below.

"The United States has received from the Greek Government an urgent appeal for financial and economic assistance....
The very existence of the Greek state is today threatened by the terrorist activities of several thousand armed men, led by Communists, who defy the government's authority at a number of points, particularly along the northern boundaries.... Greece must have assistance if it is to become a self-supporting and self-respecting democracy.... One of the primary objectives of the foreign policy of the United States is the creation of conditions in which we and other nations will be able to work out a way of life free from coercion.... This is no more than a frank recognition that totalitarian regimes imposed on free peoples, by direct or indirect aggression, undermine the foundations of international peace and hence the security of the United States....
I believe that it must be the policy of the United States to support free peoples who are resisting attempted subjugation by armed minorities or by outside pressures."

Harry Truman, speaking to a joint
session of Congress, 1947

51. In this excerpt, Truman advocates for an American doctrine of support in

   (A) international economic regulation and assistance for growing economies
   (B) isolationism and neutrality to avoid future wars
   (C) the recovery of nations destroyed in World War II
   (D) opposing the growing geopolitical influence of communism

52. Among the goals of Truman's domestic policy (dubbed the Fair Deal) was to

   (A) expand social and political rights of women and minorities
   (B) aid in the reintegration of war veterans into American society
   (C) provide financial support and resources to banks to counter an ongoing recession
   (D) provide legal protections for unions and workers' rights

53. The era of McCarthyism aligns most closely with what other period in U.S. history?

   (A) The Red Scare
   (B) Populism
   (C) The Temperance movement
   (D) Counterculture

GO ON TO THE NEXT PAGE.

Questions 54–55 refer to the excerpt below.

"Your imagination, your initiative, and your indignation will determine whether we build a society where progress is the servant of our needs, or a society where old values and new visions are buried under unbridled growth. For in your time we have the opportunity to move not only toward the rich society and the powerful society, but upward to the Great Society.

The Great Society rests on abundance and liberty for all. It demands an end to poverty and racial injustice, to which we are totally committed in our time. But that is just the beginning.

The Great Society is a place where every child can find knowledge to enrich his mind and to enlarge his talents. It is a place where leisure is a welcome chance to build and reflect, not a feared cause of boredom and restlessness. It is a place where the city of man serves not only the needs of the body and the demands of commerce but the desire for beauty and the hunger for community."

Lyndon B. Johnson, commencement speech, 1964

54. All of the following were new programs and initiatives instituted as a part of Johnson's Great Society EXCEPT

(A) the Civil Rights Act
(B) the Economic Opportunity Act
(C) the Voting Rights Act
(D) the Social Security Act

55. The domestic policy and vision of the Great Society aligns most closely with which of the following political stances today?

(A) Liberals
(B) Evangelicals
(C) Moderates
(D) Conservatives

GO ON TO THE NEXT PAGE.

UNITED STATES HISTORY
SECTION I, Part B
Time—40 minutes

Directions: Answer Question 1 **and** Question 2. Answer **either** Question 3 **or** Question 4.

Write your responses in the Section I, Part B: Short-Answer Response booklet. You must write your response to each question on the lined page designated for that response. Each response is expected to fit within the space provided.

In your responses, be sure to address all parts of the questions you answer. Use complete sentences; an outline or bulleted list alone is not acceptable. You may plan your answers in this exam booklet, but no credit will be given for notes written in this booklet.

Question 1 is based on the excerpt and map below.

"Nowhere had the Federalists exerted themselves to do battle for the administration with greater enthusiasm than at the Virginia capital where the Republicans had so forcefully launched their attack five months before. According to Randolph's eyewitness account, John Marshall had taken the lead and was constantly on the speaker's stand 'concluding every third sentence with the horrors of war.' Two weeks of petitioning and public meetings were climaxed on April 25 with an all-day demonstration ending in the adoption of a series of resolutions condemning the Republican program and demanding the execution of the Jay Treaty....

A strong segment of the New York citizenry was behind his call for the Jay negotiation papers, but by the end of March nothing that the Republicans had done had roused public opinion to the proportions that would be necessary to drive Federalism from power in November. The great ground swell only made its appearance after Washington's call to battle, and if the petition struggle of April, 1796, was a gauge of public opinion, as Federalists claimed it was, the radicals had made a tragic blunder in allowing the sanctity of George Washington's name to become a political football. Federalists were not slow in exploiting the mistake."

Stephen G. Kurtz, *The Presidency of John Adams: The Collapse of Federalism, 1795–1800*

GO ON TO THE NEXT PAGE.

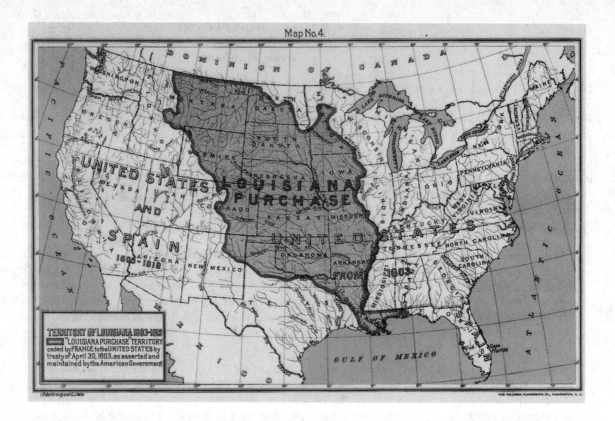

Map of the United States in 1803 from *Old Map File Manuscript and Annotated Maps of the United States and Its Territories, 1790–1946,* U.S. National Archives and Records Administration

1. Using the excerpt and the map above, answer parts (a), (b), and (c).

   a) Briefly outline the main characteristics of both Federalists and Anti-Federalists during this time period.

   b) Explain the effect of factionalism on ONE of the following events.
      - Washington's Farewell Address
      - The Federalist Papers
      - The Sedition Act

   c) Analyze the reasons for the decline of Federalism in the following decades. Use at least ONE specific piece of evidence.

GO ON TO THE NEXT PAGE.

Question 2 is based on the following excerpt.

"The situation was inescapable. Germany was unable to make the payments due on July 1, and without these payments made to them our debtors, under the stress of the depression, could hardly have paid us…. It was clear that financial disaster at this vulnerable spot might well drag down some of the surrounding countries. It did not appear that Germany was permanently down and out—the Germans are not the kind to give up—and therefore the nation must be saved in order once more to take its place as one of the world's safeguards against disorder and despair. If Germany was unable to buy, there would have been further drops in the prices of such commodities as foodstuffs, cotton, and minerals. If financial disaster brought revolution, the holders of German securities the world over would suffer. In other words, Germany was a key spot. With her rescue, the tide might well turn, to the benefit of all."

William R. Castle, Under Secretary of State, address to the Women's National Republican Club, 1932

2. Using both the excerpt above and your knowledge of history, answer parts (a), (b), and (c).

   a) Outline at least ONE root cause of the Great Depression.

   b) Describe the effect of the Great Depression upon the federal government's willingness to address foreign policy issues.

   c) Explain the long-term effect of U.S. foreign policy in the 1930s.

GO ON TO THE NEXT PAGE.

Question 3 or 4

Directions: Answer **either** Question 3 **or** Question 4.

3. American domestic manufacturing took a large step forward from 1800 to 1830. Answer parts (a), (b), and (c).

    a) Briefly explain ONE of the advances in <u>manufacturing technology</u> that made this growth possible.

    b) Briefly explain ONE of the changes in <u>transportation</u> that made this growth possible.

    c) Briefly describe ONE <u>legal</u> or <u>labor</u> development that contributed to this growth.

GO ON TO THE NEXT PAGE.

4. Many historians view the 1970s as an era marked by growing distrust in government. Answer parts (a), (b), and (c).

   a) Discuss ONE reason for elevated public trust in federal government in the decades prior to the 1970s.

   b) Choose ONE of the events below and discuss why your choice represents a growing lack of faith in elected officials.
      - The exit from the Bretton-Woods Agreement
      - The Pentagon Papers
      - The Watergate scandal
      - The Iran hostage crisis

   c) Briefly explain why one of the other options is less persuasive.

END OF SECTION I

GO ON TO THE NEXT PAGE.

AP® United States History Exam

SECTION II: Free Response

DO NOT OPEN THIS BOOKLET UNTIL YOU ARE TOLD TO DO SO.

Instructions

The questions for Section II are printed in the orange Questions and Documents booklet. You may use that booklet to organize your answers and for scratch work, but you must write your answers in this Section II: Free Response booklet. No credit will be given for any work written in the Questions and Documents booklet.

The proctor will announce the beginning and end of the reading period. You are advised to spend the 15-minute period reading the question and planning your answer to Question 1, the document-based question. If you have time, you may also read Questions 2, 3, and 4. Do not begin writing in this booklet until the proctor tells you to do so.

Section II of this exam requires answers in essay form. Write clearly and legibly. Circle the number of the question you are answering at the top of each page in this booklet. Begin each answer on a new page. Do not skip lines. Cross out any errors you make; crossed-out work will not be scored.

Manage your time carefully. The proctor will announce the suggested time for each part, but you may proceed freely from one part to the next. Go on to Question 2, 3, or 4 if you finish Question 1 early. You may review your responses if you finish before the end of the exam is announced.

After the exam, you must apply the label that corresponds to the long-essay question you answered—Question 2, 3, or 4. For example, if you answered Question 2, apply the label [2]. Failure to do so may delay your score.

GO ON TO THE NEXT PAGE.

UNITED STATES HISTORY
SECTION II
Total Time—1 hour, 40 minutes

Question 1 (Document-Based Question)
Suggested reading and writing time: 1 hour

It is suggested that you spend 15 minutes reading the documents and 45 minutes writing your response.

Note: You may begin writing your response before the reading period is over.

Directions: Question 1 is based on the accompanying documents. The documents have been edited for the purpose of this exercise.

In your response, you should do the following.

- Respond to the prompt with a historically defensible thesis or claim that establishes a line of reasoning.
- Describe a broader historical context relevant to the prompt.
- Support an argument in response to the prompt using at least six documents.
- Use at least one additional piece of specific historical evidence (beyond that found in the documents) relevant to an argument about the prompt.
- For at least three documents, explain how or why the document's point of view, purpose, historical situation, and/or audience is relevant to an argument.
- Use evidence to corroborate, qualify, or modify an argument that addresses the prompt.

GO ON TO THE NEXT PAGE.

1. Describe the growth of an imperialistic U.S. foreign policy during the late 19th and early 20th centuries. Using your knowledge of the period, construct an essay that explains the roots of this policy, as well as the arguments of those who opposed it.

Document 1

Source: Charles Francis Adams, Jr., historian and great-grandson of John Adams, in a letter to Hon. Carl Schurz (December 21, 1898)

In 1862, when the United States was involved in the War of the Rebellion, the Europeans took advantage of the situation to invade Mexico, and to establish there a "stable government." They undertook to protect that people against themselves, and to erect for them a species of protectorate, such as we now propose for the Philippines. As soon as our war was over, we insisted upon the withdrawal of Europe from Mexico. What followed is matter of recent history. It is unnecessary to recall it. We did not reduce Mexico into a condition of "tutelage," or establish over it a "protectorate" of our own. We, on the contrary, insisted that it should stand on its own legs; and, by so doing, learn to stand firmly on them, just as a child learns to walk, by being compelled to try to walk, not by being kept everlastingly in "leading strings." This was the American, as contradistinguished from the European policy; and Mexico to-day walks firmly.

Finally take the case of Venezuela in 1895. I believe I am not mistaken when I say that, during the twenty-five preceding years, Venezuela had undergone almost as many revolutions. It certainly had not enjoyed a stable government. Through disputes over questions of boundary, Great Britain proposed to confer that indisputable blessing upon a considerable region. We interfered under a most questionable extension of the Monroe Doctrine, and asserted the principle of "Hands-off." Having done this—having in so far perpetuated what we now call the scandal of anarchy—we did not establish "tutelage," or a protectorate, ourselves. We wisely left Venezuela to work out its destiny in its own way, and in the fullness of time. That policy was far-seeing, beneficent, and strictly American in 1895. Why, then, make almost indecent haste to abandon it in 1898?

Instead, therefore, of finding our precedents in the experience of England, or that of any other European power, I would suggest that the true course for this country now to pursue is exactly the course we have heretofore pursued under similar conditions. Let us be true to our own traditions, and follow our own precedents. Having relieved the Spanish islands from the dominion of Spain, we should declare concerning them a policy of "Hands-off," both on our own part and on the part of other powers. We should say that the independence of those islands is morally guaranteed by us as a consequence of the treaty of Paris, and then leave them....

GO ON TO THE NEXT PAGE.

Document 2

Source: Vladimir Lenin, *Imperialism: The Last Stage of Capitalism,* 1917

In the United States, the imperialist war waged against Spain in 1898 stirred up the opposition of the "anti-imperialists," the last of the Mohicans of bourgeois democracy. They declared this war to be *"criminal"*; denounced the annexation of foreign territories as being a violation of the constitution, and they denounced the "jingo treachery" by means of which Aguinaldo, leader of the rebel native Philippinos, was deceived (first the Americans promised him the independence of his country; then they landed troops and annexed it). They quoted the words of Lincoln: "It is self-government when the white man governs himself; but when he governs himself and also governs others, it is no longer self-government, it is despotism."

But all this criticism shrank from recognizing the indissoluble bond between imperialism and the trusts, and, therefore, between imperialism and the very foundations of capitalism....

Document 3

Source: Treaty of Guadalupe Hidalgo (1848)

Article IV

Immediately after the exchange of ratifications of the present treaty all castles, forts, territories, places, and possessions, which have been taken or occupied by the forces of the United States during the present war, within the limits of the Mexican Republic, as about to be established by the following article, shall be definitely restored to the said Republic, together with all the artillery, arms, apparatus of war, munitions, and other public property, which were in the said castles and forts when captured, and which shall remain there at the time when this treaty shall be duly ratified by the Government of the Mexican Republic....

The final evacuation of the territory of the Mexican Republic, by the forces of the United States, shall be completed in three months from the said exchange of ratifications, or sooner if possible; the Mexican Government hereby engaging, as in the foregoing article to use all means in its power for facilitating such evacuation, and rendering it convenient to the troops, and for promoting a good understanding between them and the inhabitants.

Article XI

It shall not be lawful, under any pretext whatever, for any inhabitant of the United States to purchase or acquire any Mexican, or any foreigner residing in Mexico, who may have been captured by Indians inhabiting the territory of either of the two republics; nor to purchase or acquire horses, mules, cattle, or property of any kind, stolen within Mexican territory by such Indians.

Article XII

In consideration of the extension acquired by the boundaries of the United States, as defined in the fifth article of the present treaty, the Government of the United States engages to pay to that of the Mexican Republic the sum of fifteen millions of dollars....

GO ON TO THE NEXT PAGE.

Document 4

Source: Political Cartoon from the Chicago Tribune by John T. McCutcheon (1914)

GO ON TO THE NEXT PAGE.

Document 5

Source: *Industrial Liberty: Our Duty to Rescue the People of Cuba, Porto Rico, and the Philippine Islands from That Greatest of All Evils—Poverty* by Charles E. Buell, Secretary, U.S. Special Commission to Porto Rico (1900)

The Philippine Islands are west of the United States, and near the southern coast of Asia, they are in longitude 120 degrees and 130 degrees and latitude 5 and 20, and are about 6,300 miles from San Francisco, and 600 miles from Hong Kong, China.

The Island of Luzon, on which the capital city, Manila, is located, is about the size of New York State, Mindanao is nearly as large, and the next largest islands are Samar, Panay, Mindoro, Leyet, Negros, and Cebu. These are among the best known....

The published statements of W.B. Wilcox, Paymaster, U.S. Navy, and Ensign L.R. Sargent, U.S. Navy, who, in 1898, made a visit to the most distant districts of the Island of Luzon, are highly commendable to the character and ability of the natives whom they met and associated with.

They were cordial and honorable in their treatment of our men at that time, and these people were found to be comfortably situated, and enjoying life since the departure of the Spaniards. They are an intelligent and a polite people; ambitious to improve their condition every way. They are patriotic and high-minded, as described by these officers, and while they may have since entertained a mistaken idea regarding our intentions towards them, and given us battle, they are capable of being won over to a brotherly regard for our people.

With proper care and direction, these people will become happy, and a strength to our nation. There should be no desire to, in the least, encroach upon their property....

GO ON TO THE NEXT PAGE.

Document 6

Source: U.S. Census Bureau (1940)

TABLE 1.—POPULATION OF THE UNITED STATES AND ITS TERRITORIES AND POSSESSIONS: 1940, 1930, AND 1920

AREA	Gross area (land and water) in square miles, 1940	POPULATION		
		1940	1930	1920
United States and all territories and possessions	3,735,223	150,621,231	[1] 138,439,069	[2] 118,107,150
Continental United States	3,022,387	131,669,275	122,775,046	105,710,620
Territories and possessions, exclusive of the Philippines	597,236	2,477,023	2,061,570	1,680,292
Alaska	586,400	[3] 72,524	[3] 59,278	55,036
American Samoa	76	12,908	10,055	8,056
Guam	206	22,290	18,509	13,275
Hawaii [4]	6,433	423,330	368,336	255,912
Panama Canal Zone	553	51,827	39,467	22,858
Puerto Rico	3,435	1,869,255	1,543,913	1,299,809
Virgin Islands of the United States	133	24,889	22,012	[2] 25,346
The Philippines	115,600	[5] 16,356,000	[1] 13,513,000	[2] 10,599,000
Military and naval services, etc., abroad	- - - - -	118,933	80,453	117,238

GO ON TO THE NEXT PAGE.

Document 7

Source: Political cartoon by Victor Gilliam (1899)

END OF DOCUMENTS FOR QUESTION 1

GO ON TO THE NEXT PAGE.

Question 2, 3, or 4 (Long Essay)

Suggested writing time: 40 minutes

Directions: Answer Question 2 **or** Question 3 **or** Question 4.

In your response, you should do the following.

- Respond to the prompt with a historically defensible thesis or claim that establishes a line of reasoning.
- Describe a broader historical context relevant to the prompt.
- Support an argument in response to the prompt using specific and relevant examples of evidence.
- Use historical reasoning (e.g., comparison, causation, continuity or change over time) to frame or structure an argument that addresses the prompt.
- Use evidence to corroborate, qualify, or modify an argument that addresses the prompt.

2. Compare and contrast the development of the Massachusetts Bay Colony with the development of the Virginia colony in the 17th century.

3. Analyze the ways in which Prohibition led to a rise in organized crime.

4. Describe the changing role of women in the labor force from 1920 to 1960.

   In your argument, analyze both changes and continuities in the relevant time period.

WHEN YOU FINISH WRITING, CHECK YOUR WORK ON SECTION II IF TIME PERMITS.

STOP

END OF EXAM

Practice Test 2:
Answers and
Explanations

PRACTICE TEST 2 ANSWER KEY

Section I, Part A: Multiple-Choice Questions

1. C	20. A	39. B
2. B	21. B	40. A
3. C	22. B	41. C
4. D	23. A	42. C
5. B	24. B	43. C
6. A	25. C	44. D
7. B	26. B	45. D
8. D	27. D	46. C
9. D	28. C	47. B
10. B	29. D	48. C
11. C	30. C	49. D
12. C	31. C	50. A
13. A	32. D	51. D
14. A	33. C	52. B
15. A	34. C	53. A
16. B	35. A	54. D
17. D	36. B	55. A
18. A	37. C	
19. A	38. B	

SECTION I, PART A: MULTIPLE-CHOICE QUESTIONS

Questions 1–5

This excerpt is the Mayflower Compact from William Bradford's account of the earliest days of Plymouth colony. The pilgrims that rode upon the Mayflower to form a colony in Virginia were Puritans seeking freedom from persecution to practice their religion. Aboard their ship, they agreed to a compact establishing a political body to govern themselves.

1. **C** While the pilgrims were certainly fleeing persecution for their religion, they were not planning to develop a society open to many religions. The Puritan pilgrims were Calvinists, (B), who sought to purify the Anglican church of Catholic practices, (A). Both statements (A) and (B) are accurate views of Puritans, and can be ruled out. As supported by the words of the Compact, the Puritans believed in only their religion and planned to develop a society that was governed by their people consistent with their shared beliefs in God, (D). Therefore, statement (D) is also accurate and can also be ruled out.

2. **B** Roger Williams, (A), and Anne Hutchinson, (D), were both famously banished from Massachusetts Bay Colony for disagreeing with the doctrines and firmly held beliefs of the colony. William Penn, (C), was a Quaker and would have also had differing views from Puritan New England. Ruling out (A), (C), and (D), leaves John Cotton, (B), who is a famous minister in the early Massachusetts Bay Colony.

3. **C** The first Great Awakening, which occurred in the early 18th century, was a period of religious revival spurred on by the Enlightenment. It saw a substantial return to the strong Calvinist doctrines of life and predeterminism. While political activism, (A), philosophical enlightenment, (B), and increased commercialization, (D), can be found at times throughout the colonies for much of this period, the Great Awakening specifically pertains to this sudden and significant period of religious fervor in the colonies.

4. **D** The English Civil Wars during the mid-17th century led to a period between English kings (interregnum) marked largely by Puritan rule. During this period, there was less need for Puritans to flee to New England, resulting in a reduction in immigration to the colony. The English Civil War did not result in religious hysteria, (A), in New England (actually quite the opposite), nor did it result in increased taxation, (B), on the colonies as the English continued their salutary neglect of the colonies. Lastly, trade, (C), between colonists and Native Americans continued to increase as all of the colonies continued to grow and expand into new territories.

5. **B** Maryland was a proprietary colony established by Lord Cecilius Calvert as a haven for Catholics who were being persecuted in an ever changing, more Protestant England. Unlike most of the other colonies, Maryland was also far more tolerant of other religious views. The Quakers established Pennsylvania, (A); Virginia, (C), was established for primarily commercial interests and economic gain; and New York, (D), was seized from the Dutch.

Questions 6–7

Pontiac's speech and subsequent rebellion coincided with the end of the Seven Years' War (or French and Indian War) fought between the French (with many Indian allies) and the English between 1754–1763. The English victory in the war resulted in a transfer of territorial and trade rights from the French to the English, who infringed more on the land and rights of the Native Americans (including the Ottawa).

6. **A** The Huron were mostly found in and around the Great Lakes (in present day Ontario) and, like the Ottawa, were also sympathetic to the French during the war. The Iroquois, (B), were one of the few tribes that sided with the British and would not have heard this speech. The Seminoles, (C), and Cherokee, (D), were found in Florida and the Carolinas, respectively, and were not involved in the conflict.

7. **B** Pontiac's rebellion resulted in attacks on colonial outposts and prompted the British government to pass the Proclamation of 1763, forbidding settlement west of the Appalachian Mountains out of fear of further unrest because of encroachment upon Native American lands.

Questions 8–9

The Stamp Act of 1765 was a strictly revenue-generating measure passed by the British on the American colonies to help pay for the high costs associated with the Seven Years' War. Since the measure targeted all legal documents and licenses, it had a particularly strong impact on influential lawmakers and the educated wealthy in the colonies. Consequently, the Stamp Act quickly became the source of increased frustration and led to the famous calls of "taxation without representation," referring to the issue of the British passing taxation legislation without colonial representation in British Parliament.

8. **D** The French and Indian War (or Seven Years' War) was a highly costly affair for the British. To reimburse the crown for the costs associated with this war, the British began passing revenue-generating acts such as the Stamp Act. While the British would continue to have to support the defense of the colonies, they would not maintain a significant force, (B), in the American colonies until later, with measures such as the Quartering Act of 1770. Furthermore, in comparison to the true costs of the French and Indian War, these defense costs were insignificant. Indian removal and resettlement was not a practice until much later, (C), and the costs to produce and import paper were not significant, (A).

9. **D** During the mid-18th century (and even up to and during the revolution), there remained a strong sense of loyalty towards the British. Very few at this time were calling for separation or independence, as it remained the hope for reform and greater representation in Parliament. The taxation and revenue-generating measures did highlight the lack of colonial representation in Parliament, (A), and interfered with the rights of the colonies to set their own taxes and self-govern, (B), both of these major points of contention among the colonies. In addition, the French and Indian War did lead to an economic depression, which only exasperated the impact of these new taxes and levies, (C), on the colonies.

Questions 10–13

The famous "Join, or Die" political cartoon by Benjamin Franklin and the "Liberty or Death" speech by Patrick Henry have now become synonymous with the cause of the American Revolution. However, these symbols both speak to the growing need for unity among the colonies. In 1754 (around the time of this first publication of his cartoon), Benjamin Franklin urged the colonies to unite with the Albany Plan. His sentiments are displayed in this cartoon where he shows that only when united will the colonies have the ability to survive. While the Albany Plan was not adopted, it represented an early push for colonial unity. Patrick Henry's speech, while still calling for unity, now advocated for liberty and survival in the face of possible war with the British.

10. **B** Franklin's cartoon, which was later adopted in response to calls for independence and unity of the American colonies against the British, actually dates back to much earlier, at a time when conflict with the French and their Indian interests over territorial and trading rights on the frontier of the growing colonies existed. The colonies, which remained both loyal and dedicated to the British at the time, were enveloped in the French and Indian War and Franklin viewed colonial unity under a single body and the ability to raise and maintain a single source of funds vital to the survival of the colonies. Both increased anti-British sentiments, (A), and the subsequent economic downturn, (D), would not hit the colonies until much later, after the war was over. Conflict over religion, (C), was less of an issue by the mid-18th century in the colonies and most armed conflict at this time was between the French and English factions rather than religious groups.

11. **C** Even in 1775 at the brink of the American Revolution, most colonists were not calling for war and independence with Great Britain. Patrick Henry would have been considered a radical at this time.

12. **C** At the start of the war, most colonists remained indifferent or on the fence regarding unity and independence from Great Britain. Much smaller fractions were true patriots (consistent with the statement in A) or loyalists, (B), who remained loyal to the British and opposed war and independence. While many slaves, (D), were found within the colonies by this time, they still represented a minority of the American population.

13. **A** The Boston Tea Party was a protest against the passage of the British Tea Act and other policies, which favored British imports over domestic production. As a response to the Boston Tea Party, Britain passed the Intolerable (or Coercive) Acts to punish the colony for its actions.

Questions 14–16

The Declaration of Independence (1776) was a statement declaring to Great Britain that the 13 colonies were independent of Great Britain and united in their common principles as one. The Declaration also included language to establish why the colonies sought independence from Great Britain and their grievances against the crown. John Trumbull "has been called the "Painter of the Revolution" and was commissioned to paint this presentation of the draft of the Declaration of Independence to the Second Continental Congress.

14. **A** While the Declaration did state the common principles of individual liberties and the rights of people, (B), grievances against the British crown, (C), and justification for self-governance of the United States, (D), it did not actually address how the states would self-govern. The governance of the early United States was addressed first in the Articles of Confederation and later with the ratification of the U.S. Constitution.

15.   **A**   The 13th Amendment formally abolished slavery in the United States and was symbolic in recognizing that rights of all peoples to liberty regardless of their skin color. Many Northern abolitionists used the phrasing of "all men are created equal" as a founding principle of the United States and justification for the adoption of the 13th Amendment. The Articles of Confederation, (C), and the U.S. Constitution, (D), while establishing how the states would govern themselves, largely avoided addressing enforcement of personal liberties (hence the later push for the Bill of Rights). The much later 19th Amendment, (B), granted the right to vote to women.

16.   **B**   The Articles of Confederation failed to address the right of the new government to raise taxes and impose tariffs. Consequently, efforts to raise funds during the war were limited, leading to rampant inflation and the later incapacity to regulate foreign trade. The Articles did support the governance, (A), of the young nation primarily through the formation of a legislation body, (C), which was able to adopt and pass resolution, (D), such as the Northwest Ordinance of 1787.

Questions 17–19

The Federalists supported adoption of the new U.S. Constitution, as it was desperately needed to address the shortfalls of the existing Articles of Confederation. The Federalist Papers were a series of anonymous letters published in newspapers by leading Federalists such as Alexander Hamilton, James Madison, and John Jay to justify and promote favor for ratification of the U.S. Constitution.

17.   **D**   The Federalists felt that the U.S. Constitution was needed and should be adopted as proposed. One issue raised by the anti-Federalists was the lack of a Bill of Rights protecting the rights of citizens in the new nation. The Federalists felt this was unnecessary, would delay ratification, and in fact would restrict the rights of the people. Choices (A), (B), and (C) are all consistent with different views held by anti-Federalists at the time.

18.   **A**   Of the options listed, only Alexander Hamilton was a known and established leader of the Federalists. The excerpt provided is from *The Federalist Papers* and has been attributed to Alexander Hamilton. Patrick Henry, Thomas Jefferson, and Samuel Adams were all leaders of the anti-Federalist movement.

19.   **A**   The Federalist Party (which did not completely overlap with the Federalist movement promoting the U.S. Constitution) favored the formation of a strong national government and national bank. In addition, they were generally more pro-British, opposed the War of 1812, and wanted to repay national debts to encourage foreign investment. Related to foreign investment, the Federalists also favored policies that promoted merchants and urban economic development. The Democratic-Republicans (or Anti-Federalists) favored a strict and narrow interpretation, (B), of the U.S. Constitution, opposed the formation of a national bank, were strong supporters of farmers and agriculture, (D), and were generally more pro-French, (C).

Questions 20–21

The location of New Orleans at the mouth of the Mississippi River gave it high strategic value in the regulation of trade in the interior of the North American continent. In 1802, a deal between France and Spain led to the transfer of New Orleans from the Spanish to the French. Thomas Jefferson, the president at the time and a French sympathizer, feared that American economic growth and commercial trade could and would be restricted by the French. In this excerpt, Jefferson implored his ambassador (Livingston) to either secure access or acquire New Orleans to protect American interests.

20.   **A**   As Jefferson points out in this letter, three-eighths of American produce must pass through the port of New Orleans. New Orleans was a major center of trade and economic growth and therefore a lucrative possession in the New World. French concerns over the slave revolt uprising in Haiti, (C), pushes for American expansionism into the interior of the continent at the cost of war, (D), and need for funds with the onset of war in Europe, (B), all contributed to Napoleon (and France's) decision to sell New Orleans and the Louisiana Territory.

21.   **B**   The Quids were a faction within Jefferson's own party (the Democratic-Republicans) led by John Randolph of Virginia. The Quids believed that Jefferson's decision to purchase Louisiana without congressional approval was betrayal of his Republican ideals to strictly adhere to the interpretation of the rights and responsibilities of the president as outlined in the U.S. Constitution. One of the leading Federalist arguments against the purchase was that Jefferson had actually paid too much for the land, (A), and that the purchase would simply lead to war with Spain, (C). The New England Federalists were concerned that with the new territory, use of Atlantic ports for trade would diminish and Western states, (D), sympathetic to Republican interests, would soon form and therefore further restrict Federalist power.

Questions 22–24

Henry Clay was a famous War Hawk who in his early days in the House of Representatives advocated for war with Great Britain to preserve American shipping interests. This excerpt is from a speech that he delivered in the House of Representatives advocating for expansion of the U.S. Navy. The War of 1812 would see an ill-prepared U.S. military suffer numerous defeats against the British before both sides came to a stalemate with the Treaty of Ghent.

22.   **B**   Henry Clay was a noted War Hawk and his sentiments to go to war to protect foreign commerce were a common stance of fellow War Hawks. Federalists, (A), were opposed to war with Great Britain. Neither the British, (C), nor the French, (D), wanted the United States to continue to develop its military.

23.   **A**   The Federalists were largely against the War of 1812 and felt that open war with Great Britain would stifle foreign trade and commerce. Ultimately, the War of 1812 led to fervent nationalism and the downfall of the opposition Federalist Party. As a result of the war, the United States saw a massive boost in domestic manufacturing due to lessened trade with Britain and France, (B). The war did not directly lead to an increase in American territorial possessions, (C), nor did it directly lead to the Monroe Doctrine, (D).

24. **B** The Missouri Compromise of 1820 saw the admission of Maine as a free state and Missouri as a slave state to maintain the balance of free and slave states. New states under the compromise would be admitted as free or slave based on whether they were located north or south of the 36°30' parallel.

Questions 25–26

The Election of 1824 saw four major candidates of the same political party (Democratic-Republicans) run for the presidency. While Andrew Jackson, quoted here, won the most Electoral College votes, he failed to garner a majority to win the presidency, resulting in the decision being turned over to the House of Representatives. In what has been dubbed the "Corrupt Bargain," Henry Clay, who had previously opposed John Quincy Adams, pledged his support to Adams in exchange for being selected as his secretary of state. This excerpt describes Jackson's personal views on the situation.

25. **C** Having failed to win a majority of Electoral College votes (or even the most Electoral College votes), John Quincy Adams became president by a vote of the House of Representatives. During the Election of 1824, Andrew Jackson actually won the most popular votes, (B), and Electoral College votes, (A), but failed to garner the required majority to win the presidency, which triggered the vote by the House of Representatives. The previous president, James Monroe, completed his entire presidency.

26. **B** All of the major candidates for president in the Election of 1824 were from the same political party (the Democratic-Republicans).

Questions 27–30

Andrew Jackson won the presidency in the Election of 1828 backed by a strong campaign. Soon after ascending to the presidency, he replaced government officials with those loyal to his views and, unlike his predecessors, was the first president to use his executive powers and influence to challenge the will of the legislative and judicial branches of government. In this political cartoon, he is satirized as a monarch who wields the power of veto and the will to trample on the powers provided to him by the U.S. Constitution.

27. **D** Andrew Jackson's new political party was called the Democratic Party and strongly supported his policy decisions. The Whigs, (A), National Republicans, (B), and Anti-Masonic, (C), all rose in direct opposition to Democratic policies.

28. **C** *McCulloch v. Maryland* (1819) was a landmark case that established the legitimacy of the Second National Bank and stated that states could not tax the national bank. *Gibbons v. Ogden* (1824) held that congress could regulate navigation as an extension of the constitutionally given right to regulate commerce. *Marbury v. Madison* (1803) justified the process of judicial review. *Chisholm v. Georgia* (1793) outlined the jurisdiction of the U.S. Supreme Court on both state and federal cases.

29. **D** The Nullification Crisis developed as a response to the passage of the "Tariffs of Abomination," which saw tariffs being levied on goods which were in greater demand in the agrarian South. In response, Southern states (such as South Carolina) aimed to nullify the federal tariffs as unconstitutional, thus challenging the authority of federal powers over states rights.

30. **C** The Gold Rush in California helped relieve the financial pressures stemming from the Panic of 1837 by infusing the American economy with much needed gold and financial support. Jackson's Bank Wars, (A), and policy of Specie Circular, (B), as well as overspeculation, (D), led to a sudden money shortage and the onset of the panic.

Questions 31–34

Manifest Destiny was the commonly held view among many Americans that it was their God-given right to expand the shared vision of democracy and expand and colonize the West. Much of this belief came from the view that American virtues of democracy and liberty were in alignment with the mission of God. These two excerpts are from two U.S. presidents describing the "Divine Providence" and the "aid of that Almighty Ruler" in supporting the destiny of the United States in governance.

31. **C** The vision that the "whole continent of North America…be peopled by one nation, speaking, one language" aligns closely with the commonly held 19th-century view of Manifest Destiny. Laissez-faire economics, (A), was a policy of keeping economic regulation and policy out of politics. This approach to the American economy was far more common in the late 19th century during the Gilded Age. Social Darwinism, (B), was a view that only the "fittest" and strongest should see their power and wealth increase at the expense of the weak. Nativism, (D), which also extolled the vision of the United States, was more concerned with the superiority of existing Americans over the rights and influence of immigrants.

32. **D** The Polk presidency marked a period of significant westward expansion in U.S. history. Annexation of Texas, (A), and war with Mexico, (C), led to the Mexican Cession and the addition of much of the western part to the United States. The Gold Rush, which occurred late in Polk's presidency, provided the financial support and westward population expansion to aid in the formation of California, (B), and Oregon territories. The Compromise of 1850 is not associated with the presidency of President Polk (as he died in office before its passage).

33. **C** The Wilmot Proviso (1846) was an unsuccessful proposed congressional bill to outlaw slavery in any territory acquired from Mexico. Unlike most bills, this proviso saw a vote strictly along sectional or regional lines. Nearly all Northerners voted in favor of the bill and nearly all Southerners voted in opposition to the bill, largely regardless of party lines. The Wilmot Proviso was significant because it revealed the deep-rooted sectionalism over slavery and states' rights that would ultimately lead to the Civil War. The Wilmot Proviso was not unique in addressing slavery, (A), in new states and territories as the Missouri Compromise and the later Compromise of 1850 would also address slavery. Furthermore, it did not advocate for popular sovereignty, (B), which would have granted the new Mexican territories the right to choose, nor did it address the legal rights of slaves, (D).

34. **C** The Republic of Texas applied for annexation into the United States in 1836, the same year that it had been granted independence from Mexico. However, sociopolitical pressures on the issue of slavery (II) in new territories had yet to be resolved out of fear of tipping the balance of power and the legality of slavery in Congress. Unresolved border disputes between Texas and Mexico (III)

were also of concern to the United States as fears of open war with Mexico seemed more certain with the annexation of Texas. There was far less opposition to growth and expansion westward, in part because of the commonly held beliefs of Manifest Destiny.

Questions 35–37

Irish immigration into the United States hit its peak in the 1840s during which time nearly half of all immigrants entering the United States came from Ireland. As shown in this image from the 1890 census, most Irish immigrants settled in the North.

35. **A** From the population density of Irish natives in the 1890 census, most immigrants settled in Northern cities and towns where the economy was far more dependent upon industrialization. Plantations and agrarian society, (B), was far more common in the South, which saw comparatively little Irish immigration. The American west, (C), would see more immigration from central and eastern Europe during the mid- to late 19th century. While American port cities in New England saw massive populations of Irish immigrants, there was little immigration of Irish peoples into Southern ports such as New Orleans and Charleston.

36. **B** The majority of immigrants to the United States during the 1840s and 1850s were from northern and western Europe, whereas later immigrants during the 1890s–1920s, were more frequently from southern and eastern Europe. The educational levels, (D), and religions of immigrants, (C), differ from the specific parts of the regions that they came from and their decision to immigrate to the United States by the 19th century was largely due to financial hardships and higher promise of jobs rather than religious persecution, (A).

37. **C** The Quota Act of 1924 saw the United States set effective limits based on quotas for all immigration into the United States. The passage of this act led to a significant reduction in immigration for all groups.

Questions 38–41

The Emancipation Proclamation (1863) declared that all slaves in states of open rebellion were henceforth free. However, this freedom was neither guaranteed by the U.S. Constitution (which would take the later Reconstruction Amendments) nor could it take effect in any form until those territories came under Union jurisdiction, which were technically not in open rebellion and therefore not covered under the proclamation. This excerpt by Booker T. Washington describes the impact and legacy of the proclamation on slave communities, as freedom for slaves became a reality across the American South.

38. **B** The Emancipation Proclamation was meant to undermine the strength of the Confederate economies by encouraging slaves to flee and strengthened Union military support (many would go on to fight in the war). It did not grant citizen rights, (A), to freed slaves nor impact legality, (C) and (D), of slavery in free states (as largely a measure not to push away border states, which remained in the Union, but were dependent upon slavery).

39. **B** Copperheads were anti-war Democrats who opposed the ongoing war, (A), with the Confederacy and felt that President Lincoln was abusing his power of office. They viewed the Emancipation Proclamation as unnecessary and as an attempt by Lincoln to push his personal abolitionist views and social agenda to limit the power of the South, (D). Copperheads emerged after the war had already begun, (C).

40. **A** The 13th Amendment to the Constitution officially abolished slavery and involuntary servitude (except for punishment of a crime) in the United States. Passage of the 13th Amendment legitimized the decree of the Emancipation Proclamation and expanded its influence to the entirety of the country.

41. **C** The Freedmen's Bureau was established to aid former slaves in their transition to freedom. Among the impacts of the Freedmen's Bureau was the development of institutions of higher learning for African Americans, (A), public assistance with job hunting and housing, (B), and providing financial support and food to those in desperate need, (D). Although it was the hope of the Freedmen's Bureau to provide land and property, this was largely not achieved.

Questions 42–45

The Sherman Antitrust Act was passed at a time when large monopolies, trusts, and corporations were eliminating competition and growing in power and influence. The Sherman Antitrust Act aimed to restrict monopolies and trusts from anti-competitive measures that might lead to abuses on consumers and the public. While far more effective later, the Sherman Antitrust Act was the first major step by the government to regulate the nature of the capitalist market.

42. **C** Andrew Carnegie was a business magnate who oversaw the steel industry and became one of the wealthiest industrialists in his time. He was a strong supporter of the principle of Social Darwinism and viewed the Sherman Antitrust Act negatively as it stifled capitalism.

43. **C** Teddy Roosevelt took a strong anti-trust stance and sought to regulate the policies of big businesses. Through his policies, he was dubbed a "trust-buster." He effectively used the Sherman Antitrust Act to enact changes in the regulation of big businesses.

44. **D** The McKinley Tariff (1890) imposed a high tariff on imports to protect domestic production and economic growth. However, this tariff had very little impact on the legality of the Sherman Antitrust Act and would have simply aided the existing big businesses in expanding their influence by reducing foreign competition. The Clayton Antitrust Act (1914), (A), Interstate Commerce Act (1887), (B), and formation of the FTC (1914), (C), all helped reign in abuses by big businesses and regulate domestic capitalism.

45. **D** John Jacob Aster made his millions in the fur industry. While Vanderbilt, Morgan, and Rockefeller made their millions in different ventures of industry. Vanderbilt, (A) made his fortune in railroads. Morgan, (B) made his fortune in banking, and Rockefeller, (C) made his millions in oil.

Questions 46–48

The Square Deal (1903–1909) was Roosevelt's domestic program, which aimed to collectively address what was often called his three C's: conservation, control of corporations, and consumer protections. As a progressive, he would go on to pass several key measures in these primary areas, many of which remain active parts of our regulation today. The excerpt shown is from his famous Square Deal speech.

46. **C** Remember that the cornerstone to Roosevelt's Square Deal was his three C's: conservation of natural resources, control of corporations, and protection of consumers.

47. **B** Upton Sinclair's *The Jungle* exposed poverty, poor working conditions of the working class, and exploitation of immigrants. His work is credited with driving up public support for reform and likely played a major role in the passage of both the Meat Inspection Act and the Pure Food and Drug Act.

48. **C** FDR's First New Deal came at a time when the Great Recession crippled the United States and there remained fear of insecurity of banks and financial institutions. Much of his program aimed to restore confidence in banks and was successful in returning much needed money to banks to help stabilize the economy.

Questions 49–50

The Treaty of Versailles was the peace agreement that brought the formal end to World War I. As evidenced in this excerpt, the Allied powers rest the entire blame for the confrontation on the German government. This caused significant embarrassment and resentment among the German people, who felt that the Allies were at least partially culpable for the war. As part of the treaty, Germany would be required to pay war reparations for the damage they had caused. Included in the treaty, at the recommendation of President Wilson, was the formation of the League of Nations, which would serve as an international body to resolve future disputes through diplomacy.

49. **D** Following the First World War, there was fear that the standing alliances and formalized treaties that had led to the flair-up of the first war might ignite a second conflagration. Therefore, much more attention was applied towards diplomacy and negotiation through channels such as the League of Nations. Rampant inflation in Germany, (A), the fall of the monarchy, (C), and existing indignation towards the rest of Europe, (B), have all been credited with leading to the rise of Nazism in the 1920s and 1930s.

50. **A** Wilson's League of Nations proposal was meant to provide an international body to maintain peace and resolve conflicts through dialogue, diplomacy, and arbitration rather than armed conflict. The League of Nations would serve as a precursor to the United Nations that we have today.

Questions 51–53

The Truman Doctrine laid out U.S. foreign policy advocating for opposition to the rising spread and influence of communism in Europe and elsewhere through financial and economic support. This excerpt from his speech to a joint session of Congress is in reference to a request for support to be given to Greece to resist the influences of communism in its weakened state.

51. **D** Truman's request for support in Greece stemmed from his stance that U.S. should oppose the growing geopolitical influence of communism sweeping through Europe and elsewhere in the world. While the U.S. did advocate for recovery of nations destroyed during World War II, (C) and improved economic regulation, (A), these concerns were minimal compared to the rising fears of communism.

52. **B** During the Truman presidency, World War II came to a close and millions of soldiers returned from the battlefront. A key part of his Fair Deal domestic policies was aimed to help veterans reintegrate into American society with support for higher education (G.I. Bill) and work opportunities.

53. **A** McCarthyism is a period of paranoia riddled with accusations of collusion and treason over fears of communism within the United States. These fears and impacts on society closely resembled similar fears during the Red Scare of the late 1910s.

Questions 54–55

Johnson's Great Society was a set of widespread domestic policies and programs aimed at sweeping reform of the socioeconomic inequities of American society. Many of the acts and initiatives established during the mid-1960s had significant impacts on the poor and minorities. This excerpt is from one of his famous speeches about his grand vision in a commencement speech at the University of Michigan.

54. **D** While much of his attention was aimed at several of the same goals as the Social Security Act, this legislation was actually passed during the presidency of FDR. The Civil Rights Act, (A), Economic Opportunity Act, (B), and Voting Rights Act, (C) were all major acts passed during the Johnson presidency that had major impacts on American society.

55. **A** President Johnson was a Democrat and a liberal. His policies of greater government involvement in socioeconomic reforms and social change align far more closely to modern liberals.

SECTION I, PART B: SHORT-ANSWER QUESTIONS

Question 1

a) Despite the best efforts of the Founding Fathers to warn against factionalism (political parties), the political body of the new United States soon divided itself into two camps—the Federalists and the anti-Federalists.

The Federalists:
- believed in a centralized national government
- were popular in the Northeast
- consisted of mostly urban merchants and businessmen
- supported the National Bank
- stayed close to the British
- headed by Washington and Hamilton, among others

The Anti-Federalists:
- believed in decentralized state governments
- were popular in the South and Southwest
- consisted mostly of rural people
- opposed the National Bank
- stayed close to the French
- headed by Jefferson

b) Factionalism, and the movement against it, was expressed in multiple ways throughout the earliest years of the republic. You could choose from any of the following:

- George Washington's farewell address, delivered shortly before he left office, is renowned even today. In it, he warned against many dangers to the fledgling republic, such as entangling foreign alliances, regional sectionalism, and—most importantly for the purposes of this question—the dangers of political parties.
- The anonymous Federalist Papers were published in 1787 and 1788 in a series of newspapers and journals. Secretly authored mostly by Hamilton, Madison, and Jay, this collection of 85 articles and essays argue for many things, including passage of the new Constitution (minus a Bill of Rights), the principle of judicial review, the need for checks and balances, and the desirability of federalism.
- The Sedition Act was passed as part of the Alien and Sedition Acts, and it criminalized making false statements that were critical of federal government. This power was quickly used by President John Adams (a Federalist) to imprison newspaper publishers, primarily in the South, who were anti-Federalist. Standing in fierce opposition to the Act, Thomas Jefferson and James Madison anonymously authored the Virginia and Kentucky Resolutions, urging those states to nullify the Alien and Sedition Acts.
- The nation was divided over the Jay Treaty (1795), as mentioned in the passage. It avoided war with England, ironed out issues that were over a decade old, and set the stage for successful trade with England for the future. Anti-Federalists intensely opposed this treaty, believing that closer ties with England would strength the Federalists and create an aristocracy.
- The Louisiana Purchase, the largest expenditure of money made by the federal government up to that point, doubled the size of the United States. This was an expression of federal power—and

yet it was accomplished by Thomas Jefferson, a Democratic-Republican president! There are a few ways to analyze this. One way is to note that anti-Federalists weren't as pure in their opposition to national power as they would like to believe. Another way is that the Federalist Party essentially had its beliefs stolen by the Democratic-Republicans, and you could argue that this was one factor in the collapse of the Federalists. A third way is to argue that making a deal with the French was attractive to Jefferson and the anti-Federalists, owing to their closeness.

c) In the years after 1800, the Federalist Party declined for several reasons:

- Federalists opposed the War of 1812, cautioning that it couldn't be won, that it would bankrupt the new nation, and that their own merchant businesses would suffer. It didn't bankrupt or tear apart the U.S., and the Federalists were left looking a bit selfish, and even a bit traitorous.
- British behavior towards the U.S., particularly the impressment of U.S. sailors, made the anti-Federalists (who were called Democratic-Republicans by this point) very resentful of the British. Because the Federalists were so closely tied to the British, it made them resentful of the Federalists by association.
- The Federalist-led Hartford Convention of 1814 was an unmitigated disaster, given the talk of secession that occurred there. It was viewed as treasonous, failed to result in almost any nominees, and became a final black mark against the party. The Federalists never recovered.
- Whatever the reason, the Democratic-Republicans eventually enjoyed a couple of decades of single-party rule during the Era of Good Feelings.

Question 2

Analyzing geopolitics and juggling foreign policy has never been an easy task, and the 1930s was extra challenging due to the arrival of the global Great Depression. Furthermore, thanks to the punitive terms of the Treaty of Versailles after World War I, Germany was suffering quite badly, having been saddled with a nearly unpayable amount of debt.

a) Historians have argued for decades whether or not there is is single root cause of the Great Depression. Either way, they largely agree on several contenders:

- World War I—It shocked the world, shattered the global financial system, and changed the entire global balance of power.
- A historically overextended stock market that resulted in Black Friday, the 1929 stock-market crash.
- Decreased international lending because of high U.S. interest rates. This contributed to economic contraction in countries that really needed growth, such as Germany. This is precisely what Under-Secretary Castle was trying to explain in the primary source material.
- Banking panics—Worried people ran to the banks to withdraw their money, but banks didn't carry enough cash to give all clients all their money back.
- The difficulty with the gold standard in major European nations. Abandoning the gold standard would allow more flexibility in setting exchange rates, which could help nations pay off war debts more easily. Clinging to the gold standard caused more problems than it was worth.

b) The Great Depression changed U.S. foreign policy quite a bit, turning the nation inward, towards its historically typical isolationism.

- World War I was the first foreign entanglement the U.S. had allowed itself in the century since the Monroe Doctrine was issued. There was backlash, and it was partly psychological, partly financial.
  - Psychological: Over a hundred thousand members of the American military had died in a foreign continent for the first time, making the citizens less likely to want to interfere elsewhere.
  - Financial: Because of the depression, the U.S wanted to get its own house in order before helping others. Again, this isolationist tendency is what Castle was so strenuously trying to rebut in the speech.
- To that end, the Roosevelt administration instituted a Good Neighbor Policy in Latin America. This was largely the principle of non-interventionism, first promoted by Wilson. This policy promoted gentle reciprocity and rejected Teddy Roosevelt's big-stick policy, which threatened both intervention and the use of force if necessary. The Good Neighbor Policy avoided the wave of small revolutions occurring in Latin America and also reduced U.S. military presence there.

c) The U.S. trend towards isolationism remained in full force throughout the 1930s, when it was finally knee-capped by the undeniable aggression of Nazi Germany and the Japanese:

- The Neutrality Acts were passed by a Republican Congress intended to maintain U.S. isolationism. Roosevelt opposed them.
- The America First Committee, chaired by the famous aviator Charles Lindbergh, successfully lobbied Congress throughout the 1930s to resist Roosevelt's desire to provide European allies with war materials.
- The cracks in the wall of isolationism finally began to show at the end of the decade, as Europe plunged into another enormous war instituted by Germany. In 1939, Congress overturned the Neutrality Acts and allowed cash-and-carry deals, in which foreign countries could purchase arms from the U.S., but only if they 1) paid in cash and 2) picked up the materials themselves, assuming all risk.
- In early 1941, Congress passed the Lend-Lease Act, which Roosevelt took full advantage of, as it permitted him to transfer arms and other materials to any country whose defense he deemed necessary to U.S. national security.
- Ironically, after the U.S. entered World War II (thus dropping its isolationist stance), the economic success and growth generated by the war effort pulled the nation out of the same economic depression that had been keeping it isolated. In other words, the virtuous circle was more like a vicious cycle, and participating in a foreign war helped break that cycle.

Question 3

The first decades of the 19th century saw the rise of domestic manufacturing in the United States. Prior to this period—and during this period as well—Americans purchased most of their goods from foreign manufacturers. That changed for many reasons.

a) The technological changes that ushered in the rise of domestic manufacturing were many. Here are three major ones:

- Oliver Evans developed a high-pressure steam engine in 1804 that was used in ships, mills, factories, and other industrial locations.
- Eli Whitney invented a system of production using interchangeable parts. It was intended for the weapons industry but came to be applied universally to all production.

- Eli Whitney also developed the cotton gin, which allowed more cotton to be processed at a faster rate, allowing the production of more textiles. This also stimulated the need for more slaves to pick the cotton, since it could be processed more quickly.

Other advances could be discussed as well.

b) Changes in transportation technology allowed for finished goods to be carried more efficiently around the nation:

- The canal system was built. Because this was the era of the Democratic-Republicans, the states took up the responsibility for constructing them, which resulted in famous state and municipal entities such as the C & O Canal (standing for Chesapeake & Ohio), the Erie Canal, and others. At one point, Pennsylvania alone had a thousand miles of canals! This system turned previously isolated river towns into national shipping centers.
- As time went on, railroads slowly replaced the canals, rendering them unprofitable. Though the golden age of the railroad wouldn't arrive until the second half of the century—the first transcontinental railroad wasn't finished until 1869—the first half of the century saw growth in local industrial railroads, mostly linking ports to rivers, where canals had not been dug. Early examples were found in Massachusetts, Baltimore, and elsewhere.

c) Growth in domestic manufacturing doesn't occur in a vacuum. It is accomplished with the help of a lot of other factors.

Legal factors:
- Tariffs—These surcharges on imported goods helped domestic manufacturers to sell their own competing goods at a cheaper price. Remember also that not all Americans wanted to support domestic manufacturing, since it was mostly a Northern phenomenon; South Caroline nearly seceded from the Union over the Tariff of Abominations (1828).
- State governments created expanded systems of credit to give entrepreneurs the loans they needed to start a business.
- Private corporations were granted special state charters and given the same rights as people.

Labor factors:
- A wave of immigration from Ireland, Germany, and China brought low-cost labor to the U.S. They lived in dedicated mill towns such as Lowell, Massachusetts.
- The rise of wage labor—While the old system of piecework labor had been paid per piece of textile delivered, the new system paid workers hourly, daily, or weekly, regardless of amount finished.

Question 4

It's often remarked that the history of public opinion is like a pendulum, swinging back and forth between opposing ideas every generation or two. This is particularly apt in popular U.S. attitude towards our federal government.

a) Prior to the 1970s, the American public came to trust their government for a few big reasons:

- World War II—To stop the German and Japanese menace, defending one's country through military service had become a mark of virtue. The military was part of the government, and the government was, therefore, a facilitator of this patriotism.

- The growth of all institutions in the postwar period—Banks, schools, courts because it was a time of civic participation and high public trust.
- Lingering good feelings toward the New Deal programs of the 1930s—the alphabet soup programs put a lot of people's parents and grandparents to work during the Great Depression, and that generosity from the federal government hadn't been forgotten.
- Cold War fears—In the dawn of the nuclear age, people bought and constructed bomb shelters in their backyards, believing that the Soviets or their proxies were going to rain atomic bombs upon us. These people often placed their faith in our federal government to protect them.

b) Yes, the various assassinations and civil unrest of the 1960s played a large role in loss of public trust. But this prompt asks about the 1970s, a decade that played a less dramatic but no less important role in the same trend. Here is a brief explanation of the four events that damaged public trust in government:

- The exit from the Bretton-Woods agreement—Perhaps the most obscure of the four listed events, this was the unilateral cancellation of the international convertibility of the U.S. dollar to gold. Though it was done to better combat inflation, the move shook people's faith in the power of the dollar.
- The Pentagon Papers was a scandal in which Daniel Ellsberg, a military analyst, leaked a classified government document to the press. The document proved that the government knew that the Vietnam War was unwinnable—even as it continued escalating the conflict, and even as it continued to ask its soldiers to sacrifice their lives for the cause.
- The Watergate scandal hit home for a lot of people who'd supported Richard Nixon. In two-and-a-half years of dogged investigation, a pair of reporters from *The Washington Post* discovered that the president himself had authorized a burglary of the Democratic National Committee headquarters in the Watergate Hotel. Nixon resigned just before impeachment, shaking the body politic, since it had been many decades since such obvious corruption had been uncovered in the executive branch.
- The Iran hostage crisis—In the last year of the decade, a group of 55 Americans were held hostage for 444 days by a religious Iranian group who were upset at President Jimmy Carter for having backed the previous leader, the shah, in their recent revolution. The hostages were released minutes after Carter left office, humiliating him, and weakening Americans' faith in the power of the office of the president.

c) Which of these four events did NOT represent a loss in public trust? That's a judgment call on your part. Here are some of the arguments that you could make:

- The reasons for the exit from the Bretton-Woods agreement were simply too abstract and too complicated for most ordinary people to understand. Therefore, this event couldn't make a real dent in public opinion.
- The Pentagon Papers could be viewed as confirmation of what people had known all along—that the government had a different private agenda from what it was publicly stating. This had been discussed for years prior to the publication of the Pentagon Papers.
- The Watergate scandal was a slow-moving admission of guilt that never featured a shocking moment that moved public opinion. Plus, the resignation of a president paled in comparison with the assassination of a president eleven years earlier.
- The U.S. government is not all powerful. Expecting our government to be able to control the decisions that our enemies make, on their own territory and in secret, is unreasonable. From personal experience, most people understand that you can't negotiate with people if they don't want to negotiate.

SECTION II, QUESTION 1: THE DOCUMENT-BASED QUESTION

The Document-Based Question (DBQ) section begins with a 15-minute reading period. During those 15 minutes, you'll want to 1) come up with some information not included in the given documents (from your outside knowledge), 2) get an overview of what each document means and the point of view of each author, 3) decide what opinion you're going to argue, and 4) write an outline of your essay.

This DBQ concerns the issue of the growth in imperialistic foreign policy in the late 19th and early 20th century. You should be prepared to discuss several different aspects of this change. You should also remember the famous PERSIA method of organizing characteristics of any historical time period—Political, Economic, Religious, Social, Intellectual, and Artistic. The first three tend to be more useful than the last three, but in this case you could use all six categories, more or less.

The first thing you want to do, *before you look at the documents*, is to brainstorm for a minute or two. Try to list everything you know (from class lectures or outside reading or documentaries) about U.S. foreign policy from, say, roughly 1850 to 1930. Since this prompt doesn't provide a very specific time period, feel free to be flexible with dates. For example, if there is a policy in the early 19th century that serves as foundation for later imperialism, add it to the list. Or if there is an event that existed much later that was a direct consequence of imperialism, add that too. You could mention these things briefly in the essay, or even discuss it at minor length. In any event, this list will serve as your reference to the outside information you must provide to earn a top grade.

Pro tip: You can always put outside-the-time-period information in the introduction or conclusion, depending on whether the information is before or after the period indicated by the prompt. This also helps you knit the prompt into the wider fabric of history.

Next, read over the documents. As you read them, take notes in the margins and underline those passages that you are certain you are going to use in your essay. Make note of the opinions and position of the document's author. If a document helps you remember a piece of outside information, add that outside information to your brainstorming list. Also remember that you do not need to mention every document to score well on the DBQ.

Here is what you might assess in the time you have to look over the documents.

The Documents

Document 1: A historian uses the examples of Mexico and Venezuela to argue that American intervention leads to better lives for the conquered. This, he says, occurs because of America's insistence that those nations eventually assume self-governance. He recommends that America do the same for the Philippines, arguing for a benevolent imperialism that benefits the acquired people: the we-conquer-them-for-their-own-good argument. Potential bias: The author is the great-grandson of President Adams. It could be argued that he was inclined towards the same belief in self-governance that his ancestor shared with other Founding Fathers.

Document 2: Vladimir Lenin, the father of Soviet communism, argues that anti-imperialists in the U.S. never fought hard against imperialism because of the strength of the bonds between imperialism and capitalism. This is an important document. It gives a clue to the type of opposition that imperialism faced. It should also give a strong idea about the underlying reason why the United States decided to put on its Darth Vader mask and start sneakily conquering neighboring lands.

Document 3: The Treaty of Guadalupe Hidalgo was signed in 1848 and finalized the Mexican-American War. This document enumerates some of the terms of surrender, including (in Article XII) a forced sale of Mexican territory for fifteen million dollars. This reflects the "hard" side of imperialism (e.g., the bullying stance that imperialistic nations often take towards conquered peoples).

Document 4: This political cartoon depicts a rosy view of imperialism. Prior to conquest, the people of the Philippines, Hawaii, Porto Rico, Cuba, and Panama were burdened under the unfair weight of the Spanish rule. Under American imperial power, however, they are well-dressed, healthy, and self-governing (note the *Filipino Assembly* paper on the far left). This is another entry in the benevolent imperialistic power argument. Also, by 1914, many of the major events of the era have already passed, so this cartoon could be interpreted as merely justifying the past.

Document 5: This document is another entry in the we-conquer-them-for-their-own-good argument. (It's especially apparent in the subtitle of the book.) However, this passage is notable for two other reasons. One: the compliments it pays to the people of the Philippines are quite extensive—and these can be interpreted in both sincere and insincere ways. Two: the warning in the last line about how *There should be no desire to, in the least, encroach upon their property* indicates that a sizable number of people must have viewed the Philippines as a piggy bank to be raided.

Document 6: This table of data from the U.S. Census demonstrates how quickly the continental United States was growing—as were its possessions, particularly the Philippines. In fact, as of 1940, the total population of American possessions numbered nearly 19 million, while the total population of the continent was just over 131 million. That means that the population of the territories accounted for about 13% of the total population of the American "empire". This is sizable, representing about 1 in 8 people.

This data shows just how vital imperialistic properties were to the United States, despite the perceived second-class status of their people. To the prompt, it could be used to support hardline imperialistic policies.

Document 7: This cartoon from 1899 shows President McKinley astride the continent, pickaxe in hand, preparing to finish the canal across the isthmus of Panama. Significantly, cargo ships are lined up on either side, waiting to pass. Note also the U.S. flags staked out on various other pieces of land, including Hawaii, the Philippines, Cuba, and Porto Rico.

This document can be used to emphasize the economic pressures that undergirded imperialistic policies. The Panama Canal was being built, after all, because it was advantageous for trade.

Outside Information

First, some early roots of imperialism—some specific, some general—that merit discussion:

General Concepts

- George Washington's farewell address, in which he promoted non-interventionism.
- Manifest Destiny—This was the concept that the United States was anointed by God to geographically spread out. However, just because we ran out of room on our continent—a.k.a. *the closing of the American frontier*—doesn't mean that this impulse disappeared.
- The Monroe Doctrine—Formulated in the early 19th century, it created separate spheres of European and American influence. A distant precursor to imperialism.

- White ethnocentrism—Imperial nations often believe that their cultural values or beliefs are superior to those of other groups. "The White Man's Burden" (1899) by Rudyard Kipling is exhibit A: a poem about the Philippine-American War, exhorting the U.S. to take control of the islands.
- Social Darwinism—Proponents often applied the theory of evolution to "less fit" cultures as justification for imperialism.
- The desire to expand and control foreign trade—With American corporations producing more goods than Americans could buy, finding new markets was paramount.

But it's the politicians who make policy. To form an imperialistic foreign policy, America needed to elect politicians who would pursue or at least sign policies that were favorable to them. They also needed friends in the media to cheerlead those policies. Here are some examples of those events and people:

Specific Events
- The election of 1896—In an all-out brawl, William McKinley defeated William Jennings Bryant. By openly stating his alliance with American industry, he ushered in a new period for the Republican Party, and for imperialism.
- The sinking of the U.S.S. Maine, in Havana, which was used as a pretext to start a war with Spain
- Yellow journalism—The American playboy publisher William Randolph Hearst pushed for war with Spain, the conflict that yielded several new territories.
- The American sugar industrials who fomented instability in Hawaii to justify a political takeover

There are four presidents who pursued policies of imperialism:

Specific People
- William McKinley (1896–1900)
  - Spanish-American War
  - Acquired control of the Philippines, Puerto Rico, and Cuba as a result
- Teddy Roosevelt (1900–1908)
  - Defended the acquisition of the Philippines, prolonging the conflict
  - As a result of the Roosevelt Corollary, U.S. began policing Latin American republics
  - Big-stick diplomacy, a.k.a. gunboat diplomacy
  - The Platt Amendment gave the U.S. both Guantanamo Bay as well as power over Cuba's sugar industry. It retained this control until 1934, when the amendment was overturned
- William H. Taft (1908–1912)
  - Continued long-running construction of the Panama Canal, which opened in 1914
  - Instituted policy of Dollar Diplomacy, which replaced big-stick diplomacy. It sought control over Latin American countries by guaranteeing loans for them
- Woodrow Wilson (1912–1920)
  - His push for U.S. involvement in World War I can be viewed as an attempt to open new foreign markets to surplus U.S. goods
  - Invaded Haiti to supposedly bring political stability
  - His personal point of view was unabashedly white and ethnocentric

Franklin D. Roosevelt likewise instituted a Good Neighbor Policy that was non-interventional and promoted reciprocal agreements between the U.S. and its neighbors.

And the opposition to imperialism existed, though not in great numbers:

- The American Anti-Imperialist League—This group formed in 1898 to oppose the annexation of the Philippines. They invoked the republicanism of the Declaration of Independence and speeches by Washington and Lincoln. The group disbanded as public opinion turned against them.
- John Hobson and his book *Imperialism: A Study*.
- Various socialist and communist groups.

The bigger question: How to organize this essay?

Choosing a Side

You can choose a variety of thesis statements, but the one that is best supported by the documents—and by history—says that the policy of imperialism rolled on despite minor protests.

There are many ways to organize. For a prompt like this, using PERSIA (Political, Economic, Religious, Social, Intellectual, Artistic) will be the most direct and most valuable method of organization. Another possible method of organization is by nation. Still another possibility is to create a chronology, but because the key events all happened in slow motion over a span of 15 years, you might find it hard to keep them separate in your head.

Let's start with PERSIA. You should always try to use at least three letters of that particular mnemonic device. In this case, there are *political* documents, a couple of *economic* ones, and some *social* or *intellectual* ones as well. (There's nothing about art or religion.)

Paragraph 1 (political): Sources 1 and 3
Paragraph 2 (economic): Sources 2 and 7
Paragraph 3 (social/intellectual): Sources 4, 5, and 6

Another possible method of organization is by conquered nation. This will be best for those who have a lot of outside knowledge.

Paragraph 1: Panama (Source 7)
Paragraph 2: Hawaii (none)
Paragraph 3: The Philippines (Sources 2, 5, and 6)
Paragraph 4: Cuba and Puerto Rico (Sources 1 and 4)

A third possible method of organization is by chronology.

Paragraph 1: Mexican-American War (Source 3)
Paragraph 2: Hawaii (no source)
Paragraph 3: Spanish-American War (Sources 1, 4, and 5)
Paragraph 4: Panama Canal (Source 7)

Again, PERSIA would work best for most people, but doing it a different way could be a fun exercise for those who enjoy that sort of thing. There are still other ways to organize, but again, with only 45 minutes to write, it's often better to go the obvious route.

Once you choose one of these structures, go down your list of outside information and think of ways to integrate each one into the essay. It won't always be possible, but every outside idea you can add will lend weight to your essay, as long as it can be fitted into your thesis statement. Remember that an obvious, desperate stretch will only hurt your score. However, history is by nature intricate and the readers of your exam want to see that you respect the intrinsic complexity behind many historical events.

Planning Your Essay

Unless you read extremely quickly, you probably will not have time to write a detailed outline for your essay during the 15-minute reading period. However, it is worth taking several minutes to jot down a loose structure of your essay because it will actually save you time when you write. First, decide on your thesis and write it down in the test booklet. (There is usually some blank space below the documents.) Then, take a minute or two to brainstorm all the points you might put in your essay. Choose the strongest points and number them in the order you plan to present them. Lastly, note which documents and outside information you plan to use in conjunction with each point. If you organize your essay before you start writing, the actual writing process will go much more smoothly. More importantly, you will not write yourself into a corner, suddenly finding yourself making a point you cannot support or heading toward a weak conclusion (or, worse still, no conclusion at all).

What You Should Have Discussed

Your first thought may be that this particular prompt seems quite broad, and in sheer number of years, you'd be right. However, in other ways, it's not as broad as you might think. There are few people, professional historians or otherwise, who deny that America underwent a period of imperialism during this era. So your task is not so much to choose a side, unless you have such exceptionally deep knowledge of U.S. foreign policy in this era that you could somehow argue against the existence of an imperialistic policy. Your task instead, as the prompt states, is to simply *describe the growth of that policy*.

That said, while ideas about the growth of the imperialistic policy are wonderful, you'll need to illustrate your ideas with knowledge of concrete events. Some of the significant ones are mentioned in the documents, while others are not.

To get a top score on this DBQ, your essay will likely not be considered complete unless you either analyze or at the very least mention U.S. involvement in all of the following from 1890 to 1930:

- Hawaii
- The construction of the Panama Canal
- The Spanish-American War
- The Philippines
- Cuba
- Puerto Rico

This is considered the classic era of U.S. imperialism, and these are its "greatest hits." (Document 4, a cartoon, mentioned all of them but one.) There is one document that mentions a different imperialistic moment—Document 3, the end of the Mexican-American War—but this is outside that highlighted range of the classic years. Again, that doesn't mean you *can't* analyze Document 3—in fact, you *should*, briefly, because your essay will be deepened by its inclusion.

SECTION II: THE LONG ESSAY QUESTION

Question 2

Compare and contrast the development of the Massachusetts Bay Colony with the development of the Virginia colony in the 17th century.

While Massachusetts Bay and Virginia were both North American colonies, they had very little in common. Your essay should touch upon some or all of the following differences:

- Jamestown, Virginia, was established first, in 1607. Massachusetts Bay was established 22 years later, in 1629.
- Virginia was founded primarily for economic reasons: to make money from tobacco, indigo, rice, etc. Massachusetts Bay was founded for religious reasons: The Puritans, tired of persecution in England, had fled to the New World to practice their Protestantism peacefully.
- Virginia was initially a settlement of the Virginia Company, which operated under a royal charter sponsored by King James I. Eventually the company disbanded and the king converted Virginia into a colony. Massachusetts Bay had no such relationship with the king of England; the Puritans fled to North America to escape English society!
- The soil of Virginia was rich and bountiful, but the soil of Massachusetts was hard and difficult to farm.
- Virginia's economy was built upon agriculture, whereas Massachusetts Bay's economy was built upon fishing and, later, industry.
- The immigrants to Virginia were largely young men looking to make a fortune; the immigrants to Massachusetts Bay were largely families looking for peace and religious freedom.
- The headright system in Virginia—by which a person sponsoring an indentured servant received a plot of land equal to the one that the indentured servant received—created vast inequality as time went on. Massachusetts Bay did adopt a headright system, but to a much lesser extent. It also managed to remain more equitable and community-minded, as evidenced by its long history of democratic town meetings.
- The settlements in Virginia were more spread out, whereas the settlements in Massachusetts Bay were more clustered.

The similarities between the colonies:

- Through the Virginia Company, Virginia imported indentured servants; in return for their passage, the indentured servants worked for their sponsor for seven years. At the end of their term, they received freedom and land. This system of indentured servitude also existed in Massachusetts Bay, though not to the same extent.
- Both colonies imported African slaves early in the 17th century, even though their attitudes towards slavery quickly took very divergent paths.
- Both colonies had conflict with native Americans. Virginians faced continual attacks from natives, which led to Bacon's Rebellion, when white settlers grew tired of the attacks and rose up against Governor William Berkeley. In Massachusetts Bay, the Puritan colonists feared the natives but felt it was their mission to convert them to Christianity. Pequot's War (in which the colonists massacred the natives) and King Philip's War (in which the natives massacred the colonists) are evidence of this constant conflict.

This is a partial list. There are many other aspects of life in these colonies that can be written about.

Question 3

Analyze the ways in which Prohibition led to a rise in organized crime.

It may be hard to believe, but the term "organized crime" didn't exist in the United States before the 1920s. Most professional criminals were small-time crooks, thugs, numbers runners, and extortion artists. They operated mostly in their own small immigrant communities.

That all changed with the passage of the 18th Amendment in 1919. With the prohibition of the sale of alcohol across the nation—a ban that went into effect the next year—the nation's thirst for alcohol needed to be illegally filled. Into that void stepped the pre-existing criminal element, and it grew quickly.

- Small-time gangs that had been employed by political machines in the 19th century to intimidate voters now turned to a different job—smuggling alcohol. That required changing tactics. Instead of fighting one another in service of their bosses (such as Boss Tweed and Tammany Hall), these mobsters began to cooperate instead, forming mutual protection pacts.
- Significantly, the gangs began cooperating across ethnic lines. For instance, the Purple Gang in Detroit, which was Jewish, began cooperating with non-Jewish groups elsewhere. In fact, it could be argued that organized crime helped the melting pot of America melt a little more.
- Despite this cooperation, there were turf wars. Gangsters like Lucky Luciano and Al Capone were willing to slaughter other mobsters, and their affiliates, in an effort to control prime territory. In Chicago, the St. Valentine's Day Massacre is a good example of this savagery.
- Because much alcohol was smuggled from Canada, organized crime needed to organize on an international level as well. They did this well, often running boats of rum and whiskey across the Great Lakes in the summer—and in the winter, running sleds full of booze across the frozen ice.
- With monthly income running over $10 million (which would be ten times that in today's dollars), these criminals also had to get organized in what to do with the money. Many turned to large-scale money laundering, which meant using criminal intermediaries like Meyer Lansky to invest their dirty money in legitimate lawful businesses such as casinos and hotels. The city of Las Vegas was built on laundered criminal money.
- Prohibition ended in 1933 with the repeal of the 18th Amendement, but organized crime had built itself into a well-organized syndicate with national reach. They simply ended their alcohol business and pursued other criminal enterprises such as drug smuggling, prostitution, gambling, and loan-sharking. The temperance movement, begun by law-abiding middle-class Protestant women in the 19th century, had ironically resulted in a national network of syndicated crime.

Question 4

Describe the changing role of women in the labor force from 1920 to 1960.

For women in the 20th century, labor force participation has followed an irregular, nonlinear path. Such a winding road is nothing new—in the 18th-century colonial era, women often owned businesses with their husbands, but by the middle of the 19th century, they'd been pushed almost totally out of the workforce by the Victorian era and its emphasis on public and private spheres. This idea could be easily placed in the introduction, as a backdrop for the question.

In the 20th century, however, the story of women's labor was complicated by many outside factors, including discrimination, technological change, the changing nature of the economy itself, and their own individual choices.

The easiest way to answer this question is to chronologically address each of the four decades covered in the prompt:

- The 1920s—This decade saw women's participation in the labor force (and public life in general) climbing, as it had been for a few decades since the low point of the 1890s. A large number of these working women were poor, uneducated, and single. They labored as piece workers in manufacturing, or they were employed as servants in other people's homes. A few were teachers or clerical workers. Most women exited the work force once they were married.

- The 1930s—The effects of the Great Depression reached wide and deep into every aspect of society, including this one.
  - With unemployment passing 30% at the height of the Depression, employers often made tough choices about laying off workers—and many chose to lay off women instead of men. The reasoning was that a man's employment was more important to the survival of a family than a woman's employment.
  - On the other hand, another change that began in this decade was that married women began to work outside the home, albeit slowly, often to compensate for a depressed spouse who'd lost his job. (Interestingly, the unemployment rate for men and women was exactly equal during this time.)
  - In many states, women were still prohibited by law from working outside of the home.
  - New Deal work-relief programs such as the Civilian Conservation Corps (CCC) relied almost totally on manual labor—and hired men almost exclusively. Women were not seen as able to perform manual labor.
  - Most social security benefits went to a man and his dependent wife. A single woman was not usually eligible for those benefits.
  - Socially, there were many brassy female celebrities playing on the movie screen—seeing movies was a favorite Depression-era pastime—and women modeled their own behavior after these icons, including actress Katharine Hepburn.

- The 1940s—Because of World War II, women began working outside of the house in much greater numbers.
  - Because of the shortage of male workers—many were off at war—women were encouraged by the government to work outside the home. Many propaganda films urged women to do so.
  - Women held new types of jobs, such as making munitions for the war effort. The famous Rosie the Riveter was a symbol of this female laborer.
  - It wasn't just the war effort. Other new types of jobs that women held included telephone operators and sales positions. The number of women in traditional "caring" jobs such as nursing, teaching, and clerical positions also increased.
  - It may be worth mentioning the fact that human behavior doesn't align easily with numbers that end in 0. The next era, the 1950s, actually began in 1946 and 1947, as the GIs returned home from war.

- The 1950s—Images of the traditional roles—female homemaker and male breadwinner—were rife in this decade. But the reality was slightly different.
  - It's true that women left their factory jobs as men returned from the war and claimed those jobs instead.
  - As in previous decades, women left the workforce to become full-time mothers. The difference was the size of this movement: The average age of marriage plummeted for women, to age 19! The Baby Boom gripped the nation.
  - In this decade, the national economic success meant that an American family could be supported on one salary only. The popular view was that there was no need for a woman to hold a job outside the home.

o The women who did work outside the home served as secretaries, bank tellers, clerical workers, teachers, and nurses. They were viewed as supplemental workers, because many of them were married with children and had limited hours. The range of positions available to them was reduced from the previous decade, and many businesses even instituted salary caps upon female employees.

o This was a sea change from the 1920s. Whereas the typical female employee a few decades earlier had been young and single, the typical female employee now was older and married. Contrary to popular image, in absolute numbers, there were more women in the workforce in 1952 than there were during World War II.

o Gendered job classification was part of every level of the economy.

o Female members of the workforce were viewed as expendable by increased corporate standardization and technological advances.

Practice Test 3

AP® United States History Exam

SECTION I, PART A: Multiple Choice

DO NOT OPEN THIS BOOKLET UNTIL YOU ARE TOLD TO DO SO.

At a Glance

Time
55 minutes
Number of Questions
55
Percent of Total Score
40%
Writing Instrument
Pencil required

Instructions

Section I, Part A of this exam contains 55 multiple-choice questions. Fill in only the ovals for numbers 1 through 55 on your answer sheet. Because this section offers only four answer options for each question, do not mark the (E) answer circle for any question.

Indicate all of your answers to the multiple-choice questions on the answer sheet. No credit will be given for anything written in this exam booklet, but you may use the booklet for notes or scratch work. After you have decided which of the suggested answers is best, completely fill in the corresponding oval on the answer sheet. Give only one answer to each question. If you change an answer, be sure that the previous mark is erased completely. Here is a sample question and answer.

Sample Question   Sample Answer

The first president of the United States was   Ⓐ ● Ⓒ Ⓓ
(A) Millard Fillmore
(B) George Washington
(C) Benjamin Franklin
(D) Andrew Jackson

Use your time effectively, working as rapidly as you can without losing accuracy. Do not spend too much time on any one question. Go on to other questions and come back to the ones you have not answered if you have time. It is not expected that everyone will know the answers to all of the multiple-choice questions.

Your total score on the multiple-choice section is based only on the number of questions answered correctly. Points are not deducted for incorrect answers or unanswered questions.

SECTION I, PART B: Short Answer

At a Glance

Time
40 minutes
Number of Questions
3
Percent of Total Score
20%
Writing Instrument
Pen with black or dark blue ink
Questions 1 and 2
Mandatory
Question 3 or 4
Choose one question

Instructions

For Section I, Part B of this exam, answer Question 1 and Question 2 and **either** Question 3 **or** Question 4. Write your responses in the Section I, Part B: Short-Answer Response booklet. You must write your response to each question on the lined page designated for that response. Each response is expected to fit within its designated page. Fill in the circle on the Section I, Part B: Short-Answer Response booklet indicating whether you answered Question 3 or Question 4. Failure to do so may delay your score.

GO ON TO THE NEXT PAGE.

**UNITED STATES HISTORY
SECTION I, Part A
Time—55 minutes
55 Questions**

Directions: Each of the questions or incomplete statements below is followed by four suggested answers or completions. Select the one that is best in each case and then blacken the corresponding space on the answer sheet.

Questions 1–3 refer to the illustration and excerpt below.

THE BURNING OF JAMESTOWN, 1676

"Whereas complaint has been made to this Board by Capt. William Pierce, Esq., that six of his servants and a negro of Mr. Reginald's has plotted to run away unto the Dutch plantation from their said masters,…the court taking the same into consideration as a dangerous precedent for the future time (if left unpunished), did order that Christopher Miller, a Dutchman (a prime agent in the business), should receive the punishment of whipping,…the said Peter Milcocke to receive thirty stripes and to be Burnt in the cheek with the letter R,…said Richard Cockson, after his full time Expired with his master, to serve the colony for two years and a half, and the said Richard Hill to remain upon his good behavior until the next offense, and the said Andrew Noxe to receive thirty stripes, and the said John Williams, a Dutchman and a [surgeon] after his full time of service is Expired with his master, to serve the colony for seven years, and Emanuel, the Negro, to receive thirty stripes and to be burnt in the cheek with the letter R and to work in shackles one year or more as his master shall see cause."

Decisions of the General Court, 1640

GO ON TO THE NEXT PAGE.

1. The excerpt best supports which one of the following conclusions?

   (A) English colonists sought to control the native populations through missions and religious conversions.

   (B) Trade alliances with American Indians promoted the economic health of early Chesapeake settlements.

   (C) A shortage of indentured servants led to the emergence of the African slave trade.

   (D) The Chesapeake colonies relied on labor-intensive agriculture, a system that utilized both white and African indentured servants.

2. Why were confrontations such as those in the excerpt rare in the New England colonies?

   (A) New England populations were largely homogenous with economies based on subsistence farming, rather than cash crops.

   (B) Puritan law forbade the sale or ownership of slaves.

   (C) Indentured servants in New England were largely treated fairly, serving for short terms before gaining freedom.

   (D) Negotiations after King Philip's War had ensured the return of indentured servants back to Europe.

3. Which of the following protests is most similar to the burning of Jamestown shown in the picture?

   (A) The Whiskey Rebellion
   (B) The Montgomery Bus Boycott
   (C) Nat Turner's Rebellion
   (D) The Bonus Expeditionary Force march on Washington

GO ON TO THE NEXT PAGE.

Questions 4–6 refer to the illustration below.

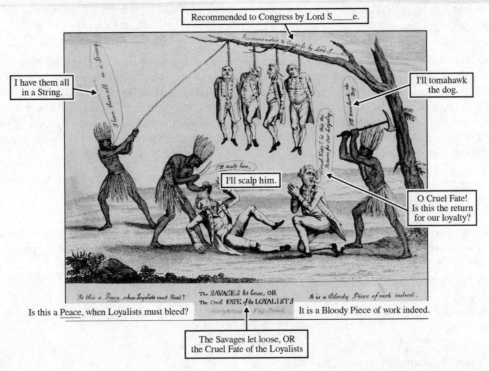

Recommended to Congress by Lord S____e.

I have them all in a String.

I'll tomahawk the dog.

I'll scalp him.

O Cruel Fate! Is this the return for our loyalty?

Is this a <u>Peace</u>, when Loyalists must bleed?

It is a Bloody Piece of work indeed.

The Savages let loose, OR the Cruel Fate of the Loyalists

4. The cartoon above supports which one of the following conclusions?

   (A) After the British victory in the Seven Years' War, many Indians sought revenge on British aristocrats.
   (B) The French withdrawal from North America after the Seven Years' War led to various conflicts between Indians and colonial settlers.
   (C) During and after the Revolutionary War, American sentiment toward those loyal to Britain became increasingly hostile.
   (D) Indian warriors were eager to fight alongside American patriots during the American Revolution.

5. The Seven Years' War is also popularly labeled the "French and Indian War." Why?

   (A) The French fought various Indian tribes throughout the Northeast for control of trapping rights and major waterways.
   (B) The French were aided throughout the war by various Indian tribes fighting in alliance with them.
   (C) Most Indian tribes sided with the British, defending their lands against French invaders from the North.
   (D) Many French settlers, particularly in the Maritime provinces of Canada, intermarried with native peoples, and thus were allied against the British in subsequent territorial conflicts.

6. Which of the following best describes the causal link between the Seven Years' War and the Revolutionary War?

   (A) Britain's defeat after the Seven Years' War led to massive debt for the crown, prompting an effort to collect taxes from the Thirteen Colonies.
   (B) Emboldened by their victories during the Seven Years' War, colonial elites challenged the crown, pushing for independence before the working-class populace was ready to accept it.
   (C) Britain's massive debt after the Seven Years' War resulted in a push for greater control over the Thirteen Colonies, sparking debate among colonists over the pursuit of independence.
   (D) Disillusioned by their experiences in the Seven Years' War, colonial militia members formed the Sons of Liberty, a radical group calling for independence from the crown.

GO ON TO THE NEXT PAGE.

Questions 7–9 refer to the excerpt below.

"…Let me now take a more comprehensive view, and warn you in the most solemn manner against the baneful effects of the spirit of party generally.

"There is an opinion that parties in free countries are useful checks upon the administration of government, and serve to keep alive the spirit of liberty. This within certain limits is probably true; and in governments of a monarchical cast patriotism may look with indulgence, if not with favor, upon the spirit of party. But in those of the popular character, in governments purely elective, it is a spirit not to be encouraged. From their natural tendency it is certain there will always be enough of that spirit for every salutary purpose; and there being constant danger of excess, the effort ought to be by force of public opinion to mitigate and assuage it. A fire not to be quenched, it demands a uniform vigilance to prevent its bursting into a flame, lest, instead of warming, it should consume."

President George Washington, Farewell Address, 1796

7. The sentiments expressed by Washington in his Farewell Address most warn against partisan divisions that occurred before which of the following conflicts?

   (A) The War of 1812
   (B) The Civil War
   (C) The Nullification Crisis of 1832
   (D) The Korean War

8. Washington's Farewell Address best exemplifies which of the following political philosophies?

   (A) Federalism
   (B) Anti-Federalism
   (C) Republicanism
   (D) Sectionalism

9. Elsewhere in the Address, Washington promotes which of the following approaches to foreign policy?

   (A) Neutrality
   (B) Imperialism
   (C) Isolationism
   (D) Dollar Diplomacy

GO ON TO THE NEXT PAGE.

Questions 10–12 refer to the excerpt below.

"Some men look at constitutions with sanctimonious reverence, and deem them like the ark of the covenant, too sacred to be touched. They ascribe to the men of the preceding age a wisdom more than human, and suppose what they did to be beyond amendment.... But I know also, that laws and institutions must go hand in hand with the progress of the human mind. As that becomes more developed, more enlightened, as new discoveries are made, new truths disclosed, and manners and opinions change with the change of circumstances, institutions must advance also, and keep pace with the times."

Thomas Jefferson, 1816

10. Which of following Amendments to the Constitution is most directly an example of the sentiments expressed above?

    (A) The First Amendment, which guaranteed the right to free speech
    (B) The Tenth Amendment, which allows powers not granted to the federal government be granted to the states
    (C) The Nineteenth Amendment, which guaranteed all women the right to vote
    (D) The Twenty-first Amendment, which repealed the prohibition of alcohol

11. Which of the following best describes a contributing factor in the crafting of the United States Constitution?

    (A) Individual state constitutions written at the time of the Revolution tended to cede too much power to the federal government, leading to a call for reform on the part of Anti-Federalists.
    (B) The weaknesses of the Articles of Confederation led James Madison to question their efficacy and prompted a formation of the Constitutional Congress in 1787.
    (C) Difficulties over trade and foreign relations led to a repeal of overly restrictive tariffs required by the Articles of Confederation.
    (D) Washington's embarrassing failure at the Whiskey Rebellion led to Federalist demands for a new framework for federal power.

12. Which of the following statements is most accurate regarding the existence of political parties in the early United States?

    (A) After the drafting of the Constitution, continued debates about states' rights and competing economic interests led to the formation of political parties, such as the Federalists and the Democratic-Republicans.
    (B) Although Washington warned against the influence of political parties, he reluctantly accepted the endorsement of the Federalist Party.
    (C) Political parties did not exist until the War of 1812, when Federalists asserted control over foreign policies with France and Britain.
    (D) Two major political parties dominated early presidential elections until John Quincy Adams founded the Whig Party in 1824.

GO ON TO THE NEXT PAGE.

Questions 13–17 refer to the excerpt below.

"Is there no danger to our liberty and independence in a bank that in its nature has so little to bind it to our country? The president of the bank has told us that most of the State banks exist by its forbearance. Should its influence become concentrated, as it may under the operation of such an act as this, in the hands of a self-elected directory whose interests are identified with those of the foreign stockholders, will there not be cause to tremble for the purity of our elections in peace and for the independence of our country in war? Their power would be great whenever they might choose to exert it; but if this monopoly were regularly renewed every fifteen or twenty years on terms proposed by themselves, they might seldom in peace put forth their strength to influence elections or control the affairs of the nation. But if any private citizen or public functionary should interpose to curtail its powers or prevent a renewal of its privileges, it cannot be doubted that he would be made to feel its influence."

President Andrew Jackson, Veto of the Bank of the United States, 1832

13. In the excerpt above, which quote best explains why Jackson chose to veto the recharter of the Second Bank?

   (A) "but if any private citizen"
   (B) "the president of the bank"
   (C) "this monopoly"
   (D) "interests are identified with those of the foreign stockholders"

14. Which of the following events most directly caused the formation of the Second Bank of the United States?

   (A) The failure of the Specie Circular
   (B) Unregulated currency and federal debts after the War of 1812
   (C) Efforts by Alexander Hamilton to stabilize the national economy
   (D) Federalist counter-reaction to the extreme budget-cutting under Jefferson

15. The debate over the First Bank of the United States was significant because it raised the issue of

   (A) whether the new government should issue paper currency
   (B) how strictly the Constitution should be interpreted
   (C) whether the United States should pay back its war debt to France
   (D) whether the president had the power to act unilaterally on important economic issues

16. The election of 1824 marked a turning point in presidential politics because, for the first time,

   (A) the presidency was won by someone who was not a member of the Federalist Party
   (B) a presidential and vice-presidential candidate ran together on one ticket
   (C) all the candidates campaigned widely throughout the states
   (D) the system of choosing nominees by congressional caucus failed

17. John Taylor of Caroline was a Virginia senator who served in office from 1792 to 1824. He distrusted large banking institutions and generally defended the institution of slavery. He was once quoted as saying that "...if Congress could incorporate a bank, it might emancipate a slave." Taylor is best categorized as

   (A) a Jeffersonian Democrat
   (B) a Jacksonian Democrat
   (C) a Republican
   (D) a Whig

GO ON TO THE NEXT PAGE.

Questions 18–21 refer to the map below.

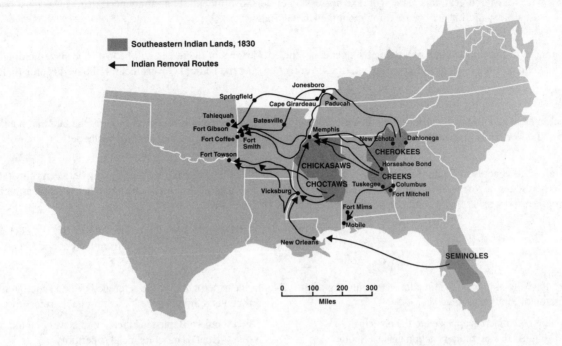

Southeastern Indian Lands, 1830

← Indian Removal Routes

18. Supreme Court decisions concerning American Indian tribes in 1831 and 1832

    (A) reinforced the rights of states to remove Indians from disputed lands
    (B) denied them the right to sue in federal court but affirmed their rights to land that was traditionally theirs
    (C) voided previous treaties between Indian tribes and the United States on the grounds that the treaties were unfair
    (D) ruled that the federal government had a unilateral right to relocate Indians to lands west of the Mississippi

19. Which of the following factors are most likely to have caused the migration shown in the map above?

    (A) Federal Executive branch mandates
    (B) Supreme Court judicial decisions
    (C) Legislative incentives for homesteading in the West
    (D) State legislative mandates for Indian removal

20. Which event in Native American history is LEAST similar to the migration depicted in the map above?

    (A) The Trail of Tears
    (B) King Philip's War
    (C) The Pequot War
    (D) The Battle of Little Big Horn

21. Which of the following is true of the Dawes Severalty Act of 1887?

    (A) In honoring communal landholdings, it reflected an appreciation of Indian culture.
    (B) It was an attempt to assimilate the Indians into American society through individual land grants.
    (C) It compensated Indians for the land they had lost at the Battle of Wounded Knee.
    (D) It outlawed individual land ownership by Indian leaders.

GO ON TO THE NEXT PAGE.

Questions 22–25 refer to the excerpt below.

"On the 4th day of March next, this party will take possession of the Government. It has announced that...a war must be waged against slavery until it shall cease throughout the United States.

The guaranties of the Constitution will then no longer exist; the equal rights of the States will be lost. The slave-holding States will no longer have the power of self-government, or self-protection, and the Federal Government will have become their enemy.

Sectional interest and animosity will deepen the irritation, and all hope of remedy is rendered vain, by the fact that public opinion at the North has invested a great political error with the sanction of more erroneous religious belief.

We, therefore, the People of South Carolina...have solemnly declared that the Union heretofore existing between this State and the other States of North America, is dissolved, and that the State of South Carolina has resumed her position among the nations of the world, as a separate and independent State."

"Declaration of the Immediate Causes Which Induce and Justify the Secession of South Carolina from the Federal Union," 1860

22. Which of the following was an immediate consequence of the secession of South Carolina?

(A) Southern Democrats appealed to the powers of Congress to stop military action against South Carolina.
(B) Abraham Lincoln signed the Emancipation Proclamation.
(C) Other Southern states seceded from the Union, forming the Confederacy.
(D) Jefferson Davis drafted Confederate soldiers into war, defending the siege on Fort Sumter.

23. The sentiments above are most consistent with which of the following ideologies?

(A) States' rights
(B) Nullification
(C) Neutrality
(D) Civil disobedience

24. In the excerpt above, the reference to "the sanction of more erroneous religious belief" most probably refers to

(A) Southern Baptist justification of slavery on the grounds of white racial superiority
(B) the Puritan abolition of slavery in New England states
(C) Jewish acceptance of slavery in the Torah
(D) Christian abolitionist rejection of slavery on moral grounds

25. Which of the following best explains why South Carolina chose to secede from the Union in 1860?

(A) The failures of the Compromise of 1850 hindered South Carolina's trade relationships with Western states, leading to severe economic recession.
(B) The Battle of Fort Sumter occurred in Charleston, prompting public outrage over Union aggression.
(C) President Lincoln signed the Emancipation Proclamation, thus undermining slavery in the South.
(D) Lincoln's election on a Free-Soil platform led Southern politicians to conclude that secession was necessary.

GO ON TO THE NEXT PAGE.

Questions 26–28 refer to the excerpt below.

"The Opposition tells us that we ought not to govern a people without their consent. I answer, the rule of liberty that all just government derives its authority from the consent of the governed, applies only to those who are capable of self-government. We govern the Indians without their consent, we govern our territories without their consent, we govern our children without their consent. How do they know that our government would be without their consent? Would not the people of the Philippines prefer the just, human, civilizing government of this Republic to the savage, bloody rule of pillage and extortion from which we have rescued them? And, regardless of this formula of words made only for enlightened, self-governing people, do we owe no duty to the world? Shall we turn these peoples back to the reeking hands from which we have taken them? Shall we abandon them, with Germany, England, Japan, hungering for them? Shall we save them from those nations, to give them a self-rule of tragedy? …Then, like men and not like children, let us on to our tasks, our mission, and our destiny."

Albert J. Beveridge, "The March of the Flag," 1898

26. The sentiment expressed by Beveridge best exemplifies which of the following?

   (A) Imperialism
   (B) Anti-imperialism
   (C) Isolationism
   (D) Manifest Destiny

27. The United States became politically engaged with the Philippines after what military conflict?

   (A) Mexican-American War
   (B) World War II
   (C) Spanish-American War
   (D) The Boxer Rebellion

28. Which of the following rationales does Beveridge employ in his argument?

   (A) The closing of the western frontier impels the United States to expand its territory overseas.
   (B) Governing territories confers economic benefits to both European and nonwhite nations.
   (C) Powerful nations have a moral duty to govern less-developed nations.
   (D) Racial superiority confers responsibility to the United States and Europe over the affairs of developing nations.

GO ON TO THE NEXT PAGE.

Questions 29–33 refer to the excerpt below.

"Whereas the laws and treaties of the United States, without interfering with the free expression of opinion and sympathy, or with the commercial manufacture or sale of arms or munitions of war, nevertheless impose upon all persons who may be within their territory and jurisdiction the duty of an impartial neutrality during the existence of the contest; And Whereas it is the duty of a neutral government not to permit or suffer the making of its waters subservient to the purposes of war...."

"Now, Therefore, I, Woodrow Wilson, President of the United States of America, in order to preserve the neutrality of the United States...do hereby declare and proclaim...."

"That the statutes and the treaties of the United States and the law of nations alike require that no person, within the territory and jurisdiction of the United States, shall take part, directly or indirectly, in the said wars, but shall remain at peace with all of the said belligerents, and shall maintain a strict and impartial neutrality...."

Woodrow Wilson, 1914

29. The statement above was most likely prompted by which of the following world events?

(A) Cuban revolt against Spanish control
(B) Adolph Hitler's invasion of Poland
(C) Austria-Hungary's declaration of war against Serbia
(D) Mussolini's invasion of Ethiopia

30. The statement above is most in harmony with the sentiments in which of the following speeches?

(A) Washington's Farewell Address
(B) George H. W. Bush's "A Thousand Points of Light"
(C) Lincoln's Gettysburg Address
(D) Franklin D. Roosevelt's "Day of Infamy"

31. All of the following increased federal government power during World War I EXCEPT the

(A) War Industries Board
(B) Food Administration
(C) Espionage Act
(D) Dawes Plan

32. Which of the following statements about the Treaty of Versailles is true?

(A) The United States Senate rejected it because it treated Germany too leniently.
(B) The United States Senate rejected it because it required increased American involvement in European affairs.
(C) The United States Senate approved it, with reservations concerning the division of Eastern Europe.
(D) It was never voted on by the United States Senate.

33. Which of the following statements is most accurate?

(A) After World War I, debates intensified over American involvement overseas.
(B) After World War I, Americans generally favored the new era of American involvement overseas.
(C) American involvement in World War I was an extension of a long tradition of involvement overseas.
(D) American involvement in World War I was a direct result of "dollar diplomacy."

GO ON TO THE NEXT PAGE.

Questions 34–36 refer to the excerpt below.

"Since the foundations of the American commonwealth were laid in colonial times over 300 years ago, vigorous complaint and more or less bitter persecution have been aimed at newcomers to our shores. Also the congressional reports of about 1840 are full of abuse of English, Scotch, Welsh immigrants as paupers, criminals, and so forth. Old citizens in Detroit of Irish and German descent have told me of the fierce tirades and propaganda directed against the great waves of Irish and Germans who came over from 1840 on for a few decades to escape civil, racial, and religious persecution in their native lands. The "Know-Nothings," lineal ancestors of the Ku-Klux Klan, bitterly denounced the Irish and Germans as mongrels, scum, foreigners, and a menace to our institutions, much as other great branches of the Caucasian race of glorious history and antecedents are berated to-day.... But to-day it is the Italians, Spanish, Poles, Jews, Greeks, Russians, Balkanians, and so forth, who are the racial lepers.... In this bill we find racial discrimination at its worst—a deliberate attempt to go back 84 years in our census taken every 10 years so that a blow may be aimed at peoples of eastern and southern Europe, particularly at our recent allies in the Great War—Poland and Italy."

Robert H. Clancy, *Congressional Record*, 68th Congress, 1st Session, 1924

34. The excerpt above is most likely a response to

    (A) World War I patriotism
    (B) immigration quotas
    (C) labor strikes
    (D) the Red Scare

35. What best accounts for the sharp increase of immigrants during the period 1880–1910?

    (A) Many Southern and Eastern Europeans turned to America for financial gain and political freedom.
    (B) Irish farmers were forced to leave their homes due to agricultural disasters.
    (C) Germans were seeking ways to avoid military conscription.
    (D) The United States welcomed immigrants by providing housing and employment.

36. Which one of the following legislative acts is most closely an example of nativism?

    (A) The Wagner Act of 1935
    (B) The Alien and Sedition Acts of 1798
    (C) The Espionage Act of 1917
    (D) The Immigration and Nationality Act of 1965

GO ON TO THE NEXT PAGE.

Questions 37–41 refer to the graph below.

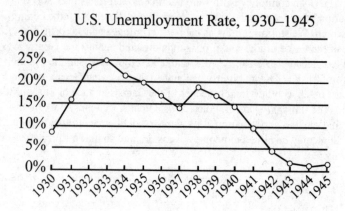

U.S. Unemployment Rate, 1930–1945

37. The graph above is consistent with which of the following statements about the era portrayed?

(A) Unemployment rates began to drop with the election of Herbert Hoover in 1933.

(B) Franklin D. Roosevelt's New Deal produced a constant decrease in U.S. unemployment rates.

(C) A full economic recovery did not occur until the U.S. involvement in World War II.

(D) A brief economic recovery in 1937 sparked a sudden increase in U.S. employment.

38. Which of the following was NOT a major contributing factor to the onset of the Great Depression?

(A) Technological advances had allowed farmers and manufacturers to overproduce, creating large inventories.

(B) The federal government interfered too frequently with the economy, causing investors to lose confidence.

(C) Stock investors had been allowed to speculate wildly, creating an unstable and volatile stock market.

(D) Major businesses were controlled by so few producers that the failure of any one had a considerable effect on the national economy.

39. The Agricultural Adjustment Act of 1933 sought to lessen the effects of the Depression by

(A) paying farmers to cut production and, in some cases, destroy crops

(B) purchasing farms and turning them into government collectives

(C) instituting an early retirement program for farmers over the age of 50

(D) encouraging farmers to increase production

40. The dismal plight of the "Dust Bowl" refugees was captured in

(A) Harriet Beecher Stowes' *Uncle Tom's Cabin*

(B) F. Scott Fitzgerald's *The Great Gatsby*

(C) Theodore Dreiser's *An American Tragedy*

(D) John Steinbeck's *The Grapes of Wrath*

41. In response to several unfavorable Supreme Court rulings concerning New Deal programs, Franklin Roosevelt

(A) urged the voting public to write letters of protest to Supreme Court justices

(B) submitted four separate Constitutional amendments broadening the powers of the presidency

(C) abandoned the New Deal and replaced it with a laissez-faire policy

(D) proposed legislation that would allow him to appoint new federal and Supreme Court judges

GO ON TO THE NEXT PAGE.

Questions 42–46 refer to the excerpt below.

"We found that not only was it a civil war, an effort by a people who had for years been seeking their liberation from any colonial influence whatsoever, but also we found that the Vietnamese whom we had enthusiastically molded after our own image were hard put to take up the fight against the threat we were supposedly saving them from.

"We found most people didn't even know the difference between communism and democracy. They only wanted to work in rice paddies without helicopters strafing them and bombs with napalm burning their villages and tearing their country apart. They wanted everything to do with the war, particularly with this foreign presence of the United States of America, to leave them alone in peace, and they practiced the art of survival by siding with whichever military force was present at a particular time, be it Viet Cong, North Vietnamese or American."

John Kerry, 1971

42. The conflict described above is most likely a result of which of the following doctrines?

   (A) Imperialism
   (B) Containment
   (C) "Big-stick" diplomacy
   (D) Isolationism

43. The most important factor in the defeat of Democratic presidential candidates in the elections of 1952 and 1968 was

   (A) the American public's desire to avoid conflict and return to a more conservative political and social life
   (B) the Democratic Party platform pledge to increase taxes in order to pay off the national debt
   (C) the Democratic candidates' controversial positions on civil rights legislation
   (D) the Democratic Party's unequivocal support of the Equal Rights Amendment

44. The two political issues that most concerned the counterculture movement of the 1960s were

   (A) U.S. involvement in Vietnam and flag burning
   (B) the civil rights movement and censorship
   (C) U.S. involvement in Vietnam and the civil rights movement
   (D) censorship and the draft

45. Which of the following best characterizes the policy of *détente*?

   (A) Direct confrontation
   (B) Covert sabotage
   (C) Decolonization
   (D) Mutual coexistence

46. From the quote above, it is reasonable to infer that

   (A) many Vietnamese viewed the United States as a colonial influence
   (B) most Vietnamese were opposed to Communism
   (C) most Vietnamese favored Communism
   (D) some Viet Cong fought alongside American troops in opposition to North Vietnam

GO ON TO THE NEXT PAGE.

Questions 47–50 refer to the excerpt below.

"Yesterday, December 7, 1941—a date which will live in infamy—the United States of America was suddenly and deliberately attacked by naval and air forces of the Empire of Japan. The United States was at peace with that nation and, at the solicitation of Japan, was still in conversation with its Government and its Emperor looking toward the maintenance of peace in the Pacific. Indeed, one hour after Japanese air squadrons had commenced bombing...the Japanese Ambassador to the United States and his colleague delivered to the Secretary of State a formal reply to a recent American message. While this reply stated that it seemed useless to continue the existing diplomatic negotiations, it contained no threat or hint of war or armed attack.... The attack yesterday...has caused severe damage to American naval and military forces. Very many American lives have been lost. In addition American ships have been reported torpedoed on the high seas.... As Commander-in-Chief of the Army and Navy, I have directed that all measures be taken for our defense."

President Franklin D. Roosevelt, radio address, December 8, 1941

47. Which of the following best describes the relationship between the United States and the Empire of Japan in the years leading up to this speech?

(A) Japan and the United States maintained an alliance against Nazi Germany.

(B) The United States and Japan developed tensions over which country rightfully controlled Hawaii.

(C) The United States depended on loans from Japan to stay afloat during the Great Depression.

(D) Japan resented the economic embargoes placed against it by the United States.

48. The above statements were most likely made after which major event?

(A) The bombing of Pearl Harbor

(B) The sinking of the *U.S.S Maine*

(C) The bombing of the *U.S.S. Liberty*

(D) The Boxer Rebellion

49. Which of the following was the most immediate consequence of the events described in the excerpt above?

(A) Trade embargoes with Japan extending up through the 1980s

(B) The Battle of Normandy

(C) The internment of Japanese-Americans

(D) The bombing of Nagasaki

50. Which of the following statements best characterizes the economic consequences of the declaration of war described above?

(A) Decreased trade with Asian nations precipitated economic recession in both the United States and Europe.

(B) The war-ravaged condition of Asia and Europe allowed the United States to emerge as one of the most prosperous nations on Earth.

(C) Cold War tensions isolated the economies of both the Soviet Union and the United States, leading to economic struggle for both nations.

(D) Japan was subsequently required to pay reparations to the United States, forcing it into a prolonged depression.

GO ON TO THE NEXT PAGE.

Questions 51–53 refer to the excerpts below.

"In the new Code of Laws which I suppose it will be necessary for you to make I desire you would Remember the Ladies, and be more generous and favorable to them than your ancestors. Do not put such unlimited power into the hands of the Husbands. Remember all Men would be tyrants if they could. If particular care and attention is not paid to the Ladies we are determined to foment a Rebellion, and will not hold ourselves bound by any Laws in which we have no voice, or Representation."

Abigail Adams, in a letter to John Adams, 1776

"Special legislation for woman has placed us in a most anomalous position. Women invested with the rights of citizens in one section—voters, jurors, office-holders—crossing an imaginary line, are subjects in the next. In some States, a married woman may hold property and transact business in her own name; in others, her earnings belong to her husband. In some States, a woman may testify against her husband, sue and be sued in the courts; in others, she has no redress in case of damage to person, property, or character. In case of divorce on account of adultery in the husband, the innocent wife is held to possess no right to children or property, unless by special decree of the court. But in no State of the Union has the wife the right to her own person, or to any part of the joint earnings of the co-partnership during the life of her husband. In some States women may enter the law schools and practice in the courts; in others they are forbidden. In some universities girls enjoy equal educational advantages with boys, while many of the proudest institutions in the land deny them admittance, though the sons of China, Japan and Africa are welcomed there. But the privileges already granted in the several States are by no means secure."

Susan B. Anthony, "Declaration of Rights for Women," July 4, 1876

51. The sentiments expressed in the first excerpt by Abigail Adams best exemplify which of the following ideologies?

(A) Second-wave feminism
(B) Jeffersonian democracy
(C) Republican motherhood
(D) Libertarianism

52. The sentiments expressed in the second excerpt by Susan B. Anthony are most likely in support of

(A) the Equal Rights Amendment
(B) universal suffrage
(C) states' rights
(D) prohibition

53. The excerpts above best support which of the following conclusions?

(A) The Second Great Awakening, along with various social reform movements, secured full rights for women by the turn of the 19th century.
(B) Before 1876, American women had no right to own property or vote in national elections.
(C) Women's rights movements flourished in response to inconsistent legislation and unequal distributions of power throughout the nation.
(D) American feminists in the 19th century largely focused on suffrage, shunning other social issues such as abolition and prison reform.

GO ON TO THE NEXT PAGE.

Questions 54 and 55 refer to the excerpt below.

"The violent tendencies of dangerous cults can be classified into two general categories—defensive violence and offensive violence. Defensive violence is utilized by cults to defend a compound or enclave that was created specifically to eliminate most contact with the dominant culture. The 1993 clash in Waco, Texas at the Branch Davidian complex is an illustration of such defensive violence. History has shown that groups that seek to withdraw from the dominant culture seldom act on their beliefs that the endtime has come unless provoked."

"Project Megiddo," U.S. Department of Justice, 2000

"Madam Attorney General, I am extremely disappointed in the decisions that have been made out of the Department of Justice, the Federal Bureau of Investigation, and the Bureau of Alcohol, Tobacco and Firearms. In Philadelphia, we had a mayor that bombed people out of an eviction. In Jonestown, we lost the life of my colleague, Congressman Ryan,...because of a miscalculation about cult people. We had Patty Hearst and the Symbionese Liberation Army. We had Wounded Knee with the Indians. Now, when in God's name is the law enforcement at the Federal level going to understand that these are very sensitive events that you cannot put barbed wire, guns, FBI, Secret Service around them, send in sound 24 hours a day and night and then wonder why they do something unstable? The root cause of this problem was that it was considered a military operation, and it wasn't. This is a profound disgrace to law enforcement in the United States of America, and you did the right thing by offering to resign...."

U.S. Representative John Conyers, Events Surrounding the Branch Davidian Cult Standoff in Waco, Texas: Hearing Before the Committee on the Judiciary, House of Representatives, 1993

54. The above excerpts most closely support which of the following inferences?

(A) In the 1990s, antigovernment sentiment, in response to excessive uses of federal power to resolve domestic conflicts, inspired dangerous cults such as the Branch Davidians.

(B) In 1993, Attorney General Janet Reno launched an offensive against the Branch Davidian cult, later drawing criticism from Congress for her heavy-handed approach.

(C) Fearing the offensive violence perpetrated by the Branch Davidian cult, Attorney General Janet Reno sent troops to quell the subsequent standoff and later faced congressional criticism.

(D) Attorney General Janet Reno resigned from office in part due to Congressional pressure put on President Clinton by Representative John Conyers.

55. In the second excerpt, Representative Conyers refers to "Wounded Knee" as an example of

(A) a violent cult
(B) a federal misuse of power
(C) the site of a bombing
(D) a recent conflict between federal agents and Lakota Indians

GO ON TO THE NEXT PAGE.

UNITED STATES HISTORY
SECTION I, Part B
Time—40 minutes

Directions: Answer Question 1 **and** Question 2. Answer **either** Question 3 **or** Question 4.

Write your responses in the Section I, Part B: Short-Answer Response booklet. You must write your response to each question on the lined page designated for that response. Each response is expected to fit within the space provided.

In your responses, be sure to address all parts of the questions you answer. Use complete sentences; an outline or bulleted list alone is not acceptable. You may plan your answers in this exam booklet, but no credit will be given for notes written in this booklet.

Question 1 is based on the excerpts below.

"The Democrats represented a wide range of views but shared a fundamental commitment to the Jeffersonian concept of an agrarian society. They viewed the central government as the enemy of individual liberty.... They believed that government intervention in the economy benefited special-interest groups and created corporate monopolies that favored the rich. They sought to restore the independence of the individual—the artisan and the ordinary farmer—by ending federal support of banks and corporations and restricting the use of paper currency, which they distrusted. Their definition of the proper role of government tended to be negative.... Reformers eager to turn their programs into legislation called for a more active government. But Democrats tended to oppose programs like educational reform mid the establishment of a public education system. They believed, for instance, that public schools restricted individual liberty by interfering with parental responsibility and undermined freedom of religion by replacing church schools.

> Mary Beth Norton, historian, *A People and a Nation, Volume I: to 1877* (2007)

"FREE-SOIL PARTY—a political party in the United States, which was organized in 1847–1848 to oppose the extension of slavery into the Territories. It was a combination of the political abolitionists many of whom had formerly been identified with the...Whigs, and the faction of the Democratic party...who favoured the prohibition of slavery,...in the territory acquired from Mexico. The party was prominent in the presidential campaigns of 1848 and 1852.

> Encyclopedia Britannica, 1911

1. Using the excerpts above, answer parts (a), (b), and (c).

    a) Briefly explain ONE additional characteristic of the Democratic Party not explicitly mentioned in the excerpts above.

    b) Briefly explain one historical event from the time period in question that could support Norton's interpretation.

    c) Briefly explain ONE piece of evidence regarding the Free-Soil Party not directly mentioned in the excerpt.

GO ON TO THE NEXT PAGE.

Question 2 is based on the following image.

2. Use the image above and your knowledge of history to answer parts (a), (b), and (c).

a) Explain the point of view in the image regarding ONE of the following:
    - Family life
    - The role of women
    - Social class

b) Explain how ONE element of the image expresses the point of view you identified in part (a).

c) Explain how the point of view you identified in part (a) helped to shape ONE significant historical event prior to 1800.

GO ON TO THE NEXT PAGE.

Question 3 **or** 4

Directions: Answer **either** Question 3 **or** Question 4.

3. United States historians have debated the role of Jeffersonian democracy during the period 1800–1824.

   Answer parts (a), (b), and (c).

   a) Briefly explain the basic principles of Jeffersonian democracy.

   b) Choose ONE of the events listed below and explain why your choice represents a shift in the ideals of Jeffersonian democracy during the period 1800–1824. Provide at least ONE piece of evidence to support your explanation.
   - The Louisiana Purchase
   - *Marbury v. Madison*
   - The War of 1812
   - The Monroe Doctrine

   c) Briefly explain why ONE of the other options is not as persuasive as the one you chose.

4. Answer parts (a), (b), and (c).

   a) Briefly explain ONE reason for the popularity of the Progressive movement during the first two decades of the 20th century.

   b) Briefly explain a SECOND reason for the popularity of the Progressive movement during the same period.

   c) Briefly explain ONE example of how the American people resisted changes brought about by the Progressive movement during the same period.

END OF SECTION I

GO ON TO THE NEXT PAGE.

AP® United States History Exam

SECTION II: Free Response

DO NOT OPEN THIS BOOKLET UNTIL YOU ARE TOLD TO DO SO.

At a Glance

Total Time
1 hour, 40 minutes
Number of Questions
2
Percent of Total Score
40%
Writing Instrument
Pen with black or dark blue ink

Question 1 (DBQ): Mandatory

Suggested Reading and Writing Time

60 minutes
Reading Period
15 minutes. Use this time to read Question 1 and plan your answer. You may begin writing your response before the reading period is over.
Suggested Writing Time
45 minutes
Percent of Total Score
25%

Question 2, 3, or 4: Choose One Question

Answer Question 2, Question 3, or Question 4
Suggested Writing Time
40 minutes
Percent of Total Score
15%

Instructions

The questions for Section II are printed in the orange Questions and Documents booklet. You may use that booklet to organize your answers and for scratch work, but you must write your answers in this Section II: Free Response booklet. No credit will be given for any work written in the Questions and Documents booklet.

The proctor will announce the beginning and end of the reading period. You are advised to spend the 15-minute period reading the question and planning your answer to Question 1, the document-based question. If you have time, you may also read Questions 2, 3, and 4. Do not begin writing in this booklet until the proctor tells you to do so.

Section II of this exam requires answers in essay form. Write clearly and legibly. Circle the number of the question you are answering at the top of each page in this booklet. Begin each answer on a new page. Do not skip lines. Cross out any errors you make; crossed-out work will not be scored.

Manage your time carefully. The proctor will announce the suggested time for each part, but you may proceed freely from one part to the next. Go on to Question 2, 3, or 4 if you finish Question 1 early. You may review your responses if you finish before the end of the exam is announced.

After the exam, you must apply the label that corresponds to the long-essay question you answered—Question 2, 3, or 4. For example, if you answered Question 2, apply the label 2. Failure to do so may delay your score.

GO ON TO THE NEXT PAGE.

UNITED STATES HISTORY
SECTION II
Total Time—1 hour, 40 minutes

Question 1 (Document-Based Question)
Suggested reading and writing time: 1 hour

It is suggested that you spend 15 minutes reading the documents and 45 minutes writing your response.

Note: You may begin writing your response before the reading period is over.

Directions: Question 1 is based on the accompanying documents. The documents have been edited for the purpose of this exercise.

In your response, you should do the following.

- Respond to the prompt with a historically defensible thesis or claim that establishes a line of reasoning.
- Describe a broader historical context relevant to the prompt.
- Support an argument in response to the prompt using at least six documents.
- Use at least one additional piece of specific historical evidence (beyond that found in the documents) relevant to an argument about the prompt.
- For at least three documents, explain how or why the document's point of view, purpose, historical situation, and/or audience is relevant to an argument.
- Use evidence to corroborate, qualify, or modify an argument that addresses the prompt.

GO ON TO THE NEXT PAGE.

1. To what extent was the breakup of the Union in 1861 a result of the conflict over slavery and to what extent was it due to other factors? Using your knowledge of the antebellum period, construct an essay that explains the reasons the nation went to war and what circumstances led to this point of national crisis.

   Use the documents and your knowledge of the time period 1844–1861 to construct your answer.

Document 1

Source: "Annexation," by John L. O'Sullivan, *United States Magazine and Democratic Review*, July 1845

Why, were other reasoning wanting, in favor of now elevating this question of the reception of Texas into the Union, out of the lower region of our past party dissension, up to its proper level of a high and broad nationality, it surely is to be found, found abundantly, in the manner in which other nations have undertaken to intrude themselves into it, between us and the proper parties to the case, in a spirit of hostile interference against us, for the avowed object of thwarting our policy and hampering our power, limiting our greatness and checking the fulfillment of our manifest destiny to overspread the continent allotted by Providence for the free development of our yearly multiplying millions.

Document 2

Source: President James K. Polk's War Message to Congress, May 11, 1846

As war exists, and notwithstanding all our efforts to avoid it, exists by the act of Mexico herself, we are called upon by every consideration of duty and patriotism to vindicate with decision the honor, rights and dignity of this country.

Document 3

Source: Representative David Wilmot, from the Congressional Globe, 29th Congress, 2nd session, Appendix, February 8, 1847

But, sir, the issue now presented is not whether slavery shall exist unmolested where it now is, but whether it shall be carried to new and distant regions, now free, where the footprint of a slave cannot be found. This, sir, is the issue. Upon it I take my stand, and from it I cannot be frightened or driven by idle charges of abolitionism.

I ask not that slavery be abolished, I demand that this government preserve the integrity of free territory against the aggressions of slavery—against its wrongful usurpations.

Sir, I was in favor of the annexation of Texas.... Yes, sir, here was an empire larger than France given up to slavery. Shall further concessions be made by the North? Shall we give up free territory, the inheritance of free labor? Must we yield this also?

…But, sir, we are told that the joint blood and treasure of the whole country being expended in this acquisition, therefore it should be divided, and slavery should be allowed to take its share. Sir, the South has her share already.

…Now, sir, we are told that California is ours, that New Mexico is ours—won by the valor of our arms. They are free. Shall they remain free? Shall these fair provinces be the inheritance and homes of the white labor of freemen or the black labor of slaves? This, sir, is the issue.

GO ON TO THE NEXT PAGE.

Document 4

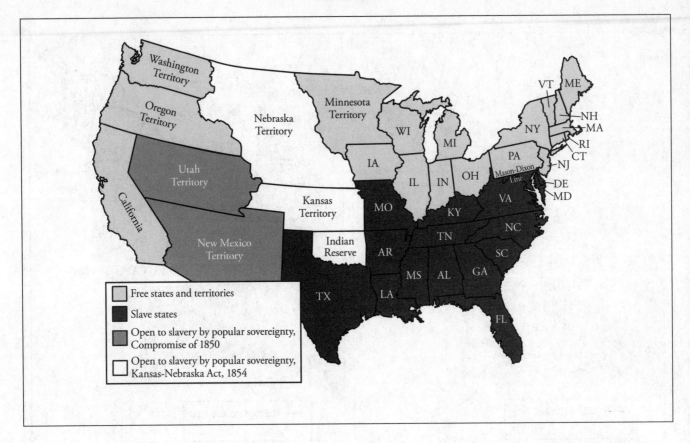

Free states and territories

Slave states

Open to slavery by popular sovereignty, Compromise of 1850

Open to slavery by popular sovereignty, Kansas-Nebraska Act, 1854

Document 5

Source: Roger Taney, in the Supreme Court opinion in *Dred Scott v. Sandford*, 1857

The right of property in a slave is distinctly and expressly affirmed in the Constitution…. No word can be found in the Constitution which gives Congress a greater power over the slave property or which entitles property of that kind to less protection than property of any other description.

GO ON TO THE NEXT PAGE.

Document 6

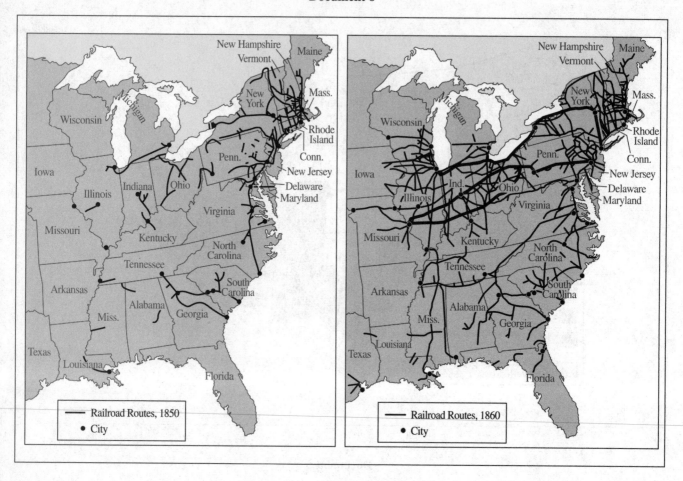

GO ON TO THE NEXT PAGE.

Document 7

END OF DOCUMENTS FOR QUESTION 1

GO ON TO THE NEXT PAGE.

Question 2, 3, or 4 (Long Essay)

Suggested writing time: 40 minutes

Directions: Answer Question 2 **or** Question 3 **or** Question 4.

In your response, you should do the following.

- Respond to the prompt with a historically defensible thesis or claim that establishes a line of reasoning.
- Describe a broader historical context relevant to the prompt.
- Support an argument in response to the prompt using specific and relevant examples of evidence.
- Use historical reasoning (e.g., comparison, causation, continuity or change over time) to frame or structure an argument that addresses the prompt.
- Use evidence to corroborate, qualify, or modify an argument that addresses the prompt.

2. Evaluate the extent to which the first Great Awakening marked a turning point in the development of an American identity.

   In the development of your argument, explain what changed and what stayed the same from the period immediately before the Great Awakening (early 1700s) to the period immediately after the Great Awakening (1750s).

3. Evaluate the extent to which farmers and factory workers did not easily adapt to changes stemming from industrialization in the years 1865–1900.

4. Evaluate the extent to which it was social and economic issues within the United States that influenced U.S. foreign policy in the 1920s.

WHEN YOU FINISH WRITING, CHECK YOUR WORK ON SECTION II IF TIME PERMITS.

STOP

END OF EXAM

Practice Test 3:
Answers and
Explanations

PRACTICE TEST 3 ANSWER KEY

Section I, Part A: Multiple-Choice Questions

1. D	20. B	39. A
2. A	21. B	40. D
3. C	22. C	41. D
4. C	23. A	42. B
5. B	24. D	43. A
6. C	25. D	44. C
7. A	26. A	45. D
8. C	27. C	46. A
9. A	28. C	47. D
10. D	29. C	48. A
11. B	30. A	49. C
12. B	31. D	50. B
13. D	32. B	51. C
14. B	33. A	52. B
15. B	34. B	53. C
16. D	35. A	54. B
17. A	36. B	55. B
18. B	37. C	
19. A	38. B	

SECTION I, PART A: MULTIPLE-CHOICE QUESTIONS

Questions 1–3

The introduction of tobacco would lead to the development of plantation slavery. As new settlements sprang up around Jamestown, the entire area came to be known as the Chesapeake (named after the bay). That area today is comprised mostly of Virginia and Maryland. Many who migrated to the Chesapeake did so for financial reasons. Overpopulation in England had led to widespread famine, disease, and poverty. Chances for improving one's lot were minimal. Thus, many were attracted to the New World by the opportunity provided by indentured servitude. In return for free passage, indentured servants promised seven years' labor, after which they received their freedom.

1. **D** The excerpt mentions only one of the servants as Negro (Emanuel), so we can logically infer that both whites and blacks served in this capacity. Choices (A), (B), and (C) are all unsupported by the excerpt.

2. **A** The lives of English settlers in New England and the Chesapeake differed considerably. Entire families tended to emigrate to New England; in the Chesapeake, immigrants were often single males. The climate in New England was more hospitable, and so New Englanders tended to live longer and have larger families than Chesapeake residents. A stronger sense of community, and the absence of tobacco as a cash crop, led New Englanders to settle in larger towns that were closer to one another; those in the Chesapeake lived in smaller, more spread-out farming communities.

3. **C** The South experienced several slave revolts, which resulted in the use of more brutal disciplinary measures by slaveholders. The most famous of the insurrections was Nat Turner's Rebellion. Turner, a well-read preacher, had a vision, and he took this vision as a sign from God that a black liberation movement would succeed. As a result, he rallied a gang that proceeded to kill and then mutilate the corpses of 60 whites. In retaliation, 200 slaves were executed, some with no connection at all to the rebellion. Choice (A), the Whiskey Rebellion, was a dispute over taxes, not labor. Choice (B), Montgomery Bus Boycott, was not related to disgruntled laborers, either. And (D), the Bonus Expeditionary March, was about unpaid compensation for veterans.

Questions 4–6

Loyalists were American colonists who remained loyal to the British Empire and the British monarchy during the Revolutionary War. They were opposed by the Patriots, those who supported the revolution. When their cause was defeated, about 15 percent of the Loyalists fled to other parts of the British Empire.

4. **C** The key to understanding this cartoon is in recognizing the reference to "Loyalists." Loyalists had no relevance during the Seven Years' War, so rule out (A) and (B). As for the Indians, they are not meant to be taken too literally, so rule out (D). The Indians represent the "savage" new country, which will not tolerate loyalty to the British crown.

5.   **B**   In fact, the Seven Years' War lasted for 10 years. It is also called the French and Indian War, which is almost equally confusing because the French and Indians fought on the same side, not against each other (for the most part). The Seven Years' War was the British name for the war. The colonists called it the "French and Indian War" because that's who they were fighting. It was actually one of several "wars for empire."

6.   **C**   Great Britain's massive debt from the Seven Years' War resulted in renewed efforts to consolidate imperial control over North American markets, taxes, and political institutions—actions that were supported by some colonists but resisted by others. Be careful—Britain was not defeated in this war, so rule out (A). Choice (B) is incorrect because many working-class people favored revolution. Choice (D) is unsupportable.

Questions 7–9

The end of Washington's presidency was as monumental as its beginning. Wishing to set a final precedent, Washington declined to run for a third term. In his famous farewell address, composed in part by Alexander Hamilton, he warned future presidents to "steer clear of permanent alliances with any portion of the foreign world." Washington's call for neutrality defined American foreign policy from 1800 until the late 1890s (during which the United States pursued a policy of imperialism) and then again from the end of World War I until 1941.

7.   **A**   In the excerpt, Washington warns against the "baneful effects" of political parties. During the War of 1812, the War Hawks, largely Anti-Federalists, saw war as an opportunity to grab new territories to the west and southwest. Their leaders were Henry Clay and John C. Calhoun. Federalists, on the other hand, opposed to the war because it disrupted trade and unaware that its end was coming, met in Hartford, Connecticut, to consider a massive overhaul of the Constitution or, failing that, secession. When the war ended soon after, most people considered the Federalists to be traitors, and their national party dissolved soon after the Hartford Convention. If you chose (B), you were close, but the Civil War involved more than just partisan divisions; it was fueled by geographical, economic, and ideological differences too. Choices (C), the Nullification Crisis of 1832, and (D), the Korean War, were not primarily partisan conflicts.

8.   **C**   Washington was not explicitly a Federalist, so rule out (A), and he was certainly not an Anti-Federalist, so rule out (B). He preaches *against* sectionalism, so rule out (D). Washington's political views most embody Republicanism—which stresses liberty and "unalienable" rights as central values, makes the people as a whole sovereign, rejects aristocracy, expects citizens to be independent in their performance of civic duties, and vilifies corruption.

9.   **A**   A key message in the address is the necessity of neutrality regarding foreign affairs. Choice (C), isolationism, is close but too extreme. Choice (A) is the best answer.

Questions 10–12

Although Jefferson was a strict constructionist, he did favor providing a means for the American people to amend their Constitution, as shown in this excerpt: "As new discoveries are made, new truths disclosed, and manners and opinions change with the change of circumstances, institutions must advance also, and keep pace with the times."

10. **D** Although all of the Constitutional Amendments represent changes to the original document, the Twenty-first Amendment best exemplifies the sentiment in Jefferson's quote. After only 15 years of banning alcohol, the Eighteenth Amendment (Prohibition) was repealed by the Twenty-first.

11. **B** James Madison led the charge to form a Constitutional Congress and draft the Constitution. It was primarily the weaknesses of the Articles of Confederation that led to their rejection. They did not impose tariffs, so rule out (C). Choice (A) is incorrect because the federal government was weak in 1787. Choice (D) is wrong because Washington responded to the Whiskey Rebellion with much force. (If you picked (D), you are confusing Shays's Rebellion with the Whiskey Rebellion.)

12. **B** In Washington's Farewell address, he denounces political parties. So, Washington was the one president who was not officially affiliated with any party, although he was endorsed by the Federalists. Choice (A) is a tempting answer, but political parties existed *before* the drafting of the Constitution. That also rules out (C). Choice (D) is incorrect because the Whig Party formed in reaction to Jackson's policies, well after John Quincy Adams left office.

Questions 13–17

Jackson's economic policies demonstrated his distrust of both big government and Northeastern power brokers. He fought the Second Bank of the United States because he felt it protected Northeastern interests at the expense of the West. He was wary of creating an unconstitutional monopoly and of dealing with the mostly British investors. He was also suspicious of paper money, preferring "hard currency" such as gold or silver. His Specie Circular, which ended the policy of selling government land on credit (buyers now had to pay "hard cash"), caused a money shortage, a sharp decrease in the treasury, and overall economic hardship. Congress overturned the circular in the final days of Jackson's final term.

13. **D** Jackson was not opposed to a bank run by private citizens per se, as in (A), but he was wary of allowing foreign shareholders to control American economic interests.

14. **B** In the aftermath of the War of 1812, the federal government suffered from the disarray of an unregulated currency and a lack of fiscal order; business interests sought security for their government bonds. A national alliance arose to create a central bank to address these needs. Choice (C) is tempting, but it refers to the First Bank, not the Second.

15. **B** As the United States' first secretary of the treasury, Alexander Hamilton had to handle the nation's considerable war debt. His solution included the formation of a national bank, modeled on the Bank of England. Through the bank, Hamilton hoped to consolidate and manage the nation's debt and provide an agency through which a national currency could be circulated. He also wished to broaden the powers of the federal government (Hamilton, a Federalist, favored a strong central government). Both houses of Congress approved Hamilton's plan, but Washington (then president) was reluctant to sign the bill because he was uncertain of its constitutionality. (Note: Washington performed very conservatively as president, aware that any action he took would set a precedent for his followers. Accordingly, he used his veto only when he was certain that a bill was unconstitutional.) The debate that followed defined the two main schools of thought on constitutional law. On one side were the strict constructionists, led

by Jefferson and Madison. Both were wary of a strong central government and interpreted the Constitution accordingly. The strict constructionists argued that the Constitution allowed Congress only those powers specifically granted it or those "necessary and proper" to the execution of its enumerated powers. While a bank might be convenient and perhaps beneficial, they argued, it was not necessary, and thus its creation was beyond the powers of the national government. Hamilton, not surprisingly, disagreed. In his "Defense of the Constitutionality of the Bank," he proposed what has come to be known as the broad-constructionist view. He argued that the creation of a bank was an implied power of the government, because it already had explicit power to coin money, borrow money, and collect taxes. Hamilton argued that the government could do anything in the execution of those enumerated powers—including creating a bank—that was not explicitly forbidden by the Constitution. Washington agreed with Hamilton and signed the bill.

16. **D**   Between 1800 and 1820, party nominees to the presidency were chosen by congressional caucus and then approved by state electors (delegates to a state nominating convention). Before 1824, electors were chosen by a variety of methods. Many electors were chosen by state legislatures, which chose electors who agreed with the choices of the caucus (often they were the same men who had participated in the caucus). By 1824, however, a majority of states allowed voters to choose their presidential electors directly. When the Republican caucus chose William H. Crawford in 1824, others, among them John Quincy Adams, Henry Clay, and Andrew Jackson, decided to challenge the nomination. Their opposition, along with their accusations that the caucuses were undemocratic, brought about the demise of the caucus system.

17. **A**   Jeffersonian Democrats believed in a republican government and equality of political opportunity, with a priority for the "yeoman farmer," "planters," and the "plain folk." They were antagonistic to the aristocratic elitism of merchants and bankers and generally favored, or tolerated, slavery. Choice (B) is incorrect because there were some Free-Soil Jacksonians.

Questions 18–21

When the state of Georgia tried to relocate the Cherokee tribe, Chief Justice John Marshall ruled that only the federal government, not the states, had authority over Native Americans within the boundaries of the United States. President Jackson didn't like Marshall's rulings and simply ignored them, pursuing an aggressive policy aimed at pushing tribes farther and farther west. The result was the Trail of Tears, the involuntary westward migration of the Cherokees. Over one-quarter died of disease and exhaustion during the three- to four-month forced march (supervised by the U.S. Army).

18. **B**   In the 1831 case *Cherokee Nation v. Georgia*, Chief Justice John Marshall ruled that American Indian tribes were neither foreign nations nor states, and as such had no standing in federal court. In short, he ruled they had no right to sue. He argued further, however, that the tribes had a right to their lands and could not be forced to give them up by anyone, including the federal government. The 1832 case *Worcester v. Georgia* reaffirmed that position.

19. **A** As noted above, it was President Jackson who was largely responsible for relocating the Cherokees, not the Supreme Court or the Legislature.

20. **B** King Philip's War was an armed conflict between Indian inhabitants of present-day New England and English colonists. The war is named after the Indian chief, Metacomet, known to the English as "King Philip." This war is least like the migration depicted in the map—the Cherokee Trail of Tears, as in (A)—because it did not lead to a forced migration. King Phillip's warriors prevailed over the short term. Choice (D), the Battle of Little Big Horn, is a tempting answer, but ultimately the Lakota Sioux were forced to leave their territories and migrate to reservations.

21. **B** In the 1860s, the government initiated its "reservation policy," by which Native Americans were granted (usually less desirable) portions of the lands they inhabited. The policy failed on many fronts, and by the 1880s, the government was searching for a different tack. Congress struck on the Dawes Severalty Act, which offered individual Native Americans 160-acre plots in return for leaving their reservations; through this program, Congress hoped to hasten the assimilation of Native Americans, whose cultures most congressmen held in contempt. The results were not good. Most American Indians preferred to remain among their tribes and did not accept the offer. Those who did accept usually ended up selling their land to whites, who often placed considerable pressure on them to do so.

Questions 22–25

After the election of Lincoln was announced, South Carolina seceded from the Union and was soon joined by Alabama, Mississippi, Florida, Georgia, Louisiana, and Texas. Several months later the other four states—Virginia, North Carolina, Arkansas, and Tennessee—joined the secession, and the Confederacy was formed.

22. **C** This is a question of chronology. There was no Confederacy until South Carolina seceded first, so rule out (D). By the time the Civil War started, Southern Democrats appealed more to Jefferson Davis than to Washington, D.C., so rule out (A). Lincoln did not sign the Emancipation Proclamation until much later in the War, so rule out (B).

23. **A** In the excerpt, South Carolina is protesting the violation of "the equal rights of the states." Choice (B), nullification, is a good trap answer because South Carolina did attempt to nullify the Whiskey Tariff under President Jackson. Choice (D), civil disobedience, cannot be right because that sort of protest is nonviolent in nature.

24. **D** The Quakers believed slavery to be morally wrong and argued for its end. More generally, the religious and moral fervor that accompanied the Second Great Awakening persuaded many Northern whites that slavery was a great evil. Southern Baptists, (A), were not strongly abolitionist or supporters of slavery. Puritans disapproved of slavery, as in (B), but they did not successfully ban it from the Massachusetts Bay Colony. Choice (C), Jews, is irrelevant to this question.

25. **D** Again, an issue of chronology. Choices (B) and (C) occurred after South Carolina's secession. Trade issues, as in (A), were not a primary reason for South Carolina's exit.

Questions 26–28

Albert Beveridge was a U.S. Senator from 1899 to 1911 and was an intellectual leader of the Progressive movement. Beveridge is known as one of the great American imperialists. He supported the annexation of the Philippines.

26. **A** In the excerpt, Beveridge is arguing that America is justified in ruling over less-developed nations with or without their consent, but that those nations would surely appreciate the "just, human, civilizing" influence of the West. These sentiments are the hallmark of Imperialism. Choice (D), Manifest Destiny, pertains more to domestic expansion, rather than international affairs.

27. **C** During the Spanish-American War, the United States not only drove Spain out of Cuba, but also sent a fleet to the Spanish-controlled Philippines and drove the Spanish out of there too. In the Treaty of Paris, Spain granted Cuba independence and ceded the Philippines, Puerto Rico, and Guam to the United States.

28. **C** Beveridge uses largely moral arguments, stating that less-developed nations must be "rescued" from "the savage, bloody rule of pillage and extortion." There is no mention of economic benefits, or racial superiority, so rule out (B) and (D), respectively. Choice (A) is describing Manifest Destiny, not Progressive Imperialism.

Questions 29–33

When war broke out in Europe in August 1914, Wilson immediately declared the U.S. policy of neutrality. Neutrality called for America to treat all the belligerents fairly and without favoritism. It was Wilson's hope that the United States would help settle the conflict and emerge as the world's arbiter. However, the neutrality policy posed several immediate problems, owing to America's close relationship with England and relatively distant relationship with Germany and Austria-Hungary. A number of Wilson's advisors openly favored the Allies (led by the British).

29. **C** Since 1914 was the beginning of World War I, only (C) is relevant. All the other answers represent conflicts in a different era.

30. **A** Washington's Farewell Address advocated neutrality in foreign affairs. Choice (D), Roosevelt's speech, is a declaration of war against Japan. Choice (B) is largely unrelated to war. The Gettysburg Address, (C), was a speech given during the Civil War, so is unrelated to issues of neutrality.

31. **D** The Dawes Plan (1924) attempted to facilitate German reparation payments. By loaning $200 million in gold bullion to Germany, the United States hoped to stabilize the German economy and enable Germany to pay off its debts.

32. **B** Many Americans supported the U.S. war effort only grudgingly, and then only after German (and, to a lesser extent, British) interference with American shipping had provoked the United States to take action. Many argued that America should stick to the foreign policy suggested in both George Washington's farewell address and the Monroe Doctrine, and therefore (1) avoid political alliances with other countries and (2) remain neutral regarding European conflicts. Wilson negotiated the Treaty of Versailles (the peace treaty following World War I) for the United States. He

was unable to get a treaty that reflected his conciliatory Fourteen Points, as the Allies demanded a treaty that punished Germany harshly. Nonetheless, Wilson did the best he could and returned with a document he was ready to present to the Senate. The treaty included provisions for the League of Nations (which Wilson had fought hard for) and contained a clause that could have been interpreted as committing the American military to the defense of European borders. Wilson, a Democrat, tried to sell this treaty to the Republican Senate, but he could not muster the two-thirds majority required for ratification, and so the treaty was never approved by the United States.

33.　**A**　The global ramifications of World War I and wartime patriotism and xenophobia, combined with social tensions created by increased international migration, resulted in a general sentiment of isolationism in America.

Questions 34–36

The Emergency Quota Act of 1921 restricted immigration into the United States. The Immigration Act of 1924 was federal law that limited the annual number of immigrants who could be admitted from any country to 2% of the number of people from that country who were already living in the United States in 1890, down from the 3% cap set by the Immigration Restriction Act of 1921, according to the Census of 1890. The law was aimed at further restricting immigration of Southern Europeans, Eastern Europeans, and Jews, in addition to prohibiting the immigration of Arabs, East Asians, and Indians. According to the U.S. Department of State Office of the Historian, the purpose of the act was "to preserve the ideal of American homogeneity." Congressional opposition was minimal.

34.　**B**　Clancy is denouncing immigration quotas as "racial discrimination at its worst." Choice (A) is far too positive for the tone of this excerpt. Choice (C), labor strikes, are not mentioned. Choice (D), the Red Scare, is a tempting choice, but the excerpt does not mention Communism specifically. Many of the ethnic groups mentioned are wholly unconnected to Communism.

35.　**A**　The largest wave of immigration to this country occurred during this period and was a result of political and economic upheaval. This so-called "new immigration" brought immigrants from Southern and Eastern Europe as well as Asia. Between 1880 and 1910, approximately 12 million people came to the United States, many to escape poverty or political persecution.

36.　**B**　The Alien and Sedition Acts were four bills that were passed by the Federalists and signed into law by President John Adams in 1798 in the aftermath of the French Revolution and during an undeclared naval war with France. The Naturalization Act increased the residency requirement for American citizenship from 5 to 14 years, and it allowed the president to imprison or deport aliens who were considered "dangerous to the peace and safety of the United States." This act was repealed in 1802 by the Naturalization Law of 1802. Choice (D) is a good trap answer, but the Immigration and Nationality Act actually encouraged immigration, rather than discouraged it.

Questions 37–41

The New Deal was a series of domestic programs enacted in the United States between 1933 and 1936 and a few that came later. The programs were in response to the Great Depression, and they focused on what historians call the "3 Rs": Relief, Recovery, and Reform. That is, Relief for the unemployed and poor; Recovery of the economy to normal levels; and Reform of the financial system to prevent a repeat depression.

37. **C** According to the graph, unemployment generally decreased from 1933 onward, but it did not decrease in 1937, so rule out (B). Hoover was not elected in 1933, nor did his administration successfully decrease unemployment, so rule out (A). Careful with (D)—unemployment increased in 1937; therefore, employment *decreased*. Since the United States entered World War II in the early 1940s, (C) is a reasonable inference.

38. **B** In fact, the federal government did almost nothing to regulate the economy even though many within the government foresaw the potential for economic disaster. Many possible remedies—an income tax to redistribute wealth, a tighter money supply to discourage speculation, aggressive enforcement of antitrust regulations—were rejected. Meanwhile, manufacturers were overproducing, causing them to stockpile large inventories and lay off workers; consumers weren't making enough money to buy what, in some cases, they built at work; and the wealth of the nation was concentrated in very few, often irresponsible, hands. The system was too fragile, and when it started to tumble, it fell entirely to pieces very quickly.

39. **A** As he began his first term, Roosevelt was faced with an agricultural market in which the bottom had dropped out; farmers had so overproduced that their crops were worth virtually nothing. Roosevelt's solution, the Agricultural Adjustment Act (AAA), provided payments to farmers in return for their agreement to cut production by up to one-half. The money to cover this program came from increased taxes on meat packers, millers, and other food processors. The program stabilized agricultural prices and increased American income from imports, but it came to an end when the Supreme Court declared it unconstitutional in 1936. A second AAA in 1938 served much the same purpose while avoiding those aspects that voided the first AAA.

40. **D** John Steinbeck's 1939 best-selling novel, *The Grapes of Wrath*, depicts the lives of farmers forced to flee the drought-ridden Midwest during the Depression years. About 350,000 Oklahomans and Arkansans trekked to southern California in search of work.

41. **D** The question refers to Roosevelt's notorious "court packing" plan. Unhappy with the Supreme Court and the federal judiciary, whose conservatism frequently resulted in the nullification of New Deal programs, Roosevelt proposed that he be allowed to name a new federal judge for every sitting judge who had reached the age of 70 and not retired. The plan would have allowed Roosevelt to add six new Supreme Court justices and more than 40 other federal judges. The proposal was not at all popular and was roundly defeated in the Senate. It also helped fuel the arguments of those who contended that FDR had grown too powerful. Not long after the "court packing" incident, several conservative justices retired and FDR replaced them with liberals, so he achieved his goal despite the failure of his plan.

Questions 42–46

The United States sought to "contain" Soviet-dominated communism through a variety of measures, including military engagements in Korea and Vietnam. The Vietnam War, in particular, saw the rise of sizable, passionate, and sometimes violent antiwar protests that became more numerous as the war escalated. Young Americans debated the merits of a large nuclear arsenal, the "military industrial complex," and the appropriate power of the executive branch in conducting foreign and military policy. The antiwar movement reached its apex in the mid-1960s and generated a variety of political and cultural responses.

42. **B** The conflict in Vietnam was an attempt to contain the spread of Communism in Southeast Asia. It was not an attempt to control the Vietnamese government over the long-term, so rule out (A). Choice (C), "big-stick" diplomacy, may involve the threat of force, but it does not necessarily lead to war. Choice (D), isolationism, would have prevented American involvement in Vietnam.

43. **A** The election of Eisenhower in 1952 reflected the desire of many Americans to disentangle the country from the Korean War and to return to a more conservative economic policy, which they hoped would lead to an economic boom that could keep pace with the baby boom. The election of Nixon in 1968 also reflected a desire for a return to a more conservative social and political approach. George Wallace, running as a third-party candidate, received almost 10 million votes in this election by appealing to those who believed in segregation, states' rights, and "law and order." Democratic candidate Hubert Humphrey suffered from his close ties to President Lyndon Johnson, who had escalated the Vietnam War. It also didn't help that the Democratic National Convention of 1968 was the scene of bitter riots and violence in the streets of Chicago, whereas the Republican convention that year ran without a hitch. In both the elections of 1952 and 1968, Americans were tired of conflict and wanted to return to good times. The more conservative Republican Party was the answer to their wishes.

44. **C** The two largest issues that concerned the counterculture movement were the civil rights of minorities and the war in Vietnam. The many demonstrations that took place during this period (such as the civil rights march on Washington in 1963 and the antiwar "moratoriums" in Washington during 1968 and 1969) had these two issues as their primary focus. Choice (A), flag-burning, was practiced, but was not a major political issue. Censorship, as mentioned in (B) and (D), was not a major issue either.

45. **D** President Nixon and Henry Kissinger formulated an approach called *détente*, which called for countries to respect each other's differences and cooperate more closely. *Détente* ushered in a brief period of relaxed tensions between the two superpowers but ended when the Soviet Union invaded Afghanistan in 1979. The Nixon Doctrine announced that the United States would withdraw from many of its overseas troop commitments, relying instead on alliances with local governments to check the spread of communism.

46. **A** In the excerpt, Kerry states that the Vietnamese were "a people who had for years been seeking their liberation from *any colonial influence whatsoever*," but they were also "hard put to take up the fight against the threat we were supposedly saving them from." Thus, it is fair to infer that the Vietnamese did not welcome U.S. involvement in their affairs. Since "most people didn't even know the difference between communism and democracy," rule out (B) and (C). Choice (D) is false and unsupported by the excerpt.

Questions 47–50

The "Day of Infamy" Speech was a speech delivered by President Franklin D. Roosevelt one day after the Empire of Japan's attack on the Pearl Harbor Naval Base in Hawaii. Within an hour of the speech, Congress passed a formal declaration of war against Japan and officially brought the United States into World War II. The address is regarded as one of the most famous American political speeches of the 20th century.

47. **D** Japan's invasion of China led the United States to place economic sanctions on Japan. Despite negotiations between the two countries to end the embargoes, no satisfactory progress was made and Japan decided to attack the naval base in Hawaii. Choice (D) is correct. Japan held an alliance with Germany, but neither held one with the United States. Eliminate (A). Hawaii was unquestionably United States territory, so (B) is incorrect. While the United States was in a deep recession during the years leading up to the attack on Pearl Harbor, it received no financial aid from Japan. Eliminate (C).

48. **A** The date, 1941, places this speech at the beginning of World War II, so only (A) is in the right era.

49. **C** Normandy is irrelevant to Japan, so rule out (B). Choice (A) might sound tempting, but it is false; trade relationships with Japan were healthy after World War II. Choice (D) is likewise tempting, but it occurred at the end of World War II. President Truman dropped the bombs, not FDR.

50. **B** There are many red herrings here. You can rule out (A), (C), and (D) by simply remembering that the American economy was very strong after World War II and that Japan was not punished for its actions in the War. In fact, General Douglas MacArthur aided in the rebuilding of Japan, and Japan developed a very strong economy, particularly throughout the 1970s and 1980s.

Questions 51–53

The history of the modern western feminist movement is divided into three "waves." Each wave dealt with different aspects of the same feminist issues. The first wave comprised women's suffrage movements of the 19th and early 20th centuries, promoting women's right to vote. The second wave was associated with the ideas and actions of the women's liberation movement beginning in the 1960s. The second wave campaigned for legal and social equality for women. The third wave is a continuation of, and a reaction to, the perceived failures of second-wave feminism, beginning in the 1990s.

51. **C** Abigail Adams, the wife of John Adams, was not a feminist in the strictest sense, but the sentiments in this excerpt do embody the precepts of Republican Motherhood, which called on white women to maintain and teach republican values within the family and granted women a new importance in American political culture. The Adamses were not Jeffersonian Democrats or libertarians, in the modern sense, so rule out (B) and (D), respectively.

52. **B** 1876 puts this excerpt squarely in the realm of first-wave feminism, which largely campaigned for universal suffrage for all, including women. Choice (A), the Equal Rights Amendment, is a good trap answer, but it was not proposed (and it never passed!) until the 20th century.

53. **C** Susan B. Anthony's quote clearly shows that women's rights varied wildly by state of residence. Choice (B) is too extreme. Choice (A) is likewise too extreme because women did not have "full rights" until the 1970s. Choice (D) is untrue because many first-wave feminists did champion other causes, such as abolition and prohibition.

Questions 54–55

The 1993 Waco Incident was a violent siege launched by American federal agents against a civilian religious group. The Branch Davidians were led by David Koresh and lived in a commune near Waco, Texas. After suspecting Koresh of child molestation and weapons violations, Attorney General Janet Reno organized a full-scale military assault on the compound. Seventy-six people died in the siege, mostly women and children. Public opinion turned sour on Reno after this heavy-handed use of federal power. This incident, along with the Ruby Ridge incident in 1992, fueled antigovernment sentiment in radical conservative militia circles.

54.   **B**   A careful reading of the excerpts can help you to use POE. We have no evidence that the Branch Davidians were "antigovernment," (A). According to the first excerpt, they were employing "defensive" measures in response to perceived threats by the federal government, not "offensive" tactics. This likewise rules out (C). Choice (D) is tempting, but notice that Conyers says the Attorney General "offered" to resign. It does not say that she did. (In fact, she did not.)

55.   **B**   It helps if you remember that the Wounded Knee incident occurred in 1890, a heavy-handed assault by the U.S. Army against the Lakota Indians. Choice (A) is a good trap, but an Indian tribe is not a cult. There was no bombing, so rule out (C), and Wounded Knee was not a recent conflict, so rule out (D).

SECTION I, PART B: SHORT-ANSWER QUESTIONS

Question 1

a) The easiest way to answer this question is to focus on the broad acceptance of slavery within most of the Democratic Party before the Civil War. You may have mentioned some of the following facts:

- The Democrats held the presidency during Polk's administration from 1844 to 1848, and then again during Pierce's and Buchanan's administrations from 1852 to 1860. As a national party, the Democrats tried their hardest to straddle both sides of the slavery issue. Polk's acquisition of new territory, however, heightened tensions on the slavery issue.
- The Democrats considered Pierce a "safe" nominee for president in 1852 because nobody knew who he was. Also, the Democrats hoped that the Compromise of 1850 had laid the slavery issue to rest for a while. In 1856, they chose Buchanan because he had been out of the country on diplomatic service and therefore had not been muddied by the slavery debate.
- By 1860, the party had split, literally. It held two conventions and nominated two candidates, one a Southerner (John C. Breckinridge), the other a Midwesterner (Stephen Douglas). Slavery had torn the party apart, into regional divisions.
- The Wilmot Proviso, authored by Democrat David Wilmot, would have banned slavery in the southwestern territories annexed from Mexico. John C. Calhoun, also a Democrat, fought the Wilmot Proviso strenuously. He argued that the federal government had no right to regulate slavery in the territories; most other Southern politicians soon picked up his argument.
- Antislavery Democrats called pro-slavery Democrats "hunkers," implying that they were so hungry for political power that they would court slave owners. Pro-slavery Democrats called antislavery Democrats "barn burners" because, they said, such folks would burn down the barn in order to kill the rats.

b) This question is asking you to provide a historical event to support Norton's interpretation. You can use one of the points outlined in part (a) as long as you link it to a statement made in Norton's quote. For instance, you can establish that Democrats saw the right to own slaves as a matter of "personal liberty" for those in an "agrarian society." Aside from the issue of slavery, you may also have used one of the following:

- The "Corrupt Bargain" of the Election of 1824 had convinced Jacksonian Democrats that the established government was run by elites who could not be trusted to adhere to the will of the people.
- Jackson, the first Democrat President, exercised the veto more often than all other presidents combined.
- Jackson opposed Reformers on other issues, too, such as the rights of the Cherokee Indians during the Trail of Tears.

c) For this question, you may have used some of the following:

- The Free-Soil Party formed around a single issue—preventing slavery in the territories annexed from Mexico.
- The Compromise of 1850, and particularly its stricter fugitive slave law, helped the party gain support in the North. It attracted antislavery Democrats and "Conscience Whigs."
- The Republican Party eventually absorbed much of the Free-Soil Party. The two parties had virtually identical policies on slavery. Because the Republicans appealed to a wider range of voters, many Free-Soilers felt they could better accomplish their objectives in the larger Republican Party.

Give yourself extra points if you mentioned the following:

- The Free-Soil Party elected nine congressmen in 1848.
- The *Dred Scott* decision killed the Free-Soil Party once and for all by taking away its one issue. Free-Soilers wanted the federal government to regulate slavery; *Dred Scott* ruled that it could not.

Question 2

This is a painting called *The Copley Family* from 1776. The Revolutionary Era was interesting not only because it changed the nation's form of government but also because America was forming its own distinctive style in architecture, clothing styles, and the family.

a) For this question, you may have mentioned some of the following:

- Family life is joyful and idealized in this picture.
- "Republican Motherhood" describes women's roles present in the emerging United States before, during, and after the American Revolution. The belief was that women should uphold the ideals of republicanism, in order to pass on republican values to their children. The "Republican Mother" was considered responsible for upholding the morality of her husband and children.
- The family in this photo is part of the upper class and is surrounded by lavish furnishings.

b) For this question, you may have mentioned some of the following:

- The overall scene is one which depicts family harmony. Three generations sit in close proximity. The younger children climb joyfully over their mother and grandfather. One daughter stares in a serious manner at the viewer, suggesting that she is reserved in the presence of an "outsider."
- In the background is a scene depicting perfect natural beauty, suggesting that the harmony of the family is part of the harmony of the natural world.

- The male members of the family look much like the Founding Fathers, reminding the viewer that the ideals of family life echo the ideals of the new Republic.
- The wealth of the family reminds the viewer of the prosperity of the new American nation.
- The mother in the photo is serene and immersed in the needs of her children, thus embodying the spirit of Republican Motherhood.
- The children are the center of attention in the picture, while the male members of the family are more reserved and take the back chairs. The children are the future of the new Republic.
- The oldest man looks to the side, perhaps representing the past, while the younger father looks at the viewer, perhaps representing the present. The mother looks at her children, representing the future.

c) The most obvious events to focus on here would be either the Revolution or the founding of the new Republic.

- As noted above, the ideal of Republican Motherhood was meant to create children with a strong foundation in the morals and ideals of America. This would be instrumental in the crafting of the Constitution and the unity of the states.
- As for social class, the Revolution was organized by members of the upper class after their bold signing of the Declaration of Independence. The picture reinforces the idea of their nobility.
- It required strong families to settle in the New World, creating communities and state governments from an uncharted wilderness. Fathers and sons fought together in the Revolution, while mothers sacrificed their sons to the cause.

Question 3

Note the dates. The years given are 1800–1824. You know that Jefferson served two terms as president, from 1800–1808, and that he was succeeded by James Madison (1809–1816) and then James Monroe (1817–1824). These three were known as the "Virginia Dynasty," and it was only with the 1824 election of former Federalist John Quincy Adams of Massachusetts that the "Dynasty" ended. So remember that you are not limiting yourself to Jefferson in this essay. You are being asked to address all three presidencies.

a) Your answer to this question may have included some of the following:

- Jeffersonian Democracy stood for a limited central government, states' rights rather than federal rights, strict construction of the Constitution, a devotion to agricultural interests, a restricted military, and support of the Bill of Rights.
- Jefferson was followed by Madison and then Monroe, and they were all Virginian Republicans who shared the same basic ideals.
- During this period, Republicans started to act like Federalists.

Give yourself extra credit for mentioning the following:

- It was common practice for the secretary of state to become president after serving in the previous cabinet. Madison was Jefferson's secretary of state before assuming the presidency, and Monroe was Madison's secretary of state before he became president.
- The election of 1800 was viewed as "The Revolution of 1800" because (a) the Republicans replaced the Federalists in the executive branch, and (b) no blood was shed in this transfer of power from one political party to the other.
- Jefferson stated in his inaugural address: "We are all Republicans, we are all Federalists."

b) Your answer to this question may have included some of the following:

The Louisiana Purchase

- There was no provision in the Constitution for the purchase of the Louisiana Territory, and Jefferson was acting like a "loose constructionist" when he purchased it.
- The Louisiana Purchase doubled the size of this country and was sold to us by France for $15 million.
- Although Jefferson had doubts about whether the United States had the authority to accept the offer, he agreed to it by reasoning that it would benefit the entire country, and it had the support of Congress.
- The Louisiana Purchase provided the country with national unity and boosted the popularity of the Republicans.

Give yourself extra credit for mentioning the following:

- The decline of the Federalists as a result of the Louisiana Purchase

Marbury v. Madison

- The court case of 1803 established the power of Judicial Review.
- John Marshall was the Supreme Court Justice who ruled on this case.
- This case, like the Louisiana Purchase, extended the power of the judiciary, and thus the federal government.

Give yourself extra credit for mentioning the following:

- While the case itself was over a minor issue (the power of the court to force the delivery of a commission), it actually gave the Supreme Court the enormous power of being able to nullify an act of Congress.
- This case was over the "midnight appointments" of John Adams, which the newly elected Jefferson was trying to block.
- Jefferson also tried to block other Federalist judicial measures by supporting the impeachment of Federalist Justice Samuel Chase.

The War of 1812

- The Jeffersonians were acting like Federalists in the expansionist and militaristic venture known as the War of 1812.
- The war called into question the classic Republican commitments to limited federal power and peace.
- The war was conducted during the presidency of James Madison.

Give yourself extra credit for mentioning the following:

- The United States started the fight because it felt the British were violating American neutrality rights at sea and also stirring up trouble on the western frontier.
- The "War Hawks" in Congress were led by Henry Clay of Kentucky and John C. Calhoun of South Carolina, representing the support of the West and South.
- The country was divided on this war, both by region and by political alliances.
- Jefferson's Embargo Act of 1807, which prohibited our trade with foreign nations, harmed the nation's economy and plunged us into a depression.

- The Embargo Act was followed by the Non-Intercourse Act of 1809 and then Macon's Bill No. 2, in 1810. All three acts aimed at settling the violation of neutral shipping rights peacefully.
- Madison, like Jefferson, attempted a combination of economic pressure and diplomacy to deal with Britain, but ultimately brought us into war.
- The New England Federalists were so opposed to "Mr. Madison's War" that they came close to secession at the Hartford Convention of 1814. (You would really make a reader's day if you included this one!)
- Tecumseh, and his brother "The Prophet," of the Shawnee tribe attempted to unite all Indians east of the Mississippi River but were destroyed by General William Henry Harrison at the Battle of Tippecanoe. (What does this say about the Jeffersonian ideal of all men being endowed by their creator with inalienable rights to life, liberty, and the pursuit of happiness?)

The Monroe Doctrine

- The Monroe Doctrine warned European nations not to interfere in the affairs of the Western Hemisphere and also claimed for us the right to intervene anywhere in our own hemisphere if we felt our security was threatened.
- The Monroe Doctrine represented bold nationalism and was applauded by the American public, though its full impact wasn't felt for quite some time, when it was later viewed as the cornerstone of our foreign policy. Nationalism signified quite a shift in Jeffersonian ideals and later took the form of economic growth and expansionism.
- The Monroe Doctrine, although issued under President James Monroe, was written by his secretary of state, John Quincy Adams. During Monroe's presidency, Adams helped to usher in a new wave of westward expansion, which was followed by our recognition of new nations in Central and South America.

Give yourself extra credit for mentioning the following:

- At the time of the Monroe Doctrine, the Republican Party was the only organized force in American politics because the Federalists had ceased running candidates after 1816.
- Even though we proclaimed neutrality in the wars between Spain and its rebellious colonies, we were selling ships and supplies to the insurgents, and when Monroe established diplomatic relations with Latin American countries, we became the first nation to do so.
- The Monroe Doctrine gave us the appearance of isolationism because we had "warned" European nations to stay out of our affairs, but in reality we had merely stated our nationalistic and patriotic fervor of the time.

c) For this question, you may have used some of the points listed under part (b), while focusing on the lack of "seismic shift" inherent in each event.

Here are some examples:

- The Louisiana Purchase was largely noncontroversial and a bargain piece of territory for the amount of land acquired. The territories acquired were not developed until after the age of Jeffersonian democracy had expired.
- *Marbury v. Madison* would not have cumulative effect until well after the time period in question. It set a precedent for greater consolidation of power at the federal level, but did not represent a shift within this time period.
- Since Anti-Federalist Democratic-Republicans prevailed in the War of 1812, it affected Federalists and not the Jeffersonian democrats themselves. It was the outgrowth of their influence, not its instigator.
- The Monroe Doctrine pertained to strictly foreign policy, so would not have represented a strong shift within the party ideals, which were largely concerned with domestic issues.

Question 4

a) and b) This essay gives you an opportunity to discuss the causes of the Progressive movement and its achievements. The following is a list of facts and concepts you might have included in your essay.

- Public disenchantment with business practices—By 1900, many major businesses were controlled by virtual monopolies. Those who controlled the businesses were fabulously wealthy; those who worked for them were impoverished. Businesses had little regard for the welfare of their workers or their customers. The government and judiciary proved to be shamelessly pro-business in their policies and rulings.
- Public horror at city conditions—Business's abuses adversely influenced the state of the cities. Urban dwellers lived under cramped, unsanitary conditions. Often entire families, including children, worked in factories for sub-living wages. City governments were controlled by political machines, who helped their impoverished patrons survive but did nothing for their long-term welfare.
- Growth of the middle class—During this time, the U.S. middle class was growing. With their new-found comfort and respectability, many middle-class Americans wanted to increase their political power. They formed associations such as the lawyers' American Bar Association and the women's National Woman Suffrage Association. The groups served as interest groups that lobbied for progressive reform. Many in the middle class, outraged by the excesses of business and the corruption of government, fought to correct them.
- Progressivism built on the foundation laid by the Populist movement of the 1890s—Populism had fought for moral causes, sought to counter the trend toward monopoly, and worked to widen access to the democratic process. Progressivism picked up these traditions, and so inherited the farmers and clergy who had made up the Populist coalition.
- Journalists helped the spread of Progressivism—With magazine articles and books like Upton Sinclair's *The Jungle*, American "muckrakers" broadened public awareness of corporate excesses.
- Teddy Roosevelt's presidency—Roosevelt used the office of the presidency as a "bully pulpit" to popularize Progressive ideals. During his tenure, he filed numerous antitrust suits against large corporations, tightened food and drug regulations, created national parks, and broadened the government's power to protect land from overdevelopment. Roosevelt took many of the cues from the book *The Promise of American Life* by Herbert Croly. The book argues forcefully for using the power of the central government to effect progressive reform.

Give yourself extra points if you mentioned the following:

- Other Progressive successes broadened the movement's appeal. On the state and local level, many new regulations were enacted, including child labor laws, limits on the lengths of the work day, minimum wage requirements, corrupt-practices acts, and housing codes. Many states adopted the initiative, referendum, and recall, thus empowering voters. Cities improved public transportation, adopted stricter health codes, and converted to a city-manager system. States introduced income taxes to redistribute wealth and provide public services.
- Wisconsin governor Robert La Follette led the way for many Progressive state leaders. He initiated such reforms as direct primaries, equitable tax structures, and the regulation of railways, all later adopted by many other states.
- Taft and Wilson continued the Progressive tradition in the White House. Taft strengthened anti-trust law and expanded conservation efforts. During his term, two Progressive amendments, the national income tax and the direct election of senators, were added to the Constitution. Wilson created the Federal Trade Commission, lobbied for and enforced the Clayton Antitrust Act, and helped create the Federal Reserve, which gave the government greater control over the nation's finances. During his term, the Nineteenth Amendment gave women the right to vote.

c) For this question, you may have mentioned some of the following:

- The many successes of Progressivism actually helped bring about its downfall. Each success satisfied a portion of the Progressive coalition, and once satisfied, these people tended not to work as hard for Progressive goals.
- World War I also split the Progressive coalition. Some supported the war while others opposed it, but the feelings on both sides of the issue were strong. When the war ended, with Americans tired of crusading for justice, the Progressive movement petered out.
- Businesses or those who objected to bigger government involvement in the lives of its citizens would have worked to stop or dismantle the goals of Progressives.
- Republican Presidents of the 1920s, such as Harding and Coolidge, deliberately failed to enforce some of the laws and initiatives passed by Progressives, thus undermining their agenda.

SECTION II, QUESTION 1: THE DOCUMENT-BASED QUESTION

The document-based question begins with a mandatory 15-minute reading period. During these 15 minutes, you should (1) come up with some information not included in the given documents (your outside knowledge) to include in your essay, (2) get an overview of what each document means, (3) decide what opinion you are going to argue, and (4) write an outline of your essay.

The first thing you will be inclined to do, after reading the question, is to look at the documents. Resist temptation. Instead, the first thing you should do is brainstorm for several minutes about what the question is asking of you. Try to list everything you remember about the causes of the Civil War. This list will serve as your reference to the outside information you must provide in order to earn a top grade.

Then, and only then, read over the documents. As you read them, take notes in the margins and underline those passages that you are certain you are going to refer to in your essay. If a document helps you remember a piece of outside information, add that information to your brainstorming list. If you cannot make sense of a document, don't worry. You may omit mention of <u>one</u> of the documents and still score well on the DBQ.

Here is what you need to look for in each document to get the most out of it:

- The author
- The date
- The audience (for whom was the document intended?)
- The significance

Remember: You are being asked to write 50 percent document interpretation and 50 percent outside information. Don't get so lost in the documents that you forget to bring in outside information. Readers will not be able to give you a high score unless you have both! What readers really don't like is a laundry list of documents: that is, a paper in which the student merely goes through the documents, explaining each one. Those students are often the ones who forget to bring in outside information, because they are so focused on going through the documents.

So, what is this DBQ all about?

This DBQ asks you two things: (1) to what extent was the Civil War caused by slavery and to what extent was it caused by other factors, and (2) what circumstances led to the breakup of the Union? In the first part, you are actually being asked to identify factors *other than slavery* that caused the breakup of the Union, although you aren't being asked to rule out slavery as a cause. Your job is to decide how much of the Civil War was caused by slavery and how much was caused by other factors. In those other factors, you might find ideas that will help you answer the second part.

Note that the question asks, "to what extent." That means you are being asked to rank the causes of the Civil War. You might state that slavery was the leading cause, but there were other causes. You might state that slavery was only one of several equally important causes leading up to the war. You might state that all the other causes had slavery at the root, or you might state that too much weight has been given to slavery as the single cause of the war. There is no right answer. You could earn a top score by writing about how slavery was only a fraction of the issue, and the student sitting across the room from you could also earn a top score by stating that slavery was the only issue!

The Documents

Document 1 is the article from which the famous phrase "Manifest Destiny" was taken. O'Sullivan states that it is the American destiny, ordained by God, to populate the country from coast to coast, in order to provide "for the free development of our yearly multiplying millions." The use of the word "free" should not be overlooked, and the idea that we should challenge any foreign power who attempts to "thwart our policy," "hamper our power," or "limit our greatness" also needs to be addressed. As stated earlier, the Mexican War and cession, which rested upon Manifest Destiny, should not be overlooked in any discussion about the Civil War.

Document 2: This declaration of war against Mexico links that war with the war that followed (like we saw in Document 1). Note the use of the words "honor, rights and dignity of this country." Clearly, in Polk's opinion, it was our right and responsibility to thwart Mexico in territorial expansion, but these words also sound like abolitionist words, so the issue of slavery also fits in well here. An astute student might also relate this document to the "spot" resolutions, in which Congressman Abraham Lincoln asked President James K. Polk to identify the exact "spot" where "American blood had been shed on American soil."

Document 3 is taken from Pennsylvania Representative David Wilmot's proposal before Congress. The Wilmot Proviso proposed that Congress award President Polk the $2 million he asked for while the United States was fighting the Mexican War, and in return that any land we wrested from Mexico remain free from slavery. If you were going to argue that U.S. territorial expansion, or the Mexican War, was a major factor in the breakup of the Union, you would certainly want to use this document to support your thesis. The Wilmot Proviso passed the House twice but was defeated in the Senate. Clearly, the argument over the acquisition of vast western lands added to the sectional debate over the extension of slavery. If you were going to argue that slavery was the most significant reason for the breakup of the Union, you could still use this document in that context. If it weren't for the issue of slavery, the issue of what to do with the Mexican cession wouldn't have been so heated.

Document 4, which shows the territorial changes of the Compromise of 1850, can be used in a multitude of ways. First, it speaks to the issue of what efforts were made to keep the Union together. Second, it displays the precarious state of the Union, with free and slave states vying for power. Third, it covers the issue of popular sovereignty in the Utah and New Mexico territories. Lastly, it shows California entering the Union as a free state. An astute student would also want to point out the aspects of the compromise that the map does not show: namely, that it was crafted by Mr. Compromise himself, Henry Clay, and that, in addition to territorial matters, it endorsed a tougher Fugitive Slave Law to pacify the South. It should be pointed out that the compromise bought time for the nation, and that while it was far from perfect, it held up the Union for another 11 shaky years. Another way this document could be used would be if your thesis includes the failure of the era's compromises, and/or ineffectual or misguided politicians.

Document 5: This well-known, unfortunate Supreme Court case turned a man into property. Dred Scott, a slave in Missouri, was taken to the free state of Illinois and then to the free territory of Wisconsin, where he lived for several years before returning to Missouri. Once he returned to Missouri, he sued for his freedom, arguing that his period of residence on free soil made him a free citizen. After he lost in the Missouri Court, he appealed to the Supreme Court, where Southern Democrat Chief Justice Roger Taney ruled against Scott. Abolitionists felt that he should be free under the Missouri Compromise, because Scott had lived in free land, above the 36°30′ line. If he lost his freedom once he returned, then didn't that nullify the Missouri Compromise? This document is filled with goodies. The slavery issue is front and center, as is the issue of political endeavor, whether successful or not. If you are arguing that slavery was at the center of our disunion, clearly the Supreme Court decision illustrates that fact. If you are arguing that the political climate, leaders, laws, court cases, and resolutions were behind the breakup of the union, this document serves you well, too.

Document 6 illustrates the differences between the North and South in terms of industrial development. In the 1850s, there was an explosion of new railroad construction, most of which was concentrated in the North. The many miles of track that existed in the North highlight the economic struggle that took place between the agricultural South and the industrial North. In Charles and Mary Beard's interpretation of what caused the Civil War, they argue that the war was not fought over slavery per se, but that it represented a deeply rooted economic struggle, akin to the American Revolution, that brought about major changes in class relations and power. The North wielded its industrial might over the less-advanced agrarian South, with the effect of destroying the cotton economy and plantation system.

Document 7: This cartoon shows the Democratic Party headed for disaster in the election of 1860. The party is not only split internally, represented by the politicians in the cart headed in different directions, but also about to be rammed by the oncoming train of the Republican Party (note that a train is a much more modern form of transportation!). The Democrats, splintered into two, offered the presidential candidacies of both Stephen Douglas, who had the support of the North, and John Breckinridge (President James Buchanan's vice president) of Kentucky, who had the support of the South. The Republicans ran Abraham Lincoln, and the Constitutional Union Party ran John Bell of Tennessee. The election of Lincoln sealed the fate of the Union. Because he would not compromise on the issue of slavery in the territories, and perhaps because he underestimated the secession movement of the South, the Union fell apart. This document can be used to illustrate the political breakdown leading to the war, and it could also be used to demonstrate the power of the slavery issue.

Outside Information

We have already discussed much more than you could possibly include in a 45-minute essay. Do not worry. You will not be expected to mention everything or even most of what we have covered in the section above. You will, however, be expected to include some outside information—that is, information not mentioned directly in the documents.

Here is some outside information you might have used in your essay. The information is divided into two groups: general concepts and specific events.

General Concepts

- One thing to keep in mind when looking toward the catalyst that began the Civil War is the settling of new territory. Think about the conflicts caused by whether or not new territory is to become free land or allow slavery.

- With old parties fracturing, new parties began to emerge. The redrawing of the political lines created a new way of looking at the parties' electoral strongholds.
- An age-old argument over the causes of the Civil War involves the claim of "states rights." This claim views slavery as a symptom of a larger critique of federal overreach, if not an outright rejection of federalism. It should be noted that this idea was popularized in the 20th century during the emergence of the "Lost Cause" defense of the Confederacy.
- The economic disparity between the rapidly industrializing North and the agrarian South was the source of consternation. In the early years of the republic, both sides had a dependence on one another. With the emergence of new technologies, the North was able to thrive with less dependence on the South.
- On a related note, cultural differences between the two sides, no doubt related to economics, but also religion and social norms, in many ways, created two de facto separate nations.

Specific Events

- The acquisition of new territory following the Mexican-American War led to consternation over which states would be free and which would allow slavery. The Compromise of 1850 was put forth by Henry Clay and Stephen Douglas to try to appease both sides: the Fugitive Slave Act would be strengthened, but California would enter the union as a free state and Utah would be a free territory. Further, the slave trade in Washington, D.C. (though not slavery) was banned. The Compromise of 1850, passed as smaller bills, shows us that the slavery issue was not close to being resolved by the middle of the 19th century.
- The Whigs split into two parties over the slavery issue, the Democrats became even more dominant in the South, and the new Free-Soil Party emerged to stop the spread of slavery—though the aims of this latter group were selfish, as white settlers did not want to compete with slave labor.
- The Kansas-Nebraska Act, which repealed the Missouri Compromise, allowing slavery to be left up to the residents of the two territories erupted into violence in a series of events that led the territory to be known as Bleeding Kansas.
- John Brown's raids in both Kansas and Harper's Ferry led him to be seen as a martyr to the cause of abolition.
- The Election of 1860 saw the Democrats split along geographical lines, as well as Southern states begin a process of secession with the election of Republican Abraham Lincoln.
- Fort Sumter
- During the war, border states (Delaware, Maryland, Kentucky, Missouri) were slave states that nonetheless fought for the Union. This is the kind of thing that makes you wonder whether the war went deeper than the slavery issue.

Choosing a Side

The first thing you want to do is to decide what kind of a statement you are going to make. You have already brainstormed all your outside information, made some notes or a quick outline, and decided where to plug in the documents. Because there is no right way to answer this, and many ways to make your argument, here are some positions you might want to argue.

- Slavery was an issue in the breakup of the Union, but it wasn't the only one. There were other equally important factors, such as

    1) the differences in regional lifestyles, with the North being more industrial and the South being more agricultural
    2) the erosion of the traditional party system, including the splintering of the Democratic and Whig parties, which paved the way for the Republican Party

3) a generation of blundering political leaders, from Polk to Buchanan

4) the passions of a few zealous reformers

5) the effect of the Mexican War and the popular sovereignty crisis that ensued over the territories

- Slavery was the underlying issue from which all other issues flowed. If it hadn't been for slavery, the issue of territorial expansion, political alignments, and differences in economies wouldn't have been enough to rip the Union apart.

- Politics tore the country apart. The laws and compromises made by a well-intentioned government backfired on the nation. If it hadn't been for the Missouri Compromise, the Compromise of 1850, and the Kansas-Nebraska Act, the North and South may have stayed united, accepting their differences.

- The Civil War was caused by the idea of Manifest Destiny, the belief that it was the nation's God-given right to expand across the continent, gobbling up all available land. If Americans hadn't held these beliefs, the issue of slavery may not have extended to such a widespread area.

Planning Your Essay

Unless you read extremely quickly, you probably won't have time to write a detailed outline for your essay during the 15-minute reading period. However, it is worth taking several minutes to jot down a loose structure of your essay, because it will actually save you time when you write. First, decide on your thesis and write it down in the test booklet. Then take a few minutes to brainstorm all the points you might put in your essay. Choose the strongest points and number them in the order you plan to present them. Lastly, note which documents and outside information you plan to use in conjunction with each point. If you organize before you write, the actual writing process will go much more smoothly. More important, you will not write yourself into a corner, and suddenly find yourself making a point you cannot support or heading toward a weak conclusion (or worse still, no conclusion at all).

What You Should Have Discussed

Regardless of which thesis you choose, your essay should discuss all of the following:

- the issue of slavery
- the Mexican War and cession
- the *Dred Scott* decision
- the Northern industrial economy versus the Southern agricultural one
- the issue of popular sovereignty in the territories
- the Compromises of 1820 and 1850
- abolitionists
- the Kansas-Nebraska Act

Give yourself very high marks for outside knowledge if you mention any five of the following:

- the Lincoln-Douglas debates
- the Freeport Doctrine
- John Brown
- "Bleeding Kansas"
- the Fugitive Slave Act
- personal liberty laws
- Harriet Beecher Stowe's *Uncle Tom's Cabin*

- the Republican Party
- Whigs
- Free-Soilers
- spot resolution
- the Tallmadge Amendment
- William Lloyd Garrison's *The Liberator*
- the Brooks-Sumner affair
- the Gadsden Purchase

Give yourself a pat on the back if you mention any of the following:

- the Ostend Manifesto
- Hinton Helper's *Impending Crisis of the South*
- the Know-Nothing Party
- the Lecompton Constitution
- the Crittenden Compromise
- Conscience Whigs
- Cotton Whigs
- "Barn burners"
- Henry Clay
- Franklin Pierce
- James K. Polk
- James Buchanan
- Millard Fillmore
- Lewis Cass
- Roger Taney
- John C. Calhoun

SECTION II: THE LONG ESSAY QUESTION

Question 2

The first Great Awakening lasted for only a couple decades, but went on to influence the way many Americans, both the faithful and the skeptical, see religion. The period of the 1730s and 1740s saw a religious revival that was influenced by a variety of factors, but perhaps most strikingly, the Enlightenment. European ideals of rationalism and scientific inquiry had begun to take hold in the colonies to the chagrin of those who saw the world through a more spiritual lens. After a period of waning religiosity in much of the colonies, the Great Awakening was spurred by those turning toward an emotional religious experience, in sharp contrast to the Enlightenment thinkers of the day. It is no accident that a similar movement took place concurrently in Europe.

The part of the prompt that asks about an American identity can seem somewhat vague—use this to your advantage. How do you see the American relationship with religion? Tie this inseparable part of the American identity to that brief period in the 18th century.

Important facts to mention about the Great Awakening:

- While some of the earliest settlers of the American colonies were quite religious (the Puritans come to mind), subsequent generations were less so. In this regard, the Great Awakening was seen as necessary by many religious leaders.
- The gatherings, or revivals, had their earliest occurrences in New England in the 1710s.
- Jonathan Edwards's harsh brand of Calvinism ("Sinners in the Hands of an Angry God," anyone?) gained traction during this period.
- George Whitefield, rejecting the Enlightenment trends of his native England, popularized the connection between Christianity and emotionalism in the American colonies.
- While the Great Awakening radically transformed Christianity in the United States, denominations such as Catholics, Quakers, and Lutherans were largely unaffected.

Give yourself extra points for mentioning the following:

- The Great Awakening was transdenominational: it crossed over the various Protestant denominations to create an evangelical Christianity.
- John Wesley helped create Methodism and gained traction with his charismatic, outdoor preaching. His insistence on repentance was in stark contrast to the predestination theology of Edwards.
- Many of the framers of the United States (Thomas Jefferson, John Quincy Adams, Benjamin Franklin, Thomas Paine) held a religious belief—deism—that was in stark contrast to the emotional fervor of evangelism.

Ways the Great Awakening impacted the American identity:

- Subsequent awakenings followed throughout the 19th and 20th centuries, evidence of a consistent presence of this brand of Christianity in American culture.
- The Evangelical movement grew and remained a permanent part of American identity, impacting voting blocs up to the present day.
- The Great Awakening created a common identity for Christians in the United States.
- Culture wars that have recurred throughout United States history (slavery, Scopes trial, civil rights, abortion, and same-sex marriage, to name a few) are underpinned by evangelical thought.

Give yourself extra points for mentioning the following:

- The appeal to the law of God, rather than on political authority, inspired radical uprisings, including the American Revolution. Jefferson, though a deist, nonetheless referenced the colonists' authority to rebel as given by the "Supreme Judge of the World."
- Many evangelicals (particularly Methodists) held abolitionist views informed by their religious convictions. Conversely, many evangelicals also used their faith to justify the institution of slavery. This same dichotomy existed during the civil rights movement of the 20th century.

About the Structure of Your Essay

Begin the essay with some background information to introduce the Great Awakening. Make sure you mention your definition of "American identity" for the purposes of this essay, and include a claim that clearly articulates the impact that this time period had on the American identity. To fully develop your analysis, you want to make sure your body paragraphs connect the people and events from the Great Awakening to a more long-term legacy. You want to show your grader that you understand events from this early period of American history and can see how they affect the country for years to come.

Question 3

This is a nice prompt to work with because you can easily support or refute the prompt by using many of the same examples. Either you can argue that farmers and factory workers DID adapt by pushing for certain changes OR you can simply argue that the solutions farmers and factory workers sought did not come easily; therefore, they did not adapt effectively. Many of these key points can be used for either side of the issue, therefore a good candidate for the "modify" approach. The "modify" approach will allow you to adjust the prompt in your own words to argue a third possible stance, which can pull evidence from both sides of the issue and offer a more nuanced argument.

Farmers

- Thanks to the Homestead Act and the Transcontinental Railroad, Eastern farmers were able to move their cash-crop farming westward. On the flip-side, the Homestead Act attracted so many new farmers that there was a gradual loss of land available for homesteading.
- Farmers started to view agriculture more as a business than as a way of life. Transportation and marketing made farming more lucrative.
- Many farmers readily adopted mechanization to improve overall productivity. On the downside, much of this machinery was bought on credit. (Cue the Grangers and the Populists.)
- Founded in 1867 as a social organization, the Grange established cooperatively owned stores, grain elevators, and warehouses for farming members. Grangers also experimented with cooperative marketing of farm products and cooperative purchasing of seed, fertilizer, machinery, and other commodities.
- Farmers generally supported the Interstate Commerce Act of 1887, which cleaned up some of the corruption in the railroad industry.
- *Munn v. Illinois* likewise regulated railroads as utilities.
- Populists demanded a silver-standard currency in order to increase the amount of money in circulation and prevent deflation. Later, Populists appealed to urban factory workers. Populists "spoke truth to power" by challenging the established two-party system.

Industrial Workers

- The big point here would be labor unions: National Labor Union (1866), Knights of Labor (1869), American Federation of Labor (1886)
- Famous strikes: Molly McGuires (1876), Great Railroad Strike (1877), Haymarket Riot (1886), Homestead (1892), Pullman Strike (1894)
- Children were sent to work in mills and factories to increase family income (an adaptation, though an unfortunate one).
- In the later years of this period, single women entered the paid labor force in increasing numbers, also an adaptation.
- Pullman Strike—a nationwide railroad strike in the United States in the summer of 1894

About the Structure of Your Essay

Whether you decide to support, refute, or modify, start with a broad overview of the Industrial Revolution. Then choose three examples to focus on in more depth. It's okay—in fact, very good— to make brief references to lots of names, dates, and events, but be sure to provide analysis, not just factual data.

Question 4

This essay asks you to delve into U.S. foreign policy in the post–World War I period. You will need to be clear on what our foreign policy was, and then select two or three main examples to explain what influenced our policy. The first thing you need to do in this essay is explain our foreign policy during the 1920s. Contrary to common belief, the United States was not entirely isolationist at that time, although we did refuse to join the League of Nations. Yes, we were fearful of being pulled into another world war, but we did make arrangements with other nations that would advance our interests while also aiming for peace.

Social Issues

- The Red Scare—This was the time of the Palmer raids, rising nativism, a resurgence of the Klan, anti-unionism, and restrictive immigration laws.
- Fundamentalism—You should include the Scopes Monkey Trial and the Prohibition movement, and, of course, Harding's "return to normalcy" pledge, which kicked off the decade.
- Cultural modernism, including women getting the right to vote, a loosening of morals, and the Lindbergh flight
- In terms of the economy, you would have to mention the boom years (1922–1928), which were followed by the stock market crash and the Depression. You should also mention the concepts of consumerism and materialism.
- Because this essay asks you to concentrate on U.S. foreign policy, you need to be sure to connect all these aspects of the social climate with the views toward international involvement. The prevalence of xenophobia during this time obviously influenced the will to involve the United States in the affairs of other countries. The United States was, however, willing to deal with other countries for economic gain, rather than for political or social reasons.

Give yourself extra points for mentioning the following:

- Attorney General A. Mitchell Palmer's raids on suspected radicals, his assistant J. Edgar Hoover, the bombs that went off in the spring of 1919, and the anti-union and antistrike activities of the U.S. government during Palmer's tenure
- The attack on IWW members, the attack on "radical" newspapers and literature, the "100 Percent Americanism" movement, the rise in Klan membership and lynching, the stand taken against feminist demands, and the general xenophobia that gripped the nation
- The trial and execution of two radical immigrants, Sacco and Vanzetti; the Emergency Quota Act of 1921; and the Johnson-Reed Immigration Act of 1924
- Henry Ford and the automobile, leisure-time activities, sports, movies, the "Jazz Age," and any other subjects

Economic Issues

- Before World War I, the United States had been a debtor nation, and after the war it emerged as a creditor nation, having lent over $10 billion to the Allies.
- Under the Treaty of Versailles, Germany was required to pay $30 billion in reparations to the Allies, but was bankrupt and couldn't pay.
- The Dawes Plan of 1924 established a flow of payments from the United States to Germany and from Germany to the Allies.
- Tariff walls resulted in international and domestic economic distress.

Give yourself extra points for mentioning the following:

- The Fordney-McCumber Tariff of 1922 created a high tariff barrier around the United States and resulted in economic dislocation here and abroad.
- Charles Dawes, an American banker, became Coolidge's vice president and was the mastermind behind the Dawes plan. He also won the Nobel Peace Prize for his efforts, even though the plan didn't solve the international economic crisis.
- The United States was not only lending money overseas, but also investing in European industry and in Latin American ventures as well.

Political Ideology

- The three Republican presidents of the 1920s—Harding (1921–1923), Coolidge (1923–1929), and Hoover (1929–1933)—all had pro-business views.
- The Washington Conference of 1921 aimed to promote peace, cut military spending, and endorse world disarmament.
- The Kellogg-Briand Pact renounced war as an instrument of national policy.
- The Republican Congress refused to permit the United States to join the League of Nations and sign the Treaty of Versailles.

Give yourself extra points for mentioning the following:

- The Nine-Power Treaty, the Five-Power Treaty, and the Four-Power Treaty resulted from the Washington Conference and dealt with issues of territorial integrity and disarmament.
- The Harding scandals and his unexpected death in 1923
- Harding's appointments of Hoover as secretary of commerce and Mellon as secretary of the treasury
- Coolidge's attitude toward the economy ("The business of America is business") and his belief in limited government
- Coolidge's refusal to pay World War I veterans their bonuses early
- Coolidge's veto of the McNary-Haugen Bill of 1928 to help farmers
- Hoover's work during World War I as head of the Food Administration and his campaign against Al Smith of New York in 1928
- Hoover's suggestion that poverty was eliminated and his belief in self-help
- The influence of Henry Cabot Lodge, chairman of the Senate Foreign Relations Committee, on U.S. foreign policy

About the Structure of Your Essay

You would have to begin with an explanation of U.S. foreign policy during the 1920s and follow with a discussion of what influenced this policy. Your essay would then include an analysis of the social, economic, and political pressures of the postwar period, focusing on the two or three main points about which you know the most. In sum, your essay would outline the varying forces that defined our international relations in the 1920s.

Practice Test 4

AP® United States History Exam

SECTION I, PART A: Multiple Choice

DO NOT OPEN THIS BOOKLET UNTIL YOU ARE TOLD TO DO SO.

At a Glance

Time
55 minutes
Number of Questions
55
Percent of Total Score
40%
Writing Instrument
Pencil required

Instructions

Section I, Part A of this exam contains 55 multiple-choice questions. Fill in only the ovals for numbers 1 through 55 on your answer sheet. Because this section offers only four answer options for each question, do not mark the (E) answer circle for any question.

Indicate all of your answers to the multiple-choice questions on the answer sheet. No credit will be given for anything written in this exam booklet, but you may use the booklet for notes or scratch work. After you have decided which of the suggested answers is best, completely fill in the corresponding oval on the answer sheet. Give only one answer to each question. If you change an answer, be sure that the previous mark is erased completely. Here is a sample question and answer.

Sample Question

The first president of the United States was
(A) Millard Fillmore
(B) George Washington
(C) Benjamin Franklin
(D) Andrew Jackson

Sample Answer

Ⓐ ● Ⓒ Ⓓ

Use your time effectively, working as rapidly as you can without losing accuracy. Do not spend too much time on any one question. Go on to other questions and come back to the ones you have not answered if you have time. It is not expected that everyone will know the answers to all of the multiple-choice questions.

Your total score on the multiple-choice section is based only on the number of questions answered correctly. Points are not deducted for incorrect answers or unanswered questions.

SECTION I, PART B: Short Answer

At a Glance

Time
40 minutes
Number of Questions
3
Percent of Total Score
20%
Writing Instrument
Pen with black or dark blue ink
Questions 1 and 2
Mandatory
Question 3 or 4
Choose one question

Instructions

For Section I, Part B of this exam, answer Question 1 and Question 2 and **either** Question 3 **or** Question 4. Write your responses in the Section I, Part B: Short-Answer Response booklet. You must write your response to each question on the lined page designated for that response. Each response is expected to fit within its designated page. Fill in the circle on the Section I, Part B: Short-Answer Response booklet indicating whether you answered Question 3 or Question 4. Failure to do so may delay your score.

GO ON TO THE NEXT PAGE.

UNITED STATES HISTORY
SECTION I, Part A
Time—55 minutes
55 Questions

Directions: Each of the questions or incomplete statements below is followed by four suggested answers or completions. Select the one that is best in each case and then blacken the corresponding space on the answer sheet.

Questions 1–3 refer to the excerpt below.

"From the large body of poor drifters, many of them diseased, feckless, or given to crime, came a great part of the labor supply of the rich sugar islands and the American mainland. From the London of Pepys and then of Hogarth, as well as from many lesser ports and inland towns, the English poor, lured, seduced, or forced into the emigrant stream, kept coming to America for the better part of two centuries. It is safe to guess that few of them, and indeed few persons from the other sources of emigration, knew very much about what they were doing when they committed themselves to life in America."

Richard Hofstadter, historian, *America at 1750: A Social Portrait,* 1971

1. The people described in the above quote were most likely

   (A) slaves
   (B) indentured servants
   (C) inmates in a penal colony
   (D) fugitives seeking religious freedom

2. The need for labor on the American mainland in 1750 was most directly the result of

   (A) the cultivation of tobacco
   (B) expansion of Northern manufacturing
   (C) the invention of the cotton gin
   (D) the decline of slavery after Bacon's Rebellion

3. The people described in the quote above most likely emigrated to

   (A) Northern New England
   (B) New Amsterdam
   (C) The Chesapeake
   (D) St. Augustine

GO ON TO THE NEXT PAGE.

Questions 4–6 refer to the excerpt below.

"I think the authors of that notable instrument intended to include all men, but they did not mean to declare all men equal in all respects. They did not mean to say all men were equal in color, size, intellect, moral development, or social capacity. They defined with tolerable distinctness in what they did consider all men created equal—equal in 'certain inalienable rights, among which are life, liberty, and the pursuit of happiness.' This they said, and this they meant. They did not mean to assert the obvious untruth that all were then actually enjoying that equality, or yet that they were about to confer it immediately upon them. In fact, they had no power to confer such a boon. They meant simply to declare the right, so that the enforcement of it might follow as fast as circumstances should permit."

Abraham Lincoln, October 15, 1858

4. The excerpt directly quotes which of the following historical documents?

   (A) The Magna Carta
   (B) The Declaration of the Rights of Man
   (C) The Declaration of Independence
   (D) The U.S. Constitution

5. At that time of Lincoln's speech, the ideas expressed in the excerpt would have been directly opposed by

   (A) Daniel Webster
   (B) Stephen Douglas
   (C) William Lloyd Garrison
   (D) Andrew Johnson

6. The excerpt best reflects which of the following?

   (A) Disagreement over the application of the phrase "all men are created equal" to people of certain racial groups
   (B) Fear that the United States would be split by a civil war
   (C) Conflicts over how slavery could be contained to the Southern states
   (D) Beliefs that the secession of South Carolina was imminent

GO ON TO THE NEXT PAGE.

Questions 7–10 refer to the excerpts below.

"The United States hereby agrees and stipulates that the country north of the North Platte river and east of the summits of the Big Horn mountains [in South Dakota] shall be held and considered to be un-ceded Indian territory, and also stipulates and agrees that no white person or persons shall be permitted to settle upon or occupy any portion of the same; or without the consent of the Indians, first had and obtained, to pass through the same."

Treaty of Fort Laramie Article XVI, 1868

"[General George A.] Custer's journey began at Fort Abraham Lincoln on the Missouri River on July 2, 1874. By the end of that month they had reached the Black Hills [of South Dakota], and by mid-August had confirmed the presence of gold fields in that region. The discovery of gold was widely reported in newspapers across the country. Custer's florid descriptions of the mineral and timber resources of the Black Hills, and the land's suitability for grazing and cultivation…received wide circulation, and had the effect of creating an intense popular demand for the 'opening' of the Hills for settlement."

United States v. Sioux Nation of Indians, 1980

7. Based on the wording of the Treaty of Fort Laramie, white settlement of the Black Hills in the 1870s

   (A) was a violation of the terms of the treaty
   (B) was justified, since gold prospecting was not mentioned in the treaty
   (C) was a threat to Indian interests in the region, though not illegal
   (D) was beneficial to the economic interests of both Indian tribes and white settlers in the region

8. Which of the following generalizations can be correctly inferred from the above excerpts?

   (A) Treaties such as Fort Laramie successfully controlled the incursion of white settlers into Sioux Indian territories in the years following the Civil War.
   (B) Treaties between the U.S. government and American Indians after the Civil War generally encouraged the formation of strong, independent tribes.
   (C) Treaties such as Fort Laramie were often short-lived, leading to future conflict between the U.S. government and the affected Indian tribes.
   (D) The Treaty of Fort Laramie was in place for over one hundred years until the U.S. Supreme Court finally ruled it unconstitutional.

9. Article 16 of the treaty most likely reflected which of the following sentiments?

   (A) A desire by many American Indians to peacefully share land with white settlers
   (B) A desire by many in the U.S. government to peacefully share land with native Indian tribes
   (C) A desire by many American Indians to legally establish claim to their native lands
   (D) A desire by many American Indians to forever ban white trespass onto their native lands

10. The 1980 decision in *United States v. Sioux Nation of Indians* most likely stated that

   (A) the seizure of land for gold prospecting in the 1870s was a violation of the Treaty of Fort Laramie
   (B) Custer's seizure of land for gold prospecting was justified under the Fourth Amendment to the U.S. Constitution
   (C) the Sioux Nation had failed to establish its claim to the Black Hills region and had thus no rights to compensation for any prior seizures of land
   (D) the 1868 Treaty of Fort Laramie made no provision for the undisturbed use of land by the Sioux Nation

GO ON TO THE NEXT PAGE.

Questions 11–14 refer to the table below.

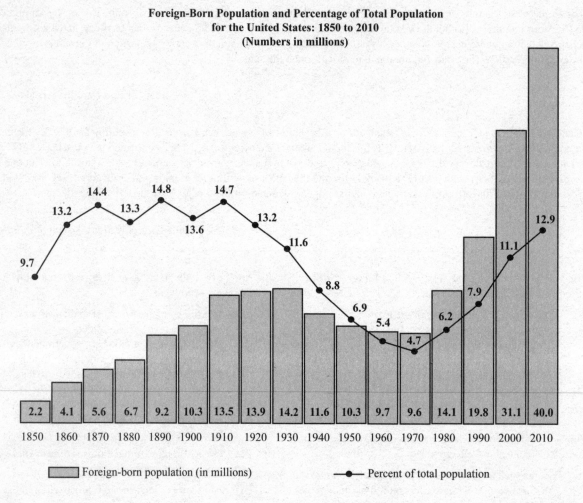

**Foreign-Born Population and Percentage of Total Population
for the United States: 1850 to 2010
(Numbers in millions)**

Source: U.S. Census Bureau

11. Which of the following most directly contributed to the overall trend depicted in the table?

 (A) Worldwide economic and banking crises
 (B) The progressive industrialization of the United States after the Civil War
 (C) The rise of the Populist Party
 (D) A rise in refugees following major wars in Europe and Asia

12. According to the table, the total foreign-born population was dramatically lower in 1970. This is most likely due in part to

 (A) a decline in the need for agricultural labor
 (B) the internment of Japanese Americans during World War II
 (C) immigration acts passed in the 1920s which limited the number of immigrants from certain countries
 (D) the Chinese Exclusion Act of 1882

GO ON TO THE NEXT PAGE.

13. Nativist sentiment in the time periods depicted in the table manifested in all of the following ways EXCEPT

    (A) establishment of settlement houses
    (B) mandatory literacy tests
    (C) the rise of the eugenics movement
    (D) increased membership in the Ku Klux Klan

14. The majority of immigrants who arrived in the United States between 1960 and 1990 settled in the

    (A) Northwest
    (B) Midwest
    (C) South
    (D) Southwest

GO ON TO THE NEXT PAGE.

Questions 15–17 refer to the excerpt below.

"Under free trade the trader is the master and the producer the slave. Protection is but the law of nature, the law of self-preservation, of self-development, of securing the highest and best destiny of the race of man. [It is said] that protection is immoral.... Why, if protection builds up and elevates 63,000,000 [the U.S. population] of people, the influence of those 63,000,000 of people elevates the rest of the world. We cannot take a step in the pathway of progress without benefitting mankind everywhere. Well, they say, 'Buy where you can buy the cheapest'.... Of course, that applies to labor as to everything else. Let me give you a maxim that is a thousand times better than that, and it is the protection maxim: 'Buy where you can pay the easiest.' And that spot of earth is where labor wins its highest rewards."

President William McKinley, 1892

15. Protectionism, as defined by McKinley's quote, is

    (A) opposed to free trade
    (B) supportive of free trade
    (C) designed to lower prices on consumer goods
    (D) harmful to organized labor unions

16. Which political party would have opposed McKinley's argument in this excerpt?

    (A) Republicans
    (B) Democrats
    (C) Know-Nothings
    (D) Whigs

17. In order to achieve his goals, President McKinley would be most likely to support

    (A) raising tariffs on imported goods
    (B) raising taxes on American corporations
    (C) raising prices on retail goods
    (D) lowering tariffs on imported goods

GO ON TO THE NEXT PAGE.

Questions 18 –20 refer to the excerpt below.

"At the end of its war for independence, the United States comprised thirteen separate provinces on the coast of North America. Nearly all of 3.9 million people made their living through agriculture while a small merchant class traded tobacco, timber, and foodstuffs for tropical goods, useful manufactures, and luxuries in the Atlantic community. By the time of the civil war, eight decades later, the United States sprawled across the North American continent. Nearly 32 million people labored not just on farms, but in shops and factories making iron and steel products, boots and shoes, textiles, paper, packaged foodstuffs, firearms, farm machinery, furniture, tools, and all sorts of housewares. Civil War–era Americans borrowed money from banks; bought insurance against fire, theft, shipwreck, commercial losses, and even premature death; traveled on steamboats and in railway carriages; and produced 2 to 3 billion of goods and services, including exports of 400 million. This dramatic transformation is what some historians of the U.S. call the market revolution."

John Lauritz Larson, historian, *The Market Revolution in America,* 2009

18. Before the Civil War, which of the following resulted most directly from the trends described in the excerpt?

    (A) A decline in sectional tensions between the North and South
    (B) A strengthening of traditional gender roles
    (C) Greater equality among wealthy and poorer classes
    (D) An increased need for slavery in the South

19. In what other time period did the United States see similar economic growth?

    (A) The Revolutionary War era
    (B) The Gilded Age
    (C) The Progressive Era
    (D) The Great Depression

20. Which of the following contributed most directly to the Market Revolution?

    (A) Improvements in transportation
    (B) Increased immigration
    (C) The rise of the abolition movement
    (D) An increase in federal tariffs on imported goods

GO ON TO THE NEXT PAGE.

Questions 21–23 refer to the excerpt below.

"Real obstructions of the law, giving real aid and comfort to the enemy, I should have been glad to see punished more summarily and severely than they sometimes were. But I think that our intention to put out all our powers in aid of success in war should not hurry us into intolerance of opinions and speech that could not be imagined to do harm, although opposed to our own. It is better for those who have unquestioned and almost unlimited power in their hands to err on the side of freedom."

Supreme Court Justice Oliver Wendell Holmes, dissenting opinion in *Baltzer v. United States,* 1919

21. Ideas which correlate with the sentiments of Justice Holmes in the excerpt quoted above are mostly found in

(A) the Declaration of Independence
(B) the First Amendment to the U.S. Constitution
(C) the Federalist Papers
(D) the Civil Rights Act of 1964

22. Justice Holmes's statement in the excerpt was most likely a reaction to

(A) the Wilson Administration's prosecution of antiwar protestors during World War I
(B) the Great Migration of African Americans from the South to the North
(C) the successes of the women's suffrage movement
(D) nativism after World War I

23. Which of the following actions is most directly opposed to the values expressed in the excerpt?

(A) Efforts to detect communists in the federal government during the 1950s
(B) Antiwar protests during the early 1970s
(C) Nuclear disarmament treaties during the 1980s
(D) Military interventions in the Middle East after September 2001

Questions 24 and 25 refer to the excerpt below.

"Actual or potential resistance was a main factor in the development of Britain's southern strategy. Influenced in part by slaves' combative and aggressive behavior, British military leaders and Crown officials seized upon the idea of intimidating independence-minded white southerners with the threat of a slave rising without, however, actually inciting one. In the end the British strategy of manipulating conflict between the races became a rallying cry for white southern unity and impelled the South toward independence. The need to weaken slaves' zeal for service with the British, which threatened to expose the moral absurdity of a society of slaveholders proclaiming the concepts of natural rights, equality, and liberty, formed part of the complex interaction of events that constituted the revolutionary war in the South. To that extent, the American Revolution in the South was a war about slavery, if not a war over slavery."

Sylvia R. Frey, historian, *Water from the Rock: Black Resistance in a Revolutionary Age,* 1991

24. Which of the following primary sources would most likely support Frey's argument in the excerpt?

(A) Statistics measuring the growth of the slave population in the South throughout the 18th century
(B) The number of slave uprisings in the late 18th century
(C) Eighteenth-century purchase and sales records of slaves by the largest plantations in the South
(D) An 18th-century slaveholder's diary documenting daily life on a plantation

25. Which of the following contributed most to the increased use of slave labor in the South during the 18th century?

(A) The Spanish Mission system's promotion of Catholicism
(B) Sustained cultivation and demand for tobacco and cotton
(C) The spread of ideas associated with European Enlightenment
(D) The policy of "salutary neglect" practiced by British monarchs

GO ON TO THE NEXT PAGE.

Questions 26–28 refer to the excerpt below.

"Even after Emancipation, courts and legislatures struggled to determine what the end of slavery meant. Clearly African-Americans could no longer be treated as property, to be bought and sold. But, in 1865, it was not clear what rights ex-slaves would have.... Sadly, within half a century of the end of the Civil War most blacks in the United States, ninety percent of whom still lived in the former slave states, had been segregated, reduced to dire poverty, and denied access to the nation's political institutions. It would take [time] to fulfill some of these promises laid out in the Thirteenth Amendment of the United States Constitution."

Paul Finkelman, historian, "Slavery in the United States: Persons or Property?" from
The Legal Understanding of Slavery: From the Historical to the Contemporary, 2012

26. The excerpt most strongly supports which of the following statements?

   (A) The Thirteenth Amendment guaranteed full human rights to emancipated slaves.
   (B) After the Civil War, African Americans continued to be treated as property.
   (C) The Thirteenth Amendment abolished the institution of slavery.
   (D) Most African Americans in the United States continue to live in dire poverty.

27. Which of the following factors most directly fulfilled "some of the promises laid out in the Thirteenth Amendment" as mentioned in the excerpt?

   (A) The success of the Populist Party in the late 19th century
   (B) A rise in Progressive reform movements in the early 20th century
   (C) The resurgence of the Ku Klux Klan in the early 20th century
   (D) The Civil Rights Movement of the mid-20th century

28. Which of the following statements best explains the uncertainty regarding the legal status of former slaves after the Civil War?

   (A) The American Constitution did not mention slavery until the adoption of the Thirteenth Amendment.
   (B) Widespread racism prevented the Supreme Court from ruling favorably on the issue of African American civil rights.
   (C) The Three-Fifths Compromise had previously established the idea that slaves possess only a fraction of the rights of non-slaves.
   (D) The Emancipation Proclamation merely freed slaves but did not bestow upon them any specific rights or freedoms.

GO ON TO THE NEXT PAGE.

Questions 29–32 refer to the image below.

Domino Theory

Source: Tony Auth, "Domino Theory," *The Philadelphia Inquirer*, ©1976

29. The image most closely reflects the political results of which of the following opinion trends in U.S. political and foreign policy in the 20th century?

   (A) A decline in public support for the Korean War
   (B) An increase in public support for the Vietnam War
   (C) The inability to achieve a clear victory during World War II
   (D) The desire to contain communism in developing parts of the world

30. The image most directly supports the idea that U.S. foreign policy during the 20th century emphasized

   (A) stopping the spread of communism in Asia
   (B) a Cold War arms race with the Soviet Union
   (C) the desire to defend human rights in developing nations
   (D) supporting the Non-Aligned Movement in Asia

31. Which of the following is the most direct result of the situation portrayed in the cartoon?

   (A) President Ford pursued nuclear disarmament treaties with the Soviet Union in the mid-1970s.
   (B) U.S. involvement in World War II brought an end to military conflict in Europe.
   (C) Because of the unpopularity of the Vietnam War, there was widespread public resistance to the passage of the War Powers Resolution of 1973.
   (D) In 1975, President Ford officially ended U.S. involvement in the Vietnam War.

32. Which of the following conflicts was most influenced by the "domino theory" mentioned in the cartoon?

   (A) The Revolutionary War, since it motivated other countries to push for independence and political reform
   (B) The Civil War, since the Confederate states left the Union in quick succession
   (C) World War II, since multiple countries around the world ultimately joined the conflict
   (D) The Korean War, since it involved the attempt to contain communism

GO ON TO THE NEXT PAGE.

Questions 33–36 refer to the excerpts below.

"The wisest among my race understand that the agitation of questions of social equality is the extremest folly, and that progress in the enjoyment of all the privileges that will come to us must be the result of severe and constant struggle rather than of artificial forcing. No race that has anything to contribute to the markets of the world is long in any degree ostracized. It is important and right that all privileges of the law be ours, but it is vastly more important that we be prepared for the exercise of these privileges. The opportunity to earn a dollar in a factory just now is worth infinitely more than the opportunity to spend a dollar in an opera-house."

Booker T. Washington, "Atlanta Compromise" speech, 1895

"This group of men honor Mr. Washington for his attitude of conciliation toward the white South; they accept the "Atlanta Compromise" in its broadest interpretation.... But, nevertheless, they insist that the way to truth and right lies in straightforward honesty, not in indiscriminate flattery; in praising those of the South who do well and criticizing uncompromisingly those who do ill; in taking advantage of the opportunities at hand and urging their fellows to do the same, but at the same time in remembering that only a firm adherence to their higher ideals and aspirations will ever keep those ideals within the realm of possibility."

W.E.B. Dubois, "Of Mr. Booker T. Washington and Others," 1903

33. Which of the following actions by people living in the late 19th century would be an example of "artificial forcing" as mentioned in the Booker T. Washington excerpt?

   (A) An African American buys property from a white landowner and starts a successful business.
   (B) An African American runs for state elected office.
   (C) A group of African Americans organize politically to challenge Jim Crow laws.
   (D) African Americans in the South start a school for poor children in their community.

34. Booker T. Washington and W.E.B. Dubois most disagreed on whether

   (A) confrontation of the white majority was the most effective means of creating social change
   (B) the most desirable goal was equal rights for African Americans
   (C) inequalities in wealth had their roots in slavery
   (D) African Americans had opportunities for bettering their social standing

35. It can be demonstrated from the excerpts that Booker T. Washington and W.E.B. Dubois shared the view that

   (A) the movement for advancement of African Americans was part of a broader effort for social change in other segments of society
   (B) desegregation of schools was a desirable goal
   (C) violence was a necessary part of any movement for social change
   (D) African Americans should enjoy greater rights and social privileges than they had previously been given

36. W.E.B. Dubois's statements suggest that he most disagreed with

   (A) the sentiments expressed in the Atlanta Compromise
   (B) the notion that expanded rights and privileges for African Americans would happen slowly over time
   (C) the idea that expanded rights and privileges for African Americans would happen naturally without direct political action
   (D) the folly of agitation regarding questions of social equality

GO ON TO THE NEXT PAGE.

Questions 37–39 refer to the map below.

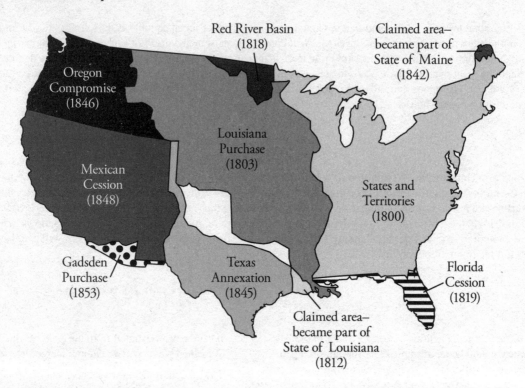

37. The territorial acquisitions shown in the southwestern region of the map most directly resulted from

    (A) treaties made with Indian tribes
    (B) the Louisiana Purchase
    (C) the Mexican-American War
    (D) the Spanish-American War

38. Which of the following provided the philosophical basis for the acquisition of land in the West during the time periods reflected on the map?

    (A) The abolition movement
    (B) The belief in Manifest Destiny
    (C) Popular Sovereignty implemented under the Kansas-Nebraska Act
    (D) The policy of Containment

39. The acquisition of territory in the time periods shown in the map exacerbated debates regarding

    (A) the Homestead Act
    (B) the sharing of mineral rights with native Indian tribes
    (C) the extension of citizenship rights to Indians
    (D) the expansion of slavery in newly acquired territories

GO ON TO THE NEXT PAGE.

Questions 40 and 41 refer to the excerpts below.

"Under a government which imprisons any unjustly, the true place for a just man is also a prison.... Cast your whole vote, not a strip of paper merely, but your whole influence. A minority is powerless while it conforms to the majority; it is not even a minority then; but it is irresistible when it clogs by its whole weight. If the alternative is to keep all just men in prison, or give up war and slavery, the State will not hesitate which to choose. If a thousand men were not to pay their tax bills this year, that would...be...the definition of a peaceable revolution, if any such is possible."

Henry David Thoreau, "Resistance to Civil Government," 1849

" [I] heard Thoreau's lecture before the Lyceum on the relation of the individual to the State—an admirable statement of the rights of the individual to self-government, and an attentive audience. His allusions to the Mexican War, to Mr. Hoar's expulsion from Carolina, his own imprisonment in Concord Jail for refusal to pay his tax, Mr. Hoar's payment of mine when taken to prison for a similar refusal, were all pertinent, well considered, and reasoned. I took great pleasure in this deed of Thoreau's."

Bronson Alcott, *Journals,* 1848

40. Thoreau's remarks in the excerpt most clearly demonstrate his support of which of the following ideas or events?

(A) The Revolutionary War
(B) The Second Great Awakening
(C) Civil disobedience
(D) Transcendentalism

41. Henry David Thoreau's actions later influence which of the following leaders

(A) Theodore Roosevelt
(B) Martin Luther King, Jr.
(C) Huey Long
(D) Gloria Steinem

GO ON TO THE NEXT PAGE.

Questions 42 and 43 refer to the excerpt below.

"The only proper basis for the protection of...all animals is an economic one, and must be based upon carefully constructed and properly enforced laws for the conservation of all species for the benefit of future generations of our citizens, rather than based on local opinion.... This expenditure for the protection of fish and game is clearly a wise economy, tending to prevent the annihilation of birds and other animals valuable to mankind which might otherwise become extinct."

Massachusetts Commission on Economy and Efficiency, 1912

42. Which of the following developments may have contributed most directly to the opinions reflected in the excerpt?

(A) A decrease in numbers of commercial fish in coastal and inland waters of the United States

(B) The erosion of agricultural soil during the Dust Bowl

(C) The growth of suburban housing in land previously held as wilderness

(D) The near extinction of the buffalo

43. What president encouraged the ideas of conservation and preservation during the early 20th century?

(A) Theodore Roosevelt

(B) William McKinley

(C) Woodrow Wilson

(D) Warren G. Harding

GO ON TO THE NEXT PAGE.

Questions 44–46 refer to the excerpt below.

"Unlike its apparent strength in current times, conservatism not so long ago was a decidedly unpopular and much-derided philosophy. As recently as the late 1970s, conservatism was seen as a permanent minority philosophy in America; in fact, it was so much in the minority that there was a question as to whether the conservative cause would even survive. Within mainstream political culture, conservative ideals had been marginalized for half a century, since the late 1920s. Thus, for conservatives, the story of that long hiatus from popular embrace, which reached its peak in the 1960s, is a story of dogged perseverance—a story of unrelenting commitment to a set of ideals rooted in three centuries of American history."

Patrick M. Garry, historian, "A Turning Point for Modern Conservatism," 2007

44. All of the following could support Garry's assertions about conservatism EXCEPT

(A) the defeat of Barry Goldwater in the Election of 1964
(B) the continued expansion of Great Society programs from the 1960s onward
(C) the election of Ronald Reagan in 1980
(D) the fall of the Berlin Wall in 1989

45. One way in which conservatism stands in opposition to liberal principles is by claiming that

(A) liberalism threatens traditional family values
(B) liberals tend to engage in futile military interventions abroad
(C) liberals ignore the concerns of minority racial groups
(D) liberals devote too little money to social programs for the poor

46. Christian evangelicals in the late 20th century would be most likely to oppose

(A) spending on social welfare programs
(B) federal tax cuts
(C) the Persian Gulf War
(D) national abortion rights

GO ON TO THE NEXT PAGE.

Questions 47–49 refer to the excerpts below.

"I have at length the pleasure to enclose you the favorable result of the Convention at Boston. The amendments are a blemish, but are in the least Offensive form.... The Convention of New Hampshire is now sitting. There seems to be no question that the issue there will add a seventh pillar, as the phrase now is, to the Federal Temple."

James Madison, letter to George Washington, 1788

"The adjournment of New Hampshire, the small majority of Massachusetts, a certainty of rejection in Rhode Island, the formidable opposition in the state of New York, the convulsions and committee meetings in Pennsylvania, and above all the antipathy of Virginia to the system, operating together, I am apprehensive will prevent the noble fabric from being enacted."

Cyrus Griffin, letter to James Madison, 1788

47. The "pillar," "temple," and "noble fabric" mentioned in the excerpts above most closely refer to

   (A) the rise of sectionalism in the early Republic
   (B) unity of the states in the ratification of the U.S. Constitution
   (C) the proliferation of political parties in the early Republic
   (D) the victory of George Washington in early presidential elections

48. In 1788, political disagreements typically centered on

   (A) balance of power between the states and federal government
   (B) abolition of slavery
   (C) westward expansion
   (D) the election of George Washington

49. Which of the following political parties expressed the most opposition to the excessive use of federal power?

   (A) Federalists
   (B) Democratic-Republicans
   (C) Whigs
   (D) Populists

GO ON TO THE NEXT PAGE.

Questions 50–52 refer to the excerpt below.

"Whereas it is expedient that new provisions and regulations should be established for improving the revenue of this kingdom, and for extending and securing the navigation and commerce between Great Britain and your Majesty's dominions in America, which, by the peace, have been so happily enlarged: and whereas it is just and necessary, that a revenue be raised, in your Majesty's said dominions in America, for defraying the expenses of defending, protecting, and securing the same; we, your Majesty's most dutiful and loyal subjects, the commons of Great Britain, in parliament assembled, being desirous to make some provision, in this present session of parliament, towards raising the said revenue in America, have resolved to give and grant unto your Majesty the several rates and duties herein after-mentioned...."

English Parliament, Sugar Act, 1764

50. According to the excerpt, the Sugar Act was passed for which of the following reasons?

(A) To promote the interests of colonial manufacturers

(B) To raise money for the kingdom of Great Britain

(C) To establish an economic system based on mercantilism

(D) To promote peace with neighboring European colonies

51. One eventual effect of the Sugar Act was that it

(A) was never enforced due to widespread colonial smuggling

(B) contributed to colonial unrest, thus fostering a move toward independence

(C) created tensions with France

(D) led to the Boston Tea Party

52. Which historical event prompted the need for the Sugar Act?

(A) The Seven Years' War (French and Indian War)

(B) The Boston Tea Party

(C) The Boston Massacre

(D) The Proclamation of 1763

GO ON TO THE NEXT PAGE.

Questions 53–55 refer to the excerpt below.

"Income inequality, moreover, had declined since the 1930s and was historically modest as of 1965 for a variety of reasons. Corporate salaries, while enabling a very comfortable lifestyle for those near the top, were far less remunerative than in later years.... To be sure, the United States was by no means an egalitarian society: in 1964, 34.6 million people (more than 17 percent of the population) lived below the government's official poverty lines. For a family of four, this was $3,130 a year. America's social safety net, having expanded only slowly since World War II, remained more porous than those in northern European nations. Labor unions, which had grown substantially since the 1930s, were starting to weaken. Still, income inequality was as low in early 1965 as it ever had been in the modern history of the country."

James T. Patterson, historian, *The Eve of Destruction: How 1965 Transformed America*, 2012

53. All of the following actions by the federal government could have served to lessen income inequality EXCEPT

   (A) the creation of a national minimum wage
   (B) the desegregation of the military
   (C) the creation of the Securities and Exchange Commission
   (D) the creation of the Federal Housing Authority

54. One significant result of the economic trend described in the excerpt was the

   (A) weakening of the civil rights movement
   (B) decrease in the number of immigrants seeking entry to the United States
   (C) increase in the number of Americans living in suburban areas
   (D) decrease in the number of women in the workforce

55. President Lyndon Johnson's Great Society initiatives passed in the 1960s were designed to address which of the following issues mentioned in the excerpt?

   (A) Growing affluence had exaggerated the effects of racial discrimination.
   (B) Pockets of poverty persisted despite overall affluence.
   (C) A rising standard of living encouraged increased union membership among the working class.
   (D) Private industry boomed in spite of a corporate tax rate.

GO ON TO THE NEXT PAGE.

UNITED STATES HISTORY
SECTION I, Part B
Time—40 minutes

Directions: Answer Question 1 **and** Question 2. Answer **either** Question 3 **or** Question 4.

Write your responses in the Section I, Part B: Short-Answer Response booklet. You must write your response to each question on the lined page designated for that response. Each response is expected to fit within the space provided.

In your responses, be sure to address all parts of the questions you answer. Use complete sentences; an outline or bulleted list alone is not acceptable. You may plan your answers in this exam booklet, but no credit will be given for notes written in this booklet.

Question 1 is based on the excerpts below.

"John Brown's effort was peculiar. It was not a slave insurrection. It was an attempt by white men to get up a revolt among slaves, in which the slaves refused to participate. In fact, it was so absurd that the slaves, with all their ignorance, saw plainly enough it could not succeed. That affair, in its philosophy, corresponds with the many attempts, related in history, at the assassination of kings and emperors. An enthusiast broods over the oppression of a people till he fancies himself commissioned by Heaven to liberate them. He ventures the attempt, which ends in little else than his own execution."

Abraham Lincoln, speech given in 1860

"I said John Brown was an idealist. He believed in his ideas to that extent that he existed to put them all into action; he said 'he did not believe in moral suasion, he believed in putting the thing through.' He saw how deceptive the forms are. We fancy, in Massachusetts, that we are free; yet it seems the government is quite unreliable. Great wealth, great population, men of talent in the executive, on the bench—all the forms right,—and yet, life and freedom are not safe. Why? Because the judges rely on the forms, and do not, like John Brown, use their eyes to see the fact behind the forms."

Ralph Waldo Emerson, "Remarks At a Meeting for the Relief of the Family of John Brown, at Tremont Temple, Boston," 1859

1. Using the excerpts above, answer parts (a), (b), and (c).

    a) Briefly explain ONE major historical difference between Lincoln's and Emerson's interpretations of the actions of John Brown.

    b) Briefly explain ONE other specific historical event or development that is not explicitly mentioned in the excerpts that could be used to support Lincoln's interpretation.

    c) Briefly explain ONE other specific historical event or development that is not explicitly mentioned in the excerpts that could be used to support Emerson's interpretation.

GO ON TO THE NEXT PAGE.

Question 2 is based on the following images.

Image 1: "Family in room in tenement house," Jessie Tarbox Beals, 1910

Image 2: "Cornelia Stewart's Bedroom," late 1800s.
Cornelia Stewart was the wife of A.T. Stewart of Stewart's Department Store.

GO ON TO THE NEXT PAGE.

2. Using the images above, answer parts (a), (b), and (c).

    a) Briefly explain the social and economic conditions of the people who lived in conditions similar to those in Image 1.

    b) Briefly explain the social and economic conditions of the people who lived in conditions similar to those in Image 2.

    c) Briefly explain ONE development in the period 1865 to 1940 that could be interpreted as a reaction to the discrepancies in the two lifestyles pictured in each photograph.

GO ON TO THE NEXT PAGE.

Question 3 or 4

Directions: Answer **either** Question 3 **or** Question 4.

3. Answer parts (a), (b), and (c).

    a)   Briefly explain ONE of the historical developments that led to the creation of the Compromise of 1850.

    b)   Briefly explain ONE of the components of the Compromise of 1850.

    c)   Briefly explain ONE outcome of the Compromise of 1850.

GO ON TO THE NEXT PAGE.

4. Answer parts (a), (b), and (c).

   a) Briefly explain ONE important way in which the Vietnam War (1955–1975) marked a change in the relationship between the United States and the rest of the world.

   b) Briefly explain ONE important way in which the Vietnam War transformed United States society.

   c) Briefly explain ANOTHER important way in which the Vietnam War transformed United States society.

END OF SECTION I

AP® United States History Exam

SECTION II: Free Response

DO NOT OPEN THIS BOOKLET UNTIL YOU ARE TOLD TO DO SO.

At a Glance

Total Time
1 hour, 40 minutes
Number of Questions
2
Percent of Total Score
40%
Writing Instrument
Pen with black or dark blue ink

Question 1 (DBQ): Mandatory

Suggested Reading and Writing Time
60 minutes
Reading Period
15 minutes. Use this time to read Question 1 and plan your answer. You may begin writing your response before the reading period is over.
Suggested Writing Time
45 minutes
Percent of Total Score
25%

Question 2, 3, or 4: Choose One Question

Answer Question 2, Question 3, or Question 4
Suggested Writing Time
40 minutes
Percent of Total Score
15%

Instructions

The questions for Section II are printed in the orange Questions and Documents booklet. You may use that booklet to organize your answers and for scratch work, but you must write your answers in this Section II: Free Response booklet. No credit will be given for any work written in the Questions and Documents booklet.

The proctor will announce the beginning and end of the reading period. You are advised to spend the 15-minute period reading the question and planning your answer to Question 1, the document-based question. If you have time, you may also read Questions 2, 3, and 4. Do not begin writing in this booklet until the proctor tells you to do so.

Section II of this exam requires answers in essay form. Write clearly and legibly. Circle the number of the question you are answering at the top of each page in this booklet. Begin each answer on a new page. Do not skip lines. Cross out any errors you make; crossed-out work will not be scored.

Manage your time carefully. The proctor will announce the suggested time for each part, but you may proceed freely from one part to the next. Go on to Question 2, 3, or 4 if you finish Question 1 early. You may review your responses if you finish before the end of the exam is announced.

After the exam, you must apply the label that corresponds to the long-essay question you answered—Question 2, 3, or 4. For example, if you answered Question 2, apply the label ②. Failure to do so may delay your score.

GO ON TO THE NEXT PAGE.

UNITED STATES HISTORY
SECTION II
Total Time—1 hour, 40 minutes

Question 1 (Document-Based Question)
Suggested reading and writing time: 1 hour

It is suggested that you spend 15 minutes reading the documents and 45 minutes writing your response.

Note: You may begin writing your response before the reading period is over.

Directions: Question 1 is based on the accompanying documents. The documents have been edited for the purpose of this exercise.

In your response, you should do the following.

- Respond to the prompt with a historically defensible thesis or claim that establishes a line of reasoning.
- Describe a broader historical context relevant to the prompt.
- Support an argument in response to the prompt using at least six documents.
- Use at least one additional piece of specific historical evidence (beyond that found in the documents) relevant to an argument about the prompt.
- For at least three documents, explain how or why the document's point of view, purpose, historical situation, and/or audience is relevant to an argument.
- Use evidence to corroborate, qualify, or modify an argument that addresses the prompt.

GO ON TO THE NEXT PAGE.

1. Analyze the extent to which the social and economic experiences of African Americans who migrated within the United States represented both change and continuity in the 20th century.

Document 1

Source: *The Promised Land: The Great Black Migration and How it Changed America,* by Nicholas Lemann, 1991

[The Great Migration] was one of the largest and most rapid mass internal movements in history—perhaps the greatest not caused by the immediate threat of execution or starvation. In sheer numbers it outranks the migration of any other ethnic group—Italians or Irish or Jews or Poles—to [the United States]. For blacks, the migration meant leaving what had always been their economic and social base in America, and finding a new one.

Document 2

Source: U.S. Census

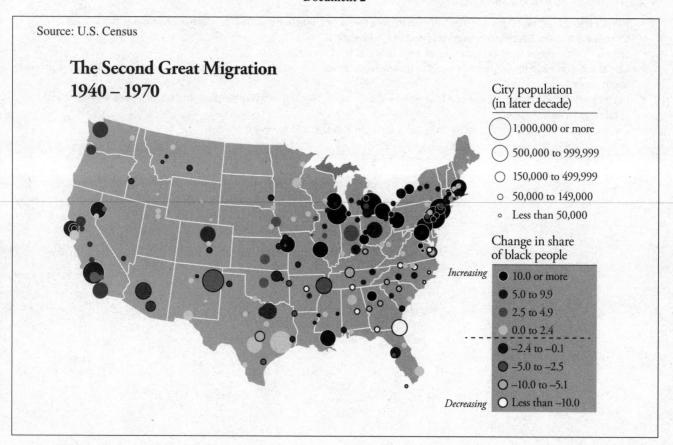

The Second Great Migration 1940 – 1970

City population (in later decade)
- 1,000,000 or more
- 500,000 to 999,999
- 150,000 to 499,999
- 50,000 to 149,000
- Less than 50,000

Change in share of black people

Increasing
- 10.0 or more
- 5.0 to 9.9
- 2.5 to 4.9
- 0.0 to 2.4
- −2.4 to −0.1
- −5.0 to −2.5
- −10.0 to −5.1

Decreasing Less than −10.0

GO ON TO THE NEXT PAGE.

Document 3

Source: A sign outside the Sojourner Truth housing project in Detroit, 1942

GO ON TO THE NEXT PAGE.

Document 4

Source: Table 14. Illinois—Race and Hispanic Origin for Selected Large Cities and Other Places: Earliest Census to 1990, United States Census Bureau

Census year (national rank through 100, state rank through 3) [1]	Total population		Race										Hispanic origin (of any race)		White, not of Hispanic origin	
			White		Black		American Indian, Eskimo, and Aleut		Asian and Pacific Islander		Other race					
	Number	Percent	Number	Percent	Number	Percent	Number	Percent	Number	Percent	Number	Percent	Number	Percent	Number	Percent
Chicago																
1980 (2, 1)	3 005 072	100.0	1 490 216	49.6	1 197 000	39.8	6 072	0.2	69 191	2.3	242 593	8.1	422 063	14.0	1 299 557	43.2
Sample.......................	3 005 078	100.0	1 512 411	50.3	1 197 174	39.8	6 804	0.2	73 745	2.5	214 944	7.2	423 357	14.1	1 311 808	43.7
1970 (2, 1)	3 366 957	100.0	2 207 767	65.6	1 102 620	32.7	6 575	0.2	29 687	0.9	20 308	0.6	(NA)	(NA)	(NA)	(NA)
15% sample.................	3 362 947	100.0	2 219 145	66.0	1 098 824	32.7	44 978			1.3			247 343	7.4	1 985 295	59.0
5% sample...................	3 366 805	100.0	2 217 712	65.9	1 102 457	32.7	46 636			1.4			247 857	7.4	1 992 024	59.2
1960 (2, 1)	3 550 404	100.0	2 712 748	76.4	812 637	22.9	3 394	0.1	19 182	0.5	2 443	0.1	(NA)	(NA)	(NA)	(NA)
1950 (2, 1)	3 620 962	100.0	3 111 525	85.9	492 265	13.6	775	-	14 163	0.4	2 234	0.1	(NA)	(NA)	(NA)	(NA)
1940 (2, 1)	3 396 808	100.0	3 114 564	91.7	277 731	8.2	274	-	4 239	0.1	(X)	(X)	16 438	0.5	3 098 126	91.2
5% sample...................	(NA)	100.0	3 118 680	91.8	(NA)	(NA)	(NA)	(NA)	(NA)	(NA)	(X)	(X)	16 460	0.5	3 102 220	91.3
1930	3 376 438	100.0	3 137 093	92.9	233 903	6.9	246	-	5 196	0.2	(X)	(X)	(NA)	(NA)	(NA)	(NA)
"Mexican" in Other race ...	3 376 438	100.0	3 117 731	92.3	233 903	6.9	246	-	5 196	0.2	19 362	0.6	(NA)	(NA)	(NA)	(NA)
1920 (2, 1)	2 701 705	100.0	2 589 169	95.8	109 458	4.1	94	-	2 984	0.1	(X)	(X)	(NA)	(NA)	(NA)	(NA)
1910 (2, 1)	2 185 283	100.0	2 139 057	97.9	44 103	2.0	108	-	2 015	0.1	(X)	(X)	(NA)	(NA)	(NA)	(NA)
1900 (2, 1)	1 698 575	100.0	1 667 140	98.1	30 150	1.8	8	-	1 277	0.1	(X)	(X)	(NA)	(NA)	(NA)	(NA)
1890 (2, 1)	1 099 850	100.0	1 084 998	98.6	14 271	1.3	14	-	567	0.1	(X)	(X)	(NA)	(NA)	(NA)	(NA)
1880 (4, 1)	503 185	100.0	496 495	98.7	6 480	1.3	37	-	173	-						
1870 (5, 1)	298 977	100.0	295 281	98.8	3 691	1.2	5	-	-	-						
1860 (9, 1)	112 172	100.0	111 214	99.1	958	0.9	-	-	-	-						
1850 (24, 1)	29 963	100.0	29 640	98.9	323	1.1	(NA)	(NA)	(NA)	(NA)						
1840 (92, 1)	4 470	100.0	4 417	98.8	53	1.2	(NA)	(NA)	(NA)	(NA)						

	Black		
	Total	Free	Slave
	955	100.0	955	100.0	-	-
	323	100.0	323	100.0	-	-
	53	100.0	53	100.0	-	-

Document 5

Source: "The New Great Migration: Black Americans' Return to the South, 1965–2000," by William H. Frey

The list of metro areas that experienced the largest net losses of black migrants changed most abruptly between the late 1960s and late 1970s…with the exception of Pittsburgh, the 10 largest net losses at the metropolitan level between 1965 and 1970 occurred in the South, and mostly in Deep South areas, including three each in Alabama (Birmingham, Mobile, and Montgomery) and Louisiana (New Orleans, Lafayette, and Shreveport). But in the late 1970s, industrial shake-outs in the Northeast and Midwest fueled a new migration of blacks out of several metropolitan areas that were their major destinations in earlier decades…. In fact, only New Orleans—a metro that continues to lose black migrants today—represents the South on the "bottom 10" list in the late 1970s….

Now, more educated blacks are migrating to Southern destinations at higher rates than those with lower educational levels … [this] pattern is mirrored in white migration to the South during the same period. As with the black population, the South gained whites at all education levels, though net gains were larger for higher-educated whites.

GO ON TO THE NEXT PAGE.

Document 6

Source: "The New Great Migration: Black Americans' Return to the South, 1965–2000" by William H. Frey

Top 10 States for Black Net Migration Gains, 1965–1970 and 1995–2000

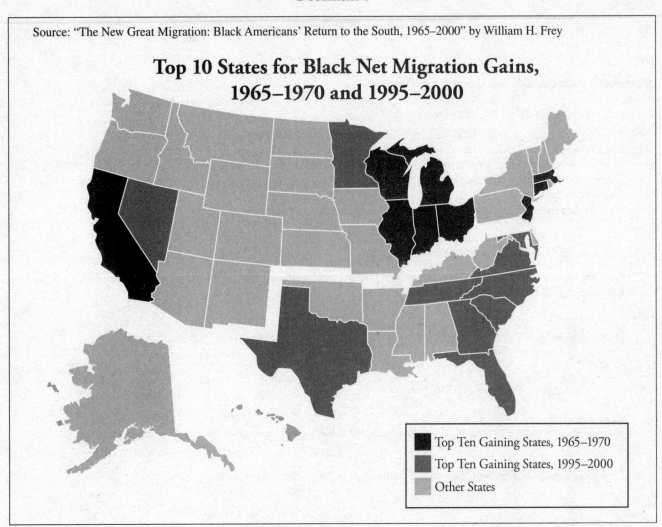

Top Ten Gaining States, 1965–1970
Top Ten Gaining States, 1995–2000
Other States

END OF DOCUMENTS FOR QUESTION 1

GO ON TO THE NEXT PAGE.

Question 2, 3, or 4 (Long Essay)

Suggested writing time: 40 minutes

Directions: Answer Question 2 **or** Question 3 **or** Question 4.

In your response, you should do the following.

- Respond to the prompt with a historically defensible thesis or claim that establishes a line of reasoning.
- Describe a broader historical context relevant to the prompt.
- Support an argument in response to the prompt using specific and relevant examples of evidence.
- Use historical reasoning (e.g., comparison, causation, continuity or change over time) to frame or structure an argument that addresses the prompt.
- Use evidence to corroborate, qualify, or modify an argument that addresses the prompt.

2. Evaluate the extent to which the Seven Years' War (French and Indian War, 1754–1763) was a contributing factor leading to the American Revolution.

   In your argument, analyze both changes and continuities in the relevant time period.

3. Evaluate the extent to which the Mexican-American War (1846–1848) was a contributing factor leading to the Civil War.

   In your argument, analyze both changes and continuities in the relevant time period.

4. Evaluate the extent to which World War I was a contributing factor leading to the first Red Scare.

   In your argument, analyze both changes and continuities in the relevant time period.

WHEN YOU FINISH WRITING, CHECK YOUR WORK ON SECTION II IF TIME PERMITS.

STOP

END OF EXAM

Practice Test 4:
Answers and
Explanations

PRACTICE TEST 4 ANSWER KEY

Section I, Part A: Multiple-Choice Questions

1. B	20. A	39. D
2. A	21. B	40. C
3. C	22. A	41. B
4. C	23. A	42. A
5. B	24. B	43. A
6. A	25. B	44. D
7. A	26. C	45. A
8. C	27. D	46. D
9. C	28. A	47. B
10. A	29. D	48. A
11. B	30. A	49. B
12. C	31. D	50. B
13. A	32. D	51. B
14. D	33. C	52. A
15. A	34. A	53. B
16. B	35. D	54. C
17. A	36. C	55. B
18. D	37. C	
19. B	38. B	

SECTION I, PART A: MULTIPLE-CHOICE QUESTIONS

Questions 1–3

Beginning in the 17th century, early British colonies, such as in the Chesapeake and North Carolina, became wealthy through the cultivation of tobacco, a lucrative export business targeted to European merchants. Although slavery would later become the preferred mode of labor, early workers were indentured servants. Indentured servants were largely poor people from England, Ireland, and France who were lured across the Atlantic by the promise of a new life, freedom, adventure, and job security. Most indentured servants were young males, some were children, and some who were not persuaded to go willingly would be kidnapped and taken to America. Once on American soil, they signed 5- to 10-year contracts, committing to a term of labor. The lives of indentured servants were often harsh and dangerous; some died before their contracts expired.

1. **B** We can find clues within Hofstadter's quote: the "labor supply" is from England (not Africa) and they "committed themselves," so they cannot be slaves, (A). Although some of them may have been "given to crime," there is no evidence that they were convicted inmates, (C). There is no mention of religious freedom, so rule out (D).

2. **A** Using the clues described above, we know that these workers are indentured servants. Indentured servants were hired to work in agriculture. "Manufacturing" as we now know it would not have existed in 1750, so rule out (B). Choice (D) is testing your knowledge of Bacon's Rebellion, an uprising by indentured servants in Virginia in 1676. It did not lead to a decline in slavery; in fact, many slaves were brought in to replace the indentured servants after 1676. So, we are left with (A) and (C). As you may know, the cotton gin was not invented until 1793. Cotton production is linked to slavery. The indentured servants of the 17th and 18th centuries were more likely hired to work in Southern tobacco plantations.

3. **C** We know that the people described in the quote are indentured servants, since they came from England and "committed themselves" to labor in America and the West Indies. So where was labor most needed in 1750? Not in Northern New England, (A), since the harsh climate and rocky soil allowed for only small subsistence farms. New Amsterdam, (B), was a small Dutch settlement created to protect Dutch interest in the fur trade. St. Augustine in 1750 was controlled by Spain, (D). That leaves us with (C). The Chesapeake region was known for its cultivation of tobacco and import of indentured servants.

Questions 4–6

During the Lincoln-Douglas debates of 1858, Abraham Lincoln appeared on the national scene as an antislavery Republican. He ran against the incumbent Senator Stephen Douglas in the U.S. Senate race in Illinois. Lincoln challenged Douglas to a series of debates in which he deftly explained his belief that the nation's opposition to slavery could not be grounds for compromise, and challenged the fundamental morality of Douglas's support of the Dred Scott decision and the Kansas-Nebraska Act.

4. **C** The phrase "life, liberty, and the pursuit of happiness" occurs in the Preamble to the Declaration of Independence. The meaning of the Declaration was a heated topic in the Lincoln-Douglas debates. Lincoln thought that the language of the Declaration was universal. In the excerpt, Lincoln clarifies this perspective by noting that "all men are created equal," although they do not all currently enjoy equal rights.

5.   **B**   Douglas argued that the phrase "all men are created equal" in the Declaration referred to white men only.

6.   **A**   Toward the end of the excerpt, Lincoln mentions "all people, of all colors, everywhere," so he is explicitly talking about race. He does not explicitly mention slavery, (C), and South Carolina's secession, (D), does not occur until 1860. Choice (B) may seem close, but the excerpt is about human rights, not the threat of war.

Questions 7–10

The Treaty of Fort Laramie was an agreement between the United States and the Sioux Nation signed in 1868, which purported to grant ownership of the Black Hills, South Dakota area to the Sioux, thus denying the possibility of white settlement in the area. As with other treaties of its kind, the Treaty of Fort Laramie was broken, in part due to the discovery of gold in the Black Hills. The excerpt from the ruling in *United States v. Sioux Nation of Indians* documents the fact that General George A. Custer was instrumental in luring whites to the Black Hills region and thus violating the terms of the treaty.

7.   **A**   The Treaty states that "no white person or persons shall be permitted to settle upon or occupy any portion of" the land in question, so white settlement of this area in the 1870s was a clear violation of the treaty. After whites began to prospect for gold in the Black Hills, General Custer was defeated by the Sioux at the Battle of Little Bighorn, one in a series of battles instigated by the violation of the treaty.

8.   **C**   The Treaty of Fort Laramie was signed in 1868, while Custer's journey from Fort Abraham Lincoln commenced in 1874. We can infer from these dates that it was only a few short years from the signing of the treaty before whites began to enter the Black Hills region. This directly contradicts answer (A). Choice (B) is unlikely, since the violations of treaties led to more uncertainty for Indians. Choice (D) is unsupported by the information given, and is incorrect. In fact, *United States v. Sioux Nation of Indians* ruled that the Sioux nation had incurred damages from the violation of the treaty and awarded it several million dollars in compensation.

9.   **C**   The Treaty states that "no white person or persons shall be permitted to settle upon or occupy any portion of" the land in question, so rule out (A) and (B). Choice (D) is too extreme, since there is a provision in Article XVI for whites to travel through the region "with consent."

10.   **A**   The wording of Article XVI is unambiguous and clearly contradicts (D). The Sioux *could establish a claim under Article XVI,* so rule out (C). Choice (B) is incorrect, since the Fourth Amendment prohibits the search and seizure of private property without just cause.

Questions 11–14

The table measures the foreign-born population of the United States every 10 years (census years) from 1850 to 1910. The trend is toward a general increase in foreign-born residents, but with a sharp decline from 1930 to 1970. Thus, we see a clear indication that immigration trends must have changed in the years previous to 1970. We can infer that the children of foreign-born people were then citizens, thus not accounted for in this table, but we can also infer that there must have been a decrease in immigration, thus no displacement of the foreign-born numbers. Then we see a spike in foreign-born residents from 1980 onward.

11. **B**   The *overall* trend is toward greater immigration from all areas of the world. The one constant in the United States since 1870 has been progressive industrialization.

12. **C**   The question is asking about the *total* foreign-born population, so (B) is too narrow. Choice (D) is also too narrow and occurred too early to affect the population in 1960. Choice (A) is incorrect. The need for agricultural labor likely increased in the 20th century and would not have affected all ethnic groups.

13. **A**   Nativism is a term that refers to a native population's desire to limit foreign immigration and promote the interests of the native-born. Literacy tests, (B), were used by labor unions throughout the 1890s to 1920s to exclude non-English-speaking immigrants from the labor pool. Eugenics, (C), was popular following World War I. Eugenicists sought to maintain the genetic purity of the United States; thus they would have been skeptical of immigration. The Ku Klux Klan, (D), was a white nationalist group based largely in the South. Although it started as a reaction to the emancipation of the slaves after the Civil War, the KKK quickly expanded as a reaction to foreign immigration, including anti-Semitism and anti-Catholicism within its milieu. That leaves us with settlement houses, (A). Settlement houses, such as Hull House started by Jane Addams, sought to help immigrants in major cities by providing them with financial assistance, education, and healthcare.

14. **D**   According to the table, immigration from Latin America exploded during the latter half of the 20th century. Most of these immigrants settled in California and other areas of the Southwest. Numbers of immigrants have always been high in New York City, but California has experienced a higher number of newcomers than even this melting pot.

Questions 15–17

President William McKinley was a powerful, pro-business Republican. He sponsored the legislation that created the eponymous McKinley Tariff, which raised taxes on many goods by about 50 percent. The primary purpose of tariffs was not to raise revenue, but to boost American businesses by giving them a price advantage over foreign competitors.

15. **A**   According to McKinley's quote, "Under free trade the trader is the master and the producer the slave…" and "protection…is where labor wins its highest rewards." So, in McKinley's view, free trade is disadvantageous to both American businesses and their employees. Protectionism does not lower prices on goods, (C), since McKinley believes there is a "maxim…a thousand times better" than "Buy where you can buy the cheapest."

16. **B**   Since McKinley was a Republican, rule out (A). Know-Nothings, (C), were concerned with immigration issues. Whigs, (D), disbanded before the Civil War.

17. **A**   McKinley does not mention tariffs in the excerpt, but he is well known for the protective McKinley tariff, along with some minor tariffs designed to give American businesses a boost over foreign competition. Choice (B) would not be helpful to American businesses. While (C) may be a by-product of tariffs, this answer is too broad and does not differentiate between American and foreign goods.

Questions 18–20

Larson's quote explains in detail what comprised the Market Revolution: a transition throughout the 19th century from an agricultural economy to an industrial one. The North was developed first, where new factories sprang up, using new methods of production such as interchangeable parts (parts made to a standard so that they can be easily replaced). Urban centers grew as people migrated from the farmlands to the cities. Improvements in transportation and communication systems were in demand to keep pace with industrial expansion. Railroad networks were built throughout the North, and the use of the telegraph aided in running this sprawling network. In time, the South caught up to these changes, and today the United States is a largely industrial nation.

18. **D** Use Process of Elimination. Sectional tensions, (A), would have been high before the Civil War, due to divisions over slavery. Choices (B) and (C) were not natural outgrowths of the Market Revolution, since many young women worked in factories and industrialization created deeper divisions between the wealthy factory owners and poorer factory workers. Choice (D) is correct, since the invention of the cotton gin by Eli Whitney allowed for the efficient removal of seeds from cotton tufts. Coupled with enormous English demand for huge quantities of cotton, this encouraged the South to continue to focus on cotton production, which in turn fueled increased demand for slave labor.

19. **B** Following the Civil War, many factors contributed to the rapid rise of industrialization and manufacturing. Remember these important ones: abundant natural resources, a large and available pool of labor (ex-soldiers, freed slaves, immigrants, women, and children), improved transportation (railroads), and other new technologies (such as the telegraph).

20. **A** Improvements in transportation, such as the building of railroads, invention of the steamship for river trade, and improvements to roads and canals, all allowed for more efficient trade. Choice (B) occurred during the same time, but was not a direct cause of industrialization. If anything, it may have been a result, since many immigrants came to America to take the jobs that had already become available in city factories. Abolition, (C), is unrelated to the Market Revolution, and (D) is in the wrong time period: tariffs came in *after* American industry had already established itself.

Questions 21–23

Baltzer v. United States (1919) and *Schenck v. United States* (1919) were landmark Supreme Court cases which ruled that speech which is intended to result in a crime and that poses a "clear and present" danger in its expression is not protected speech under the First Amendment. Justice Oliver Wendell Holmes was one of the dissenters in the Baltzer case, and the excerpt here expresses his opinion that there is danger in the impulse to suppress unpopular speech and that "it is better for those who have unquestioned and almost unlimited power in their hands to err on the side of freedom."

21. **B** Since Holmes's quote is concerned with the tendency toward "intolerance of opinions and speech" and "freedom," the First Amendment is most relevant to these sentiments. The First Amendment guarantees freedom of speech.

22. **A** Holmes is addressing the need to tolerate opinions and speech that might be "opposed to our own." Choice (B) does not involve speech, so eliminate it. Although the speech of activists associated with women's suffrage, (C), or nativism, (D), may have been unpopular with some, these people were

never arrested by the government for their divergent views. President Wilson did, however, authorize the arrest of many antiwar protestors under the Espionage Act of 1917. The protestors distributed literature encouraging draft dodging, thus leading to the *Baltzer v. United States* and *Schenck v. United States* decisions, which ruled that speech encouraging illegal activity was not protected under the First Amendment.

23. **A** Since Holmes's quote addresses the issue of freedom of speech, an action which seeks to limit speech or beliefs would be the most directly opposed to his sentiments. In the vanguard of the deep anti-communist sentiment in the 1950s was Senator Joseph R. McCarthy, who led a crusade to rid the government of supposed communists, and their "fellow travelers," or "sympathizers." McCarthy's tactics, which became known as McCarthyism, were ruthless, and his claims were often unsubstantiated. Choice (B) is the opposite of what we are looking for, since antiwar protestors are employing freedom of speech, not denouncing it. Choices (C) and (D) are unrelated to freedom of speech.

Questions 24–25

This may initially sound like a description of the Civil War, but a careful reading of the excerpt reveals that it is actually describing the British strategy of attempting to manipulate the Southern colonies before the American Revolution. According to Frey, "the British strategy of manipulating conflict between the races became a rallying cry for white southern unity and impelled the South toward independence."

24. **B** According to Frey, "British military leaders and Crown officials seized upon the idea of intimidating independence-minded white southerners with the threat of a slave rising," so knowing the prevalence (or lack thereof) of slave uprisings would help to evaluate the relevance of this statement. Choices (A) and (C) may help to establish raw numbers of slaves, but do not give us any insight into their proclivity to rebel, or white plantation owners' fears of such rebellions. Choice (D) is vague and irrelevant to Frey's argument.

25. **B** Plantation systems developed to produce single crops, such as tobacco, rice, indigo, and, later, cotton—also known as cash crops, because they were sold as well as consumed by the growers. This type of farming was labor-intensive and opened the door for the slave trade, which had been carried on by English merchants since at least the 16th century, and which increased steadily throughout the 17th, 18th, and the first half of the 19th centuries.

Questions 26–28

For newly emancipated slaves, Reconstruction brought good news and bad. The good news was that the Thirteenth Amendment, which prohibited slavery, was passed. The bad news was that Southerners passed the Black Codes, rules that restricted African Americans from many rights of citizenship.

26. **C** There are several tempting answers here, but we must pick the choice that is most *definitely* true based on Finkelman's statements. The Thirteenth Amendment did abolish slavery, though it did not guarantee full human rights for the emancipated slaves, (A), as supported by Finkelman's quote. Choice (B) is directly contradicted by the quote. Choice (D) is a good trap answer, but this statement is worded in the present tense and is unsupported by the excerpt.

27. **D** The Populist Party, (A), did not work explicitly toward expanded rights for African Americans. Since Finkelman's quote includes fulfilling "some of these promises laid out in the Thirteenth Amendment," (C) cannot be correct. Choice (B) is close, but Progressive reformers were more focused on securing rights for workers, women, and the poor. Only the civil rights movement, (D), would fully ensure equal legal protections for African Americans.

28. **A** Use Process of Elimination. The Emancipation Proclamation, (D), was not a legal document per se. The Thirteenth Amendment was the formal legal measure imposed by Congress to free the slaves. Choice (B) is not supported by any specific facts; the Supreme Court would not have been necessary to secure rights for African Americans had Congress and the States done that job. Choices (A) and (C) are very close choices, but (A) is better. The Three-Fifths Compromise was used to apportion Congressional representation at the founding of the Republic, but it did not, strictly speaking, limit the rights of African Americans. The uncertainty regarding their rights is more clearly due to the lack of explicit mention of slavery in the Constitution.

Questions 29–32

This set of questions is asking you to interpret a cartoon which depicts five presidents (Eisenhower "Ike," Kennedy "JFK," Johnson "LBJ," Nixon, and Ford) lined up like dominoes toppling each other. The caption reads "Domino Theory." To understand this cartoon, you need to know that all five of these presidents involved U.S. troops in the Vietnam War, spanning from the 1950s to 1975. The term "domino theory" typically refers to the fear that once a certain country adopts a communist form of government, that other countries around it will "fall like dominoes" and become communist, too. Here, the cartoonist is parodying this notion by showing that the presidents "fell like dominoes," too, probably because the conflict was transferred from one administration to the next, with increasing public dissatisfaction with the results of the war.

The nation's approach to Vietnam was the ultimate Cold War policy gone awry. Although the Vietnam War is at its core a story of anticommunists versus communists, the full narrative is much more complicated. The war was waged between the communist North Vietnamese, with support from their Chinese, Soviet, and Viet Cong allies, and the government of South Vietnam, supported by its primary ally, the United States. Following the military defeat and subsequent withdrawal of the French from Indochina, Vietnam was partitioned into Northern and Southern states. The government of North Vietnam and their Viet Kong allies in the South sought to reunify Vietnam under a single communist government. The United States justified its involvement in Vietnam as part of a larger containment strategy, the crux of which was to stop the expansion of communism on a state-by-state basis, wherever revolutionary elements pursued the establishment of communist rule. This containment doctrine had at its intellectual heart domino theory, which held that if one country in a region fell to communism, all of the nations in that region were then put at risk of falling.

29. **D** The cartoon portrays the five U.S. presidents who were directly involved in executing military decisions for the Vietnam War. The cartoon is unrelated to the Korean War, (A), or World War II, (C). Choice (B) is incorrect, since public sentiment toward the Vietnam War tended to turn more negative, not toward greater support. Choice (D) is the best choice.

30. **A** The Vietnam War was an attempt to contain the spread of communism in Asia. It was not rooted in a desire to defend human rights, per se, (C). Choice (B) is irrelevant to the cartoon. The Non-Aligned Movement, (D), pertains to a group of smaller countries who have attempted to maintain

independence from major countries, so the United States would not have supported this effort, nor was Vietnam a member of this group until 1976, after the war ended.

31. **D** The Tet Offensive failed in its goal of overthrowing the South Vietnamese government, but it turned the tide of the war nonetheless, as it persuaded many American voters that despite extra-ordinary effort and enormous sacrifice, the United States was no closer to victory than when the war began. A significant antiwar movement grew throughout the 1960s, which was both a reflection of and a stimulus for the larger countercultural movement of the decade. A growing sense that the United States was mired in a quagmire in Southeast Asia, along with increasingly vocal public opposition to the war, led to a slow but steady reduction in American force levels until President Ford officially ended the war in 1975, (D). Choice (C) may look tempting, but the War Powers Resolution was, in fact, an attempt to curb the executive power to commit troops to war without the consent of Congress. Anti-war activists would not have opposed this idea.

32. **D** The Korean War, which occurred under Truman, became a stage on which Cold War hostilities were played out. After World War II, Korea had been divided into North Korea, under Soviet control, and South Korea, under American occupation. Following the withdrawal of both Soviet and U.S. troops at the end of World War II, North Korea, led by Soviet-trained military leaders and equipped with Soviet arms, attacked South Korea without provocation, with the declared intention of unifying the Korean peninsula. The initial North Korean invasion across the 38th parallel into South Korea pushed overwhelmed South Korean defenders back to the so-called Pusan Perimeter. Led by America, the United Nations Security Council declared North Korea an aggressor and sent a force led by General MacArthur to the region under orders to defend South Korea.

Questions 33–36

Many strong African American leaders emerged during the Progressive Era. The National Association for the Advancement of Colored People (NAACP) and the National Urban League were multiracial groups founded to combat racial discrimination and pursue political, educational, social, and economic equality for all people. While most African Americans were in favor of racial equality, they were split as to how this could best be achieved. Booker T. Washington, an educator who founded the Tuskegee Institute, an all-black vocational school (and later, a university), advocated that, rather than fight for political rights, African Americans should strive for economic equality through job training and hard work. Washington presented these views at the Atlanta Exposition in 1895 in a speech known as the Atlanta Compromise. Whites welcomed Washington's views as they advised African Americans to work quietly rather than to agitate openly for equality. In sharp contrast to Washington, W.E.B. DuBois, who helped found the NAACP, argued that African Americans should aggressively pursue political, social, and economic rights. DuBois believed that a "Talented Tenth" of the African American population should assume roles of academic and community leadership, advancing the race through intellect and skill.

33. **C** According to Washington's statements, "artificial forcing" is political action that leads to "agitation of questions of social equality." Choice (C) involves the most direct political action. All of the other answers involve more indirect or individual actions that Washington would support as beneficial to the African American community.

34.   **A**   Washington and Dubois did not disagree upon the roots of African American suffering, (C), or the worthiness of equal rights for all, (B). They did, however, disagree upon the means by which to achieve these goals, (A). Choice (D) is incorrect, since Dubois does mention that there is a "way for a people to gain their reasonable rights."

35.   **D**   Neither speaker mentions desegregation, (B), or violence, (C). They also do not mention other types of social change, (A). Choice (D) is the most reasonable answer and would be a sentiment shared by every civil rights activist of the era.

36.   **C**   According to Dubois's statements, he does "accept the Atlanta Compromise" in its broadest interpretation," (A) and does "not expect that the free right to vote, to enjoy civic rights, and to be educated, will come in a moment," (B). Choice (D) is something with which Washington would disagree, not Dubois.

Questions 37–39

The map portrays a number of territorial acquisitions, including the Louisiana Purchase, Florida, Oregon Territory, and the lands ceded by Mexico after the Mexican-American War.

37.   **C**   The Mexican-American War officially began after Mexican troops crossed the Rio Grande into disputed territory, and President James K. Polk secured a declaration of war. While the progression of the war was neither as easy nor as swift (the war dragged on for more than a year and a half) as Polk had hoped, its outcome was everything that he had desired. With the Treaty of Guadalupe-Hidalgo (1848), Mexico acknowledged the Rio Grande as the southern border of Texas and ceded the territories of California and New Mexico to the United States.

38.   **B**   Generally, Westerners supported territorial expansion and subscribed to the notion of Manifest Destiny, which held that it was America's destiny to expand beyond its current boundaries across the North American continent.

39.   **D**   These new territories increased the tension between free and slave states in the populace and in Congress. Even as the Mexican-American War was being fought, representatives from the North and the South began disputing how this new territory would be organized, slave or free. The Homestead Act, (A), did not occur until after the Civil War and was not broadly controversial. Choices (B) and (C) were not concerns during the time periods depicted on the map.

Questions 40–41

In this excerpt, Thoreau explicitly advocates the nonpayment of taxes. Specifically, Thoreau protested the Mexican-American War by failing to pay a small poll tax and was subsequently jailed for his actions. The excerpt from Bronson Alcott's *Journals* demonstrates that Thoreau's actions were inspiring to other intellectuals of his time.

40.   **C**   Henry David Thoreau pioneered the practice of civil disobedience—that is, nonviolent resistance of authorities who enforce unjust laws. Although he was a transcendentalist, (D), a movement associated with The Second Great Awakening, (B), this excerpt is focused on political action, not spirituality.

41. **B** Thoreau advocated nonviolent resistance of authorities who enforce unjust laws (civil disobedience). This philosophy inspired activists like Martin Luther King, Jr. and formed the basis for many of the tactics of the civil rights movement.

Questions 42–43

The conservation movement came to prominence during the Progressive Era. While some conservationists, such as John Muir, sought to preserve nature on idealistic grounds, believing that a minimum of human interference with natural resources was always preferable, some conservationists took a more pragmatic approach, believing that conservation of resources was necessary in order to ensure the continued use of those resources by humans.

42. **A** Choosing the best answer is a matter of recognizing that the excerpt was written in 1912 (well before the growth of suburban developments, (C)) and is by a commission in Massachusetts, far from the Dust Bowl, (B), or buffalo, (D).

43. **A** President Theodore Roosevelt was an environmentalist. He was instrumental in the establishment of the National Park system and he advocated for federal management of natural resources through the National Conservation Commission.

Questions 44–46

In Garry's view, conservatism was "marginalized" from the Great Depression to the 1970s, overshadowed by the New Deal, Great Society, and 1960s countercultural revolution. Conservative ideas survived through "dogged perseverance—a story of unrelenting commitment to a set of ideals rooted in three centuries of American history."

44. **D** Barry Goldwater, (A), was a conservative presidential candidate in 1964. His loss to Lyndon Johnson (Democrat) could certainly support Garry's argument that conservatives were the underdogs for 50 years. Conservatives would have opposed Great Society programs, (B), designed to raise taxes and spend money on poverty programs. Choice (C) is a tricky answer, but notice that Garry acknowledges the "strength" of conservatism in "current times." He mentions that "conservatism was seen as a permanent minority philosophy in America" "as recently as the late 1970s," implying that the 1980s may have reversed the trend. Choice (D) is the best answer, since the fall of the Berlin Wall is less relevant to American conservatism than the election of a president.

45. **A** Social conservatives care deeply about traditional family values. They do not usually blame liberals for needless wars, (B), or promote government programs targeted to racial or social groups, (C) and (D).

46. **D** Christian evangelicals are often conservatives who focus their political energies on social issues regarding traditional family values. Possibly the most divisive issue since the 1970s has been the national legalization of abortion in all 50 states following the *Roe v. Wade* Supreme Court decision. Christian evangelicals are less focused on spending issues, (A) than are secular conservatives and they have not been vocally opposed to most wars, (C). Tax cuts, (B), would not be opposed by most Christian evangelicals.

Questions 47–49

In 1787, our newly independent nation convened a Constitutional Convention during which the U.S. Constitution, the foundation for the government of the United States, was written. The Constitution was ratified and passed in 1788, the date in which both of the excerpts were written. Griffin's letter helps to establish that there was some wrangling and uncertainty regarding the various states and whether they would ratify.

47. **B** The letter from Griffin lists the states that had yet to ratify the Constitution. Madison's letter confirms that the "Convention" had convened and that there were "amendments" to the document. Both speakers are referring to the states about to ratify.

48. **A** Eliminate (B) and (C), since they occur in the wrong time period. George Washington's presidency, (D), was not controversial. The degree to which states and the federal government would share power is known as federalism, (A), and was the most controversial issue of this time period.

49. **B** Federalists supported a strong central government, while Jeffersonian anti-Federalists were suspicious of such a government. Jefferson's party was known as the Democratic-Republicans.

Questions 50–52

Directly following the French and Indian War, George Grenville was appointed Prime Minister of the colonies. He sought tighter control over the American Colonies in order to raise revenues for Great Britain. In addition to stricter enforcement of existing trade laws, Grenville passed other unpopular laws. The Sugar Act (also known as the Revenue Act), which placed new duties on certain foreign goods (not just sugar), basically forced the colonies to conduct all trade through England. Although the Sugar Act resembled the Navigation Acts, by which the colonists had long abided, the fact that it was explicitly designed to raise revenue upset the colonists, who felt as if the mother country was trying to take advantage of them. Colonial legislatures sent petitions to Parliament, arguing that the act would hurt trade for Britain as well as the colonies and that the colonists had not consented to the act's passage. Grenville ignored the colonists' pleas as he proceeded with his plans to increase Britain's revenue.

50. **B** The excerpt mentions "improving the revenue of this kingdom," "that a revenue be raised...for defraying...expenses." So, raising money was the primary purpose of the Sugar Act.

51. **B** Laws such as the Sugar Act contributed to colonial unrest, since it reinforced the notion that the colonists were victims of "taxation without representation." Choice (A) may have looked tempting, but this was actually true of the Molasses Act. The Sugar Act was indeed enforced. France, (C), would not have been affected by the Sugar Act, and (D) was true of the Tea Act, not the Sugar Act.

52. **A** The French and Indian War had been enormously expensive for the British, and they felt that the American colonists did not share equally the burden of the war costs. This led to a cascade of Acts, such as the Sugar Act, designed to raise revenue for the Mother Country.

Questions 53–55

The decade following World War II brought general affluence and an improved standard of living for most Americans. The excerpt by James Patterson points out that there was a relatively low level of income inequality in America in the 1950s and 1960s compared to the soaring wealth of the rich in the 1920s and the booming economy of the 1980s and 1990s.

53. **B** A national minimum wage, (A), would ensure that even the lowest-paid workers in America earn an income beyond a set threshold. The creation of the Securities and Exchange Commission, (C), helped to regulate Wall Street, thus reining in potential corruption at the top. The creation of the Federal Housing Authority (FHA), (D), helped low- and middle-income Americans to more easily purchase a home. The desegregation of the military, (B), would have virtually no impact on income inequality.

54. **C** This is entirely a test of your knowledge of the era. After World War II, the civil rights movement, (A) experienced some notable victories (*Brown vs. Board of Education,* the Civil Rights Act, etc.). Immigration, (B), began to increase and more women joined the workforce, (D). Choice (C) is the best answer, since the proliferation of the automobile and reliable jobs encouraged many Americans to live in the suburbs.

55. **B** When Lyndon B. Johnson assumed the presidency, he outlined ambitious goals for the nation, arguing that government should play a greater role in people's lives. He called his vision the Great Society, promising a country in which poverty, disease, and lack of education, could and should be eliminated. His most important legislation was the Economic Opportunity Act (1964), which was billed as "The War on Poverty."

SECTION I, PART B: SHORT-ANSWER QUESTIONS

Question 1

The Kansas-Nebraska Act helped set the stage for one of the first violent confrontations stemming from the slavery issue. Because the fate of each locality in the Kansas-Nebraska Act hinged on a popular vote, hundreds of pro-slavery and antislavery activists poured into the territories in hopes of swaying the outcome of the referendum. Often armed and ready to fight, Kansas became a literal battleground between pro-slavery and antislavery factions. "Bleeding Kansas," as the region came to be known, was the site of several prominent attacks on opposing groups' settlements. The most famous incident was John Brown's raid, where Brown, a radical slavery opponent, led a group that murdered pro-slavery settlers. Later John Brown led a separate raid on the U.S. arsenal at Harper's Ferry (then in the state of Virginia) hoping to seize a cache of weapons with which to arm a slave uprising. Brown's raid failed and Brown himself was captured by a detachment of Marines under the command of then Col. Robert E. Lee, tried for treason, and hanged.

Many Republicans, such as Abraham Lincoln, sought to distance themselves from the actions of John Brown. In the excerpt cited, Lincoln denies that Brown's efforts were successful or supported by the slaves themselves. He calls his actions "absurd" and merely leading to Brown's own demise.

Many committed abolitionists, on the other hand, maintained that Brown's actions were the natural result of the moral desperation brought on by the continuation of slavery, and praised Brown as a kind of martyr for the cause of abolition. In Emerson's speech, he labels Brown an "idealist" who saw the necessity of action. Emerson refers to the "forms," or social and political institutions which perpetuated slavery, contrasted with the "facts" of moral reality.

a) An effective answer to part (a) will highlight differences between Lincoln's and Emerson's positions on John Brown including:

- Whether he was misguided or heroic
- Whether or not he accomplished anything useful
- Whether or not his actions were destined for failure
- Whether Brown was egocentric or self-sacrificing
- Whether or not violence is effective in promoting a just cause

b) Lincoln's view is that John Brown was misguided and ineffective and an example of a revolutionary who thought too highly of his own place in history, thus leading to his own demise. This question is asking for an event or development to support his view. You could have used one of the following, being sure to highlight the unsuccessful aspects of these events:

- Bacon's Rebellion
- Stono Rebellion
- Nat Turner's Rebellion
- The seizure of *La Amistad*
- Bleeding Kansas

c) Emerson's view is that John Brown was an idealist whose actions were noble and motivated by the knowledge of truth. This question is asking for an event or development to support his view. You could have used one of the following, or even events from the part (b) list, being sure to highlight the successful or idealistic aspects of these events:

- 1733 slave insurrection on St. John, Virgin Islands
- Haitian Revolution
- Civil War

Question 2

In Image 1, we see a family of seven living in a very small room that contains one bed, a crib, and shabby furnishings. The family is dressed in such a manner that we would assume they are low-paid workers, perhaps in a factory. "Tenements" were city apartments for the poor, and in 1910 there would have been little to no government assistance for the poor. Child labor was common in such communities and this family might be recent immigrants.

In Image 2, we see a lavishly appointed bedroom, typical of that of a wealthy family in the Gilded Age. According to the caption, this is the bedroom of the wife of A.T. Stewart, owner of a successful department store in New York City in the late 1800s. Notice that her bedroom is larger than the tenement family's one room, so we can infer that her house is massive in comparison to their dwelling. The two pictures illustrate the great disparities in wealth between the rich and the poor during the height of the Industrial Revolution.

a) Your answer to this question should mention several of the following:

- A move away from agricultural work and rural living to urban factory work
- A large increase in unskilled and semi-literate workers, largely immigrants
- Child labor
- A large number of female workers, especially in textile mills
- Laissez-faire economics
- Social Darwinism
- Virtually no government safety net for the poor (welfare benefits, food stamps, subsidized housing, Medicaid, etc.)
- Little workplace safety regulations
- The rise of labor unions

b) Your answer to this question should mention several of the following:

- The flowering of industry after the Civil War
- "Robber barons"/captains of industry: Carnegie, Rockefeller, Vanderbilt, etc.
- Increased mechanization of industry and assembly-line production leading to the need for large numbers of factory workers
- Low federal income tax rates, encouraging the accumulation of wealth at the top of society
- Laissez-faire economics
- Social Darwinism
- The Gospel of Wealth
- Intermarriage within wealthy families, encouraging a consolidation of wealth
- Inexpensive labor, which allowed for lavish home building among the wealthy

c) Your answer to this question may have focused on one of the following:

- Rise of the Progressive Party
- Muckraking journalism: McClure's magazine, Ida M. Tarbell's *The History of the Standard Oil Company,* Upton Sinclair's *The Jungle,* Jacob Riis's *How the Other Half Lives*
- The Sherman Antitrust Act of 1890 and Clayton Antitrust Act
- Settlement houses (Jane Addams's Hull House in Chicago)
- Interstate Commerce Act of 1887
- The growth of labor unions: Knights of Labor; the American Federation of Labor (AFL), led by Samuel Gompers; and the Industrial Workers of the World (IWW), referred to as "Wobblies," a militant anti-capitalist group
- Union strikes
- State Workmen's Compensation laws
- Child labor laws
- New Deal reforms: regulation of banks, Social Security, government work programs

Question 3

a) Territorial expansion increased the tension between free and slave states in Congress. Even as the Mexican-American War was being fought, representatives from the North and the South began disputing how this new territory would be organized, slave or free. The Gold Rush forced the decision; in 1849, California petitioned Congress for admittance into the Union as a free state. President Zachary Taylor, a Whig, supported admittance. Serious talk of secession circulated among Southerners.

b) and c) Henry Clay, by then an elder statesman, proposed a series of resolutions in hopes of preserving the free/slave state balance and avert the impending threat of Southern secession. Congressional squabbling followed, but included a number of notable Senate floor speeches, The Great Debate, by Clay, Daniel Webster, and John C. Calhoun. With the help of Stephen Douglas, a senator from Illinois, a deal that became known as the Compromise of 1850 was struck. The compromise admitted California as a free state and maintained Texas as a slave state. The rest of the territory in question was divided at the 37th parallel into New Mexico and Utah. These two territories would be "unrestricted"—each locality would decide its own status. The compromise also abolished the slave trade in the District of Columbia.

Henry Clay

- Whig Senator from Kentucky
- Drafted and formally proposed the Compromise of 1850
- Helped to clarify the final boundaries of Texas
- Originally proposed banning slavery in the entire Mexican Cession
- Wanted a stringent Fugitive Slave Act

John Calhoun

- Democrat Senator from South Carolina
- Defender of slavery
- Opposed the Compromise of 1850
- Advocate for states' rights and secession
- Spurred notion of popular sovereignty for Mexican Cession territories

Daniel Webster

- Whig Senator from Massachusetts
- Supported the Compromise in order to preserve the Union and avert Civil War
- In the *Seventh of March* speech, characterized himself "not as a Massachusetts man, nor as a Northern man, but as an American...."
- Risked offending his abolitionist voter base by accepting the Compromise

Question 4

This question calls for a brief overview of the history of the Vietnam War, along with a discussion of some of its impacts on American society.

a) Although the Vietnam War is at its core a story of anticommunists versus communists—not an especially unique one in the annals of Cold War geopolitics—the full narrative is much more complicated. The war was waged between the communist North Vietnamese, with support from their Chinese, Soviet, and Viet Cong (a South Vietnamese communist guerilla group) allies, and the government of South Vietnam, supported by its primary ally, the United States. The United States justified its involvement in Vietnam as part of a larger containment strategy, the crux of which was to stop the expansion of communism on a state-by-state basis, wherever revolutionary elements pursued the establishment of communist rule. This containment doctrine had at its intellectual heart domino theory, which held that if one country in a region fell to communism, all of the nations in that region were then put at risk of falling. The U.S. military presence in Vietnam increased dramatically following the 1964 Gulf of Tonkin incident. Be sure to mention that:

- Unlike the Korean War, U.S. casualty rates were much higher.
- Depending on your point of view, you could argue that the failures of the Vietnam War created more caution in American interventionism (it was not as smooth-sailing as the Korean War) OR that it ended interventionism on grounds of containment (no major conflicts over communism after 1975).

b) and c) Effective answers to parts (b) and (c) should mention some of the following:

- Protest of the draft, draft-dodging, emigrations to Canada
- Military draft not used since the Vietnam War
- Intense war protests (i.e., Kent State Massacre)
- The Pentagon Papers
- First war to be televised
- Nixon's policy of détente

SECTION II, QUESTION 1: THE DOCUMENT-BASED QUESTION

The document-based question begins with a mandatory 15-minute reading period. During these 15 minutes, you should (1) come up with some information not included in the given documents (your outside knowledge) to include in your essay, (2) get an overview of what each document means, (3) decide what opinion you are going to argue, and (4) write an outline of your essay.

The first thing you will be inclined to do, after reading the question, is to look at the documents. Resist that temptation. Instead, the first thing you should do is brainstorm for several minutes about what the question is asking of you. Try to list everything you remember about the Great Migrations. This list will serve as your reference to the outside information you must provide in order to earn a top grade.

Then, and only then, read over the documents. As you read them, take notes in the margins and underline those passages that you are certain you are going to refer to in your essay. If a document helps you remember a piece of outside information, add that information to your brainstorming list. If you cannot make sense of a document, don't worry. You may omit mention of <u>one</u> of the documents and still score well on the DBQ.

Here is what you need to look for in each document to get the most out of it:

- The author
- The date
- The audience (for whom was the document intended?)
- The significance

Remember: You are being asked to write 50 percent document interpretation and 50 percent outside information. Don't get so lost in the documents that you forget to bring in outside information. Readers will not be able to give you a high score unless you have both! What readers really don't like is a laundry list of documents: that is, a paper in which the student merely goes through the documents, explaining each one. Those students are often the ones who forget to bring in outside information, because they are so focused on going through the documents.

So, what is this DBQ all about?

This DBQ can be seen in three parts: (1) What motivated the Great Migrations? (2) What were the outcomes of the Great Migrations? And (3) How have the reasons for African American migration changed over time? For the first part, discuss slavery in the South, the end of the Civil War, Jim Crow laws, industrialization in the North, and urbanization. For the second part, discuss economic growth, the establishment of large African American communities in Northern cities, and subsequent discrimination in housing ordinances, hiring practices, etc.

In the final part of the essay, use Documents 5 and 6 to demonstrate that the migration patterns of African Americans have recently shifted from "South to North" to "North to South." Some African Americans are seeking to return to the home of their ancestors and are responding, in part, to the recent manufacturing boom and growth of suburbs in Southern cities. This net southern migration is, in large part, supported by increased opportunities for those with higher education and continued systemic racism presenting difficulties for African Americans in the workplace in both the North and South.

The Documents

In **Document 1,** Lemann establishes that the Great Migration of African Americans was significant on a scale that shadows immigration to the United States during this same period. Historians often distinguish between two periods of the Great Migration: the First Great Migration from the end of World War I up to the Great Depression, which involved African Americans moving from Southern rural areas to northern industrial cities, and a Second Great Migration after World War II, which brought African Americans not only to the north, but also to the West. The motivations for migration were largely economic, but also social: the attitudes of those in the North were thought to be less racist than those in the South.

Document 2 shows that the Second Great Migration led to decreasing numbers of African Americans in Southern cities such as Jacksonville, Nashville, and Birmingham, while many Northern and Western cities experienced a sharp increase in African Americans. It is important to consider the social and economic issues faced by the United States during these decades in order to find underlying causes of the Second Great Migration. For one, the 1940s saw an increase in manufacturing because of the American entrance into World War II. The postwar economic boon came with an increase in manufacturing jobs, offering further economic incentives for migration. Also consider the persistence of Jim Crow era discrimination in the South, particularly before the 1954 *Brown v. Board of Education* case and the 1964 Civil Rights Act.

Document 3 establishes that not all Northern cities, in this case Detroit, welcomed African Americans with open arms. Two pieces of Lyndon Johnson's Great Society legislation connect to this image: the development of the department of Housing and Urban Development and the Housing Rights Act. The department of Housing and Urban Development provided safe, decent housing for low-income Americans. Further, the Housing Rights Act prohibited discrimination in home sales and rentals—the kind of discrimination seen in the image. Some low-income African American migrants moved into government-sponsored housing projects, while others were free to purchase or rent housing anywhere they could afford. This migration led some whites to fear the demographic changes in their city and brought up decidedly ugly intimidation techniques.

Document 4 shows the increase in population in Chicago over a 150-year time period. A careful study of the racial numbers demonstrates that the numbers of African Americans increased by over 300% after World War II with a slight decrease or stabilization during the 1980s. Note the dramatic jumps. By 1950, following World War II's industrial boon, the African American population in Chicago increased by over 5%. Over the next decade, that percentage increased by another 10% as U.S. manufacturing continued to grow following the war. Numbers of whites in Chicago declined noticeably during this same time period, likely because of "white flight."

Document 5 discussed the change in migration patterns in metro areas from a northward trend during and shortly after the civil rights movement of the 1960s to a more recent southward trend due to systemic racism and changes in job opportunities in the North during the late 1970s. This document is helpful in understanding the motivation for the shift in migration towards the southward trend we see today.

Document 6 confirms that the Second Great Migration meant significant increases in the population of African Americans in Northern and Western states, while the trend in the 1990s was toward increases in Southern states. There are many factors at play, including manufacturing jobs disappearing, business moving to the "Sun Belt," deterioration of urban neighborhoods, and greater opportunities in the workplace for those with higher education in the South.

Outside Information

We have already discussed much more than you could possibly include in a 45-minute essay. Do not worry. You will not be expected to mention everything or even most of what we have covered in the section above. You will, however, be expected to include some outside information—that is, information not mentioned directly in the documents.

Here is some outside information you might have used in your essay. The information is divided into two groups: general concepts and specific events.

General Concepts

- In American history, the movement of African Americans has been both about survival and opportunity. The Great Migration of the early 20th century saw an escape from a violent South, as well as the search for decent industrial jobs in the North. What we want to consider in this essay is the extent to which African Americans found either the security or economic opportunity promised in the North.
- The migration of African Americans brought with it competition for jobs. Working-class whites, including immigrants, often showed intolerance toward African Americans due to this competition. The dream of a more tolerant North with economic opportunities did not necessarily pan out for all African American migrants.
- One constant from life in the South for African Americans was religious instructions. In the South, Christian churches provided a social infrastructure and organizing vehicle in African American communities. Those institutions were retained following the move to northern cities, often in ad hoc "store-front" churches. Other African Americans found social and economic support in a renewed interest in Islam. The Nation of Islam, for instance, maintained a focus on personal decorum and responsibility in the black community.
- As occurred in the early days of Reconstruction, African American political representation once again became a reality. In cities that became increasingly African American, some of the first black mayors were elected. The phenomenon of "white flight" left a primarily black voting bloc in many regions. Nonetheless, the black franchise was still not absolute, particularly before the 24th Amendment and the 1965 Voting Rights Act.
- The hope that African American migrants would escape the discrimination and bigotry of the South by moving to the North was dashed by housing discrimination, voter intimidation, job discrimination, and random acts of violence.

Specific Events

- You should be familiar with the Great Migration. Beginning at the start of the First World War, the Great Migration saw a swell of African American migrants moving to northern cities until the Great Depression, though some historians document the event as lasting through the 1960s (in reality, the migration appears to have occurred in a couple waves). While less than 10% of African Americans lived in the North in the first decade of the 20th century, the onset of World War I saw migrants moving to northern cities for manufacturing job opportunities created by the war effort.
- The Harlem Renaissance was a flowering of black culture and art. Located in New York City, writers and artists such as Langston Hughes, Zora Neale Hurston, and Louis Armstrong created an artistic "rebirth" that coincided with the Great Migration. The hope was that this movement would create social and economic opportunities for northern blacks. The reality was more complex—Duke Ellington, star musician on the stage of the Cotton Club, was not allowed to sit in the audience due to the club's policy of racial discrimination.

- The landmark case *Brown v. Board of Education* prohibited discrimination in school, presumably creating equal opportunities for children of all races. The implementation of this ruling caused much difficulty, with some schools openly defying the Court ruling in the South. In the North, school integration was promoted through a process known as "bussing," allowing students in the inner city to attend schools in white neighborhoods. This program was met with resistance in white communities, including a riot in Boston in the 1970s.

- The Civil Rights Acts (1964, 1965, and 1968) created a *de jure* equality for African Americans. No longer would Jim Crow laws stand in the way of a person's access to public accommodations. More significant to northern blacks, who were less likely to face Jim Crow laws, was the 1968 legislation that prohibited housing discrimination.

- In response to integrated schools and the new housing equality, whites left cities for the suburbs in a phenomenon sociologists call "white flight." This created a de facto segregation in schools and neighborhoods and also affected property values.

- By the 1960s, African Americans continued to face poverty at disproportional rates. The plans of Lyndon Johnson's Great Society attempted to combat poverty and create opportunity. Some of these programs included the Economic Opportunity Act, Head Start, Upward Bound, Job Corps, VISTA, and the Department of Housing and Urban Development.

- Black nationalism and black pride movements saw urban African Americans look to provide for their community through education, food programs, healthcare, and dozens of initiatives carried out by the Black Panthers.

Choosing a Side

The first thing you want to do is to decide what kind of a statement you are going to make. You have already brainstormed all your outside information, made some notes or a quick outline, and decided where to plug in the documents. Because there is no right way to answer this, and many ways to make your argument, here are some positions you might want to argue.

- Since the end of the Civil War, African Americans have always been more mobile than whites, tending to follow economic opportunities and seeking homes with others like them.

- African American migration in the past 20 years represents a radical departure from the migrations of the 20th century, since African Americans are moving from North to South. According to Document 5, they tend to be better educated than their migrant predecessors. We can infer that this shift may represent a different perception regarding racism and geography.

- Northern economies have become hostile to the needs of African Americans (high levels of unemployment, high cost of living, urban racial tensions), while the South is now more embracing (a growth in manufacturing, historically black communities and colleges, less disparity in the quality of public schools).

Planning Your Essay

Unless you read extremely quickly, you probably won't have time to write a detailed outline for your essay during the 15-minute reading period. However, it is worth taking several minutes to jot down a loose structure of your essay, because it will actually save you time when you write. First, decide on your thesis and write it down in the test booklet. Then, take a few minutes to brainstorm all the points you might put in your essay. Choose the strongest points and number them in the order you plan to present them. Lastly, note which documents and outside information you plan to use in conjunction with each point. If you organize before you write, the actual writing process will go much more smoothly. More important, you will not write yourself into a corner, and suddenly find yourself making a point you cannot support or heading toward a weak conclusion (or worse still, no conclusion at all).

What You Should Have Discussed

Regardless of which thesis you choose, your essay should discuss all of the following:

- Since the prompt asks you to analyze "change and continuity," you should note that the regions of the country affected by the Great Migration have remained fairly constant: the urban Northeast, Great Lakes region, and California.
- The reasons for migration have always revolved around economic and social concerns.
- The "change" has been in the direction of migration: only recently have African Americans been moving South instead of North.
- Document 5 suggests that the new migrants are better educated and placed within the economy compared with their sharecropping ancestors.
- Regardless of time period or motivation, African Americans have tended to migrate to certain areas rather than disbursing evenly throughout the country (no major changes in parts of the rural Midwest, Plains, Rocky Mountains, Northern New England, Alaska).
- Racial tensions are highest in areas affected by migration.
- Migration slowed after the 1960s.

SECTION II: THE LONG ESSAY QUESTION

Your task here is to choose ONE of the prompts and present a historically defensible thesis backed up with relevant evidence. For each of the prompts, your thesis is likely to either make the case that the Seven Years' War did or did not contribute to the Revolution, that the Mexican-American War did or did not contribute to the Civil War, OR that World War I did or did not contribute to the Red Scare. Saying that these events *did* contribute to their respective wars is likely to be the easier position for most students taking this test, although it would be possible to qualify this position with relevant exceptions.

Question 2

If your thesis maintains that the Seven Years' War *did* largely contribute to the Revolution, you may have mentioned some of the following:

- British debt following the Seven Years' War directly led to heavier taxation of the colonies (e.g., Sugar Act, Stamp Act).
- The heavier taxation that followed the Seven Years' War affected the wealthy, elite colonists who later provided the structure and organization to launch the Revolution. The Founding Fathers were plantation owners and merchants whose interests were directly tied to the changes wrought by the Seven Years' War.
- The Albany Plan of Union proved to colonists that they were capable of organizing for a common cause.
- The Proclamation of 1763 was issued after Britain's victory in the Seven Years' War. It forbade all settlement west of the Appalachian Mountains. Any previously issued land grants were now worthless, thus angering American colonists and leading to a spirit of revolution.

- Before the Seven Years' War, colonists were largely self-sufficient, running their own affairs through local governments and militias. After the War, the British took a more active role in governing and policing the colonies, leading to such incidents as the Boston Massacre, the revocation of the charter of Massachusetts, and quartering of soldiers. This led to colonial discontent and eventual revolution.
- France may have been more inclined to help the colonists during the Revolution as revenge for its prior losses during the Seven Years' War.
- Despite its victory, Britain was weakened financially by the War, possibly leading to an increased boldness on the part of colonists who saw Britain as vulnerable.

If your thesis maintains that the Seven Years' War *did not* contribute much to the start of the Revolution, you may have mentioned some of the following:

- Life did not change significantly for the masses of poor and middle-class colonists who later went on to form the backbone of the Continental Army. Especially those living in Southern colonies would have been indifferent to the effects of the Seven Years' War.
- Taxation and regulation of trade existed before the Seven Years' War.
- It was really the shift from Salutary Neglect to tighter control that prompted independence, not the Seven Years' War itself.
- The true impetus for revolution was philosophical: republicanism, natural rights, the Enlightenment, Hobbes, Locke, perhaps even the First Great Awakening.
- Mercantilism had become unduly burdensome and had existed long before the Seven Years' War.
- Colonists *were* largely British, thus culturally tied to the Motherland, and saw themselves as dependent on Britain economically.
- The Seven Years' War demonstrated to colonists that they needed the protection of a strong military power.
- There were always Loyalists who resisted the notion of pursuing independence from the Crown. The Seven Years' War had no effect on the sentiments of those disinclined to the Revolution.

Question 3

If your thesis maintains that the Mexican-American War *did* do much to launch the Civil War, you may have mentioned some of the following:

- The lands acquired under the Mexican Cession were fertile and viable for cotton production, thus leading to the possible need for slave labor.
- The Civil War was inextricably linked to debates about slavery. The Mexican-American War gave the United States access and control to new territories that would later seek statehood. Whether these territories and states would have legal slavery became the most hotly debated issue in Congress at this time.
- "Popular sovereignty" was cited by many as the easiest way to settle the free-state/slave-state conundrum. Most dramatically in the case of the Kansas-Nebraska Act, popular sovereignty tacitly assumed the rights of particular localities to determine their own destinies, thus contributing to notions of secession on the part of disgruntled Southern states.
- Southern Democrats had explicitly supported the war for the express purpose of expanding slavery (a jab in the eye to Northern Whigs).

If your thesis maintains that the Mexican-American War *did not* contribute significantly to the Civil War, you may have mentioned some of the following:

- The slave-state/free-state debate existed long before the Mexican-American War, at least as far back as the Missouri Compromise.
- The Compromise of 1850 was, in fact, "the straw that broke the [Southern] camel's back," not the Mexican-American War. In other words, it was the way the Mexican Cession was handled that enhanced tensions between North and South, not the war itself.
- Slavery was already a highly controversial issue well before the Mexican-American War. William Lloyd Garrison published "The Liberator" as early as 1831.
- The Gag Rule prevented Congress from settling the issue of slavery by legislative (peaceful) means.
- Fugitive slave laws and *Dred Scott v. Sandford* did more to heighten tensions over slavery than merely the acquisition of new territories.
- The Civil War also revolved around issues of states' rights and the uses of nullification, issues that reared their heads under President Andrew Jackson and were unconnected to slavery per se.

About the Structure of Your Essay

As you compose your essay, you want to stay focused on cause and effect. Therefore, the analysis of the earlier event has to come back to your claim about whether or not that event was a factor leading to the latter event. An effective way to do this would be to include a component from each event in a particular body paragraph and flesh out the link (or lack thereof) between the two. Remember you are not just listing facts but also directly addressing the cause-and-effect question.

Question 4

Your task in this essay is an analysis of both World War I and the Red Scare, a frenzied time in which government officials searched for Communists within the United States, in order to establish the connection between the two. Due to the contemporaneous nature of the time period (U.S. involvement in World War I lasted from 1917 until 1918 and the first Red Scare lasted from 1917 until 1920), the connections may seem obvious. However, you need to be careful to not just list events that may have happened concurrently. Rather, you should establish a link between the two to best highlight the cause-and-effect relationship. World War I, which the United States entered reluctantly several years after Europe commenced fighting, not only created a wave of anti-German hysteria in the United States, but also fears of Communism. Russia, after all, had withdrawn from the war due to the chaotic communist revolution happening on its home front.

Begin your essay with a short overview of the two events mentioned in the prompt. Make sure that you quickly move the discussion into a clear claim about the relationship between the First World War and the first Red Scare. You can, of course, claim that the wheels of the Red Scare were set in motion before World War I began, but you will find rich opportunities for connections between the two events, as well.

Things you may want to mention about World War I:

- Isolationist foreign policy characterized the Wilson Administration.
- German submarine attacks killed American citizens, fomenting an anti-German sentiment in the United States.
- Eugene Debs was imprisoned for his opposition to the war. His arrest highlights the connection between Socialist political activity and opposition to the war.

- The Espionage Act prevented anyone from using the U.S. mail system to interfere with the war effort or with the draft. The act helped stoke a suspicion that would become a normal part of American life during the Red Scare.
- The Sedition Act furthered that suspicion by making it illegal to try to prevent the sale of war bonds or to speak disparagingly of the government, the flag, the military, or the Constitution.
- *Schenck v. United States* was a Supreme Court case that challenged the constitutionality of the Espionage Act. Schenck was a prominent socialist and ardent critic of American capitalism, who was arrested and convicted when he printed and mailed leaflets urging men to resist the draft. The Court upheld the Espionage Act.

Give yourself extra points for mentioning the following:

- The government helped create this frenzied atmosphere through its wartime propaganda arm, the Committee on Public Information. Germans were portrayed as bloodthirsty and decidedly anti-American.
- Anti-German sentiment progressed during the war. Violence persisted against German immigrants. Schools largely stopped teaching the German language, while streets with German names changed their signs. Even innocuous references to German culture were rejected: sauerkraut became "liberty cabbage."

Things you might want to mention about the Red Scare:

- One fear of communism in the United States was how it would impact the war effort: the Russian Revolution forced the nation's withdrawal from World War I in order to deal with matters on the home front.
- The Bolshevik control of Russia created tensions among U.S. government officials about what would happen in the United States if a popular Communist movement gained steam.
- Federal and local governments held deep suspicions against union activities. Closely associated with Marxist ideas, organizations of laborers also fell victim due to xenophobia: many members were German and Russian. This period saw business assume greater power, while unions lost power.
- The Federal Bureau of Investigation, headed by J. Edgar Hoover, was created to keep radicals at bay.
- The Palmer Raids saw the government and its agents raid union halls, pool halls, social clubs, and residences. Over 10,000 union members were arrested in over 30 cities, but very few weapons or bombs were found. About 500 immigrants were eventually deported at the conclusion of the Palmer Raids.

Give yourself extra points for mentioning the following:

- The Progressive Party, a one-time advocate for unions, had begun to split between left wing and moderates over the war and the Red Scare.
- Sacco and Vanzetti's sham trial stands as an illustration of the anti-immigrant and anti-union sentiment of the late 1910s and early 1920s. The Red Scare, like the anti-German sentiment during World War I, was kept alive through widespread xenophobia.
- The Emergency Quota Act of 1924 also shows the influence of xenophobia on federal policy. The quotas discriminated against the "new immigrants" who came from Southern and Eastern Europe—hotbeds for socialist activity.

About the Structure of Your Essay

The task on this question is to find a cause and effect between two events that happened nearly simultaneously. For your claim, make it clear in your introductory paragraph whether the feelings of World War I led to the Red Scare or the two events happened concurrently due to common factors in each. No matter what you argue, to tackle the body paragraphs, look for undercurrents that were common to both events. There seems to be plenty of opportunity to discuss how xenophobia played into both events. Further, a distrust of Socialists could be the topic of another body paragraph. Be consistently deliberate with your analysis as you explain whether the relationships between the events are parallel occurrences or cause and effect.

The **Princeton Review®**

1. YOUR NAME:
(Print)   Last   First   M.I.

SIGNATURE: _____ DATE: ___ / ___ / ___

HOME ADDRESS: _____
(Print)   Number and Street

City   State   Zip Code

PHONE NO. : _____
(Print)

IMPORTANT: Please fill in these boxes exactly as shown on the back cover of your test book.

2. TEST FORM

3. TEST CODE

4. REGISTRATION NUMBER

5. YOUR NAME

First 4 letters of last name | FIRST INIT | MID INIT

6. DATE OF BIRTH

Month	Day	Year
JAN		
FEB		
MAR		
APR		
MAY		
JUN		
JUL		
AUG		
SEP		
OCT		
NOV		
DEC		

7. SEX
MALE
FEMALE

The **Princeton Review®**

Section I

Start with number 1 for each new section.
If a section has fewer questions than answer spaces, leave the extra answer spaces blank.

1. A B C D
2. A B C D
3. A B C D
4. A B C D
5. A B C D
6. A B C D
7. A B C D
8. A B C D
9. A B C D
10. A B C D
11. A B C D
12. A B C D
13. A B C D
14. A B C D
15. A B C D

16. A B C D
17. A B C D
18. A B C D
19. A B C D
20. A B C D
21. A B C D
22. A B C D
23. A B C D
24. A B C D
25. A B C D
26. A B C D
27. A B C D
28. A B C D
29. A B C D
30. A B C D

31. A B C D
32. A B C D
33. A B C D
34. A B C D
35. A B C D
36. A B C D
37. A B C D
38. A B C D
39. A B C D
40. A B C D
41. A B C D
42. A B C D
43. A B C D
44. A B C D
45. A B C D

46. A B C D
47. A B C D
48. A B C D
49. A B C D
50. A B C D
51. A B C D
52. A B C D
53. A B C D
54. A B C D
55. A B C D

Completely darken bubbles with a No. 2 pencil. If you make a mistake, be sure to erase mark completely. Erase all stray marks.

1. YOUR NAME:

(Print)

Last   First   M.I.

SIGNATURE: DATE: ___ / ___ / ___

HOME ADDRESS:

(Print)

Number and Street

City   State   Zip Code

PHONE NO. :

(Print)

IMPORTANT: Please fill in these boxes exactly as shown on the back cover of your test book.

5. YOUR NAME

First 4 letters of last name | FIRST INIT | MID INIT

2. TEST FORM

3. TEST CODE

4. REGISTRATION NUMBER

6. DATE OF BIRTH

Month	Day		Year	
JAN				
FEB				
MAR	0 0	0 0		
APR	1 1	1 1		
MAY	2 2	2 2		
JUN	3 3	3 3		
JUL	4 4	4		
AUG	5 5	5		
SEP	6 6	6		
OCT	7 7	7		
NOV	8 8	8		
DEC	9 9	9		

7. SEX

○ MALE
○ FEMALE

Section I

Start with number 1 for each new section.
If a section has fewer questions than answer spaces, leave the extra answer spaces blank.

1. A B C D
2. A B C D
3. A B C D
4. A B C D
5. A B C D
6. A B C D
7. A B C D
8. A B C D
9. A B C D
10. A B C D
11. A B C D
12. A B C D
13. A B C D
14. A B C D
15. A B C D
16. A B C D
17. A B C D
18. A B C D
19. A B C D
20. A B C D
21. A B C D
22. A B C D
23. A B C D
24. A B C D
25. A B C D
26. A B C D
27. A B C D
28. A B C D
29. A B C D
30. A B C D
31. A B C D
32. A B C D
33. A B C D
34. A B C D
35. A B C D
36. A B C D
37. A B C D
38. A B C D
39. A B C D
40. A B C D
41. A B C D
42. A B C D
43. A B C D
44. A B C D
45. A B C D
46. A B C D
47. A B C D
48. A B C D
49. A B C D
50. A B C D
51. A B C D
52. A B C D
53. A B C D
54. A B C D
55. A B C D

1. YOUR NAME: _____
(Print)   Last   First   M.I.

SIGNATURE: _____   DATE: ___ / ___ / ___

HOME ADDRESS: _____
(Print)   Number and Street

_____
City   State   Zip Code

PHONE NO. : _____
(Print)

IMPORTANT: Please fill in these boxes exactly as shown on the back cover of your test book.

2. TEST FORM

3. TEST CODE

4. REGISTRATION NUMBER

5. YOUR NAME

First 4 letters of last name | FIRST INIT | MID INIT

6. DATE OF BIRTH

Month	Day		Year	
○ JAN				
○ FEB				
○ MAR	⓪	⓪	⓪	⓪
○ APR	①	①	①	①
○ MAY	②	②	②	②
○ JUN	③	③	③	③
○ JUL		④	④	④
○ AUG		⑤	⑤	⑤
○ SEP		⑥	⑥	⑥
○ OCT		⑦	⑦	⑦
○ NOV		⑧	⑧	⑧
○ DEC		⑨	⑨	⑨

7. SEX

○ MALE
○ FEMALE

The Princeton Review®

Section I

Start with number 1 for each new section.
If a section has fewer questions than answer spaces, leave the extra answer spaces blank.

1. Ⓐ Ⓑ Ⓒ Ⓓ
2. Ⓐ Ⓑ Ⓒ Ⓓ
3. Ⓐ Ⓑ Ⓒ Ⓓ
4. Ⓐ Ⓑ Ⓒ Ⓓ
5. Ⓐ Ⓑ Ⓒ Ⓓ
6. Ⓐ Ⓑ Ⓒ Ⓓ
7. Ⓐ Ⓑ Ⓒ Ⓓ
8. Ⓐ Ⓑ Ⓒ Ⓓ
9. Ⓐ Ⓑ Ⓒ Ⓓ
10. Ⓐ Ⓑ Ⓒ Ⓓ
11. Ⓐ Ⓑ Ⓒ Ⓓ
12. Ⓐ Ⓑ Ⓒ Ⓓ
13. Ⓐ Ⓑ Ⓒ Ⓓ
14. Ⓐ Ⓑ Ⓒ Ⓓ
15. Ⓐ Ⓑ Ⓒ Ⓓ

16. Ⓐ Ⓑ Ⓒ Ⓓ
17. Ⓐ Ⓑ Ⓒ Ⓓ
18. Ⓐ Ⓑ Ⓒ Ⓓ
19. Ⓐ Ⓑ Ⓒ Ⓓ
20. Ⓐ Ⓑ Ⓒ Ⓓ
21. Ⓐ Ⓑ Ⓒ Ⓓ
22. Ⓐ Ⓑ Ⓒ Ⓓ
23. Ⓐ Ⓑ Ⓒ Ⓓ
24. Ⓐ Ⓑ Ⓒ Ⓓ
25. Ⓐ Ⓑ Ⓒ Ⓓ
26. Ⓐ Ⓑ Ⓒ Ⓓ
27. Ⓐ Ⓑ Ⓒ Ⓓ
28. Ⓐ Ⓑ Ⓒ Ⓓ
29. Ⓐ Ⓑ Ⓒ Ⓓ
30. Ⓐ Ⓑ Ⓒ Ⓓ

31. Ⓐ Ⓑ Ⓒ Ⓓ
32. Ⓐ Ⓑ Ⓒ Ⓓ
33. Ⓐ Ⓑ Ⓒ Ⓓ
34. Ⓐ Ⓑ Ⓒ Ⓓ
35. Ⓐ Ⓑ Ⓒ Ⓓ
36. Ⓐ Ⓑ Ⓒ Ⓓ
37. Ⓐ Ⓑ Ⓒ Ⓓ
38. Ⓐ Ⓑ Ⓒ Ⓓ
39. Ⓐ Ⓑ Ⓒ Ⓓ
40. Ⓐ Ⓑ Ⓒ Ⓓ
41. Ⓐ Ⓑ Ⓒ Ⓓ
42. Ⓐ Ⓑ Ⓒ Ⓓ
43. Ⓐ Ⓑ Ⓒ Ⓓ
44. Ⓐ Ⓑ Ⓒ Ⓓ
45. Ⓐ Ⓑ Ⓒ Ⓓ

46. Ⓐ Ⓑ Ⓒ Ⓓ
47. Ⓐ Ⓑ Ⓒ Ⓓ
48. Ⓐ Ⓑ Ⓒ Ⓓ
49. Ⓐ Ⓑ Ⓒ Ⓓ
50. Ⓐ Ⓑ Ⓒ Ⓓ
51. Ⓐ Ⓑ Ⓒ Ⓓ
52. Ⓐ Ⓑ Ⓒ Ⓓ
53. Ⓐ Ⓑ Ⓒ Ⓓ
54. Ⓐ Ⓑ Ⓒ Ⓓ
55. Ⓐ Ⓑ Ⓒ Ⓓ

1. YOUR NAME:
(Print)　　　　　Last　　　　　First　　　　　M.I.

SIGNATURE: _____　DATE: ___ / ___ / ___

HOME ADDRESS:
(Print)　　　　　Number and Street

　　　　　City　　　　　State　　　　　Zip Code

PHONE NO. :
(Print)

5. YOUR NAME

First 4 letters of last name				FIRST INIT	MID INIT

IMPORTANT: Please fill in these boxes exactly as shown on the back cover of your test book.

2. TEST FORM

3. TEST CODE

4. REGISTRATION NUMBER

6. DATE OF BIRTH

Month	Day		Year	
JAN				
FEB				
MAR	0	0	0	0
APR	1	1	1	1
MAY	2	2	2	2
JUN	3	3	3	3
JUL		4	4	4
AUG		5	5	5
SEP		6	6	6
OCT		7	7	7
NOV		8	8	8
DEC		9	9	9

7. SEX
MALE
FEMALE

The **Princeton** Review®

Section I

Start with number 1 for each new section.
If a section has fewer questions than answer spaces, leave the extra answer spaces blank.

1. A B C D
2. A B C D
3. A B C D
4. A B C D
5. A B C D
6. A B C D
7. A B C D
8. A B C D
9. A B C D
10. A B C D
11. A B C D
12. A B C D
13. A B C D
14. A B C D
15. A B C D

16. A B C D
17. A B C D
18. A B C D
19. A B C D
20. A B C D
21. A B C D
22. A B C D
23. A B C D
24. A B C D
25. A B C D
26. A B C D
27. A B C D
28. A B C D
29. A B C D
30. A B C D

31. A B C D
32. A B C D
33. A B C D
34. A B C D
35. A B C D
36. A B C D
37. A B C D
38. A B C D
39. A B C D
40. A B C D
41. A B C D
42. A B C D
43. A B C D
44. A B C D
45. A B C D

46. A B C D
47. A B C D
48. A B C D
49. A B C D
50. A B C D
51. A B C D
52. A B C D
53. A B C D
54. A B C D
55. A B C D

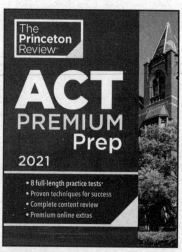
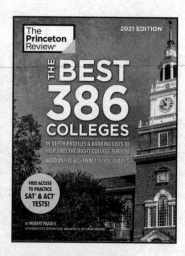
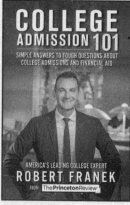